THE MAKING OF MEDIEVAL PANJAB

This book seeks to reconstruct the past of undivided Panjab during five medieval centuries. It opens with a narrative of the efforts of Turkish warlords to achieve control in the face of tribal resistance, internal dissensions and external invasions. It examines the linkages of the ruling class with Zamindars and Sufis, paving the way for canal irrigation and agrarian expansion, thus strengthening the roots of the state in the region. While focusing on the post-Timur phase, it tries to make sense of the new ways of acquiring political power.

This work uncovers the perpetual attempts of Zamindars to achieve local dominance, particularly in the context of declining presence of the state in the countryside. In this ambitious enterprise, they resorted to the support of their clans, adherence to hallowed customs and recurrent use of violence, all applied through a system of collective and participatory decision-making.

The volume traces the growth of Sufi lineages built on training disciples, writing books, composing poetry and claiming miraculous powers. Besides delving into the relations of the Sufis with the state and different sections of the society, it offers an account of the rituals at a prominent shrine. Paying equal attention to the southeastern region, it deals with engagement of the Sabiris, among other exemplars, with the Islamic spirituality. Inclusive in approach and lucid in expression, the work relies on a wide range of evidence from Persian chronicles, Sufi literature and folklore, some of which have been used for the first time.

Surinder Singh has taught at the Department of History, Panjab University, Chandigarh. His main interest is Medieval India. In nearly 55 research papers, he has explored themes of state formation, social structure, religious practices, Persian texts and popular culture. His publications include *Sufism in Panjab: Mystics, Literature and Shrines* (2009) and *Popular Literature and Pre-Modern Societies in South Asia* (2008), both edited with I.D. Gaur; *Political Memoirs of an Indian Revolutionary: Naina Singh Dhoot* (2005).

The Making of Medieval Panjab
Politics, Society and Culture
c. 1000–c. 1500

SURINDER SINGH

LONDON AND NEW YORK

MANOHAR
2019

First published 2020
by Routledge
2 Park Square, Milton Park, Abingdon, Oxon OX14 4RN

and by Routledge
52 Vanderbilt Avenue, New York, NY 10017

Routledge is an imprint of the Taylor & Francis Group, an informa business

© 2020 Surinder Singh and Manohar Publishers & Distributors

The right of Surinder Singh to be identified as author of this work has been asserted by him in accordance with sections 77 and 78 of the Copyright, Designs and Patents Act 1988.

All rights reserved. No part of this book may be reprinted or reproduced or utilised in any form or by any electronic, mechanical, or other means, now known or hereafter invented, including photocopying and recording, or in any information storage or retrieval system, without permission in writing from the publishers.

Trademark notice: Product or corporate names may be trademarks or registered trademarks, and are used only for identification and explanation without intent to infringe.

Print edition not for sale in South Asia (India, Sri Lanka, Nepal, Bangladesh, Pakistan or Bhutan)

British Library Cataloguing-in-Publication Data
A catalogue record for this book is available from the British Library

Library of Congress Cataloging-in-Publication Data
A catalog record for this book has been requested

ISBN: 978-0-367-43745-9 (hbk)
ISBN: 978-1-003-00542-1 (ebk)

Typeset in Minion Pro 11/13
by Ravi Shanker, Delhi 110 095

MANOHAR

Contents

Preface	7
1. Introduction	11
2. Warfare, Territory and Resistance	39
3. The Establishment of Sufi Orders	127
4. New Strategies of State Formation	221
5. Piety Submits to the State	297
6. Making and Breaking of Political Structures	369
7. Islamic Spirituality in Southeast Panjab	435
8. The World of the Zamindars	509
9. Conclusion	578
Bibliography	609
Index	623

Preface

At the outset, I would try to trace the genesis of this book. A decade ago, the Department of Punjab Historical Studies, Punjabi University, Patiala, invited me to present the Presidential Address (Medieval Section) at the fortieth session of the Punjab History Conference. In the ensuing attempt, I analysed the major historical developments in Panjab, with particular reference to its politics and economy, focusing on the thirteenth and fourteenth century. Subsequently, I availed the opportunities of presenting seminars on this subject and related themes at New Delhi, Patna, Santiniketan, Gandhinagar, Vadodara, Lahore and Prague (Czech Republic). I also tested the viability of my understanding at Refresher Courses and Extension Programmes at different venues. Apart from critical appreciation, I received a number of constructive suggestions. More significantly, a number of scholars advised me to develop my thoughts into a book. Keeping in mind the suggestions as well as my own rethinking, I began to explore the ideas originally laid out in the Presidential Address in greater depth and wider scope. The effort resulted in a few research papers, preparing the ground for putting together a book. A number of factors have shaped this endeavour. First, the approach to the historiography of medieval India has undergone a sea change in the last half a century, so that these advances demanded due consideration. Second, a long-term view of historical evolution that straddled several centuries promised the developing of a holistic perspective. Third, this study tends to be flexible as regards its geographical scope because the political currents and cultural traditions often crossed perceived boundaries. Fourth, this attempt calls for evidence from Persian chronicles, Sufi literature (biographies, discourses and poetry) and Panjabi folklore.

Preface

It is my pleasant duty to express my gratitude to the staff at the libraries where I worked. These institutions are: Department of History and A.C. Joshi Library at the Panjab University, Chandigarh; the Centre of Advanced Study in Medieval Indian History and the Maulana Azad Library at the Aligarh Muslim University, Aligarh; the Jamia Millia Islamia and the Institute of Islamic Studies (Jamia Hamdard) at New Delhi; the Indian Institute of Advanced Study, Shimla; Shri Natnagar Shodh Samsthan, Sitamau, Madhya Pardesh; the Rampur Raza Library, Rampur, Uttar Pardesh; Maulana Azad Arabic and Persian Research Institute, Tonk, Rajasthan; Khuda Bakhsh Oriental Public Library, Patna; the National Library and Asiatic Society of Bengal at Kolkata; the Department of History and the Bhai Gurdas Library at the Guru Nanak Dev University, Amritsar; the Punjabi Reference Library at the Punjabi University, Patiala; and Gore Meadows Community Centre at Brampton (Ontario, Canada).

I am indebted to a number of scholars, colleagues and friends who helped me in my academic pursuits. The late Iqtidar Husain Siddiqui took a keen interest in my studies and showered his affection on me. Harbans Mukhia illumined a difficult path and provided me with opportunities to learn. Navtej Singh shared with me his deep concerns for Panjab. Subhash Parihar not only offered hospitality but also allowed me to ransack his vast collection of books. Ishwar Dayal Gaur gave me insights into the growth of Panjabi literature. The late Iqbal Sabir looked after me during my visits to Aligarh and treated me as a member of his family. Virinder Kalra brought books for me from Lahore. Priyatosh Sharma, while feeling concerned about my welfare, has offered valuable advice to me. Ashish Kumar lent his books to me with grace. Mohan Singh, Senior Scientific Officer at the Centre of Advanced Study in Geography, Panjab University, Chandigarh, has prepared the map in accordance with the needs of this book. Moral support came from S. Azizuddin Husain, Raj Kumar Hans, Supriya Varma and S. Zaheer Husain Jafri. However, I alone am responsible for the views expressed here.

On the home front, my dear ones – mother, sister, wife and daughter – have been extending unconditional support to me over the decades. In particular, my daughter Jasmine ensured that I continued to pursue my studies during my stay in Canada. My nephew Lakhprit took charge of my responsibilities as and when I was away from home. My son-in-law Pawan introduced me to the libraries in Brampton (Ontario) and created conditions conducive to my interests. In the neighbouring city of Markham, my friend Balvinder S. Jassar set aside in his house a room for me where I could work in peace. The completion of this book coincided with the birth of my granddaughter Saisha, who brought unlimited joy through her innocent ways.

I record my deep appreciation for Manohar Publishers & Distributors, who decided to publish this book. Ramesh Jain took a personal interest in the task with the aim of achieving a high degree of perfection. Ajay Jain selected books of my interest and passed them on, sparing me of numerous difficulties. I am grateful to them.

SURINDER SINGH

CHAPTER 1

Introduction

Panjab has played a crucial role in the history of South Asia. Strategically placed, it often became a battleground of warlords contending for larger areas. Its subjugation opened the gates to territorial gains in different directions. It appears to have assimilated the bulk of people, who migrated to the east in the wake of the Mongol irruption in Central Asia. The new Turkish rulers faced multiple challenges. After overcoming internal strife and suppressing tribal resistance, the new ruling classes built defenses against fresh invasions and developed mechanisms to extract tributes. In view of the peculiarities of our evidence, the local tribes appeared to resist the Turkish state with courage, but their opposition was sporadic. Same was true of the smaller potentates, zamindars, whose importance was recognized when the state spread its tentacles into the countryside. The rivers and streams, even if swollen in a part of the year, did not hamper the movement of armies, caravans and pilgrims. The needs of the growing Muslim communities, particularly in several administrative centres, were met by the emergence of mosques and services of preachers. The Sufis, whether associated with orders (*silsilahs*) or worked individually, came to acquire great influence among all sections of the society. The cultural landscape underwent a gradual transformation with the emergence of new forms of architecture, literature and folklore.

Trends in Historical Writing

The early interest in the history of medieval India may be traced to the English translations of *Tarikh-i Firishtah* by Alexander

Dow, Jonathan Scott, and John Briggs. A more serious interest in the subject began with the publication of Elliot and Dowson's translations of extracts from Persian chronicles.¹ Fortunately, the Asiatic Society of Bengal (Calcutta) and Munshi Newal Kishore (Lucknow) started bringing out texts of the Persian works. Similar attempts were made from Delhi, Aligarh, and Baroda. With the establishment of universities and colleges during the colonial era, professional historians turned their energies to the study of medieval India. Almost without exception, the early writings focused on the ruling dynasties and kings. Full scale studies appeared on the Mamluks, Khaljis, Tughluqs and Lodis.² Relying on a close examination of Persian chronicles, they exclusively dealt with the politics of the ruling class. Starting with the circumstances in which a particular dynasty or king assumed power, they narrated the military achievements in terms of conquests, invasions, and rebellions. In some cases, there was a brief reference to the administrative changes and patronage of arts. As a departure from the strongly entrenched pattern, attention was given to the political structures and governmental departments, with reference to the functions of ministers and officials. A concern with the extraction of land tax brought to light the divisions in the rural society – chiefs, intermediaries and peasantry.³ Broadly speaking, this was the state of historiography in the first half of the twentieth century.

As the growing Indian middle classes responded to the withdrawal of colonialism and the dissemination of Marxist ideas, historiography did not remain immune from changing intellectual currents. Themes shifted to the material conditions of the people, with reference to the privileges of the nobility and features of ordinary lives.⁴ Against the backdrop of the religious beliefs of the Hindus on the eve of the Ghorid invasions, social change was seen in terms of a rural and urban revolution, wherein the artisan groups in the towns as well as the peasant in the countryside made substantive gains.⁵ Disagreeing with this formulation, Irfan Habib argued that there was indeed an increase in craft production, urbanization and commerce. However, these developments did not bring about the liberation of any section of the society.

According to his understanding, the new economy involved the use of slave labour, regressive agrarian taxation and parasitic urban growth.[6] Further investigation has revealed that the diffusion of new technological devices, by increasing production and lowering costs, benefited the artisans who had been accorded a low social rank. The monotheistic (Bhakti) movement, by advocating the rejection of caste prejudices, brought to the fore teachers from artisan and lowly classes: Kabir was a weaver; Namdev, a calico printer; Ravidas, a tanner; Sain, a barber; Dadu, a cotton carder, and so on.[7]

A contributory volume on medieval Panjab, appearing from the Punjabi University of Patiala, viewed an intolerant Muslim state unleashing ruthless persecution on a vast majority of the people (Hindus), who offered an unflinching resistance to the alien conquerors and creed, and displayed dogged persistence in shunning contact with them and maintaining their own exclusiveness.[8] Such an approach was quickly supplanted by a non-partisan methodology that called for a critical use of contemporary documentation. Besides a large volume sponsored by the Indian History Congress, the writings of Nizami, Siddiqui, and Jackson gained wide acceptance.[9] However, new questions kept on appearing on the scholarly horizon. Simon Digby has attributed the military superiority of the Delhi Sultanate to its ability to control the supply of warhorses and elephants and, at the same time, deprive its rival kingdoms of such crucial military resources.[10] Andre Wink has proposed a merger of two societies – frontier world of nomadic mobility and long distance trade on the one hand and settled agriculture on the other – in the eleventh to thirteenth centuries. In his view, such a fusion took place in the garrison towns (*khitta*), which, in conjunction with the dependant areas (*muzafat*) and minor crown holdings (*khalisa*), constituted the Delhi Sultanate.[11] With the major intervention of Sunil Kumar, a decisive shift has come about in our understanding of the early history of the Delhi Sultanate. It showed that the internal structure of successive dispensations remained fluid. After the death of Sultan Muizzuddin, the select Turkish slaves transformed their appanages into Sultanates which in turn were ultimately absorbed into a paramount unit under Shamsuddin Iltutmish. The careers of Shamsi slaves were not governed by professional service regulations but by the dyadic master-slave bonds. In the post-Iltutmish period, changing political trends reflected the conflicting interests of Shamsi slaves who differed because of length of service and rank. Drawing a distinction between core areas and outlying provinces, the study uncovers patterns of state formation linked in subtle ways to the theologians and mystics.[12] However, Blain H. Auer has revived the question of the real basis (religious or secular) of the Delhi Sultanate. A fresh reading of the works of three major historians (Juzjani, Barani, and Afif) shows that, in order to claim legitimacy for the state, they portrayed the Sultans in terms of symbols derived from pre-Islamic traditions, Prophetic example, and Quranic verses. This overpowering quest for legitimacy became understandable in the context of the demise (1258) of the Caliphate and looming threat of Mongol onslaught to a fledgling Delhi Sultanate.[13]

Next only to Sind, Panjab had been the first region in South Asia to receive Islam. If tradition is any indication, the earliest sign of the new creed was traced to the times of Prophet Muhammad. Islamic influences might have travelled up through Sind and Multan, where the Qarmathian sect (an offshoot of the Ismaili Shias) had been present for many centuries and created a syncretic cultural environment. In strictly religious terms, the establishment of the Ghaznavid rule in Panjab, complete with its army, bureaucracy and dependants, meant the 'rooting' of the Islamic religious institutions. One is on a more concrete ground regarding the pioneer role of Shaikh Ali bin Usman Hujwiri (d. 1072) who left an abiding legacy in the form of a mosque, a shrine and a treatise on Sufism. Towards the middle of the thirteenth century, Panjab witnessed the establishment of two Sufi orders, Chishtis and Suhrawardis. In an early attempt to comprehend these historical changes, Mohammad Habib has placed them in the larger context of Islamic mysticism in west Asia, besides uncovering the difficulties posed by spurious Chishti discourses (*malfuzat*).[14] Avoiding use of these compilations, Khaliq Ahmad Nizami has examined the growth of the Chishtis and Suhrawardis in Panjab during the mid-thirteenth century. While exploring the management of the Sufi establishments (*khanqahs*) and their attitudes to the medieval state, Nizami underscored the fundamental differences between the two principal orders.[15] In his attempt to widen the scope of the study of Indian Sufism, Rizvi went beyond the confines of major Sufi lineages of northwestern India and, in the process, explored the Indian response to the philosophy of unity of being (*wahdat ul-wujud*) and the interface between the Sufis and Hindu mystic traditions.[16] Shuja Alhaq has hailed the Chishtis as forerunners in establishing the Unitarian world view as the heart of Sufism in India, because the works of Ibn-i Arabi and Jalaluddin Rumi were introduced here only by the latter half of the fourteenth century.[17] In an insightful work on the Chishti order, which extends from its foundation to the colonial times, Ernst and Lawrence have subjected the contemporary Sufi texts to a penetrating analysis.[18] Riazul Islam, departing from the biographical model of Sufi studies and discounting the boundaries between Sufi orders, has discussed the attitude of principal Sufi masters towards working for livelihood, receiving charity, making families and expressing political concerns. Tanvir Anjum has re-examined the relations between the Chishtis and the Sultans of Delhi in terms of a contention over space.[19] Raziuddin Aquil, while rejecting the distinction between genuine and spurious Sufi texts, shows that the Chishtis converted non-Muslims to Islam by performing miracles that were a device to claim legitimacy.[20]

The Jat tribals, who offered a stiff resistance to the Ghaznavids and Ghorids, assumed a considerable significance in medieval Panjab. Irfan Habib, in a seminal study, traced their history through a millennium from the seventh to the seventeenth century, taking into account the geographical peculiarities of Panjab and linguistic features of its subregions. Relying on the early account of Hieun Tsang and *Chachnama*, it notices the presence of the Jats in central Sind, where they were marked by a pastoral economy and egalitarian social structure. By the eleventh century, they had migrated to Multan and clashed with Sultan Mahmud of Ghazni. By the end of the sixteenth century, they had migrated beyond the Satluj and Jamuna. During this migration, they settled as sedentary cultivators with the help of the Persian wheel and went on to acquire zamindari rights in a vast area. Motivated by the urge for social equality as warranted by their newly gained social position, they entered the widening ranks of Sikhism.[21] Richard M. Eaton argued that the Jat clans were also slowly converting to Islam owing to their association with the shrine of Baba Farid at Pakpattan. The complex had grown as a popular centre of devotion, because the spiritual charisma (*baraka*) of the saint was believed to abide in his tomb as well as his descendants. Alongside the institutionalization of a series of rituals, the place received land grants from Muhammad bin Tughluq. As the spiritual head (*sajjadah nishin*), who was known as the Diwan, developed agriculture in these lands, the Jat and Rajput clans settled as farmers, benefiting from the availability of the Persian wheel. The clans, owing to their integration in the devotional world of the shrine, underwent the slow process of Islamization.[22] At present, there is nothing to suggest that other Sufi shrines in Panjab played a similar role with regard to the diverse pastoral-agricultural groups.

During the last decade and a half, the Suhrawardis have attracted a considerable scholarly attention. As many as four major studies have altered the existing understanding on the subject. Qamar ul-Huda has shown that the Suhrawardis of Multan could not be seen in isolation from their counterparts in Baghdad. Moving beyond the dichotomous model of 'official' *versus* 'popular' religion and delving into Shaikh Abu Hafs Umar Suhrawardi's classic *Awarif ul-Maarif*, he stresses the incorporation of the Prophetic traditions and memorization of Quranic verses into its spiritual path. While pointing to the destruction of Suhrawardi sources in Multan owing to political turmoil, it underlines the significance of Shaikh Bahauddin Zakariya's works, *Khulasat ul-Arifin* and *Al-Aurad*, in the making of the order in a specific political context in the region.[23] Amina M. Steinfels, in her biography of Syed Jalaluddin Bokhari, emphasizes the role of Sufism in the making of Indo-Islamic culture, which could not be cut off from the Islamic traditions in the rest of the Islamic world. Relying on the four compilations of the discourses of the saint, she focuses on his education in Hejaz and affiliation to several Sufi orders. She argues that the Shaikh, who combined in himself the dual role of a Sufi and scholar, gave precedence to the knowledge of canonical law over acts of devotion.[24] Hasan Ali Khan reveals the cryptic metaphysical links between the Suhrawardis and Nizari Ismailis (Satpanth) in the middle Indus region. Drawing on the iconography of the Suhrawardi monuments, the astronomical implications of Ali's spiritual authority and a long existing religious syncretism, he reveals the secret Shia inclination of the Suhrawardis and, by implication, the Sufi garb of the Shias for dissimulation.[25] Anna Bigelow shows that the cult of another Suhrawardi saint Shaikh Sadruddin (1434-1508) took on a different hue. She explains the identity of Malerkotla as a shared sacred space due to a collective memory comprising the piety of Shaikh Sadruddin, the blessings of Guru Gobind Singh to the Nawab of the principality, and peace during partition riots.[26]

As modern scholarship on Sufism indicated, efforts have been mainly directed to the Chishti lineage extending from Khwaja Muinuddin Chishti to Shaikh Nasiruddin Mahmud. The pioneering work of the Sabiris, a branch of the Chishtis in the vast plains of northern India, has remained largely concealed from view, owing to the lack of contemporary evidence.[27] The Sabiri hagiographical literature, which appeared in the heyday of the Mughal empire, was said to lack credibility and authenticity.[28] This might be true of the early history of the Sabiris, while the evidence was quite satisfactory from the opening of the fifteenth century onwards. The Sabiris acquired a considerable prominence on account of the diligence of a line of modern exemplars – Haji Imdad Allah (d. 1899), Ashraf Ali Thanvi (d. 1943), Zauqi Shah (d. 1953) and Captain Wahid Bakhsh Siyal (d. 1955). In particular, Siyal has brought out a number of Sabiri texts for the benefit of scholars and followers. Ernst and Lawrence, in their influential work on the Chishtis, have recognized the tremendous contribution of Sabiri masters in the colonial and post-colonial periods. More recently, Moin Ahmad Nizami has examined the same subject in greater depth. In these circumstances, the early history of the Sabiris, which pertained to southeast Panjab, could no longer be marginalized, even if one had to rely on later hagiographies of Allah Diya Chishti, Abdul Rahman Chishti and Muhammad Akram Quddusi.

One would be curious to know the fate of Sufi cults that have survived to the present. In a film (2012) entitled *Milange Babey Rattan De Mele Te* (Let's Meet at Baba Rattan's Fair), Ajay Bharadwaj has treated the cult of this saint as integral to the popular culture of the post-partition Panjab. Over the medieval centuries, the shrine at Bathinda has emerged as an important sacred centre. In spite of the migration of Muslims to Pakistan in 1947, devotees belonging to all religious communities continued to have faith in the charisma of the saint. On any festive day, steady streams of devotees arrived in the midst of beating of drums. They purchased a number of articles – embroidered sheets, mustard oil, brooms, and sweets – to offer at the grave. They prayed for the Baba's intercession for the fulfilment of their wishes. While the food was cooked in the open for the community meals (*langar*), the Qawwals regaled the gathering with devotional lyrics steeped in Islamic spirituality. Knowledgeable devotees understood the oneness of God and diversity of paths leading to Him. Believing that Prophet Muhammad was the beloved of God, they were also conversant with the message of Bulle Shah and Waris Shah. They also recognized the supreme sacrifices of legendary lovers like Laila-Majnu, Hir-Ranjha, Sassi-Punnu and Sohni-Mahiwal. If they knew the mystical verses of Daya Singh Arif, they also cherished the poetry of Babu Rajab Ali, the famous balladeer (*kavishar*) of the Malwa region, who paid rich tributes to Baba Haji Rattan even after shifting to Pakistan. Older inhabitants of Bathinda preserved fond memories of the great fair held at the shrine before 1947, when Sufis and Qawwals arrived from distant places. At the same time, they were nostalgic about their affectionate relations with the local Muslims, who were forced to leave the place during partition. It was amazing that the spirit of non-denominational spirituality, which emanated from the Baba's shrine at Bathinda, remained unaffected by the phases of partition, terrorism and polarization. As the film showed, this very spirit prevailed at the

Introduction

mausoleum of Haidar Shaikh at Malerkotla and smaller shrines at Atalan, Bhundari and Chhpaar.

Primary Sources

Though the Ghaznavids were intimately associated with Panjab for nearly two centuries,[29] contemporary evidence on this experience remains inadequate. Abu Nasr Muhammad Utbi, who has penned the *Tarikh-i Yamini*, served as a secretary at the court in Ghazni. This work described the military expeditions of Sultan Subuktigin and Sultan Mahmud up to 1020. Written in difficult Arabic and unclear about dates and places, it took more interest in western parts of the Ghaznavid empire than in India.[30] However, later writers like Khwaja Nizamuddin Ahmad and Muhammad Qasim Hindu Shah Firishta have benefited from it. Far superior to Utbi as a chronicler was Abul Fazl Baihaqi (d. 1077). He produced a comprehensive account of the Ghaznavids in thirty volumes. Only a small portion, *Tarikh-i Masudi*, which was devoted to the reign of Sultan Masud (r. 1030-41), has survived.[31] The author, having served in the department of correspondence at the Ghaznavid court, had access to official documents. An eyewitness to a number of events, he observed the functioning of the polity from close quarters.[32] He has offered valuable evidence on the problems of the Ghaznavid rule in Panjab. He has revealed the failure of the bifurcation of administration under a civil officer and military commander. He has provided details of the dominant thinking at the royal court in Ghazni, which received regular reports from Panjab through different sources. Besides the machinations of Qazi Shirazi, he describes the revolts of Ali Aryaruq and Ahmad Niyaltigin. Equally significant is his account of the success of a Hindu general, Tilak, in quelling the disturbances in Panjab, particularly in winning over the Jats from the side of the rebels. The writer shows that positive results followed the appointment of a single governor and the Sultan's personal intervention in the region. Abu Raihan Alberuni (973-1049), the author of the classic *Kitab ul-Hind*, spent a major part of his life at Ghazni and lived for some time in parts of Panjab. Other than noting the latitudes of some towns of the region and the diplomatic exchange between the Hindushahis and Sultan Mahmud,[33] he did not say anything about the political changes in Ghaznavid Panjab. By inclination, he was more interested in Indian astronomy, social structure and religious practices.

The *Taj ul-Maasir*, which was the first chronicle written in the Delhi Sultanate, came from the pen of Tajuddin Hasan Nizami. A migrant from Nishapur to Delhi, he employed a highly ornate language to narrate the military achievements (1191-1217) of the new rulers.[34] Besides describing the stiff opposition of the Jats and Khokhars to the Turkish rule, it threw light on the functions of the governor of Lahore, Prince Nasiruddin Mahmud. The *Tabaqat-i Nasiri* of Minhaj-i Siraj Juzjani describes the fortunes of the rulers of the Delhi Sultanate from the Ghorid conquest to the twelfth regnal year of Sultan Nasiruddin Mahmud. Keeping a close watch on the internal strife in the new ruling class, he traced the careers of twenty-five Shamsi nobles, among whom Ulugh Khan (Ghiasuddin Balban) was accorded the maximum space. Ziauddin Barani, in his celebrated *Tarikh-i Firoz Shahi*, has recorded the political history of nearly a century from the accession of Ghiasuddin Balban to the sixth regnal year of Firoz Shah Tughluq. In spite of his hostility to the low-born elements in the bureaucracy and inclusion of some doubtful conversations between powerful individuals, Barani remains unique for his attention to state policies affecting the peasantry. While pointing towards the benefits of canal irrigation in southeast Panjab, he has highlighted the growing influence of the Sufis, with reference to popularization of devotional practices and demand for Sufi literature. Amir Khusrau has left a day-to-day poetic account of the march of Ghazi Malik (Ghiasuddin Tughluq) from Dipalpur to Delhi and his correspondence with the nobles posted in Panjab. In a chronicle of the military campaigns of Alauddin Khalji, his references to the Mongol invasions were high on rhetoric and low on facts. Abdul Malik Isami has revealed the crucial role of the Khokhars in bringing the Tughluqs to the seat of power, besides offering some valuable information about the Mongol inroads. The family of Shams-i Siraj Afif had intimate ties with the Tughluqs as well as the town of Abohar. In his celebratory history of the reign of Firoz Shah Tughluq, he has described a number of administrative reforms revolving around the patronage of Sufi establishments, provision of canal irrigation and founding of new urban centres. He has also narrated the Sultan's hunting expeditions in southeast Panjab, when he appeared to have accompanied the royal entourage.

Ain ul-Mulk Mahru, as the governor of Multan during the mid-fourteenth century, has recorded accurate information on the state attempts to revive the agrarian economy of the region. In addition to the reorganization of land grants, it draws attention to the digging of canals with the support of local elements, regulation of the prices of essential commodities and complaints against subordinate officers.[35] Sharfuddin Ali Yazdi, apparently present in the army of Timur, offers a useful testimony on the march of the invaders through several places in Panjab, Delhi and northern hills. Not trying to conceal the enormity of destruction and displacement, he has dutifully noted the contents of the rich booty including grain, cattle and human captives. Yahya Ahmad Sirhindi, in his useful account of the quarter of a century following Timur's departure, has exposed the unending warfare in the different pockets of Panjab and, in the process, focused on the revolts of district officials and varying attitudes of the local chiefs. Abdullah and Shaikh Rizqullah Mushtaqi have described the manner in which Bahlol Lodi developed the nucleus of Afghan power in Sirhind and ultimately acquired sovereign status in Delhi. Khwaja Nizamuddin Ahmad, in his ambitious project on the history of nine regions until their annexation under Akbar, has dealt with the establishment of the Langah kingdom in Multan amidst the failure of a Suhrawardi saint to hold on to the reins of the government, while the Delhi Sultanate withdrew from the region.

Ali bin Usman Hujwiri, who was one of the earliest Sufis of Panjab, produced a comprehensive work on the history and philosophy of Islamic spirituality. Starting with the pious caliphs and Prophet's companions, he has traced the history of early Sufi orders and biographies of prominent spiritual leaders. Equally significant was his discussions on the doctrines and practices of Sufism, with particular emphasis on the multiplicity of interpretations and contentious debates in the Sufi circles. Baba Farid, who was instrumental in establishing the Chishtis in Panjab and neighbouring areas, composed several mystical verses (*shaloks*) in the Lehandi dialect of Panjabi. These compositions have survived the vicissitudes of time and, travelling across centuries, found a place in the Sikh scripture. His close disciple, Shaikh Jamaluddin Hansavi, wrote a short treatise in Arabic entitled *Mulhimat* (Inspirations), wherein he explained the basic principles of Sufism. While examining the nature of seeker's love for God, he drew attention to the inner significance of Islamic rituals. Shaikh Bahauddin Zakariya prepared two manuals, *Khulasat ul-Arifin* and *Al-Aurad*, wherein he formulated the content of spiritual exercises and supplications for the benefit of Suhrawardi aspirants. His close pupil and son-in-law Shaikh Fakhruddin Iraqi, who developed his ideas on divine love during a long stay in Multan, appeared to have given them a formal shape in the *Ushaqnama* during 1282-4. Employing a skilful combination of Masnavi and Ghazal, he has elaborated the complexities of divine love in sensuous and passionate ways.[36] To an extent, this very ground was covered in a long poem (*masnavi*) of Bu Ali Qalandar. This composition saw the presence of God in all forms of creation and uncovered the numerous hues of divine love. At the same time, it exposed the dangers of carnal love as well as the doings of fake Sufis. Some strands of the mysticism of Bu Ali Qalandar could also be gleaned from his advice to the novice, as noted in the *Akhbar ul-Akhyar* of Shaikh Abdul Haq Muhaddis Dehalvi.

The *Fawaid ul-Fuad*, which has preserved the sermons of Shaikh Nizamuddin Auliya, is undoubtedly the finest specimen in the genre of Sufi discourses (*malfuzat*). The Shaikh's disciple Amir Hasan Sijzi, who took on the onerous task of its compilation, was famous as a poet. Along with Amir Khusrau, he displayed his poetic talent for five years (1280-5) at the court of Prince Sultan Muhammad in Multan. The work comprised an account of 188 assemblies held in five different phases from 1308 to 1322. Checked closely by the Shaikh himself, it became a literary masterpiece and a guiding spirit for the lovers of God. In general, it is an authentic elaboration of the Chishti mode of Islamic spirituality. In particular, it is indispensible to reconstruct the life of Baba Farid as a leading Chishti master. The narrator, Shaikh Nizamuddin Auliya, visited Ajodhan three times and, during each sojourn spanning several months, participated in the activities of the hospice. With regard to Baba Farid, he has focused his attention on the training of disciples, teaching of religious texts, performance of austerities, interest in musical sessions and distribution of amulets. He has made significant observations on the popularity of Baba Farid among the different sections of the society. The work provides valuable evidence on the Suhrawardi exemplar Shaikh Bahauddin Zakariya, whose spiritual path was seen as entirely different from that of Baba Farid. In addition to a plethora of facts on numerous Sufis of the period, the *Fawaid ul-Fuad* has a wide scope as it was deeply rooted in the socio-cultural milieu of northwestern India. It often turned to the concerns of the ordinary people in their daily lives.[37] It frequently quoted the mystical literature (*Qut ul-Qulub, Ruh ul-Arwah, Nawadir ul-Usul* and *Ihya Ulum ul-Din*) produced outside South Asia. It contained anecdotes from the lives of eminent Sufis like Bayazid Bistami, Ainu ul-Quzat, Saifuddin Bakharzi, Abu Said Abul Khair, and Ahmad Ghazzali.

In the *Khair ul-Majalis*, Hamid Qalandar has recorded one hundred conversations of Shaikh Nasiruddin Mahmud Chiragh-i Delhi (d. 1356), who headed the Chishti order after the demise of his mentor Shaikh Nizamuddin Auliya. The compiler began his spiritual journey with the blessings of Shaikh Nizamuddin Auliya and, during his stay in the Deccan, attached himself to Shaikh Burhanuddin Gharib. On returning to Delhi, he entered the tutelage of Shaikh Nasiruddin Mahmud and, with his consent, began compiling a record of his assemblies held during a year (1353-4). The Shaikh examined portions of the output and made editorial changes to exclude improbable happenings. The final text has included a dozen events from the life of Baba Farid. Some of them revolve around the simple life of Baba Farid and his work of guiding disciples. Some others describe his power of working miracles. In one case, he ensured the restoration of an oil-seller's wife; in another, he punished a revenue officer who oppressed his sons and, in still another, he helped in the recovery of a missing falcon. In an episode, Hamid Qalandar has narrated Baba Farid's illness owing to the evil designs of a magician and the ultimate diffusion of the cause at the hands of Shaikh Nizamuddin Auliya. In spite of its limitations, the *Khair ul-Majalis* went on to acquire a degree of credibility and its passages entered the writings of Burhanuddin Gharib, Hamid bin Fazlullah Jamali, Amir Khurd and Abdul Haq Muhaddis Dehalvi.[38]

Sometime in the penultimate decade of the fourteenth century, Amir Khurd completed his *Siyar ul-Auliya*, a voluminous work on the Chishtis. The author was eminently suited to undertake this stupendous task. His grandfather Syed Muhammad Mahmud Kirmani, a trader who frequently travelled from Kirman to Multan, gave up his worldly pursuit and entered the hospice of Baba Farid at Ajodhan. Amir Khurd and his elders – his grandfather, father and uncles – shifted to Delhi and attached themselves to Shaikh Nizamuddin Auliya.[39] He was on intimate terms with the disciples of both, Baba Farid and Shaikh Nizamuddin Auliya. Against a backdrop of tributes to Prophet Muhammad and the pious caliphs, *Siyar ul-Auliya* notes the genealogical tree of the Chishtis. It was rich in detail regarding the lives of Khwaja Muinuddin Chishti, Khwaja Qutbuddin Bakhtiyar Kaki and Baba Farid. In writing the *Siyar ul-Auliya*, the author was inspired by his loving devotion to Shaikh Nizamuddin Auliya and, therefore, a bulk of the work revolved around the saint and his pupils. It is true that the author has freely picked up material from the *Fawaid ul-Fuad* and has inserted poetry at every conceivable place in his prose. But, Amir Khurd had no dearth of facts. Besides his own reminiscences and experiences of the members of his extended family, Amir Khurd could always fall back upon his friendship with the inmates of the Chishti establishments at Ajodhan, Hansi and Delhi. In this light, the strength of the *Siyar ul-Auliya* outweighs its weakness.

Shaikh Hamid bin Fazlullah Kamboh Jamali (d. 1536) was a disciple of Shaikh Samauddin (d. 1496), a leading Suhrawardi saint of Delhi. Jamali was a traveller, poet, and historian.[40] Apart from Mecca and Madina, he had travelled across Egypt, Palestine, Turkey, Syria, Iraq, Iran, Khurasan and even Ceylon. He availed the opportunity of paying homage at the mausoleum of Shaikh Bahauddin Zakariya in Multan and held discussions with Abdul Rahman Jami in Herat. He earned the respect of Sikandar Lodi (r. 1489-1517) and corrected his verses. The Mughal emperor Humayun not only visited his prayer cell several times, but also took him along on the military expedition to Gujarat. A profilic poet, Jamali composed a large corpus of poetry, which included the tragic love story of a prince of Badakhshan.[41] In the *Siyar ul-Arifin*, he has written the biographies of thirteen saints, most of whom were associated with Panjab. Paying equal attention to the Chishtis and Suhrawardis, he has begun his narrative with Khwaja Muinuddin Chishti and concluded with Shaikh Samauddin. He has depended heavily on the acclaimed Chishti works (*Fawaid ul-Fuad*, *Khair ul-Majalis* and *Siyar ul-Auliya*). He was the only writer to describe the dispute between Shaikh Sadruddin Arif and Prince Sultan Muhammad, besides narrating a massive public protest against the ban on music under Ghiasuddin Tughluq (r. 1320-5). In his attempt to demonstrate the superiority of the Suhrawardis, he often resorted to description of miracles. In the words of Lawrence, 'Jamali has sometimes been criticised for relying on oral evidence to supplement the sparse biographic data in earlier literary sources, but *Siyar ul-Arifin* is a masterpiece. Not only does its author make an objective assessment of saints from both the *silsilahs* dominant in pre-Mughal India, but he writes in a fluid style punctuated with humorous, often poetical anecdotes.'[42]

Shaikh Abdul Haq Muhaddis Dehalvi (1551-1642) was one of the finest scholars of his times. A staunch supporter of Shaikh Abdul Qadir Jilani and the philosophy of Unity of Being (*wahdat ul-wujud*), he headed a Qadiri hospice at Delhi. During a stay (1588-91) in Mecca and Madina, he specialized in the study of Prophetic traditions (*hadis*). Keeping aloof from the ideological debates at the Mughal court, he wrote over sixty books on different Islamic sciences. Though he was open to influences of several Sufi orders, he tried to reconcile canonical law with mystical discipline. In his celebrated biographical dictionary of Indian Sufis, *Akhbar ul-Akhyar*, he tried to fill gaps in the knowledge about them.[43] For example, he unearthed a rare source (*Maktubat*) of Bu Ali Qalandar's advice to a novice regarding the spiritual quest. While elaborating the teachings of Shaikh Sadruddin Arif and Shaikh Ruknuddin Abul Fateh, he retrieved information from their works no longer extant. Similarly, he stated that the mausoleum of Shaikh Alauddin Ali Ahmad Sabir was found at Kaliyar Sharif, that he was the son-in-law and spiritual successor of Baba Farid, and that his lineage led to Shaikh Abdul Quddus Gangohi. He was surprised that Amir Khurd had omitted any reference to him and wondered if he was the same person as one Shaikh Sabir noted in the *Siyar ul-Auliya*. However, he was on sure ground regarding two distinguished Sabiris, Shaikh Ahmad Abdul Haq and Shaikh Abdul Quddus Gangohi. Having studied Shaikh Gangohi's work *Anwar ul-Uyun*, he has brought to light his thoughts on various kinds of hunger.

From the middle of the seventeenth century, the Sabiris began to figure in the Sufi hagiographies. Allah Diya Chishti, who penned the *Siyar ul-Aqtab*, was a disciple of the Sabiri saint Shah Aala (d. 1623). The author hailed from Kirana, a village near the town of Karnal in southeastern Panjab. He took two decades (1626-46) to complete the work, having spent the time in collecting little known material. The author claimed a supernatural aspect for his book on two counts. First, it did not absorb moisture when it fell accidently into water. Second, the book received praise from Khwaja Muinuddin Chishti, who appeared to the author in a dream. Small in volume, it contained biographies of twenty-eight saints from Prophet Muhammad onwards. Of the last twelve, nine were Sabiris who lived from the mid-thirteenth to the early seventeenth century. Loaded with miraculous stories, it describes the relations of Sabiris with Bu Ali Qalandar, the revival of the Chishti seat of Hansi, and the procedure of nominating a spiritual successor. For unknown reasons, the work fails to record the lives of two prominent Sabiris, Shaikh Ahmad Abdul Haq and Shaikh Abdul Quddus Gangohi. This gap has been filled in Abdul Rahman

Chishti's *Mirat ul-Asrar*, which was prepared between 1635 and 1654. Substantially different from the *Siyar ul-Aqtab* in content and object, it is a massive encyclopaedia of over 260 saints who lived in the previous eleven centuries of Islam. Despite the chronological discrepancies, he drew attention to the pre-eminent Sufi authority known as the *Qutb* (axis of the age). From the perspective of the author, the *Qutb* of each age, since the appearance of Shaikh Alauddin Ali Ahmad Sabir had to be and had been a Sabiri Chishti master. The *Qutb* of each generation was situated among other Sufi masters, particularly those from the classical Persian Sufism tradition.[44]

The story of Hir Ranjha, as versified in Panjabi by Damodar Gulati, falls in a class of its own. For centuries this love tale has been the most popular folktale in Panjab. It was assimilated into the Sufi discourse from Shah Husain (1539-99) onwards. It entered the compositions of Bhai Gurdas and Guru Gobind Singh. Up to the middle of the twentieth century, nearly fifty renditions had appeared in Panjabi. The version of the story, which was composed by Waris Shah in 1766, surpassed all others in popularity. However, Damodar was the first to versify it in Panjabi. Having performed the task two centuries ahead of Waris Shah, he was closer in time to the events described in it. However, Damodar enjoyed another advantage, which somehow escaped the notice of literary critics. He had a deep knowledge of the internal dynamics of the rural society that flourished in western Panjab and, what is even more important, he was ever keen to bring it into sharp relief. More than the travails of the protagonists, Hir and Ranjha, Damodar was interested in the social context in which they struggled. He has thrown a flood of light on the powerful zamindars, who survived in a highly competitive scenario with the active support of their respective clans. It reveals their mode of taking decisions in different situations, ranging from agrarian entrepreneurship to undoing a wrong. It deals with the cherished zamindari aim of local dominance, which explains the rationale behind the pervasive violence and the remote presence of governmental authority in the rural areas.

Task in Hand

Panjab, for the purpose of the present study, comprises the area enclosed between the Indus and Jamuna. At first look, it appears as a monotonous and undifferentiated vast plain. In fact, it is marked by diverse topographical features. On its east, a submontane tract runs along the southern flanks of the lesser Himalayas from the Jamuna to Jhelam. Varying from 100 to 200 miles in breadth, its outlying hills either merge with the Himalayas or separate from it by longitudinal valleys known as Duns.[45] The plain itself may be divided into two parts, Indo-Panjab Plain and Ghaggar Plain. The former is shaped like a vast triangle, with the Siwaliks as its base, and the Satluj and Indus as its sides. It was drained by the waters of the Beas, Ravi, Chenab, and Jhelam. Its flatness induced the rivers to flow slowly and thus fertilize the country with alluvial deposits, and affording facilities for waterways and irrigation channels. The plain, leaving the submontane tract and moving southwest, slopes gradually so that the gradient seldom exceeds two feet in a mile. As the snow melts at the onset of summer, the rivers begin to swell and, during the monsoons, they are in flood and heavily charged with silt. Narrow in the mountains, the valleys widened out in the low country and carrying power of the rivers wanes with the reduction in the velocity of the current.[46] In the Indo-Panjab plain, the rivers flow in wide and deep valleys that are lower than the general level of the plain. The low plain, known as the Khaddars, through which the rivers flow, are amenable to annual floods, besides erosion and reformation. Distinct from the Khaddars stand the central uplands, the Bars. Unaffected by the inundations, they were extensive waste lands covered with grass before the arrival of modern irrigation networks.[47]

On the southeast of the Panjab Plain lies the Ghaggar Plain. A transition area between the Indus and Ganga plains, it is different from both in its characteristics. In the northeast it is bordered by the Siwaliks, while on the west it merged in the desert of Rajputana. Along the Siwalik foothills it is 75 miles wide and gradually widens towards the west, so that it achieves a width of 230 miles from Delhi to the Satluj. During the monsoons, the entire area is inundated by a dozen torrents that bring large volumes of water from the Siwaliks. More important of these are the Ghaggar, Markanda and Saraswati. They lose their water to evaporation and soakage before leaving the western border of the plain.[48] On the west of the Panjab Plain and the Jhelam, the Salt Range spreads towards the Indus. In spite of erosion suffered during the past, its western extremity rises to a height of 5,000 feet at Sakesar. Though its aridity does not allow much vegetation, its jagged hills include some fertile valleys. Tilla Balnath, famed for a monastery of the Jogis, is perched on a projection of the range running towards the northeast. North of the Salt Range is found the northwestern upland, a tract comprising a wide range of features – ravines, valleys, and sandy beds of torrents. Varying from 1,000 to 2,000 feet above the sea level, its chief hill ranges are Margalla, Kalachitta and Khairimurat. Margalla pass, which is situated on the road from Rawalpindi to Attock, commands a lot of strategic importance.[49] The distinct sandy tract of Bahawalpur, stretching from Firozpur to the border of Sind, includes the town of Uch. The annual rainfall in Panjab varied from place to place. During the early decades of the twentieth century, Hissar received 16 inches and Karnal 30, while Lahore got 21 inches, Sialkot 35 and Multan 7 only.[50]

Chapter 2 of this book covers a period of nearly three centuries, extending from the Ghaznavid invasions to the stabilization of the Delhi Sultanate. Though the roots of the Ghaznavid and Ghorid power in Panjab were separated by a long span of time, their experiences appeared to be largely the same. Here, an attempt is being made to examine the challenges faced by the Ghaznavid rule in the form of meeting local resistance, developing structures of governance, and preparing conditions for further expansion towards the east. Following an account of the opposition of the Jats and Khokhars to the Ghorid occupation, it delves into the power struggles among the slave officers of Sultan Muizzuddin. It seeks to understand the objectives of the new government as laid out in a royal order for Prince Nasiruddin Mahmud, who was posted in Lahore as the governor. While dealing with the recurring rebellions of the governors holding large territories (*muqtis*), it goes into the complexities engendered by the dogged presence of new ethnic elements – Khwarizmians, Qarlughs, and Mongols. It gives a particular attention to an important governor of Multan, whose fight against the Mongols ended in a disaster, even though he was portrayed as a martyr in the cause of Islam. It points to the efforts to strengthen the frontier lines of defence, whereas their success in the long-run was open to question, particularly during the first decade of the fourteenth century.

Chapter 3 examines the growth of Islamic spirituality in a long span of time, which, to an extent, coincides with the above political developments. It begins with the cult of Baba Haji Rattan of Bathinda, who has been linked with diverse religious traditions through oral testimonies. Since little was known about Shaikh Ali bin Usman Hujwiri (d. 1072) other than his travels and migration to Lahore, an attempt has been made to analyse his *Kashf ul-Mahjub* in order to identify the basic postulates of Sufism, both doctrinal and practical. What is disappointing, there is a big gap of nearly 150 years in our evidence on the activities of Muslim mystics. However, this chapter discusses the establishment of two major Sufi orders, Chishtis and Suhrawardis, with reference to the contribution of Baba Farid and Shaikh Bahauddin Zakariya. Besides looking at two diverse ways of spiritual endeavour, which revolved around the interface between the mentors and their disciples, it seeks to analyse their writings, both in poetry and prose, in order to have a clearer picture of their respective spiritual paths. What is significant, the chapter traces the eventful career of Shaikh Fakhruddin Iraqi in Multan and goes on to search for his mystical ideas in his verses. The exercise promises to add a new dimension to the study of Sufism in general, and alter the image of the Suhrawardis in particular.

Chapter 4 examines the new strategies of state formation adopted in the Tughluq regime. In what constitutes a major departure from the previous dispensations, the Tughluqs assimilated powerful local elements into the political structure to consolidate the foundations of their power. The change not only occurred gradually, but happened in a specific context that did not obtain during the thirteenth century. As this chapter shows, definite signs of change became visible when Ghazi Malik served in western Panjab before occupying the throne of Delhi. Evidence indicates that zamindars and Sufis, having shed their earlier aloofness, reached out to the state and made compromises in return for material gains. This chapter explores the connection between Firoz Shah Tughluq's patronage of zamindars and Sufi shrines on the one hand and the canal-based irrigation on the other. Further, relying exclusively on the letters of Ain ul-Mulk Mahru, it highlights the agrarian expansion in Multan based on the reorganization of land grants, repopulation of deserted areas and excavation of canals. It would be interesting to assess the role of village headmen and local beneficiaries in this ambitious project. Here, we are in a position to look at the lowest rungs of the administration, with reference to the complaints against local functionaries, who came into direct contact with the subjects. This chapter also takes into account the observations of Ibn Battuta that revolve around the functions of the provincial government, the state of urban centres, and the influence of the eminent Sufi masters.

Chapter 5 traces the fortunes of the Chishtis and Suhrawardis during the next phase of their evolution. Spanning nearly a hundred years from the late thirteenth to the late fourteenth century, it explores the new features in Sufism, as disseminated through the bigger of the establishments. The incumbent spiritual heads were seen facing a big challenge in continuing the legacy of their illustrious founding fathers. It seeks to identify the different paths adopted by the lineal descendants of Baba Farid, many of whom shifted to Delhi and then migrated to the Deccan. As the shrine of Baba Farid emerged as a leading centre of pilgrimage, it is imperative to describe the profusion of rituals that were held on ordinary days and festive occasions. The intimate relation of the shrine with the surrounding milieu becomes clear from a table listing marital alliances between the family of the Diwan (spiritual head) and the clan chiefs. With regard to the Suhrawardis of Multan, the testimonies of *Akhbar ul-Akhyar* and *Siyar ul-Arifin* have been combined in order to present a fuller picture. This chapter draws attention to the relations between the Suhrawardi saints and the Delhi Sultans, with reference to close collaboration and bitter confrontation. Syed Jalaluddin Bokhari, owing to his alterations in the training of disciples and emphasis on Islamic jurisprudence added a new dimension to the Suhrawardi path and, as a result of his resounding success, raised the order to the pinnacle of prestige. After this, the Sufi establishments in southwest Panjab began to fade into oblivion until a Suhrawardi saint was temporarily raised to the seat of power in Multan.

Chapter 6 concerns itself with the invasion of Timur and political transitions during the subsequent century. Pursuing the trail of the invader in three distinct zones – southwest Panjab, cis-Satluj tract and the chain of northern hills – it exposes the widespread plunder of wealth and dislocation of settlements. During the following decades, the political structure of the Delhi Sultanate began to crumble and Panjab witnessed unprecedented political convulsions, as the revenue assignees (*muqtis*) revolted, the local chiefs acquired autonomy, and foreign invaders occupied chunks of territory. Old methods of attaining political power became redundant and, therefore, new ways were put in practice with varying degrees of success. Whereas Khizr Khan won over prominent nobles holding assignments, Bahlol Lodi relied on the assistance of the fellow Afghan migrants settled in and around Sirhind. Jasrath Khokhar, who was seen as ravaging the plains of Panjab and undermining the support base of the state, remained content with sporadic gains and frequently changed his allies. This chapter describes the political rise of two Suhrawardi saints, Shaikh Haidar in Malerkotla and Shaikh Yusuf Qureshi in Multan. Both were related to Bahlol Lodi through marriage. But their success in holding on to power appeared to depend on the support of powerful local chiefs.

Chapter 7 examines the various strands of Islamic spirituality in southeast Panjab. Chronologically parallel to the better-known developments in southwest Panjab, these shades were never lighter than elsewhere. They possessed their own specificities and challenges. The Chishti seat of Hansi grew under the care of Shaikh Jamaluddin Hansavi and his lineal descendants. They neither succumbed to the pressure of the state nor lured by offers of material benefits. Remaining true to the pristine Chishti ideals, they chalked an independent course for themselves, while their better placed counterparts were gradually sucked into the widening web of the state. This chapter examines the contents of Shaikh Hansavi's *Mulhimat*, which went a long way in meeting the needs of spiritual aspirants. It discusses the mystical ideas of Bu Ali Qalandar that were lying forgotten in the pages of his compositions. It brings to light the unbroken line of the Sabiri branch of the Chishtis that worked from Kaliyar, Panipat, and Shahabad. This effort is unhampered by the apparent lack of evidence in contemporary sources and profusion of miraculous stories in later writings. What is worthy of note, the Sabiris were actively engaged in propagating the teachings of the great Sufi masters and that too at a time when the established Sufi establishments were slipping into oblivion or getting entangled in organizational problems. The Sabiris continued to gain momentum even during the tussle between the Lodis and Mughals for control over north India.

Chapter 8 undertakes a detailed study of the role of zamindars in the medieval society. It is exclusively based on Damodar's narrative of the love tale of Hir and Ranjha. Different sections of this work are structured in a manner that they uncover the various aspects of the life of zamindars. Inhabiting the tract on the banks of the Chenab, the zamindars were rich, powerful and influential. However, these possessions could be of use only if the zamindars enjoyed the loyal support of the clans to which they belonged. In the present case, the zamindars were Jats who hailed from different clans – Siyal, Ranjha, Waraich, Nahar, and Chaddar. Their well-defined enclaves comprised agricultural lands and moors, enabling them to cultivate crops and maintain herds of cattle. It appears that the zamindars were obsessed with the desire of local dominance, which was coupled with a strong sense of survival and an avid fervour for honour. In practical terms, this amounted to a perpetual urge for self-aggrandizement. Since a zamindar took all decisions in consultation with his clansmen, he was backed to the hilt by the latter. The prestige of the clan was uppermost in his mind when he distributed alms during a marriage or offered shelter to an individual in distress. In other words, any enquiry into the actions of a zamindar, in fact, meant an enquiry into the actions of his clan. Damodar's narrative has also exposed the negative characteristics of the Jat clans, owing to their patriarchal approach to love, marriage, and sexuality.

NOTES

1. For a strong criticism of the approach of H.M. Elliot in choosing extracts from Persian sources, see Mohammad Habib, 'An Introduction to the Study of Medieval India (AD 1000-1400),' in *Politics and Society during the Early Medieval Period: Collected Works of Professor Mohammad Habib*, vol. I, ed. Khaliq Ahmad Nizami, New Delhi: People's Publishing House, 1974, pp. 3-16.
2. These writings were associated with historians like Muhammad Nazim, Mohammad Habib, Muhammad Aziz Ahmad, Agha Mahdi Husain, Ishwari Prasad, Kishori Saran Lal, A.B.M. Habibullah, R.C. Jauhri, Awadh Bihari Pandey, and Abdul Halim.
3. R.P. Tripathi, *Some Aspects of Muslim Administration*, Allahabad: Central Book Depot, rpt., 1974; W.H. Moreland, *The Agrarian System of Moslem India*, New Delhi: Oriental Books Reprint Corporation, 2nd edn., 1968; Ishtiyaq Husain Qureshi, *The Administration of the Sultanate of Dehli*, New Delhi: Oriental Books Reprint Corporation, rpt., 1971. For a incisive analysis of the rural society of northern India, see Tapan Raychaudhuri and Irfan Habib, eds., *The Cambridge Economic History of India*, vol. I: *(c. 1200 – c. 1750)*, Hyderabad: Orient Longman, rpt., 1984, pp. 53-60.
4. Kanwar Muhammad Ashraf, *Life and Conditions of the People of Hindustan*, New Delhi: Munshiram Manoharlal, Second edition, 1970; A. Rashid, *Society and Culture in Medieval India (1206 – 1556 AD)*, Calcutta: Firma K.L. Mukhopadhyay, 1969; Kishori Prasad Sahu, *Some Aspects of North Indian Social Life (1000-1526 AD)*, Calcutta: Punthi Pustak, 1973.
5. Mohammad Habib, 'Introduction' to Elliot and Dowson's *History of India*, vol. II, in *Politics and Society during the Early Medieval Period: Collected Works of Professor Mohammad Habib*, vol. I, pp. 69-94.
6. Irfan Habib, 'Economic History of the Delhi Sultanate: An Essay in Interpretation,' *The Indian Historical Review*, vol. IV, no. 2, 1978, pp. 287-303.
7. Irfan Habib, 'Technological Changes and Society: 13th and 14th Centuries,' Presidential Address, Section II, *Proceedings of the Indian History Congress*, Varanasi, 1969; Irfan Habib, 'Society and Economic Change: 1200-1500,' Paper presented at Seminar on 'Social and Economic Change in Northern India' (Typescript), University of Kurukshetra, Kurukshetra, 1981.
8. Fauja Singh, ed., *History of the Punjab (AD 1000-1526)*, vol. III, Patiala: Punjabi University, 1972, p. 208.
9. Mohammad Habib and Khaliq Ahmad Nizami, ed., *A Comprehensive History of India*, vol. V: *The Delhi Sultanate (AD 1206-1526)*, rpt., New

Delhi: People's Publishing House, 1982; Khaliq Ahmad Nizami, *Religion and Politics in India during the Thirteenth Century*, New edition, New Delhi: Oxford University Press, 2002; Peter Jackson, *The Delhi Sultanate: A Political and Military History*, Cambridge: Cambridge University Press, 1999; Iqtidar Husain Siddiqui, *Authority and Kingship under the Sultans of Delhi, (Thirteenth – Fourteenth Centuries)*, New Delhi: Manohar, 2006.

10. Simon Digby, *War Horse and Elephant in the Delhi Sultanate: A Study of Military Supplies*, Oxford: Oxford Monographs, 1971.
11. Andre Wink, *Al-Hind: The Making of the Indo-Islamic World*, vol. II: *The Slave Kings and the Islamic Conquest, 11th-13th Centuries*, New Delhi: Oxford University Press, rpt., 1999, pp. 121, 382.
12. Surinder Singh, 'Book Review,' Sunil Kumar, *The Emergence of the Delhi Sultanate, 1192-1286*, Ranikhet: Permanent Black, 2007, *The Medieval History Journal*, vol. 13, no. 1, April 2010, pp. 144-9.
13. In the words of the author, 'Ultimately, we will never know if the Delhi Sultanate was ninety percent image or action. Whatever the answer, there is no doubt that historians played a major role in producing and sustaining ideas about power, justice, and Islamic rule of the premodern empire.' Blain H. Auer, *Symbols of Authority in Medieval Islam: History, Religion and Muslim Legitimacy in the Delhi Sultanate*, New Delhi: Viva Books, 2013, p. 160.
14. Mohammad Habib, 'Early Muslim Mysticism,' and 'Chishti Mystics Records of the Sultanate Period,' in *Politics and Society during the Early Medieval Period: Collected Works of Professor Mohammad Habib*, vol. I, pp. 251-90 and 385-433.
15. Nizami, *Religion and Politics in India during the Thirteenth Century*, pp. 186-245.
16. Saiyid Athar Abbas Rizvi, *A History of Sufism in India*, vol. I, New Delhi: Munshiram Manoharlal, 1978.
17. Shuja Alhaq, *A Forgotten Vision: A Study of Human Spirituality in the Light of the Islamic Tradition*, vol. I, New Delhi: Vikas Publishing House, 1997, p. 280.
18. Carl W. Ernst and Bruce B. Lawrence, *The Chishti Order in South Asia and Beyond*, New York: Palgrave Macmillan, 2002.
19. Tanvir Anjum, *Chishti Sufis in the Sultanate of Delhi 1190-1400: From Restrained Indifference to Calculated Defiance*, Karachi: Oxford University Press, 2011; a close examination of the discursive statements of Sultan Alauddin Khalji and Shaikh Nizamuddin Auliya points to a vigorous competition between the two for moral right to authority. Sunil Kumar, 'Assertions of Authority: A Study of the Discursive Statements of Two Sultans of Delhi,' in *The Making of Indo-Persian Culture: Indian and French Studies*, eds., Muzaffar Alam, Francoise Nalini Delvoye and Marc Gaborieau, New Delhi: Manohar, 2000, pp. 37-62.

20. Raziuddin Aquil, 'Conversion in Chishti Sufi Literature: 13th-14th Centuries,' *The Indian Historical Review*, vol. XXIV, nos. 1-2, 1997-8; 'Miracles, Authority and Benevolence: Stories of *Karamat* in Sufi Literature of the Delhi Sultanate,' in *Sufi Cults and the Evolution of Medieval Indian Culture*, ed., Anup Taneja, New Delhi: Indian Council of Historical Research & Northern Book Centre, 2003.
21. Irfan Habib, 'Jatts of Punjab and Sind,' in *Essays in Honour of Dr. Ganda Singh*, ed. Harbans Singh and N. Gerald Barrier, Patiala: Punjabi University, 1976, pp. 92-103.
22. Richard M. Eaton, 'The Political and Religious Authority of the Shrine of Baba Farid,' in *Essays on Islam and Indian History*, New Delhi: Oxford University Press, 2000, pp. 203-24.
23. Qamar ul-Huda, *Striving for Divine Union: Spiritual Exercises for Suhrawardi Sufis*, London and New York: Routledge Curzon, 2003.
24. Amina M. Steinfels, *Knowledge before Action: Islamic Learning and Sufi Practice in the Life of Sayyid Jalal al-Din Bukhari Makhdum-i Jahaniyan*, Columbia: University of California Press, 2012.
25. Hasan Ali Khan, *Constructing Islam on the Indus: The Material History of the Suhrawardi Sufi Order, 1200-1500 AD*, New Delhi: Cambridge University Press, 2016.
26. Anna Bigelow, *Sharing the Sacred: Practicing Pluralism in Muslim North India*, New York: Oxford University Press, 2010.
27. Khaliq Ahmad Nizami, *Tarikh-i Mashaikh-i Chisht*, vol. I, Karachi: Oxford University Press, rpt., 2007, pp. 251-2.
28. Anecdotes of saintly wrath and vindictive anger attributed to early generation of the Sabiris figured in the seventeenth century works of doubtful authenticity and these were uncritically copied by hagiographers of the nineteenth century. However, such stories went against our understanding of Chishti norms and attitudes. These harrowing accounts might be attributed to the understandable zeal of the *tazkira* writers who, by elaborating miraculous stories, tended to create the impression that the Sabiris were endowed with miraculous powers and able to defeat the spiritual power of their competitors or challengers. Moin Ahmad Nizami, *Reform and Renewal in South Asian Islam: The Chishti Sabris in 18th-19th Century North India*, New Delhi: Oxford University Press, 2016, pp. 40-2.
29. Since the Persian chronicles of the Delhi Sultanate have already been subjected to critical analyses, I have confined myself only to their relevance for the present study. For details, see Peter Hardy, *Historians of Medieval India: Studies in Indo-Muslim Historical Writing*, New Delhi: Munshiram Manoharlal, rpt., 1983; Mohibbul Hasan, ed., *Historians of Medieval India*, Meerut and New Delhi: Meenakshi Prakashan, rpt., 1983; Khaliq Ahmad Nizami, *On History and Historians of Medieval India*, New Delhi: Munshiram Manoharlal, 1983; Iqtidar Husain Siddiqui, *Perso-Arabic Sources of Information on the Life and Conditions in the Sultanate*

of *Delhi*, New Delhi: Munshiram Manoharlal, 1992; idem, *Indo-Persian Historiography: Upto the Thirteenth Century*, New Delhi: Primus, 2010.
30. Clifford Edmund Bosworth, *The Later Ghaznavids: Splendour and Decay, (The Dynasty in Afghanistan & Northern India 1040-1186)*, Edinburgh: Edinburgh University Press, 1963, pp. 9-10.
31. H.M. Elliot and John Dowson, ed., *The History of India as Told by its Own Historians*, vol. II, Allahabad: Kitab Mahal, rpt., n.d. p. 53.
32. In the words of a modern writer, 'Baihaqi's approach reveals his superiority as a historian to the turgidity of Utbi and jejuneness of Gardizi; his mind was balanced and judicious, he was able critically to weigh up conflicting evidence, and his narrative is fresh because he was a personal witness of many of the events he describes.' Bosworth, op. cit., p. 10.
33. Abu Raihan Alberuni, *Kitab ul-Hind*, English translation (*Alberuni's India*), Edward C. Sachau, New Delhi: Rupa, 2002, pp. 308, 416.
34. For details, see Nizami, *On History and Historians of Medieval India*, pp. 55-70; Siddiqui, *Indo-Persian Historiography: Upto the Thirteenth Century*, pp. 40-52.
35. Surinder Singh, 'Dynamics of Statecraft in the Delhi Sultanate: A Reconstruction from the Letters of Ainul Mulk Mahru,' *Proceedings of the Indian History Congress*, 61st Session, Calcutta, 2001.
36. According to the editor of the compendium of his poetry, Iraqi's verses indicated the impact of the Qalandari path as well as the thoughts of Attar and Sanai. Regarded as a source of instructions for the seekers, the *Ushaqnama* acquired a high place in the literary history. It became a model for poets like Auhaduddin Marghi, Ubaidullah Zakani, Imaduddin Kirmani, Ibn Imad Shirazi, Humam Tabrezi Hangami, and Ruknuddin Saiyin Simnani. Nasreen Muhtshim, ed., *Kulliyat Fakhruddin Iraqi*, (Introduction), Persian Text, Tehran: Intsharat Zawwar, 1392 AH, pp. 51-3.
37. For more details on the characteristics of *Fawaid ul-Fuad*, particularly with reference to contemporary evidence on various aspects of Islamic spirituality, see the Introduction to the two English translations contributed by Khaliq Ahmad Nizami and Ziya ul-Hasan Faruqi.
38. Khaliq Ahmad Nizami, 'Introduction,' in Hamid Qalandar, *Khair ul-Majalis*, Persian text, Aligarh: Aligarh Muslim University, 1959, pp. 10-18.
39. Amir Khurd, *Siyar ul-Auliya*, Persian text, Delhi: Matba-i Muhibb-i Hind, 1885, pp. 208-20.
40. Jamali lies buried in the Jamali-Kamali mosque and tomb, which was situated on a hill, a short distance south of the Qutb Minar, near the mausoleum of Khwaja Qutbuddin Bakhtiar Kaki. Built during the early years of the Mughal rule, its exterior was decorated with fragments of coloured tiles, while its interior was marked by the most perfect painted plaster. The two graves belonged to Jamali and Kamali. Oral tradition held the second person to be Jamali's homosexual lover, while he was also identified as wife,

a sister, a poet or disciple. Karen Chase, *Jamali-Kamali: A Tale of Passion in Mughal India*, Ahmedabad: Mapin Publishing House, 2011, pp. 8, 76.
41. Saiyid Athar Abbas Rizvi, *A History of Sufism in India*, vol. I, New Delhi: Munshiram Manoharlal, 1978, pp. 287-8.
42. Bruce B. Lawrence, *Notes From A Distant Flute: Sufi Literature in Pre-Mughal India*, Tehran: Imperial Iranian Academy of Philosophy, 1978, p. 71; for a favourable assessment of the work, see Mohammad Habib, 'Chishti Mystics Records of the Sultanate Period,' in *Politics and Society during the Early Medieval Period: Collected Works of Professor Mohammad Habib*, vol. I, pp. 394-7.
43. For a brief discussion on the approach of the author to his work, see Khaliq Ahmad Nizami, *Hayat Abdul Haq Muhaddis Dehalvi*, Delhi: Nudwat ul-Musanifin, 1964, pp. 200-5.
44. 'By this ingenious artifice the author of *Mirat ul-Asrar* accomplishes a double purpose: He makes clear how vital the connection to a Persian Sufi tradition was for all Sabiri Chishtis while at the same time conferring the highest spiritual rank on a handful of obscure saints, most of whom lived and toiled and died in northern India.' Ernst and Bruce B. Lawrence, *Sufi Martyrs of Love: The Chishti Order in South Asia and Beyond*, p. 61.
45. Ibadur Rahman Khan, 'Historical Geography of the Panjab and Sind, *Muslim University Journal*, vol. I, no. 1, July 1931, p. 100.
46. For details of the changing course of rivers in Panjab, see H.G. Raverty, 'The Mihran of Sind and its Tributaries,' *Journal of the Asiatic Society of Bengal*, vol. LXI, pt. 1, no. 3, 1897, pp. 478-508; Tapan Raychaudhuri and Irfan Habib, eds., *The Cambridge Economic History of India*, vol. I: *c. 1200-c. 1750*, Hyderabad: Orient Longman, rpt., 1982, pp. 2-3; Irfan Habib, *Man and Environment: The Ecological History of India*, New Delhi: Tulika Books, 2010, pp. 77-8.
47. Ibadur Rahman Khan, op. cit., pp. 103-4.
48. Such a stream begins in the hills with a well-defined boulder-strewn bed, which is never dry. Reaching the plains the bed of a *cho* becomes a wide expanse of white sand, hardly below the level of the adjoining country, with a thread of water passing down it in the cold weather. But from time to time in the rainy season the channel is full from bank to bank and the waters spill far and wide over the fields. Sudden spates sometimes sweep away men and cattle before they can get across. James Douie, *The Panjab, North-West Frontier Province and Kashmir*, Delhi: Low Price Publications, rpt., 1994, pp. 47-8.
49. Ibid., p. 30.
50. Ibid., p. 360.

CHAPTER 2

Warfare, Territory and Resistance

On the eve of Ghaznavid invasions, Panjab was politically fragmented. There were a number of kingdoms with varying territorial resources, their political boundaries fluid and uncertain. The most powerful of them, the Hindushahis, ruled over an area extending from Lamghan to the Chenab and from the foothills of Kashmir to Multan.[1] They had kinship ties with the ruling dynasty of Kashmir which, owing to its power and wealth, often intervened in the politics of Panjab. To the south, stood the principalities of Bhera, Lahore and Bathinda that appeared to be tributaries of powerful neighbours. Multan, having separated from the Habari kingdom of Sind, flourished under the rule of the Ismaili Qaramthians, who owed allegiance to the Fatimid caliphate of Egypt. Faced with the expansionist pressure of the Pratiharas in the east, Multan found it expedient to tilt towards the Hindushahis. The kingdom of Jalandhar, which could not withstand the onslaught of Kashmir in the north and Pratiharas in the east, was reduced to insignificance.[2] Southeastern Panjab was ruled by the Tomars who, as faithful vassals of the Pratiharas, struggled against the Chauhans of Sakambari from the south and Ghaznavid incursions from the northwest.[3] Despite their vulnerability, the Tomars displayed military vigour and diplomatic skill in erasing the Ghaznavid strongholds and establishing their control over major sacred centres. The northern Himalaya witnessed the rise of autonomous states in Jammu, Chamba and Kullu that remained aloof from the military conflicts in the plains of Panjab.

The Nature of the Ghaznavid Rule

During the last quarter of the tenth century, the Hindushahi king Jaipal faced intrusion of the Ghaznavids from southern Afghanistan. In order to relieve this pressure on his kingdom, he joined hands with Abu Ali Lawik (a scion of the former ruling family of Ghazni) and Shaikh Hamid Lawi, the ruler of Multan. Subuktgin (r. 977-97), who had assumed power in Ghazni, turned his attention to the Hindushahis. At the outset, he neutralized the chief of Multan with an assurance that his territories would remain intact. Jaipal, who had lost a number of forts to Subuktgin, marched towards Ghazni to meet the challenge. Hostilities broke out (987) near the hill of Ghuzak, which was situated between Ghazni and Lamghan. The fight continued for several days. A sudden snowstorm threw the Hindushahi forces into confusion,[4] forcing Jaipal to sue for peace with an offer of ransom, elephants and territory. Subuktgin, owing to his sympathy for his vassals, gave his consent for a settlement. However, Mahmud's insistence on a complete victory prevented agreement. Jaipal, alluding to the Rajput rite of *jauhar*, threatened to launch a fierce counter-attack after burning his own possessions – property, women and children. Subuktgin accepted terms of peace that bound Jaipal to pay an indemnity of 10 lakh *dirhams*, and 50 elephants, besides the surrender of some forts and towns on the frontier. As a guarantee for the fulfilment of these conditions, he left behind a few kinsmen as hostages. On reaching the safety of his kingdom, however, he repudiated the agreement and imprisoned the Ghaznavid officers who had been sent to take charge of their acquisitions.[5] Apparently, this action was designed to secure the release of his own kinsmen in Ghaznavid custody.

As could be expected, Subuktgin took the offensive and, in an act of revenge, ravaged the territories of the Hindushahis. Advancing beyond Kabul, he reached Lamghan, famous for its strength and wealth. All along the way, he plundered towns, killed people, and carried away booty. For his part, Jaipal mobilized the rulers of Delhi, Ajmer, Kalinjar, and Kanauj. Having mustered a vast army of 1,00,000 troopers, he penetrated Afghanistan and reached a place near Lamghan. Subuktgin took up his position on a high peak and, preparing several detachments of 500 soldiers, sent them to attack in succession. They drove a wedge in the Hindushahi ranks and made a concerted assault after uniting the smaller contingents. The Hindushahis scattered and fled, leaving behind all possessions – horses, elephants, weapons, property, provisions and utensils. Jaipal surrendered a vast area extending from Lamghan to Peshawar. Apart from paying a large tribute, he surrendered wealth and 200 elephants to the victors. Subuktgin placed Peshawar under a commander of 1,000 horsemen. He also received the allegiance of Afghans and Khaljis who inhabited the conquered tracts. In fact, thousands of them were recruited in the Ghaznavid armed forces.

Jaipal compensated himself for his losses in trans-Indus lands by making territorial gains in the east. In 991, the chief of Lahore, Bharat, attacked the Hindushahi dominions with the aim of occupying the districts of Nanadanah and Jhelam. Advancing at the head of a formidable army, he crossed the Chenab that formed the boundary between the two kingdoms. Jaipal's son Anandpal scattered the troops of Bharat and gained an entry into Lahore. The notables of the town promised to pay a tribute and, thus, secured the restoration of Bharat. Shortly after the withdrawal of Anandpal, Bharat was deposed by his son Chandardat who was hostile to Jaipal. In 999, Jaipal again deputed Anandpal to punish the challenger. Chandardat made vigorous preparations for defence and marched out of Lahore to meet the Hindushahi commander. One day, on a hunt he rode far from his camp and was captured in an ambush. The sons of Chandardat took refuge with the neighbouring Raja of Jalandhar. Jaipal annexed the kingdom of the vanquished that probably extended upto the Beas and placed it under the governorship of Anandpal.[6]

During the first three decades of the eleventh century, the petty principalities of Panjab were exposed to the formidable Ghaznavid onslaught from the northwestern direction. In the winter of 1001, Jaipal fought a fierce battle against Sultan Mahmud near Peshawar. He not only lost nearly 5,000 soldiers in the encounter, but he was also taken prisoner along with fifteen princes. He purchased his freedom by paying a huge ransom, besides agreeing to send a grandson as hostage. Within two years, he burnt himself to death, being unable to bear the humiliation. His son and successor Anandpal made an attempt (April 1006) to block the passage of the Ghaznavid troops that were bound for Multan. Abul Fateh Daud, the Qarmathian ruler of Multan, who had offended Sultan Mahmud by assisting the chief of Bhera, fled to an island on the Indus. His garrison resisted the siege for seven days before surrendering the fort to the invaders. The inhabitants offered a fine of 20 lakh *dirhams*, but could not prevent the killing of hundreds of Qarmathians, nor the destruction of their place of worship.[7] The next year (1006-7) Biji Rai, the ruler of Bhera, emerging out of his fort, came out to fight the Ghaznavid aggression. He fought for three days in the open and then fortified his position in the fort. When forced to leave the garrison, he escaped to a forest and killed himself with a dagger. Sultan Mahmud occupied Bhera and placed it under Sukhpal (the son of Anandpal), who had converted to Islam in a gesture of loyalty. The arrangement turned out to be fragile, as Sukhpal revolted against his new masters and abjured his new faith. He was defeated and captured (1007) by the Ghaznavids who imprisoned him for life. His father Anandpal, in an attempt to secure the release of his son and to reduce the Ghaznavid pressure on his kingdom, made an offer of military assistance to his enemies who were then fighting against Kashghar. He prepared to send 5,000 cavalry, 10,000 foot soldiers, and 100 elephants with the possibility of doubling this number. It appeared that the proposal was not pursued.[8]

By now, three principalities of Panjab – Waihind, Bhera and Multan – had been severely weakened owing to the Ghaznavid invasions, though they had provided some support to one another in this crisis. Having learnt their lesson in real politic, the Hindushahis now mobilized a large number of Indian states –Delhi, Ajmer, Kanauj, Kalinjar, Gwalior and Ujjain – in order to meet a common threat. In addition to 30,000 Gakkhars and other tribes, the Hindu women gave their ornaments as a contribution to the war effort. In the battle fought (1009) near Peshawar, the Gakkhars penetrated the Ghaznavid ranks with their bare hands and feet, accounting for the deaths of nearly 5,000 enemy troopers. But the sudden withdrawal of Anandpal's elephant, owing to the effect of naphtha balls, caused a panic among the Indian army. In the course of its disorderly flight, nearly 20,000 soldiers were killed.[9] Sultan Mahmud followed up his success by effecting the final subjugation of Multan. In this attack (1010), thousands of Qarmathians were either killed or taken as prisoners to different forts. As the resistance of western and central Panjab was wiped out, the principalities of Kangra and Thanesar, which included two prominent sacred centres famed for the wealth of their temples, were exposed to Ghaznavid incursions. In fact, Kangra could offer little opposition as its troops had not yet returned from Peshawar. The Brahmins, having withstood a siege for seven days, surrendered the fort to the Ghaznavids, who acquired thousands of maunds of precious metals from its ancient shrine.[10] After two years, when Sultan Mahmud marched towards Thanesar, he benefited from an agreement with the Hindushahis. Anandpal not only provided safe passage to the Ghaznavid troops as well as material supplies, but also sent his brother with a contingent of 2,000 horsemen. However, his offer of an annual tribute of 50 elephants and jewels in return for the safety of the temple of Thanesar, was rejected. The Hindus, owing to their devotion to the idol of Chakraswami, had the same veneration for the place as the Muslims had for Mecca. During the course of its advance towards Thanesar, the Ghaznavid army overcame stiff resistance put up by the chief of Dera on the Satluj near the hills.[11] The invaders entered Thanesar unopposed and, as the local Rai had fled, they plundered the town and carried away the idol as a trophy.[12]

With the accession of Trilochanpal (r. 1013-21), the Hindushahis amended their relation with the Ghaznavids. Owing to the assertive intervention of prince Bhimpal, they adopted an aggressive stance towards the Ghaznavids and turned towards Kashmir for mutual support. In the winter of 1013, Sultan Mahmud marched to Nandanah, a strong fort at the junction of two hills in the Salt Range, where Bhimpal had entrenched himself. After several days of fighting, the invaders drew Bhimpal out and, neutralizing a line of elephants and laying mines under the ramparts, occupied the fort. Sultan Mahmud sealed his victory by placing a garrison in the citadel.[13] Trilochanpal, who met with a major reverse in the upper reaches of the Jhelam even with the military aid from Kashmir, withdrew eastwards to seek shelter in the hills. Sultan Mahmud, having swept away the defences of all the principalities in Panjab, penetrated the rich lands beyond the Jamuna. He could dispatch plundering expeditions into these areas only if he could exercise a firm control over Panjab, which lay between Afghanistan and the Gangetic plains. The political situation in northern India favoured the realization of this object. Trilochanpal, who had formed alliances with the chiefs of Sherwa and Kalinjar, failed to withstand the Ghaznavid expansion and died after the battle of Rahib, while his son Bhimpal took shelter in Ajmer. Therefore, Sultan Mahmud annexed (1021) Panjab to the Ghaznavid empire. In order to establish a regular administration in the region, he posted a governor in Lahore, appointed officers in other places, and assigned garrisons for military strongholds.[14] The city of Lahore was entrusted to the care of Sultan's favourite Malik Ayaz, who rebuilt the fort and beautified the urban space. In the newly struck coins, the following Kufic inscription renamed Lahore as Mahmudpur.[15]

Al Qadir
There is no god but God and Muhammad the Prophet of God
The right hand of the state and asylum of faith Mahmud
In the name of God this dirham was struck at Mahmudpur in 418 AH

Such measures formalized the extinction of the Hindushahis, who earned a respectful tribute from Alberuni: 'The Hindu Shahiya dynasty is now extinct, and of the whole house there is no longer the slightest remnant in existence. We must say that, in all their grandeur, they never slackened in the ardent desire of doing that which is good and right, that they were men of noble sentiment and noble bearing.' Alberuni's admiration was based on Anandpal's offer of military assistance to Sultan Mahmud, even while the relations between them were strained,[16] so that the Ghaznavid ruler could stand up against his Turkish rivals in Khurasan.

The new Ghaznavid rulers of Panjab, after enjoying five years of peace, faced opposition from the Jats of Multan, who had harassed the Ghaznavid army returning from Somnath laden with a rich booty. Since their country was intersected by several rivers and they were known for their expertise in river warfare,[17] Sultan Mahmud made adequate preparations for a punitive expedition. On approaching the Indus, he ordered the construction of 1,400 boats, each of which was provided with six iron spikes on the prows and sides, so as to prevent the enemy from boarding. Each boat was manned by twenty archers and five men, armed with naphtha balls. The Jats, having received the intelligence of the Ghaznavid mobilization, equipped themselves for the impending confrontation. They sent their wives, children and goods to the safety of distant islands in the Indus and launched as many as 4,000 boats that were properly manned and armed. Sultan Mahmud blocked the upper course of the Indus with a flotilla of boats and placed two detachments of cavalry, supported by elephants, to guard the banks.[18] As the two fleets met, a terrible conflict followed. The Jats fought with courage, but their boats were overturned owing to the impact of projecting spikes. Not only this, they were mowed down by showers of arrows. Some of their boats caught fire, while others sank into the water. The Jats tried to escape by land, but their path was blocked by enemy detachments and, as a result, they were pushed back to the river. A majority of them were killed, while the remaining were either captured or managed to escape. Their families, which had been sheltered in the islands, fell into the hands of the victors along with the spoils of war.

Identifying the factors underlying Sultan Mahmud's Indian invasions, Mohammad Habib observed, 'His real aim was the establishment of a Turko-Persian empire and the Indian expeditions were a means to that end.' First, they gave him the prestige of a holy warrior that enabled him to outclass a large number of Ajami princes. Second, the wealth of Indian temples secured the financial position of his kingdom and enabled him to raise a vast army, which could not be resisted by minor rivals. Moreover, he understood that the conquest of Indian territories was not possible without the support of a native Muslim population. He carried away all that centuries of Indian industries had accumulated, leaving the Indians to rebuild as best as they could 'the ruined fortifications of their cities and the fallen altars of their gods'. In Habib's view, the annexation of Panjab to the Ghaznavid empire as late as 1021-2 proved his non-territorial ambitions. In the beginning of his military enterprise in India, he expected that his alliance with Anandpal would enable him to penetrate the Indo-Gangetic plain. Since the alliance failed owing to Anadpal's death, he felt the necessity of a foothold elsewhere. Though Panjab could be the only such region, Sultan Mahmud appeared to have looked at Lahore and Multan simply as robber's perches, from where he could plunge into Hindustan and Gujarat at will. In contrast, his campaigns in Central Asia revealed evidence of a different policy, as they always led to annexations, followed by the establishment of his government over conquered territories, very often under his personal supervision.[19] However, as it unfolded, Ghaznavid rule over Panjab across the century and a half, showed that the cities of the region turned out to be much more than robber's perches, a situation that could not have been anticipated even by the genius of Sultan Mahmud.

During the early Ghaznavid period, there was no permanent civil administration in India. Incomes of the state, both plunder and tribute, were irregular and often extacted by force. The payment usually stipulated in peace treaties between Sultan Mahmud and the princes, assumed the form of elephants and indigo, besides cash. Towards the end of his reign, the Sultan tried to establish a more permanent control over Panjab.[20] Keeping in view the unique geographical position of the region, the administrative functions were bifurcated to prevent concentration of power in a single hand. The civil administration, including financial matters, was entrusted to a Persian officer, Qazi Shirazi. Essentially manned by Turkish slave captains, the army, was placed under the command of a distinguished general, Aryaruq. The two officers were made independent of each other, so that they directly reported to Ghazni. Bul Qasim Hakim was appointed the chief news writer (*sahib barid*) to keep the central government informed about important happenings and, thus, to act as a check on the two officers. However, the arrangement did not work. Qazi Shirazi and Aryaruq could not agree on the demarcation of their respective jurisdictions and each felt free to encroach on the authority of the other. From the perspective of the Sultan, Aryaruq had not only become disobedient and arrogant, he had also shed innocent blood. The news writers did not dare to report his oppressive acts, as they feared losing their own lives. Since he had taken possession of the roads, no one could pass without his permission. He did not report to Ghazni even when he had been summoned by the Sultan. When any coercive measure was taken against him, he reacted by creating a great disturbance. The kingdom's *wazir* Khwaja Hasan Maimandi managed to allure Aryaruq back to Balkh where he was arrested and thrown (1031) into prison. His property was confiscated, and it took three days to make an inventory of his possessions. His slaves of the first grade were imprisoned, while those of the second grade were distributed among other commanders. Special auditors were dispatched to Panjab to bring his reputed stock of wealth.[21]

Sultan Masud (r. 1030-41) held detailed discussions with Maimandi on choosing a suitable successor to Aryaruq. Hindustan could not be left without a governor, as the office carried importance and honour. Since Aryaruq had maintained a great retinue and commanded much prestige, his successor had to be a trained and experienced general. The Sultan proposed the name of Ahmad Niyaltigin. Though this man had not trained under generals, he had served Sultan Mahmud as a treasurer and, having accompanied him in all his journeys, knew the ways of the late king. The Wazir had no choice but to give his consent, though he had reservations about Niyaltigin, as he had failed to submit his accounts for several years and had been slapped with a fine. Accordingly, it was felt that Niyaltigin must give a promise on oath and leave his son at Ghazni as a surety. Equally important, he had to understand the circumstances in which he was being deputed to Panjab. Qazi Shirazi, who regarded himself as self sufficient, wished the generals to be under his command. Since he dealt with a weak man like Abdullah Karatigin, he managed to monopolize all authority. He was unnerved at the arrival of a tough officer like Aryaruq. He requested Ghazni to depute a revenue collector and accountant general to Lahore. In response, Ghazni sent a team of Abul Fateh, Damghani and Abul Farj Kirmani, but they could not cope with Aryaruq. For his part, Aryaruq paid the price for conducting official matters for his personal benefit.[22]

The new officer was given instructions about his new role, which was different from that of Shirazi, who wore a soldier's uniform without being a commander. Panjab needed a general, a man of renown and dignity, to lead the army and exact tribute. The functions of Shirazi were confined to oversee civil affairs and collect revenue. But the general was required to make war, take tribute, seize elephants, and chastise refractory elements. Once Niyaltigin had understood the demands of his office, he was granted a robe of honour which was more magnificent than the one given to Aryaruq. It comprised a golden girdle and a cap with two points, besides kettledrums, flags, and other symbols given to generals of the army. He was handed two documents, viz., the letter of appointment and a solemn oath that was duly signed by him. He was directed to avoid any interference in political and revenue matters, and to confine himself to military work, so that he did not provide any excuse to Shirazi for pulling him down. He must have been aware that Bul Qasim Hakim, the superintendent of the newswriters, reported all occurrences in due time and all royal orders were routed through him. What ever Niyaltigin had to report to Ghazni, he was expected to do so in detail, so that a categorical response could be sent to him. His retinue included three distinct elements – some Dailami chiefs, who being strangers, had to be kept away from the court; nobles about whom there were some apprehensions; and slaves who had been convicted of misconduct, but had been freed for their rehabilitation. These slaves were to be treated with kindness, but none of them could go beyond the Chenab without permission or the orders of the Sultan. They had to be taken along on any military expedition, but could not be allowed to mingle with the army of Lahore, nor allowed to drink wine or play polo (*chaughan*).

Niyaltigin was directed to deploy spies and observers to keep a watch over them. He was to treat this duty as essential, not to be neglected in any case. He would receive the assistance of the chief news writer Bul Qasim Hakim in the discharge of his functions. On reaching his post, he was asked to report all events, including the response of his subordinates to royal orders. He was allowed to take along with him his wife and children. His son was left at home under the care of a tutor, a friend, and a confidential person. This arrangement, it was hoped, would prevent the son from associating with bodyguards, and provide a lot of liberty to his father. On the occasion of Niyaltigin's departure for Panjab, his large retinue – military captains, Dailamis and 130 slaves – was inspected by the Sultan. The contingent of slaves, who marched under three officers of the Sultan, had three flags with the device of lions and spears according to the fashion of royal slaves. They were followed by the general's kettledrums and banners that were made of red cloth and had gilded balls on their tops. This section was accompanied by seventy-five slaves and richly caparisoned camels and dromedaries.[23]

Armed with the support and advice of Sultan Masud and Wazir Maimandi, Niyaltigin arrived in Lahore and began to function as the army commander of Hindustan. He maintained his troops, including a detachment of sturdy slaves, in an impressive state. He discharged his official duties with conspicuous boldness and pride, but did not yield any space to his civilian counterpart, Shirazi. Not surprisingly, differences surfaced between the two officers regarding command of the army. Shirazi declared that the command belonged to Abdullah Karatigin as laid in the royal decree. But Niyaltigin rejected this because the office had been conferred on him by the Sultan and he was superior to Abdullah Karatigin in every respect. Every soldier, including the person in reference, had to march under his banner. Since the army of Lahore and the warriors were solidly behind Niyaltigin, he did not hesitate to irritate Shirazi and planned a military expedition to a distant place. Shirazi lost no time in preparing a complaint, which was delivered by his messengers to Sultan Masud at Bust on the route to Herat and Nishapur. In consultation with the Wazir, the Sultan examined the complaint and sent a stern response, reiterating the demarcation between civil and military affairs in

Panjab. The job of Shirazi was to manage revenue affairs and he had nothing to do with the command of the army. At the same time, Niyaltigin was advised to undertake military expeditions, to extract tribute from the Thakurs and, thus, to bring large sums into the treasury. In support of the official position, the letter quoted a proverb, 'There must be no contention between the door and the house.' Niyaltigin marched out of Lahore and, crossing the Ganga, reached as far as Benares. All along the route, he extracted tribute from the Thakurs. The troops plundered the markets of drapers, perfumers and jewellers. The soldiers grabbed gold, silver, jewels and perfume for themselves.[24]

Shirazi, driven by sheer jealousy, sent his messengers to Nishapur with the report that Niyaltigin had obtained immense wealth and, having concealed a bulk of it, had sent only a small portion to the court. He claimed to have prepared this report based on the information collected by his agents (including accountants and the chief of couriers) who secretly accompanied the army. In addition to this, Shirazi levelled a number of other allegations against Niyaltigin. The general was said to have secretly dispatched his men to Turkistan to procure Turkish slaves for him. He had acquired seventy slaves by then and more were expected to arrive. He had also developed friendly relations with the Turkomans who were disloyal towards the Ghaznavid state. Since he called himself the son of Sultan Mahmud, there were doubts about his intentions. The mind of Sultan Masud was poisoned against the general, while the news of the gains of the Benares campaign failed to neutralize the false suspicions. In fact, the Sultan learnt from fresh letters that Niyaltigin had reached Lahore and a large number of turbulent men of all classes, including the Turkomans, had flocked around him. Since his power and dignity were increasing by the day, the central government was asked to intervene before the situation went out of hand. The Sultan convened a meeting of his commanders to discuss the means of suppressing the rebellion of Niyaltigin. Most of them were reluctant to march to Lahore in the hot weather, even though a strong body of troops was present in the city.[25]

In these circumstances, Tilak volunteered for the task,

because he wished to make some return for the favours he had received from the Ghaznavid regime. Moreover, being a native of Hindustan, he would not be troubled by the hot weather and could travel across Panjab with ease. Those present regarded Tilak as fit for the job, a famous man who could wield the sword and possessed both men and material. Sultan Masud readily accepted Tilak's offer which, in his view, had shamed numerous grandees who themselves would not do anything. He promised to provide a strong army, ample finances and other necessities to Tilak, so that he could put an end to the rebellion in Panjab. He also vowed to raise his rank in the official hierarchy, despite the opposition of other nobles. Tilak drew up a plan of his military expedition, which was promptly approved by the Sultan. He was also authorized to take all steps that were needed to secure the allegiance of the Hindu soldiers. The secretary of state, who drafted the official documents in Persian, prepared the papers regarding Tilak's appointment, authority and privileges.[26]

It would be appropriate to trace the career of this remarkable man. The son of a barber, Tilak was handsome in appearance and eloquent in speech. He wrote an excellent hand, both in Hindi and Persian. He had lived for a long time in Kashmir where he acquired proficiency in disguise, eroticism and witchcraft. He entered the service of Qazi Shirazi but, owing to differences with him, wished to leave him. He was assisted by Wazir Maimandi to present himself before Sultan Mahmud and also heard his complaint against Shirazi. He became a confidant of the Wazir, who employed him as his secretary and interpreter in dealings with Hindus. He acquired a considerable importance in the Wazir's office where he exchanged messages and handled difficult matters. Even after the temporary eclipse of his master, he remained in the good books of Sultan Mahmud, who attached him as an interpreter with Prince Bahram. During the reign of Sultan Masud (r. 1030-41), he brought Hindu chiefs under the Ghaznavid rule. He was promoted as the commander of an army and was granted a gold embroidered robe and a jeweled necklace, besides a tent and umbrella. Kettledrums were beaten at his abode in accordance with the custom of Hindu chiefs, while his banners were ornamented with gilded tops. Being elevated to a high position, he sat amidst nobles in the privy council and was assigned administrative duties. Baihaqi has argued that Tilak did not suffer any setback on account of his being the son of a barber. If with his character and wisdom, he had been gifted with a good social background, he would have risen still further in the bureaucratic structure. After all, the nobility of birth was of no use without learning, propriety and spirit.[27]

The conflict between Tilak and Niyaltigin in the heart of Panjab assumed significance owing to two factors – the crucial role of the Jats, and regular correspondence between Lahore and Ghazni. In the middle of 1033, it was learnt that Niyaltigin had returned from Benares to Lahore at the head of his troops. Along with his counsellors and followers, Shirazi took shelter in the fort of Mandkakur. Owing to the perpetual fighting between the combatants, the entire neighbourhood was in a state of turmoil. When Sultan Masud was preoccupied with celebrations of Id, he received a dispatch from Lahore, informing that Niyaltigin had occupied the fort. It was also reported that Tilak had mustered a powerful army from every quarter and, advancing to the site of the military action, reached within a distance of 2 *kos* of the rebel force. The Sultan sent a letter to Tilak directing him to proceed with all speed. Adding a postscript with his own hand in his characteristic style, he gave fresh instructions to Tilak that were concealed even from his confidential secretary.[28] The Sultan ordered Tilak to expedite the operations against Niyaltigin, who should be driven out of Lahore. Shirazi was asked to leave the fort, but continue his exertions so that the Sultan's anxiety about the rebellion was relieved. In September 1034, the Sultan received letters from three independent sources – Tilak, Shirazi, and his secret service – informing him that Niyaltigin had been slain, his son had been taken prisoner, and his Turkoman followers had been subdued. The letters provided the following details of the punitive measures.

As soon as Tilak arrived at Lahore, he assumed the offensive. He captured several Muslims who were followers of Niyaltigin. He ordered their hands to be cut off. This draconian step sent a wave of terror among Niyaltigin's men, who deserted their master and appealed for mercy. In a follow up measure, Tilak organized matters relating to revenue and police. He sent a big detachment, comprising largely of Hindus, to pursue the rebels. During the course of the pursuit, a number of skirmishes took place. Niyaltigin, having suffered numerous reverses, took to flight and, in the process, suffered from desertions. The Turkomans left him in a body and, pleading for forgiveness, managed to save their lives. Tilak sent letters to the Jats, who had earlier joined the ranks of the rebels, to give up a lost cause. He announced a reward of 50,000 *dirhams* to any person who would bring the rebellious governor or his head. The announcement had the desired effect. The Jats abandoned their recent alliance with Niyaltigin and, joined by every kind of malcontent, merged with the pursuers. The situation came to such a pass that Niyaltigin was left with only 300 followers, including his personal attendants. One day he arrived on the bank of a river and intended to cross it on his elephants. He was accompanied by 200 men, while 2,000 or 3,000 mounted Jats closed in upon him. As he plunged into the water, the Jats attacked him from two or three sides, largely with the object of seizing his money and possessions. Reduced to dire straits, Niyaltigin tried to kill his son with his own hands. The Jats prevented him from doing so and, in a swift move, carried away the son who was riding an elephant. Not only this, they fell upon Niyaltigin with arrows, swords and spears. Though Niyaltigin defended himself with exemplary valour, he was killed and his head was cut off. His followers were slain or made captive, while a huge amount of wealth fell into the hands of the Jats.

The Jat chief sent his messengers to Tilak, who was present close by, and conveyed the news of the occurrence. Tilak was delighted and sent some men to demand the head of Niyaltigin and the custody of his son. However, the Jats asked for the reward of 50,000 *dirhams* as agreed upon. Tilak wanted the Jats to give up their demand, as they had already acquired a huge stock of wealth belonging to Niyaltigin. The two sides negotiated through their messengers, who twice went forward and backward. Ultimately, Tilak agreed to send a sum of 10,000 *dirhams* to the Jats. The stipulated amount of money was delivered to the Jats, who handed over

Niyaltigin's head and his son to the victors. Tilak, having achieved his object, returned to Lahore and took measures to settle the country after the recent turmoil. Sultan Masud sent congratulatory letters to Tilak and his associates, who were asked to come to the Ghaznavid court along with the trophies of war.[29]

The Ghaznavid regime, having learnt a lesson from the recent disturbances, undertook two steps: the abolition of dual government, and occupation of the fort of Hansi – to consolidate its rule in Panjab. The practice of bifurcating the administrative functions between a military commander and a revenue officer was given up, as it had led to dissension and rebellion. Sultan Masud appointed (September 1036) his son Prince Majdud as the governor of Panjab, with supreme authority over both military and civil affairs. The new governor was to be assisted by three chamberlains – Mansur as his secretary, Sarhang Muhammad as the paymaster of the troops, and Sad Salman (the father of the poet Masud Sad Salman) as accountant and treasurer. As the symbols of his exalted office, Prince Majdud was honoured with a standard, kettledrum, elephant and seat. He also received a dress from the Sultan while taking the permission to join his duties. On his way to Panjab, he took along Rashid (the son of Khwarizm Shah), so that he could be kept under his surveillance in the city of Lahore.[30] Equipped with an impressive entourage of officers and soldiers personally loyal to him,[31] Prince Majdud aimed at building a power base for himself. He held the governorship for nearly five years till his death (11 August 1041), though he visited Ghazni a number of times. A year before his demise, he led a force of 2,000 soldiers to secure Multan.

In 1037 Sultan Masud marched to Panjab in order to occupy the fort of Hansi. His leading ministers did not favour the campaign owing to the disturbed state of Khurasan, Ray and Jubbal. They felt that if the Turkomans conquered a province or even a village, then this loss could not be compensated even by ten victories over Hansi. However, the Sultan rejected the unanimous advice of his counsellors on the ground that he had taken a vow to occupy Hansi and, therefore, he was bound to accomplish this task in all circumstances. Travelling via Kabul (mid November

1037), he camped at Dinarkotah on the banks of the Jhelam. He stayed there for two weeks due to sickness. During this period, he abstained from the consumption of alcohol and ordered the entire stock of wine to be thrown in the Jhelam, besides the destruction of all other instruments of pleasure. A detachment was sent to capture the fort of Chakki Hindu, the exact location of which was uncertain. After marching for three weeks, the Sultan reached Hansi and, setting up camp at the foot of the fort, laid a siege. The two sides engaged in frequent armed encounters that were quite intense in severity. The garrison made desperate attempts to defend its position without relaxing any effort. On the other hand, slaves of the Ghaznavid royal household displayed conspicuous gallantry. Ultimately the invaders planted mines at five spots and thus brought down the boundary wall. They stormed into the fort wielding their swords. The Brahmins and other notables were slain, while women and children were made captives. Treasure was distributed among the soldiers. The occupation of the fort of Hansi – reputed in Hindustan as the 'The Virgin' because no one had succeeded in occupying it[32] – opened the path of the Ghaznavids into the neighbouring principalities. Placing the fort under a trusted captain, Sultan Masud marched against Sonepat. Since the local chief Dipal Hari fled into the jungle, his treasure fell into the hands of the invaders. Dipal Hari managed to escape with his life, but most of his retinue was taken prisoner. The Sultan proceeded against another chief, Ram Rai, who sent a large ransom of gold and elephants, but excused himself from personal appearance on account of old age.[33] As a result of these military gains, the eastern boundary of the Ghaznavid empire reached as far as the Jamuna, while the position of Prince Majdud in Lahore was significantly strengthened.

Unnerved by the Ghaznavid defeat at Dandanqan and the rise of the Saljuqids in Khurasan, Sultan Masud failed to stay put in Ghazni. Towards the close of 1040, he decided to leave for India along with his family and treasure. He intended to spend the winter at a number of places, Waihind, Marminara, Peshawar and Giri, and return in the spring after mobilizing a fresh army. His ministers tried to dissuade him because his Indian soldiers and slave troops could not be relied upon for the safe transport of the royal family and valuable cargo. The Sultan remained adamant and, loading his wealth and goods on hundreds of camels, marched towards Panjab. When a part of the cavalcade crossed the Indus, a section of the army comprising the palace slaves and led by the Turkish commander Anushtigin Balkhi, broke into a mutiny. The rebels plundered the royal treasure and overpowered the loyalists in an armed encounter at Marigalah. They captured Sultan Masud and sent him to the fort of Giri, where he was put to death (17 January 1041) within a month.[34] Muhammad, the brother of the deceased, was proclaimed ruler, but he could retain his position only for a short time during which his son exercised the real power.

Sultan Maudud (r. 1041-9), the son of Sultan Masud, returned from Tukharistan to Ghazni and initiated a movement of revenge. In a battle (19 March 1041) fought at Nangrahar, Prince Maudud overwhelmed the forces of the new regime. He captured all his rivals – Muhammad, his sons and military commanders – and punished them with death. Prince Maudud assumed the reins of the government in his hands, but his writ was challenged in Panjab by Prince Majdud, who ruled over a vast area extending eastwards upto Thanesar and Hansi. Sultan Maudud marched to Lahore to contend with his brother who, however, died (14 August 1041) before the eruption of hostilities. Ayaz, the chief advisor of Prince Majdud, also expired soon after. Faqih Saliti, the new governor of Lahore, was joined by the local garrison and the Ghaznavid troops. The combined force suppressed a rebellion of the erstwhile Qarmathian rulers and retrieved Multan for the Ghaznavids. Appointing Muhammad Halimi as the governor of Multan, Faqih Saliti returned to Lahore and, on the way, chastised the Jats and other local elements on the middle Indus.[35]

In spite of these gains, the Ghaznavid hold on Panjab remained weak. The local chiefs, taking advantage of the dissensions in the Ghaznavid ruling family, made a resolute attempt to recover their principalities and power. The ruler of Delhi, having garnered the support of other chiefs, ousted the Ghaznavid officers from Thanesar and Hansi. The united force followed up this success and, penetrating into the hills, besieged the fort of Nagarkot, held by a Ghaznavid garrison. During a blockade of four months, the defenders suffered from a scarcity of provisions and lack of reinforcements from Lahore, and were forced to capitulate. The ruler of Nagarkot recovered his sovereignty and, installing a new idol at the famous temple, revived the traditional pilgrimage of the Hindus. As the next logical step, the confederacy of three rulers mustered an army of 10,000 horsemen and innumerable foot soldiers. They placed the city of Lahore under a siege which continued for seven months. Since the boundary wall had been pulled down, the defenders exerted themselves to protect the townships and streets. According to Ibn-i Asir, the defenders succeeded in sowing the seeds of discord among the besiegers. One of the chiefs returned to Ghaznavid allegiance, the second was besieged in a fortress until he surrendered, and the third was slain in battle along with 5,000 of his men.[36] In this manner, the Ghaznavid regime overpowered the combined military strength of the local chiefs and managed to survive in the western and central parts of Panjab.

A historian of the early seventeenth century has attributed the recovery of Nagarkot by the local rulers to the clever manipulation of Hindu religious sentiments. According to this narrative, the Raja of Delhi, encouraged by the decline of the Ghaznavid state and instigation of a Brahmin advisor, cooked up a fantastic story. Having summoned his nobles and officers, he related a vision in which he saw the idol of Nagarkot. The idol told him that it had been staying in Ghazni where it succeeded in weakening the Muslims; its present aim was to return to its original home and assist the Hindus in ousting the Muslims from there. The Raja's speech had the desired effect among the gathering who celebrated the news like a major festival. He ordered the sculptors to carve an idol similar to the one belonging to Nagarkot. Equipped with this idol, he went to Hansi and Thanesar and, accompanied by other Hindu rulers, reached Nagarkot. The cunning Brahmin advisor installed the new idol in a garden and, through the gardeners, the news spread about the return of the idol. People began to pay obeisance to the idol and made offerings of precious metals and jewels, as if the troubled soul of Sultan Mahmud had come all the way from Ghazni. The Brahmin whispered to every devotee that the idol had ordered the Hindus to expel the Muslims from the fort, its sacred abode. Thus inspired, the Hindus redoubled their efforts at the siege. The long enduring Muslims, failing to get any aid from Lahore, relinquished the fort. The temple, which had been pulled down by Sultan Mahmud, was repaired and the idol was installed in it. A wave of religious fervour spread in all directions, attracting Hindu pilgrims in droves. So strong was the faith of the Hindus in the idol that they did not start any work without its permission. Following suit, ignorant Muslims also made offerings to the idol and saw it as the agency for fulfilling their desires.[37]

The death (18 December 1049) of Sultan Maudud inaugurated a phase of political instability when, owing to palace intrigues, four Sultans ascended the throne of Ghazni in ten years. Emboldened by this crisis in the royal household, a prominent military commander Ali bin Rabia gave shape to his ambitious designs on Panjab. He plundered the treasury and, carrying as much gold and jewels as he could, collected a band of household troops and also won over a number of petty chiefs. Leading this armed brigade, he marched to Peshawar where numerous local inhabitants joined him, so that he was able to raise a sizeable army. He entered the vast plains of Panjab and attacked the Afghans, who had ravaged Multan and Sind, besides assuming autonomy in other areas. The chastisement of the Afghans enabled Ali bin Rabia to establish his own rule in these two provinces till the accession of Sultan Abdul Rashid (r. 1049-52). When the Sultan was securely placed on the throne, he persuaded Ali bin Rabia to return to Ghazni and reiterate his former allegiance. In his place, the Sultan deputed Anushtigin Hajib to administer the territories lying on the east of the Indus. This governor, being equipped with an armed force, arrived at Lahore. Soon after, he marched to Nagarkot and besieged the fort. On the sixth day, he scaled the walls and, gaining entry, occupied the place by assault. The governor displayed his strength, both political and military, by successfully intervening in the politics of the royal court at Ghazni, as indicated by the following development.

At this time, Sultan Abdul Rashid and nine members of the royal family were killed by Tughril Hajib, who had been sent to occupy Sistan. The usurper not only ascended the throne, but also forcibly married a princess who was the daughter of Sultan Masud. He wrote a letter to Anushtigin Hajib, seeking his allegiance to his authority. But Anushtigin Hajib rejected the proposal outright and, instead, developed contacts with all the people – nobles and the daughter of Sultan Masud – who were loyal to the ruling family and urged them to avenge the murder of the late Sultan. In response to the appeal, the partisans of the previous regime formulated a plan which led to the assassination of Tughril Hajib after a rule of just forty days. Anushtigin Hajib returned to Ghazni with his troops. Owing to his efforts, a meeting of the nobles was convened. Three princes from the line of Subuktgin were released from a prison and one of them Farrukhzad was enthroned. Anushtigin Hajib, who was promoted as the head of the administration, won important victories against the Saljuqids and thus stabilized the Ghaznavid empire.[38]

Sultan Ibrahim (r. 1059-99), who enjoyed a long reign of four decades, personally led a military expedition to Panjab and targeted three places. In the summer of 1079, he besieged the fortress of Ajodhan, a town which later on acquired fame as the ferry of Shaikh Fariduddin Ganj-i Shakar. Located at a distance of 120 *farsakhs* from Lahore, it was well fortified and inaccessible. It was large in size and boasted of 10,000 warriors who offered a prolonged resistance from the base of the fortress. The Sultan led several sharp attacks on the defenders who were forced to surrender (13 August 1079) the fortress. Thereafter, the Sultan advanced towards the outlying regions of India and reached the fortress of Rubal. Situated on the summit of a lofty hill, it had a jungle below it and a river behind it. It could be attacked only through a narrow defile, defended by war elephants. The fortress was garrisoned by several thousand warriors. The invaders cut their way through the jungle and imposed a blockade. Since the citadel stood on a soft rock, miners built passages under the walls and thus brought them down. The Sultan, having exerted pressure through all methods of warfare, captured the fortress and brought out the defenders. After this victory, he proceeded to the neighbouring town of Darrah, which was inhabited by people of Khwarizmian origin and whose ancestors had been banished here by Afrasiyab, the Turk. The fortress had a lake with a circumference of a mile (half a *farsakh*) and a depth beyond measure. Its water, which fulfilled the needs of the inhabitants and cattle, did not diminish in any weather. The invaders could not approach the place for three months on account of heavy rains and, as a result, faced great hardship. At the end of this period, the Sultan took the town by assault amidst intense fighting and heavy casualties. In addition to a large quantity of valuables, the Sultan carried away innumerable captives as slaves.[39]

Masud Sad Salman (1046-1121), the distinguished poet, was intimately associated with Panjab as well as the Ghaznavid ruling elite. His father Sad Salman came to Lahore as an accountant (*mustaufi*) in the staff of Prince Majdud, who had been sent as the governor of Panjab by Sultan Masud in 1935-6. He was reputed to have served the Ghaznavid regime for over fifty years and to have acquired a landed estate through hard work. Masud Sad Salman, during his long and chequered career, served as a panegyrist to his first patron Prince Mahmud and five Ghaznavid rulers – Ibrahim, Masud III, Shirzad, Arsalan Shah and Bahram Shah. During two phases, he fell from favour and, as a consequence, suffered long terms of exile and imprisonment. It was difficult to identify the causes of his punishment. It appeared that, during a visit to Ghazni, he managed to rouse the jealousy of the poet Rashidi, whose partisans started a slanderous campaign against him. Prince Mahmud, being influenced by this propaganda, ordered punitive action against Salman. His house was pulled down, while his property and belongings were confiscated. He was denied the permission to leave for Haj, as it was seen as an excuse to defect to the court of the Saljuqids in Khurasan. The beleaguered poet travelled all the way to Ghazni and, appealing to Sultan Ibrahim, sought redressal for the injustice inflicted by Prince Mahmud. His appeal was rejected by the Sultan, who ordered him to be thrown in prison. He spent the next ten years (1088-98) in three Ghaznavid fortresses – Dahak, Su, and Nay. He was released only at the death of Sultan Ibrahim. On returning to Panjab, he entered the service of Prince Shirzad, the new governor of Hindustan. He was favoured by the deputy governor Abu Nasr Parsi, who facilitated his appointment as the administrator of Jalandhar. He held this post for a short time. He was condemned to imprisonment along with the dependants of Abu Nasr Parsi, who had been dismissed from his office. Salman spent the next seven years (until 1107) in the prison of Maranj. Following his release he served four Ghaznavid rulers as a panegyrist and librarian. Thus, he spent the last fifteen years of his life at Ghazni, enjoying the fruit of his restoration to office and dignity.[40]

The nostalgia of Salman for the two Ghaznavid cities, Lahore and Ghazni, was relative, owing to the instability of time and space. When he was in Lahore, he longed to be in Ghazni. But when he was posted in Jalandhar, he felt attracted to Lahore. During his short stay at Jalandhar, he composed an ode (*masnavi*) describing a courtly gathering of his patron Prince Shirzad, the governor of Hindustan from 1099 to 1114. Comparing this assembly with paradise, he underscored its opulence and liveliness. While lamenting his own absence from the scene, he hoped to lessen his sadness by coming to Lahore and witnessing the boisterous assembly of his master.[41] Notwithstanding his love for Lahore, he was not satisfied with his life at the provincial court and, therefore, nursed an ambition of shifting to the central court at Ghazni. This was possible as he was conscious of his superiority over the poets of Ghazni and he could merely follow his master to that city in the wake of his enthronement. He was willing to suffer the hazards of the journey from Lahore to Ghazni for the sake of joining his master, who was seen as a beloved.[42] In one of his most poignant poems, composed in prison, he visualized Lahore as a mother who had been separated from her child. He could not understand how such a city could exist without its bright sun and beautiful flowers.[43] In another prison poem, Salman imagined Lahore as his beloved who alone was capable of understanding his painful ordeal. When incarcerated in the darkness of prison in distant lands, he expressed his longing for this city.[44]

During the reign of Sultan Masud III (r. 1099-1115), the governorship of Hindustan was bestowed on Hajib Tughantigin. This officer advanced from Lahore and, crossing the Ganga, plundered the cities that had been targeted by Sultan Mahmud a century ago.[45] After the demise of the Sultan, his three sons were locked in a power struggle and, in the process, facilitated the intervention of the Saljuqids and the rise of the Ghorids. Malik Arsalan (r. 1116-17), who replaced his brother Shirzad on the throne, failed to prevent the Saljuqid expansion and, therefore, retreated to Lahore.[46] He mobilized troops from the region and succeeded in recovering Ghazni. He was defeated by the Saljuqids and killed by his brother Bahram Shah. The new ruler Bahram Shah (r. 1117-57), having received the assistance of the Saljuqids, accepted their overlordship.[47] But his writ did not run in Panjab, because the Ghaznavid governor Muhammad Bahalim (who had supported Malik Arsalan in the power struggle) refused to recognize his accession to the throne. The Sultan was forced to suppress two rebellions of this officer. Early in his reign, Bahram Shah marched to Panjab and captured (11 January 1119) Bahalim after a decisive battle. However, he reinstated the governor in view of his bright reputation as a military commander and his unrivalled experience of conditions in India.[48] However, this submission turned out to be short lived. Rising up in revolt, Bahalim transferred his treasure to Nagaur in the Siwaliks and gathered an army of Arabs, Persians, Afghans and Khaljis. He also garnered support from numerous Indian chiefs, so that he managed to collect 70,000 men including Hindus and Muslims. He took position in a marshy tract, which was created by flooding, somewhere on the confluence of rivers near Multan. The Sultan expressed his willingness to confirm Bahalim in his office in view of the faithful service of his family to the Ghaznavids, provided he returned to obedience. Since the Sultan did not receive any response to his overture, he prepared to give battle. He crossed the Indus on long boats and, clashing with the rival force in a marshy terrain, killed Bahalim along with a number of his sons. The Sultan appointed Salar Hasan Alavi as the new governor and returned to Ghazni.[49] The son of this officer succeeded his father in the same position and commanded the

Indian contingent which was summoned by Bahram Shah to fight (1149) against the Ghorid, Saifuddin Suri.

It might be recalled that Bahram Shah himself took shelter (1135) in Lahore, while temporarily shaking off the suzerainty of the Saljuqids. Following the sack (1149) of Ghazni at the hands of Alauddin Husain, he again withdrew to Panjab. He stayed here for a year and returned only when Alauddin Husain had been defeated by Sultan Sanjar. At his death (1157), he was succeeded by his son Khusrau Shah. Fresh attacks from Alauddin Husain deprived the Ghaznavids of Ghazni, Bust, Zamindawar and Tiginabad. The Ghuzz tribesmen, after annexing Khurasan from the Saljuqids and killing (1157) Sultan Sanjar, marched on Ghazni. Unable to resist the Ghuzz onslaught, Khusrau Shah retired to Lahore where he died (1160) after ruling for seven years.[50] His son and successor Khusrau Malik (r. 1160-1186) turned out to be the last Ghaznavid ruler. Early in his reign, he failed to consolidate his hold over Ghazni and was forced to remain content with parts of Panjab. According to Juzjani, the affairs of the government had fallen into disorder, because the governors and officials, who had been posted in the provinces and districts, had begun to exercise independent power. This negative judgement did not find favour with Bosworth on the grounds that Khusrau Malik gave ample proof of his political abilities. The Sultan enjoyed a long reign of twenty-six years, had a firm grip over the Ghaznavid territories in Panjab and led a military campaign against the Gahadvala kingdom in the Gangetic plain. He also extended his authority to the hills of northern Panjab and fringes of Kashmir, where he allied with the Khokhars against the principality of Jammu.[51] His struggle against the Ghorids for control over Panjab formed a part of the discussion on the beginning of Ghorid conquests in Panjab.

Jat and Khokhar Resistance to the Ghorids

Sultan Muizzuddin's military expeditions,[52] which resulted in the establishment of the Delhi Sultanate, were spread across a period of three decades (1175-1206). The advance was slow, and marked by alterations in military strategy and chosen targets. In 1175 the Sultan gained a foothold in southwestern Panjab by occupying Multan and Uch,[53] as he did not encounter much resistance from the Qarmathians. He placed the conquered territories under Ali Karmakh, indicating a long term interest in the region. In 1178 he marched across western Rajasthan and suffered a humiliating defeat at the hands of the Chalukyas of Anhilwara.[54] This reverse induced him to focus on the Ghaznavid kingdom of Panjab, with its capital at Lahore. He managed to achieve his aim in stages that lasted six years (1181-6). As a first step, he descended through the Khaibar Pass and occupied Peshawar (1179), a Ghaznavid possession. After two years, he led an assault on Lahore. Khusrau Malik, the last Ghaznavid ruler, did not put up a fight and opened negotiations for peace. He also sent one of his sons to the rival camp as a guarantee of his sincere intent. Sultan Muizzuddin, being satisfied with this limited gain, postponed further hostilities and returned to Ghazni. The next year (1182), he marched against the Sumra kingdom of Sind and occupied the entire area upto the port of Debal. The stage was set for the final showdown between the Shansbanis and Yaminis for control over central Panjab. Khusrau Malik formed an alliance with the Khokhars of Koh-i Jud, while Sultan Muizzuddin secured the promise of support from the chief of Jammu. In 1185, the Ghorids laid siege to the fort of Lahore and, failing to break the defence, ravaged the environs of the city. Sultan Muizzuddin occupied the fort of Sialkot and, placing it under Husain bin Kharmil, returned to Ghazni. Khusrau Malik made an attempt to retrieve the fort, with the help of the Khokhars, but failed.

In 1186 Sultan Muizzuddin again appeared in Panjab and laid siege to Lahore.[55] Since he did not anticipate an early success, he sought to trap his opponent in a web of deception. He sent a proposal to Khusrau Malik, asking him to surrender and include the name of Sultan Ghiasuddin in the Friday sermon (*khutba*). In return, it was offered that his family and treasure would be secured, that he would be given suitable *iqtas* for his maintenance, and that his son would be married to a daughter of Sultan Muizzuddin. Khusrau Malik, owing to his weakening military and political resources, accepted the terms of the proposal. Sultan Muizzuddin, acting in violation of the agreement, took Khusrau Malik and his son Bahram Shah into custody, sending them away to Firozkoh. The prisoners, who were kept in the forts of Balaram and Saifrud respectively, were put to death in 1191 when hostilities erupted between the Shansbanis and Khwarizmians. Sultan Muizzuddin acquired control over all the military posts from Sialkot to Debal and from Peshawar to Lahore. In other words, the Ghorids succeeded in consolidating their rule in large parts of Panjab and Sind. For the purpose of administering this vast area, the military and executive functions were given to Ali Karmakh (who was earlier posted in Multan and Uch), while the judicial administration was entrusted to Maulana Sirajuddin, the father of the historian Minhaj-i Siraj Juzjani.

The next object of Sultan Muizzuddin was to annexe the cis-Satluj tract extending up to Delhi. In pursuit of this aim, he occupied the citadel of Bathinda and placed it under Malik Ziauddin Tulaki. A band of 1,200 horsemen, who had been selected from the forces of Ghazni and Hindustan, joined this garrison. Tulaki was directed to hold the citadel for eight months until the arrival of Sultan Muizzuddin from Ghazni. Prithviraj Chauhan,[56] the ruler of Ajmer, perceived this as a serious threat to his kingdom. Supported by a number of feudatory chiefs and a vast army (comprising 200,000 horsemen and 30,000 elephants according to Firishta), he marched north to dislodge the Ghorids from their strategic positions. On hearing the news, Sultan Muizzuddin turned back to meet the challenge. The two armies clashed at Tarain situated between Bathinda and Sarsuti. The Ghorid commanders on the left and right wings fled, while the vanguard comprising Afghans and Khaljis were found absent. Sultan Muizzuddin rejected a proposal for withdrawing to Lahore and, displaying exemplary courage, inflicted a severe wound on Gobind Rai's face with a lance. In a counter attack by his rival, Sultan Muizzuddin was dislodged from his horse in the midst of a total rout of his troops. His life was saved on account of the presence of mind of a Khalji soldier, but his temporary absence caused a panic and lamentation among his rank and file. Once he was recognized, the nobles and troopers gathered around him and, improvising a litter and stretcher by breaking their spears, carried him to safety. As a consequence of this setback, the invading army retreated to Ghazni. As a saving grace, Tulaki succeeded in holding the fort of Bathinda for thirteen months before surrendering it to Prithviraj Chauhan.[57]

After a gap of a year spent in vigorous military preparations Sultan Muizzuddin marched to Tarain to avenge his defeat. On this occasion (1192), he relied on numbers and tactics. His vast army, which included 120,000 horsemen in defensive armour, was positioned with care. The central division – baggage, banners, canopy and elephants – was left several miles in the rear. The light armed and unencumbered horsemen were divided into four companies so as to attack from the four directions. A special detachment of 10,000 mounted archers was instructed to engage the opposing force in battle, keeping a distance of a horse's course ahead of them.[58] Once their opponents were exhausted in defending themselves, the four companies of cavalry were to fall on them from different sides.

On the other hand, Prithviraj Chauhan had mobilized an army of 300,000 men and enjoyed the support of 150 feudatory chiefs. The Sultan launched the attack at dawn when the Rajputs were not ready for battle. The Turks enacted the ruse of retreat from the battlefield. As soon as the Rajputs rushed out in pursuit, the Turks turned back to attack with full force. In a final assault, which was delivered by 120,000 men armed with swords and spears, the Rajputs scattered.[59] Gobind Rai of Delhi was killed in action, while Prithviraj Chauhan fled from Tarain only to be captured near Sarsuti. As a result of this victory, the Sultan occupied an area lying between the Satluj and the Jamuna and such important places as Hansi and Sarsuti. He assigned the districts of Kuhram and Samana to Qutbuddin Aibak. By doing so, the Sultan aimed at restoring peace and order in the region. According to the author of *Taj ul-Maasir*, he was guided by the principle, 'Provide means of prosperity in the areas which have been robbed.'[60]

The Jats of Hansi did not accept the newly established Turkish rule, which was manifested in the appointment of administrative officers in the conquered areas and posting of garrisons in the local forts. According to Tajuddin Hasan Nizami, satanic pride had filled the head of the accursed Jat chief, who had put on the cap of insubordination and independent suzerainty. The object of the Jat resistance was to oust Nusratuddin, who had been placed in the fort of Hansi along with an armed contingent. The Jats were reported to be engaged in fierce fighting at the foot of the fort. Swarms of soldiers of opposing sides converged in the countryside.[61] Aibak, who was then engaged in hunting somewhere near Kuhram, rushed to Hansi so that the Turkish garrison could be relieved. He covered a distance of 12 *farsangs* during the night and reached the scene of action by daybreak. When the Jat chief learnt about the arrival of the Turkish force, he raised the siege and fled southwards to the dry tract of Bagar. Aibak rushed after the Jats in hot pursuit and managed to attack their rear. The two armies encountered each other in the vicinity of Bagar. Amidst the loud clamour of battle cries and the beating of drums, the two armies became locked in a bloody conflict. Aibak succeeded in overwhelming the resistance and, it has been claimed, he perpetrated so much carnage that blood tinged hoofs of his horse became red like the rubies of Badakhshan and he scattered on the ground the heads of his rival commanders like balls hit by a polo stick.[62] He forced the Jat chief to surrender and put him to death. The Turkish soldiers acquired an enormous booty. Aibak turned back to Hansi and, after staying for a few days to supervise the reconstruction of the fort, went back to his post at Kuhram. He regarded his success against the Jats as an embroidery on his previous conquests, an ornament on the body of the bride of the empire and a gift of divine grace and heavenly felicity. In view of the significance of this event, letters of victory were dispatched to Ghazni as well as the cities of Hind and Sind, whether near and far.[63]

The news of the defeat of Sultan Muizzuddin and his subsequent retreat from Khwarizm was a rude shock to the Ghorid dominion in Panjab. The author of *Taj ul-Maasir* has alleged that Qutbuddin Aibak made use of the opportunity to chalk out an independent course for himself and, in doing so, forcibly occupied Multan and murdered its administrator Amirdad Hasan. The Khokhars, who had earlier supported Khusrau Malik in his attempt to recover the fort of Sialkot from Sultan Muizzuddin, revived their opposition to the Ghorid regime. Led by the sons of Khokhar Bhikan and Sarki, they planned to annex Lahore. They occupied the territory between the Jhelam and Chenab, devastated villages, and drove out the cattle belonging to the inhabitants. Bahauddin Muhammad, the governor of Sehwan, along with his brothers who had fiefs in the vicinity of Multan, undertook punitive measures to quell the Khokhar uprising. Tajuddin Hasan Nizami would have us believe that the troops of the Khokhars were as numerous as the leaves of a tree and had been receiving innumerable reinforcements.[64] The Khokhars outnumbered the opposing army under Sulaiman, who was forced to flee to Ghazni. The Khokhar ascendancy posed a serious threat to the fledgling Ghorid kingdom. Sultan Muizzuddin himself marched from Ghazni to Koh-i Jud and, at his summons, Aibak also started from Delhi to the scene of confrontation. The Ghorid generals met on the bank of the Jhelam and formulated a strategy for the impending conflict. The two armies were arrayed at a ferry on the Jhelam. Impressed with the turnout of the Khokhars in the battlefield, Tajuddin Hasan Nizami expressed himself in the following words:[65]

Against the army of Islam, there stood like a mountain a hard stone, the troops of Hindus of incredible strength, so numerous that they could not be computed. Their centre and sides were in correct position. In the wide battlefield they were something like the waves in the ocean. Each one of them held a shield like the sky and drew his sword from the scabbard. They had put their fiery arrows on the bow for the fight and kept their serpent like lassos ready for the conflict. They were holding dragon like spears with the poison of hatred. Mounted on swift horses, they were ready for the engagement. They were all attention to hear the order to start the conflict.

In a battle fought on the ferry of the Jhelam, the three Ghorid commanders – Sultan Muizzuddin, Qutbuddin Aibak and Shamsuddin Iltutmish – performed exemplary deeds of valour. The Khokhars suffered massive casualties. The heaps of corpses turned the level ground into a hill and the blood of the wounded flowed on the dead like the water of logwood. Waves of blood rose from the Jhelam to the great sky. The heads of the Khokhar commanders hung on the spears of Khatt like flags. All the people of the city were killed, so that there was not a single soul left in a house to kindle the fire. One of the sons of the Khokhar chief, after failing to withstand the Ghorid onslaught, jumped into the river and thereafter took shelter in the fort of Nandanah. Besides the large number of their soldiers, the Khokhars had depended on the impregnability of the fort, 'the peak of which was higher than the battlements of the palace of the moon and the top of the zodiacal sign of the sun and the bottom of whose moat touched the back of the bull and the fish on which the earth rests'. It was asserted that the battlements of its rampart touched the girdle of the Gemini. The top of its tower was so high that it placed its feet on the heads of the sign of Leo and the star Farqad. It was an impregnable edifice, the strength and inaccessibility of its walls could claim equality with the mountains of Judi and Shahlan. Its moat was as deep and unfathomable as the depth of the ocean. Neither the swift moving northern and southern winds could catch the fringe of its skirt, nor were the eastern breeze and western wind capable of crossing its threshold.[66]

In spite of their defeat at the ferry the Khokhars were not demoralized. They closed their ranks, prepared themselves to defend the citadel and, if the situation demanded, to lay down their lives in the effort. The state of their minds at this critical hour has been captured by Tajuddin Hasan Nizami:

> The Hindu warriors drew into battle array. All of them were singing like the nightingales on the rose tree of valour. Like a woodpigeon they were playing a Rud on the bough of bravery. They were happy like a pheasant on the verdure of sharp swords and daggers. Like a Francoline, they were taking pride in the tulips of sharp javelins and spears. In the garden of the battlefield they were displaying their elegance like peacocks. Like a dove, they were singing in the mansion of name and fame. On the rocks of manliness, they were strutting like a partridge on the tulips of lance and spear. They were blowing pipes like turtledoves in the meadow of wisdom. In the market of plunder and war, they were displaying eloquence of a parrot. They were violent like an eagle in the air of combat with spears and swords. They were cautious and scared at the time of

fleeing. When fighting they were alert and circumspect like a crane. On the day of battle and skirmish, they could be dependable guides like Qata (a bird of the tetra ride or grouse family, flying in large flocks, and knowing where water is to be found at a great distance). They could find their way in the dark night like a bat. In drawing the bow of treachery and attacking from ambush each was as farsighted as a vulture. In the battlefield, they appeared wise like an intelligent raven. They shared the nature of owl in desire for ruins and evil. They were a compeer of a cock ever keen to fight and subdue. Resembling an ugly looking crow, they were as quick as a falcon when attacking, and were well informed.[67]

The Ghorids followed up their success on the ferry of the Jhelam by besieging the fort of Nandanah and destroying its ramparts. The defenders rushed out of the bastion and engaged in close combat. The Khokhar chief realized the futility of further resistance, sought a peaceful settlement and offered to accept the position of a vassal. 'He put on the robe of Brahmins, kissed the surface of the ground like a slave and placed his head at the hoof of the swift steed of the king.' His life was spared, but he was forced to surrender the fort and part with an enormous booty consisting of horses, slaves and arms. The defeat was a severe blow to Khokhar pride. Refusing to accept the outcome of the battle, they hatched a conspiracy to kill Sultan Muizzuddin. A group of Khokhar assassins entered the royal tent at night, killed a few guards and murdered the Ghorid ruler in his sleep.

Triangular Contest

During his active political career, Sultan Muizzuddin chose his elite Turkish military officers (*bandgan-i khas*) to administer the newly conquered territories in the Indo-Gangetic plain.[68] He did not formalize any fragmentation of his territorial possessions, which would function after his death. Therefore, his demise triggered a major conflict among the three of them, Qutbuddin Aibak, Nasiruddin Qubacha and Tajuddin Yaldoz – each seeking to establish his control over Panjab. It must be understood that the late Sultan had entrusted small places to them as revenue assignments (*iqtas*), but they were left free to bring much larger areas under their respective jurisdictions. Aibak was assigned Kuhram and Samana, but exercised his authority over central and south-eastern Panjab, Delhi, eastern Rajasthan and the Gangetic plain. Qubacha was given Uch, but he established his sway over Multan and Sind. Yaldoz was conferred Karman and Sanquran, but was allowed to govern a large part of central Afghanistan including Ghazni. It was interesting to note that these three Turkish military officers were related to one another by marriage. At the instance of the late Sultan, the two daughters of Yaldoz were married to Aibak and Qubacha. The two daughters of Aibak were married, one after the other, to Qubacha. Even otherwise, the contestants were evenly placed in terms of their military resources, legal claims, and personal capabilities. Thus, the stage was set for a triangular contest to decide Sultan Muizzuddin's political heir in northwestern India.

Anticipating the situation, Aibak shifted (25 June 1206) his headquarters from Delhi to Lahore. A large number of local inhabitants – Syeds, Sufis, judges, preachers, revenue collectors, soldiers, elite and ordinary, rich and poor – welcomed him and assured their support to him. He welded diverse ethnic groups, Turks, Ghorids, Khurasanis, Khaljis and Hindustanis, into a unified and disciplined army, so that none could deprive the commoners of their possessions. As a first administrative step, he ordered the confirmation of land grants (*imlak*) to the old beneficiaries and forbade the collection of one fifth of the produce, which was being levied like the land tax (*kharaj*). Instead, he imposed the *ushr* in some places and half of it in other places, dispatching written orders about this to different places. By undertaking this measure, he abolished a practice that was not permitted by the Shariat.[69] As a result, he won the goodwill of the Muslim religious classes and, thus, earned legitimacy for the new regime. Having consolidated his position, Aibak turned his attention to Yaldoz who, having suffered a loss of authority in Ghazni due to the intrusion of Khwarizm Shah, marched across the Indus and entered Panjab. In a quick and vigorous response, Aibak forced Yaldoz to flee to Kohistan. Aibak followed up his success by marching beyond the Indus and even occupying Ghazni. However, he could not consolidate his hold over the city, owing to the lack of support from the local inhabitants. Yaldoz succeeded in recovering his position in Ghazni within two months. Aibak retreated from Afghanistan and, having entrenched himself in Lahore,[70] took effective steps to consolidate his authority in central Panjab.

The triangular contest continued even after the death (4 November 1210) of Aibak, as his place was taken by his son-in-law Shamsuddin Iltutmish. At this stage, our attention turns to Qubacha who, taking advantage of the tussle between Iltutmish and Aram Shah, had occupied Lahore. Yaldoz, who had been worsted by the Khwarizmians, moved eastwards and snatched Lahore from the hands of Qubacha. Having gained a fresh foothold in Panjab, Yaldoz occupied the area extending up to Thanesar. Not only this, he sent a message to Iltutmish asserting his claim over the territories of Sultan Muizzuddin and, as such, demanded a complete submission to his authority. Rejecting these assertions on the ground that the days of hereditary descent were over, Iltutmish defeated (25 January 1216) Yaldoz at Tarain and later on had him executed.[71] Taking advantage of this outcome, Qubacha recovered Lahore, so that his domain extended to the Arabian Sea and the Indus Delta in the south,[72] to Nanadanah and Peshawar in the northwest and Bathinda, Kuhram and Sarsuti in the east. Iltutmish realized that Qubacha, who had acquired a formidable position in Panjab and Sind, could not be permitted any further aggrandizement. He marched west and, in a battle (1217) at Mansura on the Chenab,[73] inflicted a big defeat on Qubacha. He thus recovered Lahore and placed it under the charge of his son Nasiruddin Mahmud. Subsequently, Iltutmish was constrained to divert his attention to a new political storm that blew from Central Asia and Afghanistan. The changed circumstances enabled Qubacha to survive in the troubled waters of Panjab and Sind for another ten years.

In a brief digression, we would consider the royal order (*farman*) issued to Nasiruddin Mahmud, the son of Iltutmish, on his appointment in Panjab. Notwithstanding its ornate prose and emphasis on the ideal,[74] it laid the priorities of the new ruling class in the early stage of state formation. It stated that in the year 1217, the governorship of Lahore (including its remote and well known parts, along with its famous forts and mansions), the capital of renowned kings and seat of triumphant Sultans, was entrusted to Nasiruddin Mahmud after deliberations and the customary divination. He was lauded as a benefactor of humanity, king of the world, a celebrated champion and warrior of the world. He was in front of the army of Islam, a supporter of the troops of faith, a forearm of religion and empire. He was the arm of the kingdom and nation. He was the light of the eyes of saints and fire in the heart of the enemies. He was the signet ring of the sweetheart of kingship, ruby of the mine of success and cornelian of the crown of sovereignty. He was the middle pearl of the necklace of gallantry and a precious gem in the girdle of fame. He was the turquoise in the crown of eminence and a pearl in the oyster of mental qualities. He was like a gem in the ocean of bounty and firm like a mountain in war. From his childhood and boyhood, the fragrance of kingship had been diffused by his charming nature and magnanimous temperament. While he was still a raw youth, he displayed the potential for conquering territories and capturing enemies. The star of victory rose from his auspicious countenance and good fortune. His kingly disposition provided enough evidence that he would be a great conqueror. His numerous talents convinced every one that he possessed the signs of becoming a fortunate and invincible hero.

By conferring the governorship on the prince, Iltutmish acted according to the text, 'God has ordered us to place everyone in the rank one is worthy of.' The governor must deal with important affairs pertaining to religion and state. It was an office of eminence and dignity that God bestowed and it was the highest rank and position for any man to reach. A royal mandate was issued to the prince enjoining him to honour the commands of the Creator and follow the religious law as his primary duty. Next, he was advised to show respect and honour the Syeds, the descendants of the Prophet, who were the leaves and fruits of the sweet smelling tree of Prophethood and flowers of the bright garden of apostleship. He was called upon to honour this arrangement in the necklace of the family of Muhammad. They should be treated as the foundations of faith and the bases of Islam. He should think it necessary to look after the Imams and oversee the adulation of students, who would rise from the position of seekers of knowledge to the status of teachers. They learnt the subtleties of what was lawful and what was unlawful, besides grasping the true implications of religious laws. They had protected the path of the Shariat and drinking place of tradition from blemishes of aberration and heresy. They had adorned the hearts and minds of the people with expositions of esoteric doctrines and axioms. By their charming intonations and lucid explanations, they had performed the miracle of Jesus, i.e. resuscitation of the dead. They had displayed wonderful skill in explaining the sayings of apostles and expounding the doctrines of various religions. They had entered the sanctuary of trusteeship and the sacred enclosure of the belief according to the dictum, 'The learned man is the trustee of God on earth' with genuine sincerity. Their inner charm and perfect piety had lent eloquence and splendour to the personality of each one of them.

The new governor was directed to bear in mind the necessity of extending unstinted bounty and liberal generosity to his servants and attendants according to rank and position. He was expected to unite the hearts of all men, high and low, in their love for the great empire, which would last as long as the heavens and earth lasted. He was required to do his level best to provide leisure and comfort to the helpers of the dominion and supporters of the empire. He had to bear in mind that the banners of faith and flags of Islam could not be raised without unsheathed swords, nor would victory and conquest be gained without spears and arrows. The safety of highways and the defence of the dominions were not possible without horsemen and foot soldiers. In the battle, their stone piercing arrows and rock smashing maces forced stationary earth to move like the sky. As regards men of letters, the governor was expected to provide each one of them with all opportunities to live happily, keeping in mind their rank and position. To them, the knowledge of all secret affairs of the dominions was as clear as the day. When they wrote with the tongues of their pens, it appeared as if they were scattering rare pearls on the leaf of silver. In the matter of making speech, they had excelled *sahban vail e wail* in eloquence. In the domain of writing epistles, they had shown precedence over Sahib and Sabi.

The new governor was advised to protect the peasants and people of lower rank from calamities. He was expected to make their lives brighter and more cheerful by fulfilling their needs through his kindness and compassion. If he conferred a variety of gifts and favours on free men, he could convert them into his slaves and, by employing the same trick, he could make his slaves feel that they were free men. He was instructed to make a number of virtues – forbearance, modesty and sedateness – his inner and outer garments as well as adornment of his life. When free from work, he had to move fast like the fast moving mill of the sky. But at the time of being firm, he had to be inflexible and steadfast like the firm footed pole star. He was urged to turn all his efforts to renew charitable foundations and observance of prayers. He was expected to remove idols from the idol temples wherever they were to be found in Hindustan. He should think it obligatory to publicize his good works and take steps to spread his reputation as was done by rulers in the past. Thus, he should leave behind in the world a good name with fragrant praise. When the pillars of kingship were firmly strengthened and foundations of governance were consolidated by means of equity and uninterrupted administration of justice, then the tree of justice and equity would become fresh and bear fruit during the regime of the king (Iltutmish). Owing to the fear of punishment, all types of mischief and disturbance would be banished. Owing to the impact of royal wrath, all forms of tyranny would sink into concealment. By remaining consistently righteous and kind to the people, he would earn happiness in this world and the next. In all circumstances, he was required to follow charming and noble manners that characterized the nature of kings. He was called upon to tread the straight path that rested on the words and actions of the emperor (Iltutmish), as he must have observed with his own eyes.[75]

The entry of three political entities – Khokhars, Khwarizmians, and Mongols – added considerable complexity to the power struggle in Panjab. This development could be traced to Alauddin

Muhammad bin Tekish, the ruler of Khwarizm, who had seized much of Afghanistan from the feeble hands of the Ghorids. He assigned a large chunk of territory, Ghor, Bamiyan, Ghazni, Bust, Tiginabad and Zamindawar, to his son Jalaluddin Mangbarni who was represented at these places by a number of lieutenants. Pushing eastwards, he extended his sway upto the Indus, including Peshawar. The extensive Khwarizmian empire, however, crumbled before the rising tide of the Mongol onslaught. Chingez Khan routed (November 1221) the Khwarizmians on the banks of the Indus, forcing Mangbarni to flee across the river. He managed to elude a Mongol detachment of 20,000 soldiers led by Dorbei Doqshin, which had been sent in pursuit of the fugitive. Rana Shatra, the Khokhar chief of the Salt Range, resisted the Khwarizmian advance with a force of 6,000 men but was defeated and killed. Mangbarni's retinue swelled to 3,000 or 4,000 with the arrival of fresh contingents. The presence of the Khwarizmians filled the local rulers with awe. Qubacha's lieutenant at Nanadanah, Qamruddin Kurramani, sent gifts to Mangbarni with the object of purchasing immunity from attack. Qubacha, on his part, also made conciliatory gestures. He sent under escort a lady (the daughter of Amin Malik, the Khwarizmian governor of Herat) who was related to Mangbarni and had taken shelter in Qubacha's territory after her father's death in the battle on the Indus. The friendly relations between the two potentates did not last long. The Khwarizmians were alienated at the violent death of two important members of their entourage, the son of Amin Malik and Mangbarni's *wazir* Shaihabuddin Alp Sarakhsi, in Qubacha's domain.[76]

In these circumstances, Mangbarni formed an alliance with the Khokhar chief Rai Sangin (an enemy of Qubacha) and received his daughter in marriage. Thus strengthened, he pushed forward into Panjab and, reaching a few days journey from Delhi, sought asylum from Iltutmish and proposed an alliance against the Mongols. Iltutmish refused to provide any assistance to the fugitive, because he could neither endanger the Delhi Sultanate, nor give offence to the Mongols. Giving a clear indication of his stance, he ordered the Khwarizmian emissary Ain ul-Mulk to be put to death. In fact, he marched towards Lahore with the object of fighting against Mangbarni. The latter retreated to the Salt Range where he was joined from all sides by refugees escaping from the Mongols and thus mustered an army of 10,000 soldiers.[77] Chingez Khan, who toyed with the idea of returning to Mongolia through the Himalayan foothills of Qarachal and Kamrup, sent envoys to Iltutmish seeking permission to march through his territories. The outcome of this diplomatic exchange was not known, though Chingez Khan abandoned this plan in view of unfavorable auguries.[78] It was quite possible that the Mongol delegation ensured that the Khwarizmians did not receive any help from the Delhi Sultanate.[79]

Finding his passage towards Delhi effectively closed, Mangbarni carved out his own dominion at the expense of Qubacha. Assisted by a Khokhar contingent, he led a military expedition to Uch. His commander Uzbeg Tai, who headed a force of 7,000 soldiers, made a surprise attack at night. The rival camp of 20,000 men was scattered and Qubacha was forced to flee to Bhakkar and then to Multan. Mangbarni sent an envoy to Qubacha and demanded the return of some important adherents as well as the payment of a large indemnity. Qubacha fulfilled these demands forthwith and requested that his territories not be encroached. Mangbarni retreated to his abode in the Salt Range and, on the way, occupied the fortress of Pasrur.[80] Not long after, he received the news of the arrival of a Mongol army in his pursuit. He retraced his steps to Multan and, sending an emissary to Qubacha, notified the passage of his troops and demanded what had been termed as the Shoe Money. Qubacha refused to meet the fresh demands and came out to fight. Mangbarni left for Uch after a brief encounter. Since he met with resistance from the local inhabitants, he set fire to the town and proceeded to Sehwan. This place was held by Fakhruddin Salari on behalf of Qubacha. Mangbarni's commander Orkhan besieged the fort of Sehwan and succeeded in killing his counterpart Lachain. Mangbarni received the submission of Salari and confirmed him as the governor. After a sojourn of one month, Mangbarni proceeded to Debal and Damrila, forcing its ruler Sinanuddin Chatisar to escape into the sea. He also sent a predatory expedition to Anhilwara and, having acquired a large booty of camels, left Indian soil on way to Persia through Makran.[81]

With the final retreat (1224) of Mangbarni from the Indian subcontinent, Iltutmish and Qubacha were free to contend for supremacy over western Panjab. The contest turned out to be unequal. By this time, Iltutmish had already established his authority over Sarsuti, Bathinda, and Lahore.[82] On the other hand, Qubacha had suffered the depletion of his military and financial resources at the hands of Mangbarni. Iltutmish, anticipating the decisive nature of the conflict, roped in the services of the senior officers of the realm – Nasiruddin Aitmur (the governor of Lahore), Tajuddin Sanjar Gazlak Khan (the governor of Bathinda), Nizamul Mulk Muhammad Junaidi (the *wazir*) and Izzuddin Muhammad Salari (the *amir-i hajib*). At the commencement of military operations, Nasiruddin Aitmur marched from Lahore and besieged Multan. Iltutmish reached the walls of the fort of Uch. Qubacha, who had pitched his camp before the gate of Ahrawat, placed his baggage and followers on a fleet of boats that were stationed in the river. He did not offer any resistance and, carrying his treasure from Uch, left for Bhakkar. Iltutmish deputed Junaidi and other nobles to Bhakkar in pursuit of Qubacha. He himself supervised the siege of Uch that continued for nearly three months. On 4 May 1228, the garrison capitulated, inducing Qubacha (then stationed at Bhakkar) to send his son Alauddin Bahram Shah to negotiate the terms of peace. Overcome by frustration and fear, Qubacha jumped from the ramparts of the fort of Bhakkar into the river below. Iltutmish took charge of the treasure and followers of the deceased. Having appointed governors for Multan and Uch, he extended his sway up to the coast of Sind, as the local ruler Sinanuddin Chatisar accepted his authority.[83] With the success of Iltutmish, a curtain was drawn on the power struggle, which defined the politics of Panjab for more than two decades.

The Disaffection of Provincial Officers

In the wake of the Ghorid conquest, Panjab witnessed the emergence of several garrison towns and this marked a preliminary stage in the process of state formation. They were situated in a number of distinct geographical zones in the region. Nadanah and Sialkot were located in the northwestern zone; Lahore, Dipalpur and Bathinda in the central zone; Multan and Uch in the southwestern zone; Sunam, Samana and Kuhram in the cis-Sutlej zone and Sarsuti and Hansi in the southeastern zone. The Sultans of Delhi sought to impose their authority in the region by posting military commanders (*muqtis*) at these stations. These officers made their headquarters in the fortresses whose structure had been in existence for several centuries. They were required to maintain armed contingents of horsemen and, to meet their expenditure, extract tribute from the local chiefs of the hinterlands. Sometimes they could be placed over two or even three of these commands. The presence of hostile forces – Mongols, Khwarizmians and Qarlughs – raised the importance of the garrison towns of Lahore, Dipalpur, Bathinda, Multan and Uch. Constrained by circumstances, the Sultans of Delhi assigned these commands to senior nobles with leadership qualities and entrusted them with vast military resources. The Sultans were not in a position to keep an eye on the governor's retinue and finances. Nor did they have any mechanism that could ensure the loyalty and efficiency of these military commanders. In this nascent stage of state formation, the powers of the Sultans and nobles were ill-defined. The raw passion for grabbing high positions and lucrative assignments (*iqtas*) generated acute factionalism among the nobles.[84] In these circumstances, it was not surprising if some of them nurtured the ambition of occupying the throne at the right opportunity. Instances of disaffection of the provincial officers provide insights into the historical developments in Panjab during the thirteenth century.

The death of Sultan Shamsuddin Iltutmish (30 April 1236) marked the beginning of a series of revolts by the military commanders (*muqtis*) posted in different parts of Panjab. The seven-month rule of Ruknuddin Firoz Shah was not accepted by a number of prominent nobles, a majority of whom were associated with the revenue assignments in the region. His mother Shah Turkan, by exercising supreme authority, caused a number of negative consequences – maltreatment of members of the royal household including Princess Raziya, death of Prince Qutbuddin in Delhi and rebellion of Prince Ghiasuddin Muhammad Shah in Awadh. These developments provided an opportunity to three military commanders – Alauddin Jani of Lahore, Saifuddin Kuchi of Hansi, and Kabir Khan Ayaz of Sunam – to rise in revolt and grapple with the Delhi army for a long time. Soon after, they were joined by Izzuddin Muhammad Salari, the *muqti* of Badaun, and Nizam ul-Mulk Junaidi, the *wazir*. The Sultan marched to Kuhram to quell the revolt. In the neighbourhood of Mansurpur and Tarain, the Turkish nobles and slaves of the household, who constituted the central contingents of the army, massacred a number of Tazik officers.[85] As a result, the revolt of the military commanders, which had remained unattended, spilled over into the next reign.

Sultan Raziya (r. 1236-40) tackled a difficult situation with understanding and tact. Having won over Ayaz, she defeated Jani and Kuchi, both of whom were captured and put to death. Ayaz was rewarded with the territory of Lahore and its suburbs. However, his loyalty continued to be suspect. In 1238, Sultan Raziya marched towards Lahore in order to punish him.[86] He fled out of the city and reached Sodhra. It was impossible for him to move any further, because the territories beyond the Chenab were under the control of the Mongols and he was apprehensive about their attitude towards disaffected officers of the Delhi Sultanate. Therefore, he sought forgiveness from the Sultan. Raziya, who had earlier punished two officers of Panjab – Jani and Kuchi – with death, merely transferred Ayaz from Lahore to Multan. Ayaz served here only for two years. Taking advantage of a major Mongol invasion (1241) of Lahore, Ayaz assumed the symbols of royalty and began to rule over Multan, Uch, and Sind. After his death (1242), his son Tajuddin Abu Bakr Ayaz succeeded him.[87] The shortlived Ayazi dynasty exercised sovereign power over southwest Panjab and Sind just like Nasiruddin Qubacha in the first quarter of the thirteenth century. The Ayazi rulers were responsible for blocking the eastward expansion of the Qarlugh kingdom towards Multan and, viewed in this sense, played a role similar to that of Qubacha who had stood up against the Khwarizmians.

Precisely at this time, another officer posted in Panjab revolted. This was Akhtiaruddin Altuniya, the governor of Bathinda. Originally a slave of Iltutmish, he had served as a wine-keeper and canopy bearer. During the reign of Raziya, he was first given the assignment (*iqta*) of Baran and later on Bathinda. He was one of those Turkish nobles who were unhappy with Raziya owing to the rise of Jamaluddin Yaqut, an Abyssinian, as the superintendent of royal stables (*amir-i akhur*). Altuniya entered into a conspiracy with the most prominent noble at Delhi, Akhtiaruddin Aitigin, who held the office of royal chamberlain (*amir-i hajib*). Altuniya took advantage of Raziya's punitive expedition against Ayaz and began to make preparations for revolt in the fort of Bathinda. On learning of this development, Raziya marched from Delhi (3 April 1240) to Bathinda at the head of the central army (*hashm-i qalb*). When she reached the fort of Bathinda, the Turkish nobles broke into rebellion and, in accordance with a premeditated plan, murdered Yaqut and imprisoned Raziya in the fort. Meanwhile, a new political dispensation was put in place in Delhi. Muizzuddin Bahram Shah was crowned as the Sultan, and Aitigin was appointed deputy of the government (*naib-i mamlikat*). Within a month, the Sultan engineered the murder of Aitigin. Altuniya, having failed to get any reward for his role in the conspiracy, repudiated the new arrangement and chalked out an independent course of action. He married Raziya, secured the support of two Turkish nobles, Akhtiaruddin Qaraqash and Izzuddin Salari, and went on to mobilize 10,000 men from the local population. Altuniya and Raziya were defeated by an army from Delhi. They fell back on Kaithal where they were killed (14 October 1240) by some local people.[88]

Disaffection continued unabated into the middle of the thirteenth century. This was amply illustrated by the conduct of Izzuddin Balban Kishlu Khan and Sher Khan. The former was given the command of Nagaur during the reign of Sultan Alauddin Masud Shah (r. 1242-46).[89] In 1246, he was given charge of Multan as a reward for assisting the Sultan in defending Uch against the Mongols. Following the accession of Nasiruddin Mahmud (r. 1246-66), he was permitted to add Uch to his charge, provided he relinquish his claim over Nagaur. The Sultan marched to Nagaur and forced the recalcitrant officer to surrender the place. Kishlu Khan learnt to be satisfied with the administration of Multan and Uch. In 1249 Saifuddin Hasan Qarlugh marched to Multan. Kishlu Khan rushed from Uch to Multan, overpowered the invaders and gained an entry into the fort. Kishlu Khan was forced to open negotiations with the besiegers and, surrendering the fort, retreated to Uch. When he learnt that the Qarlugh chief had been killed, he repented his withdrawal from the fort.[90] The focus shifted to Sher Khan who, then holding the charge of Bathinda and Lahore, ousted the Qarlughs from Multan and placed it under the charge of Akhtiaruddin Kurez. This action marked the beginning of a conflict between Sher Khan and Kishlu Khan for the possession of Multan. The former not only succeeded in retaining Multan, but also snatched Uch from the latter. Sultan Nasiruddin Mahmud Shah did not approve the usurpations by Sher Khan.[91] He marched towards western Panjab, fought against the armed retinue of Sher Khan and re-established control over Bathinda, Multan and Uch. Soon after, he restored Multan and Uch to Kishlu Khan. Since Sher Khan did not see any future for himself in the Delhi Sultanate, he left for Turkistan with the intention of seeking asylum at the court of the Mongol chief Mangu Khan.[92]

Though Kishlu Khan managed to regain the charge of Multan and Uch, he began to feel insecure owing to the presence of his archrival Sher Khan in the Mongol camp and the unprecedented ascendancy of Ulugh Khan (Ghiasuddin Balban) at Delhi. While grappling with these fears, Kishlu Khan adopted a two-pronged strategy. On the one hand, he sent his son and Malik Shamsuddin Kurt Ghori to the court of the Mongol ruler Halaku, with a view to seek assistance in times of need. On the other, he joined hands with the rebel Qutlugh Khan and marched to Delhi at the head of the armed contingents of Multan and Uch, with the intention of displacing the political dispensation headed by Sultan Nasiruddin Mahmud and Ulugh Khan. Kishlu Khan's plan did not materialize as his accomplices (theologians and scholars) in the capital had been banished and his own armed retinue which he had brought from Multan and Uch, defected to the opposite side. Since his life was in danger, he mustered 200-300 horsemen and fled to Uch. Continuing his flight, he travelled to Khurasan and Iraq, ultimately presenting himself at the court of Halaku. Kishlu Khan secured the promise of support in return for agreeing to maintain a Mongol resident (*shahna*) in his territories. From then onwards (1259), he began to rule independently over Multan and Uch, which had come under the protection of the Mongols.[93]

Kishlu Khan and Sher Khan were not the only members of the ruling class who had defected to the Mongols. Jalaluddin Masud, the brother of Sultan Nasiruddin Mahmud, had also placed himself in this category. In 1248 he was appointed to the provinces of Sambhal and Badaun. For unknown reasons, he marched through the Sirmur hills and entered Lahore, then under the Mongol sphere of influence. He travelled through the frontier zone and reached Mangu Khan's court at a time when two officers of the Delhi Sultanate, Sher Khan and Qutlugh Khan, were already present there. Mangu Khan not only treated Jalaluddin Masud with honour, but also directed the Mongol commander Sali Bahadur to provide military assistance to the princely visitor. During the course of their eastward march, they were joined by the Mongol feudatory Nasiruddin Muhammad Qarlugh, who ruled over a kingdom that included Binban and Salt Range. They drove away the officers posted by the Delhi Sultanate at Lahore and Jalandhar, installing Jalaluddin Masud in their place. The latter assumed the title of Sultan Jalaluddin Masud Shah and began to rule (1254) over a vast region comprising the trans-Satluj areas as a Mongol vassal.[94] Sher Khan, at the instance of the Mongols, joined Jalaluddin Masud at Lahore. However, he fell out with Jalaluddin Masud and captured the latter's retinue. He also snatched the charge of Bathinda from Tajuddin Arsalan Khan. As a result of Delhi's intervention, Tajuddin Arsalan Khan was transferred to Awadh and Sher Khan was restored to Bathinda and other territories as before.[95] Thereafter began Sher Khan's conflict with Kishlu Khan.

At this juncture, a showdown appeared imminent between the two warring factions of nobles – the disaffected faction led by Ulugh Khan and the ruling faction led by Imaduddin Raihan, Qutlugh

Khan and Kishlu Khan. In his desperate search for allies, Ullugh Khan managed to win over Jalaluddin Masud and Sher Khan, who marched from Lahore to negotiate for political gains. Ulugh Khan's clique adopted Jalaluddin Masud as a rival candidate for the throne, while the armies of the partisans started arriving from different places in Panjab – Bathinda, Sunam, Kuhram, Kaithal and Hansi. Sultan Nasiruddin Mahmud struck a deal with Ulugh Khan, as a result of which he and his supporters were retained in their previous posts.[96] Jalaluddin Masud, disgusted at the betrayal, returned to Lahore and continued to rule from there until the end (1266) of Sultan Nasiruddin Mahmud's reign. Benefiting from the restoration of Ulugh Khan in the capital, Sher Khan was given the command of Bathinda. In order to prevent a revival of his conflict with Kishlu Khan and Jalaluddin Masud, he was transferred (1258) from Bathinda and given the charge of extensive territories in Kol, Biana, Balaram, Jalesar, Mehar, Mahaban and Gwalior.[97] While the Delhi Sultanate acquired a semblance of political stability, its northwestern boundary remained fixed at the Satluj and no attempt was made to recover the trans-Satluj areas, which were firmly in the grasp of the Mongols or their vassals.

Mongols, Khwarizmians and Qarlughs

While Jalaluddin Mangbarni finally retreated from the Indian subcontinent through Sind, a Mongol commander Dorbei Doqshin reached (1224) Panjab and, entering the Salt Range, sacked Nandanah that was held by a lieutenant of the Khwarizmians. He advanced south and invested the fort of Multan. During a siege of forty days, he quarried material for projectiles along the river and transported it to the site of confrontation on rafts.[98] Nasiruddin Qubacha not only defended the city with courage and ability, but also spent liberal amounts from his treasury and provided several benefits to the inhabitants.[99] The Mongols abandoned the siege owing to the onset of hot weather but, during their withdrawal, they ravaged the territories of Multan and Lahore.[100] Within two years of this episode, the rising Mongol pressure in Afghanistan induced a few nobles of Ghor to travel to Panjab, where they received shelter from Qubacha. This forced a body of Khalji tribesmen, who possibly constituted a part of the Khwarizmian forces under Saifuddin Hasan Qarlugh, to entrench themselves at Mansurah in Siwistan. Qubacha marched in that direction and, after killing the captain Malik Khan Khalji, cleared the region of intruders.[101]

The legacy of Mangbarni survived in Panjab in the form of the Qarlugh kingdom. On the occasion of his departure (1224) for Persia, he placed his acquisitions under the charge of two lieutenants. Saifuddin Hasan Qarlugh was appointed to govern areas lying to the west of the Indus – Nangrahar, Kurraman and Peshawar. Uzbeg Tai was posted at Nandanah in the Salt Range to control the area including Binban.[102] This development was a matter of deep concern for Iltutmish, who had made major gains in Panjab in the wake of Qubacha's death (1228). But with the removal of the buffer of Qubacha's domain, he was required to deal directly with the political successors of the Khwarizmians, the Qarlughs. In 1229, he marched to northwestern Panjab and drove out Uzbeg Tai from his stronghold in the Salt Range. However, he received the allegiance of Saifuddin Hasan Qarlugh and allowed him to rule beyond the Indus. In 1234, a Mongol general Hoqutar, after a successful raid on Kashmir, attacked the Qarlugh principality and forced its ruler to accept the suzerainty of the Mongol potentate Ogetai (r. 1229-41). As the Mongol troops moved into Kabul, Ghazni and Zabulistan, Saifuddin Hasan Qarlugh was constrained to accept a Mongol resident (*shahnah*) in his domain. This prompted Iltutmish to advance towards Binban but, owing to his death (1236), he could not chastise Saifuddin Hasan Qarlugh.[103] Qarlugh assumed a royal title and began to issue coins, including the 'bull and horseman' type with a Devanagari legend. This move, according to Siddiqui, reflected his good relations with the Hindu chiefs of Koh-i Jud, who had accepted him as their overlord instead of the Sultan of Delhi after the death of Iltutmish.[104]

The rising power Saifuddin Hasan Qarlugh did not impress his Mongol masters. In 1238-9, two Mongol commanders Anban and Negudar led a sudden attack on Saifuddin Hasan Qarlugh, who was expelled from his possessions in Ghazni, Kurraman and Binban.[105] In a bid to compensate himself for these losses, he turned to southwestern Panjab. Marching at the head of a strong body of troops, he attacked Uch. Malik Saifuddin Aibak, who held the place on behalf of the Delhi Sultanate, emerged out of the fort in battle array and, following a brilliant victory, forced the invaders to flee.[106] Motivated by the instinct of survival, Saifuddin Hasan Qarlugh, tried to secure the assistance of the Delhi Sultanate against the Mongols and, thus, followed in the footsteps of his master Mangbarni. He sent his son Muhammad to the court of Raziya, who received him with honour and conferred the fief of Baran on him. After a short time, he left the place without the permission of Raziya and joined his father.[107] The reason for this secret departure lay in Raziya's possible refusal to join hands with the Qarlugh chief against the Mongols. Underscoring the buildup of the Mongol military power in Turkistan and Afghanistan as well as the increasing Mongol pressure towards the Indus, Peter Jackson observed, 'The Mongol campaign against Hasan Qarlugh brought them to the frontiers of the Delhi Sultanate, and they now occupied the territories which had served as the springboard for the Ghorid invasions of India two generations earlier.'[108]

While advancing his designs on southwestern Panjab, Saifuddin Hasan Qarlugh subdued the chiefs of the Salt Range and secured their allegiance. He also accepted a Mongol resident at his court and, from 1241 onwards, joined the Mongol raids on the borders of India. On two occasions (1245 and 1249), he succeeded in snatching Multan from the hands of Delhi-appointed governors, but could not retain it. His son and successor Nasiruddin Muhammad maintained diplomatic ties with the Mongols and pragmatic compromise with the Delhi Sultanate. Avoiding armed conflict with both the powers, he promoted agriculture and trade as testified in the abundance of his coins found in the Salt Range. In view of his subordination to the Mongols, he collaborated with the disgrunutled elements in the Delhi Sultanate – Prince Jalaluddin Masud in Lahore and Izzuddin Balban Kishlu Khan in Multan and Sind – who had accepted (1254) the overlordship of the Mongol emperor Mongke. The Qarlugh ruler, who had acted as a mediator between the Mongols and Delhi, fell from power sometime after 1266, when Balban recovered large parts of western Panjab and eliminated the pro-Mongol warlords. The Qarlugh ruler, who was suspected of complicity by the Mongols, lost the confidence of Halaku. Balban did not extend any support to the Qarlugh kingdom, which was erased by the Mongols with the annexation of Binban and Salt Range to the Chaghtai Khanate.[109]

More than two decades earlier (1241), Tair Bahadur, who held the charge of Herat and Baghdiz, along with several Mongol commanders who controlled Ghor, Ghazni, Garmsir and Turkistan, crossed the Indus. It appeared that the vigorous preparations for defence made by Kabir Khan Ayaz, the governor of Multan, induced them to turn instead to Lahore. They besieged the fort, placed catapults (*manjniqs*) around it and destroyed the ramparts. Akhtiaruddin Qaraqash, the governor of Lahore, who offered stiff resistance at the gates of the city, fought to the limits of his capacity. But he was demoralized on account of a combination of factors.[110] First, the military garrison posted in the fort was unprepared to meet the challenge, because it did not have the required war materials and provisions. Second, a sizeable number of the inhabitants were merchants who had already travelled across Khurasan and Turkistan which were under the Mongol rule. During these journeys, they had acquired security letters promising safe passage from the Mongols and, therefore, they had little reason to fear the presence of the invaders. What was more probable, they did not wish to alienate the Mongols in view of their commercial interests in Central Asia and, therefore, did not cooperate with the administration in defending the place. Third, the notables of the city including the judge (*qazi*), who were appointed to guard the boundary walls, were guilty of negligence. Fourth, there was no hope of assistance from Delhi, as the Turkish and Ghorid nobles had fallen out with Sultan Muizuddin Bahram Shah (r. 21 April 1240-10 May 1242).[111]

Unnerved by all this, Qaraqash planned his flight from Lahore. On the pretext of making a night attack, he emerged (22 December 1241) from the fort with his followers and, piercing the Mongol cordon, rushed towards Delhi. The flight caused much confusion and loss. Several women of his household were separated, but managed to hide from the enemy. A number of fugitives were killed. Still others, taking advantage of the darkness, concealed themselves in the graveyard and ruins. When the citizens of Lahore and the defenders of the fort learnt about the flight of Qaraqash, their hearts were broken. The Mongols were emboldened to capture the city and begin a massacre in every quarter. At this stage, the remaining local officers mobilized their resources and organized a desperate resistance. Two groups of people performed incredible deeds of valour and sacrificed their lives in the effort. One group was led by Aqsanqar, the police chief (*kotwal*) of Lahore and his dependants who, according to Juzjani, surpassed the legendary Rustam in bravery by a thousand times. The other group was led by Dindar Muhammad, the master of stables (*amir-i akhur*) and his followers, who fought as if they had been blessed by Ali Murtaza and other prophets.[112]

The Mongols were reported to have massacred the entire population of Lahore and the survivors, if any, were made captive. But the Mongols too suffered heavy casualties. It was estimated that 30,000 to 40,000 Mongols were killed along with 80,000 horses. Several Mongol commanders, including Tair Bahadur, lost their lives. In fact,there was not a single Mongol who had not received a wound from the spear, sword or arrow. As a result of this setback, the invaders were forced to retreat. But the collapse of the civil administration provided an opportunity to the Khokhars and other tribals to pour into the city, which was subjected to a second round of plunder. Qaraqash, who had returned from the Beas to his post by then, found no difficulty in inflicting a severe punishment on the intruders. During the course of his flight from Lahore, his servants (wardrobe keepers or *jamadars*) had hidden gold and other valuables in a marked spot under the water of the Ravi. The governor managed to recover the wealth as it had not fallen into the hands of the Mongols.[113] The resolute defence of the city by the remainder of the garrison and the massive Mongol casualties could not have been possible without the active support of the faceless citizenry of Lahore. It might be suggested, then, that Qaraqash's assessment of the situation was wrong and, if he had led the soldiers and people like his distinguished subordinates, it would have been possible to save the city from a genocide at the hands of Mongols.

During the reign of Sultan Alauddin Masud Shah (r. 1242-6), the Delhi Sultanate had a precarious hold in western Panjab. While Lahore continued to be in a state of desolation, Multan had been wrested by Saifuddin Hasan Qarlugh after the death of Tajuddin Abu Bakr and Uch was held by Hindu Khan and his deputy Khwaja Salih. In 1245, the Mongol general Mangutah (who on entering Iran had established his base in Taliqan, Kunduz and Walwalij) penetrated into Sind and advanced towards Multan and Uch. On hearing the arrival of the Mongols up to the banks of the Indus, the Qarlugh warlord evacuated the fort of Multan and, having abandoned the city to its fate, embarked on a vessel and fled to Debal and Siwistan. Meanwhile, Mangutah reached the boundary wall of the fort of Uch and, placing it under a blockade, ravaged the environs of the town. The people of the fort not only made utmost efforts to defend the citadel, but also killed a large number of the invaders. Though the besiegers succeeded in making a breach in the rampart, they could not gain an entry through the fortification. The Mongol captains were worried by the delay in bringing the siege to a logical end. One of them, who reproached Mangutah for the failure of his tactics, volunteered to take the fort in a single assault. He planned to make a surprise attack during the third watch of the night, while the guards took rest and the inmates were asleep. The defenders had mixed a vast quantity of water with clay at the rear of the breach, thus preparing a large pit of mud as deep as a spear's length. When the Mongol captain placed his foot on the breach, which was thought to be firm ground, he fell into the quagmire and sank into it. The defenders, who were roused from their slumber, raised a shout of joy and, bringing out burning torches and grabbing their weapons, they came out to fight. The Mongol troops retreated to the base camp. Next morning, they requested the defenders to release their captain who was thought to have been made a prisoner and, in return, promised to raise the siege and depart. They were shocked to learn that their captain was not a captive, but had actually drowned in the muddy water.[114]

However, the final retreat (15 January 1246) of the Mongols from Uch was brought about by the news of the arrival of the Delhi army under the command of the Sultan Alauddin Masud Shah and Ulugh Khan. Juzjani, who was a member of the retinue, has attributed the Mongol retreat to the leadership and planning of Ulugh Khan. It was he who mobilized the troops for this military expedition, while other nobles showed indecision about the enterprise. He sent guides in advance so that the line of the route could be cleared beforehand. At every stage, he declared the intention of covering a distance of 8 *kurohs*, but actually covered 12. By employing this mode of movement, the army crossed the Beas and reached the banks of the Ravi. The withdrawal of the Mongols was triggered by a clever move of Ulugh Khan. A number of letters were drafted for the garrison of Uch, announcing the arrival of a vast army, including a sizeable cavalry and an impressive fleet of elephants, besides stressing the high morale of the soldiers. A detachment was placed in front to serve as a reconnoitering force and advance guard. The couriers carried the letters to the garrison, while some of these fell into the hands of the Mongols. As the defenders beat drums in joy, the Mongols were unnerved and decided to raise the siege. Mangutah was forced to take this decision when he learnt that the Delhi army was marching along the skirts of the hills on way to the Beas, owing to the numerous islands on the banks of the river and, thus, opted for a longer route instead of the shorter one via Sarsuti and Marut. On the one hand, he was worried about the vast size of the Delhi army and, on the other, he feared that his line of retreat might be cut off. Though he divided his troops into three divisions, they were routed and forced to flee. They released a number of their captives, both Muslim and Hindu. Ulugh Khan followed up this success by advancing upto the Chenab (March 1246) and thus asserted the authority of the Delhi Sultanate upto Sodhra.[115]

The aggressive action of the Delhi Sultanate could not deter the Mongols from another invasion soon after. In 1246, Sali Bahadur and Shamsuddin Kurt Ghori (a feudatory of the Mongols in Herat) laid siege to Multan that was held by Jankar Khan, who had been a slave of Iltutmish. On the fourteenth day of the siege, Jankar

Khan sent the Suhrawardi saint Shaikh Bahauddin Zakariya to Shamsuddin Kurt Ghori to negotiate the terms of peace in return for an indemnity. The Mongols accepted the proposal and, having raised the siege, accepted a sum of 100,000 *dinars*, thirty ass-loads of soft goods and one hundred captives.[116] Sali Bahadur marched northwards to Lahore and extracted a similar contribution from the governor, who even agreed to be a vassal of the Mongols.[117]

It appeared that the Delhi Sultanate could not take suitable retaliatory measures, as the ruling class was involved in setting up a new political dispensation. As soon as Nasiruddin Mahmud was elevated as the Sultan, Ulugh Khan convinced him of the need to send a military expedition to northwestern Panjab. Accordingly, he marched (12 November 1246) out of the capital and, travelling through the different parts of Panjab, reached Sodhra on the Chenab. He and some prominent nobles separated from the main army and entered the Koh-i Jud in order to punish the Khokhar chief Jaspal Sehra, who had acted as the guide of the Mongols in the previous year. They ravaged the entire countryside extending from the Jhelam to the Indus. They plundered the Khokhar tribesmen – families, children and dependents – in such a manner that they were forced to flee. A body of the Mongols, which observed the Delhi army from the bank of the Jhelam, was filled with awe on seeing the vast number of soldiers as well the abundance of weapons and war materials. During the winter of 1246, Ulugh Khan led his troops through the mountains, ravines and forests. By showing exemplary vigour and military organization, Ulugh Khan occupied several forts and subdued the inhabitants. The stories of his exploits, if Juzjani was trusted, spread as far as the land of Turkistan. Since the entire tract suffered from lack of cultivation and fields, the supply of provisions was not possible. This difficulty forced the Delhi army to return from the Salt Range.[118]

The increasing factional conflict among the nobles, which defined the political developments in the middle of the thirteenth century, enabled the Mongols to recast their strategies in Panjab. Instead of fitting out frequent predatory campaigns in the region, they began to support disgruntled nobles who travelled long distances to seek asylum in their courts. Such notables – Jalaluddin

Masud (brother of Sultan Nasiruddin Mahmud), Kishlu Khan, Sher Khan and Qutlugh Khan – insecure in the unprecedented ascendancy of Ulugh Khan, thought it prudent to transfer a part of their loyalty to the principal enemy of their first patron. In fact, they used their new homage to the Mongols to make political bargains with the Delhi Sultanate. Their loyalty could not be taken for granted, as they were free to tilt to any side keeping in mind their political interest at any given point of time. When Jalaluddin Masud was installed in Lahore as a vassal of the Mongols, he received the support of Sali Bahadur on the one hand and Sher Khan on the other. Both Jalaluddin Masud and Sher Khan were sponsored by the Mongols, but they did not hesitate to compromise with Ulugh Khan for a short time in their search for greater gains. Realizing that they had been merely used by Ulugh Khan as a pawn in a political game, they were quick to distance themselves from Ulugh Khan. Not only this, they also fell apart and chalked out separate political courses for themselves. Jalaluddin Masud, despite these reverses, managed to carve out a petty kingdom in Panjab that included Lahore, Sodhra and Kujah.[119] If the Delhi Sultanate did not interfere with him, it was because he continued to enjoy the protection of the Mongols until his death in 1260.

The case of Kishlu Khan was somewhat different. Being frustrated at his failure to dislodge Ulugh Khan from his dominant position and a nagging conflict with Sher Khan over Multan and Uch, he felt induced to turn to the Mongols. As noted above, he had sent Shamsuddin Kurt Ghori as his emissary to Halaku, the prince of Turkistan.[120] During a personal appearance at Halaku's court, he agreed to accept a Mongol resident in his domain of Sind and sent his grandson as a hostage in Mongol custody. On returning to Uch, he sent his agents and the Mongol resident of Sind to Delhi. Evidently, he took this step to explain his link with the Mongols and thereby preempt any punitive action against himself.[121] At the same time, he displayed his continued loyalty to the Mongols. When the Mongol commander Sali Bahadur led a predatory raid (1257-8) on Sind, Kishlu Khan was forced to join the invaders owing to the presence of the Mongol resident in the region. When the Mongols dismantled the fortifications of Multan, Kishlu Khan remained a silent spectator and, in this manner, maintained a fine balance between his two warring overlords and also paid a price for serving two masters. Juzjani, as seen above, showed that the arrival of the Delhi army forced the Mongols to retreat on this occasion.[122]

But Isami's account was somewhat different, as he has described two military expeditions (1258) of Nasiruddin Mahmud to Multan. In the first one, the Mongols were routed in an ambush and the victory was followed by the revival of agriculture. Since the Sultan had a great liking for Kishlu Khan, he was left in charge of Multan.[123] The second military campaign, which was led by Ulugh Khan, was directed against Kishlu Khan who had revolted and fled. The fort of Multan was besieged and the garrison was reduced to distress. Muhammad, the son of Kishlu Khan, sued for peace and received an amicable treatment. The Multan troops defected to the Delhi army, while Kishlu Khan took refuge at Binban in the Qarlugh kingdom. Isami has accused Kishlu Khan of twice bringing the Mongols to Multan, though they failed to capture the place.[124]

In the long run, the Delhi Sultanate could not ignore the growing affinity between its provincial governors (*muqtis*) posted in western Panjab and the Mongols (or their clients). The trend posed a serious threat to the very existence of the Delhi Sultanate and deprived it of large chunks of territory beyond the Beas. The remedy lay in exercising a more effective control over highranking officers holding commands (*iqtas*) in these areas as well as fighting out the Mongols and their satellites from there. Given the circumstances in which it was placed, the Delhi Sultanate could not apply any of these measures. Still there was one option i.e. opening negotiations with the Mongols so as to block their expansion across central and eastern Panjab. With these ideas in mind, Ulugh Khan decided to use the services of the Qarlugh chief – the Mongol vassal whose kingdom lay between the Delhi Sultanate and the Mongol Empire – as a conduit. This move was facilitated by a strategic marriage between the son of Ulugh Khan and the daughter of Nasirudin Muhammad Qarlugh.[125] Ulugh Khan deputed Jamaluddin Ali Khalji to carry his letters for Halaku. This emissary, while travelling through Panjab, secured exemption from the demands of tax collectors on the ground of his diplomatic status. When he entered the territory (Sind) of Kishlu Khan, the latter became suspicious and desired to know the contents of the letters. Jamaluddin Ali Khalji took advantage of the presence of Mongol agents and, claiming diplomatic immunity and declaring his aim of appearing before the Qarlugh chief, refused to divulge the official correspondence. Kishlu Khan, realizing his helplessness, permitted the emissary to go ahead. When he arrived at Binban, the Mongol officers and other people came to know about the mission from Delhi. The Qarlugh chief, who was obliged to facilitate the journey of the emissary to Halaku's court through Iraq and Azarbaijan, provided his own escorts, letters and gifts.[126]

The manner in which Jamaluddin Ali Khalji secured a safe passage through vast territories, which were ruled by potentates hostile to one another, indicated the depth of Mongol hegemony in Panjab, Afghanistan and Central Asia. When the emissary met Halaku at Tabrez, he was pleasantly surprised to find that Ulugh Khan, in contrast to other nobles of Hindustan and Sind, was held in high esteem as an autonomous ruler. As the emissary embarked on his return journey, Halaku ordered the Mongol resident at Baniyan to escort the visitor. The Mongol ruler also issued a stern order for his military commander Sari Nuyin, 'If the hoof of a horse of your troops enters the dominion of Sultan Nasiruddin Mahmud, you are instructed to cut off the four legs of the horse.' Evidently, the diplomatic contact between the two powers culminated in an agreement to uphold peace on the Indian frontier. Not long after, Halaku dispatched a delegation from his army, which had been stationed in Khurasan and Turkistan, to Delhi where it was given (March 1260) a warm reception.[127] In this manner, the Delhi Sultanate sought to minimize the Mongol threat and the recalcitrance of the pro-Mongol Panjab officers. Ulugh Khan found it easier to deal with the longstanding enemy of the Delhi Sultanate than its own ambitious and restless officers.[128]

Sultan Ghiasuddin Balban (r. 1266-86), who had held important positions in the Delhi Sultanate during a career of two decades as a distinguished noble (Ulugh Khan), developed his own approach towards problems on the northwestern frontier. He believed that the glory of state depended on war animals, horses and elephants. He did not rely on the lands ruled by the Mongols for the supply of horses. He had assigned the region of Sind to his elder son Sultan Muhammad, who facilitated the supply of a large number of Tatari and Bharaichi horses to Delhi. Selected horses of Indian breeds were raised in large numbers in the various places of Panjab: Sunam, Samana, Bathinda, Thanesar and the Siwaliks. The Sultan found it easy to secure an adequate number of horses at low prices from these places in order to meet the needs of his army.[129] Once he had suppressed the rebellious elements of Mewat and Doab, he led a military expedition to the Koh-i Jud, the stronghold of the Khokhars. While the mountainous tract was ravaged, his troops acquired innumerable horses from the retainers of hill men (Khokhars). Owing to the ample availability of horses among the troops, their prices fell as low as 30-40 *tankas*.[130] Two years after this success, Balban marched to Lahore and initiated several measures for its rehabilitation. The fortification (*hissar*) of the city, which had been pulled down by the Mongols, was rebuilt. Concrete steps were taken to revive normal life in all those places – the city of Lahore along with its towns and villages – which had suffered devastation at the hands of the Mongols. The Sultan appointed superintendents and builders (*gumashtgan wa maimaran*) for the task of resettlement and reconstruction.[131] However, beyond the recovery of Lahore, no attempt was made to secure large parts of Panjab that were in the firm grip of the Mongols. In fact, their presence in the region was such a potent threat that the Delhi Sultanate could not contemplate any territorial expansion in other directions. In response to a specific question on this subject, Balban underscored the enormity of the Mongol threat. His response was as follows:

The Mongol armies had established themselves on the borders of the Delhi Sultanate. They were firmly settled in Ghazni, Tirmiz, and Mawra ul-Nahr. Halaku, who was ruling from Baghdad, had occupied Iraq. Since the Mongols were aware of the wealth and prosperity of Hindustan, they had always intended to plunder it. Lahore, which formed the border of the kingdom, had often been attacked and destroyed by them. Not a year passed when they did not enter the country or failed to plunder the habitations of the Khokhars. As soon as they would hear the departure of the Sultan from Delhi, they would surely destroy the capital city, ravage the towns and plunder the Doab. The previous Sultans failed to block the entry of the Mongols, who felt free to attack any part of the kingdom and loot its wealth. In contrast, Balban claimed to spend the revenue from provinces on raising a strong army. Instead of leaving his capital, he looked forward to confronting the Mongols. If there had been no fear of the Mongol inroads and the Sultan was not burdened with the safety of India's towns, he would have led military campaigns to distant kingdoms and brought back unlimited treasures, elephants and horses.[132]

In 1270 Sher Khan, who had played a significant role in the politics of Panjab for several decades, died. His death became an occasion for Barani to pay a rich tribute to this veteran noble with reference to the situation on the northwestern frontier. According to the historian, Sher Khan had stood as a wall of Gog and Magog between the Mongols and Delhi Sultanate for thirty years since the death of Iltutmish. He was one of the forty Turki slave officers of this Sultan and, attaining the rank of Khan, held a high position among them. Since the accession of Nasiruddin Mahmud, he held the revenue assignments of Lahore, Dipalpur, Sunam and other places that were located in the direction of the Mongols. Besides raising the citadel of Bathinda, he had constructed a fort and high dome at Bhatner. He had mustered a crack force of several thousand horsemen and, in his repeated campaigns against the Monglos, inflicted crushing defeats on them. He had even succeeded in getting the Friday sermon (*khutba*) read in the name of Sultan Nasiruddin Mahmud in Ghazni. Owing to the large size of his armed contingent and his personal qualities (alertness, intrepidity, power and pomp) the Mongols did not dare to approach the borders of Hindustan. He had also forced the warlike tribes of Panjab – Jats, Khokhars, Bhattis, Minas, Mandahars and others – to withdraw into their strongholds. However, he did not visit Delhi, as the Shamsi slaves were being murdered on one pretext or the other. He maintained this posture even when his cousin

Ghiasuddin Balban ascended the throne. Unfortunately, he was poisoned by the Sultan through a cupbearer (*fuqai*).[133]

After Sher Khan's death, the *iqtas* of Samana and Sunam were assigned to Tamar Khan who was also one of the Shamsi Turkish slaves. Other *iqtas* in his charge were assigned to other officers. But his successors could not come upto his stature and failed to fight the Mongols or suppress the tribes. In fact, none of them could achieve what Sher Khan had achieved in just thirty years. Keeping this factor in mind, Sultan Ghiasuddin Balban nominated his son Sultan Muhammad, who was given the title of Qaan-i Malik and was popularly known as Khan-i Shahid, as his heir apparent and entrusted to him all the territories of Sind and its dependencies. He was sent to Multan along with several highranking nobles and dignitaries.[134] Every year the prince arrived from Multan laden with treasures, horses and gifts. He returned after staying in Delhi for a few days.[135]

When Balban deputed Sultan Muhammad to Multan with the task of defending the northwestern frontier against the Mongols, he also created a second line of defence by assigning the *iqtas* of Sunam, Samana, and neighbouring places to his younger son Bughra Khan. Since Bughra Khan lacked the intelligence and ability of his elder brother, the Sultan issued special instructions to him, so that he could acquit himself in a satisfactory manner. The prince was required to understand that the *iqta* of Samana was extensive, while numerous experienced soldiers and officers were already serving there. He was asked to keep the army of Samana properly equipped and trained under the supervision of an experienced commander, so that it was always ready to fight against the Mongols. He was directed to increase the salaries of the old servants of the state. He was instructed to undertake a fresh recruitment drive, so that the number of soldiers and officers was doubled. He was advised to patronize sincere and loyal well wishers of the state, who ought to be appointed as nobles (*amirs*) and granted suitable revenue assignments. He was expected to avoid rash decisions, but to consult confidants who had adequate knowledge of state affairs. He was urged to seek the advice of the Sultan in complicated administrative matters. He was warned to keep away from excessive drinking and wasteful activities, as these bad habits would adversely affect the administration of his extensive *iqta*. If this happened, he would be dismissed from his post and also deprived of his *iqta*, his future would be jeopardized as he would not be given any other *iqta* and he would be pushed to the rank of the unemployed. The Sultan's concerns were quite understandable as, during those days, the Mongols had become so audacious as to often cross the Beas. On these occasions, the Sultan dispatched three armies – Sultan Muhammad from Multan, Bughra Khan from Samana and Malik Barbak Bektars from Delhi – each of which comprised 17,000-18,000 horsemen. These commanders marched to the Beas and, taking up the offensive against the Mongols, secured many victories.[136] Barani's statement indicates that in spite of the numerous measures taken by Balban, the Beas was treated as the northwestern boundary of the Delhi Sultanate, the Mongol inroads occurred quite frequently and the Bari Doab up to Multan became a zone of contestation between the two powers. It might be added that, with the transfer of Bughra Khan to Lakhnauti after the suppression of the Bengal revolt, his administrative responsibilities in Panjab were handed over to Sultan Muhammad.

Life and Death of a Governor

Sultan Muhammad, who administered several areas in western Panjab, deserved a closer look for a variety of reasons. Impressed with his colourful personality, prominent nobles who had been Shamsi slaves, named their sons as Muhammad after him. The prince was known among his contemporaries for his learning, affability and sophistication. While attending to administrative matters, he sat on his knees an entire day and night without shifting his posture. He always conducted himself with great dignity. A moderate drinker, he did not get inebriated, nor did he utter a bad word.[137] His assemblies were crowded with people who were skilled in wisdom and arts. His companions recited poetry from the *Shahnama* of Firdausi, the *Khamsa* of Nizami Ganjavi and the *Diwans* of Sanai and Khaqani. They also discussed the aesthetic features of the verses of these poets. His court was a veritable galaxy of the finest literati in the Indian subcontinent. He extended patronage to Amir Khusrau and Amir Hasan Sijzi who spent five years at the governor's court in Multan. In his convivial parties, Sultan Muhammad discerned their extraordinary literary talent, both in poetry and prose. He not only treated them as his confidants, but also favoured them with lavish salaries and awards. In fact, he made two attempts to invite Saadi Shirazi to join his court in Multan. On both the occasions, he sent an emissary to the great Persian poet at Shiraz along with suitable expenses for the journey. He wished to build a hospice (*khanqah*) for the guest in Multan and endow it with the revenue of a few villages. Shirazi declined the invitations because of his old age and, while expressing his regret for his inability to come, he sent a collection of his sonnets (*ghazals*) which had been transcribed in his own hand.[138]

Besides literature and poetry, Sultan Muhammad had a passionate interest in Islamic mysticism and musical sessions (*sama*). Once an eminent saint Shaikh Usman Marwandi arrived in Multan.[139] The prince received him with great devotion and presented him a large offering (*ba-ifrat tawazo kard wa futuh basiyar dasht wa basiyar jehd kard*). Since he wished the distinguished visitor to permanently settle in Multan, he constructed a hospice (*khanqah*) and granted a few villages in maintenance. The Shaikh, owing to unknown reasons, did not settle in the city. However, he attended a musical session along with Shaikh Qudwa and some other Sufis. During the proceedings, devotional verses in Arabic (*ghazal-ha-i arabi*) were sung, as a result of which the Sufis began to dance in ecstasy. As long as the saints engaged in song and dance, Sultan Muhammad kept on standing with folded hands and wept profusely (*ta aan zaman keh darveshan dar sama wa raqs budand dast bastah istadah bud wa zarzar megreest*). He also displayed a deep emotional involvement in secular assemblies. When his companions recited devotional verses, which were imbued with advice and admonition (*waaz wa nasaih*), he abandoned all other tasks and, while listening with utmost devotion, broke into soulful weeping. The gathering was astonished at his intelligence and sensitivity.[140]

Sultan Muhammad, who was endowed with stellar personal excellences, could not face the Mongol invasions in a satisfactory manner. In fact, his troops met with humiliating defeats on two occasions. When he had spent a fairly long time in Multan, two Mongol contingents penetrated the boundary of the city and ravaged the exposed areas. On hearing the report of this incursion, he ordered his commanders to march out of Multan and to break the ranks of the intruders. This army marched towards Hind Kandhali on receiving a report about the presence of the Mongols. As the battle went underway, a terrific noise rose up. A Mongol detachment moved fiercely and, drowning the beat of the indigenous drums of war, fell upon their adversaries. In the initial stages, the Indian soldiers offered some resistance, but they were soon outnumbered and put to flight. The Indian commanders, while being aggressively pursued by their opponents, reached as far the environs of Sind. Any fugitive, who lagged behind, fell as a prisoner in the Mongol hands. While the victorious columns withdrew to the camp, the Indian commanders returned to Multan. As soon as Sultan Muhammad learnt the details of their miserable defeat, he fell into a terrible rage and even wanted to kill them. On second thoughts, he decided to issue a strong rebuke and impose a fine for their slackness, so that they did not accept defeat in the future and staked their lives in the battlefield. Accordingly, he served a notice of fine to each one of them. When the officers read the embarrassing order, they appealed for the substitution of 'fine' by another word, so that their reputation was not sullied for all times. Taking a lenient, Sultan Muhammad replaced the word 'fine' by 'offering and presentation', thus saving his army commanders from disgrace.[141]

Sultan Muhammad, in order to crush the revolt of the Sumras, marched to Sind and encamped in the vicinity of Jatral. During the course of punitive operations, he learnt through a written message that a force of 30,000 Mongol horsemen (under Tamar, according to Barani) had arrived at distance of a few miles

(3 *farsangs*) from his camp. Since the Indians had been taken by surprise, the army commanders advised Sultan Muhammad to leave for Multan, as it would not be proper for him to lead the fight against the Mongols in person and, owing to the uncertainty of the result on the battlefield, his life was extremely valuable, particularly for the ageing Sultan in Delhi. Sultan Muhammad, refusing to be demoralized by the sheer size of the Mongol contingents, rejected the advice and vowed to die like a hero in the thick of battle. Next day, his troops emerged from their camp and took up positions to fight, so that the atmosphere was filled with dust. The Mongols moved in from every side and fell upon the Indian ranks. Sultan Muhammad firmly established himself and guided a resolute resistance, which was coupled with offensive tactics. As the soldiers of the two adversaries grappled in a central place, all types of weapons were deployed. Though the fierce engagement raged from morning until afternoon, no side could overpower the other. The Mongols managed to trace a weak link (a Ghuzz chief named Mangli) among their opponents and, in a fierce attack, scattered his retinue. As the Mongols gained the upper hand, the Indian troops fell into a state of panic and fled in all directions. Some Indian soldiers stuck to their places and made a desperate use of all arms one after the other – arrows, swords, fists and teeth. But all their captains, who held different positions on the ground, were crushed. A terrible scene like the day of resurrection (*qiyamat*) was enacted.[142]

Sultan Muhammad, who had been left alone in the battlefield, drove his horse towards a rivulet. But he was killed by a sharp arrow fired by a Qaraunah. With his main artery pierced by the shot, he rolled down from his saddle and fell in the mud. The Qaraunah, who was unmindful of the identity of the fallen adversary, seized his equipment – horse, sword, bow and quiver – and joined his companions. One of the Indian prisoners (who belonged to the party of the prince's musicians), having recognized his master's horse and quiver, started wailing while throwing dust on his head, pulling his hair and scratching his face. As soon as the Mongols heard the name of Sultan Muhammad, they forced the Qaraunah to reveal the source of his valuable booty. Cornered thus, the Qaraunah led his companions to the site on the bank of the rivulet. They were astonished to see the stout physique and broad shoulders of the deceased, now lying dead in a pool of blood. They carried the body, along with the horse and armaments, to their commander. He ordered the body to be placed in a coffin and intended to send it to their own country. At this juncture, Rai Kalu, the father-in-law of Sultan Muhammad, heard the tragic news. He rushed to the scene and broke into mournful lamentations. He paid a sizeable amount of money from his *iqta* to the Mongols and redeemed the body of his son-in-law,[143] who was not only the governor of a large territory, but also the son of the reigning Sultan and heir apparent to the throne of the Delhi Sultanate. Barani has failed to provide any detail of the battle on the frontier, except that the military engagement took place somewhere between Lahore and Dipalpur. But he did mention that the death of Sultan Muhammad caused such a commotion in Multan that there was mourning in every house; all inhabitants of the city wore blue clothes and the noise of their lamentations reached the sky. Since that date, Sultan Muhammad, the governor of Multan, came to be known as Khan-i Shahid.[144]

Amir Khusrau, who was present in Multan during the tragic occurrence and even suffered captivity of the Mongols, has described the military conflict in his own way. According to him, as soon as Sultan Muhammad received the news of enemy's approach, he donned the helmet and hoisted the flag. He marched out with whatever troops were in readiness and did not wait for any reinforcements, as Rustam did not seek the aid of an army. It was inauspicious hour when he commenced on his journey from Multan and, in one swift move, reached Lahore. He was furious at the Mongols for the audacity of raising their head when he, like a lion, had reduced thousands of his foes to dust every year. He stated, 'So much of their blood have I caused to flow like water that the vultures swim in it as the duck does in the river. This year the ground shall be dyed so red with their blood that the twilight will borrow its red tinge from the earth.' On the eve of Muharram, he entered the battlefield like Husain of Karbala before the coming of Ashura and thrust his spear down the throats of his foes.[145]

At an unhappy hour, horde upon horde of the Mongols crossed the Ravi and drew close to the Prince's army. As his charger clouded the sky with dust, the Mongols scattered like chaff in a storm. The earth trembled with the swift rush of horsemen, while the sky resounded with the shouts of warriors, neighing of horses and rumbling of drums. But the Prince thought only of fighting like a man and urging his men to fight. The bright day changed into a dusky evening, but the combatants were still involved in a fierce contest. As the dead lay on the field like the figures woven into a green tapestry, the wounded struggled in agony with blood gushing out of their throats. The Prince's sword did not rest for a single moment from its slaughter of the foes. Riding on his glorious charger, he moved from place to place, arranging his men and giving them instructions. As victory appeared in his sight and Mongols awaited the opportunity to escape, the scales suddenly changed and the Prince lost his life. If Husain trod a waterless path in Karbala, the Prince was drowned in the river owing to the guile of the demons. The severed heads of the dead were strewn over the field, looking like Indian nuts chased with bright vermilion. 'Each year the Prince had to deal with the Mongols for the sake of Islam, and behold how at last he has given away his life also in that cause.'[146]

Amir Khusrau has described his experience as a prisoner in the custody of the Mongols against the backdrop of this calamity. It was difficult for him to narrate the heroic deeds of Sultan Muhammad which were similar to the valour of Hazrat Ali against the Khaibaris.[147] The terrible outcome of the battle was a divine decree which issued from God and therefore could not be averted. The blood of the martyrs drenched the soil like water, while cords tied the faces of prisoners like flowers in a wreath. Their heads jostled in the knots of the saddle straps and their throats choked in the nooses of the reins. Though Amir Khusrau was spared of this painful treatment yet, being a prisoner, the fear of death did not leave any blood in his thin and feeble body. He had to run headlong like a torrent, while the long trek caused a thousand blisters on his feet like bubbles and the skin of his feet was rent. On account of these hardships, life appeared hard like the hilt of a sword and his body became dry like wood in the handle of an axe. Like an autumn tree, his body was naked and torn into a thousand shreds by the painful lacerations of thorny bushes. Tears dropped from his eyes as pearls fell from the necks of brides. The despicable Mongol captor, who drove him in front of him, sat on his horse like a leopard on a hill. A foul stench came from his mouth and filthy moustaches hung from his chin. When the hapless prisoner was forced to slow down his pace due to exhaustion, he was threatened with death. Heaving sighs of despair, he felt that he would never be able to escape alive from his ordeal. He offered a thousand thanks to God for delivering him from an inhuman affliction, without his heart being pierced by any arrow and body unscathed by any sword. His release came at the end of a difficult journey through a desert heaped with layers of sand, where his brain boiled like a cauldron with intense heat. When they reached a stream of water, the Mongol captor and his horse drank water until they were satiated and, as a result, died instantly. Amir Khusrau, who just moistened his lips and refreshed his body, managed to save his life.[148]

On returning to Multan, Amir Khusrau was shocked to find the state of inhabitants, who were sunk in a sea of mourning. They expressed grief at the death of the Prince and their relatives who had fallen round him. In his words,

Even the sun and the moon wept for his handsome face, and the night and the day mourned his brief life. As the birds and the fish had also been in peace during his reign, the air and the water were full of moanings on his death. The inhabitants of Multan on all sides, in every alley and in each quarter, wept, rending their clothes and tearing their hair. With the loud cries of mourning and the beating of the drums, nobody could sleep that night, for in every house there was some dead to be wept for. The darkness of the Hindu and the whiteness of the Turk have both disappeared, for the two are alike dressed in deep blue. The fair ones no longer require indigo and rouge, for with slapping their cheeks are red and their eyebrows blue.

Whenever any captive secured his release from bondage and returned to the city, the people looked at his face and wept bitterly because the survivor was not the one they looked for. Though Amir Khusrau was relieved at his providential escape, yet he was extremely sad at the absence of his numerous friends who had lost their lives in the violent catastrophe. At the age of thirty-four, he could expect to live for several decades. But his long life could not bring any joy, as his friends were no longer there to add happiness to his existence.[149]

In view of the above bitter experience and sense of loss, it was understandable if Amir Khusrau has left behind a prejudiced portrait of the Mongols. According to him, the Mongols wore quiltted vests as under armour and cotton garments on their bodies. They were fire faced, flat nosed, narrow eyed, foul mouthed and dog tongued. Known for devouring dogs and pigs, they gave out a dirty stench from their armpits. They emitted sounds of 'Qarbu Qarbu' like monkeys. In battle, they were headstrong and fierce. They wore plumes of feathers on their heads, which were shorn and looked like eggs. Their caps were made of sheepskin. Their azure coloured eyes were so narrow and piercing that they looked like two crevices bored in a large brazen vessel. The stench coming out of them was worse than that from a rotten carcass. Their skin was crumpled and wrinkled like the soft leather of a bottle. Their nose extended from cheek to cheek. The hair of their nostrils, which represented an oven full of stinking water, extended as far as their lips. They had scanty beard on their sunken cheeks, as no vegetation grew on the surface of ice. Their moustaches were of inordinate length. Owing to the excess of lice on their clothes, their breasts had turned black and white like the mustard growing over barren soil. Whereas other people got oil from the bodies of the Tartars, the bodies of the Mongols were covered with rough untanned hide, which could be used for the soles of shoes. Eating dogs and pigs with their nasty teeth, they pilfered morsels of food like dogs. There was a constant flow of watery substance from their drain like nostrils. They emitted such a foul smell that nobody dared to sit near them.[150]

Winning over Opponents

Jalaluddin Khalji, who ascended the throne of Delhi on 13 June 1296 in the wake of political changes at the highest levels of the state, had served in Panjab for several years and possessed the experience of fighting against the Mongols. Sometime during the reign of Ghiasuddin Balban, he was appointed the chief of royal bodyguard (*sar-i jandar*), besides being entrusted with the administration of Samana and Kaithal. His connection with these two places has been recorded by Barani. Maulana Sirajuddin Savi, a poet of Samana, on being oppressed by local officers for land tax, complained to the governor Jalaluddin Khalji. When his complaint went unheeded, he wrote the *Khalji Nama* in which the governor was subjected to satirical criticism. As the *muqti* of Kaithal, Jalaluddin Khalji plundered a village of the Mandahars and, in an armed clash, he received deep wounds on his face by the sword of a Mandahar.[151] While holding military commands in Panjab, Jalaluddin Khalji led punitive expeditions against the Mongols as well as the frontier tribes. In fact, while exercising his authority as the Sultan and dealing with the revolt of Malik Chajju, he recalled with pride his military exploits in different areas. His fame as a military general was well known, as his conquests had reached distant places like Ghazni, Kirman, Barjand and Darband. He had converted his enemies into worms with his Kirmani sword. He had filled his cup with the blood of the Mongols and had stuck their inverted skulls on the top of his standards. He had wounded the Afghans with his spears, so that the mountains echoed with their lamentations. He had made the blood of the Janjuas flow in such large quantities that boats could glide through it in the Koh-i Jud. The local populace could not imagine how he filled hell to the brim with the dead.[152]

In addition to the appointment of his son Arkali Khan as the governor of Multan, the Sultan's intimate connection with the military campaigns against the Mongols was indicated by two pieces of evidence. In a discussion with Ahmad Chap, he offered to renounce the kingship and retire to Multan, so that he could, like Sher Khan, wage a war against the Mongols and prevent them from entering the territories of the Delhi Sultanate.[153] On another occasion, he wished his name to be recited in the Friday sermon (*khutbah*) as a crusader on the path of God (*al-mujahid fi sabil allah*), as he had been fighting against the Mongols for several years. At his suggestion, his wife Malika-i Jahan asked the leading theologians of Delhi to make a formal proposal on this issue to the Sultan. However, the Sultan changed his mind on the plea that his wars against the Mongols were aimed at exhibiting his bravery and gaining fame. He admitted that these battles had not been fought in the true spirit of a crusade (*jihad*), which was exclusively undertaken in the way of God and implied a keen desire for martyrdom.[154]

In 1292 Abdullah, the grandson of Halaku, invaded India at the head of over one lakh soldiers. Jalaluddin Khalji led his troops out of the capital Kilogarhi and, resorting to forced marches, reached Barram. Here the two armies stood facing each other, being separated by a river. As preparations were being made for a pitched battle, there were skirmishes between the advance guards of the adversaries. In these clashes, a number of Mongols were killed and some were taken as prisoners. The two sides exchanged emissaries and decided to stop further hostilities. A meeting was arranged between the Sultan and Abdullah. They addressed each other as son and father respectively, while the troops were withdrawn from the battlefield. Alaghu, a grandson of Chingez Khan, entered the service of the Sultan along with some commanders of 1,000 and 100 troopers.[155] The Sultan also gave his daughter in marriage to Alaghu. The Mongols embraced Islam by reciting the confession of faith. Alaghu and his associates, who were accompanied by their women and children, came to settle in Delhi. They received salaries for a period of one or two years. They built their houses near Kilogarhi, Ghiaspur, Indarpat, and Tiloka. The area of their settlement acquired the name of Mughalpur.[156] The climate of the country and residence in the neighbourhood of the city did not suit the immigrants. Most of them returned to their own country along with their families. Some of the leading men among them continued to stay back in the land of their domicile. They continued to receive villages and allowances and, having contracted marriages with the local Muslims, became popularly known as neo-Muslims.[157]

Last Phase of the Mongol Incursions

The first half of Alauddin Khalji's reign witnessed a manifold increase of Mongol pressure on Panjab. During a span of ten years (1296-1306), there were as many as six invasions and, on two occasions, the invaders besieged the city of Delhi. In 1296 Dava Khan, the Mongol ruler of Mawra ul-Nahr, sent Kadar at the head of a large army. This Mongol horde ravaged the Koh-i Jud and destroyed the habitations (*talwarah*) of the Khokhars. It crossed the rivers of Panjab (Jhelam, Beas, and Satluj) and, turning towards the town of Qasur, demolished its buildings. The Sultan sent Ulugh Khan and Zafar Khan at the head of an extensive force, which included several Jalali and Alai nobles. These troops swam across the Satluj and overwhelmed the invaders at Jaran Manjur (Jalandhar). In a bloody battle (9 February 1298), nearly 20,000 Mongols were killed and the survivors were sent to Delhi in chains. In the capital, the occasion was celebrated with the beating of drums and recitation of the victory letters (*fatehnamas*).[158] In 1299 when the Delhi army was engaged in the subjugation of Gujarat, Zafar Khan was directed to march to Siwistan, which had been occupied by a Mongol retinue led by Saldi. Zafar Khan besieged the invaders in the local fort, but did not employ any of the technical devices – siege engines (*manjniq*), ballistas (*arradah*), covered passages (*sabat*), ladders (*pasheb*), and movable scaffoldings (*gargaj*). In spite of a relentless barrage of arrows from the besieged, Zafar Khan succeeded in taking the fort. A large number of Mongol prisoners – including Saldi, his brother, women and children – were dispatched to Delhi in chains.[159] Zafar Khan, who was assigned the fief of Samana, remained posted in this town in order to keep a watch on the frontier. In view of his bravery and intrepidity, Zafar Khan was seen as a second Rustam who had been born in India. In fact, he acquired such a formidable reputation that even the Sultan became jealous of him and began to consider ways of eliminating him.[160]

In the wake of his victory in Siwistan, Zafar Khan sent a messenger to the unnamed Mongol ruler and, in a angry message, asserted the territorial claims of the Delhi Sultanate upto the Indus. To demoralize this opponent, he sent a gift comprising a scarf, a veil, powder, and collyrium. The Mongols appeared to have accepted this challenge, as Qutlugh Khwaja brought (1299) in an army of two lakh soldiers, including women riding on horse-backs. The successive bands of invaders crossed the Indus, but they refrained from pillaging the plains of Panjab as their prime target was Delhi.[161] A wave of fear swept across the military strongholds in different parts of Panjab, though defensive arrangements had been put in place. The officers and soldiers, who had been serving in the province of Multan, fortified themselves in every citadel. Reputed for their alacrity and nimbleness, they emerged out of their fortresses in the darkness of the night and fell upon the assailants. Besides killing anyone who was encountered, they plundered the Turki horses in such number that a hundred of them could be purchased for a coin (*shadbashi*). Since they were not inclined to fight a pitched battle, they withdrew to the safety of their respective towns in the province of Multan.

The Mongols, in spite of their reverses, pushed to the east beyond Bathinda. Zafar Khan, who was present at Kuhram, encamped outside the local fort in order to contend with the invaders. Introducing himself as the slayer of lions and the captor of demons, he sent a message to Qutlugh Khwaja and challenged him to a battle. The Mongol commander did not accept the challenge, as he intended to fight against his equal, the Sultan of Delhi. As the invaders reached the vicinity of the capital, panic spread in all directions. People of surrounding areas rushed into the city and occupied all vacant spaces in streets, bazaars and mosques. Distress became general as the merchants failed to transport essential commodities. The Sultan summoned military commanders from the provinces and, marching out of the camp at Siri, arranged the troops in battle array at Kili. Zafar Khan commanded the right wing with a detachment of seasoned Hindu warriors (probably drawn from the tribes of Panjab). What was surprising, the Sultan acceded to the request of Qutlugh Khwaja and permitted his four representatives to inspect his military columns as well as record the names of high ranking officers.[162]

As the battle commenced, Diler Khan (the son of Zafar Khan) made a fierce attack on the invaders, who were forced to contemplate withdrawing from the battlefield. On his part, Zafar Khan neutralized a resolute assault by Hajlak. Though he felt that he had gained an upper hand, yet he was worried at the Sultan's failure to deliver a formal order for a final offensive. 'Since a man of action could not afford to rely on the Sultan's word at this critical moment,' Zafar Khan took the initiative in his own hands and routed the left wing of the Mongols. Unable to resist this sharp onslaught, the Mongols released the Indian captives and fled from the battlefield. Zafar Khan pursued the fugitives for 18 *kurohs*, but did not press for an engagement because the retreating enemy could rally for a counter offensive. Ulugh Khan, who was commanding the left wing and had numerous troops in his retinue, did not go to reinforce Zafar Khan owing to personal hostility. Taking advantage of this situation, a Mongol detachment of 10,000 strong under Targhi, which was waiting for an ambush in a low lying hollow, surrounded Zafar Khan. Qutlugh Khwaja, through a message, invited Zafar Khan to switch over to the Mongols and offered a position higher than the one offered by the Sultan of Delhi. Zafar Khan not only refused to swallow the Mongol bait, but also rejected the proposal of his companions who were in favour of a retreat. He had only 1,000 soldiers at his command, but he was pitted against ten times this number. In a fierce engagement, he decimated nearly half of the enemy force and himself died fighting to the last man.[163] In spite of this success, the Mongols retreated through Panjab without any further incident. They bore the imprint of Zafar Khan's terror for several years. When their horses refused to drink water, they asked if they had seen the face of Zafar Khan.[164] Though Alauddin Khalji was aggrieved at losing a Rustam-like warrior, he blamed him for exceeding the royal mandate and rushing headlong into the danger zone.[165]

When another Mongol commander Targhi marched in 1301 through Panjab at the head of a vast army, the officers holding military commands in the region did not offer resistance. The invaders laid siege to Delhi, where the inhabitants faced scarcity of basic goods, grain, fodder, fuel and even water. Two factors had undermined the defence preparedness. No strong army had been stationed at Multan, Samana, or Dipalpur that could fight the Mongols and join the troops at the royal camp in Siri. The detachments from Hindustan were held up at Kol and Baran, being unable to advance to Delhi as all the roads and fords on the Jamuna were occupied by the Mongols. Alauddin Khalji assembled the available troops at Siri and fortified his position by building entrenchments. The Mongols carried out raids in some localities (Chabutra-i Sultani, Hauz-i Sultani, Mauri and Hudhi), but could not penetrate the defences. Following a stalemate of two months, the Mongols withdrew with some booty.[166]

After a few years in 1305, Ali Beg and Tartaq entered Panjab at the head of 50,000 soldiers and, as they took to plunder, smoke arose from towns and inhabitants fled from their houses. Alauddin Khalji nominated Malik Kafur to lead the military operations against the invaders. In addition to Ghazi Malik, he was assisted by captains like Bahram Kabra, Mahmud Sartabe, Takli, Qarmash, Tulak and Qatla. A pitched battle was fought near Hansi and Sarsuti. As the trumpets blared and swords clinked, the twang of bowstrings echoed in the sky. Malik Kafur's resolute attack trampled the centre of the Mongols who were scattered. As Mongol blood flowed in streams, two of their captains were taken prisoner along with 10,000 followers. Besides 30,000 horses the victors grabbed booty comprising slaves, maids, tents, saddles, and bridles. These vast spoils, along with cartloads of heads of the enemy killed in battle, were brought to Delhi.[167] A spectacle was organized at Chabutra-i Subhani, where the Sultan presided over the proceedings. Troops were stationed on two sides of the road leading from the royal palace to Indrapat. A vast multitude of people converged at the site, where a cup of water was sold for 20 *jitals*. The prisoners were first paraded in chains and then trampled under the feet of elephants. A tower of severed heads was raised outside the ramparts of the fort. The two Mongol commanders, who were honoured on the occasion, were allowed to live for a short time and then put to death.[168]

During the same year (1305), Kabak led a massive horde of one lakh soldiers across the Indus. Contemporary writers differ on the route taken by the invaders and location of the final military engagement. According to Amir Khusrau, the Mongols raised dust on the border of Sind, forcing the inhabitants to throw away their property and disperse like autumnal leaves. Since they failed to cause a similar damage in Kuhram and Samana, they descended southwards across the Siwaliks and reached Nagaur, overpowering the populace of the area. It was on the banks of the Ab-i Ali that they were defeated by Malik Kafur.[169] In a somewhat similar account, Barani has recorded that four Mongol commanders with 20,000-30,000 cavalry ravaged the Siwaliks and, traversing a long route, encamped on the bank of a river. Malik Kafur, who was already waiting at the site, routed the Mongols and brought the prisoners to the fort of Naraina, which was situated on the east of Nagaur near the Sambar Lake. The men were put to death, while women and children were carried to Delhi to be sold as slaves.[170]

According Isami's more detailed account, a courier from Multan reported that Kabak had invaded with one lakh cavalrymen, that the frontier guards had withdrawn into their fortresses out of fear and that there was panic all over Hindustan. At the express orders of the Sultan, Malik Kafur held a military review outside the capital and enlisted 10,000 adept horsemen from all parts of the country. A fresh muster roll was submitted to the Sultan, who sanctioned an advance salary of one year for each soldier. In addition to leading nobles like Ghazi Malik and Malik Alam, the recipients included Hindu notables who were renowned warriors. As the imperial troops marched towards Multan, it camped at Hindali Wahan for a week. Ghazi Malik,[171] who was deputed to report the movements of the Mongols and who was forced to spend a night in the enemy camp, conveyed the crucial information to Malik Kafur. During the course of a battle, Kabak made several attempts to drive a wedge through the centre of the Delhi army and then to fall upon the ranks. Nevertheless, Malik Kafur offered a stubborn resistance and, assuming the offensive, captured Kabak and dispersed his followers. The Mongol captives stooped before every victorious soldier just as people (peasants) bowed before the Hindu landed chief (*chaudhuri*). The victorious commanders, on reaching Delhi, received awards from the Sultan and paraded the prisoners, including Kabak, one by one.[172]

Shortly thereafter Iqbalmand and Taibu led another Mongol army in to Panjab. Our sources offer little information on the matter. Isami is silent, Amir Khusrau is vague and Barani is miserly. Nothing is known about the location of the areas that were attacked, the generals who confronted the invaders and details of the military encounters. Amir Khusrau's account, marked by literary flourishes, indicates that the right wing of the Indian army overwhelmed the Mongols, who fled across the Indus along the route they came. The victorious troops pursued the fugitives and, having caught up with them, removed their heads. According to a official chronicle, they enacted scenes of resurrection on innumerable bodies, so that it appeared as if the day of judgement had arrived and angels of the Lord were collecting the corpses of the stonehearted infidels to light the fire of hell. Those captured alive were put in chains and brought to Delhi for review. Some of them were hung from the ramparts with inverted heads. Others were thrown in the air by elephants and beaten into loosened wool. Their physical remains were mixed with building material and pushed into the foundations of the towers of the fort.[173] According to Barani, the battle was fought at Tanbara-i Amir Ali and Wahan. As the Indian army emerged victorious, Iqbalmand was killed and thousands of Mongols were put to the sword. The high ranking nobles, *amiran-i hazara* and *amiran-i sadah*, were captured and brought to Delhi, where they were crushed under the feet of elephants.[174]

The increased frequency of the Mongol invasions and rising threat to the capital of the Delhi Sultanate forced the ruling class to devote its attention to the matter. Before the battle against Qutlugh Khwaja and death of Zafar Khan, the Sultan had been holding discussions with his leading advisors on the means to fight the Mongol menace. However, it was after the invasion of Targhi that the Sultan discarded his indifference and implemented a slew of measures which were designed to strengthen the military infrastructure in Panjab.[175] At the outset, he raised the fortifications of Delhi and constructed the palace of Siri, which was recognized as the capital of the realm and therefore suitably populated. All the forts that were situated on the route of the Mongols and had been in a state disrepair, were to be rebuilt. Wherever the need for a new fort was felt it was to be constructed. In the forts that lay in the direction of the Mongols, prominent and efficient superintendents (*kotwals*) were appointed. These officers were directed to manufacture a large number of siege engines (*manjniqs* and *arradahs*), besides recruiting skilled artisans and stocking every kind of weapon. They were ordered to store copious quantities of grain and hay. A sizeable number of selected soldiers were to be recruited in Samana and Dipalpur. They were expected to remain ready for any exigency. Revenue assignments that lay in the direction of the Mongols were granted to senior nobles, while experienced governors and renowned commanders were posted in the area. After undertaking these measures, the Sultan summoned his counsellors and discussed the reorganization of the army. After considerable deliberations, it was decided to raise a large army that should be adept in archery and equipped with all types of armaments as well as a fine cavalry. In pursuance of these objectives, markets were regulated and prices were controlled. At the same time, the salary of a soldier was fixed at 234 *tankas*, while a trooper with two horses was paid an additional allowance of 78 *tankas*. The entire force appeared before the army minister (*arz-i mamalik*) for a test in archery. Those who were found skilled and possessed the necessary weapons were duly enrolled. Their horses were branded in accordance with their prices.[176]

Such measures, in the view of Barani at least, produced the desired results. Having suffered repeated defeats, the Mongols were so terrified of the armies of the Delhi Sultanate that they gave up the intention of attacking India. To the end of the rule of Sultan Qutbuddin Mubarak Khalji (r. 1316-20), they did not even bring the name of Hindustan on their tongue. Nor could they rest in peace because, even in their dreams, they imagined the swords of the Delhi Sultanate hanging over their heads. In contrast, the fear of the Mongols was removed from the city of Delhi and complete peace was established in other parts of the kingdom. The people, who inhabited the territories lying on the routes of the Mongol inroads, got engaged in the cultivation of land with absolute peace of mind. What was significant, Ghiasuddin Tughluq, who was then known as Ghazi Malik, acquired immense fame in Khurasan and Hindustan. Till the end of the reign of Sultan Qutbuddin Mubarak Khalji, he remained firmly entrenched in the revenue assignments of Lahore and Dipalpur, where he stood as a Chinese wall against the Mongols. In this role, he was seen as a worthy substitute of Sher Khan. Every winter, he marched out at the head of his troops from Dipalpur and carried out attacks on the borders of the Mongols. As a result, they did not dare to walk up to their own borders. In India, the fear of the Mongols was erased in such a manner that no one brought their name on his tongue.[177]

Towards the end, Barani (like all other religious minded people who were concerned about the future) did not attribute the great military achievements of the Khalji regime and corresponding public welfare to the genius of Alauddin Khalji. This was so because the Sultan was not only guilty of unpardonable sins – murder, oppression, cruelty and bloodshed – but he was singularly lacking in spirituality and piety (*kashf wa karamat*). In fact, the achievements of his reign and the contentment of the people were due to the blessings of Shaikh ul-Islam Nizamuddin Ghiaspuri (Shaikh Nizamuddin Auliya). Since the Shaikh remained absorbed in prayers and received the showers of divine kindness, he ensured that the Delhi armies always returned victorious and the desires of the people were always fulfilled.[178]

NOTES

1. With its core around Attock, it supported a minimum of agriculture and derived its income from the movement of pastoralists and trading caravans. Romila Thapar, *The Penguin History of Early India*, New Delhi: Penguin, rpt., 2002, p. 417.
2. Gurbux Singh, 'Punjab on the Eve of Muslim Invasions,' in *History of the Punjab*, vol. III *(AD 1000-1526)*, ed. Fauja Singh, Patiala: Punjabi University, 1972, p. 54.
3. Dashratha Sharma, 'The Political Condition of Northern India in 985,' in *A Comprehensive History of India*, vol. IV, pt. I, *(AD 985-1206)*, ed. R.S. Sharma and K.M. Shrimali, New Delhi: People's Publishing House, 1992, p. 316.
4. According to a popular tale, a ravine enclosed a lake of pure fountain water of the dimensions required for purification under the Hanafite law. If any filth were thrown in it, there followed dreadful consequences – black clouds collected, whirlwind arose, hilltops turned black, rain fell and the area was filled with cold blasts until death supervened. As soon as a dirty substance was actually thrown in, there was a terrible hailstorm that uprooted trees, caused invisibility, and destroyed food. Abu Nasr Muhammad bin

Muhammad al-Jabbar al-Utbi, *Tarikh-i Yamini*, English translation in *History of India as Told by its own Historians*, ed. H.M. Elliot and John Dowson, Allahabad: Kitab Mahal, n.d., rpt., vol. II, p. 20; Muhammad Qasim Hindu Shah Firishta, *Tarikh-i Firishta*, Urdu translation, Abdul Rahman and Abdul Hayy Khwaja, Lahore: Al-Mizan, 2004, vol. I, p. 52. (hereafter cited as Firishta).

5. Abu Nasr Muhammad bin Muhammad al-Jabbar al-Utbi, *Tarikh-i Yamini*, pp. 20-1; *Firishta*, I, pp. 52-3.
6. Fakhr-i Mudabbir, *Adab ul-Muluk wa Kifayat ul-Muluk*, pp. 486-93, quoted in Muhammad Nazim, *The Life and Times of Sultan Mahmud of Ghazna*, New Delhi: Munshiram Manoharlal, 2nd edn., 1971, pp. 195-96.
7. Muhammad Nazim, *The Life and Times of Sultan Mahmud of Ghazna*, p. 97; Mohammad Habib, *Sultan Mahmud of Ghaznin*, New Delhi, S. Chand & Co., 2nd edn., 1967, p. 25.
8. Abu Raihan Alberuni, *Kitab ul-Hind*, English Translation, Edward C. Sachau, entitled *Alberuni's India*, New Delhi: Rupa, rpt., 2002, p. 416.
9. Firishta, I, p. 66.
10. Ibid., p. 67.
11. Nazim, op. cit., pp. 103-4.
12. Firishta, I, pp. 67-8.
13. Nazim, op. cit., pp. 91-3.
14. Mohammad Habib, *Sultan Mahmud of Ghaznin*, p. 47.
15. Syad Muhammad Latif, *History of the Punjab: From the Remotest Antiquity to the Present Time*, New Delhi: Eurasia Publishing House, rpt., 1964, pp. 84-5; Edward Thomas, *The Chronicles of the Pathan Kings of Delhi*, New Delhi: Munshiram Manoharlal, rpt., 1967, pp. 47-8.
16. Alberuni, II, p. 416.
17. Long before the Ghaznavid invasions, the Jats were settled in central Sind on both sides of the Indus. Having no social inequalities, they were engaged in pastoralism, besides pursuing the occupations of soldiers, and boatmen. They owed allegiance to Buddhist shramans, but suffered harsh restrictions imposed by the Brahmana dynasty. By the early eleventh century, they had migrated north to Multan and Bhatiya by the Indus, as noted by the Ghaznavid historians. On the basis of his experience of Lahore, Alberuni referred to them as cattle owners and low Shudra people. Irfan Habib, 'Jatts of Punjab and Sind,' *Essays in Honour of Dr. Ganda Singh*, ed. Harbans Singh and N. Gerald Barrier, Patiala: Punjabi University, 1976, pp. 94-5.
18. Nazim, op. cit., p. 122.
19. Habib, *Sultan Mahmud of Ghaznin*, pp. 76-7.
20. Clifford Edmund Bosworth, *The Later Ghaznavids: Splendour and Decay (The Dynasty in Afghanistan and Northern India 1040-1186)*, Edinburgh: Edinburgh University Press, 1963, pp. 75-6.
21. Abul Fazl Baihaqi, *Tarikh-i Subuktgin*, English translation, in *The History of India as Told by Its Own Historians*, H.M. Elliot and John Dowson,

Allahabad: Kitab Mahal, vol. II, rpt., n.d., pp. 112-13 (hereafter cited as Baihaqi).
22. Baihaqi, pp. 116-19.
23. Ibid., pp. 120-1.
24. Ibid., pp. 122-4.
25. Ibid., pp. 124-5.
26. Ibid., pp. 127-9.
27. Ibid., pp. 127-9.
28. At this time, a Ghaznavid army under Ahmad Ali Noshtigin was defeated at Kirman and forced to retreat to Nishapur. The Hindu soldiers had turned their backs and, fleeing to Sistan, returned to Ghazni. In a series of strict actions, the Sultan dismissed them from service. Six of their officers committed suicide with their daggers. The Sultan felt that they should have used their daggers at Kirman and, treating them severely, forgave them in the end. Baihaqi, pp. 130-1.
29. Baihaqi, pp. 132-4.
30. Baihaqi, p. 134; in spite of this change, Panjab remained in a state of turmoil and disorder. In the words of Habib, 'Ghaznavide garrisons held the towns: Hinduism and freedom reigned supreme in the countryside. Nothing else was possible when the government was so incompatible with the spirit of the people.' Habib, op. cit, p. 98.
31. Clifford Edmund Bosworth, *The Ghaznavids: Their Empire in Afghanistan and Eastern Iran 994-1040*, Edinburgh: Edinburgh University Press, 1963, p. 30.
32. Baihaqi, pp. 137-40.
33. Firishta, I, pp. 103-4.
34. Baihaqi, pp. 149-53; Firishta, I, pp. 106-7.
35. Bosworth, *The Ghaznavids: Their Empire in Afghanistan and Eastern Iran 994-1040*, pp. 30-1.
36. Ibid., pp. 32-3.
37. Firishta, I, pp. 110-11.
38. Ibid., pp. 109-11.
39. Ibn-i Asir, *al-Kamil fi al-Tarikh*, quoted in Bosworth, *The Ghaznavids: Their Empire in Afghanistan and Eastern Iran 994-1040*, pp. 62-63; Firishta, I, pp. 120-1.
40. Sunil Sharma, *Persian Poetry at the Indian Frontier: Masud Sad Salman of Lahore*, New Delhi: Permanent Black, 2000, pp. 18-25.
41. Ibid., pp. 56-8.
42. Ibid., pp. 59-62.
43. Ibid., p. 63.
44. Ibid., p. 65.
45. Minhaj-i Siraj Juzjani, *Tabaqat-i Nasiri*, English translation, H.G. Raverty, New Delhi: Oriental Books, rpt., 1970, vol. I, pp. 106-7 (hereafter cited as Juzjani); it was this military achievement that appears to have been

celebrated in the poetic eulogies of Usman Mikhtari, Masud Sad Salman and Abul Farj Runi. For details, see, Bosworth, *The Ghaznavids: Their Empire in Afghanistan and Eastern Iran 994-1040*, pp. 84-6.
46. Juzjani, I, p. 109.
47. Saljuqids (1083-1194), who had been enlisted by the Ghaznavids to defend Khurasan, rose to establish their domination over Transoxiana, Iran, Iraq and Anatolia. Their rule marked the restoration of Sunni supremacy, the development of institutional and architectural model of Madrasa for the teaching of religion and jurisprudence, besides the innovative organization of Sufis into the Tariqat path. Francoise Aubin, 'The Turco-Mongol Period,' in *History of Humanity*, vol. IV: *From the Seventh to the Sixteenth Century*, ed. M.A. Al-Bakhit et al., Paris: Unesco & London: Routledge, 2000, pp. 286-7.
48. Bosworth, op. cit., p. 102.
49. Juzjani, I, p. 110; Firishta, I, p. 126; Bosworth, op. cit., 103.
50. Juzjani, I, pp. 111-12; Firishta, I, p. 130.
51. Bosworth, op. cit., pp. 125-6.
52. Sultan Muizzuddin was a descendant of the Shansbanis who ruled over Ghor, which was situated to the west of Kabul and Ghazni. Serving for long as a buffer between the Ghaznavids and Saljuqids, Ghor managed to survive under the shadow of the two archrivals. In the early twelfth century, it was fragmented among the seven sons of Izzuddin Husain (1110-46). The youngest son Alauddin Husain sacked Ghazni and forced the Ghaznavid ruler Bahram Shah to leave for Panjab. As the Ghorid fortunes were on the ascendant, the two nephews of Alauddin Husain, Ghiasuddin and Shihabuddin, rose to prominence. Shahabuddin (later known as Sultan Muizzuddin) snatched Ghazni from the Ghuzz Turks and, with the support of his brother, embarked on the conquest of northwestern India.
53. During his siege of Uch, the Sultan was said to have developed a secret contact with the queen of the local Bhatti Rajput ruler and promised to marry her. She poisoned her husband to death and delivered the fort to the Ghorids. The Sultan married the princess, but sent the queen to Ghazni as he did not trust her. This story (Firishta, I, p. 143) has not been found in any contemporary source. Uch, at this juncture, was under the Qarmathians and not Bhatti Rajputs. A.B.M. Habibullah, *The Foundation of Muslim Rule in India*, Allahabad: Central Book Depot, revd. edn., 1976, p. 28; Mohammad Habib and Khaliq Ahmad Nizami, eds., *A Comprehensive History of India*, vol. V: *The Delhi Sultanate (1206-1526)*, New Delhi: People's Publishing House, rpt., 1982, p. 156, n.2.
54. Juzjani, I, pp. 449-51.
55. Ibid., pp. 453-5.
56. The Chauhans of Sambhar began their political career as feudatories of Pratiharas and carved an autonomous principality in Ajmer during the late tenth century. By 1164, they occupied northeastern Rajasthan and eastern

Panjab. They extended their northern boundary to the Himalayas and formed a barrier between Ghaznavid Panjab and Rajasthan. Their power reached its zenith under Prithiviraj III (1180-1192), who vanquished local rivals and contended against Gahadvalas and Chandels in the east and Chalukyas in the west. Habib and Nizami, eds., *A Comprehensive History of India*, op. cit., pp. 821-2.
57. Juzjani, I, pp. 458-64; Firishta, I, pp. 144-45.
58. Juzjani, I, pp. 465-8.
59. Khwaja Nizamuddin Ahmad, *Tabaqat-i Akbari*, English translation, B. De, Calcutta: The Asiatic Society, 1973, vol. I, pp. 38-9; Firishta, I, pp. 147-8.
60. Tajuddin Hasan Nizami, *Taj ul-Maasir*, English translation, Bhagwat Saroop, Delhi: Ibn Saud Dehalvi, 1998, pp. 72-3.
61. Ibid., p. 84.
62. Ibid., pp. 92-4.
63. Ibid., pp. 97-100.
64. Ibid., pp. 253-4.
65. Ibid., pp. 260-1.
66. Ibid., pp. 264-6, 269.
67. Ibid., p. 266; the author's praise for the Khokhars (with reference to their fort, numbers and bravery) appeared to have been designed to imply the military superiority of the Turkish military organization, which ultimately overpowered the Khokhars. By employing the same idiom, he has praised the bravery of the Ghorid army and its commanders like Sultan Muizzuddin, Qutbuddin Aibak and Shamsuddin Iltutmish.
68. Following the Shansbanid tradition of coparcenary inheritance as practiced in Ghor, Sultan Muizzuddin appanaged the conquered areas in north India among his slave military commanders, who emerged as rulers of autonomous principalities –'they were given dominions, the prerogative to raise armies, wage war, construct alliances, collect tribute, disburse funds, embellish their capitals, and patronize commerce.' Sunil Kumar, *The Emergence of the Delhi Sultanate*, Ranikhet: Permanent Black, 2007, p. 117.
69. Fakhr-i Mudabbir, *Tarikh-i Fakhruddin Mubarak Shah*, Persian text, ed., E. Denison Ross, London: Royal Asiatic Society, 1927, pp. 30-2.
70. Juzjani, I, pp. 525-8.
71. Ibid., 505-6, 607-8.
72. Peter Jackson, *The Delhi Sultanate: A Political and Military History*, Cambridge: Cambridge University Press, 1999, p. 30.
73. Tajuddin Hasan Nizami has devoted a considerable space to describe the great folly of Qubacha in raising the standard of revolt, the march of Iltutmish from Delhi to Lahore, a battle on the bank of the river, the valour displayed by the forces of Iltutmish, the flight of Amir Aqsanqar Kitta and the retreat of Qubacha to Uch. The account was loaded with rhetoric, but did not yield substantive facts. Tajuddin Hasan Nizami, *Taj ul-Maasir*, pp. 323-30.

74. Iqtidar Husain Siddiqui, *Indo-Persian Historiography up to the Thirteenth Century*, New Delhi: Primus, 2010, p. 41.
75. Tajuddin Hasan Nizami, *Taj ul-Maasir*, pp. 332-7; for a comparison with similar royal orders, see Iqtidar Husain Siddiqui, *Perso-Arabic Sources of Information on the Life and Conditions in the Sultanate of Delhi*, New Delhi: Munshiram Manoharlal, 1992, pp. 167-87; .
76. This discussion is based on a seminal study by Peter Jackson, who has relied on a minute analysis of the works by Nasawi and Juwaini, besides Juzjani. Peter Jackson, 'Jalal al-Din, the Mongols and the Khwarizmian Conquest of Panjab and Sind,' in *Studies on the Mongol Empire and Early Muslim India*, Farnham: Ashgate, 2009, pp. 6-12.
77. Alauddin Ata Malik Juvaini, *Tarikh-i Jahan Gusha*, English translation, John Andrew Boyle, entiled *The History of the World Conqueror*, Manchester: Manchester University Press, 1958, vol. II, pp. 413-14.
78. Juzjani, II, pp. 1045-7.
79. Habib and Nizami, eds., op. cit., p. 216.
80. Alauddin Ata Malik Juvaini, *Tarikh-i Jahan Gusha*, vol. II, pp. 414-15.
81. Ibid., pp. 415-17.
82. Habib and Nizami, eds., op. cit., p. 219.
83. Juzjani, I, pp. 612-15.
84. According to an important study, the Turkish bureaucracy was divided into three groups – provincial governors, army oficers and household dignitaries. Each tried to dominate the Sultan and monopolize political power. The Sultan could survive only by preventing a conjunction of any two groups and playing upon their mutual rivalries. A group that was outmanoeuvred rose in revolt. These groups combined when there was a common danger from non-Turkish elements. Otherwise, every one pulled in his own direction, so that a triangular conflict became a permanent feature of the political life in the thirteenth century. Khaliq Ahmad Nizami, *Religion and Politics in India during the Thirteenth Century*, New Delhi: Oxford University Press, New Edition, 2002, p. 141; also see, S.B.P. Nigam, *Nobility under the Sultans of Delhi*, New Delhi: Munshiram Manoharlal, 1968, pp. 29-30.
85. Juzjani, I, pp. 632-5.
86. The problem in the ruling class was no longer seen as a racial conflict between the Turks and non-Turks. The acute differences have been attributed to the aspirations of junior Turkish slave officers, whose interests clashed with their senior counterparts and those regarded as outsiders including free Turkish nobles. Recently it has been argued that the middling Shamsi slave officers (as opposed to the high-ranking seniors and lowly placed domestics), who performed intermediary tasks and aspired for higher positions, often mutinied against the Sultan. Peter Jackson, *The Delhi Sultanate: A Political and Military History*, p. 70; Sunil Kumar, *The Emergence of the Delhi Sultanate*, pp. 241-3.

87. Juzjani, II, pp. 725-7.
88. Juzjani, I, pp. 645-8; II, p. 749.
89. Izzuddin Balban Kishlu Khan, a Turk of the Qipchaq tribe, had been puchased by Iltutmish from a trader at Mandor. After serving as a bartender in the royal household, he was promoted as the *muqti* of Barhamu and then Baran. An extremely ambitious man, he participated in the revolt against Ruknuddin Firoz and appeared as a strong partisan of Raziya. Having played a major role in the dethronement of Muizzuddin Bahram, he declared himself as the Sultan in a sensational move. The vigorous opposition of his peers forced him to retract. Juzjani, II, pp. 775-80; for an analysis of his failure to secure the throne, see Nizami, op. cit., pp. 147-8; S.B.P. Nigam, op. cit., p. 35.
90. Juzjani, II, pp. 781-2.
91. It was not clear if Sher Khan undertook this military action at the behest of Sultan Nasiruddin Mahmud and Ulugh Khan, to whose faction he belonged. It was possible that the Sultan and his principal advisor, after having used the services of a confederate for an unpleasant task, had second thoughts about their original decision. This change appeared to have been hastened by the visit of Kishlu Khan to Delhi, where he might have removed doubts regarding his conduct at the siege of Multan and his loyalty to the regime in power.
92. Juzjani, II, pp. 783-4, 791-2.
93. Ibid., pp. 784-6.
94. Rashiduddin Fazlullah, *Jami ut-Tawarikh*, MS, Punjab University, Lahore, f. 38a, quoted in Agha Hussain Hamadani, *The Frontier Policy of the Sultans of Delhi*, Islamabad: National Institute of Historical and Cultural Research, 1989, p. 91.
95. Juzjani, II, p. 793.
96. Juzjani, I, pp. 699-700; II, pp. 829-33.
97. Juzjani, II, pp. 793-4.
98. Peter Jackson, 'Jalal al-Din, the Mongols and the Khwarizmian Conquest of the Panjab and Sind,' in *Studies on the Mongol Empire and Early Muslim India*, p. 17.
99. Juzjani, I, pp. 534-9.
100. Habibullah, *The Foundation of Muslim Rule in India*, p. 174.
101. Juzjani, I, pp. 539-41.
102. Iqtidar Husain Siddiqui, 'The Qarlugh Kingdom in the Thirteenth Century: Liaison Between Mongols and Indian Rulers,' in *Medieval India: Essays in Diplomacy and Culture*, New Delhi: Adam Publishers & Distributors, 2009, p. 34.
103. Juzjani, I, p. 623.
104. Siddiqui, op. cit., 35.
105. Peter Jackson, *The Delhi Sultanate: A Political and Military History*, p. 105.

106. This success, in the eyes of Juzjani, was significant as, after the death of Iltutmish, the authority of the Delhi Sultanate had been undermined and its numerous enemies nurtured the vain desire of appropriating its territories. Juzjani, II, pp. 730-1.
107. Juzjani, II, pp. 1129-30.
108. Peter Jackson, *The Delhi Sultanate: A Political and Military History*, p. 105.
109. Andre Wink, *Al-Hind: The Making of the Indo-Islamic World*, vol. II: *The Slave Kings and the Islamic Conquest (11th–13th Centuries)*, New Delhi: Oxford University Press, rpt., 1999, pp. 200-1.
110. Juzjani, II, p. 1133.
111. It was in a state of intense conflict among the nobility that Sultan Muizzuddin Bahram Shah sent an army from Delhi to fight against the Mongols. When this army reached the Beas, the *wazir* Khwaja Muhazzabuddin misinformed the Sultan regading the disloyalty of nobles and Turks and sought an order for their execution. The Sultan fell in the *wazir's* trap and sent the required order. When the *wazir* showed this order to the nobles, the latter retraced their steps to dislodge the Sultan. Juzjani, I, pp. 657-8.
112. Juzjani, II, 1134-5.
113. Ibid., pp. 1135-6.
114. Ibid., pp. 1153-6.
115. Ibid., pp. 809-14.
116. Saif bin Muhammad Yaqub Haravi, *Tarikhnama-i Herat*, ed. M.Z. Siddiqui, Calcutta, 1944, pp. 157-8, quoted in Agha Husain Hamadani, *The Frontier Policy of the Sultans of Delhi*, p. 86; Khaliq Ahmad Nizami, *Religion and Politics in India during the Thirteenth Century*, p. 272.
117. Habibullah, op. cit., p. 178.
118. Juzjani, II, pp. 814-15.
119. Peter Jackson, *The Delhi Sultanate: A Political and Military History*, p. 111.
120. Halaku (r. 1256-65), a grandson of Chingez Khan, founded the Il-Khanate. One of the four divisions of the Mongol Empire, it covered a vast area comprising Persia, Iraq and Anatolia. It benefited from an intimate relation with the Great Khanate of Qublai Khan, but faced vigorous opposition from the Golden Horde of the Jochids. Adhering to religious tolerance, it encouraged non-Muslim traditions. It patronized science and scholarship. Nasiruddin Tusi founded an astronomical observatory at Maragheh, while Ata Malik Juwaini and Rashiduddin produced major works of history in Persian. Shagdaryn Bira, 'The Mongol Empire,' in *History of Humanity: Scientific and Cultural Development*, vol. IV, *From the Seventh to the Sixteenth Century*, ed. M.A. Al-Bakhit et al., pp. 476-7; Thomas T. Allsen, *Culture and Conquest in Mongol Eurasia*, Cambridge: Cambridge University Press, 2001, pp. 17-23.
121. Juzjani, II, pp. 784-6.
122. Juzjani, I, p. 711; II, pp. 844-6.

123. Abdul Malik Isami, *Futuh us-Salatin*, English translation (*Shahnama-i Hind of Isami*), Agha Mahdi Husain, Bombay: Asia Publishing House, 1976, vol. II, pp. 269-73 (hereafter cited as Isami).
124. Ibid., pp. 276-80.
125. As a faithful admirer of Ulugh Khan, Juzjani would have us believe that the initiative for the alliance was taken by Nasiruddin Muhammad Qarlugh because, by virtue of the union, he hoped that his power would increase and his prestige among his peers would rise. He wrote a confidential letter to a confidant of Ulugh Khan, so as to know the fate of his intention. Ulugh Khan accepted the proposal, because the Qarlugh chief was a renowned grandee of the times. Juzjani, II, pp. 859-63.
126. Ibid., pp. 859-61.
127. Ibid., pp. 861-3.
128. In addition to the vulnerability of the Delhi Sultanate, the internal conflict in the Mongol principalities also contributed to this conciliation. In view of the impending struggle for succession on Mongke's death, both Halaku and his cousin Berke made overtures to Delhi and established diplomatic contacts with it. This possibility remained a matter of conjecture. More probably, Halaku called a halt to campaigning in India, just as in Syria, prior to moving into Azerbaijan and waiting upon events. Attack on a gravely weakened Delhi Sultanate could be revived in a short time. But within three years, Halaku lost control over the Indian border lands. Peter Jackson, 'The Dissolution of the Mongol Empire,' in *Studies on the Mongol Empire and Early Muslim India*, 2009, p. 241.
129. Ziauddin Barani, *Tarikh-i Firoz Shahi*, Persian text, ed. Sir Syed Ahmad, Aligarh: Sir Syed Academy, Aligarh Muslim University, rpt., 2005, p. 53. (hereafter cited as Barani).
130. Ibid., pp. 59-60.
131. Ibid., p. 61.
132. Ibid., p. 51.
133. Ibid., p. 65.
134. Ibid., p. 66.
135. Ibid., p. 69.
136. Ibid., pp. 48-9.
137. The addiction of the Prince to alcohol was resented by his beautiful wife, who was a daughter of Sultan Ruknuddin Firoz. Owing to his short temper and fickle mind, he divorced her through three verbal pronouncements. On saner thoughts, he resolved to have her back. This could be done if she was married to someone else and divorced again. Through a mediator, she was married to Shaikh Sadruddin Arif, the Suhrawardi saint of Multan. However, she refused to be separated from the Shaikh. The Prince intended to punish the Shaikh with death, but died in a battle against the Mongols. Hamid bin Fazlullah Jamali, *Siyar ul-Arifin*, Persian Text, Delhi: Rizvi Press, 1893, pp. 134-6.

138. Barani, pp. 66-8.
139. Syed Usman Marwandi (d. 1274), who was famous as Lal Shahbaz Qalandar, was born at Marwand near Tabrez. His spiritual genealogy has been traced to diverse sources – Ismail bin Jafar (the sixth Shia Imam), Shaikh Bahauddin Zakariya of Multan and even Raja Bharthari of the Nathpanthi order. Opposed to institutional Sufi orders and indifferent to the Shariat, he adhered to the Qalandari path based on wandering, renunciation and antinomianism. His shrine at Sehwan Sharif attracted vast multitudes of devotees, who took a special interest in the ecstatic dance (*dhamal*). Michel Boivin, *Artefacts of Devotion: A Sufi Repertoire of the Qalandariyya in Sehwan Sharif, Sind, Pakistan*, Karachi: Oxford University Press, 2011, pp. 15-19; also see, Jurgen Wasim Frembgen, *At the Shrine of the Red Sufi: Five Days and Nights on Pilgrimage in Pakistan*, Karachi: Oxford University Press, 2011, pp. 63-141.
140. Barani, p. 68.
141. Isami, II, pp. 299-301.
142. Ibid., pp. 304-8.
143. Ibid., pp. 309-11.
144. Barani, p. 109.
145. A younger grandson of Prophet Muhammad, Husain was born to Hazrat Ali and Fatima. After the assassination of his father and abdication of his elder brother Hasan, Husain was invited by the Shias of Kufa to claim his rightful position as the caliph. As such, he led a revolt against Yazid, the son of Muawiyah. In the battle of Karbala, which was fought on 10 Muharram AH 680, he was killed along with his kin and followers. Seen as a supreme martyr in the cause of righteousness and a symbol of resistance against tyranny, his death has been commemorated in the form of passionate ritual mourning during the first ten days of Muharram by the Shias.
146. Amir Khusrau, *Wast ul-Hayat*, Adapted from the English translation in Mohammad Wahid Mirza, *The Life and Works of Amir Khusrau*, Delhi: Idarah-i Adabiyat-i Delli, rpt., 1974, pp. 56-9.
147. Cousin and son-in-law of Prophet Muhammad, Ali bin Abi Talib was first male convert to Islam. He participated in most expeditions in the Prophet's lifetime. Seen in diverse roles, he was a distinguished judge, pious believer and brave warrior. He was the first Imam of the Shias and fourth caliph of the Sunnis. He served as a paradigm for political activism aimed at redressal of social and political injustices. John L. Esposito, *The Dictionary of Islam*, Karachi: Oxford University Press, 2005, p. 15.
148. Amir Khusrau, *Wast ul-Hayat*, pp. 61-2.
149. Mohammad Wahid Mirza, op. cit., pp. 62-4; also see, Sunil Sharma, *Amir Khusrau: The Poet of Sultans and Sufis*, Oxford: One World, rpt., 2009, p. 22.
150. Amir Khusrau, *Wast ul-Hayat*, quoted in S.H. Askari, 'Wit and Humour in

the Works of Amir Khusrau,' in *Life, Times and Works of Amir Khusrau*, ed. Zoe Ansari, New Delhi: National Amir Khusrau Society, n.d., p. 153.
151. When these two persons appeared at the court to receive punishment for their crimes, the Sultan showed kindness to them and treated them with honour. He bestowed on Savi two villages along with a robe and a horse. The royal order to this effect was drawn up and sent to his sons in Samana. He praised the Mandahar for his bravery and, enrolling him in the army, fixed his salary at one lakh *jitals*. He ordered the Mandahar to be paraded in the court with his weapons along with the retinue of his new commander Malik Khurram. Barani, pp. 194-6.
152. Amir Khusrau, *Miftah ul-Futuh*, Persian text, ed. Shaikh Abdul Rashid, Aligarh: Aligarh Muslim University, 1954, p. 8.
153. Barani, p. 187.
154. Ibid., p. 196.
155. Jalaluddin Khalji was not the first to patronize the Mongols. Ghiasuddin Balban appeared to have welcomed a number of Mongol notables who, following internal upheavals in the Mongol territory after 1260, had taken refuge in the Delhi Sultanate. During Balban's reign, a whole quarter of the capital was named Chengizi after them. Under Balban and his successors, nobles of unmistakable Mongol names figured in the sources e.g. Bayanchar, Ulughchi, Turumtai and Juarchi. The Mongol officers formed a part of the coalition that raised Kaiqubad to the throne. Most of them were executed or exiled by Malik Nizamuddin. Peter Jackson, *The Delhi Sultanate: A Political and Military History*, pp. 80-1.
156. A son of Yugrush, Jalaluddin Khalji was the Mongol commander (*shahna*) of Binban, just west of the Indus. His military exploits, which were directed against the refractory Mongol and Afghan tribes of the Salt Range, might have occurred before he joined service under the Sultans of Delhi. He might have visited Delhi with a Mongol embassy in 1260. Sunil Kumar, 'Trans-regional Contacts and Relationships: Turks, Mongols and the Delhi Sultanate in the Thirteenth and Fourteenth Centuries,' in *Turks in the Indian Subcontinent, Central and West Asia: The Turkish Presence in the Islamic World*, ed. Ismail K. Poonawala, New Delhi: Oxford University Press, 2017, pp. p. 176.
157. Barani, pp. 218-19.
158. Amir Khusrau, *Khazain ul-Futuh*, English translation, in *Politics and Society during the Early Medieval Period: Collected Works of Professor Mohammad Habib*, ed. K.A. Nizami, New Delhi: People's Publishing House, 1981, vol. II, pp. 168-9; Barani, p. 250.
159. Barani, pp. 253; Isami, II, pp. 421-2; Firishta, I, p. 243.
160. The Sultan considered two ways of dealing with Zafar Khan. Either he could be dispatched at the head of a few thousand horsemen to Lakhnauti, so as to conquer new territories, besides sending elephants and tribute to

126   *The Making of Medieval Panjab*

Delhi. Alternatively, he could be removed from the presence of the Sultan by administering poison or by blinding. Barani, p. 254.
161. Barani, p. 254.
162. Barani, p. 260; Isami, II, pp. 426-33.
163. Barani, pp. 260-61; Isami, II, 434-44.
164. Barani, p. 261.
165. Isami, II, pp. 441-2.
166. Barani, pp. 300-01; Isami, II, pp. 460-1; according to another version, Targhi besieged the fort of Baran which was in the fief of Malik Fakhruddin, the Amir-i Dad. In response to Sultan's order, Malik Tughluq (Ghazi Malik) marched to Baran with a big force. The two commanders joined hands and defeated the Mongols in a night attack. Malik Tughluq carried Targhi to Delhi as a prisoner. Yahya bin Ahmad bin Abdullah Sirhindi, *Tarikh-i Mubarak Shahi*, Persian text, ed. M. Hidayat Husain, Calcutta: Asiatic Society of Bengal, 1931, p. 73 (hereafter cited as Sirhindi).
167. Amir Khusrau, *Khazain ul-Futuh*, pp. 169-70; Isami, pp. 478-82.
168. Barani, pp. 320-1.
169. Amir Khusrau, *Khazain ul-Futuh*, pp. 171-2.
170. Barani, p. 322.
171. Isami's account was singular on two counts. Firstly, it noted the presence of Hindu notables as renowned warriors among the troops mustered by Malik Kafur. Secondly, it introduced Ghazi Malik as a man of intelligence and determination, as an experienced warrior who was assigned the *iqta* of Dipalpur and as one who considered fighting a pastime and enjoyed the title of Shahna-i Bargah. Isami, II, p. 497.
172. Isami, II, pp. 495-500.
173. Amir Khusrau, *Khazain ul-Futuh*, pp. 172-4.
174. Barani, p. 322.
175. Ibid., pp. 269, 302.
176. Ibid., pp. 302-3.
177. Ibid., pp. 322-3.
178. Ibid., p. 325.

CHAPTER 3

The Establishment of Sufi Orders

Tracing Links of a Cult to the Prophet

Baba Haji Rattan, whose shrine was situated in Bathinda, appears to have been the earliest Muslim saint we know of in Panjab. He did not figure in the standard biographical compendia of Sufis. Ibn Hajar, an Arab scholar of the sixteenth century, has compiled a number of stories about him. These stories were in active circulation across the entire Islamic world straddling Central and West Asia. They recorded the experiences of religious scholars who travelled to Bathinda in order to collect the sayings (*hadis*) of Prophet Muhammad from Baba Rattan, an exceedingly old man who was reputed to have met the Prophet in Arabia. There were some differences in these accounts, but they converge on the essential points. Baba Rattan, as a young man, travelled to Arabia along with his father, a long-distance trader. When he reached the valleys of Mecca, rain fell in torrents. A local boy, who was tending camels, was separated from his animals by a flowing channel. Baba Rattan saw the predicament of the boy and, picking him up, waded across the water. The boy, while expressing his gratitude, blessed his benefactor. Baba Rattan returned to Bathinda and lived an uneventful life until he saw a miracle involving the splitting of moon into two and joining again. On inquiry, he learnt that the miracle had been performed by a man of the Hashim clan as the proof of his Prophethood. Baba Rattan travelled again to Mecca and met the Prophet, who recognized the person who had helped him decades earlier. The Prophet, having inspired the visitor to convert to Islam, blessed him to live for 700 years. According to some versions, Baba Rattan performed military service for the Prophet in the battle of Trench and also participated in the wedding procession of the Prophet's daughter Fatima. Baba Rattan retraced his steps to Bathinda and made his abode in a large basket suspended from a tree. In this strange abode, he received visitors who learnt from him anecdotes about the Prophet. Musa bin Mujalla, a Sufi, was said to have recorded as many as forty traditions of the Prophet on the authority of Baba Rattan. However, the role of Baba Rattan as a purveyor of the Prophetic traditions was challenged by Shamsuddin Zahbi (d. 1382), who even wrote a booklet in support of his contentions.[1]

According to the Nath version of the life of Baba Rattan, he was born in the fifth or sixth century at Dang, on the present Indo-Nepal border. He was the son of a local ruler Raja Manbiya Parikshak. During the course of a hunting expedition, he met the great spiritual teacher Gorakhnath who had matted hair, an ash-smeared body and large earrings. Gorakhnath advised the prince to destroy his own ego instead of killing animals. The prince became a disciple of Gorakhnath and adopted the path of the Nath Yogis. This association led to the construction of a big temple at Rattanpura, which grew into a prominent centre of the Nath Yogis known as Shaktipeeth Devipatan. It boasted of a historical connection with the famous shrine of Gorakhnath at Gorakhpur, while small Nath centres in different parts of Nepal were associated with the monastery of Rattan Nath at Dang. Meanwhile, Baba Rattan acquired mastery in yogic sciences and, at the advice of Gorakhnath, travelled as far as Afghanistan. His miraculous power impressed the ruler of Kabul, who not only conferred a land grant on him, but also permitted him to build a temple and establish a sacred fire pit (*dhoona*) in his palace. On his return, he intended to cross the Indus at Attock. Since he had no money, the boatmen refused to take him across the river. Enraged, he turned them into stone. During his stay at Bathinda, he learnt about the Prophethood of Muhammad and travelled to Mecca. He stayed with the Prophet for three years and, on coming back to Bathinda, continued to preach the yogic path till the age of 700 years. The Nath tradition claimed that Baba Rattan assisted Sultan Shihabuddin of Ghor in his war against Prithviraj Chauhan, having provided water to the Turkish army through a miracle. When the Sultan sought the blessings of the saint, the latter predicted that he would occupy Bathinda after the martyrdom of two Syed soldiers. The prophecy turned out to be correct. A variant account has named the Turkish conqueror as Sultan Mahmud of Ghazni. As asserted by the Nath tradition, Baba Rattan produced a number of religious works. Two of them, *The First Sufi Path* (*Awwal-i Suluk*) and *The Wisdom of the Unbeliever* (*Kafir Bodh*), contained esoteric explanations of Yoga in the light of Islamic teachings. Two of his verses, focusing on the role of the spiritual mentor, were found in the *Gorakhbani* which has been composed by Gorakhnath himself. The Nath tradition has sought to show that Baba Rattan had disseminated the Yogic doctrines in such distant lands as Afghanistan and Arabia.[2]

Apart from Islam and Yogic asceticism, Baba Rattan also figures in the legend of Guga. According to a legend retrieved by R.C. Temple, Guga killed his twin cousins (sons of mother's sister) during a quarrel in the jungle and, as a penitence, was directed by his grieving mother Queen Bachhal to go to Ajmer and adopt Islam at the hands of Baba Rattan, who was portrayed as a venerable Muslim saint in the same category as Khwaja Khizr. Guga,[3] who was then a follower of Gorakhnath, abided by the wishes of his mother and converted to Islam after meeting Baba Rattan. According to a legend current in Kashmir, Baba Rattan was a successor of Raja Ven. This ruler, having lost a battle against Sultan Zainul Abidin,[4] was asked to embrace Islam by the victor. A true worshipper of Shiva, he refused. He went on a pilgrimage to Lake Gagribal, and threw a letter of Prophet Muhammad into a well. However, Baba Rattan expressed his willingness to become a Muslim. Since he did not know the way to proceed in the matter, he sought the advice of Sultan Zainul Abidin. Owing to the Sultan's prayer, a Muslim saint Bulbul Shah flew over from Baghdad and converted Baba Rattan to Islam along with his subjects.[5]

The present attendants of Baba Rattan's shrine narrate a new tale regarding the antecedents of the saint: he was born into a Brahmin family and his original name was Pandit Rattan Lal. He rose to become a master astrologer and one of the nine jewels in the court of the legendary Raja Bhoj of Ujjain. This part of the story was followed by the miracle of splitting of the moon into two parts, the visit of the Pandit to Mecca, his meeting with the Prophet and conversion to Islam. He was said to have received from Abu Bakr (the Prophet's father-in-law) a female camel on which he rode back to India.[6]

The massive structure of a gurdwara, which was built in the midst of the sacred complex at Bathinda, stood next to the small shrine of Baba Rattan. The local Sikh devotees of the saint connected him with the Sikh gurus. They believed that Guru Nanak paid a visit to the place in order to wean Baba Rattan, a Muslim, from his evil ways. Baba Rattan, who was a practitioner of black magic, converted two large stones into horses and made them rush at the visitor. With the protection of God, Guru Nanak raised his hand and stopped the horses in their tracks. The Guru admonished Baba Rattan for his ego, so that he repented and lived the rest of his life as a good Muslim. Guru Gobind Singh, also said to have visited the place, underwent the same experience and delivered Baba Rattan from the cycle of rebirth. A massive stone lay there as a relic of the missile which was hurled at the Sikh gurus.[7]

At present the shrine complex comprises the tomb of Baba Haji Rattan, a small mosque, a cell (*hujra*) and a number of recent structures. The tomb is a moderate sized square building with slightly sloping walls. An archway in its southern wall gives access to the interior containing the main grave along with four others. The western wall of the interior originally had a niche (*mihrab*) indicating the direction of Mecca, the contours of which were bordered by a text (verse 17 of Chapter 3) of the Quran, being further framed by the Throne verse (*Ayat al-Kursi*). Each corner of the interior had a squinch, converting the square of the room into an octagon that supported a domed ceiling. On the exterior, each corner of the building at parapet level was marked by a turret, which was in fact a small replica of the tomb. In the centre arose a hemispherical dome sitting on a tapering circular drum and crowned it with a nipple shaped canopy. Near the western wall of the tomb was a recent grave shaped like a sitting camel, which

The Establishment of Sufi Orders 131

was said to have been gifted by Prophet Muhammad to Baba Haji Rattan. If the tomb was built, as reasonably suggested, in 1234-5, it ranks as the earliest surviving monument of the Sultanate not only of east Panjab, but also of the entire Delhi Sultanate. Four Persian and Arabic inscriptions, still extant on the eastern wall of the building, record the repairs undertaken by state officials, both Muslim and Hindu, in the heyday of the Mughal empire. In the south west of the tomb was found a mosque, the interior of which was divided into a nave and two aisles. It was believed to have been built by Sultan Raziya (r. 1236-40), though the structure, in view of its features, could have come up much later. The cell (*hujra*) associated with Baba Farid is a small chamber with a dome, the outer surface of which bore heavy moulded flutings. Around the main tomb were found five smaller tombs that were built of bricks and had lines of Arabic worked into the stucco relief. Of these smaller tombs, one was the burial site of Pir Shah Chand, who ascended the spiritual seat in the fifteenth century.[8]

Fundamentals of Sufism

During the Ghaznavid rule in Panjab, a number of scholars and mystics migrated to Lahore and made it the centre of their activities. Abul Hasan Ali bin Usman Hujwiri (d. 1072), who was popularly known as Data Ganj Bakhsh, was one such immigrant who propagated Islamic spirituality in the city. As a Syed, his ancestry was traced to Hazrat Ali through Imam Hasan.[9] In order to acquire mystical knowledge, he travelled extensively across Turkistan, Persia, Syria, Iraq and Azerbaijan. He visited Samarqand, Uzkand, Maihana, Merv, Tus, Nishapur, Kish, Ramla, Bistam, Damascus and Baghdad. During these journeys, he met prominent mystics and paid homage at sacred tombs, besides witnessing miracles and suffering misadventures.[10] A seeker of spiritual knowledge, he trained under Abul Fazl bin Muhammad Khattali. He also benefited from the scholarship of Abul Qasim Gurgani, Khwaja Muzzafar and Abul Abbas Ahmad Ashqani. According to Dara Shukoh, Hujwiri became a follower of the school of sobriety (*sahv*) founded by Junaid Baghdadi, but remained an adherent of the Hanafi school of Muslim jurisprudence.[11]

Why and in what circumstances did Hujwiri shift from Ghazni to Lahore? A categorical answer cannot be given.[12] According to a common view, it was Khattali who advised Hujwiri to go to and settle in Lahore. Hujwiri expressed his reluctance to follow the advice, as a senior disciple of Khattali (Shaikh Husain Zinjani), was already working there. However, at the insistence of Khattali, Hujwiri travelled to Lahore and witnessed a coincidence. When he entered the city, he saw the coffin of Zinjani being carried out for burial.[13] This view has not been supported by Hujwiri's own testimony. It indicates that he was brought to Lahore under duress, that he had been forced to leave his books in Ghazni and that he found himself captive among uncongenial people (*darmian-i na-jinsan*) in Lahore.[14] During his sojourn there, he undertook two long journeys through the Islamic lands beyond Afghanistan. He constructed a mosque in Lahore and, in the process, demonstrated his miraculous power. Unlike similar buildings, its niche (*mihrab*) tilted slightly towards the south. The theologians of the city raised objections on this count. Hujwiri did not respond to the complaints and, soon after the completion of construction, invited the people to the inaugural congregational prayer. After having led the prayer, he reminded the gathering of the controversy and asked it to point towards the Kaaba. As soon as the assembly looked at the niche, they were amazed to see disappearance of all physical obstacles and a clear vision of the Kaaba itself. As the fame of Hujwiri spread in all directions, he was commonly accepted as the Qutb ul-Aqtab.[15]

In addition to being an ardent Sufi and a tireless traveller, Hujwiri was a prolific writer. He had written as many as eight books on various dimensions of Islamic spirituality, besides a compendium of poetry. These books are not available, but his name has been immortalized by one extant work, *Kashf ul-Mahjub* (Revelation of the Veiled), a major treatise on theoretical and practical aspects of Sufism. This work was a literary response of the author to the issues raised by a person named Abu Saeed Hujwiri. These revolved around the meaning of the path of Sufism, nature of stations, doctrines and sayings of the Sufis, mystical allegories of the spiritual adepts, nature of the divine love and its manifestation in the human heart, inadequacy of intellect to reach the essence and withdrawal of the soul from the reality. In particular, the questioner wanted to be enlightened on the practical aspects of Sufism connected with these theories.[16] Hujwiri was constrained to frequently insert his own name in the discussion, because clever plagiarists had misappropriated two of his earlier works.[17] In its structure, the treatise has four parts. The first part, forms a background, and seeks to define Sufism and examines the issues of poverty, blame, and dress. The second part, constituting a fourth of the book, contains short biographical sketches of numerous historical figures, who practised Sufism in different ways. The third part, which also forms a fourth of the work, explains the principles of several Sufi orders: Muhasibis, Qassaris, Taifuris, Junaidis, Nuris, Sahlis, Hakimis, Kharrazis, Khalifis, Sayyaris and Hululis. The fourth part, crucial to the following discussion, uncovers theoretical and practical aspects of Sufism in eleven chapters (veils).[18] This treatise received liberal praise from Dara Shukoh in the seventeenth century. In his assessment, he has stated that none had cast any doubt about the authenticity and comprehensiveness of the work, that it commanded the status of a perfect guide among all books on Sufism and that a work of such high merit had never been written in the Persian language.[19]

Hujwiri wrote his study on the foundations of three major works already written by Abul Qasim Qushairi, Abu Nasr Sarraj, and Abu Abdul Rahman Sulami. It covered both the *tabaqat* and manual genres. His chapters on rituals, regarded as the pillars of Islam, were followed by the customs and practices specific to Sufism, creating an impression that the latter were based on the former foundational principles. While defining the content of a ritual, he ended up offering its mystical interpretation and explanation. An innovative study, it elaborated subjects not taken up elsewhere in the same level of detail. An important feature of the work was a constant aim to highlight divergent views on every issue. By accommodating numerous contentious discourses, Hujwiri has extended the boundaries of acceptability in Sufism.

On occasion, he appeared indecisive and incoherent, yet he remained consistent in his underlying object.[20]

Hujwiri felt deeply anguished at the general ignorance and flawed knowledge of Sufism. In fact, the discipline of Sufism had become obsolete, particularly in the Indian subcontinent. Its people had discarded the path of contentment. Theologians and the learned had formed a conception of Sufism quite contrary to its fundamental principles. Disciples, having neglected their ascetic practices, indulged in idle thoughts that were mistakenly designated as contemplation. High and low were content with dubious claims, while blind conformity had taken the place of spiritual enthusiasm. The vulgar claimed to know God, while the elect treated their desire for spiritual progress as ardent love. Hujwiri himself had written several books on Sufism that did not serve any purpose. Some false pretenders picked up a few passages at random to deceive the public, erasing and destroying the rest. Others did not mutilate the books, but did not read them. Still others read them, but did not understand their meaning. Others copied the text and, committing it to memory, prepared to discourse on the mystical science.[21] Negative pursuits – arrogance, hypocrisy, anger, wrangling, fanciful vision, sensuous urges, heresy, disbelief, and neglect of the Prophet's law – were misinterpreted as positive ingredients of the spiritual path. In his own words, 'In time past the works of eminent Sufis, falling into the hands of those who could not appreciate them, have been used to make lining for caps or binding for the poems of Abu Nuwas and pleasantries of Jahiz.'[22] It appeared that Hujwiri took up his pen to dispel general indifference and imperfect knowledge regarding Sufism, besides satisfying the curiosity of individuals.

It was incumbent on the seeker to comprehend the definition of Sufism. Several books had been written on the subject, but they had merely led to contention and confusion. This situation was traceable to some factors. On the one hand, God himself had veiled most people from Sufism and its votaries, having concealed its mysteries from their hearts. On the other hand, Sufism itself had undergone a decline during its evolution. In earlier times, it was a reality without a name but later acquired a name without reality.²³ The etymological roots of Sufism were traced to diverse features – the woolen garment (*jama-i suf*), the quality of purity (*safa*), being first in rank (*saf-i awwal*) and companions of the verandah (*ashab-i suffa*). The very name Sufi, argued Hujwiri, had no derivation that could meet etymological requirements, as Sufism was too exalted to have any genus from which it might have been derived. Confronted with this state, Hujwiri has quoted the definitions of Sufism as advanced by eminent mystical thinkers – Zu ul-Nun Misri, Abul Hasan Nuri, Abu Amr Dimashqi, Abu Bakr Shibli, Abu Muhammad Murtaish, Junaid Baghdadi and Muhammad bin Ahmad Muqri – who focused on different aspects of Sufism. For example, a Sufi was seen as one whose speech reflected his spiritual state. He did not have worldly possessions, nor was he possessed by anything. He saw nothing but God in the two worlds. His body and soul were in the same place. The presence of Sufism was an attribute of God and involved a destruction of human traits. It meant guarding the heart from anything other than God and keeping in concord with the Beloved. It involved behaving with propriety in every place, time and circumstance. It comprised a good nature towards God, others and self. It demanded freedom from desire and conceit of generosity. It required detachment from the phenomenal world and purification from carnal taints. It was imitation of the idea of purity, which was more splendid and conspicuous than others.²⁴

At the beginning of his spiritual journey, a seeker needed to possess the knowledge of God (*marifat allah*). Emphasized by both the Quran and Prophetic traditions (*hadis*), it was of two kinds, cognitive (*ilmi*) and emotional (*hali*). It was seen as the life of the heart through God and removed one's innermost thoughts from everything other than God. The worth of a seeker was in proportion to his knowledge of God. The theologians and lawyers assigned the name of gnosis to the right cognition (*ilm*) of God, but the Sufis applied this name to the right feeling (*hal*) towards God. The Sufis held gnosis (*marifat*) as more exalted than cognition, because the right feeling was the result of right cognition. In other words, a person who did not have cognition of God was not a gnostic (*arif*), but one could have cognition of God without being a gnostic.[25] Hujwiri subjected various modes of acquiring knowledge of God – reason, demonstration, inspiration and intuition – to critical examination, and rejected all of them as ineffective and futile. Instead, he held that knowledge of God could be acquired only through His will and favour. He stated, 'God causes man to know Him through Himself with a knowledge that is not linked to any faculty, a knowledge in which the existence of man is merely metaphorical.'[26] He argued that the knowledge of God depended entirely on information and eternal guidance of the Truth. If God so willed, He made His actions a guide that showed the path leading to Himself. On recognizing the perfection of God's attributes one experienced a state of amazement regarding the divine reality and one's own being.[27]

A seeker not only asserted the unification of God (*tauhid*), but also had perfect knowledge of this unity. In His essence, God does not have any partner or substitute. God is incapable of union and separation, does not occupy space, exists without a similar entity, does not become immanent in things, is free from imperfections, is unchangeable in His qualities, is endowed with perfection and does not procreate. Pointing towards God's outstanding traits, Hujwiri noted that He is living, knowing, forgiving, merciful, willing, powerful, seeing, speaking and subsistent. His knowledge encompasses all objects of cognition and all entities are dependent on Him. He does what He wills; He wills what he knows. His decree being an absolute fact, He is the sole predestinator of good and evil. He alone gives judgement that is all wisdom. None can behold Him face to face, though His saints enjoyed contemplating Him in this world. The Sunnis envisioned God as a single artificer who originated all forms of creation in the universe. Dualists, who held the opposite view, were refuted by Hujwiri in *Al-Riayat li-huquq Allah*. Considering the stance of the Sufis, it has found that Junaid Baghdadi drew a distinction between the eternal and phenomenal, while Husain bin Masur ascribed unification to none other than God. Thus, unification of God required denial of partnership (with God) and phenomenality. Any thought other than God raised a veil between the seeker and God. Knowledge of unification could be acquired by denying personal initiative and surrendering the will of man, whose body was a repository for the mysteries of God. The seeker could not reach God through his intellect, but could behold Him with his spiritual eyes, without comprehending His infinity. Hujwiri asserted that unification was a mystery revealed by God to His servants and that it could not be expressed in language at all, much less high sounding phrases.[28]

A seeker understood that faith was employed with reference to one's belief in God, His angels and His revealed books. Some Sufis held that faith was verbal profession, verification and practice. Others believed that it was just verbal profession and verification. Hujwiri argued that the difference between them was one of expression and not substance. The former applied the name of faith to obedience, which alone provided a man with security from punishment. On the other hand, the latter asserted that gnosis and, not obedience, was the cause of security. God is known by one of His three attributes – beauty (*jamal*), majesty (*jalal*) and perfection (*kamal*). Those who saw evidence of gnosis in the beauty of God nurtured a longing for vision, which was an effect of love. Therefore, faith and gnosis were love, while obedience was a sign of love. Anyone who denied it neglected the command of God and betrayed his ignorance of gnosis. Some thinkers believed that faith came entirely from God, while others held that it sprang entirely from man. Hujwiri perceived faith as absorption of all human attributes in the search of God. When gnosis was established in the heart of the seeker, all forms of skepticism was destroyed and he remained in the circle of its authority. In simple words, faith was absolute trust in God, which flowed from the knowledge bestowed by God.[29]

In their spiritual quest, the seekers laid a considerable emphasis on prayer, which ordinarily meant remembrance of God and submission to Him enabled them to find the entire way leading to God and revealed their spiritual states. All Muslims were bound to offer five daily prayers after meeting preliminary conditions relating to purification, garments, place, direction, posture, intention, recitation, prostration and salutation. However, a seeker discerned spiritual meanings in these conditions – purification in place of repentence, dependence on a mentor in place of the direction (*qibla*), standing for prayer in place of self-mortification, reciting the Quran in place of inward meditation, bowing the head in place of humility, prostration in place of self-knowledge, profession of faith in place of intimacy, salutation in place of detachment from the world and escape from bondage of stations.[30] According to Hujwiri, prayer was a divine command, and not a means to obtain presence with or absence from God. Seekers engaged in self-mortification or who had attained steadfastness, were advised to perform four hundred bowings in prayer day and night, so that their bodies became habituated to devotion. In case of seekers who had achieved the spiritual states, their prayers corresponded to the stations of union, so that they became united in their condition of ecstasy. However, when the condition of ecstasy was withdrawn, their prayers corresponded to the station of separation. The former Sufis, who were united in their prayers, prayed day and night, besides adding supererogatory prayers to the obligatory ones. The latter Sufis, who were separated, performed only the prayers needed by them. Some Sufis performed obligatory acts of devotion openly, while they concealed the supererogatory ones to escape the charge of ostentation. Others performed both types of devotion openly, as they held ostentation as unreal and piety as real.[31]

The role of poverty in the pursuit of spirituality was often discussed in Sufi circles. Both the Quran and Prophetic traditions accorded unconditional approval to poverty.[32] It was a mark of distinction for the poor to have renounced all external and internal possessions in order to turn entirely to God. For them, poverty had become their pride so that they lamented its departure and rejoiced its arrival. Its form was seen in destitution and indigence, while its essence was located in fortune and free choice. Those who focused on the essence withdrew from worldly objects and, while seeing only the Supreme Being, hastened towards fullness of eternal life. For a poor man, the two conditions, being wealthy or indigent, were similar. In fact, higher the degree of his poverty, more was the expanse of his spiritual state. Poverty was meritorious in the sense that it insulated his body from sinful acts and heart from evil thoughts, as his exterior was absorbed in blessings of God and his interior was protected by invisible grace. Some mystics treated wealth as superior to poverty, ascribing former to God and latter to man. But God's wealth was not only marked by independence and omnipotence, but it was also eternal. In contrast, man's wealth was subject to decay. According to another view, there was no difference between wealth and poverty as both were divine gifts. Both could be corrupted, the former by forgetfulness and latter by covetousness. If the seeker's heart was cleansed of everything except God, the difference between wealth and poverty vanished.[33] Similar to the question relating to this binary, mystics encountered a dispute on the relative merits of poverty (*faqr*) and purity (*safwat*) which, in turn, was associated with subsistence (*baqa*) and annihilation (*fana*) respectively. In Hujwiri's view, there could be no reason for superiority so long as one dealt with ideas as such; but a choice had to be made when names were given to them. This was why some mystics used the term poverty and others the term purity to express the same idea.[34]

Most Sufis seemed to prefer a distinct outward appearance by wearing a patched frock (*muraqqa*).The practice had been sanctified by Prophet Muhammad and pious caliphs.[35] Made of coarse wool and repaired with patches, the garment conformed to the Sufic principles of detachment, poverty and humility. Yet different views persisted through the ages. There were vulgar Sufis who wore a patched frock to gain public honour and spiritual reputation, but they lacked inner purity that was the hallmark of spirituality. Others felt that wearing a patched frock was unnecessary as God knew that the person was one of the elect. If the aim was to show to the people his proximity to God, then he was guilty of ostentation. In spite of these doubts, the Sufis advised their disciples to wear a patched frock so that, being marked out, they were exposed to public reprobation on committing any transgression. The garment not only provided a feeling of ease, its damaged portions were covered with a patch. Some held that the patch could be sewn at random. Others stood for neat and accurate stitches, as a sound practice indicated sound principles. The most common colour of the garment was blue, as it was not easily soiled and also symbolized mourning that emerged from the state of the world. Spiritual men bestowed a patched frock on a disciple who had completed an education of three years. The parts of a patched frock were seen as allegories for virtues required from a Sufi – collar as patience, two sleeves as fear and hope, two gussets as contraction and dilation, belt as self-abnegation, hem as soundness of faith and fringe as sincerity. If a Sufi was forced by worldly powers to tear this apparel, he was excused. If he did it deliberately, he was not permitted to wear it again. Normally, he changed his dress when graduating from one stage of the spiritual journey to the other. But a patched frock comprised all stages in the spiritual path and, therefore, discarding it meant the abandonment of the path itself.[36]

The Quran, Prophetic traditions (*hadis*), and Prophetic practice (*sunna*) enjoined the Muslims to adopt matrimony. Some mystics held marriage as desirable as a means to quell lust and free the mind from anxiety, while others felt that its object was procreation.[37] If man and wife were suited to each other, marriage provided companionship that was unmatched in reverence and security. However, if the two were not suited to each, an uncongenial wife brought unlimited torment and anxiety. A dervish was advised to weigh the relative evils associated with both marriage and celibacy. In themselves, marriage and celibacy could not ruin a man, because the mischief lay in asserting one's will and yielding to one's desires. Once a man entered into matrimony, he was expected to provide his wife with lawful food and dowry out of lawful property. But he could indulge in sensual pleasure only after fulfilling his obligations towards God. After adopting a moderate stance, Hujwiri held women to be responsible for past calamities and therefore declared celibacy as the foundation of Sufism. The problem of lust could be solved by means other than marriage. Lust could be effectively suppressed by two methods, by starving oneself or by pursuing true love that divested all senses of their sensual quality. Hujwiri recommended celibacy because, according to him, it was not possible to have a suitable wife, whose wants were limited and whose demands were reasonable.[38]

In Hujwiri's view, the seeker was bound to regulate his religious and temporal life on the basis of rules of discipline (*adab*). These rules were of three kinds and covered the seeker's attitude to God, himself and others. These were not separate from one another. Further, these rules comprised three categories – observing Prophetic practice, good manners and loving conduct – that were similarly interconnected.[39] In addition to the rules of discipline, the seeker was required to understand the role of companionship in the path of Sufism.[40] The believers cultivated companionship only for the sake of God, not for gratifying the lower self or selfish interests. If one was unable to derive any religious benefit from a friend, then he had to shun his company. He was free to associate with both a superior and inferior. He derived benefit from the former, while the benefit was mutual in the latter case. But it was advisable to abandon a friend who needed to be flattered or from whom one had to seek forgiveness for a fault. The existence of unworthy friends did not warrant a withdrawal from society, because solitude was fatal for a seeker. A principle in companionship was to treat others in accordance with their degree (age, status and experience) i.e. old men with respect like fathers, of the same age with agreeable familiarity like brothers and young men with affection like sons. It was proper to renounce hate, envy and malice, but equally befitting to use sincere admonition when needed. The biggest enemy of companionship was selfishness.[41]

Hujwiri divided Sufis into two classes, residents (*muqiman*) and travellers (*musafiran*), each treating the other as superior. The travelling ones regarded the resident ones as superior, because they themselves had adopted mobility in their own interest, while the resident ones had settled down in the service of God. The former stage was a sign of search, while the latter was a token of attainment. In a similar vein, the resident ones regarded the travelling ones as superior, because they themselves were burdened with worldly cares, while the travelling ones were detached from the world.[42] Interestingly, the resident dervishes had clear obligations towards the travelling ones. Acting as decent hosts, they were expected to treat the traveller as an honoured guest, who was met with joy and respect. They had to place before him whatever food they had. They could not enquire as to where he came from or where he was going or what was his name. They had to accept that he had come from God, that he was going to God and his name was the servant of God. They had to ascertain whether he desired to be alone or in company. In former case, they were expected to lodge him in an empty room. In the latter case, they had to interact with him in a friendly and social manner. When the traveller prepared to sleep for the night, the resident Sufi could offer to wash his feet, but act only in accordance with his wishes. Next morning, he took him to the cleanest bath available and, while waiting upon him, rubbed away stains from different parts of his body. If he had the means, he could provide a new set of clothes. During the course of his stay, he could not be invited to visit a saintly figure against his wishes. He could not be escorted to meet worldly men and their functions. In no case was he taken from house to house for begging.[43]

A travelling Sufi, on his part, was guided by a set of rules. He could travel only for the sake of God, not for pleasure. The object of his mobility was pilgrimage or war (against infidels) or to seek knowledge or to visit a venerable person or to pay homage at a tomb or holy site. During the journey, he observed his devotions, remained in a state of purity and kept away from sensual affections. He carried a number of articles – patched frock, prayer rug, bucket rope, shoes, clogs and staff. In keeping with the Prophetic custom, he carried such items of daily use like a comb, nail scissors, a needle and a box of antimony. The number of goods carried by the travelling Sufi varied with the spiritual station he had achieved. A firmly grounded adept could carry all the above articles, while for a novice every article was like a shackle, a stumbling block and a veil that merely showed conceit. When a travelling Sufi reached the house of a resident counterpart, he could not interfere with the host and should not make unreasonable demands. He was required to occupy himself with religious duties incumbent on Sufis. In no case could he speak of hardships suffered on the way or narrate idle anecdotes. Since all Sufis, travelling or resident, were engaged in the larger endeavour to please God, they made every effort to trust one another and never spoke ill of others.[44]

In Hujwiri's understanding, the subject of audition (*sama*) was intimately connected with the phenomena of the sense of hearing, role of poetry and impact of music. The sense of hearing enabled humans to comprehend the nature of God, sermons of prophets and logic of religious injunctions. Numerous examples showed that listening to the recitation of the Quran was most delightful to the ear and beneficial for the mind. Though the Quran was revealed to Prophet Muhammad, yet he was fond of hearing it being recited. The listener was more perfect in state than the reciter, for the latter might recite with or without feeling, while the former experienced the true feeling. This was so because speech denoted pride and, in contrast, hearing reflected a sort of humility.[45] Sufi masters followed the Prophet in listening to non-religious poetry, provided the words communicated lawful thoughts, which were more important than the form of expression.[46] Hujwiri was certain that both humans and animals felt the joyful impact of melodies. Traditions of the Prophet listening to songs were collected in *Kitab-i Sama* by Abu Abdul Rehman al-Sulami. Theologians also permitted the playing of musical instruments, provided they were not used for diversion and did not turn the mind towards wicked actions. The legality of audition was determined by the nature of circumstances and impact of the event. Zu ul-Nun Misri argued that those who listened spiritually attained God, while those who listened sensually fell into heresy. Audition was not required by spiritual adepts who had reached the end of their journey. But it was employed by beginners to obtain concentration when distracted by forgetfulness. Audition affected its practitioners in accordance with their grade. It augmented the remorse of the repentent, increased the longing for vision of lovers, confirmed the certainty of those having faith, clarified complex matters for novices, impelled lovers to snap worldly connections and discovered hope for the spiritually poor.[47]

It was necessary to understand the nature of three emotional states – *wajd*, *wujud* and *tawajud* – that directly flowed out of audition. The real sense of *wajd* was pain felt at the loss of the Beloved and failure to gain the object of desire. The real sense of *wujud* was removing grief from the heart and obtaining the object of desire. Inaccessible through investigation, it was a grace bestowed by the Beloved on the lover. *Wajd* was characteristic of the gnostics (*arifan*), while *wujud* was associated with novices (*muridan*). The spiritual status of gnostics being higher than that of the novices, it followed that *wajd* was more perfect than *wujud*. A person, who was overwhelmed by *wajd*, lost his sense of discrimination, but he was exempted from any punishment for any bad action. He was able to overpower his *wajd* by asserting the strength of his knowledge (*ilm*) and thus remained within the confines of divine commands. The pain, which was undertaken to produce *wajd*, was known *tawajud* and it was done by instilling in mind the bounties and evidences of God.[48] The musical sessions, owing to a variety of reasons, came to be associated with controversial acts of dancing and rending garments. Confusion arose when the ecstatic movements of those who tried to induce ecstasy resembled dancing and led frivolous imitators to excessive indulgence. Participation in an audition could lead to a condition where the heart throbbed with exhilaration, rapture became intense, ecstasy was manifested and conventional forms disappeared. But this agitation was a dissolution of the soul and could not be called dancing. A participant, who tore his clothes after losing his senses in an audition, was excused. The torn garment was bestowed on the singer or its pieces were distributed among the listeners who affixed these on their patched frocks as a blessing.[49]

Concluding his discussion on musical sessions, Hujwiri has enumerated the rules that needed to be followed. Attending an audition could not be made a frequent habit, lest one should erode the reverence for it. Such a gathering was presided over by a spiritual mentor, while the singer had to be a respectable person. The performance was attended only by those who were initiated into the discipine of Sufism, while the uninitiated and beginners were kept away. The heart of the listener had to be cleansed of worldly thoughts and his disposition could not tilt towards amusement. The listener allowed himself to be moved by the power of the audition in a natural way. He was required to feel agitated or calm in conformity with the spirit of the audition. He could not try to generate any artificial feelings in his mind. He needed to be perceptive enough to receive divine influence and doing justice to it. He could not permit anyone to interfere with his state. Nor could he himself interfere with the state of other listeners. He could not try to assess the musical abilities of the singer. He was expected to involve himself in his own time (*waqt*), so that he duly received blessings from it. Hujwiri warned that musical concerts could be dangerous and corrupting, as women looked at the listeners from roofs and other places.[50]

Hujwiri took a keen interest in a hallowed debate between the Taufuris and Junaidis on the validity of two states – intoxication (*sukr*) and sobriety (*sahw*) – and threw his weight behind the latter. Bayazid Bistami and his followers, who advocated a rapturous longing for God,[51] believed that sobriety involved fixity and equilibrium of human attributes, which became a veil between God and man. In contrast, intoxication involved the destruction of human attributes, leading to the survival of faculties that did not belong to human genus and were the most perfect. Junaid Baghdadi and his followers,[52] who stood for sobriety in relation to God, held that intoxication reflected a disturbance of one's normal state and loss of sanity and self control. The seekers sought to know the principle of things through annihilation or subsistence, but the principle of verification could not be attained unless they were sane. With the eye of subsistence, they perceived the universe as imperfect, while with the eye of annihilation they perceived the creation as non-existent. In both cases, he turned away from created things. Therefore, one was advised to pray to God (like the Prophet) so that He would show the things as they were, because whoever saw the things as such was rewarded with equanimity. However, such a vision could be obtained only in a state of sobriety. Musa, being intoxicated, failed to endure a single epiphany and fell into a swoon. But the Prophet, being sober, beheld the same glory continuously with increasing consciousness, all the way from Mecca to a space of just two bows from the Divine presence.[53]

Hujwiri recalled that his Shaikh, who was a follower of Junaid Baghdadi, often stated that intoxication was a playground of children, while sobriety was the death field of men. In line with this understanding, Hujwiri observed that the perfect state of an intoxicated man was sobriety, that the lowest stage of sobriety lay in accepting the powerlessness of humanity and that a sobriety which appeared to be an evil was better than intoxication that was really evil. In developing his approach towards Mansur al-Hallaj,[54] Hujwiri drew support from the position of Junaid Baghdadi. According to Hujwiri, Junaid Baghdadi's mystical doctrine, which was based on sobriety, became the most celebrated of all doctrines and therefore it was adopted by all the Shaikhs despite the differences in their sayings on the ethics of Sufism. Junaid Baghdadi not only rejected the request of Hallaj for association, but also denounced his ideas on sobriety and intoxication. The former denoted the soundness of one's spiritual state in relation to God, while the latter denoted excess of longing and extremes of love that could not be acquired by human effort. Junaid Baghdadi went to the extent of declaring that he saw much foolishness and nonsense in the words of Hallaj.[55]

In the above context, the judgement of Hujwiri on Hallaj assumed significance. He found that some Sufis accepted Hallaj's controversial expressions, while others rejected them. There were some who accused Hallaj of magic, trickery and heresy. But few denied the purity of his spiritual states and the abundance of his ascetic practices. He was criticized not for his mystical principles, but for his outward conduct. Hujwiri, who had examined fifty works of Hallaj in different places – Baghdad and neighbouring districts besides Khuzistan, Fars and Khurasan – adjudged all his sayings like the first visions of novices, though some of them were weaker or stronger. It appeared that if a spiritualist described a vision with the power of ecstasy and help of divine grace, his words were obscure, particularly if said in haste and self-praise. These words were repugnant to the imagination and incomprehensible to the minds of the listeners. If people of true spirituality and insight had a vision, they did not try to describe it, nor felt concerned with praise or censure. However, Hallaj could not be accused of magic as his life was based on piety, prayers, fasting, praise of God and sublime sayings on unification. His actions, that were misunderstood as magic, were in fact miracles and these were vouchsafed only to a true saint. A person, who was overcome by intoxication, did not have the ability to express himself correctly. Since the expression was difficult to comprehend, the real intention was overlooked. The sayings of Hallaj could not be taken as a model as, being an ecstatic, he was not firmly settled and therefore his sayings could not be regarded as authoritative.[56] In the final analysis of Hujwiri, the path devised by Hallaj was not established on any sound principle, his spiritual state was not fixed in any position and his experiences were largely mingled with error. Hujwiri, during the course of his own visions, derived support from the ideas of Hallaj by way of evidences. At this early stage, he even wrote a book explaining the sayings of Hallaj and demonstrated their sublimity with proofs and arguments. In another work entitled *Minhaj al-Din*, Hujwiri had reconstructed the entire life of Hallaj. Since his own understanding of Sufism had evolved over a period of time, he revised his thinking on the doctrines of Hallaj. After all, it was futile to express the reality in words.[57]

After the death of Hujwiri (1072), his tomb became a centre of pilgrimage. During his lifetime, Rai Raju, who was the deputy governor of Panjab, became a disciple of the saint and converted to Islam.[58] Since then his descendants served as attendants (*khadim wa mujawir*) of the shrine. The records available with this institution have enabled Nur Ahmad Chishti to prepare a long genealogical table of the attendants, besides identifying their income from land grants, cash stipends and offerings of the devotees. Chishti has also delved into the process that raised Hujwiri to be the patron saint of Lahore. According to a belief prevalent among the Muslims, the spiritual jurisdiction of every kingdom and city was invariably bestowed on an eminent Sufi, though the ordinary governance was in the hands of administrators. It was through this Sufi that the decrees of God and the orders of the worldly rulers were implemented. It was with the permission of this Sufi that the new saints could settle in any part of Hind and Panjab. Accordingly, Khwaja Muinuddin Chishti, before settling in Ajmer, broke his journey at Lahore and performed austerities for forty days (*chillah*) at the grave of Hujwiri.[59] This action became a precedent for the subsequent Sufis of the region. Baba Farid and Miyan Mir undertook meditation at this shrine. While Shah Husain (1539-99) actually lived in its premises, Sultan Bahu

(1631-91) and Bulleh Shah (1680-1752) mentioned Hujwiri in their mystical verses.[60] Dara Shukoh, writing in the middle of the seventeenth century, drew attention to the popularity of Hujwiri in the city of Lahore, the like of which was not found anywhere on the face of the earth. According to him, the tomb of Hujwiri was situated in the western fort. On every Thursday, thousands of people came here to pay obeisance to the Sufi. It was believed that a person, who undertook a complete circumambulation of the shrine for forty consecutive Thursdays, had all his wishes fulfilled.[61] Sujan Rai Bhandari, who has described the prominent monuments of Lahore existing at the end of the seventeenth century,[62] noted the presence of the mausoleum of Hujwiri.[63] He remembered Hujwiri as the crown among the Sufis and one who, in addition to being a saint, was perfect in his knowledge and learning. Allama Iqbal, the distinguished poet and philosopher, has paid the following tribute to Hujwiri:[64]

The saint of Hujwir was venerated by the peoples
And Pir-i Sanjar visited his tomb as a pilgrim.
With ease he broke down the mountain-barriers
And sowed the seed of Islam in India.
The age of Omar was restored by his godliness.
The fame of the Truth was exalted by his words.
He was the guardian of the honour of the Quran.
The house of falsehood fell in ruins at his gaze.
The dust of the Panjab was brought to life by his breath.
Our dawn was made splendid by his sun.
He was a lover, and, withal, a courier of Love.
The secrets of Love shone forth from his brow.
I will tell a story of his perfection
And enclose a whole rose-bed in a single bed.

The Chishti Path of Austerities

Shaikh Fariduddin Masud Ganj-i Shakar, who was popular in Panjab as Baba Farid, laid the foundation of the Chishti order in the region. His long life (1175-1265) coincided with major political changes including the decline of the Ghaznavid rule, military campaigns of the Ghorids, establishment of the Delhi Sultanate, internal conflict in the ruling class, Mongol inroads and migration of refugees from the western lands. His grandfather, Qazi Shuaib, a prominent citizen of Kabul, migrated to Lahore in the middle of the twelfth century and settled as a judge (*qazi*) in Kahtwal near Multan. As a teenager, Baba Farid adopted the mystical path under the inspiration of his mother. His sincere devotion attracted the attention of the eminent mystic Shaikh Jalaluddin Tabrezi who was on his way to Delhi. During the course of his education in Multan, he became a disciple of Khwaja Qutbuddin Bakhtiar Kaki, who had attached himself to Khwaja Muinuddin Chishti of Ajmer. Baba Farid travelled to Delhi and, entering the hospice of his mentor, began his advanced mystical training in the right earnest. Here he had the good fortune of receiving the blessings of Khwaja Muinuddinn Chishti. He undertook hard spiritual exercises that included fasting for three consecutive days and practising inverted devotion (*chilla-i makus*). After completing his training under Khwaja Kaki, Baba Farid moved to Hansi, a town on the Delhi-Multan trade route, and established here a hospice. On his departure, he was nominated as the principal successor of Khwaja Kaki. However, he received the insignia of his exalted office – cloak (*khirqa*), turban (*dastar*), and wooden sandals (*nalain-i chaubin*) – when he visited Delhi on the demise of his mentor. He returned to Hansi in response to the demand of his followers. His reputation increased manifold when he received fulsome praise from Maulana Nur Turk, who was delivering a sermon at Hansi. During his stay of two decades, he earned the unconditional love of a disciple Jamaluddin Hansavi.[65] Around 1236, he came to Ajodhan and spent here the remaining twenty years of his life, though he also toyed with the idea of settling in Lahore.[66]

Baba Farid did not permanently settle in Delhi and Hansi, because large crowds of devotees did not allow him to follow his schedule of prayers. He pined for a peaceful place where he could delve into his devotional pursuits without the distraction of visitors. He finally chose Ajodhan even though it had disadvantages. It did not boast of much cultivation owing to scanty rainfall. The local inhabitants were somewhat uncouth and did not have much faith in dervishes. Yet it afforded a peaceful environment needed for a life of spiritual engagement, the most suitable sites being a mosque in the town and a jungle of *kareel* outside the town.[67] During the season of *kareel* and *delahs*, a disciple was deputed to collect fruit. The inmates of the hospice ate it to their fill and felt as happy as on Id. When it was not available, the disciples were sent to the neighbouring localities with the begging bowls to collect food (*chun waqt delah wa kareel nabudi zanbil me gardanidand*).[68] Unlike a fellow mystic Shaikh Badruddin Ghaznavi, who attended frequent banquets at Delhi, Baba Farid asked himself, 'O Masud! You are fattening your stomach by eating oily and sweet bread. How will you meet your obligations to God?'[69]

Having established a hospice (*khanqah*) at Ajodhan, Baba Farid laid the principles for its communal living and multifarious functions. Besides providing residence to him and his family, it served as a school for grooming disciples and an open house for a variety of visitors. The hospice comprised a large hall (*jamaat khana*), which was little more than a roof standing on a number of pillars. At the foot of each pillar, a disciple resided with his bedding, books, and rosary. The disciples slept, prayed and studied on the floor, there being no discrimination on the grounds of seniority or piety. If food was available, it was shared among all and, if not, they jointly suffered hunger. Responsibilities were distributed equally, as no work was seen as undignified. The personal needs of the Shaikh were met by Syed Nuruddin Kirmani, Iqbal and Isa. Badruddin Ishaq brought wood from the forest, Jamaluddin Hansavi plucked *delah* and *kareel* from the trees, Husamuddin fetched water and cleaned the utensils, Nizamuddin Auliya cooked, and Alauddin Ali Ahmad Sabir managed the common kitchen.[70] A large amount of unasked charity (*futuh*) was received, but it was distributed among visitors and nothing was kept for the next day. In times of financial stress, Baba Farid did not permit taking loans, but introduced the practice of circulating the begging bowl (*zanbil*) in the neighbourhood, something which could be done twice a day. He normally broke his fast with the bread of this bowl. The inmates ate what was collected during the day and the remaining food was consumed at night.⁷¹ The hospice offered free access to all classes of people – rulers, nobles, soldiers, merchants, and commoners from the countryside – who sought answers to their existential and spiritual needs, besides simple blessings. Different types of roving mendicants, particularly Jogis and Qalandars, also registered their presence. The doors of the hospice remained open until midnight and food was always ready. Every visitor was offered whatever was available.⁷²

Baba Farid did not easily enrol a person as disciple. He assessed the sincerity of a candidate to traverse the spiritual path and, after satisfying himself, directed him to undergo the first step of shaving his head. Having thus admitted a person under his tutelage, he made sure that he did not deviate from the single-minded pursuit of his spiritual aim. Khwaja Wahiduddin, a grandson of Khwaja Muinuddin Chishti, met Baba Farid and expressed his desire to be enrolled as a disciple and permitted to shave his head. Baba Farid expressed his reluctance to accede to the request as he had himself taken an oath of allegiance at the hands of the Chishti saint of Ajmer. Khwaja Wahiduddin remained firm in his resolve, so that Baba Farid agreed to initiate him into his circle of disciples and gave directions for shaving his head. However, in the case of another candidate, the situation took an unfavourable turn. A student named Nasir, who wished to adopt the avocation of trade, became a disciple of Baba Farid and, in accordance with the Sufi practice, had his head shaved. One day he got in touch with a visiting Jogi and sought to learn from him the method of growing long hair. Nizamudin Auliya could not understand how a person who had registered his allegiance to a distinguished Sufi, could behave in such an objectionable manner. Since the purpose of removing one's hair was to erase all traces of arrogance and vanity, there was no point in wanting long hair again.⁷³ In normal circumstances, a disciple took the oath of allegiance to his mentor only once. However, if he so desired, he could repeat the act. In case the mentor was not present, he could place his (mentor's) garment before him and, placing his hand on it, renew the oath of allegiance. Baba Farid himself did this several times and also allowed his disciples to do so. The practice of renewal was traced to the oath of benediction (*bait ul-rizwan*) which was conducted by Prophet Muhammad before embarking on a punitive expedition against the Meccans.[74]

The spiritual progress of a disciple depended on his capacity to absorb the lessons imparted by his mentor. That this capacity varied among the disciples was indicated by the experience of Baba Farid. One of his disciples, Yusuf, complained to the Shaikh that he had been under his tutelage for several years, that all others had gained something from the Shaikh's beneficence and that he himself deserved to be honoured before the others. Baba Farid explained, 'There has been no shortcoming on my part. There must be preparedness and capability on your part. I do all that I can. But if God does not give the required capacity, what can anyone else do.' In order to elaborate his point, he took recourse to a practical example. He asked a lad to bring three bricks one after the other and place them before three persons present. The boy brought in full sized bricks to place before Baba Farid and his friend, but he placed half a brick before Yusuf. The Shaikh, while decoding the spectacle, said that he played no role in the distribution of bricks. Being fair, he had given the same direction three times. Since the disciple continued to have the same capacity that day as he had before, there was nothing left for him to do and he could not be held accountable for the outcome.[75] He was acute enough to note that disciples were not alike, as their attitudes varied from time to time. There was one disciple who professed allegiance to him but, after leaving his presence, changed. Another disciple, took his leave, but remained loyal for a fairly long period; ultimately he too changed. The third one, Nizamuddin, fell in a different category, as his disposition remained the same throughout without changing even a bit. When this disciple recalled his association with Baba Farid, he was filled with emotion and his eyes welled up with tears. Four decades after the demise of Baba Farid, he was constant in his love for his mentor and, in fact, his love for him increased with every passing day.[76]

As soon as a novice grasped the hand of a spiritual preceptor and made a pledge of loyalty to him, it amounted to making a compact with God. He was bound to remain firm in his commitment and, if he deviated from his resolve, he could not retrace his steps to the path of piety. In this context, Nizamuddin recalled his own experience after taking the oath of allegiance (*bait*) to Baba Farid. During the course of his journey from Ajodhan, he felt thirsty on the way as the air was hot and water was not available. By chance, he met an Alavi named Syed Imad, who offered his own flask to drink from. Nizamuddin refused to consume the contents of the flask, which was either wine or hemp juice. Syed Imad persisted in his offer, as he had brought the liquid to beat the thirst in a dry terrain and there was no water for a long distance to come. He warned that the newly enrolled disciple would die, if he did not drink the stuff available. Remaining firm on his refusal, Nizamuddin declared that he would die if he drank from the flask. Since he had pledged his allegiance and bound himself by oath to Baba Farid, he could in no case touch such a thing. He hurriedly departed from the place and, in a short time, reached a spot where water was available.[77]

None of the disciples of Baba Farid could match Nizamuddin in their commitment to the oath of allegiance. A disciple named Arif, who had completed his training under Baba Farid, was given the letter of succession. He was sent to Siwistan and adjacent areas with the permission to admit disciples of his own. A ruler in the area of Multan and Uch appointed Arif as a prayer leader (*imam*) or he was assigned an equivalent official position. This ruler sent a sum of 100 *tankas* for Baba Farid through Arif. Arif went to Baba Farid and, giving him only half of the amount, kept the remaining with himself. Baba Farid remarked that he had made the division on a brotherly basis, i.e. each receiving half of the whole. Arif was ashamed and handed over the balance of the offering to Baba Farid. He not only asked for forgiveness, but also requested for the renewal of the oath of allegiance. Baba Farid acceded to the request and re-admitted Arif into his circle of initiates. Arif renewed his vows by getting his head shaved. After sometime, he showed his firmness in the principles of spirituality, so that Baba Farid once again granted him the permission to enrol disciples and asked him to leave for Siwistan.[78]

During the course of their tutelage, most disciples stayed with their mentor for varying periods. Others paid visits to the mentor, the frequency being determined by their respective circumstances. Nizamuddin visited Baba Farid three times, keeping a gap of one year between each visit. After the demise of Baba Farid, he visited his tomb six or seven times, so that the total number of his visits to Ajodhan turned out to be ten. Jamaluddin Hansavi paid seven visits to Baba Farid, while Najibuddin Mutawakkil did so nineteen times.[79] Whenever Muhammad Shah Ghori, a disciple of Baba Farid who served as a soldier in the army, wished to see the Shaikh, he visualized him in a dream. Wherever he wanted to go, Baba Farid would appear to him from that direction. Once he resolved to leave for Hindustan, but instead travelled to Ajodhan, because he saw Baba Farid in a dream going towards that town. This change turned out to be beneficial, as he experienced a lot of comfort and pleasure.[80] Owing to the reverence of the disciples towards their mentor, they offered prayers to God for his recovery whenever he fell ill. However, the results were not always positive. On one such occasion when Baba Farid became sick, he asked a few disciples including Nizamuddin to pray at the graves of martyrs. On their return, Baba Farid remarked that their visit had failed to improve his condition. Though Nizamuddin was speechless, his friend Ali Bihari reasoned that their Shaikh was perfect, while they were deficient; prayers of the deficient could not produce an effect on the perfect one. The Shaikh replied that he had asked God to provide whatever they sought from Him. Handing over his staff to Nizamuddin, he directed him and Badruddin Ishaq to retire to a particular cell and engage themselves in remembering God. Both of them reached the place and spent the entire night in the task. Next morning, they appeared before the Shaikh and learnt that he was better. Only a prayer offered in the appropriate manner produced fruitful results.[81]

A disciple of Baba Farid embarked on a journey only after taking his leave of the Shaikh. When he returned, he paid his respects to the Shaikh. If the journey was put off due to some reason, he met the mentor and explained the reason for a change in the schedule. The protocol was repeated as many times as the alterations in the travel plans. Such a situation had developed in the case of a disciple of Baba Farid named Ali Makki. However, the uncertainty came to an end when Baba Farid sent two loaves of bread to him.[82] Such was the intensity of the disciple's reverence for his mentor that it was not terminated by the latter's death. The bereaved disciple continued his association with the mentor through his tomb. When Nizamuddin was overpowered by a strong urge to go on the Haj, he travelled to Ajodhan to visit the tomb of his mentor. When he paid his homage at the grave, his desire for going to the holy cities was fulfilled and nothing remained to be done. When he felt the same desire again, he again went to Ajodhan and experienced the same feeling. For him, visiting the tomb of his mentor was as meritorious as the pilgrimage to Mecca.[83] Another disciple Khwaja Hamid, who had been instructed to settle in Indrapat after the completion of his training, faced a similar situation. But he changed his mind and, having joined a group of friends who were leaving for Mecca, came back to Baba Farid and secured his permission for this change in his travel plans.[84]

Baba Farid was an erudite scholar and a diligent teacher. He was also unsurpassed in eloquence. His curriculum included the study of the Quran, Shihabuddin Suhrawardy's *Awarif ul-Maarif* and Abu Shakur Salimi's *Tamhid ul-Muhtadi*. He taught three books to Nizamuddin. He read one of these books as the pupil listened, while the other two were read together by them. He heard Nizamuddin recite the Quran in his presence every day from the noon prayer to the late afternoon prayer. In this manner, he heard the recitation of six portions (*siparahs*) of the Quran. He detected that his pupil could not pronounce the alphabet (*zad*) in the correct manner in spite of several attempts. Nizamuddin admitted that no one could pronounce this particular alphabet as his teacher. Baba Farid explained that this alphabet was revealed to Prophet Muhammad and, therefore, it was not accessible to others.[85] He also taught five chapters of *Awarif ul-Maarif* to Nizamuddin and, in the process, offered insights that were beyond the erudition of any other scholar. His expositions generated such an intense passion for God that listeners wished to die at that moment and regarded such a death as propitious. It appeared that he spoke from a high mystical station that had been graced by divine light.

When he received a copy of *Awarif ul-Maarif*, he was blessed with a son who was named Shihabuddin after its famed author.⁸⁶

In the above context, the case of Maulana Badruddin Ishaq offered interesting evidence. This young man, who belonged to Delhi, had studied Islamic sciences from the leading scholars of the city. Endowed with an insatiable hunger for knowledge, he aimed at achieving the highest level of academic progress. He encountered a few complex themes that could not be clarified by the scholars of Delhi. Therefore, he decided to travel all the way to Bokhara in order to seek answers to his questions. During the course of his journey through Panjab, he stopped at Ajodhan. At this time, the fame of Baba Farid's spiritual attainments had spread in all directions, so that people from different lands came to benefit from his perfections. On the insistence of a friend, he met Baba Farid and came under the spell of his personality – vigour of spirituality, power of oratory, breadth of vision and purity of heart – that provided insights into the future. The doubts of Maulana Ishaq were removed owing to the Shaikh's wide erudition and communicative skills. He was amazed at a Sufi, who did not keep a book in front of him and sat with a sheet wrapped around him, but spoke through divine inspiration. In his perception, the Shaikh's knowledge was not acquired by his effort but had been bestowed by God. He felt that he had gained a hundred times more than what he would have brought from Bokhara. Abandoning the idea of going to that city, he enrolled as a disciple of Baba Farid. In due course, he distinguished himself in the service of the Shaikh. He not only received the spiritual successorship of his mentor, but also became his son-in-law.⁸⁷

Though Baba Farid was perfect in his knowledge, yet he could loose his temper, if a pupil behaved with indiscretion. Once he was teaching *Awarif ul-Maarif* from a faint and defective manuscript. Nizamuddin, in his innocence, remarked that a better copy of the book was in the possession of Najibuddin Mutawakkil. Baba Farid fell into a rage and asked if he did not have the ability to correct a defective manuscript. Nizamuddin realized his mistake and asked for forgiveness, but the Shaikh's anger did not subside. Nizamuddin, owing to shame and confusion, wished to commit suicide. Baba Farid relented only when his son Shihabuddin interceded on behalf of the erring pupil. The Shaikh clarified that his action was aimed at perfecting his spiritual state and, in this sense, a mentor was a beautician (dresser of brides) for the disciple. In order to console a repentant Nizamuddin, the Shaikh bestowed on him a robe of honour and special clothes.[88]

Baba Farid issued a certificate of succession (*khilafatnama*) to a disciple on the occasion of the completion of his training. Drafted in Arabic, it mentioned the abilities of the disciple with reference to the books studied by him under his supervision. It also highlighted his qualities as a person and advised him on his conduct as a Sufi in his own right. In such a document, which was issued to Nizamuddin, Baba Farid underlined the importance of the Prophetic traditions (*hadis*), which was a difficult subject. The Shaikh had taught the best book on the theme, *Tamhid ul-Muhtadi* by Abu Shakur Salimi, to Nizamuddin. This disciple was not only an adornment among scholars, he was also meritorious and virtuous as a student. He was authorized to teach this book to his students, provided he avoided mistakes in teaching, writing and elaborating it, besides devoting his energy and knowledge in correcting the manuscripts and purifying the language. He was also permitted to teach what he had learnt from his mentor, having collected and preserved the same. He was advised to adopt isolation in a mosque where prayers were held in congregation. He was urged to embrace seclusion as laid in the Prophetic tradition, provided he controlled cravings of the flesh and abjured worldly temptations. In case he felt fatigued by the struggle, he could resort to devotion or sleep, but had to abstain from idle seclusion. Finally, Baba Farid declared Nizamuddin as his bonafide successor in both religious and worldly matters, but urged others to show him obedience and respect.[89]

Baba Farid was on intimate terms with Nizamuddin. The day he enrolled as a disciple, he decided to record the words uttered by his mentor. After attending the Shaikh's discourse he would write down in proper order all he had heard. He kept up with this practice and informed the Shaikh of his activity. Whenever the Shaikh narrated an anecdote or explained a principle, he would check if the writer was present. In case he was found absent, the Shaikh repeated the sermon. This showed that Baba Farid approved the task that Nizamuddin had taken upon himself. At that time, Nizamuddin received from a stranger some sheets of white paper that were bound in a volume. He accepted the gift and began to record the sermons of Baba Farid. At the top of each page, he inscribed, 'Glory be to God. Praise be to God. There is no god but God. God is great. There is no might nor power but with God the Magnificent, the Sublime.' Thereafter, he recorded the discourses of the Shaikh as he heard and till that day (30 March 1309) the compilation was still with him.[90] If a disciple received any gift from his mentor, he treated it with great care and preserved it in all circumstances, even if he had to pay a price. Nizamuddin received from Baba Farid a cloak (*khirqah*) which was made of a blanket of coarse wool and cut according to the design peculiar to the Chishtis. While travelling with a companion from Ajodhan to Delhi, he reached a place where a dangerous fork had been created by heavy rain. As they took shelter under a tree, a gang of robbers approached them. Nizamuddin felt so concerned about the cloak that he decided to prevent the robbers from snatching it. However, if he failed in his effort, he resolved to remain in the wilderness and never return to the city. Fortunately, the robbers dispersed in different directions without harming anyone.[91]

Baba Farid was the first Sufi to articulate his mystical ideas in the form of poetry composed in Punjabi. He did not wish to confine himself to a limited number of disciples, who studied their courses in Persian and Arabic.[92] Instead, he aimed at popularizing the teachings of the Chishti discipline to a larger circle of devotees who did not have access to learned languages that were mastered only through formal education. His poetry was originally collected by Guru Nanak and later on included in the final version of the Sikh scripture by Guru Arjan Dev in 1604.[93] At one time, some scholars like Macauliffe and Nizami doubted the attribution of this poetry to Baba Farid. Carl W. Ernst, basing himself on Zainuddin Shirazi's discourses (*Hidayat ul-Qulub*), which were compiled only a hundred years after the demise of Baba Farid, has put the controversy to rest. In his words, 'This evidence favours the strength of the oral tradition of the Punjabi poetry, and the continuity of the Sikh Farid material with the older poems of the Sufi tradition.'[94] Significantly, Baba Farid located Islamic spirituality in the context of local imagery, which encompassed not only rivers and boats, but also animals, birds, crops and plants. He explained the nuances of divine love in terms of physical intimacy between man and wife. Conscious of wide social disparities between the ruling elite and underprivileged poor, he emphasized the physical decay caused by age and the reality of death. Composed in the Lehandi dialect of Panjabi, his verses faithfully elucidate his teachings.

The seeker understood that the search for God, who is boundless and unreachable, nourished humankind.[95] God is sweeter than such eatables as jaggery, sugar, honey and creamy milk.[96] But this search for God was fraught with difficulties. On the one hand, the seeker carried a worldly baggage and, on the other, his understanding was so inadequate that the world appeared as a mysterious fire to him. Since he was led by the Satan, it was not possible for him to turn his mind (*chit*) towards God. If he longed for the lord (*sayin*) and wished to enter His door, he had to be as humble as the grass that was trampled under the feet. True love could not exist with greed, just as a crumbling thatch (*chhappar*) could not withstand rain. It was futile to wander from forest to forest, as God lived in one's heart.[97] Therefore, it was desirable to search for God in the wide ocean, rather than putting one's hand in the mud of the ponds.[98] This search did not exempt him from the observance of basic Islamic obligations. A seeker who ignored his prayers was no better than a dog. It was not a good practice to shirk going to the mosque five times a day (*panje wakht masit*). The seeker was directed to get up, perform ablutions and offer the morning prayer. This was the most essential opportunity for registering submission to God. A head that did not bow before God, deserved to be cut off and burnt under the pot in place of firewood (*balan*).[99] In view of these injunctions, it was possible only for rare individuals to traverse the spiritual path in the tradition of saints (*darvesi reet*).[100] The journey of the seeker was long, as his destination was hundreds of miles away. Endowed with short legs, the seeker walked through the long night over hills and plains, so that his body began to suffer pain.[101] Sainthood was akin to a hazardous journey, as it caused the body to burn like an oven and bones to smoulder like firewood. It involved walking on one's head when the feet suffered fatigue.[102]

A seeker was expected to cultivate numerous qualities of head and heart. If he was endowed with a sharp understanding (*aql latif*), he should not slander the deeds of others. Instead he should examine his own inner self (*girevan*). He should not seek revenge from his opponents, but treat them with respect.[103] If he met evil with good, his body would be free from disease and he would achieve his aims. He should minimize his basic needs. He should satisfy his hunger with dry bread (*rukhi sukhi*) and cold water. He should not show any greed for the buttered bread of others, as those who ate dainty foods were destined to suffer in the end.[104] He should avoid futile actions, so that he did not feel ashamed in the court of God (*sayin de darbar*). He should serve (*chakri*) the Lord quietly, as the saints were required to have the patience (*jirand*) of trees.[105] He should not merely wear the black garb of saints to attract public attention. He should rather pay attention to the purification of his inner self.[106] He should develop his sense of discrimination like the swans, who dipped their beaks in the pond, but did not drink salt water and who landed in a field of millets (*kodra*) but did not eat the grain.[107] He should keep his mind on an even keel and overcome the ups and downs (*toye tibbe*) in his path, so that he was not harmed by the fire of hell.[108] He should not surrender himself to sound sleep, lest he should fail to get his share of musk (*kathuri*) which was distributed only at night.[109] He should spend his time in wakeful meditation, as he would get flowers at first watch of the night and fruit at the last watch, whereas his rising at dawn promised gifts from God. These gifts depended entirely on God's will. Some seekers, who were awake, failed to get them. Some others, who were asleep, were awakened to receive them.[110] A seeker should shun arrogance in spite of his merits. He should be innocent even if knowledgeable and powerless (*nitana*) even if powerful. He should share even if he had nothing on him. Only then he would become a true devotee (*bhagat*).[111]

The Establishment of Sufi Orders   161

The path of the seeker was extremely difficult. It was as narrow and sharp as the edge of a dagger. The seeker was expected to commence his journey in the early hours of the morning.[112] He should be as humble as grass that grew in his path. Though it was trampled under everyone's feet, yet it led to the court of God. This attribute of humility was akin to the role of earth in human life. People saw the earth as something lowly. In reality, nothing was as sublime, because it remained below the feet of the living and covered the dead from above.[113] The seeker was advised to develop the quality of patience (*sabr*) because, like a bow and arrows, it acted as a weapon against the obstacles in the spiritual path. It enabled the seeker to discipline his body in a manner that he continuously got closer to God, but did not reveal his secret to anyone. If his patience increased, he acquired the qualities of a river and, if it decreased, he was lost in the wilderness like a rivulet.[114] A seeker should not hurt others by using harsh words, because God resided in every human being, each of whom was as precious as a gem. If he desired the love of God, he could not harm others in any way.[115] The ideal course for him was to follow the guidance of his mentor, as it would enable him to separate truth from falsehood. The role of his mentor was similar to that of a boatman who, owing to his alertness, warned the passenger about the presence of whirlpools in the long river, which washed away its own banks.[116]

The seeker desired a state of perpetual union with the divine beloved God. When this desire remained unfulfilled, the seeker suffered from physical ailments. Employing sexual imagery, Baba Farid perceived the seeker as wife and God as husband. When she failed to enjoy sexual union with her husband (*kant*), her bodily organs were twisted. Only a deserted wife (*duhagan*) understood the misery of spending the night in loneliness. A wife was unfortunate if she did not receive support in her husband's house. She was blessed if she was married (*suhagan*) in the true sense.[117] But if she was unable to experience the bliss of marriage during her youth, she lamented her marital inability even in the grave.[118] If her search for her Beloved did not bear fruit, her body smouldered like a slow fire. In view of the ever present demands of her body, she was forced to suppress her senses. Though such delicious foods as dates and honey were available, each passing day reduced the span of her life.[119] As the seasons changed, she searched the four corners for her Beloved. She had torn away her silken apparel (*patola*) and adopted the lowly blanket (*kambalri*), a garb which was likely to unite her with her Lord.[120] In order to control her husband, a wife wore the dress of three parts – the word of humility, the quality of tolerance and the charm of sweet tongue.[121]

While suffering from the pangs of separation, she wrung her hands as if driven to insanity. She wished to know her fault that had alienated her husband. She had become desperate as her youth was leaving. If she knew that her divine groom was innocent like a child, she would have shed her ego. If she had foreseen separation from her Beloved, she would have tied the bridal knot tightly.[122] Her husband had become rude because she was no longer physically attractive. She knew that there would be no milk in her breasts in the absence of sexual union with her husband.[123] Her condition was like that of the black cuckoo who had burnt in the fire of separation. She found herself at the frightening well without a friend or companion. In her frustration, she looked forward to God's grace which could enable her to unite with her beloved.[124] So strong was her passion to meet her beloved that she would not be deterred by physical obstacles like heavy rain, muddy street and wet blanket.[125] What was common, a wife bathed and dressed to meet her husband. When he did not turn up, her body lost its fragrance of musk and acquired the pungent smell of asafoetida. She did not fear the departure of her youth, provided the love of her husband remained firm. Instead of the joy of her bedstead, she was destined to see her sorrows as strings, pain as mattress and separation as coverings. Ultimately, she realized that love was inseparable from separation (*birha*). In fact, a body that did not nurture the affliction of separation was as dead as the cremation pit (*masan*).[126]

Baba Farid appreciated the difference between the rich and poor, both of whom were subject to death and destruction. Some people had plenty of flour, while others did not even have salt. But it was only after death that one would know who was ultimately punished. The members of the ruling elite travelled in large processions exuding splendour and pomp. Ornamental parasols were carried over their heads. Trumpets and drums were played, while the minstrels sang their praises. When their lives ended, they went to the graveyards and slept like orphans. During the course of their life, they constructed palaces, mansions and towers (*kothe, mandap, marhiyan*). They entered into false transactions (*koorha sauda*) and fell into their graves. The angel of death occupied their forts, plundered their wealth and extinguished their lamps. It appeared that all human beings stood in a queue, waiting for their turn to be claimed by death one after the other. This inexorable law applied equally to the spiritual preceptors (*sekh masaikh*). Some of them displayed all marks of piety like the prayer mat and woollen cloak. In reality, they were hypocrites and impostors. Outwardly they emitted light, but their inside was dark. They had jaggery in their mouths, but carried a dagger (*kati*) in their hearts. Those who were guilty of evil actions (*mande amal*) received the deserved punishment. There were a plenty of goods – cotton, sugar cane, sesame, paper, pots and coal – serving useful purposes, but even they could not escape from a harsh treatment and a final extinction.[127] Baba Farid's lesson was that one should not attach one's mind to worldly possessions like buildings and wealth. When one was buried under layers of earth, no one turned out as a friend (*mit*). Therefore, one was advised to keep in mind the powerful death as well as one's ultimate destination after death.[128]

Since everything on earth was in a flux, the trees shed their leaves with the change of seasons and caravans departed for their next station with the beating of drums.[129] Baba Farid, despite his exalted spiritual status and immense popularity, did not hesitate to apply the principle of change to himself. In his times, he held the position of a Shaikh and the society recognized him as a mystic teacher. But this position had been held by several others before him. Like them he would also leave one day. He had only played the role assigned to him and, therefore, had no intention of perpetuating himself. He had seen cranes in autumn, forest fires in summer and lightning in monsoons. Not surprisingly, the earth and sky could count on the number of spiritual guides (*khewat*) who had gone away and were lying decomposed in their graves. In fact, their conduct had inflicted pain on the society.[130] God had allotted a limited life span to every person. As a person grew from childhood to youth and then to old age, his body experienced important changes. When he was young, his limbs were strong and the faculties were sharp. At this stage, he got involved in worldly pursuits and physical gratification. He did not pay any attention to the spiritual dimension of his life, i.e. the loving submission to the Supreme Being. The span of life allotted to him was not unlimited. It was progressively reduced, as he inched closer to death with every passing day. In addition, his body began to show signs of degeneration. The hair turned gray, the eyes and ears became weak, having become tired of seeing and hearing. The eyes that charmed the world failed to attract any longer. During the youth, they were so delicate that they could not bear a line of kohl (*kajal*). But with the passage of time, these eyes had been forced to accommodate a nest of birds. As the skin started withering, it began to lose its radiant complexion. What tasted sweet like sugar became bitter like poison. The misery was compounded by one's negligence towards God. A person, who had not shown any love towards God during youth, would hardly do so during old age. Man had not attuned himself for the spiritual engagement. But he had rendered himself incapable of any spiritual advancement. He realized that he could not relate his pain (*vedan*) to anyone other than God (*sayin*).[131] His state was like a boat, which had not been anchored at the proper time, so that it could not stay afloat in a rough sea.[132]

Arguing in the same vein, Baba Farid held that man wasted four watches in wandering and another four in sleeping. He was required to submit an account to God for the work done by him. He feared impending punishment for his guilt of negligence, particularly when the innocent gong (*ghariyal*) was beaten every half hour for no fault. His state was like that of a bride, who could not unite with her husband in youth and, in the wake of her death and burial in the grave, repented her failure before her lord. Even in old age, man was engaged in futile activities.[133] Time lost could not be retrieved, just as rotted crop did not sprout again and a married woman could not become a virgin again.¹³⁴ Different organs of the body did not function, while the entire physique was permeated by pain.¹³⁵ As the end drew near, the body dried up into a skeleton, so that the crows pecked at the palms and soles. His love was not confined to life on this earth, but went beyond death. Imagining crows pecking at his corpse, he urged them not to touch his eyes as he still hoped to see his Beloved. He asked the crows not to nibble at his body as his Lord still dwelt in it.¹³⁶ Here, Baba Farid's lesson was loud and clear. A person was expected to remain attached to God throughout his life, i.e. from the time he developed higher consciousness up to the time of his death. If this was not done, he would be overwhelmed in old age by guilt and repentance that could do little to retrieve the lost opportunity.

Baba Farid exerted himself to create awareness about the inevitability of death and reflected on the state of the corpse in the grave. In his view, there was nothing strange about death, as it was a common experience. Every person saw people dying one after the other.¹³⁷ There was no certainty about human life. A living person was as vulnerable as a tree on the river bank and unbaked earthen pots (*kachhe bhande*).¹³⁸ Employing another metaphor, Baba Farid envisioned the human seeker as a bride, angel of death as a bridegroom and marriage as death. On the occasion of her engagement, the day of her marriage was fixed and, on the appointed day, the angel of death revealed his face and carried away his bride in marriage. In other words, he took away her life and, while her bones crackled, she was helpless. She cried at the thought of crossing the bridge between life and death (*pursalat*), which was thinner than hair.¹³⁹ In spite of the inevitability of death, one was troubled by its horrors and its aftermath. In fact, the boundary between life and death was similar to a river bank, as on the other side, one could hear the shrieks of pain emerging from burning hell (*dojak tapeya*). Some people understood that their actions (*amal*) on this side would bear witness in God's court (*dargah*), while others wandered without care. Death was seen as a terrible event because it could strike with suddenness. Just as a hawk (*baj*) swooped on a swan (*bagla*) sporting happily on the river bank, God's hawk struck without prior indication in a manner that all games were forgotten and an unforeseen calamity was inflicted by God. A man, who came to this world, fed on food and water and, in due course, acquired an impressive physique weighing three and a half maunds and nurtured high ambitions. When the angel of death (*malik ul-maut*) came breaking all doors,[140] the dear brothers bound him up and sent him away on four shoulders. His actions in this world would serve him in God's court (*dargah*).[141] As his colourful body collapsed, the chain of breath was snapped. None could identify the person who would be visited by the guest named the angel of death (*ajrail faresta*).[142] Even those who took pride in their rich possessions – youth, power and wealth – were subject to death. They suffered in this world and found no peace in the hereafter, because they were distant from God.[143] While buried in the grave, they spent ages lying on one side, with a brick under their head and worms eating into their flesh.[144]

In Chishti circles, the devotional aspect of spirituality comprised prayer and recitation. Regarding prayers, the seeker was guided by three ways of the Prophet – first determined by time, second by a specific cause, and third by neither of the two. Imam Ghazzali observed that a supererogatory prayer linked to time was repeated, i.e. once a day or once a week or once a month or even once a year. After the five obligatory prayers, the sixth was the late morning prayer (*chasht*), the seventh was twenty genuflections (*rakats*) after the evening prayer and the eighth prayer (*tahajjud*) was performed throughout the day and night. A weekly prayer began on Sunday and, continuing across the week, concluded on Saturday. A monthly prayer was like the twenty prostrations of the Prophet offered at the appearance of the new moon. The four yearly prayers included two prayers for the two Ids, the prayer of rest (*tarawih*) and prayer of fourteenth Shaban (*shab-i barat*). All these prayers depended on an appropriate time. Prayers associated with a just cause included the supplication beseeching rain (*istiqsa*) and connected with solar and lunar eclipse (*kusuf wa khusuf*). Prayers related neither to time nor cause (*namaz-i tasbih*) were laudatory prayers and included the greeting 'Peace (be upon you)'. As for supererogatory prayers, Baba Farid held these in congregation, as on the eve of fourteenth Shaban. Prayers were said while leaving one's house and re-entering it. Aimed at protecting oneself from affliction, they comprised two prostrations. Alternatively, one could recite the Throne Verse (*ayat al-kursi*) and recite four times 'Glory be to God and Praise be to God. There is no god but God. God is great. There is no protection nor power save with God the Sublime, the Almighty.' This could be repeated if one entered a mosque when the canonical prayer could not be offered.[145] Baba Farid intended to popularize the recitation of *Surah-i Fatiha* not only among his disciples but also outside this exclusive circle. Accordingly, he directed his disciples and their friends to recite it a thousand times and urged the friends to ask their friends to do the same. The disciples did as he commanded. Everyone recited *Surah-i Fatiha* as many times as he could – one 5,000, another 4,000 and some more or less. Nizamuddin recited it 10,000 times intoning it 1,000 or more each day. Not being directed towards any purpose, these recitations were hoped to enable the reciters to attain what they wished from God.[146]

During his days as a disciple, Baba Farid sought the permission of Shaikh Kaki to perform the inverted forty-day retreat (*chilla makus*). At first, the mentor felt it was not needed as it became the cause of fame, but later allowed his disciple to go ahead with it. Since Baba Farid was ignorant about its detail, he gained its knowledge from his mentor through a colleague Shaikh Badruddin Ghaznavi. The aspirant was suspended upside down into a well, with his feet tied with a rope. The venue preferably had to be a well in the precincts of a mosque, where a neighbouring tree had spread its branches over the mouth of the well. Baba Farid began to look for such a spot, but tried to make sure that no one came to know about it. His search at Delhi and Hansi proved futile. Ultimately, he discovered a suitable site at the Masjid Taj in Uch. Fortunately, he knew the muezzin Khwaja Rashiduddin Minai, who originally belonged to Hansi. He took Minai into his confidence and made sure that he would not reveal the purpose of his visit. At the time of the night prayer (*isha*), he performed the ablution and, with the help of Minai, lowered himself upside down into the well. In this arduous posture, he remained engaged in prayer throughout the night. At dawn, Minai pulled him out of the well. He sat down facing Mecca and immersed himself in contemplation. He observed this routine for forty days and, by doing so, abided by the instructions of his mentor and did not let anyone know about his round of austerities. His advice enabled Minai to graduate as a sermonizer (*waiz*) despite his illiteracy and, with the newly gained prosperity, cared for a family comprising many daughters. Masjid Taj, owing to its association with Baba Farid, acquired a sacred character and attracted streams of devotees, who prayed for the fulfilment of their wishes.[147]

The life of Baba Farid was marked by simplicity of the highest order. After finishing his morning prayer, he remained engrossed in remembering God. With his head prostrate on the ground, he remained in this posture for a long time. Even in severe winter, he did not have any attendant by his side, though the inmates of the hospice spread a fur garment on his body.[148] After his breakfast, he again busied himself in remembering God and offering devotion till the night prayer. During this long interval, his disciple Shams Dabir prepared some food and Baba Farid broke his fast along with two or three associates.[149] He usually broke his fast with a bowl of flavoured beverage (*sharbat*), which had some raisins in it. It was further diluted with water in a jug. Two thirds of it was distributed among those present. He kept the remaining one-third for himself, though it was often shared among select persons who considered the gesture as auspicious. In between the breaking of fast and offering prayers, two loaves of bread weighing less than 2 pounds (1 *ser*) and spread over with a layer of fat were brought. He broke one loaf into pieces that were distributed among others. He kept the other loaf for himself, though some of it was offered to select persons. From the time of sunset prayer, he immersed himself in God till dinner. For dinner, Baba Farid did not eat anything till the moment of breaking the fast next evening. Towards the end of his life, he was afflicted with a disease of the bowels that ultimately led to his death. At this juncture, he was forced to lie on a cot (*khat*). A rug was spread over the cot and, during the day, he used to sit on it. Since the rug was too small, it did not cover that part of the cot where his feet rested. A patch of cloth was improvised to cover the lower portion of the cot. When he pulled it up during the night, the lower portion of the cot again remained uncovered. He rested his head on a staff that he had received from his mentor Shaikh Kaki. Many times, he reached up to touch it and kiss it.[150] When he died (15 October 1265), it was not possible to meet the expenses of his burial. Therefore, the door of his house was pulled down, so as to extract the unburnt bricks that were used for constructing his grave.[151]

Baba Farid took a lot of delight in musical sessions (*sama*). Since the Qawwals were aware of the Shaikh's passion, they often visited his hospice. On one occasion, he desired to hear it, but there was no Qawwal. He asked a disciple Badruddin Ishaq to bring a letter written by Qazi Hamiduddin Nagauri. Badruddin Ishaq retrieved it from the bag containing letters and, as instructed by the Shaikh, began to read it. It began with the line, 'This humble, weak and worthless beggar Muhammad Ata, who is the slave of dervishes from head to toe, is as lowly as the dust of their feet.' As soon as Baba Farid heard these words, he was transported to a state of spiritual ecstasy and a closeness to God was manifested in him. Not surprisingly, he recalled a quatrain which was inscribed in this letter. He himself composed verses on the theme of mystical love. The following one was noted in a letter, which was received by Shaikh Badruddin Ghaznavi:[152]

Farid has been, for faith and the faithful, a mighty friend.
That he spend his life bestowing wonders has been my prayer.
But how I wish that my own heart could have been more composed,
For I'd have laid before him pearls of praise, layer upon layer.

A judge (*qazi*) of Ajodhan, who was always picking a quarrel with Baba Farid, went to Multan and met the local theologians. He complained that a man sat in a mosque, listened to musical performances (*sama*) and sometimes even broke into dance.[153] The theologians wished to know the name of the person concerned. As soon as they heard the name of Baba Farid, they refused to say anything about him. Nizamuddin, while referring to his own experience of a musical performance, ascribed all virtues and dispositions to Baba Farid that were depicted by the performer. Once Nizamuddin heard a Qawwal render a verse, 'Stroll not so gracefully as this, lest from the evil eye you are made distressed.' On hearing these lines, he at once recalled the laudable virtues of Baba Farid – his perfect saintliness, his extraordinary piety and his surpassing grace – and felt overwhelmed to an extent that he (Nizamuddin) was unable to describe the state of his own mind.[154] Baba Farid, by nature, was inclined towards poetry. His mind was often occupied by specific verses. Once he was powerfully attracted towards the following couplet, which was on his lips throughout the day, evening and upto the dawn next day. It was impossible to know what was going on in his mind and what induced him to recite this couplet over and over again:[155]

Oh Nizami, what secrets are these, revealed from your heart?
His secrets no one knows, bridle your tongue, bridle your tongue.

Often locked in the privacy of his cell, Baba Farid recited Persian mystical verses on the theme of loving submission to God and the desire to live and die for Him. While humming the following piece of poetry, he walked in the direction of the Kaaba and, jubilant in his ecstasy (*tawajjud*), turned back and bowed his head in the posture of surrender. So happy was he at this moment that he blessed Nizamuddin with constancy (*istiqamat*) in his spiritual pursuits. For many years after this episode, the disciple regretted his failure to ask for death in a state ecstasy induced by a musical session. While admitting the significance of such gatherings, he clarified that if someone indulged in feverish leaping every moment, this bodily movement did not constitute dance (*raqs aan nabuwad keh har zamaan bar khezi*).[156]

Khwahm keh hamesha dar hawai tu ziyam
Khaki shawam wa bazer pai tu ziyam
Maqsud man bandah ze kaunain tui
Az behar tu miram az barai tu ziyam

I always wish to live pining for you,
And to live like the dust of your feet.
Aim of this slave is to look for you in this life and hereafter,
And to live for you and die for you.

As seen above, Baba Farid abandoned the urban centres of Delhi and Hansi, preferring the quiet wilderness of Ajodhan, so that he could focus on his spiritual quest. By doing so, he chose the bread of dervishes and the fruit of the jungles, feeling content in using rough wood as his tooth brush.[157] When Sultan Nasiruddin Mahmud passed through Ajodhan on his way to Multan, Ulugh Khan (the future Sultan Ghiasuddin Balban) came to pay his respects to Baba Farid. He brought an offering of cash and a land grant of four villages – the money for the benefit of dervishes and land grant for the Shaikh. Baba Farid agreed to accept the money, which would be instantly distributed among the dervishes. But, he refused to accept the land grant, which could be given to those who longed for it.[158] He could not pull on with Sher Khan, who held the fiefs of Multan and Uch. This prominent noble, owing to unknown reasons, did not have faith in the saintly qualities of the Shaikh. Baba Farid felt that Sher Khan was unaware of his credentials and that he would repent when he learnt the truth about him (Shaikh). In his observation, Nizamudin has implied that if Sher Khan had been considerate towards Baba Farid, then the northwestern frontier would have remained safe from the Mongol invasions.[159] Baba Farid was not surprised at the woes of his brother Najibuddin Mutawakkil, who received lavish financial assistance – prayer leadership of a newly built mosque, a house and 1 lakh *jitals* on the marriage of his daughter – from a Turkish noble and then deprived of it in a whimsical act.[160] To meet the humble needs of his hospice, Baba Farid accepted unasked charity (*futuh*) in gold, silver and goods, but spent it on others, keeping nothing for himself. Once a visitor told him that there was a contemporary Shaikh who possessed extensive wealth, but who claimed that he had not been granted the divine consent to spend it. Baba Farid rightly identified this Shaikh as Bahauddin Zakariya and argued that he had made a lame excuse for not spending. He asserted that if Shaikh Zakariya authorized him to expend the wealth on his behalf, he would empty his treasury in two or three days, yet he would not give away the smallest coin without divine consent.[161]

It was not as if Baba Farid had entirely insulated himself from all political matters. Going by the claims of Chishti documentation, he went out of his way to help people in distress and, while doing so, he did not hesitate to confront the representatives of the state. It was another matter that he was reputed to have used his supernatural powers to achieve laudable objectives.[162] Let us consider the following instances.

An oil-seller (*raughan farosh*) lived in a village, which fell under the jurisdiction of Ajodhan. The local governor (*muqti*) attacked the village and imprisoned all the inhabitants. In the confusion, the oil-seller's wife went missing and was feared to have been abducted. The husband passionately loved his wife, who was extremely beautiful. He searched her in all directions, but failed to find her. Crying profusely, he went to Baba Farid and narrated his tale. Food was offered to him, but he could not swallow a morsel. Baba Farid persuaded him to stay at the hospice for three days. On the third day, a clerk (*nawisindah*), who was being carried as a prisoner to Ajodhan, appeared on the scene. This functionary was posted in a town that was in the administrative control of the above governor. He was summoned for investigation into his accounts (*muqti falan qasbah barai muhasiba talbidah ast*). Fearful of his fate, he requested Baba Farid to pray for his release. The Shaikh assured that his superior would not only be generous to him, but would also confer on him several awards including a robe. However, he placed a condition that he would give a part of the package, a slave girl (*kanizak*), to the troubled husband. At this moment, the oil-seller declared, 'God has granted to me the resources to purchase as many as 40-50 slave girls. They are of no use to me. I must have my own wife.' As directed by the Shaikh, the oil-seller and clerk left for their common destination. The governor met the clerk and, asking for forgiveness, conferred a robe on him. He also ordered that the slave girl be clothed in bright apparel and handed over to the clerk. The oil-seller recognized his wife from her gait. Though the woman was veiled, yet her uncovered eyes fell on her husband. As soon as she removed her veil, he fell at her feet and, while crying, revealed that she was indeed his wife, whom he had been searching. The entire episode ended on a happy note.[163]

A noble (*malik*), who was bloodthirsty by nature, lived in a town about 30 or 40 leagues from Ajodhan. He possessed a falcon that he dearly loved. He had given strict instructions to his chief huntsman (*mir-i shikar*) not to fly the falcon in his absence. One day, when the huntsman was wandering with his friends, he was persuaded to let the falcon chase a bird. As soon as the falcon was released, it flew high up into the sky and disappeared from sight. When the huntsman realized the violation of his master's instructions and the impending punishment, he felt utterly depressed and fell to crying. He thought of selling his horse and, becoming a Qalandar, to adopt the life of a wanderer. However, he abandoned this line of action, as the cruel Turk was likely to torture his children during his absence. In his desperation, he reached Ajodhan and, on meeting Baba Farid, described the cause of his misery. The Shaikh consoled the huntsman and offered him food. As he found it difficult to push a morsel down his throat, Baba Farid turned his attention to the falcon that was perched on the ramparts of the local fort. The huntsman easily attracted the falcon to return to its wooden trap (*khwandani*). Expressing his gratitude to the Shaikh, he presented his horse as an offering. Baba Farid asked him to return to his place on the horse and, after getting his horse evaluated, give only half of its price to him. The huntsman went back and, on meeting his master, described the miracle of the Shaikh. Amazed at the saintliness of Baba Farid, the noble (who did not have faith on him) changed his opinion. He not only sent some gold coins (*tankaha-i zar*) to the saint along with the value of the horse, but also expressed his submission and became a disciple.[164]

A revenue officer (*amil*) of Ajodhan, who was harassed by the local chief, approached Baba Farid for intercession in his favour. The Shaikh sent a man to the chief with his greetings and the man's complaint. The chief remained engrossed in his own affairs and did not pay any attention to the matter. Baba Farid observed that either the complaint was made at an inopportune time or the officer might have himself ignored the plea of a supplicant. While the Shaikh was speaking, the chief turned up and offered his apology, which was accepted.[165] In another case, a revenue official (*mutasarrif*) oppressed the sons of Baba Farid, who were engaged in cultivation of land. They often complained against him to their father, who advised them to be patient. Feeling frustrated, they declared that his spiritual eminence (*buzurgi wa karamat*) was of no use. Baba Farid picked up his staff and wielded it as if hitting someone. Instantly, the concerned official was afflicted with a severe stomachache. He was brought to the presence of Baba Farid. He sought forgiveness from the Shaikh, who expressed his helplessness as the arrow had hit the target. The man was carried back to his house where he died. On being informed of the death, Baba Farid said, 'For a period of forty years, I did what God wished me to do. For some years now, whatever comes into my mind is fulfilled by God.'[166]

In Ajodhan, there lived two brothers, both of whom were employed as clerks. One of them, driven by a sudden inner inspiration, turned to spirituality. He gave up his job and, placing his wife and children under the care of his brother, enrolled himself as a disciple of Baba Farid. Thus freed from worldly concerns, he delved into prayers and devotions. His brother, who was taking good care of his family, fell ill and even reached the brink of death. The brother, who had become a dervish, went to Baba Farid crying. If his brother died, the responsibility of his children would fall into his lot and, owing to this burden, he would cease to benefit from his prayers and devotions. Baba Farid informed him that his brother had recovered from his sickness and, with his miraculous power, saw his movements and showed the same to the troubled supplicant. Baba Farid observed, 'Just as you came to me with pain in your heart, I have been similarly engaged in the love of God, but did not lose heart.'[167] In another case of a needy person, Baba Farid used his social influence instead of relying on his supernatural prowess. One of his disciples had a large family, including five or six daughters. Since he could not meet the requirements of his household, he requested his mentor to place him under the care of someone. By chance, the grandson of Zafar Khan (apparently a man of means) appeared on the scene. Baba Farid discussed the problem with the visitor, who agreed to accommodate the poor family in his house. Owing to the Shaikh's intervention, the days of the needy began to pass in comfort.[168]

The early Chishtis followed the practice of distributing amulets (*tawiz*) among their devotees who, in turn, had faith in the efficacy of these objects as a remedy of their problems, both worldly and spiritual. However, they began the practice only after receiving the formal permission of their mentors. When people approached Baba Farid for amulets, he sought the advice of his preceptor Khwaja Qutbuddin Bakhtiar Kaki. He was told that an amulet was God's name and, therefore, it could be written and distributed as God's word. It was clarified that the impact of an amulet was not in the hands of the Sufi, whether one was a master or a disciple. A large number of people appeared at the hospice of Baba Farid to receive amulets. The task was delegated to a close disciple Badruddin Ishaq and, in his absence, the work was assigned to Nizamuddin who had been looking forward to the opportunity for this service. As soon as Baba Farid gave his permission, Nizamuddin took up the task in great earnestness. Though he kept on writing and writing, his diligence could not keep pace with the crowd that kept on swelling. Baba Farid, having noticed the state of his disciple, asked if he was tired of writing the amulets. Nizamuddin replied that he was sustained by the spiritual boon of his mentor. Impressed with his response, Baba Farid authorized him to write and give amulets on his own initiative, declaring, 'Something touched by the hands of men of piety produces an effect.'[169]

Even if a needy person was unable to come personally before a saint, he could still be provided with an amulet through someone who was known to him. When Nizamuddin lived in the city (Delhi), a neighbour, who was afflicted with intestinal tumour, urged him to convey his suffering to Baba Farid and to bring an amulet as a cure. When Nizamuddin visited Ajodhan, he spoke to the Shaikh regarding the matter. As advised by his mentor, Nizamuddin prepared the amulet. Baba Farid examined it and, in due course, it was brought to the needy person. The amulet proved to be effective, as the man never suffered from this ailment for the rest of his life. The inscription on the amulet contained invocations such as 'God alone heals, God alone suffices, God alone forgives.' However, he did not remember the remaining part of the inscription. On another occasion, Nizamuddin was permitted by Baba Farid to pick up a curl of his beard. He treated it with utmost respect and, folding it in his garment, took it home. From then onwards, he gave it to those who suffered from grief or despair. They kept it with them till they were relieved of their problem. However, Nizamuddin misplaced the curl and could not give it to a friend's son, who ultimately died. When he discovered it again, he felt that he could not find the amulet earlier as the boy was destined to die.[170]

Baba Farid began to acquire popularity even before he had established himself as a Sufi at Hansi and Ajodhan. During his sojourn at Delhi after the demise of Shaikh Kaki, he would leave for the Friday prayer a little earlier than the stipulated time in order to avoid being mobbed by the devout. In fact, so many of them rushed forward to kiss his hand that he would be caught in a circle. When he emerged from one circle, he was stranded in another. The scene was repeated so many times that he was annoyed. A similar situation developed at Ajodhan when Sultan Nasiruddin Mahmud led his army to Multan and Uch. A large number of soldiers went to pay their respects to Baba Farid, leading to a blockade in the passage to his hospice. Being perplexed at the crowd, he shifted to another house. A sleeve of his garment was hung from the balcony overlooking the main street. The troopers touched and kissed the sleeve which, as a result, was reduced to shreds. Baba Farid went to the mosque and, directing his disciples to form a cordon around him, received the greetings of the people from a distance. The disciples abided by the instructions, but an old servant (*farrash*) managed to penetrate through the cordon and, grasping the Shaikh's feet, pulled them towards himself in a bid to kiss them. The servant, on seeing the Shaikh's predicament, exclaimed, 'Oh Shaikh, do you feel annoyed? You should thank God as He could not have bestowed a greater blessing than this.' These words had a spontaneous effect on Baba Farid who, while weeping, embraced the servant and repeatedly asked for forgiveness.[171] Even the unruly mendicants (*jawaliqs*), who were not permitted to meet Shaikh Bahauddin Zakariya, enjoyed easy access to Baba Farid. This attitude conformed to a universal belief according to which there was one God's elect in the midst of every group of people.¹⁷²

When Baba Farid finally settled in Ajodhan, his fame as a mystic spread beyond Delhi. Abu Bakr, a Qawwal, who returned from Multan to Badaun, narrated his experiences to the teacher of Nizamuddin. As soon as Nizamuddin heard the virtues of Baba Farid, a sincere love for the Shaikh took root in his heart, so that he began to repeat his name ten times after every prayer. He often spoke to his friends about Baba Farid and, if ever they wanted him to vouchsafe the truth of any statement, they asked him to swear by the name of Baba Farid. When he travelled to Delhi along with a relative and feared an attack of lions or robbers, they claimed to be proceeding under the protection of Baba Farid.¹⁷³ At Ajodhan, a large number of people visited the hospice of Baba Farid, who distributed his possessions – silver, food and blessings – to all, whether one was an old acquaintance or had come for the first time. Nizamudin remarked, 'Yet no one came to the Shaikh for material assistance since he himself possessed nothing. What a marvelous power! What a splendid life! To none of the sons of Adam had such grace previously been available.'¹⁷⁴ Even the town of Abohar had come to have a community of Baba Farid's followers. These people believed that they had been absolved of any offences committed before pledging their allegiance to the Shaikh, who had forgiven them of their sins.¹⁷⁵

Centrality of Prayers Among the Suhrawardis

Shaikh Bahauddin Zakariya (1182-1262) laid the foundation of the Suhrawardi order in the early thirteenth century. His grandfather had migrated from Mecca to Multan, while his mother's family had shifted from Ghazni to Kot Karor near Multan. At an early age, he committed the Quran to memory in accordance with the seven modes of recitation. He undertook higher education in Khurasan and Bokhara. His passion for religious knowledge brought him to the holy cities of Hejaz. At Madina, he learnt the *hadis* from Maulana Kamaluddin Muhammad Yamani and, at Mecca, served as an attendant at the tomb of the Prophet. Travelling to

Baghdad, he enrolled himself as a disciple of Shaikh Shihabuddin Suhrawardi and, within seventeen days, received the certificate of succession.[176] Equipped with brilliant academic and mystical credentials, he returned to Multan and busied himself in setting up a hospice. His contribution as a Sufi master revolved around an engagement with politics and wealth, besides the outward form of Islamic observances.

Shaikh Zakariya threw the weight of his support behind Shamsuddin Iltutmish in the power struggle among the Turkish slave officers of Sultan Muizzuddin. For unknown reasons, he was opposed to Nasiruddin Qubacha who was the independent ruler of Multan and Uch. He sent a letter (like the one to *qazi* of Multan) to Iltutmish, probably assuring his support in the impending conflict. These letters fell into the hands of Qubacha, who got the *qazi* killed and summoned the Shaikh. The Shaikh went to the court and fearlessly sat on the right of Qubacha as he used to do in the past. He confirmed having written the controversial letter and that too in his own hand. He declared that what he had written was true, that he himself was free to do what he wished and that Qubacha could do nothing as he was powerless. Though Qubacha was cornered, yet he looked for a pretext to punish the Shaikh. He invited the Shaikh to join him over meals. He guessed that the Shaikh would refuse, as it was not his practice to eat at someone else's house. A refusal from the Shaikh would provide the required reason for punishment. But the Shaikh, having seen through the governor's intention, joined the others in eating the food. As a result, Qubacha's anger waned and the Shaikh returned to his lodge.[177] In the subsequent years, the two lived in peace with each other.

Shaikh Zakariya took part in the efforts to defend the city of Multan and protect the lives of its inhabitants whenever the Mongols descended on the city from the northwestern frontier. In 1224, an army of 20,000 Mongols under the command of Dorbei Doqshin marched in pursuit of the Khwarizmian prince Jalaluddin Mangbarni and besieged Multan. The local elements joined hands to offer a stiff resistance, forcing the Mongols to raise the siege and retreat. It has been suggested that three Sufis

– Shaikh Bahauddin Zakariya, Shaikh Jalaluddin Tabrezi and Khwaja Qutbuddin Bakhtiar Kaki – employed their miraculous powers to save the city. One night during the siege, Khwaja Kaki was said to have given an arrow to Qubacha and directed him to shoot in the dark. The instruction was duly obeyed. Next morning, it was found that the invaders had disappeared. The episode implied the contribution of three Sufis in protecting the city from destruction at the hands of the Mongols.[178] In 1246, the city of Multan was besieged by a Mongol army led by Malik Shamsuddin and Sali Nuyin. The local governor Chengiz Khan, who had been a slave of Iltutmish, defended the place. After resisting the invaders for a fortnight, Chengiz Khan sent Shaikh Zakariya to negotiate for the Mongol withdrawal. In a meeting held at the Gate of the Blacksmiths on the Id ul-Azha, it was agreed that Chengiz Khan would pay a ransom of one lakh dinars to the invaders. Next day Shaikh Zakariya delivered the amount to Sali Nuyin and governor's gifts to Malik Shamsuddin.[179] The Delhi Sultanate could rely on the Suhrawardy saint to diffuse a major crisis that threatened its northwestern frontier, in particular an important administrative and commercial centre.

Shaikh Zakariya was often criticized for the aristocratic character of his hospice and amplitude of his riches, though the exact sources of his income were never recorded. His wealth and granaries implied the possession of lavish land grants. Since Multan was a leading entrepot of long distance trade, he received large offerings from merchants, as shown by the following episode. Khwaja Kamaludin Masud Sherwani, an ardent follower of Shaikh Zakariya, was a famous diamond merchant. Once he was travelling on a ship from the island of Jaroli to Aden. He had some highly priced diamonds in his bag. When half the distance had been covered, strong winds started blowing, causing the vessel to crack. The passengers feared that the vessel would sink into the deep sea. In this moment of crisis, Sherwani prayed for Shaikh Zakariya to appear on the scene. Soon he saw the Shaikh on the board owing to God's command. All the passengers looked at the Shaikh with hopeful eyes, asking for his miraculous intervention. He responded with a gesture that cheered them and, within the batting of an eyelid, vanished from the scene. The stormy wind subsided and, as the ship stabilized, it safely arrived at the port of Aden. All big merchants contributed one third of their money in a common pool and requested Sherwani to deliver it to the Shaikh through any means. Sherwani added half his diamonds to the amount and, after sometime, deputed his diamond keeper Khwaja Fakhruddin Gilani to complete the task. Accordingly, Gilani travelled all the way to Multan. Though he had seen only a glimpse of the Shaikh, he was able to recognize him by his face and apparel. His devotion having increased manifold, he delivered the large collective gift which was valued at 7 lakh *tankas* and comprised both cash and goods. The Shaikh accepted the gift and, showing his reputed kindness, distributed it among the people. Gilani was deeply moved by the Shaikh's generosity. He placed all his possessions in the hands of the Shaikh, who disposed them in accordance with his practice. Renouncing the world, Gilani became a disciple of the Shaikh and received the robe of succession. He spent five years under the tutelage of the Shaikh and, during this period, remained in the service of his mentor's son Shaikh Sadruddin Arif. Securing the formal permission of the Shaikh, he left for the pilgrimage of Mecca but, on his way, died at Jedda.

Shaikh Zakariya possessed a generous disposition. When he wished to give something to anyone, he was found to be extremely liberal. While paying the teachers, who tutored his sons, he virtually poured silver into their laps. Even the local administration fell back upon his material resources in times of exigency. On one occasion, the governor of Multan requested him for some grain. Shaikh Zakariya readily acceded to the request. A group of functionaries, who were shifting the grain, were surprised to find a pitcher full of silver coins in the consignment. They reported the discovery to the governor. The latter ordered them to return the silver, as the Shaikh had provided them only with grain. When the Shaikh learnt what had transpired, he informed the governor that he knew all about the matter and that he had intentionally sent silver along with the grain.[180] On another occasion, the Shaikh asked a servant to bring a chest containing five thousand *dinars*. The servant went inside the treasury and moved the goods to different

The Establishment of Sufi Orders 181

spots, but could not find the chest. When the Shaikh learnt about the situation, he closed his eyes and, after deliberating for a while, exclaimed, 'God be praised'. After a few days, he was informed that the chest had been found lying underneath some household items. The Shaikh reflected on the matter and again exclaimed, 'God be praised'. As he sent the servant to bring the chest, he explained the same response to two opposite situations. For the people of God, the existence and non-existence of the worldly possessions were the same. There was no sorrow at their departure, nor any joy at their arrival. Soon after, he distributed 5,000 *dinars* among the needy and did not pay any further attention to the matter.[181]

Shaikh Zakariya laid considerable emphasis on the outward form of religious observances. He disapproved any deviation, howsoever minor, from any prescribed injunction. Once he found a group of his disciples performing ablutions on the bank of a river. They left their task unfinished and rushed to greet their mentor. One of them continued to perform the task till completion and only then rose to offer regards to his mentor. Shaikh Zakariya, observing the diffrence in the conduct of his disciples, declared that only one of them was a true mystic (*darvesh*).[182] While passing this judgement, the Shaikh employed the yardstick of strict conformity to ritual. In another instance, Shaikh Zakariya went to meet a devout man named Sulaiman, who was famed in Multan for his devotional exercises. He asked Sulaiman to stand up and offer two cycles (*rakats*) of prayer. Sulaiman did so, but somehow did not set his feet in the prescribed manner. The Shaikh directed him to repeat the prayer and keep the required space between his feet, not more or less. Though Sulaiman tried a number of times, he could not follow the instructions. The Shaikh asked him to leave Multan and settle in Uch and this was duly done.[183]

The Shaikh was said to have reprimanded a Qawwal, Abdullah Rumi, for wearing a black shawl (*gilim*) on the ground that it was the dress of the devil. Distressed, Rumi tried to defend himself by arguing that he (the Shaikh) had never reproached people who hoarded gold and silver and enjoyed all worldly possessions. Seeing that Rumi had lost his composure, the Shaikh reminded that he (Rumi) had been able to travel safely owing to his protection.[184] On yet another occasion, the Shaikh expressed his shock at the physical appearance of a scholar (*danishmand*) who had travelled all the way from Bokhara. He asked the visitor the purpose of appearing with two snakes, curled hair and loose ends to his turban. Upset at this remark, the scholar got his head shaved in the presence of the Shaikh.[185] The Shaikh's contempt for individuals supporting curls was shared by his companions. Some of them abruptly walked out of a feast on seeing a man (Sharf Piyadah) with curls. Shaikh Nizamuddin Auliya, who hosted the feast, held this insolence as a false sense of pride and a lustful desire for distinction among fellow beings.[186]

One hastens to point out that Shaikh Zakariya did not always have his way. There were occasions when he was confronted on equal terms and shown the infirmity of his stance. Qazi Qutbuddin Kashani, who had established a seminary (*madrasah*) in Multan, was a man of knowledge and probity. Every day Shaikh Zakariya went to the mosque attached to his seminary and offered the morning prayer behind him. Somewhat surprised at this attitude, Kashani asked him as to why did he come so far and offered prayer at that place. The Shaikh replied that his action conformed to the Prophetic tradition (*hadis*), 'One's praying behind a pious and learned man was as if one had prayed behind a prophet.' One morning, the Shaikh arrived late. Since the first cycle (*rakat*) had been completed, he joined the congregation in the second one. While Kashani was still in the midst of *tashahhud*, the Shaikh stood up and completed his prayer before Kashani could turn to the right for *salam*, denoting the completion of the *tashahhud*. Kashani asked, 'Why did you stand up before the *salam*. The *imam* may have made a mistake which could be corrected by performing the *sajdah-i sahw*. Since you stood up before the *salam*, you have missed it.' The Shaikh replied that if one learnt from inner light (*nur-i batin*) that the *imam* had not erred in observing the obligatory details of prayer, one was allowed to rise. Kashani, who would not take things lying down, observed that the light, which was not in harmony with the Shariat, was nothing but darkness. Taken aback at this assertion of authority, the Shaikh thought it prudent to terminate the confrontation at that very moment and left the place quietly. After this unseemly encounter, he never came to the mosque of the seminary for any prayer.[187]

Shaikh Zakariya had acquired proficiency in reciting the Quran and tried to improve the religious consciousness of those who came into his contact, including prominent Sufis belonging to other orders.[188] One evening, he threw a challenge to a gathering to offer two cycles of prayer and to recite the entire Quran in one of them. When no one accepted the challenge, he himself stepped forward. In the first cycle, he recited the entire Quran and four additional sections (*siparahs*), while in the second cycle he recited the Surah-i Ikhlas and completed his prayer (*namaz*). He claimed to have successfully undertaken all the prayers and invocations heard of the saints. But he admitted his failure to follow the example of a pious man who could recite the entire Quran from dawn to sunrise.[189] Yet, it was owing to his inspiration that everyone in Multan was immersed in remembering God, offering prayers and reciting invocations. The trend reached such an extent that even the slave girls, while grinding corn, chanted God's name.[190]

At an assembly of Shaikh Nizamuddin Auliya, a conversation once occurred about the nature of various commentaries on the Quran. It indicated the preference of Shaikh Zakariya on the matter. In the opinion Shaikh Nizamudin Auliya, Zamakhshari (d. 1144), the compiler of *Kashshaf*, possessed deep insight into the grammatical and rhetorical aspects, but he was guilty of innovation and unbelief.[191] Interestingly, Shaikh Zakariya too did not favour this author. Two scholars, Maulana Sadruddin Qonawi and Maulana Najmuddin Sunami, were discussing matters of mutual interest. In reply to a question, the former said that he was studying the works of Quranic exegesis, viz., *Kashshaf, Ijaz* and *Umdah*. Sunami suggested that he should continue his study of *Umdah*, but he should burn the first two. Qonawi wanted to know the reason. Sunami replied that Shaikh Zakariya also held the same opinion on the issue. Not satisfied with the explanation, Qonawi underwent a strange experience that very night. He was studying the three commentaries in front of a lamp. He had placed *Umdah* on top of the other two. While he was overcome by sleep, a fire suddenly broke out. When he woke up, he found that *Kashshaf* and *Ijaz* (which were placed underneath) had been burnt, but *Umdah* remained unscathed. After narrating this episode, Shaikh Nizamuddin Auliya came up with another story with a similar theme. Shaikh Sadruddin Arif, the son of Shaikh Zakariya, wanted to study the grammatical text *Mufassal* and sought the permission of his father. The latter asked him to be patient and wait till the night had passed. That night Shaikh Arif had a dream in which he saw a captive being dragged in chains. He asked as to who he was. The people, who were present, replied that it was Zamakhshari, the compiler of *Mufassal*, who was being carried to hell.[192] In Sufi circles, Shaikh Zakariya was recognized as a profound scholar and his views on theological literature were treated with respect. Sometimes his opinions could be rather strong and even articulated through supernatural means. Among Sufi orders, there was a free flow of information regarding teaching methods practised in the precincts of hospices.

As a matter of common practice, the Sufis provided hospitality – at least food, if not the arrangement for stay – to the people who visited them. This hospitality was in line with a Prophetic tradition (*hadis*) according to which 'Whoever visits a living person and does not taste something from him, it is as if he visited a corpse.' Whenever the companions of the Prophet visited him, they ate something – a piece of bread or a date or some other thing – before leaving. In fact, they did not leave until they had taken a bite to eat. Shaikh Badruddin Ghaznavi (a disciple of Shaikh Qutbuddin Bakhtiar Kaki) at least offered water to his visitors, if he could not offer food to them. Contrary to the Prophetic tradition and common Sufi practice, Shaikh Zakariya did not share this attitude, so that people who came to visit him left without having been offered anything to eat. Once someone reminded him of the Prophetic tradition and asked why he did not follow it. The Shaikh explained, 'People do not understand the true intent of this tradition. There are two kinds of people, the commoners and elite. I have nothing to do with the common folk. But when the elite visit me, I speak to them about God, the Prophet, norms of conduct and similar other subjects, so that they might be benefited from my instruction.'[193] As this explanation indicated, the Shaikh felt that his visitors, being prosperous and well fed, did not come to his hospice for food. Rather they had a hunger for knowledge on religious and spiritual matters. By providing appropriate answers to their queries, he offered precisely what they looked for and thus satisfied their urgent need. In this sense, he did not send them away empty handed.

Since the above discussion was largely based on Chishti documentation,[194] it showed Shaikh Zakariya in a somewhat unfavourable light. In a recent study, Qamar ul-Huda has drawn attention to the Shaikh's works that promised to develop a more balanced understanding of the theme. These two works, *Khulasat ul-Arifin* and *Al-Aurad*, constituted important steps to institutionalize the Suhrawardi order in southwestern Panjab. They were produced in specific political, social and religious contexts. The Shaikh was faced with opposition from the local ruler like Nasiruddin Qubacha and a theologian like Qazi Qutbuddin Kashani. Having received the designation of Shaikh ul-Islam from Iltutmish, his religious authority as a leading Sufi and scholar was consolidated. He was required to ensure that the members of his hospice were loyal to the new political regime and to demarcate the Suhrawardi order from other Sufi theologies in the region. However, unlike his mentor's *Awarif ul-Maarif*, his works did not reaffirm the historical, religious and legal legitimacy of Islamic mysticism. Instead, he sought to establish a balance between the domain of Islamic law and the world of Islamic mysticism, so that a person in the Suhrawardi order could become a law-obeying spiritual seeker. He laid down specific details of spiritual exercises that were incorporated by the Suhrawardis in their lives. In addition to the ritualistic prayers and fasts, he prescribed a series of spiritual exercises that were basically composed of remembrance of God (*zikr*). In his view, *zikr* brought about a connection between the mind and spirit, thereby creating a moment when the heart was in movement with the spirit of God. He believed that *zikr* cleansed the heart of impurities and redirected the seeker towards God's path. He recommended specific forms of *zikr* for each of the twelve months in the yearly calendars as well as occasions like pre-dawn prayers, Prophet's heavenly ascension, funerals and pilgrimages to mausoleums. The repetition of specific words was not an irrational and mindless religious practice, but the process of cleansing the heart of the seeker and underscoring the close relationship of language, sound and spirit. It employed all human senses to experience the love of God.[195]

In his work entitled *Khulasat ul-Arifin*, Shaikh Zakariya has elaborated the fundamental ideas of Suhrawardi mysticism and laid guidelines for seekers who chose the path of inner enlightenment. Considerably inspired by his mentor's *Awarif ul-Maarif*, this treatise was liberally interspersed with Quranic verses. A seeker was enjoined to prepare himself to meet the challenges on the spiritual path, so that he could achieve higher levels of inner knowledge. This preliminary task comprised as many as ten steps. The seeker learnt that true knowledge emerged from the heart, which had to maintain absolute purity by insulating itself from extraneous influences. He endeavoured to connect himself to the moment of union with God. He could attain this state by being humble in front of the Creator, distancing himself from temptation and seeking solitude. He should expect neither any reward for accomplishment, nor should he allow emotion to control his actions. The Shaikh, continuing the legacy of his mentor, held that the human heart was the main organ for spiritual cleansing, inner awareness and a primary site for comprehending God's presence. The Shaikh laid great emphasis on the heart because the Suhrawardi order was heavily rooted in the Quran and Prophetic traditions *hadis*. The Shaikh perceived mysticism as a long arduous path that required a constant struggle with purifying the heart in order to encounter God. In his view, the seeker's heart could be cured of maladies and he could remain firmly entrenched on the spiritual path leading to God by adopting a combination of prayers (*salat*), spiritual exercises (*zikr*) and pure intentions (*niyat*).[196]

Citing Sura 58: 22, Shaikh Zakariya held that the seeker's heart was spiritually inspired by God, provided suitable conditions were created. This spiritual inspiration was not a momentary emotional stimulation triggered by intense exhilaration. The moment was as if the heart moved from deep slumber and was awakened by a touch of divine illumination. When the heart was in prayer and in remembrance of God, it began to cleanse away worldly concerns and, opening itself as a divine presence, made itself known to the seeker. At this moment, the heart was like a patient lover who was waiting for affection from a partner and would receive divine illumination if he understood the vulnerability of the heart. If this did not happen, then the seeker was advised to repeat the spiritual exercises of the heart. Citing Sura 64: 11, 'Whoever believes in God, He will guide his heart,' the Shaikh observed that the seeker was assured of real guidance, if his heart was guided towards patience through the practice of daily exercises. By citing Sura 4: 63, 'God knows what is in their hearts,' the Shaikh suggested that God waits for the proper time to be invited to the seeker's heart so as to disclose His love for him. In other words, the invitation came from God, but the seeker needed to prepare for the glorious moment by undertaking specific cleansing exercises. By citing Sura 50: 16, 'We are nearer to him than the jugular vein', the Shaikh assured the seeker not only God's proximity to him, but also His active presence in His body. However, if the seeker was guilty of evil actions, his heart ceased to receive future blessings and invitations from God. Such a situation had been anticipated in Quranic verses (Sura 7: 101, 2: 7, 3: 167 and 6: 25) stating that God had set seal on the hearts of such people. It was possible for him to return to the path of God by undertaking sincere repentance (*tauba*) and satisfactory inner cleansing (*mutmaina*). For the Shaikh, the Quran not only guided the seeker to mould his outward conduct on the Shariat, but also illuminated his inner life and spiritual journey leading to God.[197]

In his *Al-Aurad*, Shaikh Zakariya designed the structure of a number of *zikrs*, each meant for a particular occasion. By way of illustration, it was possible to consider the remembrance of prayer (*zikr-i namaz*). He believed that God had established the daily ritualistic prayer (*namaz*), so that the creation worshipped Him and understood the connection between the outer world and spiritual world. The physical movement of the bodily parts – hands, legs and forehead – leading to prostration was accompanied by a parallel movement of the heart, which released its impurities and prepared a clean purified place for the presence of God. As the forehead led the rest of the body in prostration before God, the action was similar to the seeker's preparation to be mentally alert and physically strong for the spiritual quest. Between the two ritualistic prayers, the seeker was asked to perform the *zikr-i Quran*, i.e. to recite the Throne Verse (*Ayat ul-Kursi*) which enabled the seeker to focus on God and affirm His omnipotence. This recitation was followed by two cycles (*rakats*) of prayer that were similar to the ritualistic prayers, though they were not tied to specified prayer times. The *zikr* concluded with *Surah-i Fatiha* and a supplication (*dua*). In a similar exercise after the sunset prayer (*maghrib*), the seeker was instructed to continue *zikr-i Quran* by reciting the *Surah-i Kafirun* and *Surah-i Ikhlas*. This exercise culminated in a supplication, which reaffirmed unconditional belief in the profession of faith (*kalima*), showered fulsome praise on the Supreme Being and His messenger Muhammad, accepted God as merciful and compassionate towards earthly creatures, sought forgiveness for human shortcomings and testified Heaven and Hell as true places. While formulating the content of *zikr* for different occasions – ritualistic prayers, twelve months of the calendar and other commemorative days – Shaikh Zakariya specified the Quranic verses that were to be recited with the respective prayers and laid down the order in which this recitation was to be done. The seeker was directed to contemplate on the inner meaning of the Quanic verses, so that he achieved a new state of being and his heart established a new identity with the Quran and its message.[198]

Shaikh Zakariya was not averse to attending a musical session (*sama*). Once a Qawwal named Abdullah Rumi arrived at the Suhrawardi hospice in Multan and, appearing before the Shaikh, revealed that he had performed in the presence of Shaikh Shihabuddin Suhrawardi. Instantly, Shaikh Zakariya expressed his desire to follow in the footsteps of his spiritual master. He had the visitors stay till the evening and, with the onset of darkness, sent Rumi and his companion to a cell (*hujra*) along with an attendant. He made sure that only two persons were present in the cell. After offering the night prayer (*isha*) and reciting invocations (*aurad*), he entered the cell. He sat down and immersed himself in invocations and then recited half a section (*siparah*) of the Quran. He bolted the door of the cell and asked Rumi to sing. As the audition got underway, there was a movement in the body of the Shaikh, who stood up and extinguished the lamp. It became pitch dark and the singing progressed. The singers could feel that the Shaikh, who had been moved to ecstasy, broke into a whirling movement. They could see the lower edge of his garment whenever he came closer. Owing to the darkness, they could not discern if the movement synchronized with the beat (*darb*) of music. As soon as the audition ended, the Shaikh opened the door and returned to his own place. The two singers, who spent the night in the cell, were not offered any food or drink. At daybreak, a servant appeared and, giving them a fine garment and 20 *tankas* in cash, asked them to accept the gifts from the Shaikh and leave. This episode, which was narrated by Abdullah Rumi to Baba Farid, raised many questions about the attitude of Shaikh Zakariya to spiritual music.[199] It was not clear why he held the audition in the strict privacy of a dark cell and not in the public space of his extensive establishment. Perhaps he was assessing the musical skills of the Qawwals as well as his own response to audition before they could be presented before a larger gathering. It might be added, Rumi came to Multan again after paying a visit to Baba Farid at Ajodhan.

Abdullah Rumi was not the only Qawwal to have visited the Suhrawardi hospice in Multan. Another Qawwal named Abu Bakr Kharrat had also come to the city and performed audition in the presence of Shaikh Zakariya. Our source has not described the circumstances in which the musical session was held. It could not be ascertained if the event was held in private or in public. However, our source did give an idea of the kind of lyrics that were sung. The verses, which were in Arabic, related the suffering of the lover who was separated from his beloved. The lover was afflicted with an ailment, which could not be cured by any physician or charmer; his desire could be fulfilled only if the beloved chose to do so.[200]

Each morning and again each evening,
My eyes, due to love of you, keep weeping.
My liver, bitten by the snake of desire,

No doctor or charmer has the means of curing.
For none but he who enflames me with desire
Can, if he chooses, quench that raging fire.

Shaikh Zakariya took pride in the merits of his disciple Hasan Afghan, who was regarded as a pillar of saintliness. Regarding his high spiritual states, the Shaikh used to say, 'If tomorrow they ask me to bring forward one person from my household (*dargah*) as a representative to face judgement on behalf of all others, I would present Hasan Afghan.' Sufi masters narrated several stories regarding Hasan Afghan, with a view either to highlight his spiritual eminence or to elaborate principles of mysticism. Once Hasan Afghan, while passing through a street, reached a mosque in time for prayer. The *muazzin* called out the *takbir*, the *imam* led the prayer and people stood in rows. Hasan Afghan also joined the congregation. As the prayer came to an end and people dispersed, Hasan Afghan went up to the *imam* and admonished him for the lack of concentration of his heart on the prayer. He said, 'Oh Khwaja, you began the prayer and I joined you. You went from here to Delhi and bought some slaves. Then you came back and took the slaves to Khurasan. After this transaction, you returned to Multan and entered the mosque. I got my neck twisted in an attempt to catch up with you. What has all this to do with prayer?' On one occasion, Hasan Afghan reached a place where a mosque was being constructed. He advised the builders to fashion the prayer niche (*mihrab*) in a manner that it pointed towards Mecca and also indicated the orientation of the Kaaba. A scholar (*danishmand*) disagreed with him and argued that the Kaaba was in a different direction. The two exchanged arguments for some time. Finally Hasan Afghan asked the scholar to face the direction pointed by him and note it well. The scholar complied with the suggestion and, after due verification, found that the Kaaba was indeed in the direction indicated by Hasan Afghan. This man was endowed with some extraordinary abilities. Though he was entirely illitrate, yet he could identify the verses from the Quran. People came to him and, placing a paper and tablet before him, wrote lines of poetry or prose, some in Arabic and some in Persian. Having done this, they would insert a line from the verses of the Quran and asked him to identify the same. Hasan Afghan invariably made the correct identification. How could he, they asked, pinpoint the Quranic verse when he was unable to read the holy book. He would explain that he discerned a unique light in the particular lines, which he did not see in the other lines of writing.[201]

Singing of Love in the Taverns

Fakhruddin Ibrahim Iraqi (1213-89), a close disciple of Shaikh Zakariya, contributed to the popularity of the Suhrawardi order in Multan. He developed his spiritual ideas on the foundation of physical love and expressed them through emotional verses. Born in village Kamajan in district Hamadan, he memorized the Quran soon after joining the school. His soulful recitation from the holy book made him famous in the region and even inspired the conversion of some non-Muslims to Islam. Before entering his twenties, he mastered the religious subjects and adopted the avocation of teaching. One day, he attended an assembly of wandering Qalandars and, overwhelmed by their chanting of love-laden muse and infatuated by the beauty of a boy among them, he discarded his apparel and threw away his books. Leaving his home, he caught up with the Qalandars who had left for Isfahan. He formally joined their fraternity and, as a symbol of his conversion, shaved his hair and eyebrows. He wandered along with the Qalandars across Persia and ultimately reached Multan.[202] Thus began a new phase in the life this maverick.

The Qalandars enjoyed the hospitality of the Suhrawardi hospice. Shaikh Zakariya, prompted by his intuition, wished to take Iraqi under his tutelage, as the young man was found fully prepared for spiritual advancement. Iraqi, who was impressed with the Shaikh, could not snap his association with the Qalandars. He accompanied them to Delhi and, owing to a storm, separated from them. Finding himself alone in unfamiliar surroundings, he returned to Multan where he was destined to live for the next twenty five years. He enrolled himself as a disciple of Shaikh Zakariya, who weaned the youth away from his Qalandari affiliation. At the direction of his mentor, he withdrew into a forty-day retreat and sang in praise of love, beauty and wine. Outraged at these ecstatic outpourings, the inmates of the hospice complained to the Suhrawardi master. The Shaikh declared that such behaviour was forbidden to them, but not to Iraqi. Soon it was learnt that Iraqi's songs were being sung to the accompaniment of musical instruments in the bazaar and taverns of the city. Perturbed at this musical spillover, the Shaikh asked Iraqi if he said his prayers in the taverns. Iraqi emerged out of his cell and, while weeping, placed his head at the feet of his mentor. The Shaikh instantly nominated Iraqi as his successor (*khalifa*) and, conferring his own robe on him, married his daughter to him. In due course, this union produced a son who was named Kabiruddin. After the death of Shaikh Zakariya in 1262, his disciples, motivated by sheer jealousy, complained to the Sultan (probably Prince Sultan Muhammad, the governor of Multan) that Iraqi had deviated from the established rules and spent his time in reciting poetry in the company of young boys. The Sultan, who was suspicious of the Suhrawardi order, decided to take punitive action and assert his authority. He sent an order for Iraqi to appear at the court. Iraqi, having anticipated his fate, left for Oman via the sea along with a few trusted friends.[203]

Jamali took keen interest in the career of Iraqi, particularly with reference to the poet's association with the Suhrawardis of Multan. To Shaikh Zakariya, he has given the credit of detaching Iraqi from a group of Qalandars and assimilating him into the Suhrawardi lineage. Not surprisingly, Iraqi acknowledged his gratitude to Shaikh Zakariya by composing several panegyrics in his adulation. After the death of Iraqi's first wife, Shaikh Zakariya wished the younger sister of the deceased to be married to his pupil. However, the son of the Shaikh, Sadruddin Arif, scuttled the move on the ground of Iraqi's allegedly crude behaviour and submission to his lower self.[204]

Iraqi and his party disembarked at Oman, where his fame as a mystic had already reached. The visitors were received by the political and religious elite with immense enthusiasm. The local ruler treated Iraqi as a state guest and, appointing him as the Shaikh ul-Islam, wished him to settle on a permanent basis. Iraqi refused to accept any further material assistance and went to Mecca, where he performed the Haj. Travelling via Damascus, he arrived at Konya in Rum (Turkey). Here, he entered the tutelage of Shaikh Sadruddin Qonawi (d. 1274), who had been a pupil of the great Sufi ideologue Ibn-i Arabi and a Suhrawardi master Shaikh Auhaduddin Kirmani. Iraqi developed a bond of friendship with the famous Sufi poet Maulana Jalaluddin Rumi and often attended his sessions of music, poetry and dancing. Inspired by the lectures of Qonawi on Ibn-i Arabi's *Fasus ul-Hikam* (Bezels of Wisdom), Iraqi produced its interpretive commentary entitled *Lamaat* (Flashes). In the eyes of Qonawi, this work was in fact the pith of *Fasus al-Hikam* and therefore articulated the secrets of spiritual discourses.[205] Iraqi earned the devotion of the local administrastor Amir Muinuddin Parwanah, who built a hospice for the master in Tuqat. After the death of Parwanah in a political purge, Iraqi travelled to Cairo and, after meeting the Sultan, secured the release of Parwanah's son from prison. The Sultan, who was deeply influenced by Iraqi's mystical knowledge, ensured that he was conferred numerous honours at Damascus. Here, his son Kabiruddin, who had travelled all the way from Multan, joined him. Following the death of Iraqi (23 November 1289), Kabiruddin was chosen as his spiritual successor.

Jamali did not give the credit of Iraqi's *Lamaat* to the mentorship of Qonawi; he indirectly attributed the treatise to the blessings of Shaikh Zakariya. This was indicated by Jamali's account of his meeting with Abdul Rahman Jami at Herat. Jami, while referring to *Lamaat*, praised Qonawi whose guidance had enabled Iraqi to produce the treatise. At this remark, Jamali felt offended without justification and exclaimed that the state of every person was fully known to God. As Jamali would have us believe, Jami saw a dream that night and observed Shaikh Sadruddin Arif (who then headed the Suhrawardi hospice of Multan) sitting in the midst of a number of Sufis. At this moment, Iraqi kept standing and held the shoes of Shaikh Arif in his hands. Jamali also appeared in the assembly and kissed the hands of Shaikh Arif. Jami, who was overawed by the presence of Shaikh Arif, admitted that Jamali's stance was true.[206]

Iraqi has indicated that he composed mystical poetry under divine inspiration, which was conveyed to him through supernatural means. He has described the visit of an angel and a conversation revolving around his work as a poet. The angel, while assessing a fresh poem, exclaimed that Iraqi's passion was deep and his thoughts flew swiftly like an arrow to its target.[207] He hoped that God would intensify the wisdom of Iraqi's love, so that he composed pearls that gave delight to others. He asked Iraqi to shun self-praise, as poetry was only a plaything in this world of men and a sport for children. He also urged Iraqi to engage himself in the acquisition of knowledge, to cast himself in the furnace of love and to create music for the benefit of true lovers. Since a number of poets had employed a variety of genres – sonnets, odes and elegies – to sing of lust (*hawas*), Iraqi was urged to focus on some original theme. He was told that the speech of the heart was different from what was understood as poetry. It was prose in rhyme or rhyme in prose. Its origin could be traced to love which, in turn, was moved by the beauty of form. All humans possessed a body and soul, but not all of them grasped the inner meaning embedded in the words. The angel assured Iraqi that he was adequately equipped for the task. His thought was robed in light; he did not stand with the idolaters; he was not moved by outward form; he could distinguish love from lust (*farq dani miyan ishq wa hawas*); he knew the reality of love and he had traversed the path of love (*tariqat ishq*). Finally, he was advised to improve his natural abilities to the level of perfection and to live in the midst of lovers, so that his initial efforts were brought to a logical conclusion by the blessings of God.[208]

In the eyes of Iraqi, the spiritual quest began by comprehending the nature of God. All human beings reserved unlimited praise for Him owing to a variety of reasons. God is everlasting, though He is neither born nor brought up. Pure in essence and free from flaw, He had vanquished all rival forces. Being omnipotent and sovereign, He knew both the seen and unseen. As the supreme artificer, He employed His creative power for forty days and uttering, 'Be, and it is' (*kun fayakun*), produced a number of species that were true to their types. Employing the principle of being and decay, He fashioned life with the hope that every species, being born of Him, shall return to Him. He achieved this purpose through the basic elements of earth, water, air and fire. He shaped human frames out of opposites, body and soul. He cast the clay of body from the dark earth and, associating it with outer darkness, illumined it with the light of spirit. He assigned a quickening power to the soul and, being associated with light, it aspired for a communion with Him. He sculpted man in a manner that he was receptive to knowledge and, owing to this faculty, distinguished between good and evil.[209] Since God transcends time and space, the wondrous work of creation was beyond description and imagination. All forms of creation traced their life to Him and, therefore, all was He. When a person's soul was ignited by divine light, his heart burst into a flame. When a person surrendered himself to God, all his actions were undertaken through Him, while he himself had no autonomy in relation to Him. For example, when the sun shone in its full brightness, the light of the stars faded into darkness. In spite of elaborating the unlimited powers of God, Iraqi admitted his inability to praise the Infinite.[210]

Alongside comprehending the nature of God, a seeker was required to appreciate the distinct position of Prophet Muhammad and the pious caliphs. Muhammad was the last of the Prophets. A confidant of God, he was a companion of Jibrail and messenger of guidance (*khatim anbiya rasul hadi / sahib jibrail amin khuda*). He was the first in creation, but he was born last in time. He was the preserver of the page where the meaning of the heart was inscribed. An anchorite of God's own cloister, he possessed the entire knowledge of the Quran. Only he wore the divine apparel, so that even the heaven bowed in his obeisance. He reached within a distance of just two bows from God. His holy law scattered a hundred sciences across the world. His spiritual state was so exalted that the sky served as his slave, the sun his servant, the dawn his face and the night his hair. He had four companions (the pious caliphs) who, after him, provided leadership to the faith. During his lifetime, they were his friends and, after him, they followed his example without any fault. It was wrong to treat one of them as the Prophet's friend and another as his enemy. Such an approach was born out of ignorance and conceit. A companion, who had been chosen by the Prophet himself, could only be right in his actions. The four companions were worthy of approbation, as their secret resting places opened a thousand gates to heaven.[211]

At the commencement of his spiritual quest, a seeker did not have the perfect vision and, therefore, could not distinguish between union and separation. He was advised to awaken from his slumber and discard the undeserving teacher as well as foolish superstitions. He was not entirely made of flesh and, unlike cows and sheep, did not confine himself to eating and sleeping. He was bound to look beyond his physical existence and turn his soul towards God. These high truths were the exclusive preserve of true lovers and not everyone. Such a person converted his heart into a mirror, where the beauty of God was reflected. He was expected to polish away the rust which stained the mirror of his heart, so that he entered the palace of the king of beauty (God). If he transformed his entire body into an eye and suppressed his selfhood, he could see God face to face as in a mirror. The light of God was reflected on the mirror of the lover's heart in the same manner as the light of the sun was reflected by the moon. His eye served as the door of the heart. If the eye did not have the ability to see, it would not absorb the light emanating from God, just as a bat remained blind in broad daylight. An eye, which possessed the ability to see, developed a connection with God and served as a coin in the bazaar of God's unlimited kingdom. A seeker needed to understand that love did not require intellect, as it dwelt beyond the intelligible world. If he wished to unravel the mysteries of love, he had to shake off the bonds of reason and proof and, freeing his brain from barren intellectual exercises, soar beyond the summit of imagination.[212]

A lover could not be held guilty of falling in love. Even prophets were afflicted with this ailment, while lovers (like Yusuf and Zulaikha) were held in its overpowering spell.[213] A lover's heart could stray owing to faulty guidance and his soul could fail to respond to the desire of the Beloved. But on seeing the simurgh's feathered plume, a lover's heart began to beat like David on the door of love. Even if the lover happened to be a saint, love overthrew his faith and pulled him into apostasy. The holiest man, while treading the path of love, did not shrink from tending swine for the love of a gazelle.[214] What the lover guarded as a secret was his identity as a neophyte of love and his ultimate desire was to die as a martyr of love (*shahid ishq*).[215] The lovers were set apart from other sections of the society. Their company constituted an earthly paradise, while their friendship emitted heavenly light. It was for their sake that God created the universe including the sun and stars. They possessed a variety of virtues like knowledge, abstinence, clemency and righteousness. Yet they attributed these adornments to God's grace. They sought nothing but love and, having lost their selfhood, experienced true love. They were the first to whom the reality of love was revealed. When love made its way into a heart, it gripped this heart as a captive. Even if the lover held a low social rank, he could make the highest spiritual gains. When love was stirred in a heart, it became a recipient of God's bounty, as God states in the Quran, 'This is affection cast in thee by Me.' In case of a heart which had been rendered distraught by beauty, affection grew to perfection and attained the stage of absolute absorption (*istaghraq*), so that the intimate passion was defined as love. If a lover drowned himself in the ocean of love, he could become a master of the spiritual path. Even if he was familiar with its fame and took a bold plunge in it, he could still comprehend its mysteries.[216]

The lover was a victim who, having sacrificed himself to love, was thrown at the door of the Beloved. Though he had been burnt in the furnace of love, yet his heart continued to throb for love. If he sacrificed himself at the altar of love, it was because he knew the worth of the Beloved in the manner of legendary lovers. Wamiq was aware of the beauty of Azra; Khusro could wax eloquent on the qualities of Shireen; Majnu bore the stamp of Laila's love; Parwana burnt in the desire of Parvin; enticement of Ramin had been embedded in the sadness of Wisa. Life was dear to Farhad, but dearer to him was to die for Shireen. If the entire world overflowed with passion, the gnat would be content in their yearning for Hind. A person, who possessed a heart, perforce possessed a sweetheart. Those who were unaware of the mysteries of love ended up wasting their lives. A heart, which was averse to love, was not a heart but a devil's chamber. A heart, which did not have love in sight, was like an eye without eyesight. The lover treaded the path leading to the Beloved, as this threshold was his sole destination. Though his reason was rendered blind by love, yet he could not be treated as one having lost his mind. A person, who was not experienced in love, was like an ass who carried sugar cane on his back and preserved straw in his heart.[217] Love was a joy that was identical with life itself. In fact, love was more alive than the heart and soul. It reigned supreme in the realm of spirit. It lay hidden in the soul of the soul. The life, which animated the soul, sprang from love. If soul was seen as soil, then love was the plant. Love was liquor flowing in the fruit of mind. Love was the very fount of life.[218]

Charmed by the beauty of the Beloved, the lover underwent a long period of suffering in order to achieve the ultimate union. What appeared strange, the Beloved could become instrumental in a tragic death of the lover.[219] In this sense, the Beloved acted like a hunter, who attracted His prey by several ruses and, when His target came within reach, shot a fatal arrow which pierced its body. In this game of love, the Beloved was not held guilty of any crime. At the same time, the lover was seen as afflicted by a mysterious ailment, which made his mind distraught and destroyed his body. Since the lover was aware of the fatal trait of his affliction, he continued his quest in a fearless manner and did not regard the Beloved's arrow as a threat to his life. In fact, the lover willingly offered himself as a target for the Beloved's arrow. He firmly believed that the fatal arrow would not pierce his flesh till he had seen the Beloved's face. He could not figure out why the Beloved chose to shoot the fatal arrow in a sudden move when he himself had placed his heart on the gallows long back. Moreover, the fatal arrow could not cause any fresh pain to the lover, because his heart was already suffering from the pain of love. In these circumstances, the lover found a new life in the Beloved, even after meeting his death at the hands of the beautiful charmer. The lover drew a distinction between his body and soul. The former was as valueless as a dunghill (*mazbala*), while the latter was as valuable

The Establishment of Sufi Orders 199

as a jewel. The body could be compared to a furnace (*gilkhan*) and the soul to a stoker (*gilkhani*) who tended the furnace. When the seeds of the soul were planted in the lover, his body was rendered irrelevant. So long as the lover was a prisoner of his body, his soul was unable to gaze at the Beloved. When he was freed from the prison of his body, he surrendered his soul and saw the face of the Beloved. In other words, the lover had to die in order to unite with his Beloved.[220]

The lovers felt happy on realizing that they were in love with God, who represented a world that was purer than this world. Unmindful of their own existence and treating themselves as dead, they happily treaded the path leading to God. For the lovers, love was a sweet anguish and they gladly bore its pain. It was like a sickness that affected both the heart and soul. The ailment of love could not be cured, as the lovers did not know its remedy. Though they suffered from this incurable malady, yet they did not falter in their loyalty to God, nor did they complain regarding their pitiable condition. Ever since the lovers consumed the cup of primaeval covenant,[221] they became eternal worshippers of the wine of love. As this wine of love flowed through their veins and they felt intoxicated by its unique effect, they reeled on the road leading to the heart of the Beloved. Their heart and soul were illumined by the same love, which constrained God to create the world. As the lover erased his self and sipped the wine of love, he snapped his attachment to everything except God. Once he learnt the alphabet of love, the tablet of his mind was cleansed of all he had learnt in the past. His heart became the abode of God, while his love was manifested in yearning. The Beloved warmly reciprocated his love by whispering sweet messages and thus accepted the fact that he (lover) was absolutely dedicated to his Beloved and that his (lover's) heart played a generous host to the Beloved. Sometimes love sprang from the heart like the herbs springing from dust, while at other times it descended on the heart like rain. Whatever the reality, love just arrived and conquered the heart, even as the lover remained ignorant of the manner in which this wonderful event took place.[222]

The lovers were fond of listening to the songs of love for several reasons. The plaintive melody of the singer (*mutrib*) had a tender impact on souls and uncovered the secrets concealed in hearts. A lover on the verge of death owing to his malady of separation, could be revived by the life-giving stream of melody. On hearing the soulful songs, the lover became oblivious of himself and, passing to the realm of intoxication, began to dance. In such a state, the lover raised the cry of his yearning for the Beloved. The lover shook his wings like the sacrificial bird and flew from the empty world to true reality, so that he was able to describe the beauty of the Beloved.[223] The lovers dwelt in the threshold of the Beloved and, like the nightingales in His garden (*andalib bostan tuyem*), sang only of Him. There was no escape for the lovers, as they were captives in the net of the Beloved. Since they drew their breath from His affection, they could not think of leaving His threshold and turning towards strangers. Since they had quaffed the cup of His love, they had surrendered their hearts to Him and treated their lives as His ransom. Their souls were bound to serve Him, as they had killed their selfhood. Having become the captives of His, they did not have the strength to flee. Their hearts had been burnt by a flame that had been lit by the beauty of the Beloved. Their bodies had been set ablaze by the lamps of His love, so that the smoke of their inner glow had risen to the heaven. They had staked their possessions for winning His love, as they could not think of a better move in this game of gambling. Though they knew that their quest would lead to their death, yet they were not willing to retreat. Ever since they entered His circle in a state of ecstasy, they became weary of their earthly existence. They did not need the light of the sun and moon as the radiance of His face could transform their dark night into a bright day. Yet the lovers did not boast of a sole claim over His love, as a thousand hearts were engaged in plying their trade in His bazaar of love.[224]

The lover lamented that his heart was close to the Beloved, whereas he was physically distant from Him. His heart had been pierced like an arrow by the charming glance of the Beloved. His injurious affliction could be cured by the Beloved (*tu tabibi wa ma chunin bimar / tu maluli wa ma chunin mushtaq*), who could act as a leech and suck away the impure blood from his wound. He felt intoxicated by the yearning for the Beloved, but the separation threatened to sink the ship of his life in the sea of pain. Even as his patience seemed to crumble, he longed to see the Beloved's face and hear His sweet voice. Though love was an incurable distress, yet the remedy lay with the Beloved. As the tales of Beloved's beauty spread across the world, the lover ran all around in His pursuit. Instead of seeking an end to His travails, he prayed for the aggravation of his sickly condition in order to prove his fidelity (*gar cheh dardi ast ishq be darman / hast darman dard ma janan*).[225] Since the lover was unable to establish any contact with the Beloved, he was unaware of the Beloved's attitude to himself. This ignorance had compounded his suffering, which had been caused by the pangs of separation. In his desperation, the lover turned to the breeze of dawn which could answer the numerous questions assailing his mind. Since the lover's soul was occupied with Him, he did not know the distinction between union and separation. He felt like a prisoner in His noose and had lost the will to be released from His bondage. In spite of his misery, he longed to see His beauty that still stirred his thoughts.[226] He could not let the Beloved depart from his life, though he was doomed to suffer. This emotion indicated his undying commitment, just as a spark betrayed the glow of ember. He had no alternative but to offer obedience to the Beloved, who ruled the world as a sovereign. Since his heart was set to suffer in the quest of the Beloved, his desires had become the same as those of the Beloved. The sole joy of his heart lay in His punishment, while the sole object of his soul coincided with this purpose. He could not leave the street of the Beloved, though thousands of lovers were engaged in a similar pursuit (*aankeh dur az tu man nadanam zeest / gar cheh dari cho man hazar hazar*).[227]

Iraqi has imagined meeting his Beloved in person and expressing the sentiments accumulating in his heart. Since his love for the Beloved had opened his spirit, his heart longed for Him. His night of grief had not turned into a day, as the face of the Beloved had turned away. The Beloved was unmindful of poor supplicants who had placed the petitions of their hearts at His door. The lover's soul, like a bird, had flown out of its nest and would rest only in His street. He hoped that his absence from the Beloved's thoughts might end, lest the veil of his love should be torn to shreds. Whatever be his ultimate fate, he entreated the Beloved not to ignore him. Every moment of his separation was marked by the desire of heart and pain of spirit. The pangs of separation were ever present in his heart, so that he had gained nothing from destiny except grief. Paradoxically, he treated his suffering as a boon, as the gradual augmentation of pain transformed the shadow of love into a concrete reality. Still he was apprehensive, because in love the truest fidelity could prove to be hypocrisy (*nur ikhlas shud riya dar ishq*).[228] When his heart was filled with sadness owing to separation from the Beloved, his weary brain demanded wine to sooth his troubled nerves. But when the pigeon of love flew to his heart with a message from the Beloved, he felt like sacrificing his life due to sheer happiness.[229] It was easy to surrender his heart to the Beloved, but it was not possible to part from Him. Since it was impossible to conceal his love for the Beloved, he was inclined to proclaim it far and wide. Though the lover was not fortunate enough to win his love, yet he sought the pain that flowed from the Beloved. He entreated God to fling open the gate and show the path of the destination. He was desperate to see the face of the Beloved and, in lieu of this boon, offered to sacrifice his possessions in both the worlds.[230]

Iraqi visualized the Beloved as a woman and described her beauty in sensuous terms. Her fairness and grace had stolen his heart, while his mind went into a rapture by gazing on her face. Her loveliness had put the sun to shame. Her grace was manifest whether her face was uncovered or veiled. Her elegance was so fine that it could not be discerned by the sharpest eye. Her countenance was so fair that it could not be described by any human tongue. Her gleaming forehead looked like the moon and acted like a moth-consuming candle. Her eyelashes were murderous and her glances were langourous. The softness of her ruby lips had put the petals to shame. In response to her beauty, the lovers had staked their lives on a throw and royal falcons had become her passion's prey.[231] The mole on her face caused unlimited enchantment. Her mirthful eyes tried a new blandishment every moment to steal the beholder's heart. Her mouth was so delicately carved that it could not speak. Her waist was so thin that it was visible only due to the girdle.²³² The radiance of her face cheered the heart and loveliness of her form turned the night into day. A person, who was not stirred by the comeliness of her physique, was a body without soul. A look at her beauty produced the same effect as mead.²³³ Only a beholder who possessed a pure vision (*deeda-i pak*), could see her beauty in its true loveliness. Faced with such a spectacle, most beholders lost control over their senses. As soon as a person saw her majestic form, including a tall stature and flowing locks, he surrendered his body, heart and soul. In fact, he was overcome by the desire to become an idolator (*hamchu man dil aseer u shuwadat / but prasteedan arzu shuwadat*). The slender grace, which reflected the charm of her beauty, had ensnared even the hearts of the spiritual men (*aan latafat keh husn u darad / dil sahib dilan beh dam arad*).²³⁴

In some Sufi circles, seekers drew spiritual inspiration from the looks of handsome boys. Iraqi has explained the phenomenon through three examples. When Imam Ghazzali heard about the beauty (*husn u dilfreb wa shorangez*) of the son of the prefect (*shahna*) of Tabrez,²³⁵ he lost his self restraint and rode all the way from Ray to see the fair one. As his intention became known to people, he was condemned as a hypocrite and idolator (*suratprast wa zarraq*). The prefect forbade Ghazzali's entry into Tabrez. Ghazzali pitched his tent in the outskirts of the town and spent the night. The prefect, on being directed by Prophet Muhammad in a dream, reversed his order. Ghazzali entered Tabrez and, having shown a miracle in the mosque, delivered a sermon which established his credentials as a gnostic.²³⁶ In another poem, Iraqi has described this episode in a slightly different manner. What was relevant for us was the mystic principle which has been asserted through the two narratives. Ghazzali was absolutely clear in his mind that a person, who attracted the attention of others owing to his beauty, was required to be treated as an incomparable work of God. The experience of its vision reminded us of the creative power of God, which remained unmatched and unreplicated. It was true that when the human vision attained perfection, its pleasure lay in seeing the beauty.²³⁷ But it was equally true that the beauty did not lie in the form. An object of beauty was there to be admired, not to be plucked and eaten.²³⁸

When a true seeker beheld a beautiful face, which exuded a lovely radiance and divine grace, he was amazed in the first instance and immediately saw the form of the Supreme Beloved. As he gazed at the sight, holding his heart and soul in place, he discerned a new face every moment. Employing the beauty of form as an instrument, he engaged in his spiritual quest. Those who were swayed only by their senses and did not heed their soul, focused only on the beauty of the outward form. Those who possessed the superior ability of seeing beyond the skin and discovering the hidden kernel, succeeded in seeing a flashing ray in the light of the Beloved (*maghaz khud ze andrun post ba-been / ze-an shuai beh nur dost ba-been*). He who sought the Beloved found that His essence could not destroy His attributes. The seeker's eye merely caught the first glimpse of the Beloved, but it remained for his heart to perceive the ultimate reality. Till he succeeded in achieving this, his heart continued to suffer in yearning.²³⁹

Ruzbihan Baqli, an eminent mystic of Shiraz who was famed for his learning and piety,²⁴⁰ fell in love with a handsome boy. Tales of their mutual attraction and physical intimacy caused a scandal. The ruler Saad Zangi decided to make a personal enquiry and visited the cell of the saint. He observed that the fair boy, whose face was as bright as the full moon, held Baqli's feet in his bosom. The next moment, Baqli withdrew his feet from the boy's chest and thrust them in a brazier of burning coal, exclaiming, 'Though my eyes are sorely distraught, yet I do not feel what happens to my feet.' He declared that the flame, which burnt a portion of the flesh, tried only to consume the witless brain. The two prophets of yore, Abraham and Musa,²⁴¹ were not harmed by blazing flames. Though some people felt that Baqli's gaze was sinful, yet his heart had achieved its object in the form of the spiritual fruit. Since his heart was pure, his gaze was not defiled. But the pain of love, which did not affect others, held Baqli in its stranglehold for all times (*mel dil ra natija ruhanist / nazre kez sar safa ayad / beh tabiyat magar nialayad*).²⁴²

A similar idea was reflected in a anecdote involving a saintly figure, who was spoken of as a beloved of God, a defender of the Shariat and a sun of spiritual truths. This mystic was ensnared by the beauty of Majduddin Baghdadi. He invited his beloved to his presence and engaged him in a game of chess (*shatranj*). As they sat over the chess-board for several days, he not only relished the sensual experience of gazing at the fair one, but also delved into the characteristics of God and secrets of love. He realized that love was a fire whose spark operated in the heart and consumed the veil of every accident. This love, after being stirred by spiritual desire, brought the heart to God's omnipotence and perfect beauty. Love was essentially a quality of the Creator that underscored a unity between lover, love and beauty (*ishq ausaf kardgar yakist / ashiq wa ishq wa husn yar yakist*). God's essence was revealed through the display of His numerous attributes – power, knowledge, hearing, sight, speech, will, life, beauty, affection and love – that in turn were also reflected in the lover. When the lover saw himself, he beheld God and secretly proclaimed, 'I have no other in my cloak but God'.[243]

From the demise of Hujwiri in 1072 to the rise of two Sufi orders in the early thirteenth century, there is practically no evidence on Islamic spirituality. Quite significantly, Khwaja Muinuddin Chishti, the founder of the Chishti order in the Indian subcontinent, chose the mausoleum of Hujwiri to undertake a forty days' retreat. A hundred years later, it was noted that Hujwiri's *Kashf ul-Mahjub* was one of the books the seekers demanded in the city of Delhi. Though the Chishtis and Suhrawardis were seen as substantially different from each other, yet they displayed a number of common traits. Their early history coincided with the emergence of the Delhi Sultanate as a viable political structure. Growing up in the arid zone of southwestern Panjab, they were faced with similar material conditions and socio-cultural contexts. Their founders, Baba Farid and Shaikh Bahauddin Zakariya, were scions of families that had migrated to Panjab from lands in the west. Having set up their respective Sufi lodges, they focused their energies on training novices from far and near. In addition to the Quran and Hadis, they included the *Awarif ul-Maarif* as a basic text for the education of disciples. Interestingly, both disfavoured the Quranic commentary of Zamakhshari, who was seen as a Mutazilite. Both realized the significance of intellectual engagement and produced texts revolving around the essentials of the spiritual quest and content of prayers. Their influence extended to all sections of society ranging from powerful rulers to the hapless commoners. Their fame spread to the Islamic lands beyond Afghanistan in the west and across the Jamuna in the east. If Baba Farid reached out to the unlettered devotees of the countryside through his verses in the local dialect, Fakhruddin Iraqi carried his message of love-laden spirituality out from the confines of a fortress-like Sufi lodge to the open air of the bazaars and taverns.

NOTES

1. J. Horovitz, 'Baba Ratan, the Saint of Bathinda,' in *Notes on Punjab and Mughal India: Selections from Journal of the Punjab Historical Society*, ed. Zulfiqar Ahmad, Lahore: Sang-e Meel Publications, 2002, pp. 71-7.
2. Yoginder Sikand, *Sacred Spaces: Exploring Traditions of Shared Faith in India*, New Delhi: Penguin Books, 2003, pp. 201-5.
3. A deity worshipped by diverse groups in northwestern India, Guga was invoked to guard against snakebites, though his miraculous powers were also sought to heal the blind, the deaf and the lame. In his shrines, he was depicted as a figure on horse. According to some legends, he was a Rajput from Bikaner and fought against Mahmud of Ghazni. Roshen Dalal, *Hinduism: An Alphabetical Guide*, New Delhi: Penguin Books, 2010, pp. 150-1.
4. One of the most successful rulers of Kashmir, Zain ul-Abidin (1420-70) left a deep imprint on every aspect of life in the valley. Having suppressed internal revolts and defended the frontier against foreign powers, he reformed the revenue system by measuring out land. He constructed canals, bridges and towns, besides introducing new crafts. He sponsored the translation of Hindu and Muslim classics. He not only gave high positions to the Hindus, he also revived temples, patronized Brahmins and encouraged Hindu customs. Mohammad Habib and Khaliq Ahmad Nizami, eds., *A Comprehensive History of India*, vol. V: *The Delhi Sultanate*, AD 1206-1526, pp. 751-9.
5. Horovitz, 'Baba Ratan, the Saint of Bathinda,' pp. 67-8.
6. Sikand, op. cit., p. 207.
7. Ibid., pp. 211-13.

8. Subhash Parihar, 'The Dargah of Baba Haji Ratan at Bhatinda,' *Islamic Studies*, vol. 40, no. 1, 2001, pp. 108-18.
9. Nur Ahmad Chishti, *Tahqiqat-i Chishti*, Lahore: Al-Faisal Nashiran wa Tajiran Kutb, rpt., 2001, pp. 164-5.
10. For a useful analysis of Hujwiri's experiences and encounters in different parts of the Islamic world, which was based on autobiographical references in his only extant work, see Anna Suvorova, *Muslim Saints of South Asia: The Eleventh to Fifteenth Centuries*, Abingdon, Oxon: Routledge Curzon, 2001, pp. 40-6.
11. Dara Shukoh, *Safinat ul-Auliya*, Urdu translation, Muhammad Waris Kamil, Deoband: Sabir Book Depot, n.d., p. 198.
12. Relying on a local tradition, a chronicle of the seventeenth century would have us believe that Hujwiri arrived in Lahore along with Sultan Mahmud of Ghazni, who attributed his conquest over the city to the blessings of the saint. Sujan Rai Bhandari, *Khulasat ut-Tawarikh*, Persian text, ed. M. Zafar Hasan, Delhi: G. and Sons, 1918, p. 66.
13. Nur Ahmad Chishti, *Tahqiqat-i Chishti*, p. 165.
14. Ali bin Usman al-Hujwiri, *Kashf al-Mahjub*, English translation, Reynold A. Nicholson, Delhi: Taj Company, rpt., 1982, p. 91. (hereafter cited as Hujwiri).
15. Dara Shukoh, *Safinat ul-Auliya*, p. 198.
16. Hujwiri, p. 2.
17. Ibid., pp. 6-7.
18. Mohammad Tazeem, 'Theory and Practice of Islamic Mysticism: An Exposition by Ali bin Usman Hujwiri,' in *Sufism in Punjab: Mystics, Literature and Shrines*, ed. Surinder Singh and Ishwar Dayal Gaur, New Delhi: Aaakar Books, 2009, p. 180.
19. Dara Shukoh, *Safinat ul-Auliya*, p. 198.
20. Jawid A. Mojaddedi, *The Biographical Tradition in Sufism: The Tabaqat Genre from Al-Sulami to Jami*, Richmond (Surrey): Curzon Press, 2001, pp. 126-8, 146-7.
21. Hujwiri, p. 6.
22. Ibid., p. 7.
23. Ibid., p. 44.
24. Ibid., pp. 30-44.
25. Ibid., p. 267; according to another view, a majority of Sufis regarded knowledge (*ilm*) as superior to both reason (*aql*) and gnosis (*maarifat*). Knowledge was the conception of an object as it was, reason was the capacity to distinguish between true and false, and gnosis was the experience of senses. Abu Najib Suhrawardi, *Kitab Adab-i Muridin*, English translation, (entitled, *A Sufi Rule for Novice*), Menahem Milson, Cambridge: Harvard University Press, 1975, pp. 39-41.
26. Hujwiri, p. 271.
27. Ibid., pp. 268-77.

28. Ibid., pp. 278-85.
29. Ibid., pp. 286-90.
30. Ibid., pp. 300-1; in prayer exercises (*aurad*), the confession of faith (*kalima-i shahadah*) held a special place. By confession (*iqrar*) was meant the use of tongue to recite the confession, while the deed (*amal*) denoted the use of limbs on orders of the Shariat. Both the confession and deed acted as witnesses to the existence of faith. Faith was verification by heart, confession was verfication by tongue and action was verfication by limbs. Shihabuddin Umar bin Muhammad Suhrawardi, *Awarif ul-Maarif*, English translation, H. Wilberforce Clarke, New Delhi: Taj Company, revd. edn., 1984, pp. 160-1.
31. Hujwiri, pp. 302-4.
32. It was believed that one's lower self (*nafs*), which was the source of all immoral activities, could be overpowered by the practice of austerity (*zuhd*) and poverty (*faqr*). The former signified turning away from worldly pleasures, while the latter meant the absence of property despite desire. The status of the Sufi was higher than that of the practitioners of austerity and poverty, as he was veiled from both the worlds. Shihabuddin Umar bin Muhammad Suhrawardi, *Awarif ul-Maarif*, pp. 130-4, 163-7.
33. Hujwiri, pp. 19-24.
34. Ibid., pp. 58-9
35. For the Sufis, it was part of their ethics to be satisfied with the clothes they had at any given moment without affectation or preference. They were content with clothes that covered their nakedness and protected them from cold and heat. Such clothes were not considered as worldly goods by the Prophet. Favouring only one set of clothes, he regarded cleanliness as part of faith. Abu Najib Suhrawardi, *Kitab Adab ul-Muridin*, pp. 55-6.
36. Hujwiri, pp. 45-57.
37. A seeker was advised to marry not for worldly reasons, but to comply with the established custom and preserve one's chastity. A husband was obligated to meet his wife's needs according to his capability and, if she demanded more than his power, she could choose between what she received and divorce. In the early medieval times, it was considered better to avoid marriage and suppress desire by discipline, hunger, vigil and travelling. Abu Najib Suhrawardi, *Kitab Adab ul-Muridin*, p. 67.
38. Hujwiri, pp. 360-5.
39. Ibid., pp. 334-5.
40. A seeker was required to associate with others, particularly with those who agreed with his religious beliefs. He dealt with different types of people in accordance with their roles in society. However, companionship with youngmen was reprihensible, as it was a sign of weakness and stupidity. Abu Najib Suhrawardi, *Kitab Adab ul-Muridin*, pp. 45-8.
41. Hujwiri, pp. 337-9.

The Establishment of Sufi Orders 209

42. Ibid., p. 340; a seeker was advised to undertake frequent journeys, as they acted as antidote to lust and developed the qualities of patience and ebdurance. But he had to establish the object of his endeavour – acquiring knowledge, meeting brother Shaikhs, overpowering attachment to one's abode and friends, securing solitude, reading verses on the unity of God and so on. In the normal course, he was accompanied by a friend and, in case of a group, a chief was appointed to provide leadership. Following the Prophet's example, he carried articles like a staff, water flask and girdle. Shihabuddin Umar bin Muhammad Suhrawardi, *Awarif ul-Maarif*, pp. 42-5.
43. Hujwiri, pp. 341-3.
44. Ibid., pp. 345-7.
45. Ibid., pp. 393-6.
46. Ibid., pp. 397-8.
47. Ibid., pp. 404-7.
48. Ibid., pp. 413-15.
49. Ibid., pp. 417-18.
50. Ibid., pp. 419-20.
51. Bayazid Bistami (d. 874) emphasized transcendence of human condition in order to experience the Divine and recognized Godhead as ultimate ideal of all spiritual endeavour and, in the process, recalled the Quranic ideal of acquisition of knowledge that enabled one to reach inner reality of prophets. He introduced the concept of annihilation of self (*fana*) and subsistence in God (*baqa*). He was also identified with the tendency of intoxication (*sukr*), as he advocated a greater role for the individual in religion, as his experience of divinity superseded the tradition of prophets. This position was epitomized in the ecstatic utterance, 'Glory to me, how great is my dignity.' Shuja Alhaq, *A Forgotten Vision: A Study of Human Spirituality in the Light of the Islamic Tradition*, vol. I, New Delhi: Vikas Publishing House, 1997, pp. 148-52.
52. Junaid Baghdadi (d. 910), was deeply influenced by Muhasibi, Kharraz and Saqati. He saw Sufism as a constant purification and mental struggle, a perpetual striving to return to one's origin that was embedded in God and from which everything emanated. Every thought of his was permeated with the majesty of God in His aloneness and unity. Instead of intoxication, he held sobriety (*sahw*) as preferable state, as after ecstatic intoxication, man again became aware of himself in a life in God when all his attributes were transformed, spiritualized and restored to him, so that his ultimate goal was remaining (*baqa*) in God. Opposed to expressing spiritual mysteries to the uninitiated, he refined the art of speaking in subtle allusion to truth. Annemarie Schimmel, *Mystical Dimensions of Islam*, New Delhi: Yoda Press, rpt., n.d., pp. 57-9.
53. Hujwiri, pp. 419-20.

54. Mansur al-Hallaj (d. 921), the most controversial of all Sufis, held that anyone could strive for high station where he reflected God in himself. He believed that intoxication and sobriety were essentially one, so that a permanent state of union was possible. As man could transcend his humanity for good, he could reside in God permanently. His claim to a complete identity was reflected in his bold statement, 'I am the truth'. He denied the role of canonical law in religious life, as it separated man from God. He was sentenced to death for questioning the validity of Haj and canonical law. Shuja Alhaq, op. cit., pp. 155-9.
55. Hujwiri, p. 189.
56. Ibid., pp. 150-2.
57. Ibid., pp. 152-3.
58. In another local tradition, Hujwiri and Rai Raju were portrayed as holy men who competed for the loyalty of followers. Ultimately, the former employed his miraculous power to outclass the latter, who accepted discipleship as well as Islam. Samina Qureshi *Sacred Spaces: A Journey with the Sufis of the Indus*, Ahmadabad: Mapin Publishing & New Delhi: Timeless Books, 2009, pp. 135-8.
59. Nur Ahmad Chishti, *Tahqiqat-i Chishti*, pp. 166-7.
60. Anna Suvorova, *Muslim Saints of South Asia*, p. 54.
61. Lahore was a flourishing cultural centre due to the presence of numerous saints, scholars and theologians. There were a large number of graves of Sufis, owing to which the inhabitants of Mohalla Talla remained safe during the epidemic of plague. Dara Shukoh, *Safinat ul-Auliya*, pp. 98-9.
62. Sujan Rai Bhandari, *Khulasat ut-Tawarikh*, pp. 65-6.
63. A recent study focuses on the present state of the shrine, with reference to its functional division of space, management, internal organization, finances, charitable work, modernization, political engagement and socio-economic functions. Now, the structure of the shrine has been divided into two floors. The upper one comprised the tomb, Ghulam Gardish, mosque and roof garden. The lower one comprised offices, school, library, concert hall, research centre and police station. Linus Strothmann, *Managing Piety: The Shrine of Data Ganj Bakhsh*, Karachi: Oxford University Press, 2016, pp. 106-17.
64. Anna Suvorova, *Muslim Saints of South Asia*, p. 55.
65. Amir Khurd, *Siyar ul-Auliya*, Persian text, Delhi: Matba-i Muhibb-i Hind, 1885, pp. 58-63 (hereafter cited as Amir Khurd); according to this source, Baba Farid's stay in Hansi was twelve years, but Khaliq Ahmad Nizami believes it to be nineteen or twenty years.
66. Shaikh Qutbuddin Bakhtiyar Kaki wanted his pupil to settle in Delhi. However, the latter returned from Delhi to Hansi in response to the entreaty of a devoted follower Sarhanga. Amir Khurd, p. 73; Amir Hasan Sijzi, *Fawaid ul-Fuad*, English translations, Ziyaul Hasan Faruqi, p. 346, Lawrence, p. 292 (hereafter cited as FF and followed by the names of

translators). What was more plausible, Baba Farid did not settle in Delhi, because he wished to avoid any competition or rivalry with his friend Shaikh Badruddin Ghaznavi who had been in the city for long and worked with his deceased master. Khaliq Ahmad Nizami, *The Life and Times of Shaikh Fariduddin Ganj-i Shakar*, Delhi: Idarah-i Adabiyat-i Delli, rpt., 1973, p. 34.
67. Hamid Qalandar, *Khair ul-Majalis*, Persian text, ed. Khaliq Ahmad Nizami, Aligarh: Aligarh Muslim University, 1959, p. 89.
68. Ibid., p. 150.
69. Ibid., p. 188.
70. Khaliq Ahmad Nizami, 'Some Aspects of Khanqah Life in Medieval India,' in *Studies in Medieval Indian History and Culture*, Allahabad: Kitab Mahal, 1966, pp. 85-6; Khaliq Ahmad Nizami, *The Life and Times of Shaikh Fariduddin Ganj-i Shakar*, pp. 46-9; Khaliq Ahmad Nizami, *Religion and Politics in India during the Thirteenth Century*, New Delhi: Oxford University Press, New Edition, 2002, pp. 220-5.
71. Amir Khurd, p. 66.
72. Ibid., p. 64.
73. FF, Faruqi, pp. 424-5 ; Lawrence, pp. 346-7.
74. FF, Faruqi, pp. 158-9; Lawrence, pp. 148-9.
75. FF, Faruqi, pp. 114-15; Lawrence, pp. 114-15.
76. FF, Faruqi, p. 324; Lawrence, p. 275.
77. FF, Faruqi, pp. 371-2; Lawrence, pp. 310-11. In a similar incident, Shaikh Hamiduddin Suwali, who had received the cloak of discipleship from both Khwaja Muinuddin Chishti and Shaikh Qutbuddin Bakhtiyar Kaki, was invited by his friends and neighbours to join them in some enjoyment. Shaikh Suwali replied that he would not indulge in such a pastime, because he had tied the string of his trousers so tightly that it would not loosen until the day of judgement, even if there were virgins of paradise.
78. FF, Faruqi, pp. 386-7; Lawrence, p. 322.
79. FF, Faruqi, pp. 134-5; Lawrence, pp. 128-9.
80. FF, Faruqi, pp. 166-7; Lawrence, p. p. 155.
81. FF, Faruqi, p. 160; Lawrence, p. 150. According to another version, the physicians, on examining the Shaikh's pulse, failed to ascertain the cause of his loss of appetite. His son, Badruddin Sulaiman, learnt from a dream that his father was under a spell (*sehar*) imposed by the son of Shihab, a famous magician (*sahir*). Shaikh Nizamuddin went to the graveyard and, digging near the grave of Shihab, discovered an effigy (*surat*) pierced with needles. At the Shaikh's direction, the needles were removed and he regained his health. Hamid Qalandar, *Khair ul-Majalis*, pp. 116-17.
82. FF, Faruqi, pp. 305-6; Lawrence, p. 260.
83. FF, Faruqi, p. 303; Lawrence, p. 258.
84. FF, Faruqi, pp. 371; Lawrence, p. 310.
85. FF, Faruqi, pp. 313-14; Lawrence, pp. 266-7.
86. FF, Faruqi, p. 183; Lawrence, pp. 167-8.

87. Amir Khurd, p. 180.
88. FF, Faruqi, pp. 107-8; Lawrence, p. 109. As a disciple, Baba Farid was audacious towards his mentor Shaikh Kaki only once. He sought permission for a inverted forty day retreat (*chilla makus*). The Shaikh replied that the practice was not necessary, because it merely led to publicity and had not been followed by senior Chishti masters. Baba Farid submitted that he did not intend to make himself known to the world. Shaikh Kaki kept quiet. His disciple realized his mistake of entering into an argument and, remaining repentant for the rest of his life, prayed continuously for his forgiveness.
89. Amir Khurd, pp. 117-20.
90. FF, Faruqi, pp. 112-13; Lawrence, pp. 113-14; Amir Khurd, pp. 74-6. In the middle of the fourteenth century, there was a debate in Chishti circles on books written by their Shaikhs. According to Shaikh Nasiruddin Mahmud, the manuscripts of Shaikh Usman Harwani's discourses were available, but they did not conform to his authentic views. Shaikh Nizamuddin Auliya stated that neither he nor any of the Chishti elders (Shaikh Kaki and Baba Farid) had written any book (*man hech kitabe tasneef nakarda am wa khwajgan ma neez na karda and*). In his times, the discourses of Shaikh Harwani and Shaikh Kaki were not available. Otherwise, these would have been mentioned in his discussions and would have been available. Hamid Qalandar, *Khair ul-Majalis*, pp. 52-3.
91. FF, Faruqi, p. 349; Lawrence, p. 294.
92. The use of folk language enabled the mystics to teach the core of religion without mediation of a priestly caste and without relying on the writings of erudite scholars. In order to disseminate mystical teaching among the masses, the poets resorted to an imagery taken from daily life and landscape surrounding them. Annemarie Schimmel, *As Through A Veil: Mystical Poetry in Islam*, London: Oneworld Publications, rpt., 2001, pp. 138-41.
93. Baba Farid has composed two hymns (*shabads*) in Rag Asa and two in Rag Suhi, besides a large corpus of couplets (*shaloks*). These verses are found at three different places in the holy book (pp. 488, 794 and 1377-84). Scholars have also discovered Baba Farid's poetry that has not been included in the text of Sikh holy book, besides twenty anecdotes on his life. Pritam Singh, *Sri Guru Granth Sahib Wale Sekh Farid Di Bhal*, Amritsar: Singh Brothers, 2010, pp. 274-344.
94. Carl W. Ernst, *Eternal Garden: Mysticism, History and Politics in a South Asian Sufi Centre*, New Delhi: Oxford University Press, 2nd edn., 2004, p. 168.
95. Brij Mohan Sagar, *Hymns of Sheikh Farid*, Amritsar: Guru Nanak Dev University, 1999, p. 36 (hereafter cited as Baba Farid, *Hymns*, followed by the serial number of the shalok).
96. Baba Farid, *Hymns*, Shalok no. 27, p. 26.
97. Ibid., Shalok nos. 15-20, p.25.
98. Ibid., Shalok no. 53, p. 28.

The Establishment of Sufi Orders 213

99. Ibid., Shalok nos. 70-2, pp. 29-30.
100. Ibid., Shalok no. 118, p. 34.
101. Ibid., Shalok nos. 20-1, p. 25.
102. Ibid., Shalok nos. 119, p. 34.
103. Ibid., Shalok no. 6-7, p. 24.
104. Ibid., Shalok nos. 28-9, p. 26.
105. Ibid., Shalok nos. 59-60, pp. 28-9.
106. Ibid., Shalok no. 61, p. 29.
107. Ibid., Shalok nos. 64-5, p. 29.
108. Ibid., Shalok no. 74, p. 30.
109. Ibid., Shalok no. 80, p. 30.
110. Ibid., Shalok nos. 112-13, p. 34.
111. Ibid., Shalok no. 128, p. 35.
112. Ibid., Rag Suhi, Shalok no. 1.4, p. 37.
113. Ibid., Shalok nos. 16-17, p. 25.
114. Ibid., Shalok nos. 115-17, p. 34.
115. Ibid., Shalok nos. 129-30, p. 35.
116. Ibid., Shalok nos. 85-6, p. 31; Rag Asa, Shalok no. 2.3, p. 36.
117. Ibid., Shalok nos. 30-1, p. 26.
118. Ibid., Shalok no. 54, p. 28.
119. Ibid., Shalok nos. 87-9, p. 31.
120. Ibid., Shalok nos. 102-3, p. 32.
121. Ibid., Shalok no. 127, p. 35.
122. Ibid., Shalok nos. 4-5, p. 24.
123. Ibid., Shalok Suhi Lalit, Shalok no. 2.2, p. 38.
124. Ibid., Shalok Rag Suhi, Shalok nos. 1.2-1.3, p. 37.
125. Ibid., Shalok nos. 24-6, p. 25.
126. Ibid., Shalok nos. 33-6, p. 26.
127. Ibid., Shalok nos. 44-50, pp. 27-28.
128. Ibid., Shalok nos. 57-58, p. 28.
129. Ibid., Shalok nos. 79, 102, pp. 30, 32.
130. Ibid., Rag Asa, Shalok nos. 2.5-2.8, pp. 36-7.
131. Ibid., Shalok nos. 8-12, 14, pp. 24-25.
132. Ibid., Rag Suhi Lalit, Shalok no. 2.1, p. 38.
133. Ibid., Shalok nos. 38-40, p.27.
134. Ibid., Shalok nos. 62-3, p. 29.
135. Ibid., Shalok no. 77, p. 30.
136. Ibid., Shalok nos. 90-1, p. 31.
137. Ibid., Shalok no. 94, p. 31.
138. Ibid., Shalok no. 96, p. 32.
139. Ibid., Shalok no. 1, p. 23.
140. Izrail or the angel of death (*malik ul-maut*) came to a person at the hour of death to carry his soul away from the body. According to the Quran (XXXII: 11), 'The Angel of death shall take you away, he who is given charge of you.

214 *The Making of Medieval Panjab*

Then unto your Lord shall ye return.' The Prophet is reported to have said that when the Angel of Death approaches a believer, he sits at his head and says, 'O pure soul, come forth to God's pardon and pleasure.' Then the soul comes out as gently as water from a bag. But in case of a infidel, he says, 'O impure soul, come forth to the wrath of God.' Then the Angel of Death draws it out as a hot spit is drawn out of wet wool. Thomas Patrick Hughes, *Dictionary of Islam*, pp. 222-3.

141. Baba Farid, *Hymns*, Shalok nos. 98-100, p. 32.
142. Ibid., Shalok nos. 68-9, p. 29.
143. Ibid., Shalok nos. 105-6, p. 33.
144. Ibid., Shalok no. 67, p. 29.
145. FF, Faruqi, pp. 201-2; Lawrence, pp. 181-3.
146. FF, Faruqi, p. 160; Lawrence, p. 150.
147. Amir Khurd, pp. 68-70.
148. FF, Faruqi, p. 301; Lawrence, p. 256.
149. FF, Faruqi, p. 312; Lawrence, p. 266.
150. FF, Faruqi, pp. 148-9; Lawrence, p. 140; Amir Khurd, p. 65.
151. FF, Faruqi, p. 382; Lawrence, pp. 318-19.
152. FF, Faruqi, pp. 296-7; Lawrence, pp. 252-3.
153. A number of Chishtis like Fakhruddin Zarradi, Hamiduddin Nagauri, Masud Bakk and Syed Ashraf Jahangir Simnani wrote in support of this practice. Far from being an embarrassment to them, they defended it as an essential component of the spiritual discipline. Bruce B. Lawrence, 'The Early Chishti Approach to Sama,' in *Islamic Society and Culture: Essays in Honour of Professor Aziz Ahmad*, ed. Milton Israel and N.K. Wagle, New Delhi: Manohar, 1983, pp. 73-87.
154. FF, Faruqi, pp. 217-18; Lawrence, p. 192.
155. FF, Faruqi, pp. 224-25; Lawrence, pp. 197-8.
156. Hamid Qalandar, *Khair ul-Majalis*, pp. 224-5.
157. FF, Faruqi, p. 181; Lawrence, p. 166.
158. FF, Faruqi, p. 222, Lawrence, p. 196. Since Ulugh Khan secretly aspired for the throne, he cleverly prevented the Sultan from visiting Baba Farid. He hoped that the Shaikh would throw some hint about the fate of his ambition. The Shaikh, having guessed Ulugh Khan's secret aim through his inner light, recited a couplet advising the visitor to be munificent if he wished to be a king. Amir Khurd, pp. 79-80.
159. FF, Faruqi, p. 399; Lawrence, p. 327.
160. FF, Faruqi, p. 188; Lawrence, p. 171.
161. FF, Faruqi, p. 380; Lawrence, pp. 317-18.
162. Biographical material on Baba Farid was found in two so-called apocryphal works *Asrar ul-Auliya* and *Rahat ul-Qulub* as well as later compilations like *Akhbar ul-Akhyar*, *Siyar ul-Arifin* and *Jawahar-i Faridi*. Even if these anecdotes were incredulous, they pointed towards the role of Baba Farid as a healer and protector of the people, besides his attitude to the contemporary

The Establishment of Sufi Orders 215

ruling class and religious figures. Raziuddin Aquil, 'Episodes from the Life of Shaikh Farid ud-Din Ganj-i Shakar,' *International Journal of Punjab Studies*, vol. X, nos. 1 & 2, 2007, pp. 30-7.
163. Hamid Qalandar, *Khair ul-Majalis*, pp. 236-8.
164. Ibid., pp. 147-50.
165. FF, Faruqi, p. 292; Lawrence, pp. 249-50.
166. Hamid Qalandar, *Khair ul-Majalis*, p. 182.
167. Ibid., p. 147.
168. Ibid., pp. 87-8.
169. FF, Faruqi, p. 363; Lawrence, pp. 304-5.
170. FF, Faruqi, pp. 164-65; Lawrence, pp. 153-4.
171. FF, Faruqi, pp. 289-90; Lawrence, pp. 247-8; Amir Khurd, p. 79.
172. FF, Faruqi, p. 75; Lawrence, p. 84. Once a Qalandar barged into the cell of Baba Farid and sat on his prayer carpet (*gilim sajjadah*). After taking the food that was offered, he began to crush his drugs in his begging bowl (*kachkol*), so that a few drops spilled out on the prayer rug. When Badruddin Ishaq asked him to behave, he fell into a rage and picked up his begging bowl to assault him. Baba Farid, who appeared on the scene, sought his forgiveness and asked him to turn his anger against the wall. As he flung the begging bowl on the wall, it collapsed. Hamid Qalandar, *Khair ul-Majalis*, pp. 130-1.
173. FF, Faruqi, pp. 294-5; Lawrence, pp. 251-2.
174. FF, Faruqi, p. 181, Lawrence, p. 166.
175. A man named Sirajuddin and other inhabitants of Abohar had become the disciples of Baba Farid. Once a quarrel irrupted in the town, as some people were annoyed with the family of Sirajuddin's wife and there was an exchange of harsh words. The wise lady, speaking in her defense, asked if her alleged wrong doing happened before or after their pledge of allegiance to Baba Farid. If the act occurred before, she was forgiven by the Shaikh and, therefore, exempted from any punishment. Evidently, the people attached great importance to their attachment to Baba Farid and were aware of the principle by which a seeker was absolved of all sins committed before registering his allegiance to the Shaikh. FF, Faruqi, p. 157; Lawrence, p. 147.
176. When Shaikh Zakariya was engaged in mystical exercises at the hospice of Shaikh Shihabuddin Suhrawardi, he looked forward to receive the robe of succession (*khirqah*). In a vision, he saw the Prophet in a profusely illuminated house, where Shaikh Suhrawardi was standing as a doorman and several robes were hanging from a rope. The mentor introduced his disciple to the Prophet. The Prophet directed him to confer a particular robe on the disciple. Next morning, Shaikh Suhrawardi called his disciple, who saw the robes on the line. Shaikh Suhrawardi gave him the robe that had been identified by the Prophet. The Shaikh declared that he could not adorn anyone with a robe without the permission of the Prophet. Hamid bin Fazlullah Jamali, *Siyar ul-Arifin*, Persian text, Delhi: Rizvi Press, 1893, pp. 104-5 (hereafter cited as Jamali).

177. FF, Faruqi, pp. 253-4; Lawrence, p. 219.
178. FF, Faruqi, p. 234; Lawrence, p. 205.
179. Saif bin Muhammad bin Yaqub Haravi, *Tarikh Nama-i Herat*, Persian text, ed., Zubair Ahmad, Calcutta, 1944, pp. 157-8; quoted in Khaliq Ahmad Nizami, *Religion and Politics in India during the Thirteenth Century*, p. 272.
180. FF, Faruqi, p. 493; Lawrence, pp. 330-1; Jamali, p. 113.
181. Jamali, pp. 112-13.
182. On this issue, there was a difference of opinion and practice. Shaikh Nizamuddin Auliya was sure that the disciples must complete their prayers before turning to any other activity. However, the Prophetic tradition and Baba Farid's practice was contrary to this. Baba Farid went to the extent of saying that the command of the Shaikh was like that of the Prophet. FF, Faruqi, pp. 413-14; Lawrence, pp. 338-89.
183. FF, Faruqi, pp. 399-400; Lawrence, p. 328.
184. Ibid., Faruqi, pp. 279-80; Lawrence, pp. 239-40.
185. Ibid., Faruqi, p. 399; Lawrence, pp. 327-28.
186. Ibid., Faruqi, pp. 374-5; Lawrence, p. 313.
187. Ibid., Faruqi, p. 420; Lawrence, pp. 343-4. Kashani felt sorry when he learnt that a Sufi of Kashghar, Najamuddin Yusuf, whom he held in high regard and about whom he narrated a personal experience of miraculous power, was in fact a disciple of Shaikh Zakariya. Jamali, pp. 125-6.
188. The attitude of Shaikh Zakariya to fasts and devotions was different from that of Baba Farid. The latter was seldom without fast and, while doing so, did not care if he had fever or had undergone bloodletting or cupping. In contrast, Shaikh Zakariya seldom fasted or fasted occasionally. However, he remained engrossed in devotional prayers and remembrance of God. He had moulded his life in conformity with the Hadis, 'Eat good and pure things and do good deeds'. FF, Faruqi, p. 341; Lawrence, p. 288.
189. Ibid., Faruqi, p. 77; Lawrence, pp. 85-6.
190. Ibid., Faruqi, p. 295; Lawrence, p. 251.
191. Abul Qasim Mahmud Zamakhshari (1075-1144) produced the famous commentary on the Quran entitled *Kashshaf al-Haqaiq al-Tanzil* which, in spite of its Matazila bias, was widely read in the orthodox circles. It focused on dogmatic exegesis of a philosophical nature, paying only slight attention to tradition. Besides giving purely grammatical expositions, it paid attention to rhetorical beauties and thus supported the doctrine of Ijaz of the Quran. M.T. Houtsma et. al., Eds., *The Encyclopaedia of Islam*, vol. IV, Leiden: E.J. Brill and London: Luzac & Co., 1934, p. 1205.
192. Ibid., Faruqi, pp. 235-6; Lawerence, p. 206; Jamali, p. 115.
193. FF, Faruqi, pp. 277-8; Lawrence, pp. 237-8; Jamali, p. 119.
194. Unlike the Chishti works, the Suhrawardi accounts have not survived. Multan frequently suffered from political instability. For long periods, it became peripheral to the Delhi Sultanate. During the Tughluq period,

The Establishment of Sufi Orders 217

the Suhrawardi hospice came under government control. In the fifteenth century, it lost endowments preventing sponsorship of Suhrawardi accounts. Qamar ul-Huda, *Striving for Divine Union: Spiritual Exercises for Suhrawardi Sufis*, London & New York: Routledge Curzon, 2003, pp. 111-12.
195. Ibid., pp. 153-6.
196. Ibid., pp. 148-9.
197. Ibid., pp. 150-2.
198. Ibid., pp. 157-0.
199. FF, Faruqi, pp. 278-9; Lawrence, pp. 238-9. Jamali has followed this account, but has added the following couplet. *Mastan keh sharab nab khurdand / az pehlu-i khud kabab khurdand.* Jamali, pp. 113-14.
200. FF, Faruqi, pp. 294-5; Lawrence, p. 251.
201. Ibid., Faruqi, p. 82-3; Lawrence, pp. 90-1; Jamali, pp. 110-11.
202. In the Islamic lands beyond the Indian subcontinent, the diverse strands of the Qalandari path were represented by Jamaluddin Savi, Qutbuddin Haidar and Otman Baba. In India, these were associated with Lal Shahbaz Qalandar, Bu Ali Qalandar, Shah Khizr Rumi and Abu Bakr Tusi. Antinomian in appearance and behaviour, they pursued renunciation through individual and social deviance. Ahmet T. Karamustafa, *God's Unruly Friends: Dervish Groups in the Islamic Middle Period 1200-1550*, Oxford: Oneworld Publications, rpt., 2007, pp. 13-23.
203. William C. Chittick and Peter Lamborn Wilson, *Fakhruddin Iraqi: Divine Flashes*, New York: Paulist Press, 1982, pp. 37-42.
204. Jamali, pp. 108-9.
205. William C. Chittick and Peter Lamborn Wilson, *Fakhruddin Iraqi: Divine Flashes*, pp. 42-6.
206. Jamali, pp. 138-9.
207. Fakhruddin Iraqi, *Ushaqnama*, in *Kulliyat Fakhruddin Iraqi*, Persian text, ed. Nasreen Muhatshim, Tehran: Intsharat Zawwar, 1392 AH, p. 397, (hereafter cited as Iraqi).
208. Iraqi, pp. 398-9.
209. Ibid., pp. 371-3.
210. Ibid., pp. 373-6.
211. Ibid., pp. 379-0.
212. Iraqi, pp. 381-2.
213. According to a famous tale, Yusuf, the son of Yaqub, was thrown into a well by his jealous brothers. Rescued by a caravan, he was purchased by a notable of Egypt. Zulaikha, the master's wife, fell in love with him and made an unsuccessful attempt to seduce him. Owing to false accusations, he was thrown into prison. After his release, he was appointed to high office. His parents and brothers came to stay with him, thus fulfilling his dream. This story, which has figured in the Quran (Surah XII: 1-111), has often been

seen as an exalted love tale underlining the relation between human lover and Divine Beloved. Seyyed Hossein Nasr et. al., Ed., *The Study Quran: A New Translation and Commentary*, New York: Harper One, 2015, pp. 589-90.
214. This was an allusion to the extraordinary life of Shaikh Sanan who, for fifty years kept the Kaaba and taught 400 pupils. While on a visit to Rome, he fell in love with a Christian beauty. At her bidding, he not only abjured Islam and drank wine, but also tended a herd of swine. Fariduddin Attar, *Mantiq ul-Tair*, English Translation (entitled *The Conference of the Birds*), Afkham Darbandi and Dick Davis, London: Penguin Books, Revised Edition, 2011, pp. 68-86.
215. Iraqi, p. 393.
216. Ibid., pp. 401-3.
217. Ibid., pp. 405-6;
218. Ibid., p. 409.
219. Jalaluddin Rumi (d. 1273), a distinguished contemporary of Iraqi, frequently alluded to the cruel aspects of love. It was seen as a man-eating monster, which slaughtered the lover on Id. Dragging the lover by a hook, it ate his liver and devoured him. The road to love was full of blood of those who have felt its sword. Love was dangerous like a lion, unicorn, crocodile and dragon. Annemarie Schimmel, *As Through A Veil: Mystical Poetry in Islam*, pp. 113-14.
220. Iraqi, pp. 415-17.
221. According to God's original covenant with the sons of Adam as recorded in the Quran (Surah VII: 172-74), '(Remember) when your Lord took from the sons of Adam – from their loins – their descendants, and made them bear witness about themselves: 'Am I Not your Lord?' They said, 'Yes indeed! We bear witness.' (We did that) so that you would not say on the Day of Resurrection, 'Surely we were oblivious of this,' or say, 'Our fathers were idolators before (us), and we are descendants after them. Will You destroy us for what the perpetrators of falsehood did?' In this way, We make the signs distinct, so that they will return. A.J. Droge, *The Quran: A New Annotated Translation*, New Delhi: Oxford University Press, 2013, p. 103.
222. Iraqi, pp. 390-2.
223. Ibid., pp. 409-10.
224. Ibid., pp. 423-4.
225. A greengrocer (*tirrah farosh*), while passing by a palace, fell in love with the princess. He forgot everything about himself and ran about with dogs in her street. The princess advised him to secretly withdraw into a mountain cave and, living like a saint, acquire fame. The man followed the direction in letter and spirit, so that his saintliness attracted the king and commoners. The princess went to the saint to express her love, but he refused to see her, because he was no longer the person who had fallen in love with her. The

The Establishment of Sufi Orders 219

roles being reversed, the seeker became the sought and the lover became the beloved. The princess, owing to her separation and longing, fell sick. The king, accompanied by his nobles, met the saint. In response to their collective plea, he married the princess. Iraqi, pp. 423-35.
226. Ibid., pp. 445-6.
227. Ibid., pp. 446-7.
228. Ibid., pp. 429-30.
229. Ibid., p. 443.
230. Ibid., pp. 444-5.
231. Ibid., pp. 440-1.
232. Ibid., pp. 443-4.
233. Ibid., p. 435.
234. Ibid., pp. 436-7.
235. Assuming that our poet has referred to elder of the two Ghazzali brothers, Abu Hamid Muhammad Ghazzali (1058-1111) contributed to a wide range of subjects including theology, jurisprudence, philosophy, mysticism and political theory. He abandoned his distinguished teaching position at Nizamiyya Madrasa at Baghdad. His solitary travels through Islamic lands were deliberate occasions to leave behind all societies of communal attachments and attainment of an existential and individual certitude. Hamid Dabashi, 'Historical Conditions of Persian Sufism during the Seljuk Period,' in *The Heritage of Sufism: Classical Persian Sufism from its Origin to Rumi 700-1300*, ed. Leonard Lewisohn, Oxford: Oneworld Publications, 1999, pp. 144-6.
236. Iraqi, pp. 419-22.
237. In mystical understanding, there was nothing objectionable in admiring a beautiful form. On being chided about his infatuation for a fair face, Ghazzali exclaimed that if he had not succumbed to form, he would have been Jibrail, the saddler of the skies (*gar neeftad me ba-surat zaar / bud me jibrail ghashia daar*). Iraqi, p. 441.
238. Ibid., p. 443.
239. Ibid., p. 442.
240. Ruzbihan Baqli (d. 1210) was one of the three Persian mystics (other two being Ahmad Ghazzali and Ainul Quzat), who gained popularity on account of their love theories and subtle interpretation of mystical states. His *Sharh-i Shathiyat* was a key to the theopathic utterances of early mystics, particularly Mansur al-Hallaj. He excelled in the use of pliable and colourful language, which was filled with roses and nightingales. While elaborating his mystical ideas, he drew from the Quranic tale of Yusuf and Zulaikha, besides the Prophet's reference to the red rose as manifestation of God's glory. Annemarie Schimmel, *Mystical Dimension of Islam*, pp. 294-9.
241. Abraham, the first Muslim and builder of the Kaaba, earned spiritual leadership owing to his firm faith in God. Known for his covenants with

God, he prepared to sacrifice his son at God's command. Musa, a prophet, has been mentioned in the Quran for his struggle against Pharaoh and setting God's commandments on tablets.

242. Iraqi, pp. 437-8.
243. Ibid., pp. 424-8.

CHAPTER 4

New Strategies of State Formation

The appointment of Ghazi Malik as the governor of Dipalpur marked the beginning of a process that transformed political and social life in Panjab. The first quarter of the fourteenth century witnessed the emergence of a new environment suitable to the demands of change. The Delhi Sultanate, as a political dispensation, acquired stability and maturity. Internal conflict within the ruling class was considerably reduced, particularly with the expanding social base of the nobility and the assimilation of fresh ethnic elements. A vigorous military offensive against the Mongols rendered the northwestern frontier safe from invasions. Since the rulers were better informed about conditions in the countryside, they developed close ties with diverse local elements, particularly rural intermediaries and spiritual elites. In these circumstances, the Delhi Sultanate undertook agararian expansion based on canal networks in two arid zones, the Satluj-Jamuna divide and Multan. Increased agricultural production necessitated new urban centres and administrative units. The provincial administration penetrated hitherto untouched areas for the management of land grants, the regulation of prices and working of lower rung functionaries.

The Tughluq Household

The social origin of the Tughluqs has been a theme of controversy. The question continues to retain its relevance in the context of the present discussion, which focuses on the association of the Tughluqs with the local elements in Panjab. According to Amir Khusrau, Ghazi Malik was living a nomadic life (*awara mardi*) when he entered the service of Sultan Alauddin Khalji and, in due course, became a royal confidant. Subsequently he was patronized by the Sultan's brother Ulugh Khan. He was honoured for his bravery in the attack on Ranthambhor. He gave a good account of himself in the campaigns against the Mongols at Baran and the sea coast of Banbol, besides fighting first against Tirmaq and Ali Beg and then against Haidar and Zirak. In this manner, he had been victorious in eighteen major battles.[1] Ibn Battuta learnt from Shaikh Ruknuddin Abul Fateh, the grandson of Shaikh Bahauddin Zakariya, that Ghazi Malik belonged to the Qaraunah Turks who inhabited the hills between Sind and Turkistan. He was in a humble condition when he reached Sind with a merchant for whom he was a horse keeper (*gulvaniya*). Thereafter, he was employed by Alauddin Khalji and enlisted under his brother Ulugh Khan. He began his career as a house keeper and, after serving in the infantry and cavalry, acquired the office of the master of horses (*amir ul-khail*) and thus entered the class of high nobles (*umara-i kibar*). Subsequently, he was made the governor of Dipalpur and its dependencies on the accession of Qutbuddin Mubarak Shah Khalji and, in due course, he acquired the title of Malik ul-Ghazi for defeating the Mongols in twenty-nine battles.[2] Shams Siraj Afif has stated that three brothers, Tughluq, Rajab, and Abu Bakr, arrived from Khurasan in Delhi during the reign of Alauddin Khalji. They impressed the Sultan with their loyal services to such an extent that Tughluq (Ghazi Malik) was given the administration of the famous city of Dipalpur.[3] These facts have come from three contemporaries, but it was difficult to believe that an obscure adventurer like Ghazi Malik could undergo such a meteoric rise.

The antecedents of the Tughluqs continued to be unclear for nearly four centuries. Firishtah, who wrote his history in the early seventeenth century, felt constrained to visit Lahore to discover the background of the Tughluqs from persons reputed for their knowledge of the past rulers. General belief current in those parts (central Panjab) held that Malik Tughluq, the father of Ghazi Malik, was one of the Turkish slaves of Ghiasuddin Balban, that Malik Tughluq had married into a local Jat family and that the

New Strategies of State Formation 223

first Tughluq ruler was born of this marriage.[4] Sujan Rai Bhandari, a native of central Panjab at the close of the seventeenth century, wrote that the person named Tughluq Shah (Ghazi Malik) was a ruler of Turkish descent, that he was one of the Turkish slaves of Ghiasuddin Balban and that his mother belonged to the Jat tribe of Panjab.[5] Thus, a strong tradition has persisted in medieval Panjab that pointed to the genealogical connection of the Tughluqs with the local people. The mixed parentage of the Tughluqs appeared to have paved the way for several other linkages of Ghazi Malik – the marriage of his brother Sipahsalar Rajab with the daughter of Rana Mal Bhatti of Abohar, his political alliance with the Khokhar chiefs of the Salt Range and his association with the shrine of Baba Farid at Pakpattan.[6]

Of the modern writers, Agha Mahdi Husain and Ishwari Prasad held that Ghazi Malik was the son of Ghiasudin Balban's Turkish slave and his Jat wife.[7] R.C. Jauhri has shown that Ghiasuddin Tughluq had arrived in India from Khurasan after the reign of Ghiasuddin Balban.[8] Peter Jackson has suggested that Ghiasuddin Tughluq was of Mongol or Turko-Mongol stock and may have been a follower of the Mongol chief Alaghu who took employment with Sultan Jalaluddin Khalji and settled near Delhi.[9] In line with this suggestion, Sunil Kumar viewed the rise of Ghiasuddin Tughluq in the context of political fragmentation within the Delhi Sultanate and Mongol confederacies, when relationships across the Panjab frontier were complicated. During the Mongol raids in northern India during the second half of the thirteenth century, disaffected Sultanate nobles looked for allies in the Mongol camps, while the Mongol and Turkic migrants searched for Sultanate patronage. The old tradition of slave commanders guarding the frontier underwent a slow modification to include immigrants who had intruded into the region. Ambitious military commanders on the frontier gathered large retinues and built impressive local reputations as warriors and patrons. Though they remained distant from the courtly intrigues at Delhi, they possessed sufficient assets and initiative to seize power in the capital and establish their own dynasties. It was not surprising that from 1290 to 1526 every dynasty – Khalji, Tughluq, Syed and Lodi – had frontier origins. So paradoxically, many frontiersmen patronized by the Delhi Sultans shared a history of past service and cultural affinities with the very groups who posed periodic threats to the Delhi Sultanate. Unlike the *bandagan-i khass*, they had not undergone a period of training and acculturation. As they arrived in the Delhi Sultanate with their lineage networks, they were linked to substantial parts of their retinues by shared natal, ethnic, and past service associations. Amir Khusrau and Ibn Battuta do not hesitate to highlight the Turko-Mongol antecedents of Ghiasuddin Tughluq. In contrast, Ziauddin Barani, a prominent representative of the Persian literati, not only concealed the controversial social origins of Ghiasuddin Tughluq, but also reinvented him as a saviour of Islam.[10]

Whatever be his social origin, Ghazi Malik, the administrator of Dipalpur, looked for support among rural intermediaries, tribal chiefs, and prominent Sufis. An opportunity came his way when he searched for a suitable bride for his brother Sipahsalar Rajab. On this matter, he sought the advice of Malik Saadul Mulk Shihab Afif (the great grandfather of the historian Afif), who was holding the charge of Abohar. It was learnt that Bibi Naila, the daughter of Rana Mal Bhatti, the chief (*rai*) of Abohar, was not only beautiful, but also possessed noble qualities. At this time, the tribes of Bhattis and Minhas inhabited the town of Abohar and its forested hinterland (*zamin jangal*) which was included in the administrative jurisdiction of Dipalpur. Ghazi Malik sent a marriage proposal to Rana Mal Bhatti who, owing to his alleged pride, rejected it and even used improper words. After a second round of consultations with Shihab Afif, Ghazi Malik changed his strategy. He entered the ancestral lands (*talwandi*) of the Bhatti chief and demanded the land tax in cash and that too in one single instalment (*maal salinah naqd talbeed*). Considerable pressure was exerted on the village headmen (*chaudharis* and *muqaddams*),[11] so that the entire population of Rana Mal Bhatti's domain was on the verge of destruction. But none dared to protest due to the fear of the authority wielded by Sultan Alauddin Khalji. In this crisis, the mother of Rana Mal Bhatti went to her son and narrated the tale of woes being suffered by the people of the locality. The lady told

Bibi Naila that she was the root cause of the crisis because, if she had not existed, Ghazi Malik would not have oppressed the people (*khalaiq*) in such a cruel manner. In order to diffuse the situation, Bibi Naila expressed her willingness to marry the brother of the oppressive governor and, while doing so, she urged every one to understand that the Mongols had abducted her (*bayad danist keh yak dukhtar ra mughlan burdand*). Pleased at her initiative, Rana Mal Bhatti conveyed the acceptance of the proposal through Shihab Afif. After the solemnization of the marriage, the bride was renamed Bibi Kadbanu and was escorted to Dipalpur.[12] After a few years in 1309, she gave birth to her only child, a son, who grew up to be Firoz Shah Tughluq. When he was seven, his father Sipahsalar Rajab died. Since Bibi Kadbanu was worried about the upbringing of her son, Ghazi Malik assured her that he would treat the boy as his own son and as a part of his own body until he himself was alive (*een farzand man ast wa jigar gosha man*).[13]

Since the promise was kept in its true spirit, Firoz did not suffer discrimination on account of being born of a Hindu Rajput mother. He was treated with utmost affection by his uncle, stepbrothers and cousins. He received appropriate education and training under the fraternal care of two kings, Ghiasuddin Tughluq and Muhammad bin Tughluq, so that he excelled his contemporaries in his knowledge of administrative affairs. From Ghiasuddin Tughluq, Firoz received the office of Naib Amir Hajib and the title of Naib Barbak. Muhammad bin Tughluq always kept Firoz by his side and instructed him in statecraft. When he divided his kingdom into four parts, he assigned one to Firoz so that he could understand the intricacies of governance. On account of these factors, Firoz was elevated to the throne, despite the presence of two elder step brothers, Malik Qutbuddin and Malik Naib Barbak, who were born of two other wives of Sipahsalar Rajab.[14] Firoz also enjoyed cordial relations with his mother's Rajput family. When he ascended the throne, a conspiracy was hatched by Khudawandzada Begum (the uterine sister of Muhammad bin Tughluq) to assassinate him. At this critical moment, the presence and support of his maternal uncle Rai Bhiru Bhatti was one of the factors that saved his life.[15] This little known man might have been living in the Tughluq household ever since his sister was married to Sipahsalar Rajab. When Firuz became the Sultan, he appeared to have shifted to the court in Delhi. It might be recalled that Sadhu and Sadharan, the zamindars of a locality near Thanesar, also shifted to Delhi as soon as their sister was married to Firoz, then a prince.[16]

Modern historians have attempted to understand the circumstances and implications of the above conjugal union. Agha Mahdi Husain has viewed it as a part of the trend of Muslim-Hindu marriages that occurred in the wake of territorial conquests by the Muslim rulers. He has cited the examples of the marriages of four Muslim rulers (Muhammad bin Qasim, Sultan Muizzuddin of Ghor, Alauddin Khalji and his son Khizr Khan) with the women of Hindu ruling houses. Husain observed that a combination of factors, the resolve of Muslim conquerors to settle in India, scarcity of women belonging to their own religion and a natural desire to increase their progeny, were the motives for these matrimonial alliances. Husain has hastened to point out that the marriage of Sipahsalar Rajab differed characteristically from its prototypes as it was personal and not political. He argued that the idea underlying this marriage was to overcome difficulties faced by a Muslim governor in securing the cooperation of the Hindus, to erase the causes of friction between the two religious communities and to remove from Muslim rule the stigma of being foreign. He believed that the favour conferred by Ghazi Malik on his sister-in-law was a matter of great significance.[17] Irfan Habib has viewed the entire episode as an advanced stage in the subversion of the older rural aristocracy, which was being transformed by the Delhi Sultanatate into a class of intermediaries, so essential for the extraction of agricultural surplus from the countryside.[18] I feel that the episode is understandable in the context of the agararian reforms of Alauddin Khalji – rule of measurement and yield per unit of area (*hukm-i masahat wa wafa-i biswa*) – which was imposed in a vast area extending from Dipalpur and Lahore in the west to Kara in the east. The governor could achieve this difficult task by making a demonstration of force in the countryside, taking care to minimise human suffering. He saw the measure sufficient for the implementation of the new rules of agrarian taxation, but found it expedient to blunt the sharp edge of coercion by establishing kinship with the dominant local elements.

The episode provides other interesting insights into the process of state formation in the Delhi Sultanate and social relations between the officers posted in Panjab. The relationship of mutual trust enabled them to control the rural population of peasants, headmen and chiefs. The professional and formal relations were cemented by kinship and informal ties. In this case, Shihab Afif served Ghazi Malik not only by providing information regarding the locality of Abohar, but also offered valuable advice on personal matters. He was as an intermediary in the negotiations between the district governor and the local chief, which culminated in a marriage alliance between the two. The relation between a high-ranking officer and his subordinate was extended to the woman members of the two households. It was recalled that Firoz and the son of Shihab Afif were born on the same day. The women of Shihab Afif's family often visited the Tughluq household at Dipalpur. Thus conditions were created in which Firoz was fed on her milk by the wife of Shihab Afif. This emotional bond became an integral part of the psyche of Firoz. Even after half a century, Firoz was overpowered by nostalgia when he recalled in the presence of Afif's father and uncle that he (Firoz) had been fed by their grandmother.[19] Members of the ruling class not only developed intimate personal relations with deep emotional appeal, but also nourished and cherished them with care. In return for the perennial flow of Tughluq patronage, Shams Siraj Afif performed a great service for his patrons by writing the history of Firoz Shah Tughluq's reign in an idiom of unrestrained admiration.

Role of the Khokhars

When Ghazi Malik marched out from Dipalpur to fight againt Khusrau Khan, his retinue comprised of three elements – kinsmen, the Khokhars and non-indigenous tribesmen. His kinsmen included his son Malik Fakhruddin Juna (the future Muhammad bin Tughluq), a son-in-law Malik Shadi, two nephews Asaduddin

Arslan and Bahauddin Gurshasp, and two subordinates Yusuf and Ali Haidar. The Khokhars of Koh-i-Jud, who had offered tough resistance to the Delhi Sultanate during the middle of the thirteenth century, were firmly ranged behind Ghazi Malik. Amir Khusrau merely mentions the presence of a large number of Khokhars in the army of Ghazi Malik, but Isami has described the crucial role of the Khokhars in the Dipalpur-Delhi military conflict, with particular focus on the feats of two Khokhar chiefs Gul Chand and Sahij Rai. Amir Khusrau has drawn our attention to the non-indigenous tribes. According to him, Ghazi Malik's troops were not drawn from the Hindustanis or Hindu chiefs. Instead, they came from the upper country (*iqlim-i bala*) that embraced Khurasan and Transoxiana. They comprised the Ghuzz, Turks, Mongols of Rum and Rus, besides the Khurasani Taziks of pure stock. Skilled in warfare, they were entirely devoted to their master Ghazi Malik.[20] A penetrating analysis of the social background of these tribes has provided interesting results. The Ghuzz and Turkoman pastoralists, who nomadized in the tract of Afghanistan, Transoxiana and Khurasan, were often in conflict with the Saljuqs, Ghaznavids, and Ghorids. The reference to the Turks pointed to the loose confederacy of the Qipchaq Turks who, owing to the invasions of Chingez Khan, had scattered over a vast region between eastern Europe and northwestern India. They formed the dominant Turkish group in the political dispensation of Iltutmish. The Mongols of Rum and Rus were the Mongols who had occupied the Qipchaq region, then under the rule of the Golden Horde. This large body included the Qaraunahs (Neguderids), a group to which Ghazi Malik belonged.[21] During his long service in the frontier areas, Ghazi Malik had welded diverse groups – his kinsmen, the Khokhars and non-indigenous tribes – into an efficient military machine which, under his generalship, had carried out a protracted military offensive against the Mongols.

The dependence of Ghazi Malik on the above elements increased when he failed to get the support of fellow officers posted in different parts of northwestern India. He had sent letters seeking assistance from the governors of Uch, Multan, Samana, Sind and Jalor.[22] Except Bahram Aiba of Uch, all the governors refused and showed an inclination to oppose him. Malik Mughalti, the governor of Multan, could not tolerate the audacity of the administrator of Dipalpur, which was merely a dependency of Multan. Though he had adequate treasure, he could not rise against Delhi in the absence of an army. Incensed at his bitter reply, Ghazi Malik instigated through Bahram Siraj a petty rebellion against Malik Mughalti, who tried to save his life by jumping into a canal, only to be caught and beheaded by his opponents.[23] Malik Yaklakhi, the governor of Samana, sent Ghazi Malik's letter to Khusrau Khan and marched out to fight the challenger. Defeated in the battlefield, he fell back on Samana where he was killed by some disgruntled local people.[24] Muhammad Shah Lur, the governor of Sind, was facing an insurrection from his own officers. On receiving Ghazi Malik's letter, he patched up with the rebels. He sent a promise to join the army of Ghazi Malik but, owing to the delay of his movement, reached Delhi only when the Tughluq warlord had ascended the throne. Hoshang (the son of Kamaluddin Gurg), who held the governorship of Jalor, reached Delhi only when the final battle had taken place.[25] Ain ul-Mulk Multani, who was the governor of Malwa, showed Ghazi Malik's letter to Khusrau Khan and thus proved his loyalty to the new ruler. However, he conveyed a message through an emissary that, as soon as hostilities irrupted, he would appear before Ghazi Malik who could kill him or forgive him.[26]

The attitude of the provincial governors indicated that they were not willing to challenge the new regime in Delhi, even if it was weak and unpopular. In fact, two of them fought for it and, in the process, laid down their lives. Two others initially decided to fight against the new dispensation but, on second thoughts, developed cold feet. Still another expressed his allegiance to the new government, but ultimately decided to sit on the fence. The provincial governors, driven by the instinct of survival, did not take sides until the political situation remained fluid. Ghazi Malik appreciated their predicament and, on assuming power, did not act against his former colleagues who had failed to keep their promises.

The Dipalpur rebellion assumed a clear shape as soon as Ghazi

Malik was joined by his son Malik Fakhruddin Juna, who had fled from Delhi with servants, horses, and Bahram Aiba's son.[27] While Ghazi Malik emerged from Dipalpur, he learnt that a caravan carrying the revenues of Sind and numerous horses for the Sultan of Delhi was travelling from Multan to Delhi. Ghazi Malik plundered the caravan and distributed the booty among his soldiers.[28] He established his control over the territory extending up to Sarsuti, which was placed under his trusted lieutenant Mahmud. Khusrau Khan deputed his brother Khan-i Khanan at the head of a large army to quell the challenge. Mahmud fought against the Delhi forces from within the fort, but could not prevent it from ravaging the surrounding villages.[29] Ghazi Malik, advancing via Alapur, reached Hauz-i Behat. Meanwhile Khan-i Khanan crossed a waterless jungle during the night and suddenly appeared before the opposing troops. In the plain of Sarsuti, Ghazi Malik took position in the centre of his army. The Khokhars, who were led by Gul Chand, formed the vanguard. Bahram commanded the left wing, while Asaduddin held the right wing. As soon as the action began, the Khokhars made a furious charge on the rival force, which was paralysed and scattered. The Khokhars attacked the captain of the rival vanguard and, pulling him down from his horse, cut off his head. As the Delhi army began to flee, the Khokhars wrought havoc with their swords and arrows. Gul Chand charged at the Khan-i Khanan and, killing his parasol bearer, sent his head to Ghazi Malik. In a spontaneous action, Gul Chand snatched the parasol and raised it over the head of Ghazi Malik,[30] thereby anticipating the decision of the great nobles at Delhi. In a dramatic manner, Ghazi Malik received his first symbol of royalty from the hands of a Khokhar chief, who had also distinguished himself in the battlefield.

As a result of this success, Ghazi Malik acquired firm control of the territory up to Hansi. He adopted a cautious approach and refrained from alienating any section of society. He not only forgave prisoners of war, but also returned a ransom of 6 lakh *tankas* that had been extracted by his men from a caravan of grain merchants. As he marched to Delhi, he passed through such places as Madina, Rohtak, Mandoti, and Palam. He pushed across the hills

New Strategies of State Formation 231

of Aravalli and, advancing through Kasanpur and Hauz-i Sultani, camped at the plain of Lahrawat between the Jamuna and the city of Delhi.[31] The reports of Ghazi Malik's march and the flight of the vanquished from Sarsuti to Delhi caused a breakdown of administrative order. The areas around the capital were subjected to chaos and plunder. Khusrau Khan upbraided his commanders for a poor showing against Ghazi Malik at Sarsuti.[32] He consulted his close advisors on the future course of action. Some nobles asked him to make peace with Ghazi Malik by offering him the territory north of Hansi that was, in fact, already in his control. Others urged him to act like a king and order a free distribution of treasure, so as to widen his base of support.[33] Rejecting these proposals, Khusrau Khan mustered his forces at Hauz Khas for fresh resistance.[34] His retinue comprised such prominent men as Yusuf Khan Sufi, Kamaluddin Sufi, Shaista Khan, Kafur Muhardar, Shihab and Bahauddin. Besides the Khan-i Khanan, Rai Rayan Randhol and Hatim Khan, there were officers who had risen from slavery to nobility. A strong contingent of 10,000 Baradus came out with distinctive banners under captains like Ahar Dev, Amar Dev, Narsiya, Parsiya, Harmar, Parmar and others. Looked at in totality, half of the soldiers were Hindu and the other half Muslim.[35]

The second battle between the contenders was fought in Delhi near the Bagh-i Jud. In the battlefield,[36] Ghazi Malik placed himself in the centre, while in front of him stood Ali Haidar and Sahij Rai. Gul Chand, the hero of the previous battle, led the vanguard along with all the Khokhars. Asaduddin, the nephew of Ghazi Malik, commanded the right wing along with Shadi, Malik Fakhruddin and Shihab Jashghuri. Bahauddin, the sister's son of Ghazi Malik, was stationed on the left wing with Bahram Aiba. At the outset, the Delhi army secured the upper hand, as Qabula fired a volley of arrows and a fierce Baradu charge forced two captains, Malik Fakhruddin and Shihab Jashghuri, to withdraw. Though Asaduddin overpowered Bughra Khan, the Delhi army still appeared to be moving towards victory. Shasti Khan rushed towards Ghazi Malik's camp, cut down the ropes of the tent and proclaimed the flight of the challenger. Ghazi Malik rallied his leading men – Gul Chand, Bahram Aiba and Bahauddin – to the centre and resorted to a new tactic. A contingent of one hundred warriors, headed by Gul Chand, was deputed to attack the rear of the opponents. Ghazi Malik made a sharp assault from the front and, thus, turned the tide of the battle. Khusrau Khan sought refuge in flight amidst terrible losses. Gul Chand pursued the fugitives and, while doing so, repeated the act he had performed at Sarsuti. He caught up with the rival parasol bearer (*chhatardar mukhalif*) and slashed his head from behind. He seized the parasol and presented it to Ghazi Malik. The victors acquired the keys of two forts from the police chief (*kotwal*) of Delhi.[37] Thus the Khokhar chiefs and their retinue played a decisive role in Ghazi Malik's campaign against Khusrau Khan and the establishment of the Tughluq dynasty at Delhi.

In their ongoing search for allies, the Tughluqs chose the shrine of Baba Farid (1175-1265) at Pakpattan, not far from Dipalpur where Ghazi Malik had lived for more than two decades. Apart from imparting teaching in mysticism, Baba Farid developed a tradition of Islamic devotionalism based on the *tawiz-futuh* system. A large number of devotees visited the shrine to receive amulets (*tawiz*) which were supposed to cure physical ailments, a protection against evil or a boon for good fortune. For their part, the devotees made offerings (*futuh*), generally in the form of kind that were distributed among the visitors. After the demise of Baba Farid, a series of rituals – death anniversary of the saint (*urs*), community kitchen (*langar*), devotional singing (*qawwali*), succession to the spiritual seat (*dastar bandi*) and annual entry to the sanctum sanctorum through the southern door (*bahishti darwaza*) – were gradually institutionalized.[38] The Tughluq household, which was based in the neighbouring town of Dipalpur, could not remain immune from the growing popularity of the shrine in the countryside of central and southwestern Panjab. During his governorship of Dipalpur, Ghazi Malik was reported to have visited the shrine along with his son Muhammad and nephew Firoz, both of whom were minors. At this time, Shaikh Alauddin (1281-1334), the grandson of Baba Farid, was the spiritual head of the shrine. He offered a piece of unsewn cotton cloth (*jama-i kirpas ghair dokhta*) to each of the three visitors – four and a half yards to Ghazi Malik, twenty seven yards to Muhammad and the remaining forty yards to Firoz. He directed them to tie the cloth (turbans) around their heads and prophesied that all three would be crowned as the rulers (*sahib-i taj wa takht*) of the kingdom.[39] This tradition registered that there was a long association between the Tughluq dynasty and the Chishti order, that it was the spiritual charisma (*baraka*) of the saint which had granted sovereign power to the Tughluqs and that the saint had metaphorically predicted the duration of their respective reigns by the length of the turbans given as gift.

There is no evidence about the exact nature of Ghazi Malik's patronage to the shrine of Baba Farid. During the reign of Muhammad bin Tughluq (r. 1325-51), the patronage of the shrine was increased in magnitude and diversified in form. The Sultan took pride in regarding himself as the disciple of Shaikh Alauddin. After the death of the Shaikh, he constructed a magnificent mausoleum at the grave of the deceased in the shrine complex. The Sultan also appointed a son of Shaikh Alauddin, Shaikh Muizzuddin, as the governor of Gujarat. What was more important, the Sultan bestowed the entire town of Ajodhan (Pakpattan) on the shrine as an endowment. He appointed Shaikh Alamuddin, the younger son of Shaikh Alauddin, as Shaikh ul-Islam and, in this role, supervised numerous Sufi establishments. After the demise of Shaikh Alamuddin, the Sultan conferred the office of Shaikh ul-Islam on the Shaikh's son Shaikh Mazharuddin.[40] The Sultan also patronized the Kirmani family, which was devoted to Shaikh Nizamuddin Auliya. Syed Kamaluddin Amir Ahmad, the son of Syed Muhammad Kirmani and uncle of Amir Khurd, was appointed as advisor to the Sultan with the title of Malik Muazzam. Syed Qutbuddin Husain Kirmani, another son of Syed Muhammad Kirmani, went to Daulatabad on the request of the *wazir* Khwaja-i Jahan Ahmad Ayaz. Khwaja Karimuddin Samarqandi, a disciple of Shaikh Nizamuddin Auliya, was granted the title of Shaikh ul-Islam and Anwar Rai Malik Satgaon and was deputed to Satgaon for administrative work.[41]

Observations of Ibn Battuta

At a time when the Tughluq rulers were implementing new strategies of administrative conrol, Ibn Battuta travelled through Panjab. During a period of nearly three decades (1325-53), the celebrated Arab traveller covered a vast area extending from Morocco to Java. The first eight years of his travels enabled him to move across north Africa, Egypt, Syria, Asia Minor, Arabia and Persia. Passing through Central Asia and Afghanistan, he reached Sind in the middle of 1333 and spent the next ten years on the Indian soil. He pushed northwards from Lahri and Bhakkar, entering Panjab through the southern route. He took six months (October 1333 to March 1334) to travel through Panjab on his way to Delhi. During this leg of his journey, he visited Uch, Multan, Ajodhan, Abohar, Abu Bakhar, Sarsuti, Hansi and Masudabad. He has described the mechanism developed by the Delhi Sultanate to receive distinguished foreigners and escort them to the capital. He took a keen interest in the functioning of the provincial administration under Qutb ul-Mulk. Apart from visiting the famous Sufi shrines in southwestern Panjab, he met the leading saints of the Chishti and Suhrawardi orders. He described the flora and fauna, the state of urban centres and safety of roads. Marked by richness and authenticity, his observations yielded information that was not available in any other contemporary source. Therefore, it would be appropriate to follow his account of Panjab.[42]

Travelling from the city of Bhakkar, Ibn Battuta arrived on 24 October 1333 at Uch. It was a big and well-built city, which lay on the Indus and had fine bazaars and new buildings. At that time, its governor (*amir*) was the learned Malik Sharif Jalaluddin Kiji, who was brave as well as generous. He died in this city due to a fall from his horse. A friendship grew between Ibn Battuta and this noble Sharif Jalaluddin. This relation developed into deep ties of mutual love and affection. Later they met in the capital of the Delhi Sultanate. When the Sultan (Muhammad bin Tughluq) left for Daulatabad and directed Ibn Battuta to remain at the capital, Sharif Jalaluddin said to him, 'You will need a large sum of money for your expenses and the Sultan will be absent for a long time. You should take over my village and use its revenues till I return.' Ibn Battuta did so and utilized an amount of about 5,000 *dinars* from it. He prayed that God might grant a rich recompense to the noble for this kind gesture. At Uch, he met the devout, pious and venerable Shaikh Qutbuddin Haidar Alavi, who invested him with a patched robe. This garment remained in his possession till the time it was seized by Hindu pirates on the sea.

From Uch, Ibn Battuta travelled to Multan, capital of Sind and the residence of its governor (*amir ul-umara*). On the road to Multan and ten miles distant from it ran the river called Khusrauabad. It was one of the great rivers that could not be crossed except by boat. At this spot, the passengers were subjected to a rigorous examination and their luggage was inspected. At the time of the arrival of Ibn Battuta and his party, it was the practice at Multan for the state to take one fourth of the commodities brought by the merchants and to levy a duty of 7 *dinars* for every horse.[43] Two years after their arrival in India, the Sultan remitted these taxes. He ordered that nothing should be realized from the merchants except the alms tax (*zakat*) and a tenth of the produce (*ushr*). This measure was taken when the Sultan took the oath of allegiance to Abul Abbas, the Abbasid caliph. When they were about to cross this river and the luggage began to be inspected, Ibn Battuta was aggrieved by this search of his luggage. Though it did not contain much that was valuable, it seemed a great deal in the eyes of the people. He did not like his belongings to be examined. By the grace of God, one of the principal military officers of Qutb ul-Mulk, the governor of Multan, arrived on the scene and gave orders that his luggage should not be subjected to scrutiny. It happened exactly like that. Ibn Battuta thanked God for the favours that were conferred on him. They spent the night on the bank of the river. Next morning, the postal superintendent (*malik ul-barid*) named Dihqan came to visit them. Originally hailing from Samarqand, this man used to write to the Sultan, informing him of all happenings in the city and its dependencies, including the arrival of travellers. Ibn Battuta was introduced to him and, in his company, he went to visit the governor of Multan.

The governor of Multan was Qutb ul-Mulk, who was one of the greatest and most learned of the nobles. When Ibn Battuta went up to him, Qutb ul-Mulk rose to receive him and, shaking hands with him, offered a seat to him by his side. Ibn Battuta presented him with a slave and a horse, besides some raisins and almonds. They were among the greatest of presents that could be made to an Indian noble, since they were imported from Khurasan. The governor sat on a high dais embellished by large carpets. By his side, sat a judge (*qazi*) named Salar and a preacher (*khatib*) whose name had been forgotten. On his right and left were ranged the military commanders, while armed men stood at his back. The troops passed before him in review. Many bows were found there. When anyone desirous of being enlisted as an archer appeared, he was given one of the bows to pull. The bows differed in strength and the salary of the candidate was fixed in accordance with the strength displayed by him in pulling the bow. If anyone desired to be enlisted in the cavalry, a target was set in the form of a drum. He put his horse into a run and tried to hit it with a lance. There was also a ring that was suspended from a low wall. The candidate made his horse run until he came at level with the ring. If he succeeded in lifting the ring with his lance, he was considered an excellent horseman. If the candidate desired to be enlisted as a mounted archer, a ball was placed on the ground. He galloped on horseback and aimed his arrow at the ball. His salary was fixed in proportion to his accuracy in striking the ball.

Ibn Battuta and his party waited on the governor and offered their salutations. The governor issued orders for them to be lodged outside the city in a house which belonged to the disciples of Shaikh Ruknuddin Abul Fateh. As a rule, the governor did not extend hospitality to anyone until orders were received from the Sultan to do so. Ibn Battuta has provided the names of a number of foreigners who were then present in Multan and had arrived as visitors to the court of the Sultan. Among them, the first was Khudawandzada Qiwamuddin, the *qazi* of Tirmiz, who had come with his womenfolk and children. While in Multan, he was joined by his three brothers Imaduddin, Ziauddin and Burhanuddin.

The second was Mabarak Shah, a notable of Samarqand. The third was Arun Bugha, one of the great men of Bokhara. The fourth was Malikzada, a son of the sister of Khudawandzada. The fifth was Badruddin Fassal. Each one of them had come with companions, servants and followers.

Two months after the arrival of Ibn Battuta and his party in Multan,[44] there came Shamsuddin Fushanji who was one of the chamberlains as well as Malik Muhammad Harvi who was the police chief. They had been sent by the Sultan to receive and escort Khudawandzada. They were accompanied by three waiters (eunuchs) who had been sent by Malika-i Jahan, the Sultan's mother, to receive the wife of Khudawandzada. They had also brought robes of honour for the two and their children. They had been commissioned to furnish provisions to all the visitors for the journey. All of them together came to Ibn Battuta and asked him the object of his visit. He told them that he had come to remain in the service of the master of the world (*khund alam*), the title by which the Sultan was known in his dominions. The Sultan had issued orders that no one coming from Khurasan should be allowed to enter Indian territory unless he came with the intention of staying here. When Ibn Battuta told them that he had come with the object of staying, they sent for the judge (*qazi*) and notaries (*udul*). He was made to write a bond in his name and in the names of those in his company who desired to stay.[45] However, some of his companions refused to bind themselves in an undertaking.

Ibn Battuta and his party prepared to travel to the capital, which lay at a distance of a forty days' journey through continuously inhabited (fertile) land. The chamberlain and his companion made the necessary arrangements for feeding Khudawandzada Qiwamuddin and, for this purpose, took about twenty cooks from Multan. The chamberlain used to go ahead during the night to the next station, so as to secure provisions so that when Khudawandzada arrived his meals were ready. Each of the visitors, who had been named above, used to stay in separate tents along with their companions. Sometimes they joined in the meals prepared for Khudawandzada. As for Ibn Battuta, he attended such an occasion only once. Food was served in accordance with the following order.

To begin with, loaves were served that were very thin and resembled cakes of bread. Then they cut the roasted meat into large pieces in a manner that one sheep yielded four to six pieces. One piece was served to each person. They also made round cakes of bread soaked in ghee that resembled the bread called *mushrak* in Morocco and in its midst they placed a sweet called *sabunia*. On the top of every piece of bread, they placed a sweet cake called *khishti*, meaning shaped like a brick, which was made of flour, sugar and ghee. Then they served in large porcelain bowls meat cooked in ghee, onions and green ginger. After this, they served something called *samosa* (*samusak*) which was minced meat cooked with almonds, walnuts, pistachios, onions and spices and then placed inside a thin bread and fried in ghee. They placed four or five such pieces before every person. Then was brought a dish of rice cooked in ghee on the top of which was put a roasted fowl. Next, they brought a sweet called *luqaimat-i qazi*, which was known as *hashimi* and followed it up by a pudding known as *al-qahiriya*. Before the food was served, the chamberlain stood at the head of the dinner carpet (*simat*) and performed a bow (*khidmat*) in whichever direction the Sultan was. This action was followed by all those present. In India, this homage consisted in bowing upto the knees as was done in prayer. When they had done this, they sat down to eat. Then they brought the cups of gold, silver and glass. These were filled with sugared water perfumed with rose water. They called it sherbet and drank it before eating. As soon as they consumed the *sherbet*, the chamberlain called out *Bismillah* which was a signal for them to start eating. At the end of the dinner, they were given jugs of barley water (*fuqqa*). When these had been consumed, betel leaves and areca nuts were served.[46] After the people had taken betel and areca, the chamberlain called out *Bismillah*, whereupon they stood up and, bowing in the same manner as before, retired from the spot.

Ibn Battuta and his companions travelled out from the city of

Multan and, until their arrival in the country of Hindustan, they pursued the journey in the same order as described. The first town that they entered was that of Abohar. It was the first of the towns of Hind. It was small, pretty and thickly populated, besides possessing rivers and trees. Of the trees of Morocco, there was none except the zizyphus lotus (*nabq*) which was found here. But the Indian one was very large. Its stone was equal in volume to that of the gall nut and was very sweet. The Indians had many trees that were not found in Morocco or any other country.

One of the fruits of the country was mango. Its tree was like that of orange, though bigger in size with larger number of leaves. Its shade was dense, but it was unhealthy. Who ever slept under it was seized with fever. The fruit of the tree was as large as a big pear. When the fruit was green and not yet fully ripe, the people gathered those that fell from the trees. They sprinkled salt on them and pickled them just as limes and lemons were treated in Morocco. The Indians also pickled green ginger and clusters of pepper in the same way. They ate these pickles with their food, taking after each mouthful a little of the pickles. When the mango ripened during autumn (*kharif*), its fruit became yellow and then they ate it like an apple, some cutting it with a knife and others sucking it to finish. The fruit was sweet, but its sweetness was mingled with a little sourness. It had a large stone that was sown like the orange pip and some other fruit stones, so that the trees sprouted from them.

Then there were the jack trees (*Artocarpus integrifolia*), which were known as *shaki* and *barki* and lived up to a great age. Their leaves looked like those of the walnut and the fruit grew out of the trunk of the tree. The fruit that was near the soil was called *barki*; it was sweeter and had a more agreeable flavour. The fruit that appeared on the upper part was called *shaki*; it resembled a large pumpkin with skin like the hide of a cow. When it became yellow during autumn it was plucked and split in half. Inside each fruit were found a hundred to two hundred pods resembling the cucumber, between each of which there was a thin yellow skin. Each pod had a kernel resembling a large bean and, when these kernels were roasted or boiled, they tasted like beans, though beans were not found in this country. These stone-like kernels were preserved in reddish earth and lasted till the following year. This *shaki* and *barki* was the best fruit in India.

The next fruit *tendu* (*Diospyros peregrine*) was yielded by the ebony tree. Each fruit had the size and colour of the apricot and was very sweet. Next fruit was the jambol (*jamun*). Its tree was large and the fruit resembled the olives. It was black in colour and like the olive had one stone. The sweet orange (*naranj*) was abundant in India. But the sour orange was rare. There was a third kind of orange that was midway between the sweet and sour. As large as the sweet lime, its taste was excellent and, therefore, Ibn Battuta loved to eat it. Another fruit was the *mahuwa* (*Madhuka latifolia*). Living up to a great age, its leaves were like those of the walnut, except that they were of a red and yellow colour. The fruit resembled a small pear. It was extremely sweet in taste. In the upper part of the fruit was a small hollow seed as big as that of the grape. It resembled the grape in taste, but gave a splitting headache when eaten in large numbers. What was astonishing, when its seeds were dried in the sun, they tasted like figs. Ibn Battuta ate these instead of the figs that were not found in India. They called this fruit *angur*, which in their language meant grapes. However, grape was very rare in India, being found only in some parts of Delhi and a few other provinces. As for *mahuwa*, it yielded fruit twice a year. Oil was made out of its stone that was used for lighting.

Among the Indian trees there was still another called the *kasera*. It was extracted out of the earth. It was very sweet and resembled the chestnut. Of the trees that grew in Morocco, they found the pomegranate in India. It bore fruit twice a year. In the Maldives, Ibn Battuta saw a variety that never stopped bearing fruit. The Indians called it *anar*. But according to our informant, this must be the origin of the word *julnar*, because *jul* in Persian meant a flower and *nar* stood for the pomegranate.

The Indians sowed the earth twice a year. In summer,[47] when the rains fell, they sowed the autumn crop and harvested it sixty days after sowing. Following were the autumn crops – (1) The *kudhru*, which was a kind of millet, was found most abundantly of all the grains. (2) The *qal* which was like the *anli*. (3) The *shamakh* was another crop whose seeds were smaller than those of the *qal*. It often grew without being cultivated. It was the staple food of the devout, abstainers, poor and humble who went out to gather this corn that sprang up on its own. Each of them held a huge basket in his left hand and in his right hand a whip with which he struck the corn that fell into the basket. In this way, they were able to collect enough of it to provide them with food for the whole year. The seed of the *shamakh* was very small. When it had been gathered, it was placed in the sun and pounded in wooden mortars. Its husk flew away and, with the remaining white substance, they made a gruel by cooking it with buffalo's milk. This gruel was more pleasant to eat than the bread made of the same substance. Ibn Battuta often ate it in India and relished its taste. (4) The mash was a species of peas. (5) The *mung* was a kind of *mash*, but differed from it in having a longer seed and a bright green colour. The *mung* was cooked with rice and accompanied with ghee when eaten. This dish, known as *kishri* (*khichri*), was taken for breakfast every morning. It was to the Indians what *harira* was to the people of Morocco. (6) The *lobiya* was a kind of bean. (7) The *mut* (*Cyperus rotundus*) was like *kudhru* except that its seeds were smaller. In India it formed a part of the fodder given to draught animals and they grew fat by eating the same. Since barley in this country was not regarded as nourishing, the fodder for animals consisted of *mut* or chick peas, which was fed to them after being pounded and soaked in water. Instead of the green fodder, the animals were given mash leaves after each had been fed for ten days on 3 or 4 pounds (*ratls*) of ghee per day and during this period they were not ridden. After this interval, they were given *mash* leaves to eat for a month or so.

The grains mentioned above were autumn crops. When these were harvested sixty days after being sown, the spring grains – wheat, barley chickpeas and lentils – were sown in the same soil in which the autumn crops had been raised, for their country was excellent and the soil was fertile. As for the rice, they sowed it three times a year and it was one of their principal cereals. They also cultivated sesame and sugarcane at the same time as the autumn crops that had been mentioned above.

Ibn Battuta and his party travelled from the city of Abohar through a desert that would take one day to cross.[48] Along its borders were inaccessible mountains inhabited by the Hindus, who frequently held up the travellers and made the roads unsafe. A majority of the inhabitants of India were infidels (Hindus). Some of them were subject people under the protection of the Muslim rule and lived in villages. They were placed under a Muslim officer (*hakim*) who was under a tax collector (*amil* or *khadim*) who held the village in his fief (*iqta*). Others were rebels who were at war. They fortified themselves in the mountains and waylaid the people.

At this juncture, Ibn Battuta has narrated the experience of his first armed encounter in India. When he and his entourage prepared to set out from Abohar, the main party left the town in the early morning, but he stayed there with a small group of his companions until midday. When the latter ultimately came out, they numbered twenty two horsemen, some of whom were Arabs and some non-Arabs. In that desert (open country) they were attacked by eighty infidels (Hindus) on foot and two horsemen. The companions of Ibn Battuta put up a valiant fight. They killed as many as twelve footmen and one horseman, taking away the latter's horse as booty. Ibn Battuta was struck by an arrow, while his horse was hit by another. But God in His grace rescued them, as the arrows of the attackers did not have much force. A horse belonging to one of his companions was wounded. They replaced it with a horse captured from a Hindu. The wounded horse was slaughtered by the accompanying Turks who ate it. They carried the heads of the slain to the fortress of Abu Bakhar and hung them from the city wall. They reached the fortress at midnight.

After a journey of two days from this place, Ibn Battuta and his party arrived at Ajodhan,[49] a small town belonging to the pious Shaikh Fariduddin of Badaun, about whom the pious Shaikh Burhanuddin Araj had foretold at Alexandria that the Moroccoan would meet him. Accordingly the traveller met him and thanked God for this favour. Shaikh Fariduddin was the spiritual guide of the king of India (Muhammad bin Tughluq) who had bestowed this city on him. But the Shaikh was afflicted with an apprehension of the uncleanliness of others. This was something for which Ibn Battuta sought the protection of God. He never shook hands with anyone, nor did he go near anyone. As soon as his robe brushed against the garment of any other person, he washed it.[50] Ibn Battuta entered his hospice and, having met him, conveyed to him the greetings of Shaikh Burhanuddin. The Shaikh was astonished at this and said, 'I am not worthy of the greetings you have conveyed.' Ibn Battuta also met his two virtuous sons. The elder one was Muizzuddin who, after the death of his father, succeeded to the dignity of sainthood. The younger son was Alamuddin. Ibn Battuta visited the tomb of his grandfather, the pious pole (*qutb*) of spirituality, Shaikh Fariduddin of Badaun, so called due to his connection with Badaun, the chief town of Sambhal. When Ibn Battuta was about to leave Ajodhan, Alamuddin asked him not to go without seeing his father. Ibn Battuta did so. At that time, the Shaikh was on his terrace, clothed in a white robe and wearing a big turban on his head the end of which was hanging on one side. He blessed the visitor and sent a present of some candy and refined sugar.

When he left the Shaikh (Alauddin Mauj-i Darya), Ibn Battuta saw people hurrying out of their camp along with some of his companions. He asked them what the matter was. He was told that a Hindu had died, that a fire had been kindled to burn him and that his wife was going to burn herself along with him. When both had been consumed by fire, his companions returned and told him that the woman had held the dead man in her arms until she was burnt along with him.[51] Later on, Ibn Battuta used to see in the country Hindu women adorned and seated on horseback and, being followed by the Muslims as well as Hindus. Drums and bugles played before her and the Brahmins, who were the great ones among the Hindus, accompanied her. When this happened in the territory of the Sultan, they sought his permission to burn the widow. The Sultan gave his permission and they burnt her.

After giving an account of the burning of three widows at Amjeri (Central India), Ibn Battuta returned to his original theme. He and his party set out from Ajodhan and, after a journey of four days, arrived at Sarsuti. A large city, it produced huge quantities of rice of an excellent quality that was exported to the capital, Delhi. Sarsuti yielded an enormous amount of revenue. Shamsuddin Fushanji, the chamberlain, indicated the exact amount, but Ibn Battuta could not remember it. Thereafter, the group travelled to Hansi, which was an exceedingly fine, well built and thickly populated city. It was surrounded by a huge boundary wall, whose builder was said to be one of the great infidel kings called Tura,[52] about whom a number of tales and stories were told. Kamaluddin Sadr-i Jahan, the chief justice (*qazi-ul-quzat*) of India and his brother Qutlugh Khan, who was the tutor of the Sultan (Muhammad bin Tughluq) as well as their brothers Nizamuddin and Shamsuddin traced their origin to this city. Shamsuddin, who had renounced the world and had devoted his life to the service of God, took up residence in Mecca until he died.[53] Ibn Battuta and his party journeyed from Hansi and after two days reached Masudabad, which lay at a distance of 10 miles from the capital, Delhi. They stayed there for three days. Both Hansi and Masudabad belonged to the great noble Malik Hoshang, the son of Kamaluddin Gurg. By Gurg was meant wolf. The traveller promised to offer an account of Kamaluddin Gurg later on.

The Sultan of India, whose capital Ibn Battuta and his party intended to visit, was away in the suburbs of Kanauj, ten days' march from Delhi. In the capital were present the Sultan's mother called Makhduma-i Jahan and his *wazir* Khwaja-i Jahan named Ahmad bin Ayaz, a man of Turkish (Rumi) origin. The *wazir* sent his officers to meet the visitors and nominated persons of equal rank to receive each one. Among those appointed to receive Ibn Battuta were Shaikh Bistami and Sharif Mazandrani, the chamberlain of foreigners (*hajib ul-ghuraba*) and the jurist (*faqih*) Alauddin Multani who was commonly known as Qunnara. The *wazir* sent the news of the arrival of the visitors to the Sultan in the form of a letter, which was carried by the courier post (*dawa*). This letter reached the Sultan and a reply from him came during the three days that Ibn Battuta and party spent at Masudabad.[54] After three days, a number of eminent people – judges, jurists, Sufis and some nobles (*amirs*) – came to receive the visitors. In India, the nobles were known as *maliks*, while in Egypt and other countries they were known as *amirs*. Shaikh Zahiruddin Zanjani, who held a high position in the court of the Sultan, also came to receive the visitors. Thereafter Ibn Battuta and party set out from Masudabad and encamped in the vicinity of the village called Palam, which belonged to Syed Nasiruddin Mutahr ul-Auhari, one of the confidants of the Sultan and those who enjoyed great favour with him. Next morning, the visitors reached Delhi, the imperial residence and capital of India. It was a vast and magnificent city. Its buildings were both beautiful and solid. It was surrounded by a boundary wall that was not known in any country of the world. It was the largest city in India, rather the largest of all the cities of Islam in the east.

Weaving Local Linkages

Firoz Shah Tughluq, who accepted the position of Sultan at Thatta on 24 March 1351, marched from Siwistan to Delhi. During the course of this journey, he passed through the towns of southern Panjab. He availed the opportunity to win over various sections of the society, important for him in view of the opposition of Khwaja-i Jahan to his accession in Delhi. As he entered a town, he would take measures to visit the old Sufi shrines (*mazars*), revive the crumbling hospices (*khanqahs*), give assurances of support to the descendants of the dead Sufis, confirm land grants on former beneficiaries, and provided stipends to the poor and needy in general. When he was travelling from Bhakkar to Uch, the Sultan received groups of people from Multan including Sufis, theologians, eminent citizens, rural intermediaries (*zamindars*), village headmen (*muqaddams*) and ordinary folk. Accepting their petitions, the Sultan confirmed land grants conferred in the past and issued fresh orders (*farmans*) to them. In return, the applicants prayed for the success of their royal patron and returned home in contentment. On arrival at Uch, the Sultan favoured the inhabitants with land grants, stipends, allowances and livelihood that had been cancelled years ago. He revived the hospice of Shaikh Jamaluddin that had been virtually wiped out. The sons of the late Shaikh recovered their villages and orchards that had earlier been annexed to the crown lands (*khalisa*) and this Sufi lineage regained its former prestige.⁵⁵ So too on entering the city of Multan, the Sultan honoured the Sufis with rewards and presents.⁵⁶ The royal entourage stayed in Dipalpur for a few days to provide rest to the animals of the army. The Sultan went to Ajodhan to pay homage at the shrine of Baba Farid. He organized the affairs of the saint's family, which had fallen on bad days and had scattered to different places. The descendants of Shaikh Alauddin (the grandson of Baba Farid) were favoured with land grants (*imlak*), robes of honour (*khilats*) and rewards (*inam*). The inhabitants of Ajodhan received an enormous amount of charity in the form of stipends (*wazifa*) and livelihood (*nan*). In fact, the inhabitants of all the towns lying between Dipalpur and Delhi were issued orders confirming old and new stipends and pensions (*idrarat wa wazaif qadim wa jadeed*). Not only this, mendicants and destitute people (*fuqra wa maskinan*) living in these places were given cash allowances (*sadqat naqd*). Reiterating this point, Barani has recorded that the families of eminent Sufis (most of whom were based in Panjab) – Baba Farid, Shaikh Bahauddin Zakariya, Shaikh Ruknuddin Abul Fateh, Shaikh Nizamuddin Auliya and Shaikh Jamaluddin Uch – experienced a revival owing to the grant of villages, lands and orchards.⁵⁷

When Firoz Shah Tughluq and his army reached the town of Sarsuti,⁵⁸ Shaikh Nasiruddin Chiragh-i Delhi said to him, 'I have enabled the people to travel from Thatta to this place in safety on account of my prayers to God. From this place onwards, the jurisdiction of the spiritual domain (*vilayat*) of Shaikh Qutbuddin Munawwar starts. Send a suitable request to him in writing.' The Sultan informed Shaikh Munawwar that he had been directed to his care by Shaikh Nasiruddin Mahmud.⁵⁹ In a prompt reply, the Shaikh wrote, 'Since my brother Shaikh Nasiruddin has entrusted you to the care of this frail soul, I hope that Delhi will be captured with the grace of God.' The two Shaikhs, being the disciples of Shaikh Nizamuddin Auliya, were on intimate terms with each other. Shaikh Nasiruddin Mahmud had taken this step only to show the spiritual eminence of his colleague.⁶⁰ While the Sultan was marching from Multan to Delhi, large number of people –

nobles, horsemen, troopers and individuals from all walks of life – joined him and thirty-six principalities came under his control. Yet he relied on the blessings of Shaikh Munawwar for a favourable development,[61] as the political situation was still uncertain. When the Sultan secured the submission of Khwaja-i Jahan, the prophecy of Shaikh Munawwar–Delhi itself will come out to this place with folded hands – proved true. According to Afif, the Sultan succeeded in bringing Delhi under his authority even before actually arriving at the capital.[62]

As he reached Hansi,[63] the Sultan intended to meet Shaikh Munawwar, probably to thank him for his blessings. But he did not get the kind of reception which he might have anticipated. Unfortunately, he appeared at the door of the hospice at an inopportune moment when the Shaikh was leaving for the mosque to offer the Friday prayer. The Shaikh identified two faults of the Sultan that had to be given up. First, drinking alcohol was unacceptable. Sultan could not protect the people placed under his care. Second, his indulgence in hunting was undesirable, as it was not proper to kill innocent living beings beyond a certain limit. The Sultan requested the Shaikh to pray for him, so that God kept him away from these bad habits. The Shaikh left the scene abruptly, remarking that the Sultan had ignored his advice by failing to repent. Soon after, both went to the mosque to offer the Friday prayer and occupied separate spots meant for them. The Sultan sent a costly cloak with red and black stripes as an offering to the Shaikh. The Shaikh refused to accept it as it was made of a material forbidden by the Shariat. The Sultan wished to convey his regrets, but the Shaikh was so offended by the improper gesture that he left the mosque immediately after prayers. Shaikh Nuruddin, the Shaikh's son, having realized the mood of his father, covered his departure in a manner that he was not seen. Two persons, who held the cloak by its arms as if it were a curtain, did this. The Sultan, who was looking in the direction of the Shaikh, was left helpless. Since he realized his mistake, he sent a message to Shaikh Nuruddin requesting that Shaikh Munawwar might not wear the cloak if he regarded the material unlawful.[64] Afif has stated that such kings of religion could not be expected to put on garments that were not permitted. He also suggested that, owing to the presence of such pious saints and their offspring, Hansi had remained immune from the depredations of the Mongols.[65]

Land grants and financial aid, which were advanced by Firoz Shah Tughluq during his march through Panjab, strengthened the foundations of the Delhi Sultanate and widened its support base. During the next two or three years, these measures were adopted as official policy and implemented on a large scale. Every day the officers of the Diwan-i Risalat recommended the petitions of Sufis, Syeds, theologians, students, legal experts, memorizers and reciters of the Quran, Qalandars, Haidaris, keepers of mosques, attendants of tombs, orphans, cripples and beggars. Land grants assimilated into the *khalisa* during the last 70 to 100 years, were restored and fresh documents were issued to the sons and grandsons of the beneficiaries. Barren lands were also distributed among the claimants. As the old schools and mosques were revived, the remuneration of teachers and students was increased. Sufi lodges in Delhi and provinces, which had been lying deserted, began to flourish with the help of 5,000-30,000 *tankas* each.[66] The Sultan himself claimed to have financed the construction of mosques, seminaries and hospices. Since a number of people – Sufis, scholars, puritans and devout – used these spaces, their maintenance was ensured in letters of endowment (*waqfnamas*). In particular, the mausoleum of Shaikh Nizamuddin Auliya was expanded and beautified. The doors of its domed room and the lattice-work (*gumbad wa jafriha*) were made afresh with sandal wood. From the four corners of the enclosure, golden lanterns (*qandilha-i zareen*) were suspended with the help of golden chains. A congregational hall (*jamaatkhana*), which was not there earlier, was constructed.[67]

Zamindars at Centrestage

Firoz Shah Tughluq had acquired an intimate knowledge of the countryside of Panjab. This could be attributed to his deep interest in hunting which he had been pursuing since his days as a prince, though Sultan Muhammad bin Tughluq unsuccessfully tried to dissuade him. When he ascended the throne and abjured military campaigns owing to the negative results, he turned towards hunting with renewed passion. This became evident from an account of his hunting onagers (*gorkhars*). These animals lived in forests that lacked water. Such a habitat was available in the area between Dipalpur and Sarsuti. For miles on end, there was nothing but wilderness. The land was so arid that water could not be extracted even on digging a hundred yards deep. If, during the summers, any traveller went astray, he lost his life owing to the scarcity of water. It was only at the next stage of the journey that water was available. A characteristic trait of onagers was that they lived at places where land was desolate and water was not encountered for 80 *kos*. When they were thirsty, they covered this long stretch and, having quenched their thirst, returned to their place. It was possible to hunt onagers only during the summer because, in this season, they tended to collect at one spot. During the winter and monsoons, they scattered.

When Firoz Shah Tughluq embarked on hunting onagers, he established his camp (*bungah*) between Abohar and Sarsuti. Leaving behind those with weak horses at the camp, he was accompanied by those who had stout horses. In accordance with his instructions, the nobles carried their stocks of water sufficient for three days on camels, horses, and the backs of water carriers. The Sultan rode out in the late afternoon prayer (*asr*) and, travelling throughout the night, reached the resting place of onagers at the midday prayer (*zuhr*). He organized a hunting circle (*parah*) with a radius of 15 *kos*, which was slowly contracted to just 4 *kos*, so that the onagers were trapped. After staying for the night, he spent the next day from morning to evening on the hunt. Thereafter, he broke up the hunting circle and, travelling for two days along with his companions, returned to the camp on the third day after covering a distance of 70 *kos*.[68] The common people indirectly benefited from this royal pursuit because the Sultan, who remained extremely cheerful during his hunting excursions, accepted any request made to him.[69]

In many respects a hunting expedition, which was apparently a royal diversion and pastime, was similar to a military campaign.

The Sultan had invested a lot in creating a vast establishment to supervise hunting. A large number of animals and birds – lions, tigers, dogs and falcons – were trained to assist. Two or three servants looked after each animal or bird and rode on horses during a hunt. Apart from princes and nobles, the entourage comprised forty banners and a variety of tents. The keepers of animals and birds marched on the left and right under two spears with peacock feathers, which was an invention of Ghiasuddin Tughluq. Out of five royal stables, one with 1,200 horses was set aside for the hunt. In addition to the chief of hunt (*amir-i shikar*) Malik Dailan and his deputy Malik Khizr Bahram, there were numerous officials (*faujdars* and *bazidgars*). Senior nobles worked hard to maintain different sections of this department as the Sultan was personally devoted to the pursuit.[70] The impact was seen in his forays into the jungles of Badaun and Anwala, where he hunted deer, nilgai, and asses. As many as 12,000 hunters (*bahlis*) went along. Two huge cauldrons were constructed to cook massive quantities of meat that was distributed among the people. Carried on specially fabricated carriages, the cauldrons were pulled by 120 carriers. The meat that could not be consumed was dried with a treatment of cumin seeds and carried to Delhi.[71]

During the reign of Muhammad bin Tughluq (r. 1325-51), the Delhi Sultanate formed an alliance with two zamindars of a village near Thanesar. This event took place in the context of a hunting expedition that culminated in a matrimonial union. The author of the *Mirat-i Sikandari* has provided a detailed account of the development. Once Firoz was hunting deer in the suburbs of Thanesar, and was separated from his retinue. As the sun had set, he began to look for a place to spend the night. He entered the nearest village and joined a group of local zamindars. At the request of the visitor, one of those assembled began to remove his shoes. This person happened to be an expert in chiromancy (*ilm-i qifayat wa fan-i firasat*) and seeing the underside of Firoz's feet, declared, 'None other than a king possesses such feet. It is not known if he is a king or likely to become one.' This person and his brother invited Firoz to spend the night in their house. Firoz accepted the invitation. These two brothers, Sadhu and Sadharan, busied themselves in playing the host. The wife of Sadhu, who was an intelligent woman, expressed doubts about trusting a stranger merely on the basis of his noble bearing. On her advice, a drinking party was organized in order to test the qualities of the guest. The sister of Sadhu and Sadharan, who was extremely beautiful (*jamal soorat wa kamal husn*), began to serve liquor to the guest. On seeing that the guest was entrapped in the beauty of the young maiden, Sadhu's wife sought to know the identity of the guest, who could be offered the girl in marriage. Firoz revealed that he was the cousin of Sultan Muhammad bin Tughluq and, as such, heir apparent to the throne of Delhi. Sadhu's wife proposed that the girl might be married to Firoz because the prince was enamoured by her beauty and their own family would gain material benefits from the alliance. The brothers readily agreed and the marriage ceremony (*nikah*) was performed. The marriage was consummated on the same night. The next morning, armed contingents arrived from different directions. Firoz returned to Delhi with his bride. The two brothers, Sadhu and Sadharan, remained with Firoz like a shadow and did not leave him even for a moment. Firoz fell madly in love with his wife. In a short time, the two brothers embraced Islam. Sadharan was granted the title of Wajih ul-Mulk.[72]

The author of the *Mirat-i Sikandari* would have us believe that the marriage was a culmination of love at first sight, which occurred in dramatic and accidental circumstances. However, the episode needed to be placed in the context of the process of state formation, because there was a considerable similarity between the marriages of Firoz and his father Sipahsalar Rajab. Let us recall that Ghazi Malik, as the governor of Dipalpur, had used coercion in the countryside of Abohar to (a) collect the land tax from the village headmen and to (b) force the local chief to marry his daughter to the governor's brother. These two actions were interrelated and complementary. Firoz, an offspring of this marriage, must have been conscious of the implications of political collaboration between the Delhi Sultanate and the traditional heads of agricultural communities. When he decided to wed a woman of a village near Thanesar, he must have been pleased to learn that she belonged to a family of zamindars, who were not only men of influence and exercised control over their locality, but could also muster thousands of horsemen and footmen by a mere hint.[73] They could facilitate (like Rana Mal Bhatti of Abohar) the consolidation of the Delhi Sultanate in their locality, particularly with reference to the collection of land tax from the peasantry. This also enabled us to suggest that the marriage may have been preceded by hard negotiations between the two parties.[74] The two brothers might have agreed to the proposal of their sister's marriage and their own conversion to Islam in return for high posts in Delhi, prospects of promotion in the future, and suitable jobs for their progeny. In the words of Samira Shaikh, 'From the perspective of the Taks, offering women and military allegiance to the Sultans represented a potent means of upward mobility. The transformation of the Tak peasants into independent Sultans within a generation is a prime example of the benefits that manpower-rich groups derived from association with the Sultanate.'[75]

Though the marital unions of the father and son – Sipahsalar Rajab and Prince Firoz – appear somewhat dissimilar in outward form, they are similar in content, i.e. in terms of the social classes involved, the objectives nurtured, and the results achieved. After all, the son of Sadharan rose to be the governor of Gujarat and went on to establish an independent dynasty in the region. This sequel was logical, because Sadharan enjoyed the patronage of the Tughluq rulers as well as the Suhrawardi saint of Uch, i.e worldly as well as spiritual power. Could we ignore that Syed Jalaluddin Bokhari, the famous Suhrawardi saint of Uch, and a mentor of Sultan Firoz Shah Tughluq, had bestowed the kingdom of Gujarat on Sadharan's son Zafar Khan and his twelve generations? Unsurprisingly, it was again the same source, the *Mirat-i Sikandari,* that has provided an account of the circumstances in which the boon was granted.

Sadharan, in accordance with the wishes of Sultan Firoz Shah Tughluq, became a disciple of Syed Jalaluddin Bokhari of Uch. The Sultan was pleased with this act, while Shaikh Bokhari began to shower his grace on the two brothers. One day a number of mendicants (*fuqra*) assembled in the hospice of the Shaikh, but there was no food for them. Zafar Khan, the son of Sadharan, who was also a disciple of the Shaikh, learnt about the situation. Gathering food and sweets from his house and the market, he went to the hospice and served meals to the visitors. The mendicants raised the slogan 'Allah hu Akbar' in a loud chorus. This voice reached the ears of the Shaikh, who enquired about it. His servants informed him about Zafar Khan's act of kindness. The Shaikh summoned Zafar Khan to his presence and declared, 'Oh Zafar Khan. In lieu of this feast, I confer the entire kingdom of Gujarat on you. May God make it a bliss for you.' The saint also gifted him the covering of his own bedstead (*palang posh khasa*). Zafar Khan returned home and conveyed the happy news to his wife. Not impressed, she asked her husband to seek this boon for his descendants, as he himself had become old and could not rule for a long time. She reasoned that since the Shaikh was immensely kind towards him, he would accept any request that he made to him. Zafar Khan retraced his steps to the hospice and carried a bundle of fresh gifts including flowers, fruit, perfumes, and betel leaves. The Shaikh accepted the gifts with approval and, giving a handful of dates (*khurma*) from a tray to Zafar Khan, said that his descendants would rule over Gujarat for several generations equal to the number of dates. Some people believe that the number of dates was twelve or thirteen or more.[76]

During medieval times, there were doubts about the caste of zamindars hailing from a village near Thanesar. According to Sikandar bin Manjhu, Sadharan (who was the first among the kin of the Sultans of Gujarat to embrace Islam) belonged to the caste of the Taks. Further, the annals of the Hindus indicated that the Taks had brotherly relations with the Khatris. But when the Taks took to the consumption of liquor, the Khatris expelled them from their caste. According to the Hindavi language, people who were segregated in this manner were known as Taks. With the passage of time, the Taks came to have their own set of beliefs and customs. Interestingly, Sikandar bin Manjhu has traced the genealogy of Sadharan to Lord Ramchandra who was worshipped as a deity among the Hindus.[77] When Sadharan's son Zafar Khan established his own rule in Gujarat, the doubts reappeared about his social background, which was again linked to wine. It was recalled that when Firoz Shah Tughluq ascended the throne in 1351, he had raised the ranks of Zafar Khan and his brother Shams Khan. Showing his trust in these nephews of his wife, the Sultan placed them in charge of the royal wine cellar (*sharabdari*). A few years after the death of the Sultan, Zafar Khan was sent to Gujarat to quell the rebellion of Rasti Khan. He brought the region under his control and went on to establish an independent rule.[78] At this time, some people believed that the Sultans of Gujarat belonged to the caste of wine distillers (*kalalan yani khamaran*). Sikandar bin Manjhu has pointed out that this belief was wrong and it came into circulation owing to a specific situation. On one occasion, the Sultan's household received a huge stock of grapes that could not be consumed and was on the verge of decay. He handed the fruit to the brothers, who converted it into wine. As a result, some people out of jealousy connected them with wine distillers and gave wide publicity to their lowly social background. But it had been proved by facts that they belonged to the caste of Taks. Whatever be their caste, they were known for their virtuous conduct and charitable disposition.[79] By making this statement, Sikandar bin Manjhu has tried to deflect our attention away from their ambiguous ancestry to their noble qualities.

Another zamindar, Mote Rai Chauhan of Darrera in the district of Hissar, negotiated an alliance with the Tughluq regime. The episode has been reconstructed by Kavi Jan in a poetic work.[80] According to this narrative, a young boy named Karam Chand (the son of Mote Rai Chauhan) went hunting along with a sizeable group of people. While searching for animals, the others wandered far away. The tired lad sat down under the shade of a tree and instantly fell asleep. The Sultan of Delhi, Firoz Shah Tughluq, who was also hunting in that forest, saw the boy sleeping. He was astonished to see that the lad was covered by shade that remained fixed, while the other trees did not cast any shadow at high noon. The Sultan called his companion Syed Nasir (the *faujdar* of Hissar) who declared that the boy must be a great person. They were somewhat confused to find that the boy was a Hindu. They could not understand the boy's extraordinary boon as, in their perception, Hindus did not possess miraculous power. Syed Nasir imagined that the boy would adopt the path of a Turk in the end. The Sultan renamed the boy as Qiyam Khan and took him back to Hissar. When the boy's father Mote Rai Chauhan learnt about the whereabouts of his son, he also went to Hissar. The Sultan insisted on keeping the boy and assured that he would treat him like a son and that he would be given a high official rank (a *mansab* of 5,000) on attaining maturity. The father received gifts from the Sultan and returned home. Qiyam Khan was placed under the care of Syed Nasir, who brought him up along with his own sons. When his education was completed, Syed Nasir asked him to undergo circumcision, offer prayers (*namaz*) and embrace Islam. Qiyam Khan hesitated to take any such step, as he feared that none would trust him and his family and therefore none would offer his daughter in marriage to him. Syed Nasir predicted that great kings of the future – Rao Jodha of Mandore and Bahlol Lodi of Delhi – would marry their daughters into his lineage. Thus assured, Qiyam Khan embraced Islam and became a pure and orthodox Muslim. Syed Nasir took Qiyam Khan to Delhi and presented him before the Sultan, who was much pleased. During his illness, Syed Nasir expressed a desire to bequeath his rank (*mansab*) to Qiyam Khan, as he was more capable than his own sons. The Sultan acceded to the request, so that Qiyam Khan inherited the possessions of Syed Nasir – rank, land and goods – and became a trusted noble at the court. In this manner, the Sultan fulfilled his promise to Mote Rai Chauhan.[81]

It is not possible to accept the above narrative in its entirety, because it is embellished with supernatural phenomena and violated the sequence of chronology.[82] In spite of these limitations, which might be attributed to the very nature of the heroic ballad, it does contain a substantive kernel of factual and believable information, so essential for our principal argument revolving around local linkages. By the late fourteenth century, the ruling class of the Delhi Sultanate had developed an effective mechanism – a combination of negotiation and coercion – to secure the collaboration of the powerful class of rural aristocrats. Based on the information provided by the administrator of Hissar, Firoz Shah Tughluq perceived the Rajput zamindar of Darrera, Mote Rai Chauhan, as an indispensable ally in the administrative control and economic development of Hissar. Whereas the chief might have offered to provide the necessary cooperation at the grassroots level, the state required adequate guarantees and safeguards. The possibility of a matrimonial alliance was ruled out, perhaps because the Chauhan household did not have a young maiden to be offered as a bride. The only alternative was to keep the chief's son as a hostage in the household of the local administrator of Hissar. Karam Chand Chauhan was chosen, after deep deliberation and strategic planning, to play a particular role in the process of state formation–a role which had been played earlier by the daughter of Rana Mal Bhatti in the household of Ghazi Malik and by the sister of Sadhu and Sadharan in the household of Firoz Shah Tughluq.[83]

During the later part of Firoz Shah Tughluq's reign, Qiyam Khan was military governor (*faujdar*) of Hissar and, in the absence of the Sultan, also held charge of Delhi. After the invasion of Timur, his political influence increased to such an extent that he made an abortive bid to place his candidate on the Delhi throne. During this phase, he entered into a tussle with Mallu Iqbal Khan, who had become a leading contender for political power. It has been claimed that Qiyam Khan was invited by the ministers to occupy the throne, which had been held by seven of his illustrious ancestors. Qiyam Khan declined the offer as power was transitory and its loss resulted in sorrow.[84] Subsequently, he concentrated his energies on consolidating his authority in Hissar, Hansi and Bhatner. Qiyam Khan could be identified with Qawam Khan who held the district of Hissar Firoza during the reign of Sultan Mahmud (r. 1405-12). Being a partisan of Khizr Khan, he was besieged (1408) by the Sultan in the fort of Hissar Firoza and was forced to send his son to the court for service. In 1414, he was put to death along with a few other nobles who were found guilty of conspiring against Khizr Khan.[85] His sons Taj Khan and Muhammad Khan not only held his territorial possessions in a firm grip, but also assisted Nagore in fighting against Chittor. When Bahlol Lodi (r. 1451-89) brought Hissar Firoza under his sway, Muhammad Khan and his nephew Fateh Khan (a son-in-law of Bahlol Lodi) founded respectively the principalities of Fatehpur and Jhunjhunu.[86]

Canal Network and Agrarian Expansion

Promoting agriculture in southeast Panjab through a canal network, Firoz Shah Tughluq, must have learnt from the past. During the reign of his predecessor Muhammad bin Tughluq, a widespread peasant revolt had irrupted beyond the Jamuna, forcing the state to expand cultivation through a scheme of loans. A similar revolt had also broken out in southeast Panjab. The crisis might be traced to a severe famine that raged in a vast area spreading from Malwa (central India) to Delhi, as the towns and settlements were engulfed in misery. When Muhammad bin Tughluq returned to the capital from Devagiri, he found that the city did not have a thousandth part of its population. Owing to lack of rains, cultivation disappeared and the land was devastated. The Sultan tried to ameliorate the condition of people and improve agriculture by advancing loans from the treasury. Owing to the ongoing drought, agriculture could not be revived and people continued to die. At the same time, the peasants inhabiting parts of southeastern Panjab – Sunam, Samana, Kuhram and Kaithal – rose in revolt. Having constructed fortifications (*mandal*), they refused to pay the land tax and, causing disturbances, took to highway robbery. The Sultan marched in to the affected area and, dismantling the fortifications, scattered the armed bands. The rebellious tribes were identified as Birahas, Mandahars, Jiwans, Bhattis and Manhis. These groups were expelled from their lands and their headmen were brought to Delhi, where they were placed in the custody of various nobles. They began to reside in the city along with their families, while some of them converted to Islam.[87] Peace was restored in the tract, but Firoz Shah Tughluq sought to resettle the area by providing means of artificial irrigation.

Afif's history indicated that the establishment of the city of Hissar Firoza was connected with the excavation of canals in southeast Panjab.[88] He acquired first hand information about this development from his father, who was a confidant of the Sultan and recorded the official work done by special officers at night (*shabnavisi khwasan*). The Sultan, on his return from Bengal, stayed near Hissar Firoza for nealy two and a half years and turned his attention to the welfare of the country and people. During this period, the construction of a new city took place. He visited Delhi for short intervals, but invariably returned after a few days. He decided to establish the city at the site of two large inhabited villages – Big Laras and Small Laras – that possessed fifty and forty cattle sheds (*kharaks*) respectively, indicating that the area was predominantly pastoral in character. As soon as the Sultan saw the land of Big Laras, he was so impressed that he decided to establish a city there. But the area was deficient in water. During summers, travellers from Iraq and Khurasan paid 4 *jitals* to purchase a pitcher of water. However, the Sultan felt that if he built a city for virtuous people, God would cause water to appear on the land owing to His supreme power. For many years, the Sultan and his nobles remained occupied in this work. Stones were brought from the Narsai hills and, using a mixture of slaked lime and sand, constructed a fort of enormous thickness, length and height.[89] Each noble was assigned the task of supervising the construction of a specific quarter (*alang*). When the work of construction was completed and some time had elapsed, the Sultan named the city as Hissar Firoza. A moat (*khandaq*) was dug all around the fort and, depositing the earth on its sides, a battlement was raised. A large and unmatched reservoir (*hauz buzurg wa ghadir la-nazir*) whose water lasted for one year supplied water to the moat. Inside the fort, a palace was built for the Sultan's household. Unrivalled in the world by any royal residence, it had several halls and ingenious structures, where a stranger could lose his way. A number of people, high-ranking nobles, elite and commoners, constructed houses for themselves.[90] To begin with, the Sultan aimed at providing water to the inhabitants by digging large tanks that were designed to collect the rainwater. It appears that this initial attempt turned out to be inadequate.[91] Therefore, two canals were excavated – Rajabwah and Ulughkhani – from the Satluj and Jamuna respectively. The headworks of both were situated near

Karnal and, together covering a distance of 240 kilometres (80 *kurohs*) reached Hissar Firoza.⁹²

Unlike Afif, Sirhindi has provided detail regarding the network of canals. According to him, the Sultan visited Dipalpur in 1355 and excavated a canal from the Satluj to Jahbaz (Jajner) covering a distance of 48 *kurohs*. Next year, he dug the Firozabad canal from the vicinity of Mandati and Sirmur hills. After its merger with seven streams, it was brought to Hansi. From this place it was carried to Arasan where a strong citadel (*hisar-i mustahkam*) was raised which was named as Hissar Firoza. At its base was created a large reservoir (*hauz vasih*) which was filled with the water of this canal. Another canal was excavated from the Ghaggar; it passed alongside the fort of Sarsuti and reached as far as Harni Khera. In between these canals, the fort of Firozabad was built. Another canal, which was dug from the Jamuna at Budhi, was conveyed to the reservoir at Hissar Firoza and was carried even further.⁹³ Sharafuddin Ali Yazdi has credited the Sultan with cutting a canal called Haikan from the Kali and carrying it to meet the Jamuna near Firozabad.⁹⁴

In his enthusiasm for artificial irrigation, Firoz Shah Tughluq faced natural obstacles. This was shown by an attempt to improve cultivation in the northern part of the cis-Satluj area. During the course of the Sultan's visit in 1361, it was found that the river Salima, also called the Sarsuti, consisted of two large streams that were always flowing. A high mound was situated between them. It was felt that if the mound could be dug through, the water of the Sarsuti could flow into the other stream which, then, could irrigate the tract of Sirhind, Mansurpur and Samana. This statement made sense if a minor modification was proposed. The two streams appeared to be the Sarsuti and Ghaggar, which flowed down from the Sirmur and Pinjore hills, parallel to each other, in a southwesterly direction. The mound between them could have been located somewhere at Ambala. In the mid-fourteenth century, the Sarsuti had a sufficient quantity of water and, therefore, it was possible to transfer a part of it to the Ghaggar, which was less fortunate in this regard. To achieve this aim, the Sultan enrolled the services of 50,000 labourers who, equipped with spades, began to dig through the mound. The diggers discovered several fossils of elephants and humans, indicating existence of life in these parts during the pre-historic period. Unfortunately, the Sultan's attempt ended in a failure, as the water of one stream (Sarsuti) could not be delivered to the other (Ghaggar). This failure might be attributed to inadequate knowledge of the local topography, particularly the elevations on the two sides of the mound. On this occasion, Sirhind and an area of 10 *kurohs* were constituted into a new administrative unit, which was placed under Shamsuddin Abu Rija who was ordered to construct a fort called Firozpur. [95]

Since the statements of three chroniclers (Barani, Afif and Sirhindi) on the canals of Firoz Shah Tughluq contained inaccuracies, they have caused much confusion in the minds of readers. Fortunately, a recent study has not only mapped the geographical courses of these canals, but has also reconciled contradictions found in contemporary sources. Moving from west to east, it has traced the routes of as many as seven canals. The first canal, known as the Firoz Shahi, took off from the Satluj near Ropar and flowed towards Sirhind. The second canal intended to carry the water of Sarsuti to Ghaggar, so as to flow through Sirhind, Mansurpur and Sunam. The project, as mentioned above, remained abortive. The third canal Tughluqshahi commenced from the eastern arm of the Ghaggar in the low hills of Pinjore and, receiving a diversion from the Sarsuti, reached as far as Fatehabad and Firozabad. The fourth canal Firozbah took off from Sadhaura in the mountains of Sirmur. It received the water diverted from the Sarsuti and shared the long channel of the Chutang. On reaching Dhatrat, it merged with a branch of the Rajabwah arriving from the Safedun. Flowing through Hansi and Jind, it reached Hissar. A smaller branch between Jind and Hansi, moved southwards to Bawni Khera. The fifth canal, Rajabwah, had its source in an old arm of the Jamuna above Karnal and travelled southwards as far as Rohtak. The sixth canal Ulughkhani was cut from the Jamuna in the hills of Sirmur and, merging with the Rajabwah for a part of its journey, it separated and flowed down to Wazirabad where it merged with the Jamuna. The seventh canal was the Haikan (Hindan), which was drawn from the upper Kali, and flowed into the Jamuna near Firozabad.[96] Having completed the work of construction in the new city, Firoz Shah Tughluq went to the neighbouring town of Hansi in order to pay his respects to Shaikh Nuruddin (the mentor of Afif). At this time, the Shaikh had succeeded to the spiritual seat of Hansi following the death of his father Shaikh Qutbuddin Munawwar. When the Sultan reached the hospice, he, out of respect, did not allow the Shaikh to leave his seat (*sajjadah*) and walk out to welcome him. After exchanging pleasantries and shaking hands, 'the two rulers who had been chosen by God' sat in one spot to converse. The Shaikh, following in the footsteps of eminent Sufis, delivered a sermon on spiritual matters. The Sultan, speaking like a king, said,

I have founded the city of Hissar Firoza for the benefit and comfort of the people of Islam. It would be appropriate if the Shaikh, owing to his grace, settled in Hissar Firoza. A *khanqah* will be built for the pious and the necessary funds will be provided for its maintenance. It will be easy for the people of Hansi to visit the Shaikh, as the distance was not more than ten *kos*. On account of the blessings of the Shaikh, the inhabitants of Hissar Firoza would be protected from hardships and the city would become fully populated and prosperous.

In response, the Shaikh wished to know if the proposal was a royal order or the matter was in his purview. The Sultan clarified that he could not dare to issue any command and the issue was entirely in his (Shaikh's) hands. He added that if the Shaikh himself decided to settle in Hissar Firoza, it would be good fortune for the city and its inhabitants. The Shaikh replied, 'If the decision is within my right, then my place is Hansi, which has been the spiritual domain (*vilayat*) of my grandfather (Shaikh Burhanuddin) and father (Shaikh Qutbuddin Munawwar). It had been bestowed on them by Shaikh-ul Islam Fariduddin Ganj-i Shakar and Mahbub-i Ilahi Shaikh Nizamuddin Auliya.' Overwhelmed, the Sultan conceded that it was proper for the Shaikh to continue residing in Hansi and hoped that his blessings would keep Hissar Firoza safe from all calamities. Afif would have us believe that when the cruel invaders (under Amir Timur) attacked Delhi and destroyed the property of Hindus and Muslims, the inhabitants of Hansi as well as the part of Hissar Firoza which had been included in Hansi remained safe due to the blessings of Shaikh Nuruddin.[97] It may be added that the attitude of the Shaikh towards the state was in line with that of his father Shaikh Qutbuddin Munawwar, but substantially differed from that of the descendants of Shaikh Alauddin of Pakpattan.

The Sultan took a keen interest in the working of the irrigation project. In particular, he wished to know if the canal water actually reached the fields of the peasants in the targeted areas. At the onset of every monsoon, he deputed special officers to monitor the flow of water in the canals. Afif's father and uncle were included among the functionaries who, after travelling along the canals across the countryside, collected the latest information and communicated it to the capital. The Sultan was delighted to learn that the canal water, after flowing from the east to west, had reached the destined villages. However, he reprimanded the concerned officers if he found that any village had been flooded.[98]

Since the funds on the irrigation project had been spent from the personal resources of the Sultan and the positive results of canal water had started appearing, it became necessary to develop a new mechanism to manage the income from the concerned areas. The Sultan convened a meeting of a number of scholars – including *qazis, muftis, ulama* and *mashaikh* – and sought their legal opinion (*fatwa*) on an important issue. The question was – if an individual spent his labour and money on digging canals from deep rivers and carried them to towns and villages, and the inhabitants of these places drew immense profit (*nafa basiyar*) from them, was that individual entitled to any payment in lieu of his personal contribution? According to the unanimous opinion of scholars, the one who took the trouble and made efforts was entitled to a water tax (*haq-i sharb*) which was equal to one tenth of the income of the concerned areas. In the wake of this decree, the Sultan included this tax in his personal income (*imlak*). Like previous rulers, he brought a large number of barren villages (*zamin imvat*) under the plough and added them to his personal income. The land tax from these villages was taken out of the purview of the public treasury (*bait-ul mal*) and distributed among the theologians and Sufis (*ulama wa mashaikh*). As it became evident, the Sultan's personal income comprised two sources – money from the water tax (*haq-i sharb*) and land tax from the newly settled villages. The funds of the Sultan's personal income, which amounted to 2 lakh *tankas*, turned out to be more than that of any other Sultan of Delhi. In order to administer this large amount, special officers were appointed and a separate treasury was set up.[99]

Barani completed his *Tarikh-i Firoz Shahi* six years after the accession of Firoz Shah Tughluq and thus witnessed the commencement of the project of Hissar Firoza and canals. Though he did not live long enough to see the irrigation-based agricultural transformation, he has done an impressive speculation on fairly scientific lines.[100] He has recorded that the canals laid during the reign of the Sultan were as long as 100-20 miles (50-60 *kurohs*) and as wide as the Ganga and Jamuna. They flowed through the arid wastelands and burning deserts, where there was no well or pond. It was hoped that thousands of villages would emerge on the banks of these canals and several new types of crops would be grown. Ever since Hindustan had been settled, groups of pastoralists, faced with the scarcity of water for cattle, lived in clusters of bullock carts (*talwandi*) and not in villages. Whenever they learnt about the availability of water at any place, they shifted there along with their bullock carts and cattle. For twelve months in the year, they lived under the bullock carts along with their women and children. These nomadic people, assisted by canal water, would settle as sedentary cultivators in the newly established villages and build proper houses for themselves. Whereas they raised only lentils (*moth*) and sesame (*til*) earlier, it would now be possible for them to raise superior crops like wheat, gram, and sugar cane. Agricultural production would increase and the prices of grain would fall. Cattle population would increase a thousand times. Owing to proper settlement and cultivation, the governors (*walis* and *muqtis*) would be able to collect land tax regularly, leading to a plentiful treasury. The onset of general prosperity and improved living standards would enable the people to consume superior foods – wheat, gram, and sugar – which were brought earlier by traders from Delhi and were enjoyed only on festive occasions. Since these crops would be produced in surplus, the people would store them in their houses and even send them to other areas for profit. Vast deserts, where nothing grew for miles except acacia and thorny bushes, would be covered with zones of cultivation and orchards. A variety of fruit, grapes, mangoes, pomegranates, apples, melons, figs, lemons and gooseberries, would be produced. Two varieties of sugar cane, *siyah* and *parenda*, would be raised. Trees of *peepal, jamun*, tamarind, dates and *sambal* would grow, and flowers such as *karma, baqla,* and *khashkhash*.

Continuing in the same vein, Barani has stated that the travellers in the past did not dare to set foot in these lands and some of them even lost their lives on account of acute thirst. The scarcity of water forced them to travel only during the night or carry flasks of drinking water (*mashkina wa mashk*) or hang onions from their necks. Herds of animals and flocks of birds used to die for want of water. But the arrival of canals mitigated these problems. The wayfarers forced to perform their ablutions with sand (*taiyyum*), would offer the five prayers (*namaz*) after taking proper bath. Owing to the width of the channels and the volume of water, people now would cover the distances in boats. Large armies would camp on the banks of canals for decades, without causing a decrease in the flow of water. The excavation of the canals was such an amazing achievement that thousands of boons would accrue to the people and, with the passage of time, these benefits would increase. Prophet Muhammad's understanding of perpetual charity (*sadqa-i jaria*), as an act which remained among the people for a long time, was applicable to the digging of canals that flowed all the time. Barani, who had observed the functioning of several regimes, had never witnessed anything like the digging of canals. He could not remember any other king, who combined in himself the excellent virtues possessed by Firoz Shah Tughluq. All creatures of the affected region – human beings, djinns, animals and birds – would shower eulogies on the Sultan and pray for his long life.

In contrast to Barani, Afif lived long enough to observe the fruition of the irrigation project and the consequent changes in the agrarian economy. His description is restrained and objective. He observed that before the excavation of canals, the land of Hissar Firoza produced only the monsoon crop (*kharif*). With the availability of irrigation facilities, the winter crops (*rabi*) – including wheat and different varieties of sugar cane such as the black one (*nishkar siyah*) and *paunda* could be cultivated, as they could not be produced without water. In fact, all the crops of the two seasons began to be raised. Before the reign of Firoz Shah Tughluq, this area was placed under the district (*shiq*) of Hansi. With the foundation of the new city and agrarian expansion, Hissar Firoza was constituted as a new district and it included the sub districts (*iqtas*) of Hansi, Agroha, Fatehabad, Sarsuti, Salora and Khizrabad. Malik Dailan was appointed its first administrator (*shiqdar*).[101] What was equally significant, the arrival of canals raised the subsoil water and, therefore, it became possible to dig wells and obtain water at a depth of only 4 yards. In addition to food grains and cash crops, conditions were created for the development of horticulture. A large number of orchards were planted where a variety of fruit, oranges, *sadaphal, janheri* and *sakandrawal,* was produced. In the neighbourhood of Delhi, the Sultan laid 1,200 gardens, out of which 80 were located at Band Salora and 44 at Chittoor. He also revived 30 gardens that had been originally planted by Alauddin Khalji. These gardens produced oranges, plums, and seven varieties of grapes. These gardens yielded revenues to the tune of 1,80,000 *tankas,* while that of the Doab stood at only 80 lakh *tankas*.

Afif's description was limited only to two canals (Rajabwah and Ulughkhani) with particular reference to the establishment of the cities of Hissar Firoza and Fatehabad. He stated that the towns and villages (*qasbat wa qariyat*) situated between these two canals – Hansi, Jind, Dhatrat and Tughluqpur (alias Safedun) – had benefited from the canals.[102] Keeping in view the other canals that were mentioned by Sirhindi, it appeared that a much larger area, bounded on the east by the Jamuna and on the west by the Ghaggar and Sarsuti, stood to gain from the provision of irrigation facilities. Therefore, it was possible to suggest that cultivation had also improved in such places as Ambala, Mustafabad, Shahabad, Thanesar, Kuhram, Samana, Kaithal, Tohana, Jamalpur, Ahroni, Sirsa, Khanda, Atkhera, Barwala and Agroha.

Administration and Economy of Multan

During the reign of Muhammad bin Tughluq (r. 1325-51), Ain ul-Mulk Mahru was appointed governor of Awadh and Zafarabad.[103] He came into prominence while supplying food grains and money to the Sultan, who was then staying at Sargdwari due to a famine. Forced to revolt by the move to transfer him to the Deccan, Mahru was defeated and arrested. In spite of the opposition of the nobles of foreign origin,[104] the Sultan rehabilitated Mahru in rather dramatic circumstances and appointed him superintendent of a royal garden. Firoz Shah Tughluq appointed him to the Ashraf-i Mamalik in the Diwan-i Wizarat but, owing to serious differences with the wazir, Khwaja-i Jahan, he was removed from this position. The Sultan, in view of Mahru's high stature among the nobles, conferred on him the *iqtas* of Multan, Bhakkar, and Siwistan. Mahru accepted his new job on the condition that he would submit his accounts not to the Diwan-i Wizarat, but would report directly to the Sultan. Some nobles, supporters of Mahru, complained to the Sultan about the highhandedness of the Wazir. In response, the Sultan summoned Mahru in order to gauge his feelings. Mahru, who had already covered a distance of nearly 50 miles on way to Multan, retraced his steps. On meeting the Sultan, he did not express any ill will against the Wazir, as such an attitude could weaken the foundations of the state. His good sense paved the way for his outward reconciliation with the Wazir. He clarified that his enmity with the Wazir would continue, but this enmity was too insignificant in comparison to his commitment to the interests of the state.[105] Thus, before he left for Multan again, Mahru was sure of a complete freedom of action in the discharge of his duties.

Firoz Shah Tughluq issued a royal mandate (*manshur*) to Ain ul-Mulk Mahru when the latter was appointed governor of

Multan.¹⁰⁶ This document asserted that the Delhi Sultanate sought to bestow dignity and kindness on the loyal creatures of the court, who had been raised to high ranks. It aimed at favouring great nobles and famous ministers who, on account of their knowledge and loyalty, had attained positions of trust. Such individuals had earned the confidence of the Sultan by their true faith (*husn itiqad*). By virtue of their intelligence and judgement, they had been assigned the management of the kingdom and religion. The state regarded it a prime duty to train officers who, by their skill and honesty, had illumined the country and religion. In this context, the Delhi Sultanate had showered its bounties on Ain ul-Mulk Mahru who was a conqueror of infidelity, destroyer of the rebellious, master of the sword and pen, possessor of knowledge and endurance, and commander of the Iranians who were grandees of the universe. Being a chosen one of God, he was adorned with virtues and excelled in bravery. Driven by its generosity, the state bestowed the government (*shiq*) of Multan on him and, in consequence, had conferred on him the right to arrest or release, confiscate or restore and appoint or dismiss any person. Assisted by his sound judgement and bright vision for the efficient working of the administration, he would employ these abilities in building cities and providing comfort to the common people, whose welfare had been entrusted to the government in this world and about whom the government would be answerable in the next world. Mahru was expected to act according to the requirements of knowledge, wisdom, intelligence, power and generosity. These principles constituted the pillars of the state (*arkan jahandari*) and strengthened the foundations of the kingdom, besides being in accord with the Quranic verse, 'Surely Allah enjoins the doing of justice and the doing of good (to others).' The royal mandate instructed all the people – nobles, assignees (*muqtis*), clerks (*karkunan*), chiefs (*rayan*), soldiers (*lashkariyan*) and all inhabitants – to abide by the orders inscribed in the document. In due course, they would be contented by the grace of God and His help.¹⁰⁷

Mahru's analysis of the economic crisis prevailing in Multan indicated that the provincial administration kept a close watch on settlement patterns and agricultural production.[108] He found that during the governorship of his predecessor Imad ul-Mulk, a large number of inhabitants had left for other places, so that the cultivated area had shrunk to one tenth of the better times. Despite the economic reconstruction being carried out under Firoz Shah Tughluq, few migrants returned. It was felt that unless the population reached the previous levels, there was little hope of achieving the past magnitude of revenue collection. Second, a number of taxes – *mandwah, tarkah, mal-i maujud, chahar bazaar, zaraib, guzarha* and *kharaj-i muhtarifa-i musallam* – which were bringing a considerable amount of money into the provincial coffers, had been abolished.[109] Third, a sum of 3 lakh *tankas* had been assigned as land grants (*inam*) and cash pension (*idrar*), whereas during the reign of Alauddin Khalji, when grain and cloth were cheaper, less than a tenth of the amount had been granted. Owing to a tremendous increase in expenditure, the provincial treasury did not possess even a paltry sum of 500 *tankas*.[110] Fourth, Multan had suffered in the past owing to multiple factors – negligence of officers, poor quality of land and poverty of the peasantry and villagers. Mahru, who had been serving as the governor for the last three years, had undertaken vigorous administrative measures. As a result, the economic conditions were gradually returning to normal. The local chiefs (*rangahan*), who had been brought to submission in the first year, had again risen in revolt, forcing Mahru to march against them.[111]

In addition to establishing peace in his territorial jurisdiction, the governor was required to manage the provincial finances in a manner that a reasonable balance was achieved between income and expenditure. The task involved maintaining three classes – soldiers for warfare, theologians for piety (*ifadat*) and religious opinions (*ijtihad*) and lower bureaucracy (*ahl-i qalam*) for collecting taxes. These classes had competing claims on the financial resources of the province, which were often subject to fluctuations. Mahru's attention was drawn to a particular year when prices of food grains fell to one tenth of the earlier rates. Foodgrains, which were earlier sold at 80 *jitals* per maund, slumped to 8 *jitals* per maund. As a result, the common people led a life of prosperity

New Strategies of State Formation 269

and contentment. But the revenue receipts of the province and the income of the land grantees suffered a decline, as the land which earlier yielded revenue of 50 *tankas*, offered just 5 *tankas*. It had to be understood that if the agricultural produce doubled, the revenue would not increase by five times. Since in that particular year, the land tax of eight villages in the suburbs of Multan amounted to 38,000 *tankas*, the income of the land grantees ranged in the same proportion. It was not proper for them to demand cash compensation from the land tax flowing into the treasury.

From the perspective of the provincial administration, its prime function was to maintain an efficient army. Accordingly, Mahru had set aside a separate head (*wajh*) of expenditure to organize the affairs of the army. While doing so, he did not overlook the preachers and Sufis. If a disproportionate amount of land tax was diverted to them, it would not be possible to achieve the aim of defending the territories. In other words, if a sufficient army was not in place, even the land grantees (preachers and Sufis) would not be able to gather revenue from the producers. It was only due to the fear of the army and blows of the sword (*ba mahabat-i lashkar wa zarbat-i khanjar*) that the zamindars and peasants paid their taxes and the external enemies were kept in check. Any negligence with regard to the army encouraged the zamindars to rise in revolt. In the recent past, the zamindars had acquired strength owing to an excess of wealth and weapons. Mahru could not permit the zamindars to regain their erstwhile supremacy in the countryside, nor allow the powerful enemies on the frontier to disturb peace in his territorial jurisdiction.[112] Therefore, the maintenance of the army enjoyed precedence over nourishing the religious intelligentsia.

Mahru, as per his claim, exerted himself to muster troops in accordance with his wishes and took concrete steps to ensure their welfare. Caught in a situation of falling revenue receipts, he devised a solution by which half of a soldier's salary was paid in cash and half in kind.[113] Though he himself enjoyed the privileged position of a noble (*amir*), yet he also claimed his salary in the same manner. He treated himself as equal to his soldiers, with reference to any gain or loss in their respective remunerations.

In these matters, it was futile to resort to any dishonest concealment or arrogant display.[114] Mahru was an ardent participant in a discussion on the income of the state and imposition of new taxes. Apart from the rulings of the Shariat, he relied on such legal texts as *al-Kafi*, *Siyar-i Shahan* and *al-Maheet*. At the outset, it was felt that both the income and expenditure must conform to the Shariat. But in practice, these canonical principles were not applicable. So long as war booty was available to the Muslims, there was no need to remunerate them for joining a holy war. When the Muslims faced danger, the finances could be drawn from the public treasury (*bait ul-mal*) for undertaking a crusade. If the public treasury did not include war booty, then the ruler could resort to a new tax during the course of the war. A small evil was permissible to fight against a bigger evil. In times of emergency, the Shariat allowed a ruler to levy a new tax. However, this was only a temporary expedient and, as a precaution, the task of collection had to be entrusted to officers who were guided by justice and truth. If such officers were not available, there would be injustice and oppression. In such times, one could adopt the principle that legalized even the impermissible in times of need. The ruler was advised to charge only the land tax, which was being levied since the old times and which was familiar to the people. Such a course could not cause any damage, whereas a tax on something non-existent threatened to instigate revolt. Thus, it was appropriate for the wise to adopt a course, which did the least harm. After all, some losses were less damaging than others.[115]

Despite its avowed preference for the army, the Delhi Sultanate recognized the social influence of the religious classes – Syeds, *ulama*, and Sufis – and promoted their welfare through the instrument of land grants and thus assimilated them into the political structure. The provincial governors were required to acquire complete information regarding land grants in their territorial jurisdiction: the original conferment, subsequent development, amount of income, and economic potential. They passed on these details to the finance ministry (*diwan-i wizarat*), sought clarifications on controversial legal aspects and made fresh recommendations. In this context, Mahru undertook a survey (1361-

62) in the Multan region. The exercise led to the identification of two types of land grants – the endowments made by former rulers (*auqaf salatin maziya*) to pious foundations (mosques and seminaries) since the early thirteenth century and land grants bestowed on individual scholars, Sufis and nobles (*auqaf danishmandan wa mashaikh wa umara*) who had brought about agricultural improvements. In the former category, it was found that Muizzuddin Muhammad bin Sam of Ghor had endowed the Jama Masjid of Multan with two villages. The income from these lands was spent on the maintenance of the building and providing for teachers, students, reciters of the Quran and servants who gave the call for prayers, spread the carpets and lighted the lamps. This Sultan had also endowed the Jama Masjid of Talbina with one village and its income was spent in the manner described above. Khan-i Shahid (the son of Ghiasuddin Balban) had carved a land grant in the Multan region and associated it with a prayer enclosure (*namazgah*) and mosque. The income from this source was utilized to repair the former sacred space and pay the salary of the person who gave the call for prayer. It appears that these institutions were entitled to draw funds directly from the state treasury, if the income from their respective endowments turned out to be inadequate.

Such privilege was not extended to the second category of beneficiaries, when their incomes declined owing to fall in grain prices. However, the provincial administration undertook to compensate them with grain, in direct proportion to the quantity being acquired by them before the slump. In the first place, they were placed in properly settled villages, where some lands were cultivated and others were not. Their grants were delineated in a manner that during the years of famine (*salha-i qehat*) they did not suffer owing to the rise in grain prices. They were expected to meet their household needs from the income (*mahsul*) yielded by cultivated lands. The remaining lands were supposed to be utilized for effecting improvements in the total grant. With the reclamation of barren land by the grantees, the respective claims of *waqf* and *diwani* came under dispute. Mahru recommended that the share of *diwani* be merged with that of *waqf* on the grounds that the existing income from the latter was not large. Besides, Islam had been existing in Multan for the last 700 years. The process of rehabilitation of the region had begun with the return of the former inhabitants. The concerned intellectuals and Sufis (*danishmandan wa mashaikh*) were just mendicants (*faqir*) who were particularly loyal to Firoz Shah Tughluq. Mahru had dared to make these recommendations because the rehabilitation of Multan was a personal achievement (*karnama*) of the Sultan. However, he looked forward to the central government for final orders regarding the land grants in Multan. Looked at in totality, the intention of the governor was to transfer the gains of agrarian expansion to the grantee, rather than to the state.

The kind of agrarian expansion undertaken in southeastern Panjab was replicated in the Multan region also. The project was implemented by Mahru, who was appointed as its governor during the reign of Firoz Shah Tughluq. For reasons which are not clear, Shams Siraj Afif and other contemporary writers do not mention the economic developments in Multan. As such, we are constrained to depend entirely on the letters of the governor himself. During the second half of the fourteenth century, a number of canals – Nasirwah, Qutbwah, Khizrwah, Qabulwah and Hamruwah – were excavated in the Multan region, most probably at the instance of Firoz Shah Tughluq. It is true that we know only the names of these canals, and not from where they were cut or the specific areas that they irrigated. It was probable that two rivers – the Chenab after uniting with the Jhelam at Shorkot and the Ravi which flowed to the south of Multan – offered ample scope for the development of irrigation. However, our information is quite clear on two points, viz., the financial principles governing the excavation of the canals and the role of the local beneficiaries in the enterprise. It was clarified that in case of works on large rivers – like Sihun, Jihun, Dajla, Ravi and Beas – money could be spent from the public treasury. However, if this source was short of funds, the ruler could turn to the people (*khalq*). In case of smaller canals, like Nasirwah, Qutbwah, and Khizrwah, the cost of construction and maintenance was bound to be borne by the local beneficiaries, including the peasants and chiefs (*ahali wa arbab*). Mahru advocated that the obligation be shared equally between the two classes, so that the burden of one was not shifted to the other. He condemned the refusal of land controlling elements – *mashaikh, ulama, sadrs* and *maliks* including Kamal Taj – to contribute in the repair work of Nasirwah, despite the fact that this canal passed through the villages where they had been assigned the land grants. He warned of a fall in agricultural output if both, the state treasury and local beneficiaries, failed to provide financial support for the maintenance of the canals.[116]

The provincial administration sought the active cooperation of the local community, which acted through its traditional village headmen, in the task of constructing and maintaining the canals. Those who performed this role were rewarded, while those who abstained were punished. A *muqaddam* named Babdujah had displayed much initiative and energy in digging two canals (*ju-i shahi*) – Qabulwah and Hamruwah – when the other *muqaddams* and soldiers had run away. Mahru raised the status of Babdujah from an ordinary village headman to a high ranking officer and granted to him the superintendence (*danagi*) of these canals, so that he continued to exert himself in the service of the governor. The local population comprising the village headmen and peasants of the concerned subdivision (*khutan wa muqaddaman wa riaya-i parganat*) was directed to serve and consult this new officer in the tasks related to his office (*danagi*). Those who had refused to participate in the digging of the canals and who had become fugitives were threatened with death and exile.

In a public proclamation addressed to the peasantry, Mahru declared that cultivation had made a tremendous progress owing to the ample availability of water by the grace of God. In that year, the agrarian conditions had reached a level never heard of earlier. Therefore, the peasants were encouraged to work hard. Regarding the magnitude of land revenue and its collection, Mahru assured them of adhering to the past practice (*rasm-i qadeem*), the old cultivators paying half of their dues in grain and half in cash on the basis of official grain prices (*nirkh*), while the new settlers would pay the entire amount in grain.[117] For their part, the peasants were expected to carry out cultivation in the villages where they had settled. They were not permitted to leave their traditional settlements, because such an action was bound to result in the abadonment of the existing cultivation and depriving the Delhi Sultanate of its share of the produce. As a representative of the state, the revenue assignee (*muqti*) could not exercise any control over the person of the peasants, who were free by birth. Nevertheless, he did have the right over the land tax due from them. In this regard, the order of the Sultan was final. If the landholders (*maliks*) of a neighbouring locality managed to entice away these peasants to their village, the former could not lay any claim to the said tax. Any attempt on their part to appropriate it, betrayed an ignorance of Islamic jurisprudence (*fiqh*) and made them liable to punishment. It was stipulated that lands, whose revenue had been assigned, could not be left uncultivated as these were either revenue paying (*kharaji*) or tithe paying (*ushri*).[118]

In their social gatherings (*majlis*), the members of the ruling class discussed the legality of price control by the state, particularly when such a move could ameliorate the suffering of the common people. They took into account the opinions expressed by experts in their legal texts. According to *al-Kafi*, the state must ban the regrating (*ihtikar*) of commodities, on which depended the lives of humans and animals. These goods were identified as wheat, barley, grapes, dates and apricots. This position was based on the views of Imam Abu Hanifa and Imam Muhammad Idris. Abu Yusuf defined regrating as the act of blocking and stocking of a commodity, including gold and silver, which harmed the common people. Imam Abu Hanifa and Imam Muhammad Idris did not empower a ruler to determine the prices of food items. Their argument was based on the authority of Prophet Muhammad, who had stated, 'Do not determine the prices, because it is God who determines, controls and announces the same.' Therefore, it was not proper for a ruler (*imam*) to interfere in the work of a seller. But he could intervene if the common people were harmed. For example, if a person purchased a piece of land for 50 and sold it for 100, then the ruler could stop the transaction so that the people (Muslims) did not suffer. Imam Malik advocated fixation of prices during the time of famine, so that relief could be provided to the common people. The author of *Siyar-i Shahan* argued that regrating was forbidden because it was harmful to the common people and that anyone involved in such an activity ought to be punished.

While serving as the governor of Multan, Mahru found that the merchants and artisans (*saudagaran wa muhtirfa*) were engaged in the regrating of essential commodities. He examined the dynamics of trade in four essential commodities – ghee, cloth, sugar and fuel. The merchants brought ghee from Sarsuti by paying 7 *jitals* per *ser*, but stocked it till they were able to sell it for 9 or 10 *jitals* per *ser*. They brought cloth from Huka and, having purchased at 50 *jitals* and then hoarding the stock, sold it for double the original price. They brought sugar from Lahore and Delhi, but concealed it for many years in order to make big gains. Mahru fell out with his merchant friend Khwaja Ali Kamal Dilbani who insisted on regrating even when the price of sugar started falling owing to the arrival of stocks from Lahore and Delhi. Cartloads of fuel were brought from the neighbouring countryside (*mahals*) and sold at 8 *jitals* per maund. These facts were enough to convince Mahru that the merchants and artisans resorted to hoarding and profiteering. At the outset, they were made to understand the rulings of the Shariat on the issue. However, they did not pay any heed owing to their greed. They were not reformed by the fear of punishment ordained by the Shariat. As a result, much suffering was caused to all, particularly preachers, soldiers, and destitute. In fact, the orderliness of society was disturbed.

The provincial administration could not be a mute spectator to a common problem, which had wide political and social implications. Without referring to the price regulations of Alauddin Khalji, Mahru described the mechanism by which the city of Multan was provisioned with four essential commodities – ghee, cloth, sugar, and fuel. Mahru started purchasing these goods at prices paid by the regraters, making immediate cash payments. He arranged their sale at reasonable prices, so that regrating was eliminated and some profit started flowing into the provincial treasury. The state control of trade was resented by the merchants, who wrongly termed the measure of public welfare as a harmful step. But Mahru did not care about these selfish rants, because the Shariat approved of transactions if both the buyers and sellers were satisfied. What was more important, the move benefited the common people, particularly the preachers, soldiers and destitute.[119]

With the political stabilization of the Delhi Sultanate and the expansion of trade, the mercantile class began to play an important role in the economy of northwestern India. The government functionaries – governors (*walis*), revenue assignees (*muqtis*), local officers (*ashab-i atraf*) and tax collectors (*rahdars*) – were expected to create conditions conducive for the movement of commerce, since it brought revenues for the provincial administration in the form of various taxes. On their part, the merchants were required to be honest in their dealings with the governmental functionaries. Both sides were advised to nurture with each other cordial relations that were based on mutual respect.[120] In actual practice, this ideal state of affairs could not be realized at all times. This was shown by the following two cases.

Mahru received a complaint against Muizzuddin, the administrator (*hakim*) of Uch, from a local merchant Khizr Abu Bakr. The complainant alleged that the nephew and some relatives of Muizzuddin had inflicted on him several cruelties including a beating with shoes. Mahru felt that if the charge was true, the action was a violation of the Shariat and reflected a gross inversion of wisdom. It was incumbent on Muizzuddin to have acted himself with justice, so that the dispute was brought to an end. However, there was another allegation against Muizzuddin. This officer used to issue permits (*sajal*) regarding the payment of *zakat*, which was locally known as *batta*. But he had refused to issue this document to the victim ever since the latter received some assistance from Kamal Taj. It appeared that these two officers of Uch, Muizzuddin and Kamal Taj, stood against each other in this case. Intervening in the dispute, Mahru directed Muizzuddin to look into the conduct of Kamal Taj. If his step did not show any trace of oppression, Muizzuddin should have supported him in dispensing justice. If his step reflected oppression, Muizzuddin should have reported the matter to the governor instead of passing any order. Mahru warned Muizzuddin that if he had delayed the release of the permit owing to his personal enmity, this attitude would squeeze the inflow of revenues into the provincial treasury and harm the interests of the merchants. Such a situation was neither sanctioned by the Shariat, nor did it conform to the ideal of wisdom.[121]

The second case revealed the action of a vigilant provincial administration against two merchants who had violated state regulations and made false allegation in order to grab undue financial gains. Ahmad and Yasin, the two sons of Malik Shahu, falsely claimed that they had been issued a royal order (*farman aali*) permitting them to pay *zakat* and *danganah* at Delhi and not at Multan.[122] They had also levelled an allegation against Mahru that he had ignored the royal order and had extracted a huge amount of 20,000 *tankas* as payment for the two taxes. Mahru was outraged at the false statement as well as the allegation of the two brothers. In his carefully worded response, he claimed that his subordinates had treated the two brothers with due respect. But he was deeply anguished that they, who apparently enjoyed an eminent position in the mercantile class, had failed to reciprocate in a satisfactory manner. In return for the generosity of the provincial officers, the two had acted with manipulation and deceit. Mahru, while putting the record straight, clarified that he had seen the royal order brought by them, that he had himself written to the Sultan on the matter and that he had done exactly what he was ordered to do. If he had levied a sum of 1,700 *tankas* as *zakat* and *danganah* from them, this was strictly in accordance with the specific directions of the central government.[123] In fact, the brothers were guilty of committing several illegal acts. First, they had levelled a false allegation against a highranking officer. Second, they had falsely complained of paying 20,000 *tankas* as *zakat* and *danganah*, whereas the actual amount was determined as 1,700 *tankas*. Third, they had tried to associate themselves with people, who were far superior to them in credibility and who had nothing to do with them. Fourth, they had tried to sow the seeds of dissension between provincial officers and Delhi-based bureaucrats; the differences would errupt in the open as soon as Mahru sent his report to the central government on the sordid affair. Fifth, they had included in the *bainama* slaves to be carried to Khurasan for sale and also sold horses to the local chiefs (Hindus) in violation of the state orders. Mahru took pride in claiming that he was not one of those officers who, having taken bribes, ignored the royal orders and thus connived at the illegal activities of the traders.[124]

A royal mandate (*manshur*), which was issued to a newly appointed judicial officer (*dadbeg*) of Multan, threw interesting light on the administration of justice in the region. In its first part, the document viewed the role of state in dispensing justice in the context of the commandments of religion, particularly the Quran. It was asserted that the aim of sending prophets and apostles and appointing governors and preachers was to ensure the welfare of the Muslims and protect their life and property. According to the pious caliph Hazrat Umar, a ruler was entitled to ban what the Quran had prohibited. This meant that the prohibitions of the ruler were mostly the prohibitions of the Quran and this position was derived from the Quranic verse, 'You are certainly greater in being feared in their hearts than Allah.' However, only a select few understood the Quran, deliberated over its teachings and followed them in practice. If the people did not fear the wrath of God and did not fear the authority of kings and governors, there would be violent murders and highway robberies. In these circumstances, the life, property and welfare of the people would be threatened with destruction. Since wicked men were driven by sensual desires, it was necessary to admonish such people and prevent their criminal acts, so that noble practices led to the betterment of society and the government was run in accordance with the Shariat. It was on account of these reasons that the administration of justice and moral censor (*dadbegi wa ihtisab*) was assigned to a person, who was engaged in noble deeds and promoted religious affairs by traversing the path of the Shariat and justice.[125]

Having constructed an appropriate context, the royal mandate turned the attention of the incumbent officer to a specific illegal practice prevalent in Multan. This officer was directed to deal firmly with people who transgressed the bounds of the Shariat (*daira shariat*) and acted against the precepts of religion (*khilaf mazhab*), so that they refrained from their evil acts. Some villagers of Multan took wives who had not been divorced from their previous husbands. This abominable practice, which was held illegal in all religions, was common among them. The *dadbeg* was ordered to punish the guilty and warn them in a proper manner as it was done by a judge (*qazi*). It had to be understood that God had made the legal marriage a means of strengthening one's self, producing children, and propagating the race. In this manner, the continual existence of the world was based on a pure practice. Therefore, the *dadbeg* was urged to drill the sinfulness of the practice into the ears of the adulterers, mindful of the Quranic verse, 'And go not nigh to fornication; surely it is an indecency and evil is the way.' He should admonish them with the widely known saying of Prophet Muhammad, 'Marriage is my Sunnat.' (*al-nikah man sunnati*). He should carry out a public proclamation across the villages of Multan, ordering the people to abandon the sinful practice, so that they adopted the correct religious beliefs and turned to the Creator of the world who always showed the right path. If they declared that they were following in the footsteps of their forefathers, they ought to understand that they were all misguided, except those who would die as Muslims. It was binding on the people, who were illegally keeping women in their houses, to divorce them and to observe the obligatory waiting period (*iddat*), so that their children were legitimate (*halalzadah*) and they were saved from the fire of hell. The said officer was asked to offer a period of one month to such people, so that they amended their ways and, desisting from their illegal act, returned from sin to obedience. Even after this, if a complaint was received about this evil practice and the charge was duly proved, such a person had to be given adequate punishment.[126]

In view of the prevailing political unrest in Sind and the perpetual threat of Mongol invasions, the governor of Multan was assigned the additional duties of a military commander. His status was raised above that of other nobles and he was entrusted with a vast area extending from Koh-i Jud to Multan and the river that merged into the sea. He was authorized to implement all the measures that had been applied in Delhi by the Sultan. Since the troops had been placed under his command, he was expected to suppress the rebels of Sind and fight against the Mongols.[127] In a letter to the Mustaufi-i Mamalik, Mahru reported against the activities of Banbhaniya whose revolt had assumed serious proportions.[128] The rebel was guilty of not only ravaging Sind, but also including the Mongols in his depredations. On one occasion, he had even intruded into Panjab along with the Mongols. He had also been carrying out similar activities in Gujarat. In these circumstances, Mahru urged the Mustaufi-i Mamalik (whose brother Malik Ruknuddin Hasan held the governorship of Gujarat) to mobilize the people of that province against Banbhaniya and assure them of military assistance from Delhi. In other words, the adminstrations of the two provinces, Multan and Gujarat, could join hands to meet a common threat from Sind.[129]

As the governor of a frontier province, Mahru acquired horses from different places in the region and sent them to Delhi for service in the central cavalry.[130] At one time, he sent two persons, Qazi Zahiruddin and Umaruddin, to Lahore so that they could purchase horses. Taking a personal interest in the matter, he demanded that the horses be carefully examined and particulars of the transaction (*tazkira-i kharid*) be sent to him in writing.[131] On another occasion, he sent his son Khatiruddin Nuh along with horses and camels to Delhi. The dispatch of the war animals had been delayed due to severe floods. In fact, water had overflowed from the Chenab and Ravi in such a manner that the two rivers appeared to have merged into each other. The floodwaters, having surrounded the fort, threatened to fall into the moat. There was widespread panic among the inhabitants, while the governor himself underwent intense suffering. Ultimately, the worst did not happen and the people of the city remained safe. In his letter to Wahid Qarshi (entitled Malik ul-Umara Syed ul-Hujjab) on this subject, Mahru requested him to convey his regrets to the Sultan at the delay in sending the horses.[132] In another communication, Mahru assured the Sadr us-Sudur Jalaluddin that he had not levied *zakat* or *danganah* on the horses brought for him by Shaikh Ali.[133]

Sufis and Governance

The provincial administration, motivated by its own interests, remained in contact with prominent Sufis and sought their mediation in tackling difficult problems. In an important letter to Syed Jalaluddin Bokhari, Mahru stated that it was the Shaikh's grace that could save all the Muslims (including Mahru) from inner and outer infirmities. If the state functionaries did not work in accordance with God's wishes, they would be guilty of inflicting oppression and provoking rebellion. Though Mahru prayed for freedom from the taint of oppression, yet his prayers had remained unanswered. The Sufis, owing to their numerous virtues – asceticism, faith, truth, purity and submission – were bound to pray that the state functionaries worked for justice and refrained from oppression. They were not expected to malign them in any manner, though there was concrete evidence of such an unbecoming conduct on their part. In fact, the slanderers had used bad language owing to their pride. In these circumstances, the Sufis could not remain aloof and had to come out in the field. The state functionaries were not only helpless, but they also confessed having inflicted oppression. This admission, though humiliating in itself, could pave the way for their forgiveness from God. They did try to rule in accordance with the principles of benevolence and kindness, but the people were negligent of their obligations.

In the above context, Mahru reported that the Syeds had been refusing to pay the land tax, having become used to paying the resultant penalties (*tawan*). In the previous year, they had given a written undertaking at the tomb of Shaikh Kabir to pay the land tax, but they had violated the oath. Shaikh Bokhari was requested to advise the Syeds to give up their recalcitrance, to show obedience to the regime, to pay their dues and to treat the people well. They had to understand that the collection of this amount was correctly spent on the soldiers, scholars and poor. Mahru did have the means to ensure compliance of the rules of the state. Yet he sought the mediation of Shaikh Bokhari to warn the Syeds of suitable punishment, should they persist in their indiscretion. However, if they displayed their subservience by paying the requisite land tax and meeting their financial obligations to the state, they could look forward to a variety of benefits.[134]

Mahru addressed four letters to a person named Shaikh Raziuddin. The governor's respect for him and his title of Malik ul-Mashaikh indicated that he was a prominent Sufi of Uch.[135] Mahru not only discussed administrative matters with him, but also sought his assistance in solving the problems at the grassroots. For example, a man named Maulana Haji Bihari, in his letter to Khwaja Husamuddin Junaidi, complained against the local officers (*karkuns*) of Uch, particularly the governor Khwaja Kamaluddin. It was reported that whenever they needed any work to be done, they oppressed the local inhabitants by extracting unpaid forced labour (*begar*) and using foul language. Whenever they felt the need for money, they confined the hapless people in a narrow dark cell and, thus, extracted a sum of 2,000 *tankas* or even more. They did not fear anyone. Some scholars and Sufis (*ulama wa mashaikh*) had tried to stop their oppression, but these efforts did not succeed. In these circumstances, Mahru was constrained to seek the assistance of Shaikh Raziuddin. In his letter to the Shaikh, Mahru expressed himself against the use of any threat or warning to the guilty functionaries. Instead, he suggested that the Shaikh could write to the governor Khwaja Kamaluddin, advising him in the name of God to put an end to the oppression. Mahru felt that if the governor of Uch performed his duties in a just manner, the soul of Shaikh ul-Mashaikh Qutb ul-Auliya Jamaluddin would rest in peace.[136] As the governor of Multan, Mahru felt responsible for the actions of a subordinate who was guilty of bringing a bad name to the Tughluq regime.

According to a complaint from Shaikh Raziuddin, two officers Badruddin Qimaz and Kamal Taj came from Multan to Uch and imposed a tax (*muhaddis*), subjecting the local inhabitants to great difficulty and forcing them to cry in protest. The former Sultan, Muhammad bin Tughluq (r. 1325-51), had abolished this particular tax at a time when the towns were adequately settled and people were prosperous. Therefore, the reigning Sultan, Firoz Shah Tughluq (r. 1351-88), was not expected to levy this tax on the Muslims when the inhabitants had scattered and were helpless. In fact, the entire population was finding it difficult to make both ends meet when this tax had not been levied. They could not fulfil their needs in the face of this new tax. If the government wished to increase its financial resources, it could have raised the rate of poll tax (*jaziya*) on the twenty-five Hindus, who were comfortably running their shops. Mahru expressed his ignorance about the matter, as he had not authorized the functionaries (*karkuns*) of Uch to impose any new tax. It was difficult for him to comment on the subject, as the letter was not clear about the exact nature of the tax. From his perspective, the economic adversity might be true in the case of soldiers, but not in the case of traders and artisans. According to his strong assertion, there had never been more prosperity during any period than that extending from the reign of Alauddin Khalji to his own days. The prices of food grain were low as compared to the earlier times. The artisans like weavers and tailors were making handsome earnings, as they were charging the same high rates that prevailed during the famines. After rejecting the complaint, Mahru advised Shaikh Raziuddin to pay attention to the welfare of the army, which protected the kingdom and religion, besides promoting the cause of the Shariat and Prophetic practice.[137]

It appeared from another letter that Shaikh Raziuddin, after receiving a spirited denial from Mahru, confronted Badruddin Qimaz on the question of the new tax (*muhaddis*). In order to save his own skin, Badruddin Qimaz levelled a number of allegations against the governor of Multan. Mahru was not unduly disturbed by these allegations. Since he had himself reported the matter to Delhi, he was confident that Badruddin Qimaz would not be able to substantiate his charges during an interrogation at the court. Thus, what was originally a complaint regarding the imposition of a new tax assumed the form of a dispute between the highest officer in the province and a subordinate.[138]

Mahru was anguished at the attitude of a junior officer Malik Khas Hajib, who had been posted at Dipalpur. When the latter was faced with opposition from the local population (*riaya*) and his own slaves (*bandgan*), it was Mahru who came to his rescue and took every possible step to control the situation. Due to unknown reasons, Malik Khas Hajib turned against his benefactor. He seemed to have been responsible for inciting the Kambohs of Multan to level false allegations against Mahru and to meet the Sultan, Firoz Shah Tughluq, in this connection. On his part, the

Sultan could not understand the objectionable behaviour of Malik Khas Hajib who, along with his father, had benefited from royal patronage. When Mahru went to Delhi and presented himself before the Sultan, he was conferred a robe of honour that was normally given only to eminent nobles. Made of two colours, it was embroidered with threads of gold and silver. The Sultan, while offering the gift, declared that the apparel was meant to be worn in winter and that it was splendid in quality. Mahru availed the opportunity to state that the Kambohs had levelled false allegations against him. With a view to clear his name, Mahru suggested that his troops could be inspected and the accounts of his revenue assignment (*iqta*) could be examined. The Sultan, who was convinced of Mahru's credibility, declared that the Kambohs were liars. He ordered that they should be placed in the custody of Mahru as prisoners and, after being taken to Multan, they must be given severe punishment at the gate of the city, so that those who levelled false allegations against others learnt a lesson.[139]

The Tughluq rulers, owing to their roots in Panjab, were intimately familiar with its topographical features and social structure. From the middle of the fourteenth century, they shifted the political focus from the Gangetic plain to Panjab. By this time, the dominant local elements in this region, particularly the zamindars and Sufis, had gradually shed their aloofness from the state and showed willingness to collaborate with the ruling class. As a result, the Tughluqs stitched alliances with a number of zamindars, who commanded a lot of influence in their localities. They also made it a point to pay homage at the prominent Sufi shrines and revived many such establishments with liberal endowmwnts. In this manner, they prepared the ground for agararian expansion based on canal networks in two arid zones of Panjab. The southeast Panjab, which received as many as seven canals, experienced a series of changes – the settlement of pastoral groups as sedentary cultivators, a shift in the cropping pattern and the emergence of new urban centres. In the Multan region, the governor Ainu ul-Mulk Mahru initiated a project of economic revival, which involved laying a network of canals with the active collaboration of beneficiaries including headmen and peasants. While priority was

New Strategies of State Formation 285

accorded to the maintenance of the army, the management of land grants was streamlined. The administration not only regulated the prices of essential commodities, but also checked malpractices in long distance trade. It entertained written complaints of the Sufis against the lower rung functionaries, who were accused of oppressing the ordinary people.

NOTES

1. Amir Khusrau, *Tughluq Nama*, Persian text, ed. Syed Hashmi Faridabadi, Aurangabad: Matba Urdu, 1933, pp. 136-138.
2. Ibn Battuta, *Rehla*, English translation, Mahdi Husain, (entitled *The Rehla of Ibn Battuta: India, Maldive Islands and Ceylon*), Baroda: Oriental Institute, 1976, pp. 47-8 (hereafter cited as Ibn Battuta).
3. Shams Siraj Afif, *Tarikh-i Firoz Shahi*, Persian text, ed. Maulavi Wilayat Husain, Calcutta: Bibliotheca Indica, 1890, p. 36.
4. Muhammad Qasim Hindu Shah Farishta, *Tarikh-i Firishta*, Urdu translation, Abdul Rahman and Abdul Hayy Khwaja, Lahore: Al-Mizan, 2004, vol. I, p. 293; the word 'Jat' has been wrongly printed as 'Bhat'.
5. Sujan Rai Bhandari, *Khulasat ut-Tawarikh*, Persian text, ed. M. Zafar Hasan, Delhi: G. and Sons, 1918, p. 235.
6. Surinder Singh, 'The Making of Medieval Punjab: Politics, Society and Economy c. 1200 - c. 1400,' *Proceedings of the Punjab History Conference*, Patiala: Punjabi University, 40th Session, 14-16 March 2008, p. 106.
7. Agha Mahdi Husain, *The Rise and Fall of Muhammad bin Tughluq*, Delhi: Idarah-i Adabiyat-i Delli, rpt., 1972, pp. 17-18; Ishwari Prasad, *History of the Qaraunah Turks in India*, vol. I, Allahabad: Central Book Depot, rpt., 1974, p. 7.
8. R.C. Jauhri, 'Ghiath ud-Din Tughluq: His Original Name and Descent,' in *Kunwar Mohammad Ashraf: An Indian Scholar and Revolutionary 1903-1962*, ed. Horst Kruger, New Delhi: People's Publishing House, 1969, pp. 65-6.
9. Peter Jackson, *The Delhi Sultanate: A Political and Military History*, Cambridge: Cambridge University Press, 1999, p. 178.
10. Sunil Kumar, 'The Ignored Elites: Turks, Mongols and a Persain Secretarial Class in the Early Delhi Sultanate,' in *Expanding Frontiers in South Asian and World History: Essays in Honour of John F. Richards*, ed. Richard M. Eaton et al., Delhi: Cambridge University Press, 2013, pp. 41-3.
11. Before the restructuring of the agararian economy under Alauddin Khalji, these rural intermediaries enjoyed prosperity and influence in the countryside. They did not pay tax on their lands, secured a share in the produce, appropriated the village pasture, did not recognize the authority of

the government, mobilized armed contingents and lived in great aristocratic style. Barani, p. 291.
12. In medieval France, the wife was so completely absorbed into the family of the man, who had the right to give her children, that her own name was changed. The step marked a complete break with the past and her completed capture. Yet if she was to play her part in the house and fill it with legitimate children, her blood and her womb were necessary. In her offspring that which came from her ancestors through her blood would mix with that which her husband inherited through his blood from his ancestors. Georges Duby, *The Knight, the Lady and the Priest: The Making of Modern Marrige in Medieval France*, English translation, Barbara Bray, Chicago: University of Chicago Press, 1983, pp. 44-5.
13. Afif, pp. 37-40.
14. Ibid., pp. 40-2.
15. Ibid., pp. 103-4.
16. Such marriage alliances had started much earlier. It has been nearly forgotten that Prince Sultan Muhammad, (the son of Ghiasuddin Balban), who served as the governor of Multan, had married the daughter of a chief named Rai Kalu. When the Prince was killed in a battle against the Mongols, his father-in-law expressed his deep sense of loss by resorting to the four vents of mourning - crying, shrieking, sighing and howling. Not only this, he retrieved the dead body of his son-in-law from the invaders by paying a huge ransom from the income of his assignment (*iqta*). Isami, vol. II, p. 311.
17. Agha Mahdi Husain, *The Rise and Fall of Muhammad bin Tughluq*, pp. 19-20.
18. In the hierarchy of rural society, the aristocracy, owing to the possession of military resources, was placed higher than the village headmen, who were basically associated with the collection of the land tax. Tapan Raychaudhury and Irfan Habib, eds., *The Cambridge Economic History of India*, vol. I: *c. 1200–c. 1750*, Hyderabad: Orient Longman & Cambridge University Press, rpt., 2004, pp. 55-7.
19. Afif, p. 39.
20. Amir Khusrau, *Tughluq Nama*, p. 84.
21. Sunil Kumar, 'The Ignored Elites: Turks, Mongols and a Persian Secretarial Class in the Early Delhi Sultanate,' pp. 48-9.
22. Amir Khusrau, *Tughluq Nama*, p. 57.
23. Ibid., pp. 62-4.
24. Ibid., pp. 68-70.
25. Ibid., pp. 64-5.
26. Ibid., pp. 65-7.
27. Ibid., pp. 42-3.
28. Ibid., pp. 76-7.
29. Ibid., pp. 82-3.
30. Isami, Persian Text, pp. 379-80; Eng. tr., vol. II, pp. 582-3.

New Strategies of State Formation

31. Amir Khusrau, *Tughluq Nama*, p. 115.
32. Ibid., pp. 105-6.
33. Ibid., pp. 108-9.
34. Ibid., pp. pp. 111-12.
35. Ibid., pp. 117-19.
36. Ghazi Malik ordered his commanders to tie peacock feathers (*par taoos*) to their banners, so that they could be distinguished from the flags of the opposing army. He followed this practice in his battles against the Mongols. For this particular occasion, he chose Kallah as the slogan of his forces. Amir Khusrau, *Tughluq Nama*, p.122.
37. Isami, Persian text, pp. 382-7; Eng. tr., vol. II, pp. 582-3.
38. Richard M. Eaton, 'The Political and Religious Authority of the Shrine of Baba Farid', in *Essays on Islam and Indian History*, New Delhi: Oxford University Press, 2000, pp. 204-7.
39. Afif, pp. 27-8.
40. Amir Khurd, pp. 196-7.
41. Tanvir Anjum, *Chishti Sufis in the Sultanate of Delhi 1190-1400: From Restrained Indifference to Calculated Defiance*, p. 251.
42. Ibn Battuta, pp. 11-24.
43. Since Multan was located on the land routes to Qandhar and Lahri Bandar, it was a major entrepot of trade. The chief item of import was horses, while the exports comprised slaves and indigo. A large volume of long distance trade was in the hands of persons called Multanis, who were both Hindu and Muslim. They earned interest on lending money, besides receiving direct financial assistance from Alauddin Khalji. The Sultan appointed Hamiduddin, a prominent merchant (*malik ut-tujjar*) of Multan as the chief judge of the kingdom. Raychaudhury and Habib, eds., in *The Cambridge Economic History of India*, vol. I, pp. 84-5.
44. When a newcomer arrived in the country, the newswriters sent to the Sultan a complete report, noting all particulars including his physical features, garments, number of companions, servants, slaves and horses. They also recorded his behaviour during the journey and rest, leaving out nothing pertinent. When the newcomer reached Multan, he stopped there until the arrival of royal orders for his entry and entertainment. At Multan, every person was honoured according to his conduct and ambition, without recognizing his descent and parentage. Ibn Battuta, p. 4.
45. While making recruitment to his bureaucracy, Muhammad bin Tughluq introduced three new elements – foreigners, Sufi families and socially inferior groups. Addessed as the excellent (*aizza*), the foreigners were appointed as ministers and judges, but they could not be employed indiscriminately in every part of the country owing to their limited knowledge of local conditions. However, they were quite suited for posts in the departments of justice and charity. Mohammad Habib and Khaliq

Ahmad Nizami, eds., *A Comprehensive History of India*, vol. V: *The Delhi Sultanate*, AD *1206-1526*, pp. 563-4.

46. The banquets and feasts of the old nobility were conspicuous for the large quantity of every food, as the guests were served twenty to fifty dishes. Making full allowance for huge appetites and greedy stomachs, there was terrible wastage which could only be explained in the light of their ideas of social respectability. Abundance of the dining table was an index of hospitality and wastage was immaterial, as a crowd of menials, domestics and beggars was always present to share the leavings. Kunwar Muhammad Ashraf, *Life and Conditions of the People of Hindustan*, New Delhi: Munshiram Manoharlal, 2nd edn., 1970, p. 220.

47. Conditions for two crops were created by the enormous mass of alluvium deposited by the Indus and its tributaries as well as the three sharply divided seasons. After harvesting the Rabi crop in early summer, the soil recovered its fertility during the hot months. Thereafter, it was subjected to rounds of ploughing and fertilizing with manure, so that it became ready for the Kharif crop. The peasant cultivated the land that was a ancestral legacy or acquired personally or received on hire. Hamida Khatoon Naqvi, *Agricultural, Industrial and Urban Dynamism under the Sultans of Delhi 1206-1555*, New Delhi: Munshiram Manoharlal, 1986, pp. 12-16.

48. Ibn Battuta has erred in tracing the itinerary of his journey. According to him, after leaving Multan, he reached Abohar and then arrived at Ajodhan. Since this was illogical and impossible, he, on leaving Multan, must have first stopped at Ajodhan and then proceeded to Abohar. Mahdi Husain, while preparing the itinerary in the form of a table with dates and places, has rectified the error.

49. Ibn Battuta has made two mistakes while referring to Baba Farid. He was wrong in identifying the then head of the Chishti hospice at Ajodhan as Shaikh Fariduddin. Since Baba Farid had died (15 October 1265) nearly seven decades earlier, the traveller had actually met the Shaikh's grandson Shaikh Alauddin, who was treated by the Sultan, Muhammad bin Tughluq, with great respect. Secondly, Ibn Battuta has wrongly associated Baba Farid with Badaun. He obviously confused the saint with his principal disciple Shaikh Nizamuddin Auliya who hailed from Badaun. Fortunately, he has corrected the error in the subsequent lines.

50. Amir Khurd has noted this habit of the Shaikh in a different manner. According to him, when Shaikh Ruknuddin met Shaikh Alauddin, the two saints shook hands and embraced each other. The latter, on returning to his house, took a fresh bath and changed his clothes. When Shaikh Ruknuddin received a complaint about this odd behaviour, he did not take offence. He stated that Shaikh Alauddin was entitled to act in his own way as he remained insulated from worldliness, while he himself smelt of worldly entanglements. Amir Khurd, *Siyar ul-Auliya*, p. 195.

51. This act of Sati might have been similar to the one involoving three women and observed by Ibn Battuta at Amjeri, near Dhar in central India. The act was seen as praiseworthy, as it was believed to bring glory to the kin and registered the widow's fidelity to her husband. Yet it was not obligatory. When the women agreed to burn themselves, they spent three days in eating and drinking amidst music. On the fourth day, they adorned themselves and left for the spot in procession, while the musicians played drums, bugles and timbals. People conveyed to them their messages for their dead relatives. They bathed in a pond and gave away their clothes and ornaments as alms. They wrapped themselves in unsewn cloth, but were prevented from seeing the fire. As sesame oil was poured in the pit and men stood around with poles in their hands, the women descended into the flames. Ibn Battuta, pp. 22-3.
52. Ibn Battuta was possibly referring to Rai Pithora, the popular name of Prithviraj Chauhan.
53. Hansi was a fairly important centre of the Chishti order. Baba Farid had stayed here for nearly two decades before settling in Ajodhan. His close disciple Shaikh Jamaluddin Hansavi made vigorous efforts to carry forward the legacy of his mentor. He was succeeded by his grandson Shaikh Qutbuddin Munawwar who, in his turn, was followed by his son Shaikh Nuruddin. The Tughluq rulers recognized the eminence of the Chishti saints of Hansi. It was surprising that Ibn Battuta neither paid a visit to the Chishti hospice, nor cared to mention it in his account.
54. There were two kinds of post. The horse-post (*ulaq*) was run by the royal horses that were stationed at every four miles. The foot-post (*dawa*) had three stations per mile. At every third of a mile were three pavilions, where sat the couriers with girded loins. While starting from a city, the courier held the letter in one hand and a rod with copper bells in the other. When the couriers heard the ringing of bells, one of them got ready and, receiving the letter, ran top speed until he reached the next pavilion. The foot post was faster than the horse post. It was used to transport fruit from Khurasan to India, water for the Sultan from the Ganges to Daulatabad and even criminals locked in cages. Ibn Battuta, pp. 3-4.
55. Barani, pp. 538-9.
56. Afif, p. 60.
57. Barani, p. 560.
58. At the town of Sarsuti, the Sultan received a gift of few lakh *tankahs* from the local bankers and traders. The Sultan received this amount as loan and promised to return it on reaching Delhi. He distributed this amount among his soldiers. Afif, p. 61.
59. Shaikh Nasiruddin Mahmud differed with Muhammad bin Tughluq on the issue of employing Sufis in the service of the state and, in the process, suffered harrassment at the hands of the the Sultan. However, he was one of the notables who supported the accession of Firoz Shah Tughluq in Thatta.

He advised the new Sultan to dispense justice to the people, failing which he would pray for changing the ruler. He did not identify himself with the regime, which he criticised in comparison to that of Alauddin Khalji. In view of friction with the Sultan, he resisted the state and defended the space of the Chishtis. Tanvir Anjum, *Chishti Sufis in the Sultanate of Delhi 1190-1400: From Restrained Indifference to Calculated Defiance*, pp. 272-8, 313-22.

60. Afif, pp. 60-2.
61. Ibid., p. 62-3.
62. Ibid., p. 71.
63. On this occasion, the two Chishti saints, Shaikh Nasiruddin Mahmud and Shaikh Qutbuddin Munawwar, met each other with great enthusiasm. On remembering their common mentor Shaikh Nizamuddin Auliya, they became emotional and wept. Qawwals were called, musical sessions were organized and the two listened to the mystical verses for many days. They bade farewell to each other and, after some time, both of them passed away. Afif, pp. 62-4.
64. The Sultan claimed to have banned all items forbidden by the Shariat. Firstly, he banned the use of utensils and weapons that were made of ornamented gold and silver. Secondly, he banned the pictures painted on a large number of goods including clothes, robes of honour, saddles, reins, vessels and furniture. He ordered the erasure of paintings on the walls in palaces and houses. Thirdly, he banned all clothes that were decorated with golden embroidery (*zardozi*). He outlawed the use of silken apparel and brocade, besides embroidered flags and caps. Firoz Shah Tughluq, *Futuhat-i Firoz Shahi*, Persian text, ed. Shaikh Abdul Rashid, Aligarh: Aligarh Muslim University, 1954, p. 11.
65. Afif, pp. 79-81.
66. Barani, pp. 558-61.
67. Firoz Shah Tughluq, *Futuhat-i Firoz Shahi*, pp. 11, 14.
68. Afif, pp. 319-21.
69. Ibid., p. 316.
70. Ibid., pp. 317-18.
71. Ibid., pp. 321-7.
72. Shaikh Sikandar bin Muhammad urf Manjhu bin Akbar, *Mirat-i Sikandari*, Persian text, ed. S.C. Misra and M.L. Rahman, Baroda: The Maharaja Sayajirao University of Baroda, 1961, pp. 6-10.
73. Ibid., p. 7.
74. In medieval France, society encouraged its warriors and hunters to undertake adventures. From such exploits, they brought back women. Such chance unions could be regularized, if young man's father or uncle reached an agreement with the girl's relatives. Women were introduced permanently as wives only if the advantages they brought with them were carefully weighed

and found satisfactory. Georges Duby, *The Knight, the Lady and the Priest: The Making of Modern Marriage in Medieval France*, p. 43.
75. Samira Shaikh, *Forging A Region: Sultans, Traders and Pilgrims in Gujarat 1200-1500*, New Delhi: Oxford University Press, 2010, pp. 200-1; another writer has linked the social attitude of the two brothers to their low caste. They pulled off the boots of a stranger, used their sister to beguile him, hurriedly wedded her outside their caste and abjured their earlier links by embracing Islam – all for material gains. Such practices were not current among the Rajputs, whose reaction was more accurately reflected by Rana Mal Bhatti who refused to surrender his daughter to Ghazi Malik. Hence, the two brothers were not above wine drawers, even if they were men of consequence among their own people. S.C. Misra, *The Rise of Muslim Power in Gujarat: A History of Gujarat from 1298 to 1442*, New Delhi: Munshiram Manoharlal, 2nd edn., 1982, pp. 139-40.
76. Shaikh Sikandar bin Muhammad urf Manjhu bin Akbar, *Mirat-i Sikandari*, pp. 10-11.
77. Ibid., pp. 4-5.
78. For the courtiers of the Sultans of Delhi, the governorship of Gujarat became a much coveted post and some were willing to pay substantial bribes to be appointed to Anhilvada or Cambay. By the end of the fourteenth century, the Delhi Sultanate was in a crisis following Timur's sack of Delhi and the Sultans were not in a position to control their regional governors. After a period of negotiation and uncertainty in Delhi, the last governor of Gujarat, Zafar Khan, declared his sovereignty in 1407. His descendants ruled over Gujarat for a century and a half and created institutions of governance and political articulation that had a remarkable longevity and resilience. Samira Shaikh, op. cit., pp. 5-6.
79. Shaikh Sikandar bin Muhammad urf Manjhu bin Akbar, *Mirat-i Sikandari*, p. 12.
80. The present account has been drawn from *Kayam Khan Rasa*, a poetic work in Braj Bhasha, which was composed in the second quarter of the seventeenth century. Its author Niamat Khan, who wrote under the psuedonym of Jan Kavi, was the son of Nawab Alaf Khan and, therefore, was a scion of the Qiyamkhani dynasty of Fatehpur Jhunjhunu. The work was a curious amalgamation of myth, local history and self-adulation. Its basic aim was to assert the Rajput ancestry of the dynasty, with particular reference to its Chauhan lineage.
81. Nupur Chaudhuri, 'A Vanished Supremacy: The Qiyamkhanis of Fatehpur-Jhunjhunu,' in *Popular Literature and Premodern Societies in South Asia*, ed. Surinder Singh and Ishwar Dayal Gaur, New Delhi: Pearson Longman, 2008, p. 64; Cynthia Talbot, 'Becoming Turk in the Rajput Way: Conversion and Identity in an Indian Warrior Narrative,' in *Expanding Frontiers in South Asian and World History: Essays in Honour of John F. Richards*, ed.

Richard M. Eaton et al., New York: Cambridge University Press, 2013, p. 203.
82. In his version, Nainsi mainly adopted the same sequence of the rise of the Qiyamkhanis, but rejected their claims of a Rajput ancestry. He stated that Qiyam Khan was originally a Hindu and, on becoming a Turk, suffered a loss in social stature. Far from being the mighty Turks, the Qiyamkhanis were mere slaves of Syed Nasir and, as such, they were only half men and of no use. Nainsi's disparaging remarks were understandable, as his Rathor patrons ruled over the powerful kingdom of Jodhpur, which was sometimes in conflict with the Qiyamkhanis. The factor of genealogy assumed significance when Rajput lineages were competing for political space under the Mughal dispensation. Nupur Chaudhuri, op. cit., p. 65; Cynthia Talbot, pp. 205-06.
83. Surinder Singh, 'The Making of Medieval Punjab: Politics, Society and Economy c. 1200 - c. 1400,' p. 117.
84. Talbot, op. cit., pp. 207-8.
85. Yahya bin Ahmad bin Abdullah Sirhindi, *Tarikh-i Mubarak Shahi*, Persian text, ed. M. Hidayat Husain, Calcutta: Asiatic Society of Bengal, 1931, pp. 177, 181, 189 (hereafter cited as Sirhindi).
86. Nupur Chaudhuri, op. cit., pp. 66-7.
87. Barani, pp. 483-4.
88. This area, lying between the Satluj and Jamuna, was known as the Ghaggar plain. It separated the Indus river system from that of the Ganga. During monsoon, it was inundated by a dozen torrents that brought huge volumes of water from the Siwaliks and communicated with one another. Most important of these were the Ghaggar, Markanda and Saraswati. They lost the entire volume of water by evaporation or soakage before leaving the western border of the plain, spreading sand and gravel beyond shallow channels. Ibadur Rahman Khan, 'Historical Geography of the Punjab and Sind,' *Muslim University Journal*, vol. I, no. 1, July 1931, pp. 107-8.
89. For the construction of buildings, the Sultan created a separate department, which spent countless money for the purpose. It was placed under a superintendent (*shahna mir imarat*) Malik Ghazi who was honoured with a golden mace. Different categories of artisans – stonecutters, woodcutters, ironsmiths, carpenters, saw drivers, lime crushers and masons – were placed under separate supervisors. Whenever the construction of a building started, the finance department (*diwan-i wizarat*) prepared an inventory of the material needed and provided requisite funds to the functionaries of the building department. Afif, pp. 331, 333.
90. Afif, pp. 124-7.
91. Mehardad Shokoohy and Netalie H. Shokoohy, *Hisar-i Firuza: Sultanate and Early Mughal Architecture in the District of Hisar, India*, London: Monographs on Art, Archaeology & Architecture, 1988, p. 8.
92. Afif, pp. 127.

93. Sirhindi, pp. 125-6.
94. Sharfuddin Ali Yazdi, *Zafar Nama*, vol. II, Persian text, ed. Muhammad Ilahdad, Calcutta: Asiatic Society of Bengal, 1888, p. 86.
95. Sirhindi, p. 130; Abdul Qadir Badauni, *Muntakhab-ut Tawarikh*, vol. I, English translation, George S.A. Ranking and B.P. Ambashthya, Patna: Academica Asiatica, rpt., 1973, pp. 330-1; Khwaja Nizamuddin Ahmad, *Tabqat-i Akbari*, vol. I, English translation, B. De, Calcutta: The Asiatic Society, rpt., 1973, pp. 247-8.
96. Irfan Habib and Faiz Habib, 'Mapping the Canals of Firoz Shah (1351-88),' Indian History Congress, 77th Session, University of Kerala, Thiruvananthapuram, 28-30 December 2016 (typescript), pp. 2-13.
97. Afif, pp. 131-3.
98. Ibid., pp. 130-1.
99. Ibid., pp. 129-30.
100. Barani, pp. 567-71.
101. Afif, p. 128.
102. Ibid., p. 129.
103. Ain ul-Mulk Mahru was different from Ain ul-Mulk Multani, who was a noble of the Khaljis and served in the military operations at Ranthambhore, Malwa, Devgiri and Gujarat. Multani did not join Ghazi Malik's campaign against Khusrau Khan, but took part in the Tughluq expedition (1322) to Devgiri. Subsequently, he was not heard of. Iqtidar Husain Siddiqui, *Authority and Kingship under the Sultans of Delhi (Thirteenth and Fourteenth Centuries)*, New Delhi: Manohar, 2006, pp. 283-6; Peter Jackson, *The Delhi Sultanate: A Political and Military History*, p. 329.
104. Barani, pp. 485-7; Ibn Battuta, pp. 104-09; Isami, vol. III, pp. 709-14.
105. Afif, pp. 407-18.
106. A similar royal mandate was issed to Prince Fateh Khan, the son of Firoz Shah Tughluq, when he was appointed as the governor of Sind. He was advised to exercise his authority with moderation, to promote agriculture by encouraging the tax-paying peasantry, to entrust the finance department to able officers, to dispense justice without discrimination, to care for soldiers and officials, to patronise the honest and wise, to punish those who harmed the state or people, to be generous towards the Syeds, scholars and Sufis. All the local inhabitants including nobles, chiefs and village headmen were required to abide by these orders. Ain ul-Mulk Ainuddin Mahru, *Insha-i Mahru*, Persian text, ed. Shaikh Abdul Rashid, Aligarh: Aligarh Muslim University, 1954, Letter no. 1, pp. 2-7 (hereafter cited as Mahru).
107. Mahru, *Insha-i Mahru*, Letter no. 3, pp. 10-11; for comparison, see some other royal mandates issued to provincial governors during the thirteenth and fourteenth centuries. Siddiqui, *Perso-Arabic Sources of Information on the Life and Conditions in the Sultanate of Delhi*, pp. 167-89.
108. Unlike several administrative manuals that were theoretical and normative, Mahru's letters dealt with actual historical situations on the ground and,

while focusing on a wide range of administrative problems, highlighted the rationale behind state measure in each case. Surinder Singh, 'Dynamics of Statecraft in the Delhi Sultanate: A Reconstruction from the Letters of Ainul Mulk Mahru,' *Proceedings of the Indian History Congress*, 61st. Session, Calcutta, 2001, p. 285.

109. The Sultan claimed to have abolished twenty six taxes that were not permitted by the Shariat, while Afif has mentioned only four that fell in this category. These taxes generally applied to ordinary commodities, minor crafts and petty trade. Firoz Shah Tughluq, *Futuhat-i Firoz Shahi*, pp. 5-6; Afif, pp. 375-6.
110. Mahru, Letter no. 31, pp. 67-8.
111. Ibid., Letter no. 35, pp. 75-6.
112. Ibid., Letter no. 31, pp. 63-4.
113. With the accession of Firoz Shah Tughluq, service conditions of all functionaries, from nobles to soldiers, were reversed. Estimated revenue income was fixed permanently, while offices and *iqtas* became hereditary. The Sultan instituted the practice of paying troopers by assigning them revenues (*wajh*), recreating small *iqtas* under a new name. Irfan Habib, 'The Social Distribution of Landed Property in Pre-British India: A Historical Survey,' in *Essays in Indian History: Towards A Marxist Perception*, New Delhi: Tulika, 1995, pp. 84-5.
114. Mahru, Letter no. 31, pp. 64-5.
115. Ibid., Letter no. 30, pp. 58-60.
116. Ibid., Letter no. 114, pp. 176-7.
117. Ibid., Letter no. 121, p. 184.
118. Ibid., Letter no. 28, pp. 53-4; though this clarification, as issued by Mahru in the form of a stern warning to the intermediaries (*maliks*), applied to a village in Thanesar, yet the principle must have been applicable all over the Delhi Sultanate, particularly in Multan where every effort was being made to ensure the settlement of peasants and rehabilitation of agriculture.
119. Mahru, Letter no. 30, pp. 59-60.
120. Ibid., Letter no. 120, pp. 182-3.
121. Ibid., Letter no. 26, pp. 50-1.
122. Apart from other forms of property, the *zakat* was levied on all quadrupeds, who had grazed on plains and pastures for a year or more. In case of horses, it became due if males and females had been pastured together. The owner had the option of paying a *dinar* for every horse or to appraise their value and pay 5 *dirhams* for every 200 *dirhams*. According to Imam Abu Hanifa, it was not levied if horses were all male, as they did not yield any offspring. The tax became due on camels and donkeys if they were intended for sale. The same rule might have applied to horses, as they were a high value item of import. Abdul Hamid Muharrir Ghaznavi, 'Dastur ul-Albab fi Ilm ul-Hisab,' English Translation, Shaikh Abdur Rashid, *Medieval India Quarterly*, vol. I, nos. 3 & 4, 1950, p. 63.

123. It appeared that in Multan, *zakat* and *danganah* were assessed and collected together at the same time. But in other places, the procedure was different. On the non-agricultural goods brought to the Sarai Adl, the traders first paid *zakat* on the basis of the minimum taxable limit (*nisab*). After depositing the *zakat*, their goods were carried to the office for *danganah*. Here these were weighed again and charged *danganah* at the rate of one *dang* per *tanka*. The state collected 30 lakh *tankas* from *danganah*, but the traders faced acute harrassment at the hands of the officers. The Sultan, acting on the advice of scholars, Sufis and legal experts, abolished various illegal taxes, particularly *danganah*, and made a public proclamation about it. Afif, pp. 375-8.,
124. Mahru, Letter no. 120, pp. 182-3.
125. The *dadbeg* or *amir-i dad*, who looked after the executive side of justice, ensured that the decisions of the judge were duly implemented. If he felt that there was a miscarriage of justice, he drew the attention of the *qazi* to it or delayed the execution of the decision until the matter was considered by a higher or fuller court. He supervised the work of the police chief (*kotwal*) and censor of public morals (*muhtasib*). Sometimes one person could be given the offices of *qazi*, *imam*, *muhtasib* and *dadbeg*, particularly when the Muslim population of a town was limited to its small garrison. Ishtiaq Husain Qureshi, *The Administration of the Sultanate of Dehli*, pp. 161-2, 175.
126. Mahru, Letter no. 7, pp. 15-17.
127. Ibid., Letter no. 8, pp. 17-18.
128. Jam Banbhaniya and his uncle Jam Juna, the Sammah chiefs who had established their authority in Sind, raided Panjab and Gujarat in alliance with the Mongols. Firoz Shah Tughluq, at the end of a long disastrous campaign (1365-7) in Sind, which necessitated reinforcements from Panjab (Samana, Dipalpur, Multan and Lahore) and other places in north India, managed to break the Sindi resistance. Peace was established due to the mediation of Syed Jalaluddin Bokhari, the Suhrawardi saint of Uch. Following their surrender, the Sammah chiefs were brought to Delhi, where they were settled with pensions. Jam Juna was sent to quell a rebellion in Sind. Jam Banbhaniya, who was also dispatched to the region after the death of the Sultan, died on the way. Afif, pp. 230-54.
129. Ibid., Letter no. 46, pp. 86-9.
130. In the early decades of the fourteenth century, the Mongol hordes settled in the steppes of southern Russia sent horses to India. Extremely numerous and cheap, two hundred or more horses were brought by each merchant, though many were lost due to death or theft. They were taxed in both Sind and Multan. Muhammad bin Tughluq, who abolished the duty on them, imposed *zakat* on Muslim traders and *ushr* on the non-Muslim. Still they earned handsome profit, as they fetched a price of 100-500 silver *dinars*. These horses were prized for their strength and length of pace, not for

running and racing. Simon Digby, *War-Horse and Elephant in the Delhi Sultanate: A Study of Military Supplies*, Oxford: Oxford Monographs, 1971, pp. 35-6.
131. Mahru, Letter no. 38, p. 78.
132. Ibid., Letter no. 52, p. 96.
133. Ibid., Letter no. 25, pp. 49-50.
134. Ibid., Letter no. 22, pp. 44-7.
135. Uch was an old town. It had a large number of mosques, seminaries and Sufi shrines. While Mahru felt concerned about the state of these religious institutions, he also wished to tour the bank of the river that flowed along its fort. Mahru, Letter no. 21, p. 42.
136. Mahru, Letter no. 18, pp. 35-6.
137. Ibid., Letter no. 20, pp. 41-2.
138. Ibid., Letter no. 21, pp. 42-3.
139. Ibid., Letter no. 29, pp. 54-7.

CHAPTER 5

Piety Submits to the State

Descendants and the Shrine of Baba Farid

During his last days, Baba Farid (d. 1265) nominated Shaikh Nizamuddin Auliya his principal spiritual successor and sent to him his regalia comprising a prayer rug, cloak and staff, through Syed Muhammad Kirmani.[1] However, he did not leave any instructions regarding two vital issues – the place of his burial and the headship of the hospice (*jamaatkhana*). At first, his sons decided to bury him at a pleasant site outside the boundary wall of Ajodhan, where he used to meditate near the graves of martyrs. This decision was not carried out due to the decisive intervention of Khwaja Nizamuddin, a son of Baba Farid who served as a soldier in the army of Sultan Ghiasuddin Balban. If the saint was buried outside the boundary wall, it was argued, the pilgrims would pay their homage at the tomb and return without entering the town.[2] In such a secenario, the hereditary descendants of Baba Farid would not receive the attention that was their due. Moreover, they would also be deprived of the offerings (*futuh*) that had been flowing into the hospice,[3] particularly in lieu of the amulets (*tawiz*) disributed among the devotees. Motivated by these concerns, the sons of Baba Farid buried him near the hospice that had been in a flourishing state for several decades. The exact spot was a cell meant for mendicants. It was demolished to make way for the grave, while unbaked bricks were extracted from the Shaikh's humble abode to provide a niche in the side of the tomb.[4] In due course, the lineal descendants of Baba Farid were buried near this grave.

Precisely at this time, the third son of Baba Farid, Shaikh

Badruddin Sulaiman, was chosen as the head (*sajjadah nishin*) of the Chishti hospice at Ajodhan. The decision was the outcome of a consensus among Baba Farid's sons and disciples.⁵ Shaikh Badruddin Ishaq, Baba Farid's son-in-law who managed the organizational matters of the hospice, continued to perform this duty for a short time. Owing to his differences with Shaikh Sulaiman, which were allegedly created by some jealous inmates of the establishment, Shaikh Ishaq shifted to the Jami Masjid of Ajodhan, where he taught the Quran to a number of boys.⁶ Although Shaikh Sulaiman headed the hospice for sixteen years (1265-81), contemporary sources are silent about activities during his tenure. However, Amir Khurd has described the circumstances in which Shaikh Sulaiman received the symbols of discipleship and succession from the two Chishti elders of Chisht (Afghanistan). It so happened that two Chishtis, Khwaja Zor and Khwaja Ghor, passed through Ajodhan on their way to Delhi. Baba Farid went out of the town to welcome them and escorted them to his hospice with all marks of respect. In due course, he requested the visitors to confer the discipleship and succession on his two sons, Shaikh Badruddin Sulaiman and Shaikh Shihabuddin. At first, the two guests did not think it proper to do the honours, as a spiritual adept of the eminence of Baba Farid was better equipped for the task. They gave up their reluctance, when Baba Farid submitted that he had received the headship of his shrine due to the blessings of the Chishtis of Chisht. As desired by the two Chishtis, Baba Farid called for two pieces of cloth. In this manner, they placed the turbans on the heads of the boys. Shaikh Sulaiman, while performing his functions as the head of the Chishti hospice at Ajodhan, kept in mind his formal affiliation with the foundational seat of Chisht.⁷

Shaikh Alauddin, the son of Shaikh Sulaiman, became the head of the Ajodhan hospice at the young age of sixteen and held this position for the next fifty-four years (1281-1334). Owing to his spiritual excellence and immense piety, his name was included among the most prominent mystics of the Indian subcontinent. As an infant, he was nourished with her milk by the grandmother of Amir Khurd, the author of *Siyar ul-Auliya*. He had studied the Quran from Maulana Badruddin Ishaq. Baba Farid showered his blessings on him by sharing his own betel leaf with him and allowing him to sit on his prayer rug. Throughout his life, Shaikh Alauddin cherished his proximity to Baba Farid. Whenever any aspirant came to enrol as a disciple, he was lodged at Baba Farid's tomb, where he was adorned with the distinctive Chishti cap (*kulah*). While following a strict schedule of devotional exercises, he laid much emphasis on fasting. Until the end of his life, he did not eat anything during the day, except on the two Ids and Ayyam ul-Tashriq (three days after the feast of sacrifice at Mina during Haj). He broke his fast after one watch of the night, when he ate two loaves of buttered bread with a *ser* of milk. He did not eat the semolina pudding (*halwa*), which was sent to the inmates of his choice. Twice a day, food was served to all those present in the hospice. Whenever he went to pay homage at the tomb of Baba Farid, he distributed money among the poor who lined up on the two sides of his path. He doubled the amount for anyone who begged more than once because, as a matter of principle, he would never turn down a request. He was kind to his servants, who fetched water for his ablutions or washed and sewed his clothes. Any person who dared to harass these servants, was expelled from the hospice.[8]

In an encounter with Shaikh Ruknuddin Abul Fateh, the contemporary Suhrawardi exemplar, Shaikh Alauddin underlined the Chishti ideals of spirituality. Once, Shaikh Ruknuddin, who was travelling from Delhi to Multan, stopped at Ajodhan to pay obeisance at the mausoleum of Baba Farid. After performing the ritual, he went to pay a courtesy call to Shaikh Alauddin. While the two saints shook hands and embraced, Shaikh Ruknuddin praised his Chishti counterpart by saying that God had granted him such steadfastness that no one could move him from his principles. As for himself, he did not wish to leave the sacred site. Yet he had to go, owing to the wishes of his kith and kin. He again embraced Shaikh Alauddin and left for Multan. Shaikh Alauddin, on returning to his house, took a fresh bath and changed his clothes before sitting on the prayer rug. Some people, who took offence at this, complained to Shaikh Ruknuddin about the arrogant behaviour of Shaikh Alauddin towards a fellow Sufi who was universally acknowledged for his purity. Shaikh Ruknuddin, refusing to take offence, stated that Shaikh Alauddin was entitled to act in his particular way and deserved all respect. Explaining further, he admitted that he smelt of worldly entanglements, while the saint of Ajodhan remained insulated from the taint of worldliness and thus led a pure life.[9] Ibn Battuta, who was a witness to the personal habits of Shaikh Alauddin, felt that the saint was afflicted with an apprehension of uncleanliness of others and, therefore, he did not shake hands with anyone. As soon as his garment touched anyone, he washed it. Ibn Battuta perceived the strange behaviour of the Shaikh as a personal fetish, not an ideological statement rejecting the worldliness of the Suhrawardis.[10]

In spite of an avowed distance from worldly life, Shaikh Alauddin did not practice absolute isolation from socio-political concerns. He extended his support to those who suffered from any kind of highhandedness. If any oppressed person took shelter in the congregational hall of the mausoleum of Baba Farid, he received complete protection from the oppressor. It was not possible for people wielding power, including the king, to carry away such a person by force. According to Amir Khurd, Shaikh Alauddin exercised his sway over the domains of world and religion, because of which he was feared by the rulers of the times.[11] The fame of Shaikh Alauddin spread in all directions, owing to the circulation of stories of his saintly excellence and miraculous powers. Inhabitants of a number of places – Ajodhan, Diplapur and Jabali (which was situated near Kashmir) – constructed tombs and sacred sites in his honour. Acting in the name of his mausoleum, they performed at these spots a number of rituals including giving alms and reciting the Quran.[12] Ziauddin Barani, in his account of the Khalji era, placed Shaikh Alauddin in the same class as Shaikh Nizamuddin Auliya and Shaikh Ruknuddin Abul Fateh. He was held akin to the angels (*farishtahs*) who were born only to worship God. On the authority of the attendants who had served at the mausoleum of Baba Farid for six months or a year, it was learnt that Shaikh Alauddin was perpetually engaged in prayers, the remembrance of God, and reading the Quran, besides studying books on Hadis and Sufism. If the Shaikh had not been committed to the devotion of God, it would not have been possible for him to sit in the place of a spiritual master like Baba Farid.[13] Amir Khusrau has also composed the following panegyric (*qaseedah*) in praise of Shaikh Alauddin, who has been lauded for his spiritual merit.[14]

He was the exalted Shaikh of religion and world. / He was the Shaikhzadah of the times and, in his rank, he was the deputy of Shaikh Farid. / When sweat flowed down from his face owing to the heat of divine light, his forehead outclassed thousands of suns. / If the third lunar mansion (*suraiyya*) were to behold his exalted spiritual state, it would remain happy in the sky until the resurrection. / On observing this son of the full moon (*badrzadah*), the sun would seek luster from it and would even express its submission to it. / The inhabitants of this world would cease to fear the calamities of the times and would feel as safe as the person who takes shelter under God's domain of purity. / Amir Khusrau remained awake in his praise along with people during the night and this exercise was similar to the nightlong vigil of elders during the Shab-i Qadr and of children during the Id. / The Shaikh's breath of reviving the dead (*dam-i maseehi*) has conferred a new life on this world. Therefore, the life of Khusrau is inadequate to praise him.

After his death (1334), Shaikh Alauddin was buried in the vicinity of the mausoleum of his father Baba Farid. His disciple, Sultan Muhammad bin Tughluq (r. 1325-51), constructed an impressive structure over his grave. The Sultan extended royal patronage to Shaikh Alauddin's descendants, though they had trained as spiritualists. Shaikh Muizzuddin, the elder son of Shaikh Alauddin, succeeded his father as the head of the Chishti hospice at Ajodhan. In reponse to summons from the Sultan, he went to Delhi. He was sent on an official assignment to Gujarat, where he died at the hands of some local rebels. Shaikh Alamuddin, the younger son of Shaikh Alauddin, was known for memorizing the Quran and a keen interest in musical sessions. Since he was held in high regard by the Sultan, he was nominated as the Shaikh ul-Islam of the kingdom and, in this capacity, supervised the activities of a large number of Sufis. Following his death, he was buried near the grave of his father at Ajodhan. Shaikh Afzaluddin Fuzail, the son of Shaikh Muizzuddin, took over as the head of the Chishti hospice in the town. He acquired fame on account of his constant absorption in God, renunciation and solitude. His cousin Shaikh Mazharuddin (the son of Shaikh Alamuddin) was held in high regard by Muhammad bin Tughluq and, therefore, succeeded his father as the Shaikh ul-Islam.[15]

During the stewardship of Baba Farid's descendants, the Chishti hospice of Ajodhan began to undergo a slow transformation. When Baba Farid was alive, the focus was on the performance of austerities, training of disciples, caring for the visitors and distributing the amulets. When the grave of Baba Farid was added to the hospice, the complex began to evolove as a shrine (*dargah*). According to popular belief, the spiritual charisma (*baraka*) of the late saint survived in his tomb as well as his descendants. The evergrowing number of pilgrims continued their interest in the *tawiz-futuh* system. But the celebration of the death anniversary (*urs*) of Baba Farid brought about the institutionalization of a series of rituals – tying of turban on the spiritual head (*dastar bandi*), musical sessions (*qawwali*), common kitchen (*langar*) and passing through the southern gate (*bihishti darwaza*) of the main tomb.[16] The popular cult of Baba Farid, which emanated from the shrine, attracted state patronage. Ghazi Malik, the Khalji governor of Dipalpur for two decades, sought the blessings of Shaikh Alauddin who foretold the enthronement of three Tughluq rulers. Not long after, Muhammad bin Tughluq bestowed the town of Ajodhan on the shrine.[17] Shaikh Alauddin, who managed the land grant and came to be known as the Diwan, brought the pastoral Jat clans to settle as sedentary cultivators and collected the state share of crops on which the tax was levied in kind. At the same time, the Jat clans participated in the rituals of the shrine and, gaining access to theatre-oriented Islam, slowly converted to the new creed. The evolving political and religious bond was strengthened by marriage alliances between the Diwan's family and Jat clans. Thus, the Chishti shrine of Ajodhan played the historical function of incorporating the local system of culture into a larger cultural system, having connected the rustic clans politically with Delhi and religiously with Islam.[18]

Baba Farid's lineal descendants, who had sprung from Shaikh

Badruddin Sulaiman and Shaikh Alauddin, held the guardianship of the hospice and shrine at Ajodhan in perpetuity. Since they enjoyed social influence and material resources, they were patronized by the Delhi Sultanate. On the other hand, Baba Farid's lineal descendants, who had sprung from his other sons and daughters, had little association with the Ajodhan shrine and therefore were of no use to the state. Shifting from Ajodhan to Delhi, they lived under the paternal care of Shaikh Nizamuddin Auliya and, after appropriate education and training, emerged as Sufis in their own right.

Shaikh Nizamuddin Auliya groomed Shaikhzada Azizuddin and Khwaja Qazi, the sons of Khwaja Yaqub and grandsons of Baba Farid. They established themselves respectively in Devagiri and Telengana, where they acquired large followings. Shaikhzada Kamaluddin (the son of Shaikh Bayazid, grandson of Shaikh Nasiruddin and great grandson of Baba Farid), who was trained under Shaikh Nizamuddin Auliya and served in the kitchen of the hospice at Delhi, went on to settle in Malwa. Shaikhzada Azizuddin (son of Khwaja Ibrahim, grandson of Khwaja Nizamuddin and great grandson of Baba Farid) offered prayers at meal times in the hospice at Delhi before migrating to Devagiri.[19] Khwaja Muhammad and Khwaja Musa (the sons of Shaikh Badruddin Ishaq and Bibi Fatimah and grandsons of Baba Farid) led prayers in the assemblies of Shaikh Nizamuddin Auliya. Khwaja Muhammad, who nurtured a passionate interest in musical sessions and intricacies of classical music, compiled the discourses of Shaikh Nizamuddin Auliya under the title *Anwar-i Majalis*. His younger brother Khwaja Musa was noted for his mystical poetry in Arabic and Persian.[20] Shaikhzada Azizuddin (the son of Bibi Masturah and grandson of Baba Farid) was an expert calligraphist and produced a book on the discourses of Shaikh Nizamuddin Auliya entitled *Tohfat ul-Abrar wa Karamat ul-Akhyar*. His younger brother Shaikhzada Kabiruddin spent his entire life under the loving care of Shaikh Nizamuddin Auliya and did not separate from him for a moment.[21]

In 1652, Muhammad Ali Asghar Chishti, the author of *Jawahar-i Faridi*, went on pilgrimage to the mausoleum of Baba

Farid. He availed himself of the opportunity to meet the then head of the shrine Shaikh Muhammad, who had descended from Shaikh Ibrahim, Shaikh Faizullah and Shaikh Tajuddin Mahmud. On this occasion, he acquired information about the clans settled in and around Pakpattan before the time of Baba Farid. He also collected details about the marriages and children of the descendants of Baba Farid. He has thus provided the names of nearly twenty clans, Khokhars, Khankhwanis, Bahlis, Adhkans, Jhakarvalis, Yakkan, Meharkan, Siyans, Khawalis, Sankhwalis, Siyals, Baghotis, Bartis, Dhudis, Joyeas, Naharwanis, Tobis, and Dogars. According to Ali Asghar Chishti, the Khokhars, who had migrated from the Arab lands to the tract of Pakpattan, were the earliest to have embraced Islam. They had settled in the area after occupying it by conquest. Jhakarvalis and Bartis have been specifically mentioned as Jats. Yakkans, Meharkans, and Siyans were cultivators engaged in agriculture. In earlier times, they were non-Muslims and followed the creed of the Jogi. Owing to the attention of Baba Farid, they came under his influence and became Muslims. In the wake of this conversion, the name of Jogi was changed to Qutb Kamal, while his entire community became the devotees of Baba Farid's descendants. The same was the case of the Qazis, who had earlier opposed Baba Farid. Dhudis, Joyeas and Naharwnis enjoyed prestige and influence in the areas surrounding Pakpattan. Muslims of long standing, they observed Islamic prayers and fasts. They could mobilize armed contingents comprising 10,000 horsemen and 29,000 footmen for military service. As a result, they exercised authority over clans like the Tobis and Dogars.[22]

It has been claimed that the above clans were converted to Islam by Baba Farid. Most of them gave their daughters in marriage to the families of the head of the shrine. However, the *Jawahar-i Faridi* has recorded only twenty-three such marriages: fourteen with the Khokhars, five with Bhattis, three with Rajputs and one with Dhudis.[23] The names of the Khokhar chiefs were prefixed Malik, which implied an association with political power. Two of them, Shaikhu (Shaikha) Khokhar and Jasrath Khokhar, who figured prominently in the history of the Delhi Sultanate, also formed marriage alliances with the heads of the shrine of

Pakpattan. In the following list, the name of Shaikh Tajuddin Mahmud figures as many as seven times. He himself married a woman of a Rajput clan. Three of his sons and a grandson married among the Khokhars, while another son took a bride from the Dhudi clan.

Marriages between *Sajjadah Nishin's* Family and Clan Chiefs

S. no.	Groom	Fathers-in-Law	Clan
1	Shaikh Muhammad	Shaikh Shaikhu s/o Malik Barsana Khokhar	Khokhar
2	Shaikh Ibrahim	Malik Kalu s/o Malik Shaikhu	Khokhar
3	Shaikh Faizullah	Malik Jasrath s/o Malik Hariya Khokhar	Khokhar
4	Shaikh Muhammad s/o Shaikh Ibrahim	Ismail Khan Khokhar	Khokhar
5	Shaikh Ghazanfar Ali s/o Shaikh Tajuddin Mahmud	Malik Behraj s/o Malik Kalu Khokhar	Khokhar
6	Shaikh Muhammad Makki s/o Shaikh Tajuddin Mahmud	Umar Khan s/o Shah Mansur Khokhar	Khokhar
7	Shaikh Abdullah s/o Shaikh Tajuddin Mahmud	Malik Barsana s/o Malik Jabrut	Khokhar
8	Shaikh Jan Muhammad s/o Shaikh Ahmad Qattal s/o Shaikh Tajuddin Mahmud	Malik Abdullah s/o Malik Mubarak Khokhar	Khokhar
9	Shaikh Sadruddin s/o Shaikh Habibullah	Malik Barsana s/o Malik Jasrath Khokhar	Khokhar
10	Shaikh Alauddin s/o Shaikh Dadan	Malik Theraj s/o Malik Kalu Khokhar	Khokhar
11	Shaikh Burhanuddin s/o Shaikh Ahmad	Bijli Khan Alias Sakki	Khokhar
12	Shaikh Kamal s/o Shaikh Qutbuddin	Khokhar	Khokhar
13	Shaikh Qutbuddin s/o Shaikh Ataullah	Khokhar	Khokhar

14	Shaikh Muhammad Sharif s/o Shaikh Alauddin	Khokhar	Khokhar
15	Shaikh Abdullah s/o Shaikh Tajuddin Mahmud	Rai Theraj s/o Rai Lakhmi Dhudi	Dhudi
16	Shaikh Jalaluddin s/o Shaikh Muhammad	Rai Saddu s/o Rai Allahdad Bhatti	Bhatti
17	Shaikh Qutbuddin s/o Shaikh Ataullah	Bhatti	Bhatti
18	Shaikh Kamal s/o Shaikh Qutbuddin	Bhatti	Bhatti
19	Shaikh Ahmad s/o Shaikh Allah Bakhsh	Rai Shihab Bhatti	Bhatti
20	Shaikh Allah Bakhsh s/o Shaikh Ibrahim	Nasir Khan Bhatti	Bhatti
21	Shaikh Tajuddin Mahmud	Rai Qutba s/o Rai Muhammad	Rajput
22	Shaikh Baddan s/o Shaikh Qutbuddin s/o Shaikh Ataullah	Shaikh Massi	Rajput
23	Shaikh Ahmad Qattal s/o Shaikh Tajuddin Mahmud	Shahbaz Khan s/o Rai Qutba	Rajput

In terms of its architectural layout, the shrine of Baba Farid enclosed three buildings, each of which had an entrance on the southern side. As one entered the main gate, which was located on the eastern end, one faced the first building that contained the graves of Baba Farid's grandson Shaikh Alauddin Mauj-i Darya and his lineal descendants. These were separated by a wall from the graves of Baba Farid's daughters. A mosque stood on the western edge of this edifice. The second building, which was built in the centre, sheltered the tomb of Baba Farid and his son Shaikh Badruddin Sulaiman. The Bihishti Darwaza was on southern side of this structure, while the Noori Darwaza was on its east. This was the only building that was provided with two doors. The third building contained the graves of Shaikh Shihabuddin (a son of Baba Farid), Diwan Fateh Muhammad and Diwan Allah Jiwaya.[24]

A distinct set of ceremonies have been performed in the shrine every day. An important functionary, who was known as the *chiraghi* and was entrusted with the keys of the entire complex, conducted the ritual of lighting the lamps. A number of events followed it in a specific sequence. Late in the evening, the outer gate was closed. It was opened only after midnight. The ceremony of lamps commenced fifteen minutes before the Maghrib prayer. As the devotees congregated in the courtyard, the *chiraghi* recited the *shajrah-i chiragh* in a loud voice. Drafted in Persian, it mentioned the names of Chishti masters – Shaikh Usman Harwani, Khwaja Muinuddin Chishti, Shaikh Qutbuddin Bakhtiar Kaki, Baba Farid, Shaikh Badruddin Sulaiman and Shaikh Nizamudin Auliya. Each exemplar was remembered for his particular traits. The supplicants prayed for securing their faith in Islam and attachment to the lappet of Prophet Muhammad. It was hoped that the lamp of the Chishtis would burn in spite of the stormy winds and, if anyone dared to put out its flame, his beard would be burnt. It was expected that Baba Farid, who was a darling of the prophets and a treasure of sugar, would act as a witness for the devotees under the shadow of God and, thus, would provide salvation from the sorrows of this world. For the benefit of the devotees, the recitation of the *shajrah-i chiragh* was concluded by its translation in prose. In the end of this ceremony, a popular prayer was offered. Variable in its content, the prayer relied on the wisdom of the *chiraghi* and contemporary political concerns. Through the mediation of the Chishtis, the supplicants sought firmness of their faith in Islam and help for the sick, childless, unemployed and debtors.[25]

The *chiraghi* lighted the lamps in the tombs of Baba Farid, Shaikh Alauddin and others. Five lamps were placed at the grave of Baba Farid, two at that of Shaikh Alauddin and one each at those of others. Then the *chiraghi* moved to the mosque and, serving as the *imam*, led the congregation in the Maghrib prayer. Following the lighting of lamps, the devotees were allowed to enter the tombs and this movement continued until an hour before midnight (11.00 p.m.). At this point, the Noori Darwaza was closed and electric bulbs were switched off, though the lamps continued to burn. After a gap of four hours (3.00 a.m.), the outer gate of the complex was opened. At this point, the embroidered covering on Baba Farid's tomb was replaced. The previous covering was deposited in the store and, later on, it was distributed among the devotees as a sacred gift (*tabarruk*). The precincts of the shrine were cleaned and prepared for the proceedings of the following day.

From the time of Isha prayer when the outer gate was closed, to the early morning when the door was opened, forty to fifty devotees observed vigil in the courtyard and engaged themselves in meditation. The management of the shrine did not object to the presence of these devotees in the enclosure. The shrine remained open for the devotees from pre-dawn (3.00 a.m.) to late pre-midnight (11.00 p.m.). The door was not closed during the prayers and, at these times, the number of devotees was not very large. Within the mosque, the devotees offered both the obligatory (*farz*) and supererogatory (*nafl*) prayers. This schedule was observed on six days of the week. Since there was a substantive increase in the number of devotees on Thursday, the duration for visitation was increased by two hours, so that the shrine opened one hour early and closed one hour late. This meant that the Noori Darwaza closed for only two hours on any Thursday. This arrangement provided ample opportunity to the devotees to enter the sanctum sanctorum and offer *Fatiha* and *Durood*. Minor changes in the schedule were effected in response to the change of seasons in summer and winter.[26]

On special days the schedule was modified. For example, on the day of Prophet's nocturnal journey to heaven (Miraj Sharif), which fell on 26 Rajab, there was not only a great rush of devotees, but they also offered the prayer of *Tasbih* after their obligatory prayer in congregation. During their vigil, while the Qawwals performed, some devotees recited the Quran and offered supererogatory prayers. On 14 Shaban, the Shab-i Barat was observed in the same manner. During Ramzan, the mosque remained exceptionally crowded, because the devotees offered the *Tarawih* prayers at night, usually comprising twenty cycles (*rakats*). During the last ten days of Ramzan, they reserved maximum time for devotions and, while occupying a corner in the mosque, prepared for the arrival of Shab-i Qadr. This moment came on 27 Ramzan when the shrine presented a festive look that was a treat to the eyes. On this occasion, the Diwan distributed the sacred gifts (*tabarruk*). On the Id ul-Fitr, huge crowds converged on the shrine. Before the Id prayer, the sacred relics of Baba Farid were displayed. The *chiraghi*, accompanied by devotees, carried the relics to the court of the Diwan who, in turn, conveyed them to the mosque in a procession. The relics were kept at an elevated spot, so that the devotees were able to register their reverence. After the Id prayer, the relics were brought back for safe custody. The genealogical table of the Chishtis was recited and it was followed by the recital of Khatm-i Sharif. The Diwan distributed sugar among the congregation. He went to the tomb of Shaikh Alauddin and recited the Khatm-i Sharif over sherbet. Thereafter, he moved to the tomb of Baba Farid and replaced the covering. These observances were replicated on the Id ul-Azha. On 24 Ziqad the ritual of Chillah was observed, marking the beginning of the annual death anniversary of Baba Farid.[27]

Of all the ceremonies held at the shrine of Baba Farid, the most important was his death ceremony (*urs*), which was observed from 25 Zilhijja to 6 Muharram every year. On the first date, the Khatm-i Sharif was held in memory of the martyrs Hasan and Husain, followed by that for Baba Farid. The Diwan entered the courtyard of the complex at 9.00 a.m. with his followers, while the Qawwals sang for some time. Entering the mausoleum, he sat on the west of Baba Farid's tomb and, while his followers stood around, Quranic verses and the Chishti genealogical table (*shajrah-i chiragh*) was recited. The Diwan distributed sugar on behalf of the souls of the illustrious dead. He moved to the tomb of Shaikh Alauddin and again distributed sugar. Commemoration of Hasan and Husain was recited over two small jars of *sherbet* that was distributed among the gathering. Soon he retired to the mausoleum of Baba Farid and, while recitations continued outside, he stayed for sometime and left the place. This ceremony was observed every day until 5 Muharram, the day of the demise of Baba Farid. From 1 Muharram onwards, in addition to the above ceremonies, a spiritual concert (*sama*) was held in the afternoon at 3.00 p.m.. The Qawwals sang the poetry of Baba Farid and others. Three Sufis dressed in white, who were conducted along with the Qawwals, broke into a dance at intervals and, when driven to ecstasy, rolled on the round. At the conclusion of the musical session, the Diwan flung cowries among the listeners.[28]

The great day of the festival was 5 Muharram when the Bihishti Darwaza was opened. The Khatm-i Sharif and musical session were held as usual. About an hour before sunset, the Diwan entered the courtyard. He was preceded by an escort (a Brahmin, according to Miles Irving) with a bell and another man holding palm branches to clear the way. An usher intoned the cries of 'Allah Muhammad Char Yar Haji Khwaja Qutb Farid.' A large crowd of privileged guests followed this small group. The Diwan entered the mausoleum of Baba Farid through the eastern door, accompanied by as many followers as could find room. In commemoration of the installation (*dastar bandi*) of the first successor of Baba Farid, he placed a number of strips of muslin dyed in saffron on the tomb. After rubbing them on his chest and staining his clothes with them, he tied five of these around his turban. Leaving the shrine and climbing across the Jogi's tomb, he unlocked the Bihishti Darwaza and entered the sanctum sanctorum. He emerged out of the eastern door and took his seat by the Jogi's tomb, where he distributed the remaining muslin strips and some dates. Then, preceded by music, he left the shrine. The stream of devotees began to pass through the Bihishti Darwaza and, leaving through the other door, found their way out of the town. In view of the great rush, the administration made elaborate arrangements to prevent any stampede. The movement of traffic being regulated, the devotees were admittred through the passage in batches. The flow of devotees continued throughout the night and until sunrise. It was only interrupted when a dignitary from another shrine was specially conducted with his followers. In the early twentieth century, as many as 40,000 devotees fulfilled their cherished desire of passing through the Bihishti Darwaza.[29]

On the next day, the above proceedings began to 3.00 p.m. in the afternoon. The Diwan opened the door at 11.00 p.m. and distributed a kind of bread called Kurs. As the movement of the devotees continued throughout the night, about 20,000 of them undertook the ritual of passing through the Bihishti Darwaza. On 10 Muharram, the Diwan arrived at the head of a large procession and, carrying pitchers of water, entered the mausoleum and emptied the containers over the shrine. The water, which was drained away, was regarded as holy and it was carried away in leather bags by the Diwan and other devotees. In the evenings, offerings of sandal and perfume (*ittar*) were made at the tomb. This was followed by the recitation of hymns and another distribution of sugar. Two persons associated with Baba Farid, disciple Shaikh Nizamuddin Auliya and grandson Shaikh Alauddin, were accorded a prestigious place in the celebrations. The followers of Shaikh Nizamuddin Auliya had their shrines in western and southwestern Panjab, including those at Maler and Chachran in Bahawalpur, Taunsa in Dera Ghazi Khan, Golra in Rawalpindi and Basri in Hoshiarpur. The followers of Shaikh Alauddin had their shrines towards the east in Kalyar, Gangoh and Ambatha in Saharanpur, Rudauli in Barabanki, Panipat, Thanesar and Patiala. Incumbents of these shrines brought large retinues to Pakpattan and demanded a right of private entry unto the complex. Besides the hereditary adherents of the sacred place, a sprinkling of dervishes and pilgrims was attaracted from all over India and the (northwestern) border. But a majority of devotees came from Montgomery, Multan and Bahawalpur.[30]

Legitimacy through Supernatural Acts

Shaikh Sadruddin Arif, the son of Shaikh Bahauddin Zakariya, headed the Suhrawardi establishment of Multan from 1262 to 1285. He fashioned the schedule of his activities on the lines of his illustrious father. After attending to the remembrance of God and meditative contemplation, he engaged himself in teaching the students who crowded his assemblies. For instructing the aspirants of knowledge, he produced a short work entitled *Tasrif-i Jaduli* which was studied in the seminaries for a long time. His spiritual discourses were compiled in *Kanuz ul-Fawaid* by a disciple named Khwaja Ziauddin. This work is not extant, but a few extracts have been found in prominent biographical accounts. While elaborating a Prophetic tradition (*hadis*), he opined that the profession of faith was a divine fort and whoever entered it remained safe from any calamity ordained by God. There were three different ways, external (*zahir*), internal (*batin*) and real (*haqiqat*), to approach this unique sanctuary. In the first method, the seeker placed implicit trust in none other than God. Even if the entire world turned friend or enemy, no profit or loss occurred without God's will. As laid in the Quran, if God intends to favour or punish anyone, no one can block this decision. In the second method, the seeker firmly believed before dying that all occurrences, including the future, were transitory and everything in this world was perishable. Since destruction had already been stipulated in the Quran, the seeker was advised to spend his life by denying his own existence. By the third method (*haqiqat*), the seeker overcame the desire for heaven and fear of hell by pacifying the heart through a constant engagement with God. When he attained the rank of a witness to truthfulness, the heaven itself chased him and hell ran away from him.[31]

According to another sermon of Shaikh Arif, the first condition for a follower of the Prophet was to have faith in the principles on which the Prophet had placed his faith. Thereafter, he was bound to remain steadfast in his faith and, in order to express his commitment, he verbally accepted God's uniqueness in His essence and attributes. He also believed that God is endowed with all qualities; He is beyond the understanding of reason and wisdom; He is unaffected by any occurrence and accident; He is the creator of entire world and is not comparable to any other entity. All prophets were His messengers on earth and Muhammad was the most exalted of all prophets. Whatever the Prophet had stated was absolutely true and did not betray any contradiction. Whether or not these fell within the domain of reason, they had to be accepted so that one's faith remained intact. This was so because the Prophet had rightly recognized the divine law, but did not delve into its nature and circumstances. If there was any need to explain a passage of the Quran or any Prophetic tradition, such an exercise was permissible. The strength of faith became evident when an act of kindness produced happiness in the heart. However, if a bad action was committed, one had to realize the mistake at least in one's heart. The steadfastness of faith was manifested in one's love for God and His messenger, not only with reference to one's knowledge and faith, but also on the strength of one's passion and state.[32]

In another piece of advice, Shaikh Arif asked the seeker to remember God in every breath, because Sufis believed that one who did not do so destroyed himself. While engaged in the remembrance of God (*zikr*), the seeker needed to distance himself from all satanic temptations and sensual desires. In this kind of *zikr*, all enticements and fancies that appeared in the heart were burnt to ashes. Owing to the light of this kind of *zikr*, the heart was illuminated and the reality of *zikr* was established. At this moment, the seeker (*zakir*) perceived the beauty of the remembered (God) and his heart was brightened with the light of faith. This was, in fact, the object of the seeker. Pursuing the same idea in another sermon, Shaikh Arif, quoting a Quranic verse, 'Oh believers, you must maximize the remembrance of God,' observed that when God intended to favour anyone, He inspired him to add a genuine harmony to His *zikr* with his tongue. In the next stage, God enabled the seeker to progress from *zikr* with tongue to *zikr* within heart. Even if the tongue was silent, the task was continued from the heart. Such an exercise was known as excessive remembrance (*zikr-i kasir*). The seeker reached this stage when he became immune to all forms of discord that arose owing to the contact with entities other than God and impermissible conduct. When the seeker cleansed himself of evil thoughts and forbidden acts, divine light illumined his interior and, through the *zikr*, he saw manifestations of God's beauty. For this exalted state and supreme bliss, the people of courage and intelligence surrendered themselves to God.[33]

The Suhrawardi method of training disciples has been encapsulated in the advice of Shaikh Zakariya to his son Shaikh Arif regarding a seeker named Jamal Uchi. It was stated,

There lived in Uch a saint who was highly competent and steadfast. He has not contacted any Sufi for enrollment yet. He has been destined to be attached with our family. Though he has not come to me so far, he will turn towards you after my death and will express his desire for the robe of succession (*khirqah*). At present he is immersed in spiritual intoxication. When he comes to you, do not let him meet you on the first day. Let him stay alone for three days and remain engaged in recitation of the Quran, so that he emerges out of his current state of intense intoxication to sober consciousness. By then, he will have learnt the conduct of association and will not suffer any loss while treading the spiritual path. Thereafter summon him to you. Give him only half of what you have inherited in the form of robes. Tell him that one half is yours and the other half is his. But do not give him the robe of Shaikh Shihabuddin Suhrawardi, which I have passed on to you.

It was believed that Shaikh Zakariya also advised Shaikh Arif, 'Do not embrace Jamal Uchi, lest the latter should take way all your spiritual bounties. Offer him only half of your hand. Tell him that one half of it is yours, and the other half, his.'[34]

If Jamali was relied upon, Shaikh Arif employed his miraculous power to bring Ahmad Mashuq to the spiritual path. This man was the son of a merchant, Muhammad Qandhari, and had arrived from Qandhar to Multan for the purpose of trade. Possessing a large amount of goods and wealth, he was addicted to alcohol and did not remain without liquor even for a moment. One day, he was sitting outside a shop. Shaikh Arif, who was returning from a visit to the mausoleum of his father, saw Ahmad Mashuq through the corner of his eye. He sent a servant and brought Ahmad Mashuq along with him. On reaching his residence, he called for sherbet. He drank a part of it and gave the remaining to Ahmad Mashuq. As soon as the latter took a sip, the doors of spirituality opened in his heart. He repented for his past conduct and became a disciple of Shaikh Arif. He renounced worldly life and distributed his wealth among the seekers who resided in the Suhrawardi hospice. Such was the degree of his simplicity that he wore the same set of clothes for seven years. Owing to the personal attention of his mentor, he slowly covered the successive stages of the spiritual path and reached the rank of God's beloved.[35] His spiritual attainments earned praise from Shaikh Nizamuddin Auliya. Once Ahmad Mashuq observed a forty-day penance (*chillah-i sarma*) during winter and, standing in the cold water of a river at midnight, refused to come out till God had told him who he was. A voice declared that he was the one from whom many would seek intercession on the day of resurrection to be spared from hell, that he was the one whose efforts on this day would enable many to gain entry into heaven and that if the saints and gnostics were God's lovers, he was the God's beloved. When Ahmad Mashuq emerged out of water and returned to the city, everyone greeted him as Shaikh Ahmad Mashuq. But people objected to his practice of offering prayer (*namaz*) without the Surah-i Fatiha.[36] When persuaded to recite it, he ignored the verse, 'It is You Whom we worship and it is You from whom we seek help.' After much persuasion, he agreed to recite the same in its entirety. But when he reached the above verse, blood began to ooze from the end of each hair of his body. Turning towards the people around, he declared that it was not proper for him to offer prayers, as he was a menstruating woman.[37]

Shaikh Arif's miraculous power was said to have enabled his seven-year old son Ruknuddin Abul Fateh to memorize the Quran. The Shaikh took a personal interest in the matter and took the boy along wherever he went. Once he was offering prayer on the bank of a river, while a flock of deer appeared on the scene. The boy was attracted to a calf who was running after its mother. Though he normally memorized the fourth of a section of the Quran after reading it thrice, he could not abide by this routine even after reading it ten times. Shaikh Arif learnt the real cause of his son's distraction from some people who were present there. He fixed his gaze on the direction in which the flock of deer had gone. The female deer, followed by her calf, came running to the Shaikh's presence. The boy treated the calf with love and enabled it to suckle at its mother's breast. The animals were then brought to live at the Suhrawardi hospice. It has been claimed that Ruknuddin Abul Fateh memorized half a section of the Quran that day.[38]

Jamali has provided another instance of Shaikh Arif's supernatural abilities. We were told that Shaikh Budh, having accepted the request of a neighbouring chief who was a pious man, assumed the task of measuring agricultural land and collecting taxes from his estate. While engaged in this task, he had a dream at night wherein Shaikh Arif forbade him from pursuing the work. Next day, the peasants of the locality urged Shaikh Budh to resume the measurement of land. The Shaikh, who was riding on a horse, turned towards his own house. The peasants felt that the Shaikh was leaving as he had been offended by them. Soon the Shaikh revealed the truth about the dream and returned to his house. The chief, who feared that the land revenue would not be collected, persuaded the Shaikh to resume the task. But when the Shaikh did so, Shaikh Arif appeared before him and, after admonishing him for disobedience, knocked him down so that he fell unconscious. When the sons and associates of Shaikh Budh brought him back to his senses, he excused himself from the administrative work and went on to acquire fame as a mystic.

Shaikh Arif was not only responsible for the birth of Maulana Fatehullah, but also assumed the task of training him as a Sufi. Interestingly, the Shaikh continued to play his role as mentor even after his own death. As the episode went, Maulana Qutbuddin Behram, who had memorized the Quran and remained engaged in its recitation, did not have a child. Every Friday, he paid obeisance at the tomb of Shaikh Zakariya and, dedicating the merit of a full recitation of the Quran to his soul, prayed for the blessing of a child. One Friday, he completed a recitation of the holy book and, while sleeping at the tomb during the night, he saw a dream. Shaikh Arif appeared before him and gave him two dried dates. The Shaikh asked him to eat one and give the other to his wife, who would give birth to a son endowed with good fortune. After seeing the dream, he came out of the tomb and saw a bright faced old man who gave him two dried dates. Overwhelmed with happiness at the turn of events, he returned to his house and, as directed, ate one and gave the other to his wife. Though now old, he was blessed with a son who was named Fatehullah. This boy did not study anything till the age of twenty, nor did he memorize the Quran in its entirety. As soon as he learnt about his father's dream and the circumstances of his birth, he paid homage at the tomb of Shaikh Arif and dedicated himself to the acquisition of education. One night he saw a dream wherein he found himself praying in a mosque where Shaikh Arif was also present. He offered his respects to the Shaikh and prayed that if he could not gain access to learning so far, he might still recite the Quran owing to the saint's attention. Shaikh Arif gave him some rice pudding from a pot and asked him to memorize the Surah-i Yusuf of the Quran. On waking up from sleep, he felt a strange relief and light in his heart. Next day he paid a visit to the tomb of Shaikh Arif. He also met Maulana Wajihuddin who served as the prayer leader (*imam*) of the mosque at the Suhrawardi shrine and whose recitation of the Quran could deprive the listeners of their senses. He narrated the details of his dream to the Maulana who, in turn, encouraged him to abide by the advice of Shaikh Arif. He also began to study the Quran under the tutelage of the Maulana. In just five days, Fatehullah memorized the Surah-i Yusuf and in seven months the entire holy book. At the same time, he immersed himself in learning the other subjects. He attributed his progress to the spiritual charisma of Shaikh Arif that was effective even after his death.[39]

Though Shaikh Arif kept aloof from contemporary politics, he was involved in a personal conflict with Sultan Muhammad, the governor of Multan who was the son of Sultan Ghiasuddin Balban. A man of literary tastes, the Prince was passionately interested in poetry and extended liberal patronage to poets. He was deeply attached to his beautiful wife (a daughter of Sultan Ruknuddin Firoz and granddaughter of Sultan Shamsuddin Iltutmish) who, however, was alienated from her husband owing to his excessive drinking. Once in a fit of anger, the Prince divorced her by verbal pronouncement. Within a few days, he realized that he could not bear separation from her and began to think of means to bring her back. He sought the opinion of the leading theologians of Multan. He learnt that he could remarry his former wife only if she was married to someone else and divorced again. In order to achieve this object, the Prince approved a plan mooted by his close confidant Qazi Asiruddin Khwarizmi. The Qazi, acting in the interest of expediency and keeping everything under the wraps, arranged the lady to be married to the most pious man in the city, Shaikh Arif. After a few days, the Prince secretly sent the Qazi to the Shaikh with an order seeking divorce. As the news reached her, the lady fell at the feet of the Shaikh and refused to be separated from him. The Shaikh had no alternative but to reject the proposal. Frustrated at the outcome of his move, the Prince wished to kill the Qazi who was at the root of his ultimate humiliation. On second thoughts, he decided to kill Shaikh Arif and, for this purpose, mobilized a force of 10,000 heavily armed soldiers. A wave of anxiety spread across Multan as if the day of resurrection had arrived. The next day a horde of 20,000 Mongols entered the city. The Prince succeeded in scattering the intruders, but he was killed in an ambush while offering prayers along with 500 fighting men at a reservoir. The Mongols left after collecting a rich booty. The lady, owing to her association with the Shaikh, dedicated herself to religious pursuits in a manner that she was compared with Fatima and Maryam.[40]

Sitting in the Lap of Delhi

Shaikh Ruknuddin Abul Fateh, the son of Shaikh Sadruddin Arif, headed the Suhrawardi hospice of Multan for almost half a century (1286-1335). According to Abdul Haq Muhaddis Dehalvi, a detailed account of Shaikh Ruknuddin was found in *Fatawa-i Sufiyah*, which had been penned by one of his disciples. Another work *Majmua ul-Akhyar* compiled the Shaikh's discourses and letters to his disciples. In one of these letters, he observed that man comprised two elements, form and quality, and that quality was superior to form which had no value. God does not have any interest in one's form. Rather, He focuses only on one's actions and heart. The quality assumed significance in the afterlife (*akhirat*), as in this stage every quality assumed a physical form. Since the afterlife was a reward, every quality was transformed into a corresponding physical form, which appeared in a state of decomposition and disintegration. For example, Balam Bawur, inspite of his excessive prayers and austerities, would be lifted in the form of a dog. Similarly, a cruel and rebellious person would be converted into a wolf, an arrogant person into a cheetah and a miser and greedy person into a pig. In accordance with a Quranic verse, 'Today is the day we have removed the veil from your eyes,' the people would continue to be counted among beasts till they did not expel evil thoughts from their hearts. Though the lower self of man was perpetually inclined to defiance, yet it was possible to purify the heart and suppress the baser instincts. This could be achieved by imploring God who is generous and forgiving. Without the grace of God, one could not become virtuous. As a sign of this grace, the seeker erased his personal faults and illumined his inner self, so that all the worldly pomp was rendered immaterial. In this condition, the seeker began to hate lustful beastly actions. Such a morally upright seeker wished the worldly people to assimilate angelic characteristics. Instead of negative attributes – oppression, anger, arrogance, miserliness and greed – he acquired the positive qualities of forgiveness, patience, equanimity and generosity. These standards belonged to the aspirants of afterlife, while the traits of the seekers stood at the level of perfection.[41]

While corresponding with another disciple, Shaikh Ruknuddin dealt with the issue of good and evil. On one occasion, Hazrat Ali, the son-in-law of the Prophet and the fourth pious caliph, stated that he had not done good and evil to anyone on his own. Surprised at this statement, the listeners admitted that he might not have harmed anyone, but his acts of kindness begged an explanation. Quoting a Quranic verse, 'If anyone does a good deed, its reward goes to him and if anyone does a bad deed, its punishment also goes to him,' Hazrat Ali clarified that the reward for his good or bad actions was meant only for him and had nothing to do with others, but God knows better. Since whatever was sown had to be harvested, it was advisable to sow the seeds of good. This course was proper for the wise who sought blessings in this life as well as in the hereafter. The inspiration for good and evil came from God. Regarding control over actions, the Shaikh advised the seeker to prevent, in both word and deed, his organs from all unlawful acts as decreed by the Shariat. It was proper for him to avoid the company of unscrupulous people, to distance himself from things that separated him from God and to keep away from associating with liars.[42]

According to an incident recorded in *Majmua ul-Akhyar*, Sultan Ghiasuddin Tughluq asked one Maulana Zahiruddin Lang if he had witnessed any miracle of Shaikh Ruknuddin. Replying in the affirmative, the Maulana pointed to the large number of people who visited the Shaikh every Friday to benefit from his spiritual excellence. The Maulana attributed this phenomenon to the Shaikh's overpowering qualities, whereas no one came to meet him, though he was regarded as a learned scholar. In order to test the credentials of the Shaikh, the Maulana decided to ask him the rationale behind parts of ablution – rinsing the mouth and pouring water in the nose – that were regarded as Prophetic practice (*sunnat*). That very night, the Maulana saw a dream wherein the Shaikh offered him semolina pudding, the taste of which lingered till the next morning. This could not be accepted as a miracle, as such an act could be managed even by the Satan. Next day, he went to meet the Shaikh. He was astonished to find that the Shaikh was waiting for him and immediately offered his reply to the question, which he already knew through his supernatural powers. The Maulana began to perspire while listening to the following reply:

There are two kinds of impurity, of the body and of the heart. The former is caused by having sexual intercourse with a woman and the latter by sitting in the company of bad people. The former impurity is cleansed by water and the later impurity is washed off by tears. Water is recognized as pure only if it possesses three qualities – colour, flavour and smell. In the ritual of ablution, Shariat has given preference to rinsing the mouth and pouring water in the nose, because the former reveals the flavour of water and the latter provides the smell of water. Just as the Satan cannot assume the form of Prophet Muhammad, the Satan cannot take the form of a true Shaikh. This is so because the true Shaikh follows the Prophet in letter and spirit. Maulana! You are overflowing with conventional knowledge, but you are still unfamiliar with mystical knowledge.[43]

While staying in Delhi, Shaikh Ruknuddin got an opportunity to define the characteristics of a Shaikh. The occasion arose when a group of Qalandars and Jawaliqs visited him. The Qalandars demanded *sherbet*, but the Shaikh said something and they went away. The Jawaliqs demanded expenses (*kharch*) and the Shaikh gave them something, so that they also left. Reflecting on this experience, he stated that a Shaikh ought to possess money (*mal*), knowledge (*ilm*), and spiritual states (*hal*). First, the Shaikh had to possess some resources for, if he did not have these, he would not be able to fulfil the demands of the mendicants and, then, these people felt justified in slandering him even if they became guilty for the day of judgement. Second, he ought to possess knowledge so that he was able to enter into learned discussions with the theologians. Third, he ought to possess spiritual states, so that he could swerve with the saints in response to ecstasy. Shaikh Nasiruddin Mahmud, the distinguished head of the Chishti order in Delhi, strongly disagreed with this understanding of the functions of a Sufi. In his view, a Sufi required only knowledge and spiritual states, not money. If he had nothing, he could offer water to the visiting mendicants. Even if he had no means to feed his own children on Id, he needed to desire only from God. He was likely to receive something through supernatural means, possibly by the courtesy of Khwaja Khizr. The Prophet was in favour of a person earning his livelihood by exerting with the hands and perspiring from the forehead, while simultaneously undertaking sincere devotions. As for himself, Shaikh Nasiruddin knew that wealth came only from villages, agriculture and trade. He disapproved of the Sufis who begged at the doors of rulers and rich.[44]

Besides his thoughts on mysticism, Shaikh Ruknuddin was remembered for involvement in local politics, for close relations with reigning Sultans, and for intimate friendship with Shaikh Nizamuddin Auliya. He visited the capital twice during the reign of Alauddin Khalji (r. 1296-1316) and thrice during that of Qutbuddin Mubarak Khalji (r. 1316-20). Alauddin Khalji offered to the Shaikh a sum of 2 lakh *tankas* on his arrival and 5 lakh *tankas* on his departure. The Shaikh distributed the entire amount among the needy on the same day. Whenever the Shaikh went to meet Sultan Qutbuddin Mubarak Khalji, he received applications of the people who had demands from the state. In fact, he would delay his departure until all of them had placed their applications on his palanquin. When he entered the royal palace, he was received by the Sultan at the third entrance. The Sultan, who treated the visit as a great occasion, sat on his knees before the Shaikh. The Shaikh directed his servant to place the petitions before the Sultan. The Sultan examined every application and, noting his response, affixed the royal seal. The Shaikh left the palace only when all the issues raised in the petitions had been settled to his satisfaction. Not surprisingly, Shaikh Nasiruddin Mahmud regarded the visit of Shaikh Ruknuddin as a boon for the people of Delhi because, owing to his outer and inner virtues, their days became as joyful as Id and nights as blissful as Shab-i Qadr.[45]

The Suhrawardi saints of Multan continued to maintain intimate relations with the Tughluqs and enjoyed a considerable influence at the court. Maulana Ilmuddin Ismail (a grandson of Shaikh Zakariya and a brother of Shaikh Ruknuddin) was invited to put forth his views on the legality of audition (*sama*) when Shaikh Nizamuddin Auliya was tried for his indulgence in the controversial Sufi practice. His thoughts on the subject, particularly the prevalence of audition in Rum and Sham (Turkey and Syria) went a long way in finalizing the Sultan's final verdict in the case.[46] Shaikh Ruknuddin was one of the dignitaries who went to Afghanpur on the outskirts of Delhi in order to welcome Sultan Ghiasuddin Tughluq, who was returning from Bengal to the capital. He also joined the banquet held in a newly constructed wooden pavilion. Invited by Prince Muhammad to offer the Asr prayer, he came out of the structure and thus escaped being crushed. According to Jamali, the Shaikh advised the Sultan to quickly leave the pavilion as it was new. The Sultan replied that he would come out after having lunch. The Shaikh told the Sultan that it would be appropriate to leave at the earliest. Having said this, the Shaikh walked out of the pavilion without caring to wash his hands after the meals. Before he reached the second entrance, however, the structure collapsed. The people inside, including the Sultan, died instantly.[47] Jamali has indicated that if the Sultan had heeded the warning of the Shaikh, he would not have been killed. The Shaikh, owing to his miraculous powers, had foreseen the tragedy.[48]

The family of Suhrawardi saints extended active support to Sultan Muhammad bin Tughluq during the punitive expedition against Bahram Aiba Kishlu Khan, the rebellious governor of Multan. Shaikh Ruknuddin came out of the city and, while welcoming the Sultan, offered his good wishes for the success of the campaign. In the battle, which was fought at Abohar, Shaikh Imaduddin (a brother of Shaikh Ruknuddin) who resembled the Sultan in his appearance, was positioned under the royal canopy to confuse the rival forces. Shaikh Imaduddin, mistaken as the Sultan, was killed.[49] After the defeat and execution of Kishlu Khan, the Sultan ordered a massacre of the people of Multan. On hearing this Shaikh Ruknuddin interceded with the Sultan on behalf of the inhabitants and stopped the Sultan from committing a terrible bloodbath.[50] The Shaikh and his nephew Sadruddin (the son of the deceased Shaikh Imaduddin) received grants of a hundred villages each for two purposes – as a means of their personal livelihood and to enable them to administer food in hospice of their venerable grandfather, Shaikh Zakariya.[51]

Shaikh Ruknuddin was summoned to Delhi by Sultan Qutbuddin Mubarak Khalji (r. 1316-20), who intended to pit him against Shaikh Nizamuddin Auliya.[52] The intention of the Sultan was doomed to failure as Shaikh Ruknuddin bore immense affection and respect for the preeminent Chishti saint, who warmly reciprocated these feelings. Once Shaikh Ruknuddin attended the death anniversary (*urs*) of Baba Farid that was organized by Shaikh Nizamuddin Auliya. Qawwals were invited to perform at the musical session. When they were singing, Shaikh Nizamuddin Auliya was elevated to a state of ecstasy and, in response to the intensity of his passion, tried to rise up and move in a circular motion. Shaikh Ruknuddin, who was sitting close by, held him and did not allow him to stand. After sometime, Shaikh Nizamuddin Auliya again felt ecstatic and, rising, gave physical expression to his inner feelings. This time Shaikh Ruknuddin did not stop him and, instead, stood up and joined him, as did the other Sufis. Shaikh Ruknuddin told his brother that on the first occasion, he found the Chishti saint in the astromental plane (*alam-i malkut*) where his hand reached with ease. On the second occasion, he found the Shaikh in the plane of bliss (*alam-i jabrut*)[53] and, therefore, restrained his hand. It was evident that he had a high opinion of the spiritual excellence of the Chishti master and, finding himself incapable of reaching that high level, did not interfere in his exalted spiritual state that was induced by the audition.

Whenever Shaikh Ruknuddin came to Delhi, he made it a point to meet Shaikh Nizamuddin Auliya and to exchange views on matters of common interest. Amir Khurd provides the details of five such meetings. The first took place during the reign of Sultan Qutbuddin Mubarak Khalji. When Shaikh Nizamuddin learnt about the arrival of Shaikh Ruknuddin to the capital, he went to Hauz-i Alai and welcomed the visitor near a bridge at the time of the morning prayer. In this short meeting, the two exchanged pleasantries. When the Sultan asked Shaikh Ruknuddin about the first person to meet him in Delhi, the reply was that it was the best citizen (Shaikh Nizamuddin) of the capital. The second meeting took place in the Jama Masjid of Kilokhari. Shaikh Ruknuddin, on learning that Shaikh Nizamuddin would offer the Friday prayer at this mosque, went to the place. He sat near the northern gate that was near the bank of the river. Shaikh Nizamuddin sat at his fixed spot near the southern gate. There was a lot of space between the two gates owing to the vastness of the courtyard. Shaikh Nizamuddin said his prayer, got up and sat behind Shaikh Ruknuddin who was still engaged in the exercise. At the conclusion of the prayer, they shook hands and embraced. Shaikh Ruknuddin held the hand of Shaikh Nizamuddin and walked to the southern gate where his palanquin had been brought. Each insisted that the other sit in the palanquin. Ultimately, Shaikh Nizamuddin succeeded in persuading Shaikh Ruknuddin to sit in it.[54]

The third meeting took place in the upper storey cell of Shaikh Nizamuddin at Ghiaspur. Known as the building of Khwaja Jahan Ayaz, it had been built by Shaikh Hasan Sarbarhana. As soon as Shaikh Nizamuddin was informed that Shaikh Ruknuddin was on his way to Ghiaspur, he directed his servant Iqbal to prepare food and arrange gifts. Since Shaikh Ruknuddin had a problem with his foot, he could not come out of the palanquin in spite of his best efforts. Shaikh Nizamuddin did not let his guest make any painful effort and sat in front of him. The conversation, it was hoped, would enlighten the small gathering on an academic issue. Maulana Imaduddin Ismail, the brother of Shaikh Ruknuddin, initiated a discussion on the reasons of Prophet Muhammad's migration from Mecca to Madina. Shaikh Ruknuddin replied that the perfections associated with Muhammad's prophethood could reach their culmination only at Madina. Shaikh Nizamuddin felt that the Prophet had been ordered to migrate to Madina, so that the imperfect people of the place could benefit from his teachings. At meal time, when the father of Amir Khurd spread the tablecloth between the two men, a large number of petitions were pushed aside. Shaikh Ruknuddin explained that these were the petitions of helpless sufferers, that he had placed them before the Sultan for the remedy of their problems and that the applicants did not know that he was going to meet the king of religion (Shaikh Nizamuddin) that day. In the end a purse of gold coins and pieces of fine cloth were presented to the guest. Shaikh Ruknuddin refused to take them and, at his advice, these were accepted by his brother Maulana Imaduddin Ismail.[55]

The fourth meeting took place, as Shaikh Ruknuddin went to enquire about the health of Shaikh Nizamuddin. The former expressed his feelings of reverence, saying, 'Today is the tenth of Zilhijja when the devout proceed to seek the religious merit of performing the Haj. I have tried to acquire the same blessings by visiting you.' Shaikh Nizamuddin expressed regret at his own imperfections. The fifth meeting took place when Shaikh Nizamuddin was facing his last illness, during which he repeatedly lost consciousness owing to the intensity of divine love. During these days (spring of 1325), Shaikh Ruknuddin came to see the ailing saint several times. On one occasion, Shaikh Nizamudin was too weak to rise from his cot to receive his friend. He invited Shaikh Ruknuddin to sit on his cot. Shaikh Ruknuddin, out of respect, declined the offer and instead sat on a chair. Shaikh Nizamuddin, in spite of his miserable condition, engaged in a meaningful conversation, much to the astonishment of his disciples and followers. Shaikh Ruknuddin referred to a Prophetic tradition, which allowed the prophets an option by God to live longer than their stipulated lives, if they so desired. The saints (*walis*), being the successors to the Prophet, also enjoyed the same privilege. Therefore, Shaikh Nizamuddin was urged to seek an extension of his life, so that the imperfect people could improve their existence. Bursting into tears, Shaikh Nizamuddin revealed a dream in which the Prophet had declared that he was anxiously waiting for him. At this everyone including Shaikh Ruknuddin began to weep. Thereafter, the visitor left in a state of melancholy.[56] During his last days, Shaikh Nizamuddin directed the musicians to perform audition for three days before his burial and obtained a promise to this effect from Maulana Shihabuddin. Shaikh Ruknuddin advised against it, yet he admitted that he would be responsible on the day of judgement for not carrying out the last wish of the Chishti master. Notwithstanding this lapse, Shaikh Ruknuddin played a decisive role in choosing the place of burial for the Shaikh who passed away on 3 April 1325. Accompanied by Iqbal (the servant of Shaikh Nizamuddin), he examined the garden where the late Shaikh used to come. Iqbal identified an orange tree under which the Shaikh used to sit. Shaikh Ruknuddin offered two sections (*rakats*) of prayer at the spot and oversaw the digging of the grave.[57] Shaikh Ruknuddin had the privilege of leading the funeral prayer. After performing the ritual, he declared that he understood why God had made him stay in Delhi for four years. In other words, it was God's will that he should reside in the capital for a fairly long time and maintain intimate relations with the Chishti master, so that at the proper moment he could avail of the opportunity of leading the funeral prayer of his friend.[58] This event demonstrated that Shaikh Ruknuddin commanded the respect and confidence of the disciples and followers of the deceased. It also showed that Shaikh Ruknuddin refused to toe the line of the contemporary rulers, Qutbuddin Mubarak Khalji and Ghiasuddin Tughluq, who were hostile to the Chishti master.

Following the footsteps of his Khalji predecessor, Sultan Ghiasuddin Tughluq (r. 1320-5) also summoned Shaikh Ruknuddin to Delhi. At this time, a dispute was said to have irrupted over the headship of the Suhrawardi hospice at Multan. Shaikh Ilmuddin Imamah, a son of Shaikh Bahaduddin Zakariya, advanced his claim to this high position in opposition to his nephew. Since the Sultan was inclined towards Shaikh Imamah, Shaikh Ruknuddin relinquished his claim and came to Delhi. Shortly after this change, Shaikh Imamah breathed his last.

However, Shaikh Ruknuddin continued to stay in Delhi. As such, he was present in the capital when both the Sultan and Shaikh Nizamuddin Auliya passed away.[59] The exact nature of the dispute was not known, yet it might have involved the control over the vast income that came from land grants and sundry offerings.

Around this time, Shaikh Wajihuddin Usman Siyah Sunami, who was a disciple of Shaikh Ruknuddin, led a protest against the newly established Tughluq regime. A native of the town of Sunam in Panjab, Shaikh Sunami tried hard to get a clerical job in Delhi. During these days of trial, he saw Shaikh Ruknuddin offering prayer on the bank of the Jamuna and instantly became his disciple. He came to Multan along with his mentor and spent two years at his hospice. During this period, he memorized the Quran and studied the *Awarif-ul Maarif*. Practising simplicity of an extreme kind, he did not wear anything except a loincloth and did not sport a turban. On pilgrimage to holy places, he donned the same apparel and did not carry a pot or staff. His travels spread across a period of seven years. He performed the Haj in Mecca when it was very hot. While he was circumambulating the Kaaba, he was believed to be provided shade by the legendary saint Shaikh Khizr. He also paid homage at the tomb of Prophet Muhammad at Madina and, during his return journey, visited the graves of numerous saints. When he returned to Multan, Shaikh Ruknuddin was so impressed at his simplicity and devotion that he conferred his own robe and turban on him. In response to the fresh advice of his mentor, he settled in Delhi and placed himself under the tutelage of Shaikh Nizamuddin Auliya. He received immense affection from the Chishti saint. He developed a deep interest in the musical sessions (*sama*), being often found in a state of ecstasy.[60] This attitude must be safely attributed to the influence of the Chishti practice and his personal proximity to Shaikh Nizamuddin Auliya.

Shaikh Sunami led a powerful public demonstration against the official ban on Sufi music and, in so doing, carved a permanent place for himself in the annals of Islamic spirituality in northwestern India. Before the trial (*mahzar*) of Shaikh Nizamuddin Auliya in the court of Ghiasuddin Tughluq, this ruler had imposed a ban on any form of singing. If anyone dared to open his mouth for a song, his tongue was to be pulled out by a plier. The rule was so strict that none could even recite the Quran in a melodious voice. In these circumstances, Hasan Qawwal, the chief Qawwal in the service of Shaikh Nizamuddin Auliya, visited Shaikh Sunami along with a few other singers. The Shaikh, who was fond of the visitor's singing, requested him to sing something in his typical style. Though Hasan Qawwal was aware of the Shaikh's intimate relations with Shaikh Nizamuddin Auliya, yet he expressed his inability to accede to the request in view of the Sultan's draconian ban. Seeing that the Shaikh had locked the door with a chain and no stranger was around, he agreed to sing at a low pitch. When he rendered a particular couplet in Pardah-i Ushaq, the Shaikh stood up in ecstasy and asked the singer to sing loudly. Hasan Qawwal discarded all restraint and began to sing without any inhibition. At the bidding of the Shaikh, the door was opened and a strange tumult arose. Gradually a number of people – including nearly 200 Qawwals, several Sufis and seekers of entertainment – assembled in thousands. The gathering assumed the form of a procession and, being led by Shaikh Sunami, started marching from Delhi to Tughluqabad, a distance of one league. The entire population of the city, including the elite, was filled with anxiety about the outcome of a developing situation, particularly in the light of the Sultan's harsh rule.

The Sultan, who was then sitting in the upper storey of his palace, had heard the commotion. He asked his courtiers to find the nature of the horde. Malik Shadi, the Sultan's close assistant, ran out to make an instant enquiry. He reported that Shaikh Sunami was leading a procession of innumerable Sufis and Qawwals, who were approaching and singing in ecstasy. The Sultan was deeply perplexed on seeing the resolute challenge to his authority and audacious violation of his irrational order. Much against his wishes, the Sultan could not punish a multitude of unarmed people who were asserting their right to follow a hallowed practice. He desperately looked for a pretext to take punitive action against the leader of this massive public protest, if not the prominent participants. He ordered his officers to check from an official document *Tazkira-i Khusrau Khan* if Shaikh Sunami had received any cash gift from the short-lived regime of Khusrau Khan. The courtiers held the unanimous view that Shaikh Sunami had rejected such a dubious payment. The Sultan was forced to reverse his intensions. He ordered Malik Shadi to bring Shaikh Sunami to a special suite in the palace, to send food from the royal kitchen and to reward the Qawwals. Shaikh Sunami and his companions were treated as state guests for three days. While leaving the palace, Shaikh Sunami refused to accept any cash gift and instead went to Ghiaspur in order to meet his second mentor Shaikh Nizamuddin Auliya. This episode took place after the trial in which the Chishti saint was subjected to an interrogation.[61]

A distinguished writer and ideologue, Amir Husain (Sadruddin Ahmad bin Najmuddin Syed Husaini), benefited from his association with the Suhrawardi masters.[62] Originally a native of Herat, he visited Multan in the company of his father who used to travel for the purpose of trade. After the demise of his father, he withdrew from worldly affairs and, having distributed his wealth, entered the Suhrawardi hospice in Multan. Distinguished for his expertise in mystical knowledge and severe austerities, he produced a number of works like *Kanz ul-Rumuz*, *Zad ul-Musafirin*, *Tarb-i Majalis* and *Nuzhat ul-Arwah*. An insight into his mind has been provided by the following ideas on mysticism, which were recorded in his correspondence with Saduddin Mahmud Shabistari of Tabrez.

Philosophers and theologians did not have the capacity to comprehend the nature of God, as sense and reason could not shake off the illusion of apparent reality of the world. Man perceived the reflection of all divine attributes in himself, but there was a side to his nature which was evil and non-existent. He was required to abandon realism in order to see the truth, from which all else emanated. A traveller was one who journeyed to God, but the perfect man did not rest at the ecstatic union with truth. Instead, he journeyed back to the phenomenal world, where he conformed to outward laws and, by so doing, brought forth the fruit of good works. In his phenomenal state, man could not exist without God and, aspiring to a union, was drawn magnetically towards Him. When man realized that all things were one, he died to his own self and lived in God with his regenerated soul. This was achieved by erasing all that separated God from his soul, as true mystical union could not be achieved when duality and self persisted. Since all things were one, the temporal and eternal could not be separate entities. Union meant annihilation of the phenomenal element in man, but this annihilation was a continuous process involving the erasure of phenomena. Since the law was compared to a shell and sainthood to the pearl within, a Sufi was required to retain the shell until the pearl was fully formed and ready for extraction. The Sufis, while expressing mystical beliefs and ecstatic experiences, employed unconventional terms (eye, lip, cheek, curl and mole) and even appreciated ideas from Christianity and idolatory.[63]

In the eyes of Ziauddin Barani, the presence of three eminent Sufis, Shaikh Nizamuddin Auliya, Shaikh Alauddin and Shaikh Ruknuddin Abul Fateh, two of whom belonged to Panjab, were a sublime blessing during the first two decades of the fourteenth century. Addressed with the prefix of Shaikh ul-Islam, they were reputed for occupying the exalted seat of Shaikh-hood, which was the deputyship of Prophethood. They had illumined the world with the purity of their being. A large number of people wished to enrol under their mentorship. On account of their help, thousands of people, who had been engaged in immoral activities, abandoned their evil ways. Having vowed repentance, they included prayers in their daily routines. The attitude of worldliness, which had undermined good deeds in the society, received a severe blow. The lives of these three Sufis, which revolved around arduous spiritual exercises and excellent moral chatacter, became a role model for others. Truthful seekers of God, who were immersed in prayer and devotion, began to aspire for higher stages of divine inspiration and miraculous powers (*kashf wa karamat*) and, in this manner, experienced a fundamental change in their lives. Ordinary folk began to traverse the path of truth. Such was the impact of these kings of religion (*shahan-i deen*) that the masses felt a rain of divine mercy. The fortunate contemporaries did not have to face natural calamities like drought and plague. Even the fear of Mongol invasion, regarded as a major threat, disappeared from the scene. These positive developments, which resulted from the pious personalities of these three Sufis, brought a wealth of credit to Islam. It was claimed that the rules of the Shariat and Sufism acquired immense glory, as these were observed in all the four directions.[64]

In what ways did an eminent Sufi impact society? Ziauddin Barani has answered this question with reference to the influence of Shaikh Nizamuddin Auliya in Delhi. Since two distinguished Sufis of Panjab, Shaikh Alauddin and Shaikh Ruknuddin Abul Fateh, were placed in the same cartegory, they must have exercised a similar influence in their respective domains. Shaikh Nizamuddin Auliya had opened the doors of discipleship to all social classes–nobles and mendicants, rich and poor, learned and illiterate, urbanites and villagers, crusaders and slaves–who became devout Muslims. Owing to their newly acquired allegiance to the Shaikh, they repented past sins and began to offer obligatory prayers. Sultan Alauddin Khalji and his relatives developed a deep faith in the Shaikh, while the state functionaries (nobles, clerks, soldiers and slaves), who had entered the Shaikh's tutelage, adopted a schedule of prayers and devotions. In view of the increasing number of seekers and followers, the Shaikh delegated work to his senior disciples. Between the city and the Shaikh's hospice at Ghiaspur, they raised platforms roofed with thatch, where water pots and prayer rugs were provided. At each platform, a memorizer of the Quran and a servant assisted streams of visitors in offering prayers and guiding them to meet the Shaikh. They also answered their queries related to the different kinds of prayers and recitation of sections of the Quran, besides the practices of Baba Farid and Shaikh Qutbuddin Bakhtiar Kaki. On reaching Ghiaspur, the new disciples (*muridan jadid*) met the old disciples (*muridan qadim*) and asked questions about meditation and renunciation, besides the lives of Sufis and books on Sufism.[65]

During the month of Ramzan and Fridays, many followers maintained vigils, engrossed in Tarawih prayers and reciting the Quran. In every quarter of the city, musical sessions (*sama*) were held once in twenty or thirty days, where the devotees shed tears in ecstasy. Some disciples of the Shaikh began to display miracles. Shopkeepers gave up dishonest dealings, others discarded consumption of alcohol and sexual deviations. Lovers of learning, who had entered the tutelage of the Shaikh, took to studying principles of the path and books on Sufism – *Quwat ul-Qulub, Ihya ul-Ulum, Awarif ul-Maarif, Kashf ul-Mahjub, Sharh Taaruf, Risalah Qushairi, Mirsad ul-Ibad, Maktubat Ain ul-Quzat, Lawaih* and *Lawamih* of Hamiduddin Nagauri and *Fawaid ul-Fuad* of Amir Hasan Sijzi. These books were in great demand. Interested readers often made enquiries from booksellers regarding the literature on Sufism. In fact, piety had entered all aspects of the life of devotees. There was no person, who did not tuck a toothbrush and comb (*miswak wa shanah*) in his turban. On account of the rising demand of the devotees, the price of Sufic pots and leather basins increased. The mass of people, who had begun to traverse the path of spirituality, compared Shaikh Nizamuddin Auliya with Shaikh Junaid Baghdadi and Shaikh Bayazid Bistami. On every fifth of Muharram, the death anniversary of Baba Farid was observed with great enthusiasm at the hospice of the Shaikh. A large number of people, both from within the city and different provinces, converged at the venue. They attended the musical session of a kind that was never organised again.[66]

Execution of a Suhrawardi Master

Before his death (1335), Shaikh Ruknuddin Abul Fateh nominated his grandson Shaikh Hud as the head of the Suhrawardi establishment of Multan and formalized his choice by issuing a will. However, his nephew challenged the nomination and declared that he was better suited than Shaikh Hud to inherit his uncle's legacy. Since the dispute could not be settled in Multan, the two claimants took the case to the court of Muhammad bin Tughluq (r. 1325-51). At this time, the Sultan was camping at Daulatabad and the distance between this town and Multan could be covered only in eighty days. The Sultan, having accepted the will of Shaikh Ruknuddin, upheld the claim of Shaikh Hud. While pronouncing his verdict, he might have been impressed with the advanced age of Shaikh Hud and the youth of his rival. What was surprising, the Sultan decreed that Shaikh Hud be provided with a feast at every station where he alighted on his way back to Multan. An order was issued to the inhabitants of all places, asking them to come out to meet him and prepare a feast in his honour. When Shaikh Hud arrived at Delhi, a royal banquet was arranged at a considerable expense to the state. The religious elite – theologians, Sufis, jurists and judges – went out of the city to welcome the guest. One of these dignitaries was Ibn Battuta. It was observed that Shaikh Hud was riding in a palanquin, while his horse was led by his side. Ibn Battuta said that it would have been better for him to ride a horse alongside the judges and saints who had come to greet him. Shaikh Hud heard the remark and, mounting a horse, apologized for not doing the same earlier owing to an affliction that disabled him from riding on horseback. As the cavalcade entered the capital, it was treated to a lavish feast. As customary at the end of a royal banquet, every invitee was presented money in accordance with his rank. The chief judge (*qazi ul-quzat*) received 500 *dinars*, while Ibn Battuta was given half of this amount.[67]

Shaikh Hud was escorted to Multan by Shaikh Nuruddin of Shiraz who had been deputed by the Sultan to instal the incumbent in his grandfather's hospice and to arrange a banquet for him at the expenditure of the state. No Sufi had ever been accorded such a princely treatment by the Delhi Sultanate. But the reasons were not far to seek. The first two Tughluq rulers, Ghiasuddin and Muhammad, had managed to alienate the Chishtis,[68] the most important Sufi order in northwestern India. The state, therefore, was under compulsion to bring into its fold the Suhrawardis, who were often seen as the rivals of the Chishtis.

In the above circumstances, Shaikh Hud took charge of his spiritual inheritance and occupied this position for several years. A time came when Imad ul-Mulk, the governor of Multan, sent a report to the Sultan, intimating that Shaikh Hud and his relatives were collecting money, that they were spending it on their personal needs and that they did not feed anyone in the hospice. The Sultan issued an order for the recovery of the amount which had been misappropriated. In compliance of this order, Imad ul-

Mulk demanded the money and, as a part of this action, arrested a few persons and beat some others. Every day he used to realize a sum of 20,000 *dinars*. This recovery continued for several days until they were stripped of all possessions that included enormous wealth as well as savings. Among other valuables, there was a pair of shoes studded with pearls and rubies that was sold for 7,000 *dinars*. Some people claimed that this pair of shoes belonged to the daughter of Shaikh Hud, while others believed that it belonged to one of his slave girls.

Humiliated by the persecution and fearing for his life, Shaikh Hud fled from Multan with the intention of seeking refuge somewhere in central Asia, the country of the Turks. Imad ul-Mulk captured the fugitive and, reporting his flight to the Sultan, sought further instructions. The Sultan ordered the governor to send Shaikh Hud and his captor to the capital as prisoners. As the two reached the court, the Sultan released the captor and asked the Shaikh to reveal his destination. The Shaikh had no alternative but to ask for forgiveness. Failing to extract a satisfactory answer, the Sultan alleged, 'Certainly, you intended to flee to the Turks and tell them that you were the son of Shaikh Bahauddin Zakariya and that the Sultan had done such and such thing to you and to bring them to fight me.' The Sultan ordered that head of the Shaikh be cut off, and the order was instantly carried out.[69]

Shaikh Yusuf Gardez, the next head of the Suhrawardi establishment at Multan, was honoured with the title of Shaikh ul-Islam.[70] However, the tension between the Multan hospice and the Delhi Sultanate continued well into the second half of the fourteenth century. During the course of his expedition to Thatta (1365), Firoz Shah Tughluq did not hesitate to reveal his negative attitude towards the Suhrawardis. While he made it a point to visit all the Chishti centres, he did not pay homage at any Suhrawardi hospice. Shaikh Yusuf Gardez, being offended by the Sultan's failure to visit the mausoleum of Shaikh Bahauddin Zakariya, requested him to register his presence at the Suhrawardi hospice. The episode reflected the loss of influence by the Suhrawardi order in the region. Though the Suhrawardi spiritual masters held the prestigious office of Shaikh ul-Islam, yet they could not persuade the Tughluq rulers to provide their support. As the spiritrual and poltical authority of Shaikh Yusuf Gardez was displaced, the state gradually titlted towards the Chishtis. Later in his reign, Muhammad bin Tughluq had displayed a strong interest in the Chishti order by attending the death anniversary of Khwaja Muinuddin Chishti for twelve years. Firoz Shah Tughluq also undertook a pilgrimage to the Ajmer shrine along with Shaikh Zainuddin, a prominent Chishti master. During the thirteenth and fourteenth century, the Suhrawardi order underwent a number of political, social and ideological changes. These changes influenced their standing with the state as well as the larger community. From the patronage of Iltutmish to the execution of Shaikh Hud, 'the silsilah went from being an intensely government affiliated order to an almost peripheral Sufi organization'.[71]

Some time in the early fourteenth century, the Suhrawardis attracted an Egyptian scholar, who went on to create a stir in the political and religious circles. Maulana Shamsuddin Turk arrived in Multan along with 400 books on Hadis. He wished to proceed to Delhi, but gave up the idea on learning that Sultan Alauddin Khalji did not offer routine prayers and even abstained from the Friday congregation. Instead, he stayed put in Multan and enrolled as a disciple of Shaikh Shamsuddin Fazlullah, a son of Shaikh Sadrudin Arif. During these days, he wrote a commentary on a book of Hadis, wherein he praised the reigning Sultan in superlative terms. In addition to the commentary, he wrote a letter, which was addressed to the Sultan. In this epistle (*risala*), he stated his object of visiting India and, after praising the Sultan for his administrative measures, disapproved the official indifference towards Islam. This letter deserved a closer look because, between the lines, it offered an insight into the attitude of the Suhrawardis on important matters.

Maulana Shamsuddin Turk stated that he had travelled all the way from Egypt to serve the Sultan, to establish the subject of Hadis in Delhi and, in this manner, deliver the Muslims from the dubious practices of dishonest scholars (*rivayat danishman-*

dan bediyanat). Having learnt that the Sultan did not observe the schedule of obligatory prayers and did not attend the Friday congregation, he had decided to return from Multan back to his country. In his view, the Sultan did possess a few virtues of the pious rulers (*badshahan dindar*). But some of his qualities did not conform to the conduct of such admirable kings. First, the Sultan had humiliated and impoverished the Hindus, forcing their women and children to beg at the doors of the Muslims. For thus defending the creed of Prophet Muhammad, he would be forgiven for his sins on the day of judgement. Second, the Sultan had lowered the prices of food grains and other essential commodities and, by benefiting the common people, had outclassed Muslim kings who had failed to achieve this goal despite their efforts of two or three decades. Third, the Sultan had forbidden all intoxicants and curbed all immoral activities. Fourth, the Sultan had suppressed the numerous deceitful practices of the market people and thus achieved a rare success. For implementing these four measures, the Sultan stood congratulated and deserved a place among the prophets.[72]

In the second part of the communication, Maulana Shamsuddin Turk criticized the Sultan for his failure to uphold Islam on many counts. First, the Sultan was personally responsible for a decision that was totally unacceptable not only to God and the Prophet, but also to the saints and monotheists. He had assigned the department of justice, which was one of the most sensitive positions in the government and which needed to be given to someone who had renounced the world, to Hamid Multani Bacha who had been nourished by his father and grandfather on an income from usury. Not only this, the Sultan had not taken the necessary precautions in the appointment of *qazis* and had assigned the regulation of the Shariat to the greedy and worldly. For this particular sin, the Sultan needed to fear God, because he would have no answer for the day of judgement. Second, in the city of Delhi, the Prophetic traditions were being discarded and, instead, the words of philosophers were being put into practice. It was not clear why such a city had not been struck by calamities and was not reduced to a heap of rubble. Third, in the city of Delhi, a number of ill-fated and untrustworthy scholars sat with their books in the mosques and, in lieu of money, pronounced dubious legal opinions. Through their fraudulent interpretations, they had destroyed the rights of the Muslims. They had not only doomed the claimants and respondents, but had also compromised their own consciousness. The Sultan was not aware of the last two things, because of the shameless and dishonest *qazi*, who happened to be his close confidant. Otherwise, the Sultan would not have tolerated such violation of the creed of the Prophet.[73]

Maulana Shamsuddin Turk sent his book and letter to the Sultan through Bahauddin Dabir. As could be anticipated, Dabir presented the book to the Sultan, but, owing to his anxiety of defending the interests of Hamid Multani, did not deliver the letter. The Sultan, having learnt from Sad Mantiqi about the arrival of the letter, demanded it. Since Dabir failed to produce it, the Sultan became furious and intended to punish him along with his son. Mercifully, the Sultan regretted that the Maulana had returned in frustration.[74]

Barani's narrative of the episode leaves much to be inferred. Maulana Shamsuddin Turk did not undertake the arduous journey from Egypt to Multan merely to see some places in Panjab. Since he had brought a huge stock of 400 books on Hadis, he intended taking up a job in the judicial or ecclesiastical department of the Delhi Sultanate. He resided in Multan for an extended period, with the aim of culturally attuning himself to a new environment and understanding the functioning of the political structure. By enrolling under the tutelage of a Suhrawardi master, he desired to benefit from the political influence of the Sufi network, which had a century long history of collaborating with the Delhi Sultanate. He also availed himself of the opportunity to improve his academic credentials by putting together a book. His case for a job did not find favour with the Khalji regime, owing to the negative attitude of Hamid Multani, the chief judge of the kingdom. The appointment of this man, who was the chief of merchants (*malik ut-tujjar*), as the head of the justice department had already caused widespread resentment among the religious classes. What was equally worrying, the Sultan was personally indifferent towards Islam, while freethinking philosophers like Sad Mantiqi had gained ascendancy in the corridors of power.

The Suhrawardis could not give voice to their ideological concerns, as they had been the most visible beneficiaries of state patronage in the form of land grants. Therefore, they employed the services of a frustrated job seeker to question the Sultan's commitment to Islam, highlight the incompetence of Hamid Multani and expose the dismal state of the judicial system. Since Maulana Shamsuddin Turk could not have identified the sources of his information, he repeatedly stated that he was writing what he had heard. He could not be accused of prejudice against the Sultan, as he had adequately highlighted the outstanding achievements of the Khalji regime. Since he could anticipate the impact of his sharp criticism, he avoided going to Delhi for a meeting with the Sultan. In fact, he might have left the Indian shores before his letter could reach its destination. Let us not forget, Barani had every reason to side with the Maulana and his Suhrawardi hosts on the issues at stake. Understandably, he gave prominence to an episode, which has been ignored by other contemporary writers. For his part, the Egyptian scholar would not have written such a letter without the sponsorship of his Suhrawardi hosts. Whoever was the brain behind the controversial letter, it succeeded in articulating a particular approach to issues concerning the state and religion by entering the pages of an important chronicle of the period.

The views of the Maulana were similar to those of Barani, as expressed by the historian in another part of his chronicle. According to him, Alauddin Khalji had lost his mental equilibrium during the closing years of his reign and this weakness adversely affected his choice of incumbents for high offices. Since the post of the chief judge commanded great prestige in the Delhi Sulatnate, it behoved only dignified people and their descendents who were known for their learning, lineage and piety. However, the Sultan had assigned this office to the chief of merchants Hamiduddin Multani who, as a household servant, had served as the keeper of curtains and keys of the royal palace (*chakar khana wa pardahdar wa kalid dar kushk*). It was futile to record the qualities of this chief of merchants. Instead of looking at his descent (*nasb wa hasb*), the

Sultan considered merely his services and those of his father. No one dared to bring it to his notice that mere knowledge did not constitute the requirements for the post of the Qazi. Rather the essential qualification (*lawazim shart*) was piety (*taqwa*), which meant distancing oneself from the world along with its sins and wickedness. A king could not hope for his own salvation if he did not offer the post of the chief judge to the most pious scholar of his kingdom. He would fail to play his role as the protector of the faith (*din panahi*) if he conferred this post on people who were greedy, irreligious, or worldly. Towards the end of his reign, Alauddin Khalji considered only past services in appointing the Sadr-i Jahan. The subsequent rulers followed the same practice, so that the requirement of piety was rendered unnecessary.[75]

Peak of the Suhrawardis

The punishment of a Suhrawardi master, discussed above, must have dealt a severe blow to the Sufi establishment of Multan in terms of devotional practices and financial management. Not long after this unfortunate episode, normal activities were revived at the hospice and, in fact, there was sufficient evidence of vibrancy in all spheres of the spirutrual discipline in the middle of the fourteenth century. In a work entitled *Fatawa-i Sufiyya* (Legal Judgements of the Sufis), written about 1350, Fazlullah Majawi clarified a number of regulations by referring to the practice of his teachers. According to him, visitors arrived in Multan from many lands. Sometimes they numbered a thousand at a time, apart from the permanent inhabitants of the hospice and the workers serving inside. It was stated that the hospice had roofs, courtyards, cells and terraces. All parts of the building had doors opening into the courtyard, so that everyone could follow the leader of worship. Built like a mosque for prayer and meditation, it was open to all residents as well as travellers. In addition to the service of God, it offered a number of advantages – perpetual recitation of the Quran from beginning to end, continuous remembrance of God, distribution of food and granting allowance to the family and dependants of the spiritual head of the hospice.[76]

The *Fatawa-i Sufiyya* throws interesting light on activities in the Suhrawardi establishment. Books were read in an academic setting, where a tutor instructed students in the correct transmission of the text to posterity. In a devotional setting, a Sufi elder wept profusely as he listened to literary evocations of the love of God. Extra prayers were offered that conformed to the occasions of liturgical calendar and were prescribed by the local leaders of the Suhrawardis. On Thursday nights, there was a special recitation of the Quran, which was followed by public prayers and distribution of sweet pudding (*halwa*). Once a year, food and drink was distributed. Feast days with public prayers were limited to ten in a year. On his own a Sufi could recite the whole of the Quran in his cell. Every year, a fast of six months was observed in seclusion. Seekers who undertook the arduous exercise, were served food of good quality for physical strength. Besides cash incentives, such desciples were given clothes, or the money to purchase them. Sometimes, the Sufis assembled to listen to poetry and were agitated by the experience. The leader, who presided over the function, called out to them and, in response, they regained their equipoise. The leader himself did not participate in dancing or any other form of ecstatic or automatic motion. Instead, he supervised the proceedings from a distance.[77]

From the middle of the fourteenth century the Suhrawardi seat at Uch began to gain importance in the religious, social, and political spheres. This was due to the tireless efforts of Syed Jalaluddin Bokhari, who had returned (1348) from seven years' sojourn in west Asia. His grandfather Syed Jalaluddin Surkhposh had founded the Suhrawardi establishment of Uch. Having migrated from Bokhara to Multan, Surkhposh became a disciple of Shaikh Zakariya. In response to the directions of his mentor, he shifted to Uch and began to propagate the Suhrawardi ideals of Islamic spirituality. This was not an easy task because Uch was experiencing political instability owing to the intense political conflict in the new Turkish ruling class and the recurrent Mongol invasions. Except for the close relations between the Suhrawardi seats of Uch and Multan, there was little evidence of the activities of Surkhposh and his son and successor Syed Ahmad Kabir (the father of Syed Jalaluddin Bokhari). In the words of a modern writer,

Just as Uch was often subject to Multan's authority in the political realm, so too was the case in the spiritual realm – the city's two most important khanqahs were each headed by a khalifah of Bahauddin Zakariya or his descendants. This relationship between the Sufi establishments of the two cities was carried forward in successive generations so that Jalal Surkh's son, Ahmad Kabir, and grandson, Jalaluddin Bokhari, were disciples of Bahauddin's son, Sadruddin Arif (d. 684/1286), and grandson, Ruknuddin Abul Fateh (d. 735/1334-35).[78]

Syed Jalaluddin Bokhari had his education in Uch, in Multan, and in west Asia. At Uch, he learnt the Hadis from his father Syed Ahmad Kabir and a travelling scholar. He also studied Pazdawi's *Kanz ul-Wusul* and Marghinani's *Hidaya* from the local *qazi*, Bahauddin Allama. From the age of seven onwards, he benefited from Shaikh Jamaluddin Uchi,[79] a deputy of Shaikh Sadruddin Arif of Multan. In his later life, Shaikh Bokhari preserved fond memories of Uchi's piety and unique method of solving complex issues through divine guidance. When the *qazi* of Uch died, Shaikh Bokhari went to Shaikh Ruknuddin Abul Fateh in order to complete his study of the works by Pazdawi and Marghinani. Since his object was to focus on legal texts, he was not admitted to the Suhrawardi hospice. Instead he was enrolled in a seminary (*madrasa*) under the tutelage of Shaikh Musa (a grandson of Shaikh Ruknuddin) and Maulana Majduddin. He was lodged in a room at the city gate and provided with food from the private property of Shaikh Ruknuddin. During a stay of one year, he completed his study of legal treatises. He was sent back by Shaikh Ruknuddin to Uch in a hurry, without being granted the customary affiliation (*khirqah*) and permission (*ijazat*). He was deputed to carry an urgent message to his father Syed Ahmad Kabir to place himself under the care of Shaikh Jamaluddin Uchi, so that he could be cured of his uncontrolled emotions. Shaikh Ruknuddin, who died in 1334, posthumously continued to guide Shaikh Bokhari through visions and dreams.[80]

In 1341, Shaikh Bokhari was summoned by Sultan Muhammad bin Tughluq (r. 1325-51). In the words of Steinfels, 'This encounter with the Sultan was a turning point in Bukhari's life, leading to his initiation into the Chishti lineage by Shaikh Nasiruddin Mahmud Awadhi Chiragh-i Dihli, his appointment by the Sultan to official position and his decision to perform the pilgrimage to Mecca.'[81] Before meeting the Sultan, Shaikh Bokhari met Shaikh Nasiruddin and expressed his fear at the official attempt to make the children of dervishes wear clothes that state officials wore. Shaikh Nasiruddin dressed Shaikh Bokhari in a new apparel – a robe of blessing (*khirqah-i tabarruk*), turban (*dastar*) and his own cloak (*barani-i khas*) – to protect him from the Sultan's intentions.[82] The Sultan appointed Shaikh Bokhari as the Shaikh ul-Islam of Sind and placed the Muhammadi hospice in Siwistan and forty additional Sufi lodges under his management. But he did not accept this assignment as Siwistan fell in the spiritual jurisdiction of Shaikh Ruknuddin, who had not given his affiliation (*khirqah*) to him. In these circumstances, Shaikh Nasiruddin granted a Chishti affiliation to him so that he could take up the assignment. This shows that the major Sufi orders were not exclusive and that, from the fourteenth century onwards, a person could receive affiliation from more than one Sufi lineages. However, Shaikh Bokhari was advised by Shaikh Ruknuddin in a dream to reject the assignment as it would jeopardize his spiritual pursuit and directed him to go for Haj.[83]

During the next seven years, Shaikh Bokhari visited a number of places in west Asia – Mecca, Madina, Aden, Shiraz, and Gazrun. Except the last year of his sojourn, he spent his entire time in the holy cities of the Hejaz. He interacted with profound scholars and ardent Sufis, many of whom were attached to the Suhrawardi order and followed the Shafi school of Sunni jurisprudence. He was aided in his education by his identity as a Syed, his command over Arabic, and his affiliation with Shaikh Ruknuddin and Shaikh Nasiruddin, who were noted for their miraculous presence in Hejaz. His adherence to the Hanafi school of Sunni jurisprudence did not pose a hurdle. At Madina, he studied Hadis from Afifuddin Matari and received affiliation (*khirqah*) of the

Suhrawardi and Rifai orders. At Mecca, he took spiritual training from Shaikh Abdullah Yafai and received affiliation in the Suhrawardi and Qadiri lineages. He acquired familiarity with such Sufi texts as *Rauzat-i Riahin* and *Risala-i Makkiya*, while he was kept away from the works of Ibn-i Arabi. He maintained himself by working as a copyist and earned one silver coin for producing two quires of papers. Sometimes he received food and money from his mentor Shaikh Yafai. After six years at Mecca and Madina, Shaikh Bokhari went to Aden where he met Shaikh Yafai's teacher who was popular as Faqih Bassal. He wished to take a ship from Aden to Sind,[84] but on the advice of Faqih Bassal, he stayed in Mecca till he was permitted by Shaikh Ruknuddin to return. Here he saw a vision wherein he met Shaikh Ruknuddin who bestowed a *khirqah* on him and declared him one of a great saints, and an axis of the world (*qutb-i alam*). He received a *khirqah* from Shaikh Yafai's mentor Nuruddin Ali Tawashi and another from Muhammad bin Ubaid Ghaisi.[85]

From Aden, Shaikh Bokhari returned to Madina and studied *Awarif ul-Maarif* from Afifuddin Matari. During a forty-day retreat in the Prophet's mosque, he was provided food by Matari. After spending a total of seven years in Hejaz, he travelled overland to Persia. In Shiraz, he gave lessons to a large number of people and supervised the reading of al-Baghawi's *Masabih ul-Sunna*. At Gazrun, he received two Suhrawardi *khirqahs*, one from Shaikh Qiwamudin (a deputy of Shaikh Ruknuddin) and another from Shaikh Aminuddin Baliani. During the course of his travels, Shaikh Bokhari appeared to have received nearly forty *khirqahs* that were traced to six Sufi orders – Suhrawardi, Chishti, Rifai, Kubrawi, Qadiri, and Gazruni.[86]

On retrurning to Uch in 1348, Shaikh Bokhari became head of the Suhrawardi hospice, managed in his absence by his brother Syed Raju Qattal.[87] As a preliminary step, he established a seminary in the hospice. Since the students were attracted from far and near, a number of teachers and theologians were employed here. The curriculum comprised the Quran, Hadis, and Islamic spirituality. To these subjects were added grammar and lexicography, so that learners could gain proficiency in Arabic. Shaikh

Bokhari himself delivered lectures on different Islamic sciences. While teaching Quranic exegesis, he preferred *Tafsir-i Madarak* to *Tafsir-i Kashaf* as the latter was authored by a Mutazilite. He laid stress on the teaching of Hadis and adopted a distinct pattern – reading a Hadis, explaining the meaning of difficult words, and the full interpretation. For the study of Hadis, he relied on *Sahih ul-Bokhari, Sahih Muslim, Sunan-i Abu Daud, Mishkat ul-Masabih* and *Jami ul-Saghir*. Recongnizing the significance of the Islamic jurisprudence (*fiqh*), he uncovered the differences among the four schools and, in the process, underlined the universality of the Hanafi interpretation. He also taught the recitation of the Quran, having himself mastered the seven methods during his stay in Hejaz. As the number of students was large and enough suitable teachers unavailable, senior pupils were roped in to instruct the junior batches. He employed all means to enrich the library of the seminary. From his days in Hejaz, he had brought copies of *Awarif ul-Maarif* and *Sharh Kabir Chahl Ism*, besides arranging the transcription of *Asrar-i Dawat* which belonged to Abdul Rahman Zaffari. He acquired a seven-volume Quranic commentary which was produced by a eminent jurist who visited Uch.[88] Two of his disciples produced Persian translations of the supplement to Abdullah Yafai's *Rauzat ul-Riyahin* and Qutbuddin Damishqi's *Risala-i Makkiya*. While studying at Mecca, he compiled an account of forty Sufis, *Arabain Sufiya*, which became extinct. Apart from preparing a compendium of sayings of saints and litanies, *Amal wa Ashghal*, he was believed to have done the first ever Persian translation of the Quran.[89]

For Shaikh Bokhari, the training of a novice was based on the twin foundations of knowledge (*ilm*) and action (*amal*). He gave precedence to knowledge, as it determined the legality of any action. He approved the practice in west Asia (Gazrun, Mecca and Madina), where a novice was required to study Islamic jurisprudence (*fiqh*) according to one of the four schools (*mazhabs*), which in practical terms involved the study of the Quran, Hadis, Arabic language and grammar. Once he became a master (*faqih*) of Islamic jurisprudence, he was allowed to engage in action comprising recital of litanies (*aurad*) and other devotional exercises.

In his own hospice, he might not have prescribed a two-part curriculum, but he laid a considerable emphasis on teaching various aspects of the Islamic law. Of the 200 books mentioned in his conversations (*malfuzat*), one third were compilations of legal opinions (*fatawa*) and commentaries, whereas as a quarter of the texts cited fell in the broad category of Sufism. With regard to his choice of literature, he was favourably inclined towards standard textbooks and authoritative reference works, but showed no interest in critical and speculative writings.[90]

In spite of the availability of a large number of books, it was essential for a novice to study a particular text under the supervision of a recognized authority who, in turn, granted the permission (*ijazat*) to him for further transmission of the specific content. As per the convention, a pupil read a portion of a book and, immediately thereafter, the teacher offered a detailed explanation of the passage. To his own disciples, Shaikh Bokhari taught as many as twenty-three books that pertained to different aspects of knowledge. Apart from the Quran, there were books on Hadis by Raziuddin Saghani, Abu Muhammad Baghawi and Jalaluddin Bokhari; on jurisprudence (*fiqh*) by Khatib Baghdadi, Ahmad bin Ali bin Saati, Burhanuddin Marghinani and Qaduri; on roots of law (*usul-i fiqh*) by Abul Hasan Ali bin Muhammmad Pazdawi and Husamuddin Muhammad Akhsikati; on theology (*kalam*) by Hafizuddin Abul Barkat Abdullah Nasafi and Sirajuddin Ushi Farghani Imam; on Quranic commentary (*tafsir*) by Hafizuddin Abul Barkat Abdullah Nasafi; on the mystic path (*suluk*) by Abu Hafs Umar Shihabuddin Suhrawardi, Muhammad bin Ishaq Kalabadhi and Qutbuddin Damishqi; on litanies (*aurad*) Abu Hafs Umar Shihabuddin Suhrawardi, Bahauddin Zakariya and Jalaluddin Bokhari and three compilations of divine names. Not surprisingly, in a letter of investiture (27 May 1369) to a disciple who assumed the office of a judge, Shaikh Bokhari offered instructions that indicated the way in which he embedded Sufi practice in the structures of legal orthodoxy and vice versa.[91]

Two compilations of the Shaikh Bokhari's discourses, *Khizanat ul-Fawaid* and *Siraj ul-Hidaya*, have offered important insights into his understanding of Islamic spirituality. Organized into topical chapters and not compiled as daily diary of conversations, his teachings appeared as discrete statements on different themes that were frequently interspersed with quotations from earlier works. Since the original source was often in Arabic, the quotations were translated into Persian in the explanations. The inclusion of extracts from a wide range of existing literature aimed at benefiting the readers, who did not have equal access to books as well as Arabic. Thus, the sources of South Asian Islamic tradition were traceable to central Asia. Of the books quoted in the *malfuzat* under reference, an overwhelming number belonged to the discipline of Islamic jurisprudence (*fiqh*). This proportion was more than one-third in *Khizanat ul-Fawaid* and about two-third in *Siraj ul-Hidaya*. This dilution of the distinction between a Sufi text and a legal treatise pointed towards an intermingling of two discursive traditions.[92] Shaikh Bokhari's two *malfuzat* have not only drawn extensively from the compilations of legal opinions (*fatawa*), but also shared a number of structural features with them. The two distinct categories of texts, *malfuzat and fatawa*, often relied on the same sources, particularly the basic works of the Hanafi school of jurisprudence. The boundaries between Sufism and jurisprudence seemed to crumble, even as the respective roles of the Sufi and Alim were intertwined. Bokhari's *malfuzat* tended to acknowledge the supremacy of the Shariat in the religious sphere, while he himself appeared to appropriate the authority of the legal expert. While insisting on obedience to the Shariat, Shaikh Bokhari incorporated the study of law and other religious sciences into the daily regimen of seekers.[93] He played an active role in securing punishment for holy men who violated the injunctions of the Shariat.[94]

Once the novice acquired the requisite knowledge (*ilm*) of the Islamic law, he was ready to engage in action (*amal*), which comprised a series of devotional practices. Before he could do so, he needed to cleanse himself of anything impermissible (*haram*) and to achieve absolute concentration on God (*huzur-i dil*) by keeping clear of all distracting thoughts. Such a state could also result from the correct performance of the devotional exercises. Of these, the most fundamental was remembrance of God (*zikr*) by rhythmic repetition of one of His names. Sufi orders performed *zikr* in distinct ways involving different postures of the body and pattern of breathing. In the initiatory ritual, the *zikr* was implanted in the disciple's heart by the mentor, who had received it from his elders through a chain of transmission (*isnad*). Shaikh Bokhari's *zikr* was traced back to Prophet Muhammad and Shihabuddin Suhrawardi. He used the creedal statement (*kalima*) for the purpose. The disciple sat cross-legged with his hands on his thighs. He uttered the negative portion while moving his head towards the right, while he made the affirmation of God while moving his head towards the left. While engaged in *zikr*, the disciple ensured the purity of his body and heart as well as the purity of his clothes and place. Though *zikr* could be done in silence, yet Shaikh Bokhari preferred it to be done loudly and in a group, so that the body trembled visibly and others heard it. Seen as a sign of love for God and the only way to reach Him, it had to be undertaken with sincerity and reverence. By purifying the heart, *zikr* prepared the disciple for the higher devotional exercise involving the recital of litanies (*aurad*).[95]

The regimen of devotion prescribed by Shaikh Bokhari included retreats of forty days. During this period of seclusion (*khilwat*), the practitioner detached himself from all worldly concerns and immersed himself in a variety of devotions – prayer, remembrance of God and reading the Quran, besides minimizing the physical needs of food and sleep. Shaikh Bokhari did not favour a physical withdrawal to the wilderness, as one was legally obliged to support one's family. Possibilities of error in the modes of detachment and devotion could be prevented by undertaking the retreat under the supervision of a mentor. Such an exercise could be performed three times in a year: the last ten days of Jamadi-us-Sani and entire Rajab; the last ten days of Shaban and entire Ramzan; and the entire Zialqad and first ten days of Zilhijja. An additional retreat extended from 15 Zilhijja to 25 Muharram. The disciple was permitted to undertake a shorter retreat of ten days. The ideal place of retreat was a congregational mosque. Having gone into seclusion, one could come out only for obligatory prayers or meeting emergent situations. Owing to these interruptions, one was required to reiterate one's intention (*niyat*) for the retreat every day.[96]

Shaikh Bokhari privileged obligatory prayer (*namaz*) over other forms of devotion. His spiritual discourses, as compiled in the *Khizanat-i Jawahar-i Jalaliya*, were entirely devoted to this subject. In their standard format, the five obligatory prayers comprised seventeen prostrations (*rakats*) – two of Fajr at daybreak, four of Zuhr at noon, four of Asr in the afternoon, three of Maghrib at dusk and four of Isha at night. As a matter of tradition, these obligatory prayers were doubled by the addition of extra prayers (*sunnat rakats*) which were offered in emulation of the Prophet. In addition to these, Shaikh Bokhari recommended supererogatory prayers comprising prostrations ranging from four thousand to one hundred. The last mentioned one hundred prostrations included prayers at five additional times – dawn (*ishraq*), mid morning (*chasht*), afternoon (*zawal*), twilight (*awabin*) and night after waking from sleep (*tahajjud*) – and prayers to achieve a variety of worldly and spiritual aims. Shaikh Bokhari prescribed different prayers for different purposes. Some of these could protect a practitioner from the punishment of hell and grant the bliss of heaven. Other prayers could bestow worldly benefits like health, prosperity, relief from debt and even rain. In order to attain the desired results, Shaikh Bokhari laid down the time and day of the week, besides the number of prostrations (*rakats*), recitations of Quranic verses (*suras*) and supplications (*duas*). However, a supplicant was required to be morally upright in his conduct, as he could not take a positive result of prayers for granted. Prayers held at specific times of the day – dawn, middle of the night and Friday – were most likely to be answered. It was not proper to pray for harming someone, even if such a person was a tyrant.[97]

An aspirant could achieve the desired results by reciting the Quran, offering supplications and uttering litanies (*aurad*) – all of which required an ability to engage with the Arabic language. Shaikh Bokhari prescribed readings from the Quran to ward off invaders, win over the love of a spouse and figure out future events. In the case of supplications, he used specific formulas handed down from the previous generations and traced to Muhammad or his companions. A formula was normally composed of praise for God, the Prophet and his family, the first four caliphs, the founders of Sunni schools of jurisprudence and founders of Sufi orders, and culminated in a direct request. Like the content of supplications, the Shaikh recommended litanies that were developed by himself or Shaikh Zakariya. These formulas comprised the profession of faith, the names of God, blessings on Muhammad and expressions of repentance. In some cases, the litanies were drawn from Jewish and Christian traditions that might have been assimilated by the Islamic practice in west Asia and subsequently adopted by the Muslims of India. In contrast to the Chishtis, Shaikh Bokhari showed little interest in the mystical and ecstatic experiences (*ahwal*) that were often supernatural in character. Perhaps he wished to protect his disciples from the controversial ideas of Ibn-i Arabi on the possibility of union with God and the tendency of wandering Qalandars to violate social and legal norms. However, Shaikh Bokhari has recorded cases of strong emotional responses like weeping or crying, besides autobiographical anecdotes of his encounters with distant or dead. In view of the Shaikh's belief in the efficacy of prayers and supplications in human affairs, it was implied that he approved the practice of distributing amulets (*tawiz*) inscribed with a variety of sacred verses, words, names and symbols.[98]

On meeting an aspirant, Shaikh Bokhari admitted his inability to enroll a disciple, but declared his intention of forming a bond of brotherhood in accordance a Hadis, 'Increase the good brothers, for God is noble and refrains from punishing a man in front of his brothers.' The Shaikh clasped the hand of the candidate and asked him if he accepted him as a brother. After receiving a reply in the affirmative, he made a statement of repentance. Thereafter, the two recited the following three times, 'I ask forgiveness of God, there is no god but Him, the Living, the Eternal, and I turn in repentance to Him.' The Shaikh placed his hand on the disciple's chest and beseeched God to lay open his breast. Taking a pair of scissors, he cut the hair on the disciple's forehead, while reciting, 'Oh God, shorten his expectations and protect him from sin.' After the haircut, the Shaikh sought blessings of God for Muhammad and his family. Asking for strength in their repentance and preservation from sin, he invoked the family of Muhammad as well as the names of Shaikh Bahauddin Zakariya, Shaikh Sadruddin Arif and Shaikh Ruknuddin Abul Fateh. There was no need to shave the head of the aspirant, as his repentance was enough. However, Shaikh Bokhari gave such a permission if the aspirant insisted. Putting a hat on his head, the Shaikh recited, 'My God, crown him with the crown of nobility and happiness and preserve him from sin and strengthen him in the religion of Islam.' He placed a piece of sugar in the mouth of the aspirant and prayed to God for granting him the sweetness of faith. After the haircut and supplication, the Shaikh offered instructions (*wasiyat*) in accordance with the capabilities and conditions of the aspirant. Someone was advised to study the law and Quranic recitation, another to engage in the remembrance of God (*zikr*) and still another to concern himself with the litanies of Shaikh Zakariya.[99]

The ceremony of investiture included three Quranic concepts – request for forgiveness (*istighfar*), statement of repentance (*tauba*) and request to God for opening of disciple's heart. The physical gestures, handclasp, touching the chest, clipping hair and placing sugar in the mouth, symbolized the creation of an intimate bond between the mentor and disciple. The disciple, who appeared to be passive in the hands of the master, underwent a transformation of his physical appearance and spiritual condition. However, he did participate in the verbal component of the ceremony by taking the oath of allegiance, making a statement of repentance and asking for forgiveness. These verbal expressions, according to Steinfels, placed the ritual in the context of the Islamic tradition, Prophetic example and Quranic concepts. Though the ceremony appeared to create a new relationship between the mentor and disciple, yet it invoked the express assistance of several other entities – God, Muhammad and his family, and the Suhrawardi exemplars of Multan. Since the ritualistic statements were invariably in Arabic, the aspirants who did not understand the language were given instructions in the local language and, in some cases, the conferment of hat (*kulah*) was treated as a suitable alternative.[100]

A Sufi master bestowed the Sufi robe (*khirqa*) on his disciple and it constituted an indispensable part of the institution of discipleship (*piri muridi*). It could be bestowed on two different occasions – first, when a novice was initiated into a Sufi order under the tutelage of his mentor and second, when, having completed his education and training, he was given the permission (*ijazat*) to establish himself as a Sufi master and enroll disciples. This kind of Sufi robe, which focused on discipleship, was known as the *khirqa-i iradat*. A Sufi robe could also be bestowed as a blessing and, in such cases, it was known as *khirqa-i tabarruk*. As it denoted a loose bond of affiliation and devotion, it was conferred on those who were not likely to seriously pursue the Sufi path. The *khirqa-i tahkim* was given to a disciple who had placed himself under the absolute control of his mentor, while *khirqa-i karahat* was given by a Sufi master under duress in response to the demand of a disciple. Whatever be the kind of the Sufi robe, it tried to bind the recipient with three entities – his spiritual preceptor, his peer group of fellow disciples and the initiatic lineage of the Sufi order which stretched back to Prophet Muhammad or an eminent Sufi master of the past. Shaikh Bokhari's discourses (*malfuzat*) have recorded the chains of transmission of his several Sufi robes, names of masters from whom he had received them and the circumstances in which these were conferred on him. These records have also noted similar information about his disciples along with the instructions (*wasiyat*) given to them. The *khirqas* were an authentic proof of the spiritual authority of the Sufi master in the domain of religion.[101]

When Shaikh Bokhari bestowed a *khirqah* on a disciple, it was not the one which he had actually received from his own mentor. But it was believed that the disciple had received a *khirqah* which had been transmitted from the early masters across the lineage. Shaikh Bokhari has provided lists of a variety of Sufi robes in different colours and materials, which were bestowed on different disciples in accordance with their spiritual states and virtues.[102] In actual practice, the Shaikh did not try to match a particular garment with the qualities of the recipient. The object bestowed on a disciple as *khirqah* was either a robe or more frequently a hat.

It could be accompanied by such items as a staff, scissors, prayer rug and prayer beads, all symbolizing authority in different ways. Irrespective of the form and material of the *khirqah*, it represented the recipient's affiliation to a particular Sufi order and its function as indicated by the four types mentioned above.[103]

Unlike the Chishtis, the Suhrawardis did not treat musical sessions as an essential ingredient of the spiritual pursuit. In a collection of his discourses *Khizanat-i Jawahar-i Jalaliya*, Shaikh Bokhari has expressed his sense on the subject. In his view, none of the books on Islamic jurisprudence (*fiqh*) or any jurist (*faqih*) has ever permitted ecstasy and dance. In no age any jurist has given a legal opinion in favour of an assembly for dancing. It was common knowledge that dancers, owing to their greed for easy money and sumptuous meals, indulged in acts that were heretical. In return for a small allurement, they ruined their lives and faith, besides treating the illegal as legal. Those Sufis, who approved the practice of audition, had prescribed strict conditions under which it could be held. There could be no audition without conditions, just as there could be no prayer without ablution, fast without abstinence, woman without marriage, cultivation without seed, tree without fruit, house without door and bird without feathers. If a Sufi wished to devote a part of his life to audition, he was advised to fast for three consecutive days and to keep away from food. During this period, he withdrew into a retreat, did not speak to anyone and immersed himself in meditation. After breaking this kind of fast by taking a drop of water, he could listen to a sonnet (*ghazal*) dedicated to a dervish or a dear one. In no case should the Qawwal be a stranger. Since the moment of audition was extremely sensitive, it was essential to take all precautions. While listening to spiritual music, the listener should not allow any devilish temptation to enter his heart. Any lack of concentration during the performance caused much offence. After the conclusion of audition, one must avoid taking food, which was a habit of the negligent. If one was inclined towards audition, one should not make it a habit. Instead, one should attend an audition after a gap of 80 or 120 days.[104]

In his own mystic circle, Shaikh Bokhari allowed musical sessions, but did not show any pronounced emotional response to it. According to an instance recorded in *Jami ul-Ulum*, a band of musicians and Quran reciters arrived in Shiraz and performed in the presence of Shaikh Bokhari. They began with a recitation of Quranic verses and followed it up by some poetry. When they played on the flute (*nai*), the participants began to dance and weep. Maulana Tajuddin Muhammad, who was overcome by emotion, behaved in an unusual manner. He rolled on the ground, cried aloud and foamed at the mouth, while the others tried to calm his passion. Shaikh Bokhari, who had been absorbed in meditation (*muraqba*), was disturbed by the commotion and asked for its cause. When he was informed about the situation, he led the gathering in prayer for strength to the Maulana until he regained consciousness. Meanwhile, the musicians were applauded for their performance.[105]

The Sufi establishments differed widely regarding the means of their financial support. It was known that Baba Farid lived in self-chosen poverty and rejected the state offers of land grants, while Shaikh Zakariya accumulated wealth and received large material assistance from rulers and traders. Shaikh Bokhari, according to Steinfels, adopted the middle position between these two extremes. He was inclined to receive donations, provided the source was legal (*halal*). If a Sufi received articles – food, clothing and shelter – from an illegal source (*haram*), his devotions became invalid. Not surprisingly, he refused to accept food from the hospice, which had been built for him in Uch by Malik Mardan, the governor of Multan during the 1370s. Probably, he did not impose this rule on his disciples. Since he was convinced of the piety of Firoz Shah Tughluq (r. 1351-87), he received both land grants and funds for his hospice, but only for the benefit of worshippers.[106] He consented to wear robes received from the Sultan, because it was obligatory to obey the ruler. He approved the endowment of hospices by the merchants, but such a practice (which was prevalent in Mecca) was not found in India. Before accepting a donation, the recipient was expected to assess the donor's intention. It was possible to accept four types of donations – as blessings, as votive offerings, for the removal of problems and as assistance – provided a condition was met in each case.[107] Once a donation was accepted, the recipient had to spend or distribute it immediately, failing which it would be not be proper for him to accept another donation.

For Shaikh Bokhari, the source of the donation determined the head of expenditure. The donation from merchants, farmers and artisans was spent on living expenses, children and inmates of the hospice; that from kings and officers to pay debts and feed the dervishes of the hospice and guests; from unknown sources on beggars and mendicants. The Shaikh did not want his disciples to rely on donations, but to earn their livelihood (*kasb*). He approved of four occupations – holy raid, trade, agriculture and craft.[108] But he disapproved the work of weavers (*haik*) and revenue officers (*ahl-i diwan*).[109] He also recommended borrowing money on loan, even though it involved the illegality of the interest involved. When he visited Delhi in 1379-80, he felt worried about the burden of his own debt and promised not to borrow again. Yet he did not hesitate to seek financial assistance for his disciple Syed Shamsuddin Masud, who was always short of money and constantly pestered his mentor for help.[110]

Walking in the footsteps of his Suhrawardi elders, Shaikh Bokhari took a keen interest in the contemporary politics. During a visit to Shiraz, he offered a novel interpretation of the Quranic verse (4: 59) 'Obey Allah, the Apostle, and those charged with authority among you.' The Shaikh argued that if one did not render obedience to the last one, that rendered to the first two became futile. The ruler of Shiraz, who had never heard of such an explanation of the verse, came to pay his respects to the Shaikh and made an offering of two trays of coins, one of gold and the other of silver. On this occasion, he admitted having stated only what he had heard from his teachers at Mecca.[111] He observed that the people must pray for the kings and disapproved wishing ill of them, as it could bring a disaster.[112] On another occasion, the Shaikh referred to a Hadis which held that the time spent in the company of the king was a time of grace.[113] When questioned about the unjust kings, the Shaikh again took a firm stance in favour of royalty. In his view, the kings of the world were the chosen ones of God and, therefore, it was not permitted to show disrespect to them or disobey them in matters laid by the Shariat. God had authorized the kings to conduct such acts of worship as the Friday and Id prayers, besides collecting taxes for the public treasury. These acts became valid only if organized under the authority of the king. Any opposition to the king, whether overt or covert, was not permissible. If a person received rewards (*inam*) and land grants during the time of his need and, if he did not assist the king and fight for him against his enemies, the collection and expenditure of the entire income became unlawful.[114] In his *malfuzat* entitled *Khizanat ul-Fawaid ul-Jalaliya*, Shaikh Bokhari has included a chapter on the respect due to the rulers and cited a Hadis, 'He who honours the Sultan is himself honoured by God, and he who humiliates the Sultan is humiliated by God.' He believed in expressing gratitude to God if the ruler was just and to practice patience if he was unjust.[115]

Shaikh Bokhari did not support rulers in all circumstances. On some occasions, he took a firm stance in favour of the common people and, in the process, emphasized the dispensation of justice and elimination of oppression emanating from unjust rule. Referring to the wide impact of the state administered justice, he believed that the benefit of worship was confined to the worshipper, but the benefit of justice was shared by all the people and creatures. He also held that a state could subsist with infidelity (*kufr*), but it could not subsist with injustice (*zulm*). Though he approved Shaikh Junaid Baghdadi's view to the effect that it was unlawful (*haram*) for Sufis to maintain contact with the people connected with the state, yet he permitted Sufis to meet the rulers for three objects – guidance towards good conduct, warning against evil deeds, and meeting the needs of the people. In a categorical statement, he disapproved partaking eatables and beverages offered by the Sultans of the times on the ground that the sources of income of the rulers were tainted by cruelty and injustice. In this context, he provided a long list of taxes that were unanimously held illegal by the scholars of Islam (*ulama-i din-i islam*).[116]

We have seen that Shaikh Bokhari, owing to his differences with Muhammad bin Tughluq, refused to be assimilated in the political structure and lived for seven years (1341-8) in West Asia.

In 1348, he returned to Uch and, being the head of the Suhrawardi centre, appeared to have acquired some influence among the ruling classes. At this time, he received a letter from the historian Ziauddin Barani who had fallen from grace and had been imprisoned at Bhatner. In this letter, Barani praised Shaikh Bokhari as an ideal Syed and indirectly sought his help in his misery. Since, at this stage, the Shaikh was not in a position to approach the Sultan, he sent for Barani a Meccan turban and some money, besides praying for his early release.[117] After a few years, he received a letter from Ain ul-Mulk Mahru, the governor of Multan. The Shaikh was asked to persuade some Syeds to pay their land tax, failing which they could be punished.[118] It was not known if the Shaikh intervened in this matter. However, he did intervene in the affairs of Sind, where he had gained a loyal following, particularly among the local elite. Alauddin Jam Juna and Sadruddin Banbhaniya, the two Samma chiefs of Sind, who had been reduced to straits during the second military campaign of Delhi, invited the Shaikh to intercede with Firoz Shah Tughluq on their behalf. The Shaikh, having accepted the role of a mediator, reached the scene of conflict in Thatta. As the soldiers made a beeline to pay their respects to him, he assured that an agreement would be signed in two days. When the Sultan came forward to welcome him, he revealed that the Delhi army could not subjugate Thatta, as a pious woman of the place had blocked his prayer; since she had died three days back, the Sultan would be victorious. Meanwhile, the people of Thatta sent regular messages to Shaikh Bokhari regarding their travails. The Shaikh conveyed the sad state of inhabitants to the Sultan.[119] In accordance with the terms of peace, the two Samma chiefs were sent to Delhi following their submission.[120]

In contrast to the official chronicle, Shaikh Bokhari's discourses contained a different version of the nature of his intervention. One of them, *Malfuzat-i Makhdum-i Jahaniyan*, attributed the Shaikh's intervention to his desire to prevent the repetition of bloodshed that occurred in Thatta during the reign of Muhammad bin Tughluq and to the people's expectation from him to set the things right.[121] But another record of the Shaikh's discourses, *Siraj ul-Hidaya*, has offered a different version. It indicated that the people on both sides welcomed the Shaikh's intervention, as they hoped for the establishment of peace by a descendant of the Prophet. After offering his midnight prayer (*tahajjud*), the Shaikh put on Shaikh Ruknuddin Abul Fateh's turban and prayed to God for bringing Jam Juna and Banbhaniya to the Sultan. A voice from the unseen (*awaz-i ghaib*) announced that the prayer had been accepted. Next morning Jam Juna presented himself before the Sultan. But the nobles expressed concern about the absence of Banbhaniya. Next night, the Shaikh prayed again and directed Syed Qasim to call out for Banbhaniya seven times. As a result, Banbhaniya arrived with his associates and, after submitting before Imad ul-Mulk, met the Sultan.[122] This surrender of the rebel chiefs did not bring peace to Sind. Rai Tamachi, a brother of Banbhaniya, who had been left to administer Sind, rose up in revolt. The Shaikh, who stood as a guarantee for the subservience of the local chiefs, was summoned by the Sultan to Delhi. He was deputed to Thatta along with Jam Juna and succeeded in bringing Rai Tamachi to the capital in 1371.[123]

In his dealings with state officials, Shaikh Bokhari used his spiritual power to assert his superiority. He enjoyed the patronage of Malik Mardan Daulat, who succeeded Ain ul-Mulk Mahru as the governor of Multan. The new governor not only built a hospice for the Shaikh, but also endowed it with land grants. But the Shaikh did not eat at this hospice, as the governor was found lacking in religious observances. In spite of this flaw, the Shaikh employed his spiritual power to protect Daulat from the wrath of Sultan Firoz Shah Tughluq. He also interceded with the spirit of Daulat's mentor who had been offended for some reason. He went on to establish the Syed identity of Daulat's adopted son Sulaiman, who was the father of Khizr Khan, the founder of the Syed dynasty.[124] The Shaikh's ability to puncture the ego of power drunk bureaucrats was manifested in his contact with the Sultan's *wazir* Khan-i Jahan Maqbul. For unstated reasons, Maqbul was hostile towards the Shaikh and even used bad words for him. Once Maqbul imprisoned the son of a petty officer (*maharrir*) and tortured him. Responding to the request of victim's father, the Shaikh agreed to intercede with Maqbul on the issue. When the Shaikh reached the bungalow of Maqbul, he was denied a meeting and asked not to come again with any recommendation. The Shaikh was said to have gone nineteen times to Maqbul's residence, but he received the same reply. When he went for the twentieth time, he was ridiculed for showing a lack of dignity. The Shaikh replied, 'My dear! On every visit I get a just reward, but the aim of the victim remains unmet. I wish to get him released from your custody, so that the reward of this act is credited to you.' Maqbul felt ashamed of his arrogance and, seeking forgiveness, became a devoted follower of the Shaikh. He released the prisoner and honoured him with a robe and horse. He also presented a cash offering to the Shaikh who, however, passed it on to the victim.[125]

The Shaikh did not hesitate to use his spiritual power to punish any unjust officer. Once during the month of Ramzan, he was sitting in contemplation in a mosque along with a number of Sufis and students. Sumra, the administrator of Uch, came to meet the Shaikh. He felt angry at the presence of a large number of Sufis and turned some of them out of the mosque. Incensed at this highhandedness, the Shaikh cursed Sumra in such a manner that he became insane and even had to be chained. After a few days, Sumra's old mother met the Shaikh and requested that her son be restored to her. In accordance with the Shaikh's advice, Sumra was given a bath and fresh clothes, after which he was escorted to the tomb of Shaikh Jamaluddin Uchi (a teacher of Shaikh Bokhari). Sumra returned to the mosque and, falling at the feet of the Shaikh and other Sufis, regained his sanity.[126] Thus, the Shaikh reformed an oppressive officer and converted him into a faithful disciple.

Shaikh Bokhari was on intimate terms with Firoz Shah Tughluq (r. 1351-88). Over a long period, a strong bond of affection developed between the two, each trying to strengthen it from the core of his heart. After every one or two years, the Shaikh travelled all the way from Uch to Delhi in order to meet the Sultan. During these occasions, the events were organized in accordance with a specific pattern. As soon as the Shaikh reached Firozabad, the Sultan came upto Mand and, after receiving him with great courtesy, escorted him to the city. During his visits, the Shaikh stayed in one of the three places – the palace of Firozabad, the hospital and tomb of

Prince Fateh Khan. When the Shaikh arrived at the spot meant for the chamberlains, the Sultan got up from his throne and welcomed the visitor with utmost respect. The two sat down on a carpeted floor and engaged in friendly conversation. When the Shaikh got up to leave and reached the spot for chamberlains, the Sultan also stood up and, after bidding farewell, remained standing while the Shaikh was in view. It was only at this moment that the Sultan resumed his seat on the throne.

After every second or third day, the Sultan visited the abode of the Shaikh. The two men exchanged thoughts on matters of mutual concern, while the meeting exuded a lot of warmth and cordiality. A number of people, who belonged to Uch and Delhi, put forward their requests to the Shaikh. In his turn, he directed his servants to convert the verbal demands into written applications and these were duly placed before the Sultan. The Sultan, after careful examination of the petitions, noted his orders for the fulfilment of the needs of applicants. After a few days the Shaikh left for Uch and, once again, the Sultan saw him off upto a distance of one stage. This particular arrangement between the two continued for several years and, on each occasion, the Shaikh's sojourn became longer than the previous one. During the last visit, the Shaikh told his host that this should be their last meeting as he was near the end of his life and the Sultan too had become old. He felt that it was no longer desirable for the Sultan to travel far out of Delhi on his hunting trips. This was, in fact, the Shaikh's last piece of advice to the Sultan.[127] This account, which incidentally forms the concluding portion of Afif's history, showed that the Shaikh faithfully carried forward the Suhrawardi tradition of building a mutually beneficial relationship with the highest echelons of power. The Shaikh walked in the footsteps of the senior Suhrawardi master Shaikh Ruknuddin Abul Fateh in acting as a bridge between the needy supplicants and the Delhi Sultanate.

The case of Nawahun showed Shaikh Bokhari in an unfavourable light. This man was a Hindu officer, who was posted at Uch and served as a copyist in Persian. Once he went to enquire about the health of Shaikh Bokhari during the latter's illness. As soon as he arrived and took his seat, he exclaimed, 'May God grant good health to you. You are the seal of saints just as Muhammad is the seal of Prophets.' Shaikh Bokhari understood that Nawahun, by uttering these words, had become a Muslim in accordance with the Shariat. Turning towards his brother Raju Qattal, he asked if he had heard what Nawahun had said. Raju Qattal replied in the affirmative and added that one or two Muslims, who had heard the statement, stood as witnesses. Nawahun immediately left the scene and, rushing to Delhi, narrated the occurrence to Firoz Shah Tughluq. The Sultan, who was friendly towards Nawahun, asked, 'If it is proved that you have really uttered those words, will you become a Muslim?' Nawahun replied that he would not become a Muslim, whatever the circumstances. During those days, Shaikh Bokhari passed away. After observing the last prayer, Raju Qattal travelled all the way to Delhi along with the witnesses. When the Sultan learnt about this visit, he guessed that it was related to Nawahun. He summoned a few prominent theologians and sought their advice on the ways to save Nawahun from the crisis. Acting in accordance with the suggestion of Shaikh Muhammad, the son of Qazi Abdul Muqtadar Thanesari, the Sultan asked Raju Qattal if he had come in connection with an infidel (*kafir*). Raju Qattal replied that he was concerned with that Muslim. Shaikh Muhammad intervened to assert that the fact of his religious identity had not been proved. Outraged at this remark, Raju Qattal cursed Shaikh Muhammad in a manner that he instantly developed a stomach ache and died. The Qazi pleaded for the long life of his only son, but in vain. Nawahun refused to admit that he had embraced Islam, despite the contention of the witnesses. Ultimately he was executed, while Raju Qattal returned to Uch.

Steinfels treats the incident as highly unlikely, because it did not accord with the personality of Shaikh Bokhari as documented in his conversations (*malfuzat*); it was one of the several stories in the hagiographical accounts that claimed superiority of a Sufi over the contemporary state through miraculous power. The present writer does not agree with this view and feels that Shaikh Bokhari read too much into a simple expression of courtesy. Raju Qattal pursued the case with fanatical zeal and Firoz Shah Tughluq was too weak to stand up to the undue pressure exerted by the

Suhrawardis of Uch and merely followed the principles laid out in the *Futuhat-i Firoz Shahi*. A convergence of these factors led to the execution of Nawahun.

NOTES

1. The sons of Baba Farid tried to prevent Syed Muhammad Kirmani, the grandfather of Amir Khurd, from meeting the saint who was critically ill. Kirmani virtually forced his way into the cell. The sons, being shocked at the sudden decision regarding the nomination of Shaikh Nizamuddin Auliya, directed their anger against Kirmani. They blamed him for depriving them of what they coveted the most. Kirmani tried his best to prove his non-partisan role in the decision, which had been taken solely by Baba Farid. Amir Khurd, *Siyar ul-Auliya*, Persian text, Delhi: Matba-i Muhibb-i Hind, 1885, pp. 121-2 (hereafter cited as Amir Khurd).
2. Amir Khurd, p. 90.
3. The shrine of Baba Farid was transformed into a highly profitable enterprise, since the congruence of Baba Farid's *jamaatkhana* and shrine in a single premises tremendously enhanced the sacredness of the architectural complex. Tanvir Anjum, *Chishti Sufis in the Delhi Sultanate 1190-1400: From Restrained Indifference to Calculated Defiance*, Karachi: Oxford University Press, p. 346.
4. Amir Khurd, p. 90.
5. Ibid., p. 188.
6. Ibid., pp. 171-2. Maulana Badruddin Ishaq was incomparable in his service to Baba Farid. He groomed the children of his mentor. He often remained in tears during meditation. Fond of poetry, he composed a book entitled *Tasrif-i Badri* at the instance of his intimate friend Shaikh Nizamuddin Auliya. He was held in high esteem by the elders of Amir Khurd, who has recorded a number of his miracles. He was buried in the Jama Masjid of Ajodhan, where he spent much of his time. Amir Khurd, pp. 170-8.
7. Amir Khurd, pp. 188-9.
8. Ibid., pp. 193-5.
9. Ibid., p. 195.
10. Ibn Battuta, *Rehla*, English translation, Mahdi Husain, entitled *The Rehla of Ibn Battuta: India, Maldive Islands and Ceylon*, Baroda: Oriental Institute, 1976, p. 20.
11. Amir Khurd, p. 196.
12. Ibid., p. 193.
13. Barani, p. 347.
14. Abdul Haq Muhaddis Dehalvi, *Akhbar ul-Akhyar*, Urdu translation, Subhan Mahmud and Muhammad Fazil, Delhi: Noor Publishing House, 1990, pp. 207-8.

15. Amir Khurd, pp. 196-7.
16. Richard M. Eaton, 'The Political and Religious Authority of Baba Farid,' in *Essays on Islam and Indian History*, New Delhi: Oxford University Press, 2000, pp. 206-7.
17. Ibn Battuta, *Rehla*, p. 20.
18. Eaton, op. cit., pp. 220-3.
19. Amir Khurd, p. 197-8.
20. Ibid., pp. 198-201.
21. Ibid., pp. 202-3.
22. Muhammad Ali Asghar Chishti, *Jawahar-i Faridi*, Urdu translation, Fazluddin Naqshbandi Mujaddidi, Pakpattan: Maktaba Baba Farid, n.d., pp. 488-90.
23. Ibid., pp. 390-2.
24. Pritam Singh, *Sri Guru Granth Sahib Wale Sekh Farid Di Bhaal*, Amritsar: Singh Brothers, rpt., 2010, pp. 210-12; the author of this book has acquired this information from Syed Afzal Haidar, an ardent devotee of the shrine and possibly a resident of Ajodhan, who has been visiting the sacred place regularly over several decades since the middle of the twentieth century.
25. Ibid., pp. 203-6. During the last few decades, the supplicants prayed for peace and prosperity in Pakistan, besides victory for the crusaders (*mujahidin*) who were involved in major struggles in Palestine and Afghanistan.
26. Ibid., pp. 207-8.
27. Ibid., pp. 208-10.
28. Miles Irving, 'The Shrine of Baba Farid Shakarganj at Pakpattan,' *Journal of the Punjab History Society*, no. 1, 1911; I have consulted the reprint which was published in *The Panjab Past and Present*, vol. VII, pt. 2, October 1973, pp. 410.
29. Ibid., p. 411.
30. Ibid., pp. 412-13.
31. Abdul Haq Muhaddis Dehalvi, *Akhbar ul-Akhyar*, pp. 139-40.
32. Ibid., p. 141.
33. Ibid., pp. 141-2.
34. Jamali, p. 128; Jamali did not agree with the view that a disciple could snatch spiritual bounties of his mentor, who then was rendered empty of these virtues. Such an idea did not carry any weight in the balance of Sufism. When a mentor conferred spiritual bounties on any disciple, these were in fact transferred from God's inexhaustible treasure, which never suffered from any paucity.
35. Jamali, pp. 129-30.
36. In the Quran, this chapter has been inscribed as, 'In the Name of God, the Compassionate, the Merciful. Praise be to God, Lord of the worlds, the Compassionate, the Merciful, Master of the Day of Judgement. Thee we worship and from Thee we seek help. Guide us upon the straight path, the path of those whom Thou hast blessed, not of those who incur wrath, nor

Piety Submits to the State 363

of those who are astray.' Constituting the opening of the Quran, it is recited at the beginning of each cycle of prayer, besides such diverse occasions as funeral, wedding, birth, inauguration of official event, signing of contract and beginning of individual endeavour. Seyyed Hossein Nasr et al., eds., *The Study Quran*, pp. 3-5.

37. FF, Faruqi, pp. 452-3; Lawrence, pp. 368-9.
38. Jamali, pp. 130-1.
39. Jamali, pp. 131-2; during his visit to Multan, Jamali found Maulana Fatehullah established as a teacher. The three sons of the Maulana were among his students. He had a lot of affection for Jamali.
40. Jamali, pp. 134-5.
41. Abdul Haq Muhaddis Dehalvi, *Akhbar ul-Akhyar*, pp. 142-3.
42. Ibid., pp. 144-5.
43. Ibid., pp. 145-6
44. Hamid Qalandar, *Khair ul-Majalis*, Persian text, ed. Khaliq Ahmad Nizami, Aligarh: Aligarh Muslim University, 1959, pp. 75-6. While differing with Shaikh Ruknuddin, Shaikh Nasiruddin highlighted the case of Najibuddin Mutawakkil (the brother of Baba Farid), who had settled in Delhi. He lived in a small thatched house in extreme poverty. When he had no money to feed the mendicants, he unsuccessfully tried to sell his clothes and those of his wife. When he could not feed his sons on Id, he resigned himself to the mercy of God. Compare with Khaliq Ahmad Nizami, *The Life and Times of Shaikh Nasiruddin Chiragh-i Delhi*, Delhi: Idarah-i Adabiyat-i Delhi, 1991, pp. 101-2, 114-15.
45. Jamali, pp. 140-2; in contrast, Shaikh Alauddin did not approve of Shaikh Ruknuddin's involvement with the state. After a meeting in which the two embraced, Shaikh Alauddin took a fresh bath and changed his clothes. Without feeling offended at this reaction, Shaikh Ruknuddin admitted that he himself smelt of worldliness, while his Chishti counterpart remained insulated from it. Amir Khurd, p. 195.
46. Amir Khurd, p. 530; on the basis of his travels in Turkey and Syria, Maulana Ilmuddin stated that the Shaikhs of these countries listened to audition since the times of Junaid Baghdadi (d. 910) and Shaikh Shibli (d. 945). In fact, some of them used musical instruments like the clarinet (*shabana*) and drums (*daf*), while no one stopped them from doing so.
47. Jamali, p. 143.
48. In a conversation with Shaikh Ruknuddin, Ibn Battuta learnt that the Shaikh was present at the site with Sultan Ghiasuddin Tughluq and his favourite son Mahmud. The Shaikh further related that Muhammad bin Tughluq requested him to come down from the pavilion, as it was time for the Asr prayer. As soon as the Shaikh emerged from the pavilion, the elephants entered in accordance with a premeditated plan, leading to the collapse of the structure. The Shaikh, who returned without saying his prayer, saw Muhammad bin Tughluq ordering pickaxes and shovels to be brought to

dig out the Sultan. But he signalled to the servants to delay their task, so that the implements were brought only after sunset. When the Sultan was dug out, the prince was seen bending over to save the life of the victim. Some people presumed that the Sultan was already dead, while others suspected that he was rescued alive and then finished off. Ibn Battuta, *Rehla*, p. 55.
49. Ibn Battuta, *Rehla*, p. 97.
50. Barani, p. 479; it was difficult to accept Isami's narrative of the event. According to him, Shaikh Ruknuddin, who had gone into a seclusion for a week, learnt the infliction of terrible retribution on the people whose blood flowed in torrents. Without wearing his turban or putting on his shoes, he appeared as a supplicant before the Sultan and, expressing his horror at the bloodshed, pleaded for an end to the mayhem. The Sultan accepted the plea for mercy and stopped further punishment. Isami, III, pp. 671-2.
51. Ibn Battuta, *Rehla*, p. 97.
52. The Sultan, who was hostile towards Shaikh Nizamuddin Auliya, openly spoke against him. He forbade his nobles from visiting the Shaikh at Ghiaspur. While in a state of inebriation, he offered a reward of 1,000 *tankahs* to the person who would bring the Shaikh's head. When the Sultan met the Shaikh in the hospice of Shaikh Ziauddin Rumi, he did not show any respect to him and did not even respond to his greetings. In order to harm the Shaikh, he made Shaikhzada Jam (a known detractor of the Shaikh) a royal confidant. Barani, p. 396.
53. Dara Shukoh, while elaborating the Qadiri mode of meditation, has conceived of the seeker's spiritual journey through five successive stages – physical plane (*alam-i nasut*), plane of counterparts (*alam-i misal*), astromental plane (*alam-i malkut*), plane of bliss (*alam-i jabrut*) and plane of absolute truth (*alam-i lahut*) – each of which required its own set of meditational techniques. Bikrama Jit Hasrat, *Dara Shikuh: Life and Works*, New Delhi: Munshiram Manoharlal, rpt., 2013, pp. 72-5.
54. Amir Khurd, pp. 136-7.
55. Ibid., pp. 137-40.
56. Ibid., pp. 140-1.
57. Khaliq Ahmad Nizami, *The Life and Times of Shaikh Nizamuddin Auliya*, New Delhi: Oxford University Press, New Edition, 2007, pp. 96-7.
58. Amir Khurd, p. 155.
59. Qazi Javed, *Panjab Key Sufi Danishwar*, Lahore: Fiction House, 2005, p. 98.
60. Jamali, pp. 143-4.
61. Ibid., pp. 144-6.
62. It was factually wrong to connect Amir Husain with Shaikh Zakariya, as Jamali has done. He appeared to have been born in 1272, ten years after the demise of Shaikh Zakariya. As this year of his birth seemed correct, his adulthood coincided with the life of Shaikh Ruknuddin Abul Fateh, who assumed the headship of the Suhrawardi hospice in 1285. His literary works

were written during the first quarter of the fourteenth century. Saiyid Athar Abbas Rizvi, *A History of Sufism in India*, vol. I, New Delhi: Munshiram Manoharlal, 1978, p. 206.
63. Ibid., pp. 207-9.
64. Barani, pp. 341-2.
65. Ibid., pp. 343-4.
66. Ibid., pp. 345-7
67. Ibn Battuta, *Rehla*, p. 90.
68. In a reexamination of the relations between the early Chishtis and the state, it has been shown that Muhammad bin Tughluq continued to show respect to the Chishtis, that a number of his leading nobles were disciples of Shaikh Nizamuddin Auliya and that many ordinary disciples of the Chishtis had accepted government jobs. The Sultan only sought moral support from the leading Chishtis for the implementation of his projects, but did not force them to accept official assignments. The fault lay with the Chishtis of Delhi, who were not only rigid and self-contradictory in their attitude to the state, but also failed to show resilience and adaptability to new conditions. Ishtiyaq Ahmad Zilli, 'Early Chishtis and the State,' in *Sufi Cults and the Evolution of Medieval Indian Culture*, ed. Anup Taneja, New Delhi: Indian Council of Historical Research & Northern Book Centre, 2003, pp. 75-95.
69. Ibn Battuta, *Rehla*, p. 91; this observer perceived the capital punishment of Shaikh Hud as just one of the several executions ordered by the Sultan and, by doing so, tried to prove that the Sultan was a bloodthirsty tyrant. The list of the victims included Masud Khan (the Sultan's brother), 350 army desterters, Shaikh Shihabuddin, jurist Afifuddin along with two colleagues, two jurists of Sind, sons of Shaikh Shamsuddin, Shaikh Ali Haidari, Toghan of Farghana and his brother, Ibn Malik ut-Tujjar and the chief orator. Ibn Battuta, *Rehla*, pp. 85-93.
70. A native of Ghazni, the Shaikh was forced to leave the city by his grandfather, who opposed his tendency to display miracles. After migrating to Multan, he continued his engagement with miracles. He was said to have converted stones into gems, provided instructions to djinns, enrolled disciples even after his death and worked a Persian wheel without bullocks. He would push his hand out of his grave to bless his followers. It was believed that Shaikh Sarduddin Arif, who was a strict adherent of the Shariat, stopped this practice. Farhat Multani, *Auliya-i Multan*, Multan: Kutbkhana Haji Niyaz Ahmad, 1980, pp. 58-62.
71. Qamar-ul Huda, *Striving for Divine Union: Spiritual Exercises for Suhrawardi Sufis*, pp. 128-9.
72. Barani. pp. 297-8.
73. Ibid., 298-9.
74. Ibid., p. 299.
75. Ibid., p. 352.

76. Fazlullah Majawi, *Fatawa-i Sufiyya*, MS Oxford, Bodleian Uri 321; quoted in Julian Baldick, *Mystical Islam: An Introduction to Sufism*, London: I.B. Tauris & Co., rpt., 2000, pp. 95-6.
77. Ibid., p. 96.
78. Amina M. Steinfels, *Knowledge Before Action: Islamic Learning and Sufi Practice in the Life of Sayyid Jalal al-Din Bukhari Makhdum-i Jahaniyan*, Columbia (South Carolina): The University of South Carolina Press, 2012, p. 20.
79. During their first meeting, Shaikh Jamaluddin Uchi offered dried dates to Syed Jalaluddin Bokhari, who ate them and even swallowed the seeds. On being questioned about it, the boy replied that the seeds received from eminent persons like Shaikh Jamaluddin Uchi could not be thrown away. The teacher predicted that the pupil would bring fame to his own family and those of his mentors. Jamali, p. 155.
80. Steinfels, op. cit., pp. 23-7.
81. Ibid., p. 29.
82. According to another account, the meeting between Shaikh Bokhari and Shaikh Nasiruddin did not take place before the former's sojourn in the west, but after his return (1348) to India. It was at the advice of Abdullah Yafai that Shaikh Bokhari decided to meet Shaikh Nasiruddin. During this meeting, Shaikh Bokhari received the Chishti robe of affiliation (*khirqah*). Jamali, pp. 155-6.
83. Steinfels, op. cit, pp. 30, 34-5.
84. Interestingly, there was a significant overlap between the itineraries of Shaikh Bokhari and Ibn Battuta. Every place visited by the former was visited by the latter a decade or so earlier. Many of the persons encountered (Abdullah Yafai, Afifuddin Matari and Majduddin Baghdadi) were the same. Though Ibn Battuta was an Arabic speaker from Morocco and Shaikh Bokhari was a Persian speaker from India, yet they were enculturated into a social order that spanned the Muslim world. The Muslims shared a Islamicate civilization that was characterized by three common elements -- Sunni scholarship, Arabic and Sufism. Steinfels, op. cit., p. 56.
85. Ibid., pp. 41-51.
86. Ibid., pp. 51-5.
87. Syed Raju Qattal has reported that Shaikh Bokhari, during his travels, benefited from over 300 scholars. In Mecca, Madina, Baghdad and other places, Jamali claimed to have seen the abodes where Shaikh Bokhari had stayed. He has stated that even during the middle of the sixteenth century, the attendants cleaned these places and lighted candles in them. Evidently, the memory of Shaikh Bokhari had been kept alive by the people of these localities. Jamali, pp. 155.
88. Muhammad Ayyub Qadiri, *Makhdum-i Jahaniyan Jahangasht*, Karachi: Idarah Tahqiq wa Tasnif, 1963, pp. 191-95; Aneesa Iqbal Sabir, 'Suhrawardi Mysticism in South-Western Panjab: Contribution of Syed Jalaluddin

Bukhari Makhdum-i Jahaniyan,' in *Sufism in Punjab: Mystics, Literature and Shrines*, ed. Surinder Singh and Ishwar Dayal Gaur, Delhi: Aakar Books, 2009, pp. 113-15.
89. Muhammad Ayyub Qadiri, op. cit., pp. 261-3.
90. Steinfels, op. cit., pp. 63-5.
91. Ibid., pp. 67-9.
92. Ibid., pp. 70-2.
93. Ibid., pp. 74-6, 80.
94. Ibid., p. 78.
95. Ibid., pp. 81-2.
96. Ibid., p. 83.
97. Ibid., pp. 86-8.
98. Ibid., pp. 88-90.
99. Ibid., pp. 94-5.
100. Ibid., pp. 95-7.
101. Ibid., pp. 93-4.
102. Ahmad Muin Siyahposh Alavi, *Siraj ul-Hidaya*, Persian text, ed. Qazi Sajjad Husain, Delhi: Indian Council of Historical Research, 1983, pp. 122-3. This work was transcribed by Maulana Ahmad Muin Siyahposh Alavi on the basis of a copy of the conversations of Shaikh Bokhari provided to him by the saint's son Makhdumzadah Abdullah. It is an amalgamation of the accounts by Abdullah and Siyahposh. Comprising of nine chapters, the themes included Prophetic traditions, canonical laws, jurisprudence and origin of sects. Besides the character of polity and nobility, it dealt with un-Islamic customs and the Thatta campaign of Firoz Shah Tughluq. Khaliq Ahmad Nizami, *On History and Historians of Medieval India*, New Delhi: Munshiram Manoharlal, 1983, pp. 188-92.
103. Steinfels, op. cit., pp. 100-2.
104. Muhammad Aslam, *Malfuzati Adab Ki Tarikhi Ahmiyat*, Lahore: Idarah Tahqiqat-i Pakistan, 1995, pp. 230-1.
105. Steinfels, op. cit., p. 84.
106. Alavi, *Siraj ul-Hidaya*, p. 262.
107. Steinfels, op. cit., p. 105.
108. Alavi, *Siraj ul-Hidaya*, p. 107.
109. Ibid., pp. 307, 337.
110. Steinfels, op. cit., p. 107.
111. Syed Alauddin Ali Husaini, *Jami ul-Ulum*, Persian text, ed. Qazi Sajjad Husain, New Delhi: Indian Council of Historical Reasearch, 1987, pp. 545-6.
112. Ibid., p. 647.
113. Alavi, *Siraj ul-Hidaya*, p. 86.
114. Ibid., pp. 61-2.
115. Riazul Islam, *Sufism in South Asia: Impact on Fourteenth Century Muslim Society*, Karachi: Oxford University Press, 2nd edn., 2003, pp. 280-1.

116. Alavi, *Siraj ul-Hidaya*, pp. 111-12.
117. Ahmad Baha bin Yaqub Bhatti, *Khizanat ul-Fawaid ul-Jalaliya*, ff. 196-198b, quoted in Steinfels, op.cit., pp. 126-7.
118. Ain ul-Mulk Mahru, *Insha-i Mahru*, Letter no. 22, p. 47.
119. Afif, pp. 240-2.
120. Ibid., pp. 243-6.
121. Riazul Islam, *Sufism in South Asia: Impact on Fourteenth Century Muslim Society*, p. 287.
122. Alavi, *Siraj ul-Hidaya*, pp. 360-1.
123. Riazul Islam, op. cit, p. 288.
124. Khizr Khan, the founder of the Syed dynasty, was the son of Malik Sulaiman, who was the adoptive son of Malik Mardan Daulat. Once when Syed Jalaluddin Bokhari visited Malik Daulat, the latter asked Malik Sulaiman to wash the hands of the guest. The saint did not permit Malik Sulaiman to do the errand as, being a Syed, he was not fit for the task. When the head of the Syeds testified to Malik Sulaiman's Syed origin, there could be no doubt about his pedigree. Besides, he possessed numerous qualities – bravery, generosity, humility, equanimity and adherence to his words – that were conspicuous in Prophet Muhammad. Sirhindi, p. 182.
125. Jamali, p. 156.
126. Ibid., p. 161.
127. Afif, pp. 514-16.

CHAPTER 6

Making and Breaking of Political Structures

Cracks in the Edifice

Following the death (21 September 1388) of Firoz Shah Tughluq, the political focus of the Delhi Sultanate shifted to Panjab and remained so for several decades. During the last days of the Sultan, his son Sultan Muhammad came to the throne. But the resolute opposition of Firozi slaves forced him to seek asylum in the hills of Sirmur. The new ruler, Ghiasuddin Tughluq Shah, sent a punitive expedition against the fugitive under the *wazir* Malik Firoz Ali and Bahadur Nahir. A number of nobles who held *iqtas* in Panjab – Sultan Shah Khushdil of Samana, Rai Kamaluddin Muin and others – were directed to join the campaign. Sultan Muhammad retired to the higher mountains and, passing through Baknari and Sakhet, secured himself in the fort of Nagarkot. The Delhi army entered the Sirmur hills and, marching northwards, fought minor battles against the fugitive, but ultimately gave up the pursuit.[1] At Delhi, the Firozi slaves replaced Ghiasuddin Tughluq Shah with Abu Bakr. In reaction, the *sadah amirs* of Samana threw their lot with Sultan Muhammad with promises of assistance. Encouraged by this support, Sultan Muhammad returned from Nagarkot and carried out his second coronation on 4 April 1389 at Samana, which had emerged as the centre of his growing power. He managed to garner the support of diverse elements based in Panjab – *sadah amirs* of Samana; *muqtis* like Ghalib Khan of Samana and Shams Khan of Hissar Firuza; prominent nobles like Zia ul-Mulk Abu Rija and Mubarak Khan Halajun; local chiefs like Rai Juljain Bhatti and Rai Kamaluddin Muin. He mustered a large retinue of 50,000 men and made three attempts to occupy Delhi. However, he failed to achieve his object owing to the continued opposition of the Firozi slaves. In response to his order, a large number of Firozi slaves, who were stationed in the important cities and towns of Panjab – Lahore, Multan, Samana, Hissar Firoza and Hansi – were massacred by the governors and inhabitants. With southeastern Panjab in his firm grip and Firozi slaves effectively subjugated, he succeeded in occupying Delhi on 31 August 1390, and ruled for the next three or four years. He consolidated his personal authority by expelling the Firozi slaves from the capital, putting an end to the former ruler Abu Bakr and eliminating a number of local chiefs of the Doab.[2]

Sultan Nasiruddin Mahmud Shah, who was enthroned on 23 March 1394 and ruled for twenty years, sought to establish his authority over distant provinces in the west and east. The *wazir* Khawaja-i Jahan was conferred the title of Sultan ush-Sharq and authorized to govern territories from Kanauj to Bihar. Sarang Khan, who had been placed in charge of Dipalpur, was dispatched to recover Lahore from Shaikha Khokhar. In this military expedition, Sarang Khan was joined by a few prominent local chiefs – Rai Juljain Bhatti, Rai Kamaluddin Muin of Ludhiana and Rai Daud of Jalandhar – who crossed the Satluj at Tirhara and Beas near Dohali as they advanced towards Lahore. Shaikha Khokhar, who had drawn up his forces, ravaged the suburbs of Dipalpur and besieged Ajodhan. As soon as Sarang Khan reached and plundered Bhandoit, Shaikha Khokhar fell back on Lahore. A battle was fought between the two armies at Samuthala, which was situated at a distance of 12 leagues (*kurohs*) from Lahore. As Sarang Khan emerged victorious, Shaikha Khokhar retreated towards Lahore and, taking his wife and children along, fled in the direction of Jammu hills. Sarang Khan occupied the fort of Lahore and placed the city under the charge of his brother Khandu who was given the title of Adil Khan.[3]

Not long after, a vertical division in the ruling class at Delhi manifested among the leading *muqtis* of Panjab.[4] Sarang Khan, who had recovered Lahore in 1394 from Shaikha Khokhar, attacked Khizr Khan, the governor of Multan. Having won over the slaves of Malik Mardan Bhatti, he added Multan to his charge of Dipalpur. Flushed with this success, he fell upon Ghalib Khan in order to bring Samana under his control. Ghalib Khan secured the assistance of Tatar Khan (the *wazir* of the rival king Nusrat Shah) and, having defeated Sarang Khan in a battle on 8 October 1397 at Kotla, forced the intruder to retreat to Multan. In a few weeks (December 1397), Sarang Khan was forced to surrender the fort of Multan to Pir Muhammad, the grandson of Timur, after facing a siege of six months. While he became a prisoner in the hands of the invaders, his brother Mallu Iqbal Khan fared better. By a series of clever manipulations and treacherous acts, he converted Sultan Nasiruddin Mahmud Shah into a puppet, killed Muqarrab Khan, pushed Nusrat Shah from Firozabad to the Doab and forced Tatar Khan to leave Panipat for Gujarat.[5] This was the situation when Timur crossed the Indus and entered Panjab.

Invasion of Timur

Timur had assigned a vast area,[6] which included entire Afghanistan and lands extending to the Indian border, to his grandson Pir Muhammad. As the prince utilized the resources of this large territory to muster fighting men from different places, he was deputed to subjugate southwestern Panjab. He crossed the Indus and laid siege to the fort of Uch, which fell under the jurisdiction of Sarang Khan, the *muqti* of Dipalpur. Ali Malik, who held the fort on behalf of Sarang Khan, offered resistance for one month. Sarang Khan sent a reinforcement of 4,000 cavalry under his deputy Malik Tajuddin and others to assist the garrison in defence. As this army approached Uch, Pir Muhammad raised the siege and fell upon it at Tarmtamah on the Beas. Malik Tajuddin sustained defeat, as a number of his men were killed and some others were carried away by the river. Malik Tajuddin retreated to Multan with a small force, while Pir Muhammad followed in pursuit. Sarang Khan, who did not dare to oppose the victor, withdrew into the safety of the fort. Pir Muhammad laid siege to the fort, but could not capture it for six months. When the garrison was faced with acute shortage of provisions (*ba sabab tangcheh ulf wa ghalla*), Sarang Khan initiated a move for making peace on 5 June 1398. However, he was put in prison along with a large number of dependants including his family, soldiers and ordinary people. Pir Muhammad occupied Multan and stationed an army in the city.[7]

Timur left Samarqand in March 1398 and, marching through Naghz and Banu, reached the banks of the Indus on 20 September 1398. Interestingly, he camped at the same site where Jalaluddin Mangbarni had crossed the river, and Chingez Khan had refrained from following suit. In response to the orders of Timur, a bridge of boats and bamboos was constructed in two days. The emissaries of Sikandar Shah, the ruler of Kashmir,[8] brought a message promising submission and loyalty. Timur directed Sikandar Shah to reach Dipalpur with his forces. On 24 September 1398, Timur's army crossed the Indus and set up camp at Chaul-i-Jalali, which was a vast desert (*biyaban*) without human habitation and water. This place had acquired its name from Jalaluddin Mangbarni who, after crossing the Indus and eluding his pursuers, had acquired relief from his difficulties on reaching here. Timur received the local chiefs (*muqaddaman wa rayan*) of Koh-i-Jud who offered tributes (*peshkash wa sharait malguzari wa khidmatkari*) that reflected their obedience. Timur allowed them to depart after giving instructions regarding the facilities required from them during the impending march of the invaders through their territories. A month back, these very chiefs had provided a variety of services to Timur's commander Rustam Taghi Bugha Barlas, who was marching through Koh-i-Jud on way to Multan.[9]

Timur's army travelled across Chaul-i-Jalali and reached the bank of Jhelam, where he clashed with Shihabuddin Mubarak Shah Tamimi who ruled over an island in the river. A few months back, Tamimi had expressed his obedience to Pir Muhammad as the latter marched through his domain. Soon after, he reversed his stance and began to resist the invaders. Supported by ample resources in retinue and wealth, he surrounded his fortification by a deep moat. On 26 September 1398 Timur ordered Shaikh Nuruddin to deal with Tamimi without any delay. This commander entered a large lake at the head of 10,000 cavalry and delivered a series of assaults. Tamimi failed to withstand the attacks, as several of his men jumped into the river and lost their lives. He prepared a fleet of 200 boats and, boarding them with his followers, descended down the Jhelam towards Uch. Shaikh Nuruddin continued to attack the fugitives from the bank and managed to kill several of them. When Tamimi's convoy approached Multan, its path was blocked by Pir Muhammad and his leading nobles. Tamimi's retinue was captured and put to death. He himself saved his life by crossing the river on a boat along with his family. Those of his men, who had fled into the neighbouring jungle, were pursued and killed. A large booty – grain, money and slaves – that had been loaded on boats fell into the hands of the victors.[10]

Timur's troops marched for five or six days and reached the confluence of Jhelam and Chenab on 6 October 1398. A bridge was thrown across the broad channel, a feat which could not be performed by any previous ruler including Tarmashirin Khan. The invaders moved across the bridge and encamped on 13 October 1398 near the town of Talmi (Talamba),[11] which was situated at a distance of 35 leagues from Multan. At the outset, Timur did not permit any violence. Prominent citizens – Maliks, Rais, Syeds and *ulama* – presented themselves before Timur and agreed to pay a ransom of 2 lakhs (*do lak mal ba-rasm amani*). A part of this amount had been paid when innumerable invaders poured into the streets. Since the soldiers stood in urgent need of foodgrains, they were permitted to enter houses and loot them. Some people were taken prisoner. None except the Syeds and clerics could escape from the atrocities. Meanwhile, it was learnt that the notables and chiefs (*rausa wa sardaran*) of the surrounding areas, who had offered submission to Pir Muhammad, had adopted the path of resistance. In compliance with Timur's order, Amir Shah Malik and Shaikh Muhammad Iku Timur penetrated the countryside in order to chastise the opponents. In this combing operation, nearly 2,000 people were killed and their sons were made prisoners, while an unlimited quantity of wealth and valuables was gathered (*ghanim basiyar wa nafais beshumar*).

Timur then advanced towards the Beas and set up camp at Jal. Jasrath Khokhar (the son of Shaikha Khokhar) had entrenched himself here beside a big reservoir along with 2,000 men. Anticipating an armed encounter in the open field, Timur arranged his troops in battle array – the right was placed under Shaikh Nuruddin and Allah Dad; the left was commanded by Shah Malik and Shaikh Muhammad Iku Timur; Ali Sultan Tawachi stood in the centre at the head of footmen from Khurasan. In a military engagement on the bank of the reservoir, a thousand soldiers of Jasrath Khokhar were attacked by the infantry of Ali Sultan Tawachi, who was reinforced by Shaikh Nuruddin and Allah Dad. Having emerged victorious, the invaders burnt the houses of the defenders after looting their goods. On 22 October 1398 Timur arrived at Shahnawaz, a large village conspicuous for its huge heaps of food grain (*anbar ghalla basiyar bud*). Timur permitted his troops to collect as much grain as they could and to burn whatever they could not. Timur also deputed some nobles to pursue the men who had escaped from the retinue of Jasrath Khokhar, so that there was another bout of killing and looting.[12]

On 25 October 1398, Timur left Shahnawaz and proceeded towards Jinjan on the Beas. The entire army crossed the river either by boat or by swimming across, but did not suffer any casualties. While camping at Jinjan, Timur became familiar with the affairs of Pir Muhammad. The prince had occupied Multan after a siege of six months, but an epidemic (*pisha kali azeem*) destroyed all the horses in his camp. Taking advantage of this setback, the local chiefs on the borders of India (*hukkam wa sardaran-i hudud hind wa aan hawali*) started opposing the invaders and even killed the superintendents (*daroghas*) at a few places. On 30 October 1398 Pir Muhammad hosted a banquet in honour of his grandfather and presented a number of gifts – crowns, golden belts, Tazi horses with saddles, vessels of gold and silver, costly clothes and a wide range of novelties – which had been plundered. The accountants took two days to prepare a list of these items. Timur distributed the entire stock of trophies among his nobles and officers. He also provided 30,000 horses to Pir Muhammad's soldiers, who had travelled either on bullock or on foot.[13] During the course of his march to Dipalpur, Timur passed through Sehwal, Aswan and Jehwal. The inhabitants of Dipalpur, encouraged by the epidemic in Pir Muhammad's army, had turned against the invaders and killed the prince's superintendent Musafir Kabuli along with his 1,000 soldiers. Fearing a terrible revenge they had fled towards Bhatner in order to save their lives. The arrival on 5 November 1398 of Timur at Ajodhan at the head of 10,000 horsemen caused panic among the inhabitants. On the advice of mystics like Shaikh Munawwar and Shaikh Saaduddin (the grandsons of Shaikh Nuruddin), a majority of people escaped towards Bhatner. Another group, who comprised of Syeds and theologians, relied on Timur for their safety and stayed back. Timur appointed two of them, Maulana Nasiruddin Umar and Khwaja Shihab Muhammad, as administrators (*daroghas*) of the town, with the dual function of providing protection to the people and offering facilities to the invading army. Timur paid a visit to the mausoleum of Shaikh Fariduddin Ganj-i-Shakar and, after praying for assistance, advanced towards Bhatner. Timur spared Ajodhan violence and plunder, most probably owing to its sacred character.

Crossing the large river of Ajodhan (Satluj) and encamping at Khalis Kotli, Timur covered a distance of 60 *kos* to reach Bhatner on 7 November 1398. This place had acquired fame all over Hind for its impregnable fort. It was surrounded upto a radius of 50 *kos* by a vast desert. The entire area was so dry that water was not available upto a 100 *kos*. The local inhabitants met their needs from a large lake. Yazdi would have us believe that no Indian or foreign ruler had ever led his army to this place. It was on account of this reason that the people from towns such as Dipalpur and Ajodhan – had converged here for safety. In fact, the number of fugitives was so large that it was not possible to accommodate all of them. Not only this, many of them were forced to leave their cattle and goods-laden carts behind in neighbouring places. Rai Dulchin, the ruler of the principality, commanded a sizeable army and numerous supporters. Besides a complete control over his domain, he received taxes from merchants and travellers. As the invaders approached the fort, they destroyed whatever was available outside. They surrounded the fort and, having established their control over the boundary wall, killed a number of defenders. Rai Dulchin, who stood at the gate with his commanders, wished to jump into the fray. But, on seeing his soldiers dying in action, decided to sue for peace. He sent a Syed as an emissary to Timur, with the promise of appearing in person the next day. Timur accepted the proposal and, terminating the hostilities, withdrew from the scene. When Rai Dulchin failed to fulfil his promise the next day, Timur ordered every noble to dig a trench in order to reach the base of the rampart. The defenders rained stones and arrows on the attackers, but failed to make any impact. Rai Dulchin again sought a peaceful settlement and sent his son to Timur for this purpose. He himself emerged from the fort and, accompanied by Shaikh Saaduddin of Ajodhan, surrendered before Timur.[14]

The submission of Rai Dulchin failed to save the lives of hundreds of fugitives who had arrived from different parts. Though they appeared in Timur's camp with the hope of securing forgiveness, they were handed over to his nobles in groups. Nearly 500 inhabitants of Dipalpur, who were alleged to have killed Musafir Kabuli along with 1,000 soldiers, were put to death. Of the inhabitants of Ajodhan, some were executed and others imprisoned. Shocked at these atrocities, Rai Dulchin's brother (Kamaluddin) and son resumed the resistance and closed the gate of the fort. Timur took two steps to pressurize the defenders into submission – Rai Dulchin (who was in Timur's camp) was thrown into prison and trenches were dug to demolish the boundary wall of the fort. These measures had the desired effect, as Rai Dulchin's kinsmen came out of the fort and surrendered its keys. However, this gesture failed to prevent another round of cruelties. When Timur's representatives, Shaikh Nuruddin and Allah Dad, entered the fort to collect the ransom (*mal amani*), the Rai did not appear for the payment. A fullscale battle broke out. Timur's soldiers climbed over the ramparts with the help of rope ladders (*kamand-ha wa tanab-ha*) and fell upon the people inside. Simultaneously, the gate of the fort was brought down and fierce fights erupted. The inmates consigned their women, children and property to the flames (*zan wa farzand wa mal khud ra atish zada ba-sokhtand*) and, then performed the rite of mass self-immolation (*jauhar*).

Those who claimed to be Muslim did not lag behind; they slashed the heads of their women and children as if they were goats. Hindus and Muslims showed exemplary unity and determined to fight to the last man. It was estimated that 10,000 defenders were killed, leaving behind mountains of corpses and rivers of blood. Buildings and houses were burnt to ashes or razed to the ground.[15] The magnitude of bloodshed and destruction was unprecedented.

Leaving Bhatner on 14 November 1398, Timur entered southeastern Panjab and spent nearly one month in this region. He raided small places, killed or captured the inhabitants and looted their goods, particularly grain. When he reached the town of Sarsuti the people, who reared pigs for their livelihood, fled away in panic. Many of them were chased and killed, while their horses and goods were captured. Timur covered a distance of 18 *kos* and reached Fatehabad. As people took to flight, they were pursued. Many of them were deprived of their lives as well as property. On 18 November 1398, Timur targeted Ahroni where the inhabitants were subjected to death or captivity. A large quantity of grain was looted and houses were set on fire, leaving behind heaps of ashes. Thereafter, Timur encamped at the plain of Tohana. The inhabitants, who were Rajputs and engaged in highway robbery, fled to the neighbouring jungles. In the ensuing military operations, 200 fugitives were killed, many were captured and their cattle were taken away. On 20 November 1398 Timur left Tohana and, passing through Mung, moved northwards to Samana. The invaders penetrated the jungles and killed nearly 2,000 Jats who had concealed themselves. The families of the victims were captured, while their cattle and goods were plundered. A group of Syeds, who presented themselves before Timur, were honoured as the descendants of Prophet Muhammad. The invaders proceeded to the town of Samana which was situated near the Ghaggar. On 23 November 1398 Timur left Samana and, passing through Pul Kopla and Fol Bakran, arrived at Kaithal after covering a distance of 17 *kos*. During this march, three different armed divisions – one each from Kabula, Dipalpur and Tohana – merged with the main force.[16]

Travelling through Asandi and Tughluqpur, Timur reached

Panipat on 5 December 1398. A majority of people, who inhabited the tract from Samana to Panipat, burnt their houses and rushed southwards to take shelter in Delhi. The invaders confiscated a huge stock of 10,000 maunds (160,000 *man sharai*) of wheat, which had been stored in the fort of Panipat. On 8 December 1398, Timur's right wing attacked the palace of Jahanuma, which had been constructed by Firoz Shah Tughluq on a hill near the Jamuna about 2 *farsakh* from Delhi. Two days later, Timur crossed the Jamuna and encamped at the fort of Loni, which was situated between two rivers, the Jamuna and Haikan. He overcame a feeble resistance from the local garrison and, having dug trenches for gaining access, occupied the fort. Inside the citadel, the Hindus burnt their houses along with women and children. The lives of the Muslims, particularly the Syeds, were spared, but the fort was consigned to the flames. Timur spent the next two days in identifying an appropriate spot for crossing the Jamuna and a suitable site for the impending battle against the Delhi army, besides collecting adequate quantity of grain for his forces. In two brief military encounters near Jahanuma and the Jamuna on 12 December 1398, the commanders of Timur forced Mallu Iqbal Khan (who led a detachment of 4,000 cavalry, 5,000 infantry and 27 elephants) to retreat into Delhi. Timur established himself at the fort of Loni and issued instructions regarding the placement of his troops and methods of repulsing his opponents. It was feared that nearly one lakh people, who had been captured during Timur's march from the Indus to the Jamuna and who were present in his military camp, could shift their loyalty to the Delhi Sultanate. In accordance with his orders, these people were massacred in cold blood. One-tenth of his soldiers were placed in guard over the captured women, children and animals.[17]

Timur crossed the Jamuna on 16 December 1398 and, choosing Firozabad as the site of his camp, made elaborate arrangements for its protection. A trench was dug and the earth was used to construct an embankment. Behind it a wall was raised with the help of palisades and branches of trees. In front of the trench stood a row of buffaloes, their necks and feet tied together. Tents were fixed behind the fortified wall. Having ensured the protection of his army, Timur placed his soldiers in battle array and took his position in the centre. On the other side, a similar exercise was undertaken by Sultan Nasiruddin Mahmud and Mallu Iqbal Khan, who had mustered 10,000 cavalry, 40,000 infantry and 125 elephants. The elephants were armed with several weapons of offence.[18] Poisoned knives were fastened to their trunks. On the back of each elephant was placed a wooden structure (*pushtah*) which protected an archer (*navak*) and wheel handler (*charkh andaz*). On the side of each elephant walked a rocket man (*takhshdar*) and a grenadier (*raad andaz*). The towering presence of a large number of armoured elephants caused a wave of consternation among Timur's soldiers. He took immediate steps against any onslaught of the elephants. A second fortification – comprising pillars, trenches and buffaloes with their necks and feet shackled with hides – was raised. The footmen were provided with large iron nails, which could be thrown on the ground to block the advancing elephants. At the onset of hostilities, Timur sent reinforcements to strengthen his advance guard and the right wing. As a result, they ambushed the adversaries in a manner that nearly 600 of them were killed. Targeting the elephant corps, they pulled down the drivers (*mahouts*) from their tall seats and forced the black giants to flee like oxen. Sultan Nasiruddin Mahmud and Mallu Iqbal Khan, fearing an imminent defeat, withdrew into the city and closed the gates. Since a recovery of the military fortunes was ruled out, they escaped at midnight through two different gates, Hudrani and Barka. A detachment, which was sent to pursue them, succeeded in capturing the two sons of Mallu Iqbal Khan.[19]

The next day (19 December 1398), Timur held open court near the gate of Jahanpanah and Hauz Khas. Prominent citizens – including Syeds, mystics, theologians and government officers – prayed for protection. Amidst a celebration of victory, Maulana Nasiruddin Umar recited the sermon (*khutba*) in the name of Timur. Clerical staff (*batikchiyan diwan*) prepared an account of ransom and appointed collectors (*muhasilan*) to undertake the collection. Timur permitted a group of his soldiers to enter the city and collect provisions, while another was ordered to capture those who had escaped from the battlefield. The highhanded conduct of these soldiers led to conflict and violence. Local inhabitants began to offer resistance at Siri, Jahanpanah and old Delhi. Acting out of desperation, many of them burnt their houses, property, women and children. In violation of Timur's orders, the remaining segments of his army rushed into the city and let loose an orgy of destruction that continued for two days. They inflicted cruel atrocities in the above mentioned three localities. Every soldier captured 20 to 150 persons. It was impossible to estimate the value of plunder – precious stones, vessels of gold and silver, costly cloth and Alai *tankas*. Thousands of artisans (*ahl hirfat wa peshawaran*) who had been captured were handed over to princes and nobles. Since Timur wished to construct a Jama Masjid of carved stones at Samarqand, he set aside stone cutters (*sangtarashan*) who were to be carried back to his capital. On the eve of his departure from Delhi, Timur ordered the Muslim elite – Syeds, judges, clerics and mystics – to assemble in the Jama Masjid of Jahanpanah, where they were given an assurance of safety during the withdrawal of his troops.[20]

After staying in Delhi for two weeks, Timur marched on 2 January 1399 north along the Jamuna and, passing through small places – Firozabad, Wazirabad, Maudula, Katta, Baghpat and Asar – turned east to Meerut. He deputed a detachment of 10,000 cavalry under Rustam Taghi Bugha, Shah Malik and Allah Dad to capture the famous fort of Meerut. Three local commanders – Ilyas Afghan, Safi and a son of Maulana Ahmad Thanesari – made preparations to defend the fort. The invaders, on reaching (6 January 1399) their destination, began digging trenches of 10 to 15 yards opposite the domes and towers. They gained access to the interior of the fort by climbing over the ramparts by using rope ladders (*kamand*). In the ensuing conflict, Ilyas Afghan and son of Thanesari were captured, but Safi lost his life. In a flush of victory, the invaders began to kill members of the garrison, while the women and children were made captive. The boundary wall was levelled to the ground and fire was ignited in the trenches so that the entire structure could be burnt.[21] Leaving Meerut on 10 January 1399, Timur covered a distance of 14 *kos* and crossed the Ganga near Firozpur. Having marched 15 *kos* on his way to Tughluqpur, he learnt that a group of people was advancing on 48 large boats. At Timur's orders, his archers shot arrows at the boats from the bank. Some soldiers swam through the river and, climbing into the boats, slew the inmates and captured their women and children.[22]

After the victory at Meerut, Timur appears to have divided his vast army into smaller segments, each of which was sent to ravage a particular settlement. In such a situation, it was not surprising that Timur was required to fight three battles on a single day (14 January 1399). While proceeding towards Tughluqpur, Timur learnt that a local administrator or chief Mubarak had mustered 10,000 horsemen and footmen with the intention of giving battle. Timur, who at that time had just a small group of 1,000 troopers, was fortunate to receive reinforcements from Prince Shahrukh. The invaders acquired the upper hand, a large number of their adversaries were either killed or fled into the jungles, while their women and children were captured. The second battle of the day was fought at Kopla (Haridwar),[23] a sacred place of the Hindus on the Ganga, where a large number of people had congregated. A small detachment of Timur's army, which was led by Amir Shah Malik and Ali Sultan Tawachi, defeated them and looted their property. While a group of 100 troopers were engaged in gathering the booty, a company of 100 horsemen and footmen fell upon them like a suicide squad (*fidaiyan*). It was declared without proper investigation (*tahqeeq*) that the leader of the attackers was Shaikha Khokhar. On hearing this, a part of Timur's troops left the scene for the hills, providing an opportunity to Shaikha Khokhar to kill some of his opponents. In a counter attack, Timur managed to capture this man, but he died before answering any question about his identity.[24] From this place, Timur advanced towards the pass of Kopla, where a large group of people had gathered to offer resistance. The task of the invaders became hazardous, because the short path of 2 *kos* lay through a impenetrable jungle and the number of soldiers available was too small. The unexpected arrival of a detachment under Pir Muhammad and Sulaiman Shah, which had been dispatched to a distant place three days ago, enabled

Timur to overpower and plunder the adversaries. Besides these three battles in which Timur himself participated, a successful raid was conducted at the pass of Kopla to deprive a prosperous people of their wealth and cattle.[25]

Having decided on marching back to Samarqand, Timur withdrew on 15 January 1399 from the Ganga and turned towards the Siwaliks. His object was to target the principality of Rai Bahroz, who relied on the strength of the mountain and the large size of his retinue. Timur did not meet much resistance and succeeded in collecting a considerable amount of wealth. He ordered his soldiers, who had acquired 300 or 400 cows, to share these with their weaker brethren. As a result, all categories of troops were able to benefit from the campaign. Since the army was loaded with excessive booty, it could not cover a distance of more than 4 *kos* on any single day.[26] Travelling through little known villages Timur crossed the Jamuna and thus entered another part of the Siwaliks on 23 January 1399. The local ruler, Rai Rattan, was reported to have mustered a big contingent of soldiers, many of whom had arrived from other places to join him and had taken shelter in the hills and jungles. Timur's forces exerted themselves during the night and, working under the light of burning torches, cut the trees and made a 12 *kos* long passage. On 24 January 1399, they reached a valley between the Siwaliks and Koka ranges, where Rai Rattan had organized his men in battle formation. On the arrival of the invaders, the local contingent took to flight. In the ensuing pursuit, many of them were killed. A huge amount of wealth fell into the hands of the victors, so that each soldier acquired 100 to 200 cows and 10 to 20 slaves. At the orders of Timur, Pir Muhammad and Jahan Shah raided two different passes and returned with sizeable amount of spoils.[27] Soon after on 25 January 1399 Timur advanced to a pass between two hills 15 *farsakh* this side of Nagarkot. The area was covered with a thick forest. The invaders, who were motivated by the prospect of plunder, did not hesitate to penetrate it. Timur chose two detachments who had not acquired much booty in the previous campaigns. He deputed them to attack two different targets where a large number of local inhabitants had gathered. The invaders encircled them and, having slain several of them and making the rest flee, brought back a rich catch of valuables. Though every soldier collected as much booty as he could, a special effort was made to ensure that the Syeds got their due share of the loot.[28]

During the next one month (25 January to 23 February 1399), Timur's army appeared between two mountain ranges – Siwaliks and Koka – and fought as many as twenty battles before reaching Jammu. During this period, Timur occupied seven forts, each of which was quite strong. These forts were separated by a distance of 1 or 2 *farsakhs*. But these were under the control of political masters who were opposed to each other. A majority of inhabitants of these places paid tribute (*jaziya*) to the previous Sultans, but they had stopped this payment in recent times. One of these forts belonged to Shaikha Khokhar, but it was in the possession of his kinsmen. The inhabitants, who mediated through a group of local Muslims, offered their submission. At this juncture, Timur sent an officer to receive the ransom. This man induced the inhabitants to bring out their valuables which were sold, so that they were left with little of consequence. Not only this, as many as forty of them were ordered to join the retinue of Shah Khazin, apparently the officer who had been sent to receive the ransom. A conflict erupted between the two sides, culminating in the death of a few invaders. In an elaborate act of revenge, Timur's soldiers not only occupied the fort, but also killed 2,000 people.[29]

As Timur's army approached the town of Jammu, it passed through the village of Mansar and camped on 23 February 1399 at Paila, whose inhabitants were known for their bravery and had made vigorous preparations for a military showdown. Having fortified their position in the jungle, they had constructed some temporary sheds (*chappar-ha dar kinara jangal tarteeb karda*) at the edge of the wilderness. On the arrival of Timur on the scene, they fled from the village and took refuge in the wasteland. A group of invaders destroyed the structures and, standing guard in front of the jungle, enabled the main force to march into the town of Jammu.[30] Timur's army attacked a village that was situated in the foothills. The residents burnt their houses and took to flight, while the invaders laid their hands on a large quantity of grain.

A similar attack was made on two neighbouring villages, which yielded grain as well as goods.[31]

When Timur reached the outskirts of Jammu, it was found that the cultivated fields were spread upto an expanse of 4 *farsakhs*, so that a sufficient quantity of fodder was acquired for the royal stables. Timur's army forded the Tawi on 27 February 1399 and found that the town itself lay on the foothills on the left, while the village of Mannu stood on the right. Any access into the interior was rendered difficult by a combination of mountains and jungles. The Rai had taken up a strong position on a hill and was inclined to put up a fight with the help of his retinue. In view of the impending military contest, the inhabitants had sent their women and children to the safety of the thickly wooded hills. Timur sent a body of soldiers into the forest, where they could ambush the unsuspecting opponents. Another party ravaged the village of Mannu and, having collected provisions and fodder, returned to Jammu. The next day (28 February), Timur covered a distance of 4 *kos* and set up his camp on the bank of the Chenab. The retainers of the Rai felt that invaders had retreated from the jungle and, giving up caution, emerged from their fortifications. Within no time, they were ambushed and decimated. Daulat Timur Tawachi and Husain Malik Quchin captured 50 persons including the Rai. They were brought before Timur who ordered them to be put to death. But the life of the Rai, who had been wounded in the encounter, was spared. In fact, he was provided with medical treatment, so that a ransom could be settled through negotiations. Acting under fear, the Rai converted to Islam and, in his anxiety to display his commitment to the new creed, partook of beef along with the Muslims.[32]

As Timur prepared to leave the principality of Jammu, he learnt that his commanders had achieved a major success at Lahore. They had occupied the city, extracted a ransom and even captured Shaikha Khokhar. It may be recalled that the Khokhar chief, being faced with the enmity of Sarang Khan, had submitted to Timur during the latter's entry into Panjab. Having secured the permission to travel with the royal entourage as a guide, he conducted himself in a manner that his clout grew with every passing day.

Wherever the local inhabitants declared their subordination to Shaikha Khokhar, they were given immunity from captivity and plunder. However, Shaikha Khokhar lost the goodwill of Timur on account of two controversial acts. First, he had been permitted to leave the royal camp from the Ganga-Jamuna Doab, as he promised to join Timur's army at the Beas. But he failed to keep his promise. Second, he did not pay any attention to a group of visitors from Mawra ul-Nahr comprising Maulana Abdullah Sadr, Hindu Shah Khazin and other eminent persons.[33] In these circumstances, Timur ordered that he be arrested along with his family and that his principality be ravaged. Having settled the matter regarding Shaikh Khokhar, Timur crossed the Chenab on 3 March 1399 and encamped at the edge of a forest. Since the locality possessed rich hunting grounds, he engaged himself in hunting a great variety of animals and birds. At the same time, he was joined by a number of princes and nobles, who arrived from different directions along with their contingents and presented large quantities of plundered goods. He appreciated their services during the year long military expedition and rewarded them with robes of honour (*khilats*) and gifts. At this moment, the Indian elite – nobles and Syeds – who had joined the royal camp at different points of time, were permitted to return with all marks of respect. Khizr Khan, who had transferred his allegiance to Timur, was treated with favour and given the districts (*wilayat*) of Multan and Dipalpur. Thereafter, Timur resumed his return journey on 7 March 1399 and, travelling through Koh-i Jud and Chaul-i Jalali, crossed the Indus by a bridge that was specially constructed for the purpose on 12 March 1399.[33] After the retreat of Timur, the suburbs of Delhi and all places ravaged by the invaders suffered from plague and famine (*waba wa qehat*). Many people died due to sickness, while many others died due to hunger. For many months, Delhi presented a scene of desolation and misery.[35]

Political Developments after Timur

After the retreat of Timur, Mallu Iqbal Khan began to enjoy unbridled power in Delhi as Sultan Nasiruddin Mahmud was unable to assert himself beyond the city of Kanauj and Nusrat Shah had died. In fact, the stage was set for a conflict between Mallu Iqbal Khan and Khizr Khan, with Panjab as the bone of contention. The former, after achieving a limted success against the chiefs of Doab and Gwalior, turned his attention towards Panjab. His aim was to punish the governor of Samana, Bahram Khan Turkbacha, who was a partisan of Khizr Khan and therefore hostile towards Mallu Iqbal Khan. Bahram Khan Turkbacha fled to the mountains of Harnor, while Mallu Iqbal Khan encamped in the neighbouring town of Arubar. Shaikh Ilmuddin, the grandson of Shaikh Jalaluddin Bokhari of Uch, made peace between them, so that they joined in a meeting. Mallu Iqbal Khan marched towards Multan and, on reaching Talwandi, imprisoned not only Bahram Khan Turkbacha, but also a number of local chiefs including Rai Daud, Rai Kamaluddin Muin and Rai Hinu, the son of Rai Juljain Bhatti. Soon after, he got Bahram Khan Turkbacha flayed alive and carried the others as prisoners. When he reached the bank of Dahinda near Ajodhan, Khizr Khan opposed him with a large army. In a battle fought on 12 November 1405, Mallu Iqbal Khan was defeated in the first charge. He made a desperate attempt to escape, but his wounded horse got stuck in the mire. His pursuers fell upon him and lost no time in killing him. His severed head was sent to Khizr Khan, who sent it to his headquarters at Fatehpur.[36]

Though a major hurdle in the path of Khizr Khan was removed, yet he continued to face opposition from the Delhi regime. Sultan Nasiruddin Mahmud, who was caught between the expansionist designs of the rulers of Jaunpur and Gujarat, felt threatened by the rising power of Khizr Khan in Panjab. He sent Daulat Khan to fight against Bairam Khan Turkbacha, who had replaced Bahram Khan Turkbacha in Samana and who was an ardent supporter of Khizr Khan. In a battle on 22 December 1406, fought at a distance of 2 *kurohs* from Samana, Bairam Khan Turkbacha was defeated and withdrew to Sirhind. Khizr Khan, on learning about the reverse suffered by his ally, marched against Daulat Khan at the head of a big force. As soon as he reached Fatehabad, Daulat Khan retreated across the Jamuna to the Doab. In another setback, a number of his officers transferred their loyalty to Khizr Khan. What was more significant, Khizr Khan redistributed the *iqtas* among his own partisans: Sirhind and a few *parganahs* were assigned to Bairam Khan Turkbacha, Samana and Sunam were placed under Zirak Khan and Hissar Firoza was entrusted to Qiwam Khan. Khizr Khan, by usurping what was essentially a privilege of the Sultan, had established his sovereign status in Panjab and began to perpetuate it with all the resources at his command. For example, when Sultan Nasiruddin Mahmud took Hissar Firuza on December 1408 from the hands of Qiwam Khan, Khizr Khan was so incensed that he retaliated by besieging the Sultan in Siri and Ikhtiyar Khan in Firozabad. It was true that Khizr Khan did not press the siege and withdrew to Fatehpur, he took suitable lessons from this action and applied them during the next half a decade. During this period, he occupied Rohtak after a siege of six months and, marching into Mewat, ravaged such places as Tijara, Sarhath, Kharol and others. He secured the submission of Ikhtiyar Khan, who held the fort of Firozabad. He also succeeded in making territorial gains in the Doab as well as the environs of Delhi. After the death of Sultan Nasiruddin Mahmud in October 1412, he consolidated his control over his new possessions during the next eighteenth months. He besieged the new ruler Daulat Khan in the fort of Siri for four months and, after securing his surrender, sent him to Hissar Firoza in the custody of Qiwam Khan. As a result, he occupied Delhi on 6 June 1414 and thus inaugurated the rule of the Syed dynasty.[37]

Khizr Khan,[38] who was familiar with the ground realities in Panjab, took effective measures to establish order in different parts of the region. Early in his reign, he appointed Malik Abdul Rahim (an adopted son of the late Malik Sulaiman) to the *iqtas* of Multan and Fatehpur. In 1416 he placed under Prince Mubarak the districts of Firozpur, Sirhind and the *iqtas* held by the late Bairam Khan Turkbacha. The task of administration was assigned to the prince's deputy Sadhu Nadira who was posted at Sirhind and Zirak Khan who was serving as the *amir* of Samana. The kinsmen of the late Bairam Khan Turkbacha, who treated Sirhind as their patrimonial fief, killed Sadhu Nadira and took forcible possession of the district. The Sultan deputed Zirak Khan and Daud

Khan to punish the miscreants. The Turkbachas, instead of offering resistance, fled across the Satluj and took shelter in the hills. Zirak Khan chased the rebels for two months, but discontinued the pursuit as the hills were found impregnable. After a gap of one year, Tughan Rais Turkbacha and some other Turkbachas, who had earlier killed Sadhu Nadira, again raised the standard of revolt. On this occasion, they besieged Kamal Badhan, who held the charge of Sirhind on behalf of Prince Mubarak. Zirak Khan, the *amir* of Samana, was again deputed to suppress the insurrection. As soon as he reached Samana, the rebels raised the siege of Sirhind and retreated into the hills. Zirak Khan chased them up to Pail and forced Tughan Rais Turkbacha to accept three conditions – to pay a fine, to expel from his camp those Turkbachas who had killed Sadhu Nadira, and to surrender his son as hostage. Zirak Khan returned to Samana after sending the money and hostage to Daud Khan.[39]

There was no respite, however, for the officers who had been posted in the various *iqtas* of Panjab. In early 1419, the scene of rebellion shifted from cis-Satluj tract to the foothills of Hoshiarpur. A man, who gave himself out as Sarang Khan, started rebellious activities at Bajwara, which was a dependency of Jalandhar. A number of people, who did not care to verify his real identity, joined his bandwagon. Sultan Shah Lodi, who had been assigned the *iqta* of Sirhind, was dispatched to deal with the fresh problem. As Sarang Khan and his rustic followers emerged from Bajwara and advanced towards the Satluj, the inhabitants of Ropar joined the rebels. In a military engagement at Sirhind, Sultan Shah Lodi worsted Sarang Khan who retreated to Lahori, one of the dependencies of Sirhind. Though Sarang Khan had lost the battle, yet his appearance caused much confusion within the ruling class. It was not surprising that Khwaja Ali Andrabi, the *amir* of Chhat, had a meeting with Sarang Khan along with his followers and threw his lot with the rebel. This was a signal for pro-Khizr Khan elements to close their ranks. Zirak Khan, the *amir* of Samana, and Tughan Rais Turkbacha, the *amir* of Jalandhar, began to cooperate with Sultan Shah Lodi. As the combined force approached Sirhind, Sarang Khan took to flight and turned towards Ropar. Khwaja

Ali Andrabi deserted Sarang Khan and joined the detachment of Zirak Khan. The loyalists rushed in pursuit of Sarang Khan, who disappeared into the hills. The victorious army encamped at Ropar, where it was reinforced by fresh troops under Khairuddin Khani. This large army marched into the hills in order to apprehend Sarang Khan, but the pursuit was given up owing to the obstacles posed by a difficult terrain. Sultan Shah Lodi established himself at the head of a military outpost (*thana*) at Ropar, while Zirak Khan returned to Samana and Khairuddin Khani to Delhi.[40]

Sarang Khan, who could not be brought to obedience in spite of a relentless military onslaught, met his end (1420) in dramatic circumstances. He fell into a trap laid by Tughan Rais Turkbacha, the *amir* of Jalandhar, and was murdered in a treacherous manner. Tughan Rais Turkbacha thus performed a crucial service for the Delhi Sultanate, but he himself revolted a second time.[41] He besieged the fort of Sirhind and ravaged (1420) the area lying between Mansurpur and Pail. Once again Khairuddin Khani and Zirak Khan were deputed to suppress the rebellion. Tughan Rais Turkbacha crossed the Satluj near Ludhiana, as the waters were at low ebb, but he was shocked to find himself facing the imperialists. Having met with reverses in a sharp encounter, he fled from the battlefield and rushed towards the territory of Jasrath Khokhar. The *iqta* of Jalandhar, which was held by the fugitive, was transferred to Zirak Khan, while Khairuddin Khani returned to Delhi.[42]

Rebellion of Jasrath Khokhar

Jasrath Khokhar, the son of Shaikha Khokhar, played a dominant role in Panjab for nearly two decades (1421-42). Several times, he descended from his mountainous stronghold beyond Sialkot and ravaged the plains of Panjab. In the process, he targeted the senior officers who held *iqtas* in different districts as well as the local chiefs who collaborated with them. As a result, he emerged as the most potent threat to the existence of the Delhi Sultanate. Long before a more active phase of his political career, he had made a brief appearance on the political stage of Panjab and had given adequate proof of his ambition and ability. He confronted Timur's army between Tulamba and Dipalpur, while the invader was marching through southwestern Panjab. In spite of a defeat in battle, he assisted his father in occupying Lahore. He was carried as a prisoner to Samarqand, while his father was put to death. Showing remarkable resilience and extraordinary courage, he escaped from the prison and returned to assume the leadership of the Khokhars. He began to assess the political situation in Panjab and initiated clever moves to widen his political space. First, he provided support to Tughan Rais Turkbacha (the *amir* of Jalandhar) who had twice revolted against the Syed ruler of Delhi and had given anxious moments to the pro-Delhi officers. Second, he intervened (1420) in a succession dispute in Kashmir and assisted Shahi Khan to replace his brother Ali Shah on the throne. Not only this, he imprisoned Ali Shah and plundered his baggage, while he was returning from a visit to Thatta along with a large entourage. Seen as a short sighted rustic who showed symptoms of intoxication and foolhardiness, Jasrath Khokhar was believed to be cherishing visions of conquering Delhi.[43]

Hearing the news of Khizr Khan's death, Jasrath Khokhar mustered columns of cavalry and infantry. Crossing the Beas and Satluj, he overran Talwandi Rai Kamaluddin Muin and forced Rai Firoz Muin (governor of Ludhiana) to flee towards the desert.[44] He ravaged the tract from Ropar to Ludhiana along the Satluj. After a few days, he returned back across the Satluj and besieged Zirak Khan in the fort of Jalandhar. Having set up camp on the bank of the Bein at a distance of 3 *kurohs* from Jalandhar, he started negotiations for peace. At length, it was settled that the fort of Jalandhar would be surrendered to Tughan Rais Turkbacha, that Zirak Khan would bring Turkbacha's son to Delhi and that Jasrath Khokhar would send a tribute to Delhi. In accordance with these terms, Zirak Khan emerged out of the fort of Jalandhar on 4 June 1421. But Jasrath Khokhar violated the agreement and carried Zirak Khan as a prisoner to Ludhiana. He followed up this action by besieging Sultan Shah Lodi in the fort of Sirhind, but failed to capture it. The new Sultan, in response to Lodi's request for assistance, left Delhi and, in spite of the monsoons, marched towards Sirhind. On hearing this, Jasrath Khokhar raised the siege of Sirhind and, having released Zirak Khan, advanced towards Ludhiana. He forded the Satluj and appeared before the imperial army. He secured all the boats on the bank, so as to block the movement of the opponents across the river. The two sides engaged in armed skirmishes for forty days, even while remaining entrenched in their respective positions.[45]

With the retreat of the monsoon, the Sultan marched along the Satluj towards Qabulpur, so that he could match the movement of the force on the other side. On 9 October 1421, the Sultan ordered the leading nobles – Zirak Khan, Sikandar Tohfa, Mahmud Hasan, Malik Kalu and others – to cross the Satluj at Ropar along with strong reinforcements and six elephants. The commanders forded the river, while the Sultan followed suit on the same day. The sudden appearance of this large army unnerved Jasrath Khokhar, who fell back on Jalandhar and crossed the Beas. During the course of this hasty retreat, several of his followers were killed and a large part of his baggage was captured. Rushing back across the Ravi and Chenab, he withdrew to his mountainous retreat at Tilhar. On his part, the Sultan marched in hot pursuit and, travelling along the foothills of Panjab, crossed the Beas and Ravi. He also received the submission of Rai Bhim, the chief of Jammu, who volunteered to act as a guide for the imperial troops in their westward march. In fact, Rai Bhim led the assault on Tilhar during which the fort was demolished and many defenders were captured. Laden with booty, the Sultan returned to Lahore. It was found that the city had suffered immense damage in recent times. It had been deserted by its inhabitants, while it had become the abode of inauspicious owls. The Sultan encamped at the bank of the Ravi for nearly a month and oversaw the restoration of the city, which was renamed as Mubarakabad. The fort and gates were repaired, while several buildings were reconstructed. A number of original inhabitants returned to the city and settled in their old houses. The *iqta* of Lahore was assigned to Malik ush-Sharq Mahmud Hasan, who was placed over a contingent of 2,000 horsemen. Appropriate arrangements were made for the maintenance of the fort and army.[46] Similar steps had been taken by Ghiasuddin Balban for the rehabilitation of the city of Lahore 150 years earlier.

The above military and administrative measures failed to undermine the spirit of Jasrath Khokhar. Within three months, he returned at the head of a large body of cavalry and infantry, besides some zamindars. After crossing the Chenab and Ravi, he encamped near the tomb of Shaikh Husain Zanjani. During the next five weeks, he led numerous attacks on a mud fort (*hissar kham*) which became the scene of a prolonged military conflict. Since he did not intend to lay a siege, he remained content with petty skirmishes with the royalists and destruction of the neighbouring places. Failing to make a substantial headway in Lahore, he marched to the fort of Kalanaur, where Rai Bhim of Jammu had arrived to assist the royalists. There was some fighting between the two sides, but there was no decisive result. Jasrath Khokhar retreated to the Beas in order to mobilize his Khokhar tribesmen. Sikandar Tohfa, who had arrived from Delhi at the head of a large force, crossed the Beas at Buhi and advanced to join Mahmud Hasan near Lahore. Several prominent men – Malik Rajab, the *amir* of Dipalpur, Sultan Shah Lodi, the *amir* of Sirhind, Rai Firoz Muin and some zamindars – also joined Sikandar Tohfa. The combined troops proceeded along the Ravi and, crossing the river between Kalanaur and Bhoh, reached the frontiers of Jammu, where they were joined by Raja Bhim. This strong army defeated a group of Khokhars at the bank of the Chenab and, without trying to pursue their chief, returned to Lahore. Since the Sultan was dissatisfied with the conduct of senior officers, he made a number of transfers. Sikandar Tohfa was appointed to administer the city of Lahore, with instructions to garrison the fort with an armed retinue. Mahmud Hasan was assigned the *iqta* of Jalandhar and, in view of his experience at Lahore, was directed to serve under the new governor of the city. For unknown reasons, Sikandar Tohfa was soon replaced by Malik ush-Sharq Sarwar ul-Mulk as the governor (*shahna*) of the city. The new officer was succeeded by his son in the same position.[47]

Jasrath Khokhar appeared to have felt humiliated at his failure to make any political gains in Panjab. He looked for an opportunity to retrieve his honour and to assert his power in the region. In 1423, he attacked the neighbouring principality of Jammu and killed his arch enemy Rai Bhim, who had been actively collaborating with Panjab officers in the campaign against him. He also acquired a large booty, which included horses and weapons. Encouraged by this success, he joined hands with Shaikh Ali of Kabul and ravaged the districts of Lahore and Dipalpur. Sikandar Tohfa marched out of Lahore with the intention of crushing Jasrath Khokhar, but retreated from the Chenab without achieving anything. The neighbouring governor Mahmud Hasan (who held the extensive districts of Multan, Bhakkar and Siwistan) fared somewhat better. Shaikh Ali, who had descended from Kabul with the object of attacking upper Sind, posed a serious threat to the security of Multan. Mahmud Hasan undertook the renovation of the fort of Multan and won over the local inhabitants by distributing rewards, pensions and allowances (*inam wa idrar wa mawajib*). Owing to the restoration of order and confidence, Shaikh Ali thought it prudent to retreat without any contest.[48]

Jasrath Khokhar did not rebel during the next five years (1423-8). Apparently he was engaged in consolidating his position in his own tribal domain and in garnering fresh military resources. In the middle of 1428, he emerged from Tilhar and, bypassing Lahore, laid siege to Kalanaur. Sikandar Tohfa, the *amir* of Lahore, marched to Kalanaur for providing relief to the besieged. Jasrath Khokhar retreated from Kalanaur and, in an encounter with his adversary, came out victorious. As Sikandar Tohfa fell back on Lahore, Jasrath Khokhar crossed the Beas near Jalandhar and sacked the place. Since he was unable to occupy the impregnable fort of Jalandhar, he captured some local people and withdrew to Kalanaur. When the Sultan was apprised of the latest round of the rebellion, he deputed Zirak Khan, the *amir* of Samana, and Islam Khan, the *amir* of Sirhind to proceed with their respective contingents to Lahore and assist Sikandar Tohfa. Before these reinforcements could reach their destination, Sikandar Tohfa had advanced to Kalanaur and, uniting his forces with the horsemen and footmen of local chief Rai Ghalib Kalanauri, rushed in pursuit of the rebel. Jasrath Khokhar drew up his forces near Kangra on the bank of the Beas. In the ensuing battle, his retinue faced defeat and destruction. Leaving behind the spoils that he had secured at Jalandhar, he retreated to his stronghold at Tilhar.[49] Meanwhile, Mahmud Hasan, whose *iqta* of Multan had been transferred to Rajab Nadir in 1427, was compensated with the *iqta* of Hissar Firoza. In view of his distinguished services in Biana as well as his past record against Jasrath Khokhar and Shaikh Ali in Panjab, Mahmud Hasan was conferred the *iqta* of Multan along with the title of Imad ul-Mulk in 1429. Since his presence in Panjab was regarded as indispensable, two large *iqtas*, Multan and Hissar Firoza, were placed under his charge.[50]

The span of four years (1430-3) turned out to be critical for the Delhi Sultanate because diverse anti-state elements – disaffected officers, local chiefs and foreign invaders, i.e. Faulad Turkbacha, Jasrath Khokhar and Shaikh Ali – became active at the same time and even joined hands with one another. The trouble started with the death of Syed Salim (March 1430), a senior noble who held extensive *iqtas* in Bathinda, Doab, Sarsuti and Amroha. He was reputed to have accumulated a huge amount of money and commodities in the fort of Bathinda. The Sultan, in accordance with the current practice, distributed the *iqtas* of Syed Salim between his two sons who were present in the court. Faulad Turkbacha, a slave of Syed Salim, raised the standard of revolt in Bathinda at the instigation of his master's sons. The Sultan, having placed the instigators in prison, deputed Malik Yusuf Sarwar and Rai Hinu Bhatti to win over the rebel and to confiscate the wealth piled up by Syed Salim. Faulad Turkbacha trapped the two officers in a round of negotiations but, acting with cunning and perfidy, emerged out of the fort and fell upon them. Malik Yusuf Sarwar and Rai Hinu Bhatti were forced to flee towards Sarsuti, while their baggage and cash fell into the hands of the rebel.

The Sultan set out from Delhi and, covering the distance in a prolonged march, reached Sarsuti where he was joined by the leading nobles. Faulad Turkbacha entrenched himself in the fort of Bathinda and made preparations for standing a long siege. A number of Panjab officers Zirak Khan, Islam Khan, Kamal

Khan, and Malik Kalu, the superintendent of elephants (*shahna-i feel*) besieged the citadel. Mahmud Hasan, the *amir* of Multan, arrived on the scene to advise the besiegers on technical matters in August 1430. Faulad Turkbacha expressed his willingness to meet Mahmud Hasan and negotiate the terms of his surrender. In an interview held at the gate of the fort, the two sides arrived at an agreement, which stipulated that Faulad Turkbacha would relinquish the fort and offer submission to the Sultan. Since Faulad Turkbacha suspected the designs of Mahmud Hasan, he changed his mind and determined to continue the resistance. The Sultan returned to Delhi and Mahmud Hasan left for Multan, while the Panjab officers carried on the siege. Mahmud Hasan returned to Bathinda and, providing suitable instructions to the commanders, pressed the siege to an extent that no living being could leave the fort. Satisfied at the progress of military operations, he returned to Multan after successive marches.[51]

That Faulad Turkbacha resisted the siege for six months underscored the strength of his military resources and exposed the weakness of the Delhi Sultanate. He could go to any extent to undermine the position of his employers. He sent his ambassadors to Shaikh Ali, the ruler of Kabul, and sought his assistance in return for 2 lakh silver *tankas*. Shaikh Ali, who had failed to make any gains during his incursion eight years earlier, accepted the offer and arrived at the Jhelam in February 1431. It was significant that a number of Khokhar notables (who were probably related to Jasrath Khokhar) – Ainuddin, Abul Khair and Khajeka – jumped into the fray. Having mustered a big retinue of men from Seor and Salwant, they joined hands with the invaders and began to serve as their guides. Shaikh Ali advanced along the Beas and, passing through the town of Qasur, crossed the river at Buhi. He ravaged the territory of Rai Firoz Muin, forcing him to leave Bathinda without the permission of the other nobles (*baghair ijazat umra-i deegar*), with the object of bringing in more retainers.[52] This action demoralized the commander supervising the siege. As soon as Shaikh Ali arrived within 10 *kurohs* of Bathinda, they raised the siege and retired to their homes. Faulad Turkbacha came out of the fort and, during a meeting with Shaikh Ali, paid the stipulated amount of 2 lakh *tankas*. But the invader was not satisfied. Carrying the women and children of Faulad Turkbacha as hostage, he plundered a substantial part of the territories (*wilayat*) of Rai Firoz Muin. He crossed the Satluj near the town of Tirhana and captured the inhabitants of the tract extending from Jalandhar to Jaran Manjhur. In March 1431, he crossed the Beas and reached Lahore, where Sikandar Tohfa offered the customary annual tribute (*khidami keh har sal mi dad*). Still the invader did not retrace his steps to Kabul. Instead, he marched through Qasur and reached Tilwara, which stood opposite to the famous city (*shahr mashhur*) of Dipalpur. He encamped at this place for twenty days and kept on plundering the countryside.[53]

Mahmud Hasan (now referred to as Malik ush-Sharq Imad ul-Mulk), who had been serving as the *muqti* of Multan, decided to confront the invader, particularly after learning the devastation of the territory of Rai Firoz Muin and the *iqta* of Jalandhar. He advanced to Tulamba with the intention of giving battle to Shaikh Ali. Since he was instructed by the Sultan to avoid a military encounter, he returned on 7 May 1431 for the defence of Multan. Shaikh Ali proceeded along the Ravi and passed through Tulamba and Khatibpur. Thereafter, he advanced towards Multan, now largely desolate on account of the drying up of the Ravi (*beshtar vilayat Multan ba-sabab-i khushki-i Ravi kharab bud*), he destroyed the habitations on both sides of the Jhelam and arrived at a distance of ten *kurohs* from Multan. Mahmud Hasan dispatched Sultan Shah Lodi (an uncle of Bahlol Lodi) as advance guard to assess the situation. In an encounter with the enemy, he was killed along with several companions, while the others retired to Multan. On 15 May 1431, Shaikh Ali occupied Khusrauabad and, mustering all troops for a decisive battle, penetrated as far as the prayer ground (*namazgah*) in Multan. Mahmud Hasan failed to give an adequate response to the threat. Some of his foot soldiers, who were ordered to move forward, suffered from fatigue and failed to return to the fort, being induced to retire to Khusrauabad. Not only this, his soldiers forcibly carried away cattle and grain from the people of the locality and from those living on the banks of the Jhelam. On 6 and 8 June 1431, Shaikh Ali led two assaults into the interior of

Multan. Mahmud Hasan and his troops, with the support of the inhabitants of the city, rallied out with vigour and pushed back the invaders with considerable losses.[54]

Hearing the news of these developments in western Panjab, the Sultan sent a large reinforcement under Fateh Khan (the son of Sultan Muzaffar of Gujarat), Zirak Khan, Malik Kalu, Islam Khan, Kamal Khan, Yusuf Sarwar and Rai Juljain Bhatti. This royal army reached the district (*khitta*) of Multan on 7 July 1431 and, after encamping for a week, advanced to the prayer ground and tried to enter Kotla Ala ul-Mulk. When they faced the forces of Shaikh Ali, the royalists positioned themselves in battle array -- Mahmud Hasan in the centre; Fateh Khan, Yusuf Sarwar and Rai Hinu Bhatti on the right; Zirak Khan, Malik Kalu, Islam Khan and Kamal Khan on the left. As soon as Shaikh Ali caught sight of this impressive display of military power, he lost his nerve and fled. His retreat was so hasty that it caused a stampede among his troops. The royalists fell upon the fleeing horde and succeeded in killing several commanders of Shaikh Ali, while the remnant of his forces took shelter in the fortifications (*hissar*) which had been raised round the baggage. When the royalists reached the spot, the invaders could not put up any resistance and fell back on the Jhelam. In a desperate attempt to save their lives, many were drowned in the river and those who survived the calamity were either killed or captured. Shaikh Ali and his nephew Amir Muzaffar managed to retreat across the river with a small cavalry unit to Seor, while their baggage and weapons fell into the hands of their opponents. A disaster of this magnitude, in the eyes of Sirhindi, had never struck any army on any previous occasion. Mahmud Hasan and other nobles caught up on 14 July 1431 with the fugitives at Seor and besieged the place. Shaikh Ali, who was demoralized by the series of setbacks, took the road to Kabul with a few adherents.[55] As the Sultan was dissatisfied with the handling of Shaikh Ali, he replaced Mahmud Hasan by Khairuddin Khani as the *muqti* of Multan. Sirhindi felt that this decision of transfer was imprudent and inconsiderate, as rebellions broke out in Multan in a short time.

In spite of this military success, the Delhi Sultanate could not establish peace in Panjab, because its three major opponents – Jasrath Khokhar, Faulad Turkbacha and Shaikh Ali – revived their opposition at the same time. Jasrath Khokhar, who had been lying low for almost four years between 1428 and 1431, was quick to take advantage of Faulad Turkbacha's revolt and Shaikh Ali's invasion. Descending from the northwestern hills in November 1431, he crossed the three rivers of Panjab – Jhelam, Ravi and Beas – and arrived near Jalandhar on the bank of the Bein. Sikandar Tohfa, the *muqti* of Lahore, showed negligence at the outset, but ultimately opposed the Khokhar chief with a small force. He suffered a big reverse in battle and, since his horse got stuck in the mire, he became a captive in the hands of his adversaries. Some of his men were slain, while others retreated to Jalandhar. Jasrath Khokhar, accompanied by Sikandar Tohfa and other prisoners, marched back to Lahore and laid siege to the city. The citadel was defended by Sikandar Tohfa's deputy Syed Najmuddin and his slave Khushkhabar Khan. Every day the two sides were involved in armed clashes.

It was precisely at this time that Shaikh Ali marched into Panjab and ravaged the environs of Multan. He captured the people of Khatibpur and other villages on the Jhelam. On 23 November 1431, he delivered a fierce assault on Tulamba and occupied the fort. To begin with, he made false promises of making peace with the inhabitants, but soon after put them to death and imprisoned their leaders. Even young women and children were separated from their families and dragged to the abode of Shaikh Ali. The invaders neither showed any fear of God, nor any respect for Islam. Religious leaders of the Muslim community – Syeds, theologians and *qazis* – were made prisoners. As if this was not enough, the fort of Tulamba was raised to the ground. Anguished at the terrible atrocities on the inhabitants and the destruction of the religious life of the Muslims, Sirhindi prayed for the total destruction of the accursed infidels and preservation of the ruler of the Muslims and their religion (*badshah-i musalmanan wa din Islam*).[56]

Now it was the turn of Faulad Turkbacha to fish in troubled waters. He emerged out of Bathinda and overran the country (*vilayat*) of Rai Firoz Muin. The latter encountered the intruder with a body of cavalry and infantry, but lost his life in the ensuing conflict. Faulad Turkbacha not only carried away the severed head of the Rai to Bathinda, but also captured a number of horses and stocks of grain. In retaliation for this outrageous act, the Sultan marched (January 1432) towards Lahore and Multan, besides deputing Yusuf Sarwar as an advance guard to crush the revolt. As the royal army approached Samana, Jasrath Khokhar raised the siege of the fort and, carrying Sikandar Tohfa with him, retreated to the hills of Tilhar. Shaikh Ali relinquished his interest in Multan and fell back on Bartot. On his part, the Sultan registered his displeasure at the handling of the situation by the senior officers. On the one hand, he deprived Malik ush-Sharq Shams ul-Mulk of the *iqta* of Lahore and, on the other, appointed Nusrat Khan to take charge of the fort of Lahore and the *iqta* of Jalandhar. The new commander fulfilled the Sultan's expectations by repulsing Jasrath Khokhar's fresh attack on Lahore (July 1432). Soon after, the Sultan himself marched from Delhi to Samana to contend with the disturbances caused by some unidentified rebels. At his orders, Yusuf Sarwar besieged the fort of Bathinda, where Faulad Turkbacha had secured himself with the goods and grain (*asbab wa ghalla*) acquired from his recent incursion into the territory of Rai Firoz Muin. While the siege of Bathinda was underway, Yusuf Sarwar sent the leading commanders – Zirak Khan, Islam Khan and Kahun Raj – to join the Sultan at Panipat. At this juncture, the Sultan took the *iqtas* of Lahore and Jalandhar from Nusrat Khan and assigned them to Allahdad Kaka Lodi. Having reached Jalandhar, the new officer turned towards Bajwara in order to fight against Jasrath Khokhar. But he was defeated and forced to retire to the foothills of Kothi, while the Khokhar chief continued to gain strength.[57]

In January 1433, it was reported that Shaikh Ali was marching through Panjab with the intention of attacking the nobles who were besieging the fort of Bathinda and thus to reduce the pressure on his ally Faulad Turkbacha. The Sultan decided to preempt the move, lest these nobles should get alarmed and abandon the siege, as they had done in the recent past. In response to his order, Mahmud Hasan reached Bathinda with reinforcements, so that the morale of the nobles was boosted. Shaikh Ali gave up his target of Bathinda. Instead, he overran the country from Seor to the bank of the Beas and, during this march, took a number of prisoners from Sahniwal and other places. Thereafter, he turned towards Lahore and besieged the fort which was defended by Yusuf Sarwar, Malik Ismail (a nephew of Zirak Khan) and Malik Raja, the son of Bahar Khan. Since the inhabitants of the city had failed to keep watch during the night, the commanders relinquished their duty and fled. Shaikh Ali sent a detachment in their pursuit. A number of horsemen were killed and many others were taken prisoner, including Malik Raja. Next day, he captured a big number of non-fighting inhabitants, both men and women.[58] He repaired the damaged portions of the fort and, leaving a garrison of 2,000 horse and foot for standing a siege, turned to Dipalpur. Yusuf Sarwar was willing to abandon the fort, as he had abandoned Lahore too a few days earlier. Mahmud Hasan, then occupied in the siege of Bathinda, sent his brother Malik Ahmad with a large force to defend Dipalpur. Since Shaikh Ali had escaped with great difficulty from the hands of Mahmud Hasan and, therefore, stood in fear of this general, he gave up the intention of targeting Dipalpur.[59]

At this stage, the Sultan took the affairs of Panjab in his own hands. Leaving Delhi in January 1433, he stayed at Samana for a few days and then encamped in the Talwandi of Rai Firoz Muin. He was joined by Mahmud Hasan and Islam Khan Lodi, who were besieging Bathinda, but instructed the other commanders to stick to their task in all circumstances. As he crossed the Beas at Buhi and reached the vicinity of Dipalpur, Shaikh Ali fell back across the Jhelam. The Sultan bestowed the *iqtas* of Dipalpur and Jalandhar on Sikandar Tohfa (who had been released by Jasrath Khokhar) and sent him in pursuit of Shaikh Ali. The Sultan deputed a strong force against the invaders who were entrenched in the fort of Lahore. Meanwhile, the Sultan himself proceeded to Seor, which was in the possession of Shaikh Ali. As soon as the Sultan approached Tulamba, Shaikh Ali left his nephew Amir Muzaffar in command of the fort of Seor and fled,[60] so that his horses and goods fell into the hands of his pursuers. Amir Muzaffar, after defending the fort of Seor for a month, opened negotiations for peace. In addition to paying a large tribute, he gave his daughter in marriage to a son of the Sultan. Soon after, the invaders withdrew from Lahore and the fort came into the hands of Sikandar Tohfa. The Sultan went on a pilgrimage to the tombs of eminent mystics of Lahore (*barai ziyarat mashaikh-i kibar*). While visiting Dipalpur, he provided the local officer Kamal ul-Mulk with a number of foot soldiers and elephants, besides a sizeable baggage and other necessaries, so that these could be used in any future exigency. The *iqtas* of Lahore and Jalandhar, which were held by Sikandar Tohfa, were assigned to Mahmud Hasan.[61]

After four months (November 1433), the royalists succeeded in reducing the fort of Bathinda and killing Faulad Turkbacha. The victorious nobles sent the severed head of the rebel to the Sultan, who marched back to settle the disturbed affairs of Bathinda.[62] The siege of Bathinda had continued for nearly four years. It had been besieged by the best commanders, while the Sultan also took a considerable personal interest in the matter. But the siege could not be brought to an early conclusion, as the attention of the Delhi Sultanate was often diverted towards the opposition of Shaikh Ali and Jasrath Khokhar, besides the difficulties in the Doab and Mewat. The Sultan not only led some military campaigns in person, but also asserted his authority by transferring the governors from one place to the other. By transferring the *iqtas*, he tried to prove that he was in full control of the administration. His attempt aimed at creating an aristocracy loyal to the king. But as his transfers were too rapid, they did not allow an officer to show the work of which he was capable.[63]

As for Jasrath Khokhar, ever since his victory against Allahdad Kaka Lodi (the *muqti* of Lahore and Jalandhar) at Bajwara in 1432, he had maintained a low profile till his death in 1442. During this period of ten years, he made only two appearances on the political stage of Panjab and that too after two gaps of four or five years each.[64] It was only when Sultan Muhammad Shah went on a pilgrimage to Multan in 1436 that he learnt about the disturbances caused by Jasrath Khokhar. The Sultan, on returning to Samana, dispatched an army to suppress the rebellion. The troops marched westwards and sacked the territories under the Khokhar chief.[65] However, the Delhi Sutanate was forced to change its attitude towards the arch rebel owing to the rising threat of Bahlol Lodi. Sikandar Tohfa, who was deputed to chastise Bahlol Lodi, sought the assistance of Jasrath Khokhar to meet this fresh challenge. The combined forces turned out to be so powerful that Bahlol Lodi was compelled to retire to the Siwalik foothills.[66] Ironically, the Delhi Sultanate felt constrained to alter its political choices when Bahlol Lodi forcibly occupied much of Panjab and Jasrath Khokhar rose up in revolt. In 1441, Sultan Muhammad Shah confirmed Lahore and Dipalpur on Bahlol Lodi in return for undertaking military operations against Jasrath Khokhar. The Khokhar chief made peace with Bahlol Lodi and promised to support his bid for the throne of Delhi. In return, the Lodi potentate promised not to interfere in his territories.[67] The neutrality of Jasrath Khokhar contributed, at least to some extent, in the establishment of the Lodi dynasty at Delhi. It was significant that an aspirant to the office of the Sultan regarded Khokhar support as valuable, if not indispensable. It might be recalled that, more than a century back, the Khokhar chiefs had played an active role in bringing the Tughluqs to the seat of sovereign power in Delhi.

From Sirhind to Delhi

After the departure of Timur, Panjab witnessed not only the rebellious activities of senior nobles and local chiefs, but also the unprecedented rise of the Lodi Afghans, who went on to achieve sovereign power in Delhi. The story of their progress began with an Afghan merchant Malik Bahram, who took up a job under Malik Mardan Daulat, who was appointed as the governor of Multan towards the end of Firoz Shah Tughluq's reign. Of the sons of Malik Bahram, Sultan Shah entered the service of the next governor of Multan, Khizr Khan. In a military encounter near Ajodhan, which took place between Khizr Khan and Mallu Iqbal Khan, Sultan Shah showed exemplary bravery in killing the latter. As a reward for his services, Sultan Shah received the title of Islam Khan and the governorship of Sirhind. Islam Khan never looked back. He entrenched himself firmly in Sirhind, and made it the nucleus of his power. He mobilized an armed contingent of 12,000 Afghans most of whom were his clansmen. He also managed to get suitable assignments for his brothers who also lived with him. Though he had a number of sons, yet he chose his nephew Bahlol Lodi as his successor through a will. After the death of Islam Khan in 1431, his adherents were divided into three camps that respectively supported Bahlol Lodi, Qutb Khan and Malik Firoz. Qutb Khan reported to the Syed ruler Muhammad Shah (r. 1434-1443) that the Afghans were gathering in large numbers at Sirhind with apparently bad intentions. The Sultan deputed an army under Sikandar Tohfa to send these Afghans to Delhi and, in the event of resistance, to drive them out of Sirhind. Abiding by a royal order, Jasrath Khokhar also joined the punitive expedition.

As expected, the Afghans left Sirhind and took shelter in the hills. The royalists asked them to return, as they had not committed any offence. The Afghans sought an assurance of their safety. Sikandar Tohfa and Jasrath Khokhar, while swearing in the name of faith, gave the required guarantee. Malik Firoz left his family under the care of his son Shahin Khan and nephew Bahlol Lodi and, thereafter, reached the camp of the royalists. Acting at the instigation of Qutb Khan, the two commanders violated their promise and imprisoned Malik Firoz. They also attacked the Afghans and killed Shahin Khan along with many Afghans, while many others were made captive. The severed heads of Afghans killed in action were despatched to Sirhind. Malik Firoz, while speaking to Jasrath Khokhar, gave the names of the Afghans killed. He saw the head of his son Shahin Khan, but refused to identify it. When Jasrath Khokhar's soldiers revealed that the man had fought bravely, Malik Firoz started crying. On being asked, he explained that he did not name his son, because he feared that he might have shown cowardice in military encounter. As he learnt that his son had displayed valour on the battlefield, Malik Firoz had no hesitation in owning the deceased as his son. Deeply hurt at his tragic loss, Malik Firoz now pinned his hopes on Bahlol Lodi, who was equipped to take the revenge from the adversaries.[68]

Persian chronicles have attributed the rise of Bahlol Lodi to the blessings of a dervish (*majzub*) of Samana. According to their story, which has been located in the time of Islam Khan, Bahlol Lodi visited the dervish along with his friends. The dervish wished to know if there was anyone who would purchase the throne of Delhi for 2,000 *tankas*. Bahlol Lodi offered a sum of 1,600 *tankas* that he had in his pocket. The dervish accepted the offering and conferred the kingdom of Delhi on his promising visitor. The friends of Bahlol Lodi began to make fun of him. In his response, Bahlol Lodi asserted that he had not made a bad bargain. If the prophecy of the dervish turned out to be true, he would get precious jewels at the price of peanuts. If the prophecy turned out to be false, he would not suffer any loss, as it was always meritorious to serve a holy man.[69]

A recent study seeks to place the rise of Lodis in the context of distinctive social structure of the Afghans and migrations of Afghan tribes to India. It has been argued that the Afghans were basically a pastoral nomadic society in which kinship was the main organizing principle of tribes and not territory. There was no place for a king or chief. When population outstripped resources or powerful rivals exerted pressure, tribes migrated without leaving a trace and, thus, maintained kinship solidarity. Pressure of the Ghilzais in Ghazni platueau drove the Lodis out of Roh and, joining Timur, they provided him with horsemen and also supplied horses. Being averse to agriculture, manual labour, shopkeeping and moneylending, the Afghans combined pastoral nomadism with horse trade. In fact, the Afghan tribes had monopolized the horse trade between Turan and India.[70] The Afghan warriors, who took over Delhi in the middle of the fifteenth century, hailed from a small area in the northwest frontier near the Gomal River and Sulaiman mountains. Owing possibly to disturbances in Kabul, this narrow and difficult pass became the main centre for horse caravans between two terminal points, Bokhara and the Indus plain. During the fourteenth and fifteenth centuries, the caravans arriving in north India had to be sufficiently powerful in arms and fighting tactics to be able to defeat any local ruler, who would rather confiscate their horses and other goods rather than pay for them.[71]

According to the author of the *Tarikh-i Daudi*, Bahlol Lodi (during his youth in the household of his uncle Islam Khan) engaged in the horse trade. He imported horses from the northwestern lands (*wilayat*) and, after fattening them, sold them to the buyers in northern India.[72] Once he sold a batch of horses to Sultan Muhammad Shah (r. 1434-43) in Delhi. In lieu of the price, the officers issued to him a payment order (*barat*). A fellow merchant, who reached the stipulated subdistrict (*pargana*) in Lahore to collect the requisite amount of money, failed in his aim as the locality was in a state of rebellion. On learning this, the Sultan asked Bahlol Lodi to supress the insurrection and, in return, offered the *pargana* along with the prisoners and booty. Accompanied by a group of merchants Bahlol Lodi, marched to Lahore and, entering the affected *pargana*, punished the rebels and collected the land revenue as mentioned in the payment order. When he returned to Delhi and presented himself before the Sultan, he was allowed to keep the entire booty, including the slaves and cattle, with him. Impressed with the valour of Bahlol Lodi, the Sultan began to patronise him. As a result, Bahlol Lodi came out of the class of merchants and entered that of the officers and nobles (*az hirfat-i saudagari barawardah dar zimrah-i naukaran wa umara-i khud sakht*). Bahlol Lodi was assigned a few *paraganas* in fief, so that his affairs began to progress. Every year, he mobilized a contingent of fresh troops and presented it before the Sultan. In return for this service, he claimed fresh *parganas* as remuneration for the growing body of soldiers. As a result, he came to control a majority of the *parganas* that were situated near Lahore.[73]

After the defeat of the Afghans at the hands of Sikandar Tohfa and Jasrath Khokhar, Bahlol Lodi compensated himself by plundering the highway merchants and distributed the loot among his followers. He also succeeded in winning over the other two factional leaders (Malik Firoz and Qutb Khan) and thus brought all the Afghans under his banner. He reestablished himself in Sirhind and, following in the footsteps of his uncle, made the town a fount of the rising Afghan power. He defeated the *wazir* Husam Khan in a battle near Khizrabad and occupied the area extending from Sirhind to Panipat.[74] Playing a dual game, he kept on increasing his territorial possessions and military resources and, at the same time, maintained cordial relations with the Syed ruler Muhammad Shah. He persuaded the Sultan to kill his *wazir* Husam Khan and confirm Sirhind and neighbouring areas as his fief (*jagir*). He assisted the Sultan at the head of 20,000 troops against Mahmud Khalji of Malwa and earned the title of Khan-i Khanan. On returning to Sirhind, he brought a number of important places – Lahore, Dipalpur, Sunam and others – under his control without the permission of the Sultan. He made an unsuccessful attempt to occupy Delhi. On returning to Sirhind, he assumed the title of Sultan without claiming the other symbols of royalty. When Sultan Alauddin Shah ascended the throne in 1443, Bahlol Lodi practically controlled a vast tract in Panjab comprising Lahore, Sirhind, Samana, Sunam and Hissar Firoza.[75] He made a second attempt in 1447 to occupy Delhi, but failed to achieve his aim and retraced his steps to Sirhind. Meanwhile, a tussle between the Sultan and his *wazir* Hamid Khan culminated in the retirement of the former to Badaun. Hamid Khan thought of inviting the ruler of Jaunpur or Malwa to occupy the vacant throne. Bahlol Lodi, seeing his opportunity, went to Delhi. Having learnt the right lessons from his two failures, he did not resort to any military action. Instead, he won the confidence of Hamid Khan and began to live peacefully in the city. The two political rivals appeared to have evolved a power sharing arrangement that remained in place for some time. Bahlol Lodi worked patiently according to a clever stratagem and, entering the fort with his followers, made the unsuspecting Hamid Khan a prisoner.[76] He ascended the throne on 19 April 1451 and thus inaugurated the first Afghan empire in India.

The Transformation of a Sufi as Ruler

Sometime in the second half of the fifteenth century, Shaikh Sadruddin Sadr-i Jahan (d. 1508), who was popular as Haidar Shaikh, carved out the principality of Malerkotla,[77] not far from Sirhind. Contemporary evidence on the rise of this Suhrawardi saint to political prominence is unsatisfactory. But Khwaja Niamatullah Harvi, the author of a detailed history of the Afghans, has included a brief account of Haidar Shaikh. He has stated that Shaikh Sadr-i Jahan Malneri, who was the pivot of those who had obtained divinity, was a proof of the seekers and a master of strange miracles. He was not only familiar with divine secrets, but he was also a mountain of courage and bravery. Owing to his excessive meditation and submission (*ibadat wa taat*) as well as the company of saints, he had reached the status of Qutbiyat. On account of the teachings and guidance of this spiritual mentor, a large number of people acquired nearness to God and a number of amazing miracles (*karamat ghariba wa khwariq ajeeba*) were revealed by him. It was stated that Sultan Sikandar Lodi presented a gift of one Iraqi horse and a bag of cash to the Shaikh. The latter immediately distributed the cash among mendicants and ordered the horse to be slaughtered and cooked so as to be offered as food to the dervishes. He instructed his servants to preserve different parts of the horse's body at a particular spot. The officers of the Sultan, who had brought the gifts, observed the incident with their own eyes. They returned to the Sultan and reported it as it had happened. The deeply offended Sultan wrote to the Shaikh, demanding that the horse be returned alive. After reading the letter, the Shaikh wrote back, 'I am not a merchant (*saudagar*) or soldier (*sipahi*) who could have kept an eye on the horse. It had come from God and accordingly spent in the path of God.' Outraged, the Sultan deputed a few men to bring the horse back.

One day, when the Shaikh was absorbed in a high spiritual state, the Sultan's men reached the place and demanded that the horse be sent along with them. The Shaikh, who was sitting beside a reservoir (*hauz*) in front of his abode, was immersed in meditation. He held the hand of one of the men and asked him to look for the horse in the water. Should he succeed in identifying the horse, he could untie it and carry it away. The man peered into the water and saw a stable. He observed thirty horses that were similar in colour and form to the Sultan's horse. The man descended into the tank but tried to identify the Sultan's horse unsuccessfully. He climbed out feeling ashamed of himself. The Shaikh saw the man's distraught condition and, speaking from where he stood, revealed that the Sultan's horse had been tied at the end of the row. The man descended again into the tank and brought out the Sultan's horse after putting in a great deal of effort. The Shaikh asked the men to convey his message to the Sultan, 'Do not interfere in the affairs of saints (*fuqra*). It is not proper to place them under the scanner of investigation.' When the horse was presented before the Sultan, he was amazed and instantly became a devoted follower of the Shaikh. From then onwards, the Sultan began to send gifts and offerings (*nazr wa futuh*) to the Shaikh every year. Even now a reservoir was found inside the Shaikh's house in the town (*qasbah*) of Malner. A stable has been constructed at the site. Some people believe it was the same stable that existed in the times of the Shaikh and was famous as Jhalora. Even at this juncture, the descendants of the Shaikh, who were reputed for possessing miraculous powers, were engaged in providing spiritual instructions to the people (*bar sajjada-i irshad wa hidayat*).[78]

This account is regarded as the most acceptable version of Haidar Shaikh's rise to spiritual and temporal authority. But this does not entitle us to overlook another version of the story, which was communicated by one of the descendants (*khalifas*) of Haidar Shaikh.[79] According to it, Haidar Shaikh served as a military commander before he established himself as a saint at Malerkotla. Owing to his absorption in religious devotions, he neglected his military duties. The ruler, who remained unidentified, deputed Haidar Shaikh to march to a certain place where a rebellion had raised its head. When the royal order reached him, he took it and threw it on one side, as he was immersed in the remembrance (*zikr*) of God. The followers of Haidar Shaikh, who happened to be djinns, picked up the order. Believing that the order was meant for them, the djinns marched to the scene of the insurrection and, having won a victory, brought back a large booty. The ruler was amazed at this result and wished to know how the conquest was achieved when Haidar Shaikh and his contingent did not even undertake the march. Haidar Shaikh replied, 'Your command came, but I was praying and threw it on one side, and my followers thought the command was for them, so they went there and conquered.' The perplexed king ordered that Haidar Shaikh should not be assigned any work and that he should only rest. At this,

Haidar Shaikh gave up the king's service. Since the secret of his miraculous power had been revealed, this could not be accepted in the case of a genuine Sufi. His spiritual mentor directed him to go to Malerkotla, spread Islam there and engage in prayer. At this place, there was water every where, except the spot where the shrine (*dargah*) stood. Since it was dry, he established himself there.[80]

According to Anna Bigelow, the story as narrated by the descendants of the saint encompassed multiple levels and provided insights into generally the advent of Islam in South Asia and particularly the foundation of Malerkotla. On the one hand, Haidar Shaikh possessed unlimited powers. He ignored the orders of the ruler, commanded the djinns and won battles without moving out. At the same time, he humbly obeyed his spiritual mentor and went to spread Islam in an uninhabited area. On the other hand, the narrative evoked a common trope in Sufi hagiographies: a holy man established himself in a wild forested land and became instrumental in its social and cultural development.[81] Viewed in this sense, Haidar Shaikh appeared to have played a role similar to the spiritual exemplars (Muslim *pirs*) who transformed the swampy delta of East Bengal into an agriculturally productive zone and thus triggered the twin processes of agrarian expansion and Islamization. It might be suggested that Haidar Shaikh would have been familiar with the descendants of Baba Farid who, utilizing their land grants, transformed the pastoral groups (Jat clans) of south western Panjab into sedentary cultivators. Haidar Shaikh, who had received ample land grants in Malerkotla, was mandated by the Delhi Sutanate to bring about the socio-economic development of this particular subregion in central Panjab. Since he succeeded in achieving these objectives, his name had become inseparable from the early history of Malerkotla.

A former ruler of Malerkotla had advanced a third version of the story of the rise of Haidar Shaikh.[82] We have seen that when Bahlol Lodi was the governor of Sirhind, he kept increasing his military resources and extending the areas under his control. It was precisely at this time that another Afghan, Haidar Shaikh, was rising to prominence at Malerkotla, not far from Sirhind. Haidar

Shaikh belonged to the Sherwani clan of the Afghans. Sometime during the early thirteenth century, the Sherwanis emerged from the interior of the Sulaiman Range and carved out a small principality round the town of Daraban. During the next century and a half, the Sherwanis fought against neighbouring rivals in order to maintain their existence. In these circumstances, Haidar Shaikh's grandfather Shaikh Ali Shahbaz migrated to India along with some associates. Shaikh Ahmad Zinda Pir, Haidar Shaikh's father, was employed by the Delhi Sultanate and received Chhat and Banur as revenue assignments.[83] Haidar Shaikh, who was born at Daraban in 1434, received his early education here. Thereafter, he migrated to Multan and enrolled himself as a disciple of a Suhrawardi saint, who was a descendant of Shaikh Ruknuddin Abul Fateh. After completing his spiritual training, he took the advice of his mentor and shifted to eastern Panjab. He began to live in a hut on the banks of Bhumsi, a tributary of the Satluj. As he engaged himself in spiritual pursuits, the people of the neighbourhood were attracted towards him. At this juncture, a miraculous event proved a turning point in his life. Bahlol Lodi,[84] who was firmly entrenched in Sirhind and had occupied large parts of Panjab, had encamped in the area along with his army. At night, a severe storm lashed the place, so that the tents were uprooted and the camp was thrown in disarray. What was surprising, the storm failed to damage the hut of Haidar Shaikh who kept on reading the Quran in the light of a lamp. Impressed by the miraculous power of the saint, Bahlol Lodi went to the hut next morning and sought his blessings for an impending bid for the throne of the Delhi Sultanate. He also promised to give his daughter in marriage to him if he achieved his cherished aim. Since Bahlol Lodi was met with success, he fulfilled his promise. Haidar Shaikh married the daughter (Taj Murassa Begum) of the new Sultan and received 69 villages in dowry. Two children were born out of this marriage, a son named Shaikh Hasan and a daughter called Bibi Mangi.

As far as the grant of 69 villages was concerned, what Haidar Shaikh had received was not a petty kingdom, but a land grant. According to the contemporary administrative practice, the grantee was entrusted with the right of collecting land revenue from the villages. Technically, the land grant was not permanent, as the grantee could hold it only until he enjoyed the goodwill of the sovereign power. An exception seems to have been made in the case of Haidar Shaikh, since he was an eminent mystic and a son-in-law of the reigning Sultan. Haidar Shaikh appeared to have utilized his special position in a manner that a formal land grant was converted into an informal petty kingdom. Whatever be the nature of the land grant and the status of Haidar Shaikh, he was entitled to enjoy the land revenue yielded by the grant. The only difference between the two situations was that the degree of state control was more in the former case than in the latter. In view of the autonomy enjoyed by the Shaikh, he appeared to have emerged as a zamindar.

The worldly affairs of Shaikh Haidar as a zamindar prospered in terms of power and wealth. His counterparts, who were based in different places, sought to benefit from his progress. Rai Bahram Bhatti, a powerful zamindar of Kapurthala, formed an alliance with Haidar Shaikh and, as a part of the agreement, gave his daughter in marriage to him. Two sons were born out of this marriage, who were named Isa and Musa. In due course, Haidar Shaikh's own daughter Bibi Mangi was married in the family of a prominent zamindar of Tohana. Unfortunately, the young woman became a widow just after five years of her marriage. Her parents-in-law proposed that she be married to the younger brother of her deceased husband. Bibi Mangi rejected the proposal and, as it appeared from the circumstances, could no longer live in her marital home. It has been suggested that in India, as in other oriental countries, the marital bond was regarded as strong enough to be classed as spiritual. The eastern mind made it incumbent on ladies of high families to shun the very idea of a second marriage. The stance of Bibi Mangi, therefore, was not surprising, even though it offended her parents-in-law. Haidar Shaikh intervened in the matter and asked Shaikh Hasan to bring his sister back from Tohana. For unknown reasons, Shaikh Hasan refused to obey his father on this issue. However, Shaikh Isa and Shaikh Musa (the foster brothers of Bibi Mangi) performed the delicate task with credit. They rescued her from the control of her parents-in-law and escorted her back to Malerkotla. Haidar Shaikh was delighted to meet her and showered his blessings on these two sons.[85]

According to another version, Bibi Mangi did leave Tohana along with Shaikh Isa and Shaikh Musa, but she did not reach Malerkotla alive. During the course of her journey, she implored the earth to open and receive her, which it did. Though her motivation in seeking internment in this manner was unspecified, it was assumed that she was driven by the tendency to blame widows for their husbands' deaths and to regard them as bad omens. As a pious woman and devoted daughter, she did not wish to bring shame on her father's household. There was a shrine to her at the spot where she was believed to have entered the earth. Haidar Shaikh disinherited his son Shaikh Hasan for refusing to help his sister.[86]

The above discussion indicated that there were at least three versions of the historical role of Haidar Shaikh. In the first version, Khwaja Niamatullah Harvi has accepted the Shaikh as one of the several Afghan mystics. The chronicler has portrayed him as a Sufi who, through a miracle, forced Sikandar Lodi to treat him with respect and advised the Sultan to refrain from investigating his affairs. The writer did not allude to the Shaikh's involvement in politics, with reference to Bahlol Lodi and other zamindars. The Sultan followed his advice and maintained cordial relations with the Shaikh. In the second version, narrated by a present-day descendant of Haidar Shaikh, the Shaikh was said to have begun his career as a military commander of an unnamed Sultan. Since the Shaikh was inclined towards spirituality, he neither performed his official duties, nor showed respect to the regime. His official duties were performed on his behalf by a group of djinns loyal to him. Therefore, the state was constrained to relieve him from service. The Shaikh, acting on the advice of his mentor, established himself as a Sufi in the unsettled land of Malerkotla and worked for the spread of Islam. The third version holds that Haidar Shaikh began his carrer as a Sufi at Malerkotla. He not only impressed Bahlol Lodi, the governor of Sirhind, with his miraculous powers, but gave his blessings that enabled the Lodi challenger to win the throne of Delhi. In consequence, he received the daughter of the new Sultan in marriage as well as a grant of 69 villages in dowry. As he embarked on a political career, he entered into matrimonial relations with the zamindars of Kapurthala and Tohana. Soon he converted his position as a land grantee into that of a zamindar, so that his descendants inherited this position and served the Mughal governor (*faujdar*) of Sirhind.

With his death in 1508, the dual role of Haidar Shaikh as a Sufi and zamindar was bifurcated between the male offspring of his two wives. Shaikh Hasan (the son of Bahlol Lodi's daughter Taj Murassa Begum), who had been disinherited in the lifetime of Haidar Shaikh, became the spiritual head (*sajjadah nishin*) of the Sufi establishment. His lineal descendants continued to hold this office until today. On the other hand, Shaikh Isa (the younger son of Rai Bahram Bhatti's daughter) inherited the landed estate in accordance with the will of his father. Contrary to expectations, the arrangement did not satisfy the former and he made repeated attempts to acquire a larger share of the patrimony. The history of Haidar Shaikh's household was often plagued by bad blood and acrimony. Shaikh Hasan filed a legal suit in the court of the *qazi* of Malerkotla and, some time later, his sons submitted a complaint to the governor of Sirhind. These pleas were rejected on legal grounds. Acting out of sheer frustration, the sons of Shaikh Hasan (Mirza Khan and Sulaiman Khan), assassinated Amir-i Maler who served as a representative of the Delhi Sultanate in the area. The landed estate was confiscated by the Delhi-based sovereign and it was restored in 1543 to the rightful claimant Khan Muhammad Shah only after the payment of a large sum of money.[87]

There was a positive side to the situation. Shaikh Isa and his successors employed a number of strategies to establish peace on the estate and, while doing so, they displayed a keen sense of political management and considerable sagacity. They witnessed the protracted armed conflict between the Afghans (Lodis and Surs) and Mughals, but remained scrupulously neutral and focused their attention on their own possessions. They forged alliances with prominent Rajput zamindars of central Panjab (Morinda and Nabha) and did not hesitate in accepting their daughters as wives. As Mughal rule underwent consolidation during the second half of the sixteenth century, the chiefs of Malerkotla collaborated in various administrative measures, particularly relating to the land revenue system. In their role as zamindars, they acted under the supervision of the governor (*faujdar*) of Sirhind. They diligently collected the land revenue from the estate (zamindari) and faithfully deposited it with the governor of Sirhind. They also maintained a contingent of armed retainers, which was placed at the disposal of the Mughals during any exigency. They persuaded the leading zamindars, Chain Singh of Gumti and Chaudhari Phool of Patiala, to throw in their lot with the governor of Sirhind and, in this manner, strengthened the roots of the Mughal empire in the area. Nawab Muhammad Bayazid Khan (r. 1600-59) provided escort services to Jahangir during the latter's march to Kashmir and supported Aurangzeb in his conflict with Dara Shukoh. In return, Bayazid Khan, earned a series of rewards – the titles of Asadullah Saif ul-Mulk and Nawab, additional fiefs (*jagirs*) in Qadirabad and Naugawan – besides permission to build a fort and boundary wall at Malerkotla. I hasten to point out however that, on a few occasions, the disgruntled members of the family bypassed their chief and cultivated direct relations with the Mughal governor of Sirhind, creating suspicion and dissension.[88]

In addition to the several popular stories, Haidar Shaikh has left an important legacy in the form of his shrine. The shrine has evolved over five centuries as a leading centre of pilgrimage in the cis-Satluj tract of Panjab. It is somewhat surprising that Haidar Shaikh, who acquired a lot of prominence on account of his spiritual attainment and political gains, could not be provided with a suitable tomb after his demise. On account of his multifarious commitments, he was unable to groom a group of spiritual successors (*khalifas*) who could have raised a memorial for him. At the same time, Haidar Shaikh's lineal descendants were so deeply involved in internecine conflict and struggle for survival that they could not spare a thought for their great ancestor.

Until the partition of the Indian subcontinent, the grave of Haidar Shaikh was covered merely by a tent. After 1947, a pillared structure, which appeared like a canopy, was constructed. In 2007, this small building was dismantled and a new edifice has been raised. Only two structures, the boundary wall and grave of Haidar Shaikh, have survived from pre-Mughal times. The boundary wall, constructed with boulders without any cementing material, shows all the marks of its age. At present, the shrine has been provided with two gateways, outer and inner. The outer gateway, which was located on the northern side and was built of small bricks, appears to be a century old. It can be approached by climbing fifteen steps. It is topped by a lintel which joins the roof of small rooms on two sides. Beyond it spreads a courtyard which surrounds the mausoleum on all sides. The inner gateway, which stood on the southern side, is an impressive modern structure. The arched entrance bears a marble slab on which Haidar Shaikh's name is inscribed. Its upper portion has been provided with a ornamental central canopy and flanking towers on two corners. The tomb was an octagonal structure, covered by an onion shaped dome. The inner side of the dome was decorated with multi-coloured glass work. The grave of Haidar Shaikh was raised on a three feet high platform. Made of marble and gilded with granite, it remained covered with thick embroidered sheets of cloth. This sanctum sanctorum was lit by a big chandelier that hung down from the roof. In the eastern courtyard, there was a prayer room (*ibadatgah*) where Haidar Shaikh sat for meditation. Here also are the graves of his three sons, Shaikh Musa, Shaikh Isa and Shaikh Hasan. In the eastern courtyard are the graves of Haidar Shaikh's wife Taj Murassa Begum, grandson Shaikh Sulaiman and three other relatives. Along the northern wall, there are a few rooms and a verandah. Beyond the shrine complex, two structures came up in recent times, a mosque for offering prayers and a pillared hall for accommodating pilgrims during the festivities.[89]

The shrine has, thus, emerged as an important centre of pilgrimage in central Panjab. It is managed by hereditary office holders (*khalifas*) who traced their descent from Shaikh Hasan, the eldest son of Haidar Shaikh. The attendants (*mujawirs*), descended from the original caretakers, oversee the multifarious activities at the shrine. Voluntary servants (*sewadars*) undertake a variety of duties and functions, which were related to maintenance and cleanliness, while a number of mendicants (*faqirs*) were observed in the premises at different times. Occasional visitors come to the shrine on any day of the week, but a large number of devotees registered their presence on Thursday evenings. The most significant festival is the annual fair (*mela*) which marked the death anniversary (*urs*) of Haidar Shaikh. Held during the month of May-June (Jeth), it coincides with the Hindu festival of Nirjala Ekadashi. At this particular time of the year, the peasants looked forward to a bountiful monsoon which, in turn, could guarantee the success of the paddy crop. Pilgrims arrive from different parts of Panjab as well as distant provinces. The markets of the town wear a festive look, as shops displayed household commodities, including utensils and sweetmeats. The memorabilia of Haidar Shaikh – pamphlets containing the biography and miracles of the saint, audio cassettes and CDs of Qawwalis in his praise and colourful posters depicting the shrine – are for sale. The pilgrims made obeisance at the tomb of Haidar Shaikh and, making an offering in cash or kind, seek the intercession of the saint for the fulfilment of their wishes, the birth of a son or a cure of ailment. Besides the musical assemblies where Qawwalis are presented in the traditional style, groups of singers (Toomba Parties who used a single stringed instrument) regale the audience with tales regarding Haidar Shaikh, Yusuf Zulaikha, Daud Badshah and Tota Maina.[90] A special category of devotees (*chelas*) performed the somewhat strange rite known as Haidar Shaikh Ki Chauki. These devotees worked themselves up into a state of trance and, while communicating with the spirit of Haidar Shaikh, answered the queries of people who were afflicted with physical and mental ailments.[91]

Political Turmoil in Multan

During the second half of the fifteenth century, the inhabitants of Multan and local zamindars persuaded Shaikh Yusuf Qureshi, a descendant of Shaikh Bahauddin Zakariya, to assume the reins of administration in his hands. This unprecedented development was brought about by a number of factors. In Delhi, the last Syed ruler Sultan Alauddin Shah (r. 1443-76) ascended the throne. The Syed regime, which was engulfed in a serious crisis owing to the pressure of neighbouring kingdoms and internal challenges, failed to establish its authority in Multan and could not even appoint a governor for the region. The local chiefs (Langahs and Balochis) did possess military resources, but did not show any inclination to take responsibility. The people, both high and low, thought it prudent to fill the political vacuum by turning to the descendants of Shaikh Bahauddin Zakariya, who were held in high esteem. Shaikh Yusuf Qureshi managed the affairs of the extensive Suhrawardi hospice (*khanqah*) in Multan and also exercised supervision over the area surrounding the sacred mausoleum. He began to perform his duties with enthusiasm. He ensured that the public prayers were recited in his name from the pulpits of the Suhrawardi spiritual domain (*vilayat*) which comprised Multan, Uch and other towns. He won over the local chiefs and enlarged his army by recruiting fresh retainers. In short, his rule gained strength and legitimacy with every passing day.[92]

In the above circumstances, Rai Sehra, the chief of the Langah tribe who held the town of Sewi and neighbouring areas, offered to form an alliance with the mystic turned ruler. He was reported to have sent a message in the following words,

As from the time of my ancestors, the relationship of discipleship and belief to your family has remained on firm basis; and the empire of Delhi is not free from disturbances and disorder; and they say that Malik Bahlol Lodi has taken possession of Delhi, and has had public prayers read in his name; if His Holiness the Shaikh would with utmost promptitude turn his attention to the tribe of the Langahs, and consider me among his soldiers, I shall not in every service and expedition, which may take place, consider myself excused from rendering loyal and devoted service, even to the extent of sacrificing my life. Also, at present, in order to strengthen the relationship of being disciple and of devotion and loyalty, I shall give my daughter to you (in marriage) and will accept you as my son-in-law.[93]

It is possible to draw the following inferences from the above statement. Rai Sehra had begun to feel insecure ever since Bahlol Lodi assumed sovereign power in Delhi. His position would be severely undermined, should the Lodi ruler decide to consolidate his hold in western Panjab. However, he could secure his own position by aligning himself with the new ruler of Multan.

This could be done by invoking the long standing discipleship of his family to the family of Shaikh Yusuf Qureshi, by promising to provide him military services in all future expeditions and by offering his daughter in marriage to him. Yusuf Qureshi accepted the offer of alliance with the Langah chief, while the marriage was duly solemnized. Sometimes Rai Sehra came from Sewi to Multan with the object of seeing his daughter and, on these occasions, he brought suitable presents for Yusuf Qureshi. In spite of these gestures of goodwill, Yusuf Qureshi did not have trust in his father-in-law. Acting with caution, he did not permit Rai Sehra to acquire a mansion in the city of Multan. Instead, he was required to reside outside the city and visit his daughter without any personal retinue.

Rai Sehra abided by these conditions only for some time. Thereafter, he forged an elaborate plan to usurp power from his son-in-law. It was not known if he made his daughter a party to the conspiracy. He arrived in Multan with all the members of his tribe. He requested Yusuf Qureshi to inspect these armed men, so that they could be allotted duties in accordance with their qualifications. An unsuspecting Yusuf Qureshi obliged his father-in-law, who succeeded in displaying the grandeur of his retinue. One night, he came to see his daughter escorted by a single servant. During the course of his stay in the palace, he complained of a sudden sickness and groaned loudly as if he was on the verge of death.[94] The representatives (*vakils*) of Yusuf Qureshi, being taken in by the ruse, permitted the Langah tribesmen to enter the palace and bid farewell to their master. Rai Sehra, while lying on the sick bed, deputed his trusted adherents to guard all the four gates, so that Yusuf Qureshi's men were prevented from entering the city from the outer fort. Once the entry points were sealed, Rai Sehra barged into the private apartments and, seizing his own son-in-law, brought an end to a rule of two years.[95] As he shifted from the rural hinterland of Sewi to the urbanized world of Multan and as he graduated from the rank of a tribal chief to that of a sovereign ruler of the kingdom of Multan, he discarded his non-Muslim name of Rai Sehra and adopted the Islamic name of Sultan Qutbuddin. A change in his political status was accompanied by a corresponding change in his religious identity. It was significant that his successors, who ruled over Multan till they were displaced by the Arghuns at the instance of the Mughal invader Babur, were known only by their pure Islamic names. There was no need for them to retain the non-Muslim names that corresponded well with their former occupation as tribal chiefs, who spent their lives in the rural hinterland.

As Sultan Qutbuddin was engaged in consolidating Langah rule in Multan, he was required to decide the fate of his royal prisoner. He was not in a position to treat Yusuf Qureshi in a harsh manner on account of two reasons – first, Yusuf Qureshi was his son-in-law and, second, he was a lineal descendant of Shaikh Bahauddin Zakariya who was held in high esteem by the people of Multan. Sultan Qutbuddin allowed Yusuf Qureshi to leave for Delhi through the northern gate of the fort, which was near the mausoleum of Shaikh Bahauddin Zakariya. However, he made sure that this gate was henceforth closed permanently, being sealed with burnt bricks. By undertaking this bold and unusual step, which had a considerable symbolic meaning, the new Langah ruler proclaimed that he would not permit the Suhrawardi establishment to play any role in the secular affairs of the government. Yusuf Qureshi found that his position had become so untenable that he could not even resume the headship of the Suhrawardi hospice. What was more probable, he might have been released by Sultan Qutbuddin on the condition that he would leave Multan for good. Moreover, the new Langah ruler could not feel secure when the former ruler was also staying in the city and, that too, in such close proximity to the seat of power. In these circumstances, Yusuf Qureshi had no alternative but to leave for Delhi. Bahlol Lodi not only received the fugitive with great honour, but also gave his daughter in marriage to his son, Shaikh Abdullah.[96]

Bahlol Lodi employed every possible means to boost the morale of Yusuf Qureshi and, giving repeated assurances, promised to reinstate him in Multan. However, Bahlol Lodi could not put his words into practice, as the first Langah ruler succeeded in ruling for sixteen long years and in winning the support of the local populace. However, Bahlol Lodi saw an opportunity when

Sultan Husain (the son of Sultan Qutbuddin, who assumed power in 1460) was involved in suppressing the local rebels at Shor, Khanewal, Kot Karor and Dhankot.[97] Accepting the latest request of Yusuf Qureshi for concrete action, Bahlol Lodi deputed his son Barbak Shah (the future Sikandar Lodi) and Tatar Khan Lodi (the governor of Panjab) to occupy Multan by assault. On the other side, Sultan Husain managed to defeat his rebellious brother at Kot Karor and, rushing back with speed, entered the fort of Multan. Barbak Shah and Tatar Khan Lodi, who had encamped at a prayer ground in the neighbourhood of Multan, made preparations for occupying the fort. Sultan Husain, who had returned back from Kot Karor, crossed the Indus and entered Multan. He placed a part of his army to guard the fort, while the remaining 10,000 troops, comprising both cavalry and infantry, emerged out of the citadel. Assuming the offensive, they dismounted from their horses and shot thousands of arrows simultaneously at their opponents. The Delhi army failed to withstand the deadly barrage of arrows and fled towards Khanewal, leaving behind a huge amount of war material in the hands of the defenders. The Delhi army, in an attempt to recover its credibility, attacked the fort of Khanewal and managed to kill over 300 defenders in a treacherous manner. However, it could not make any further gains in the region.[98]

On the other hand, Sultan Husain succeeded in consolidating his power in the kingdom of Multan by forging alliances with local chiefs and neighbouring principalities. He received the allegiance of the Baloch chief Malik Sohrab Dudai and his numerous adherents and, in return for their services, assigned to them the territory from Sitpur to Dhankot. He also received the allegiance of the chiefs of the Thathawa tribe[99] – Jam Bayazid and Jam Ibrahim – and assigned the tract of Shor to the former and that of Uch to the latter. What was more important, he sent condolences to Sikandar Lodi on the death of Bahlol Lodi and went on to sign a treaty of friendship and non-aggression with the Delhi Sultanate. In these circumstances, it became impossible for Yusuf Qureshi to be reinstated as the ruler of Multan. The Langah regime did not cease to respect the family of Shaikh Bahauddin Zakariya. In fact, it was grateful to God for the presence of some descendants of the saint in Multan. But, in its opinion, they were superior in all noble qualities to Yusuf Qureshi, to whose son Bahlol Lodi had given his daughter in marriage and whom he held in great honour. In the same manner, some Bokharis, the Suhrawardis who belonged to Multan and Uch, were superior in physical and mental perfections to Haji Abdul Wahab.[100] In a situation where the prominent Sufi families were represented by several descendants, it was easy for the Langah regime to develop its stance. It could favour anyone of the several successors of the Sufi masters, keeping its own political interests in view. It could not tolerate any natural or spiritual descendant of the founders of Sufi orders who, like Yusuf Qureshi, nurtured political ambitions. This message was broadcast to all stake holders when Sultan Qutbuddin bricked up the northern gate of the fort that opened towards the Suhrawardi hospice and it was so visible even as late as 1593.

Sultan Husain, owing to old age, abdicated in favour of his son Firoz Shah. The change marked the beginning of a long factional conflict from which Multan could not recover. The new ruler, driven by inexperience and anger, engineered the murder of Bilal, the son of the *wazir* Imad ul-Mulk. In retaliation, the *wazir* got his new master poisoned to death. Sultan Husain emerged from his retirement and resumed the reins of the government in his hands. He began to work for stabilizing the kingdom and avenging the death of his son. Taking the help of his maternal uncle Jam Bayazid, he imprisoned Imad ul-Mulk. He rewarded Jam Bayazid with the office of the *wizarat* along with the guardianship of Mahmud Khan, the minor son of the late Firoz Shah. After the death of Sultan Husain, Mahmud Khan ascended the throne of Multan. Since the new ruler began to differ with the *wazir* Jam Bayazid, the latter left the city and, setting up his camp on the Chenab, began to handle the administrative affairs. In an attempt to collect the land revenue, he summoned a few turbulent headmen and, getting their heads shaved, paraded them around the city. Since the Sultan regarded the headmen as loyal servants of the state, he retaliated by subjecting Alam Khan (the son of Jam Bayazid) to severe beating and humiliation. In the scuffle, the

Sultan was accidentally hit by the dagger of Alam Khan, who escaped from the scene to join his father. This episode cleared the way for the partition of the kindom of Multan.[101] Jam Bayazid had no alternative but to shift his troops to Shorkot. Sultan Mahmud sent an army in pursuit of the fugitives. In the ensuing battle, the Sultan's force was defeated. Jam Bayazid, having consolidated his position in Shorkot, had the public prayer read and coins struck in the name of Sikandar Lodi (r. 1489-1517). He also sent a petition to Delhi and explained his position. Sikandar Lodi, pleased at the prospect of recovering Multan, sent a letter of encouragement and robe of honour for Jam Bayazid. He also sent a royal order (*farman*) to his governor of Panjab, Daulat Khan Lodi, directing him to acquaint himself with the conditions prevailing in Multan and, in case of need, to provide military assistance to Jam Bayazid. Sultan Mahmud advanced to Shorkot at the head of his soldiers. Jam Bayazid and his son Alam Khan emerged out of Shorkot and, marching ten leagues, encamped on the Ravi. Daulat Khan Lodi arrived on the scene with the aim of bringing about an amicable settlement. As a result of his mediation, Daulat Khan Lodi succeeded in effecting peace by notifying the Ravi as the boundary between the warring parties. After this agreement, Daulat Khan Lodi sent Sultan Mahmud to Multan and escorted Jam Bayazid to Shorkot. In spite of the intervention by the Lodi governor of Panjab, peace was not stabilized. In the attempts to widen their respective support base, the two regimes sought the help of Baloch chiefs. Sultan Mahmud had won over Malik Sohrab Dudai, while Jam Bayazid received the allegiance of Mir Jakar Zand (along with his two sons Mir Allahdad and Mir Shahdad) who was granted a fief from the crown lands. A man of high moral character and generous disposition, Jam Bayazid attracted men of learning and piety from Multan. From Shorkot, he sent gifts by boat to the city in order to encourage distinguished persons to settle in his capital.[102]

When Babar occupied Panjab and advanced to Delhi, he bestowed Multan on Mirza Shah Husain Arghon, the ruler of Thatta. Accordingly, Mirza Arghon crossed the river near Bhakkar and marched towards Multan. Sultan Mahmud collected his troops and, marching two stages out of the city, sent two emissaries Shaikh Bahauddin Qureshi (a descendant of Shaikh Bahauddin Zakariya) and Maulana Bahlol to salvage a critical situation. Mirza Arghon, explaining the object of his arrival, stated that he had come to oversee the training of Sultan Mahmud and pay homage at the tomb of Shaikh Bahauddin Zakariya. The two representatives persuaded Mirza Arghon to put his intentions on hold. Sultan Mahmud, who suddenly died in 1524, was suspected of being poisoned by Langar Khan, a senior functionary of the kingdom. In fact, Langar Khan and Qiwam Khan Langah, the commanders of the army of Multan, transferered their loyalty to Mirza Arghon along with a number of towns. In Multan, the officers enthroned Sultan Husain, the infant son of Sultan Mahmud. The real power was exercised by the *wazir* Shaikh Shuja ul-Mulk Bokhari, who was the son-in-law of the deceased.[103] Meanwhile, Mirza Arghon laid siege to the fort and, pressing it with rigour, reduced the garrison of 3,000 soldiers to dire straits. Some defenders, who could not endure the distress, jumped from the ramparts into the ditch below. After a siege of one year and a few months, Mirza Arghon entered the fort and plundered the populace, leaving little possibility of rehabilitation of the city. As the Langah rule came to an end, Mirza Arghon placed the administration under the charge of Khwaja Shamsuddin and Langar Khan. With the establishment of the Mughal rule, Mirza Kamran was appointed as the governor of Panjab. The prince brought Multan under his control and allowed Langar Khan to reside in Lahore as a pensioner.[104]

The above discussion on the political developments during the fifteenth century would best reach its conclusion in the words of Guru Nanak (1469-1539). He took a keen interest in the structure and functioning of the contemporary political structure. He was acutely critical of the poltical system presided over by the Lodi rulers, though he did not name any individual member of the ruling class. Very often, he expressed his anguish at the negative features of the Lodi regime and suffering of the people at the hands of the Mughal invaders. He felt like living in an dark age which acted like a knife, as the kings were ruthless like butchers and righteousness had flown away. Since truth was not visible in the moonless night of falsehood, a common man was bewildered at his inability to find his path in the pervasive darkness.[105] The king sat in consultation with his ministers and bureaucrats, making dubious plans in the name of administration. They were able to have their way, because the masses, being blind and bereft of wisdom (*andhi raiyat giyan vihooni*) fed the greed of officials with bribes.[106] If the kings were rapacious like lions, the village headmen, who collaborated with the state in the collection of land revenue from the peasants, were guity of oppression. The *muqaddams* were comparable to dogs, who violently intruded into the lives of the innocent and disturbed their peaceful sleep. The king's servants (*chakar*), who behaved like ferocious dogs, inflicted wounds with their nails and licked way the oozing blood. If the conduct of these men was ever examined in the higher court, the noses of these untrustworthy persons would be chopped off.[107]

What was more disrurbing, the Lodi regime was charged with adopting discrimination on religious grounds. The practice of Islam was seen in the form of ablution pots, calls for prayer, prayer rugs and prayer, so that even the Lord seemed to appear in a blue apparel. In every house, people said that the Miyan used a different language. As God came to be designated as Allah, it was the turn of the Muslim saints to assert themselves (*adi purakh kau allah kahiye sekhan aayi*). The state began to levy a tax on temples and, thus, introduced a new practice.[108] The Brahmins felt pressurized into adopting a dual life. Inside his house, a Brahmin wore a loin cloth and, putting a frontal mark on his forehead, carried a rosary in his hands. He blew the conch and performed worship conforming to his custom. He did not allow anyone to enter his kitchen and, plastering its floor, drew boundary lines around it. If anyone dared to trespass, he forbade him from touching anything, lest it should get polluted. Once he stepped outside his house, he tried his best to be acceptable to the Muslims. He wore blue clothes and studied Islamic books. He not only ate the bread received from the Muslims, but also consumed the goat slaughtered in accordance with the Islamic injunctions.[109]

Guru Nanak's graphic description of the suffering of people at the hands of Babur's army has, by implication, exposed the failure of the Lodi regime to defend the frontier against the Mughals and protect its own subjects in the crisis. Babur, after having ravaged Khurasan, terrorized Hindustan. Descending like the agents of death, the Mughals inflicted unspeakable atrocities on the vulnerable inhabitants. When a powerful lion fell upon the defenceless herd of cattle, only God could be questioned in the absence of a competent ruler. Dogs had spoiled a priceless country, while nobody paid any attention to the dead.[110] When Babur attacked India at the head of a vast horde, even a million religious preceptors (*pir*) could not halt his advance. In the battlefield, the Mughals fired their guns and the Pathans (Afghans) fought with their elephants. The Lodi rulers lost their wits in colourful revelleries. As the princes were cut to pieces, tall edifices – palaces, gates, houses and inns – were pulled down. When Babur's rule was proclaimed, the Pathan notables could not eat their food. Some lost the time of five prayers, while others could not observe the rituals of their worship. In a moment, the victorious plundered and distributed all the wealth. All signs of power and riches – sports, stables, horses, chariots, drums, bugles, red uniforms and sword belts – were lost. Beautiful faces, shining ornaments, comfortable beds and fragrant betel leaves vanished like shadows.[111]

Women belonging to different ethnic groups, Hindus, Turks, Bhattis and Thakurs – lost their husbands. Their dwellings were converted into cremation grounds and their clothes were torn from head to foot. The Hindu women could neither bathe, nor apply their frontal marks. Some returned to their homes and enquired after the safety of their relatives, while others bewailed their losses in pain. Upper class women suffered great humiliation. At one time, they spent their lives in the lap of luxury on account of their wealth and beauty. When they were married, their bridegrooms appeared handsome besides them. They travelled in palanquins adorned with ivory. Water was sacrificed over their heads and glittering fans were waved above them. They were gifted lakhs when they sat down and offered the same amount when they stood up. They ate coconuts and dates, besides enjoying the joys of the bridal beds. Their heads were adorned with tresses and vermilion was poured in the partings. Wealth and beauty, which afforded them pleasures of life, now became their enemies. Their heads were shaven with scissors and their throats were filled with dust. Ropes were put around their necks, while their pearl strings were broken. Turned out of their places, they were not allowed to sit near their former abodes. In compliance with the royal orders, the Mughals dishonoured them and took them away.[112]

NOTES

1. Yahya bin Ahmad bin Abdullah Sirhindi, *Tarikh-i Mubarak Shahi*, Persian text, ed. M. Hidayat Hosain, Calcutta: Asiatic Society of Bengal, 1931, pp. 141-2 (hereafter cited as Sirhindi); Khwaja Nizamuddin Ahmad, *Tabaqat-i Akbari*, vol. I, English translation, B. De, Calcutta: The Asiatic Society, 1973, p. 261 (hereafter cited as Nizamuddin Ahmad); Muhammad Qasim Hindu Shah Firishta, *Tarikh-i Firishta*, Urdu translation, vol. I, Lahore: Al-Mizan, 2004, p. 330 (hereafter cited as Firishta).
2. Sirhindi, pp. 145-53; Nizamuddin Ahmad, I, pp. 267-71; Firishta, I, pp. 332-4.
3. Sirhindi, pp. 157-8.
4. A severe conflict between the factions of nobles led by Saadat Khan and Muqarrab Khan led to the emergence of two Sultans – Nasiruddin Mahmud Shah at Delhi and Nasiruddin Nusrat Shah at Firozabad. The writ of the former was confined to the forts of Delhi and Siri, while his rival controlled the *parganas* of Doab, Sambhal, Panipat, Rohtak and Jhajjar upto 20 leagues from Delhi. Every day, there were armed clashes between the partisans of the rival camps and, in spite of frequent casualties, neither could win a decisive victory. The nobles established themselves as rulers and began to appropriate tribute and taxes (*mal wa mahsul*). Such a situation prevailed for three years. Sirhindi, pp. 160-1; Nizamuddin Ahmad, I, p. 276; Firishta, I, p. 337.
5. Sirhindi, pp. 161-4; Nizamuddin Ahmad, I, pp. 276-8; Firishta, I, pp. 337-8.
6. Amir Timur (1334-1405), who was the son of a chief of the Turko-Mongol clan of Barlas, built his power on the ruins of the four Mongol Khanates. Acquiring undisputed leadership over the Ulus Chaghtai, he established his control over Transoxiana. Before invading northern India, he had carried out elaborate military campaigns in Sistan, Afghanistan, Herat, Khurasan, Mazandran, Azarbaijan, Baghdad, Anatolia, Georgia, Siberia and Southern Russia. For an analysis of his political power, see Beatrice Forbes Manz, *The Rise and Rule of Tamerlane*, Cambridge: Cambridge University Press, 1989, pp. 148-53.
7. Sirhindi, pp. 162-3.
8. Owing to the devastating conquests of Timur, a large number of Muslims from Central Asia and Persia, migrated to Kashmir. Sikandar Shah (r. 1389-1413) provided them financial support and land grants to many of them,

so that they built houses, hospices and graveyards. Mohammad Habib and Khaliq Ahmad Nizami, eds., *A Comprehensive History of India*, vol. V: *Delhi Sultanate*, AD 1206-1526, pp. 745-6.
9. Sharfuddin Ali Yazdi, *Zafar Nama*, Persian text, ed. Muhammad Ilahdad, Calcutta: Asiatic Society of Bengal, 1888, vol. II, pp. 46-8 (herafter cited as Yazdi).
10. Yazdi, pp. 49-52.
11. Talamba, a town on the left bank of the Ravi, was situated 51 miles northeast of Multan. Its fortress once possessed great strength and its antiquity was vouched for by the size of its bricks. Its ruins consisted of an open city, which was protected on the south by a lofty fortress of 1,000 feet square. The outer rampart of earth had a thickness of 200 feet and a height of 20 feet. A second rampart of earth of equal elevation stood on its summit. Both were originally faced with large bricks. When Timur plundered Talamba and massacred its inhabitants, he left the citadel untouched. According to tradition, the site was abandoned due to a change in the course of the Ravi during the time of Mahmud Langah (r. 1510-25). *Imperial Gazetteer of India, Provincial Series: Punjab*, vol. II, Calcutta: Superintendent of Government Printing, 1908, p. 244.
12. Yazdi, pp. 53-8.
13. Ibid., pp. 59-64.
14. Ibid., pp. 67-71.
15. Ibid., pp. 72-6.
16. Ibid., pp. 77-83.
17. Ibid., pp. 84-92.
18. The number of war elephants in the *pilkhana* had declined from 470 early in the reign of Firoz Shah Tughluq to 120 on the eve of Timur's invasion. The invaders, by making special arrangements, rendered them ineffective and, after their victory, captured all of them. Laden with treasure and carved stones, they were carried away to Samarqand. As a result, the ruler of Delhi stood on terms of equality with the kingdoms of Gujarat, Malwa and Jaunpur. The north Indian Sultanates had to build the *pilkhanas* from a scratch. Simon Digby, *War Horse and Elephant in the Delhi Sultanate: A Study of Military Supplies*, Oxford: Oxford Monographs, 1971, pp. 81-2.
19. Yazdi, pp. 103-16.
20. Ibid., pp. 116-24.
21. Ibid., pp. 128-31; in this manner, the fort, which could not be occupied even by Tarmashirin Khan, was reduced by Timur. Interestingly, Timur admonished the writers who, while drafting the letters of victory, tried to assert the superiority of Timur over Tarmashirin Khan as a general. Timur made it a point to alter the draft, so that the contribution of a distinguished ancestor was recognized.
22. Yazdi, pp. 139-42.

23. The pass (*darrah*) of Kopla was situated in the expanse of mountains from where the Ganga flowed out. At a distance of 15 *kos* from this spot, there was a stone which was shaped like a cow. The water of the Ganga emerged from this stone. People of India (*diyar hind*) worshipped this stone and, through this act, hoped to gain proximity to God. They cremated the dead and poured the ashes in the river, as they believed this act as a source of salvation (*vaseela najat*). They also threw gold and silver in the river. The pilgrims shaved the hair of the head and beard. They bathed in the river and poured the water over their heads. This ritual had the same sanctity in their eyes as Haj among the Muslims. Abul Nasr Utbi, the author of *Kitab-i Yamini*, had described the state of Hindus and their beliefs regarding this river. Sultan Mahmud of Ghazni, towards the end of his reign, led his army to this place. Yazdi, pp. 145-6.
24. Yazdi, pp. 139-42.
25. Ibid., pp. 143-4.
26. Ibid., pp. 149-56.
27. Ibid.
28. Ibid., pp. 157-9.
29. Ibid., pp. 160-1.
30. At this juncture, Shaikh Nuruddin, an emissary of Sikandar Shah (r. 1389-1413), the ruler of Kashmir, presented himself before Timur and conveyed a message of submission. During the ensuing negotiations, it was decided that Sikandar Shah would offer a tribute comprising 30,000 horses and one lakh Kashmiri coins weighing 2.5 *misqals* each. Timur felt that the amount of ransom was much more than could be borne by the resources of the kingdom. It appears that Sikandar Shah was given a period of four weeks to pay the tribute, when Timur's army was likely to reach the Indus on its way to Samarqand.
31. Yazdi, pp. 163-5.
32. Ibid., pp. 66-9. According to a regional history, Raja Mal Dev (r. 1360-1401), who ruled over Jammu at this time, offered to submit. As Timur invited him to embrace Islam, the negotiations collapsed and the Rajputs prepared for battle. Clad in Gulnari apparel and embroidered turbans, they applied saffron marks on their foreheads. Uttering 'Ram Ram' and carrying swords, they galloped down the hills in a dreadful appearance and overwhelming numbers. They fought so ferociously that the battlefield was strewn with corpses of Muslims like the desert of Karbala. When Timur realized that the situation had gone out of hand, he took to treachery and prayed for safety. Raja Mal Dev, having carried the day, went atop the mountain and took refuge in a jungle. Timur pursued the victors to the foot of the mountain and, at the advice of his nobles, turned back and crossed the Chenab. In a fierce attack, the Raja's army killed several invaders upto the bank and captured much booty. Several invaders perished in the flood, while the fame of the Raja spread far and wide owing to his achievements on the battle-

field. Ganeshdas Badehra, *Rajdarshani*, English Translation, Sukhdev Singh Charak and Anita K. Billawaria, Jammu: Jay Kay Book Store, 1991, pp. 101-2.
33. Yazdi, pp. 169-72.
34. Ibid., pp. 173-82.
35. Sirhindi, pp. 167.
36. Sirhindi, pp. 173-4; Nizamuddin Ahmad, vol. I, pp. 285-6.
37. Sirhindi, pp. 176-80; Nizamuddin Ahmad, vol. I, pp. 287-90.
38. Khizr Khan was the son of Malik Sulaiman, who had been adopted as a son by Malik Mardan Daulat. During the reign of Firoz Shah Tughluq, the *iqta* of Multan was assigned to Malik Mardan Daulat. After the death of this *muqti*, Multan was assigned to his adoptive son Malik Sulaiman and, following his demise, it came into the hands of Khizr Khan. The Persian chronicles have assigned a Syed identity on Khizr Khan on two grounds. Firstly, Syed Jalaluddin Bokhari (the Suhrawardi saint of Uch) declared Malik Sulaiman to be a Syed and, owing to this, did not allow him to wash his hands. Secondly, Khizr Khan possessed laudable virtues – bravery, generosity, humility, equanimity and adherence to his words – that were conspicuous in Prophet Muhammad. Sirhindi, p. 182; Nizamuddin Ahmad, vol. I, 292; Firishta, vol. II, p. 365.
39. Sirhindi, pp. 183-7; Nizamuddin Ahmad, I, pp. 293-6; Firishta, II, p. 366.
40. Sirhindi, pp. 189-90; Nizamuddin Ahmad, I, pp. 297-8; Firishta, II, p. 367.
41. During the course of his second rebellion, Tughan Rais Turkbacha joined hands with the impostor Sarang Khan. On learning that his new ally possessed a large quantitity of wealth, Tughan Rais Turkbacha was overpowered by greed and got him killed. However, only Firishta has mentioned this particular cause of the murder. Firishta, II, p. 367.
42. Sirhindi, pp. 191-92; Nizamuddin Ahmad, I, pp. 298-9; Firishta, II, p. 367.
43. Sirhindi, p. 194; Nizamuddin Ahmad, I, pp. 300-1.
44. Sirhindi, who has been followed by other writers, stated that Rai Kamaluddin Muin was attacked at Talwandi. But in the next sentence, he wrote that Rai Firoz Muin, who was the zamindar of that place, fled towards the east. Kishori Saran Lal, *Twilight of the Sultanate*, New Delhi: Munshiram Manoharlal, rpt., 1980, p. 86, fn. 15.
45. Sirhindi, pp. 195-6; Nizamuddin Ahmad, I, pp. 300-1.
46. Sirhindi, pp. 196-7; Nizamuddin Ahmad, I, pp. 301-2.
47. Sirhindi, pp. 198-9; Nizamuddin Ahmad, I, pp. 302-4.
48. Sirhindi, pp. 201-02; Nizamuddin Ahmad, I, p. 305.
49. Sirhindi, pp. 212-13; Nizamuddin Ahmad, I, pp. 310-11.
50. Sirhindi, p. 214; Nizamuddin Ahmad, I, p. 311.
51. Sirhindi, pp. 214-17; Nizamuddin Ahmad, I, pp. 312-13.
52. In pursuance of a clear strategy, Shaikh Ali took particular care to ravage the districts of the nobles, who were investing the fort of Bathinda and thus succeeded in his object. Kishori Saran Lal, *Twilight of the Sultanate*, p. 92.

53. Sirhindi, pp. 217-18; Nizamuddin Ahmad, I, pp. 313-14.
54. Sirhindi, pp. 218-20; Nizamuddin Ahmad, I, p. 314.
55. Sirhindi, pp. 220-21. Deeply influenced by the changing political fortunes, Sirhindi reflected on his times that revealed strange feats through its bicoloured sheets and multicoloured veils. As he argued, owing to the negligence of youth (*ghaflat jawani*) one should not trust this world, which was comparable to a coquettish old woman, an attractive young maiden and a deceitful whore. This woman had removed the valiant warriors from their kingdoms and powerful emperors from their thrones, pushing them into their coffins. She had also deprived numerous young damsels and newly married brides of their beauty and inflicted on them the blows of autumn, imprisoning them in the dust of extinction (*aseer khak fana*). Sirhindi, p. 222.
56. Sirhindi, pp. 223-24; Nizamuddin Ahmad, I, pp. 315-16.
57. Sirhindi, pp. 224-26; Nizamuddin Ahmad, I, 317.
58. Sirhindi has alleged that Shaikh Ali was a despicable and irreligious man, that his real object was to destroy the seat of Islam and that he achieved it by taking all the Muslims as prisoners. The writer has complained that God, who is the most high and a helper of Islam, had increased the malevolence of that accursed person. He prayed that God might assist those who helped the religion of Prophet Muhammad and disgrace those who discredited his religion. Sirhindi's narrative of the episode was in line with the familiar rhetoric that was adopted by the official chronicles in describing the Mongol invasions of northwestern India during the thirteenth and fourteenth century. Yet these lines underscored Sirhindi's deep anguish at the atrocities inflicted by the invaders on the helpless populace which had been left without defence by its own local administrators. Sirhindi, pp. 228-9.
59. Sirhindi, pp. 228-9; Nizamuddin Ahmad, I, pp. 318-19.
60. Shorkot was situated among the lowlands of the Chenab, about 4 miles from the left bank of the river and 36 miles southwest of Jhang. The modern town stood at the foot of a huge mound of ruins, marking the sight of an ancient city, which was surrounded by a wall of large antique bricks, and so high as to be visible for 8 miles around. *Imperial Gazetteer of India, Provincial Series: Punjab*, vol. II, p. 218.
61. Sirhindi, pp. 230-31; Nizamuddin Ahmad, I, p. 319.
62. Sirhindi, p. 233; Nizamuddin Ahmad, I, p. 321.
63. Mohammad Habib and Khaliq Ahmad Nizami, eds., *A Comprehensive History of India*, vol. V: *The Delhi Sultanate*, AD 1206-1526, p. 658.
64. The only contemporary source, Yahya bin Ahmad bin Abdullah Sirhindi's *Tarikh-i Mubarak Shahi*, which provided a useful account of the political developments in the early fifteenth century, terminated at 1434. The later sources, which were written in the sixteenth and seventeenth century, have

made only brief references to the role of Jasrath Khokhar in his last phase. We have no alternative but to rely on this inadequate evidence.
65. Nizamuddin Ahmad, I, p. 327; Badauni, I, p. 398; Firishta, II, p. 380.
66. Kishori Saran Lal, *Twilight of the Sultanate*, p. 118.
67. Nizamuddin Ahmad, I, p. 328; Badauni, I, p. 399; Firishta, II, p. 381.
68. Firishta, II, p. 386.
69. Ibid., p. 386; Shaikh Rizqullal Mushtaqi, *Waqiat-i Mushtaqi*, Persian text, ed. Iqtidar Husain Siddiqui and Waqar ul-Hasan Siddiqi, Rampur: Raza Library, 2002, p. 3.
70. Andre Wink, 'On the Road to Failure: The Afghans in Mughal India,' in *Islamicate Traditions in South Asia: Themes from Culture and History*, ed. Agnieszka Kuczkiewics Fras, New Delhi: Manohar, 2013, pp. 272-4, 297-8.
71. Simon Digby, 'After Timur Left: North India in the Fifteenth Century,' in *After Timur Left: Culture and Circulation in the Fifteenth Century North India*, ed. Francesca Orsini and Samira Shaikh, New Delhi: Oxford University Press, 2014, p. 51.
72. At this point in his narrative, Abdullah has inserted the story of the dervish of Samana, who conferred the kingdom of Delhi on Bahlol Lodi in return for an offering of 1,600 *tankas*.
73. Abdullah, *Tarikh-i Daudi*, Persian text, ed. Shaikh Abdur Rashid and Iqtidar Husain Siddiqui, Aligarh: Aligarh Muslim University, 1969, pp. 3-5; Shaikh Rizqullah Mushtaqi, *Waqiat-i Mushtaqi*, p. 4. However, Nizamuddin Ahmad and Fririshta did not support the statement regarding the involvement of Bahlol Lodi in horse trade.
74. Abdullah, *Tarikh-i Daudi*, 5-6; Nizamuddin Ahmad, I, pp. 332-3; Firishta, II, p. 386.
75. Abdullah, *Tarikh-i Daudi*, pp. 6-7; Nizamuddin Ahmad, I, p. 334; Firishta, II, p. 387.
76. In a banquet hosted by Hamid Khan, Bahlol Lodi was accompanied by a group of Afghans. According to a premeditated plan, these Afghans began to behave in a crude and comical manner. Hamid Khan became convinced that the Afghans were a bunch of simpletons who would not harm him in any way. He permitted a free access to the Afghans in his quarters and, falling into a trap, became a prisoner in their hands. Bahlol Lodi achieved his aim in a bloodless drama. Abdullah, *Tarikh-i Daudi*, pp. 8-10; Shaikh Rizqullah Mushtaqi, *Waqiat-i Mushtaqi*, pp. 5-7; Firishta, II, pp. 387-8.
77. The princely state of Malerkotla was bounded by the district of Ludhiana on the north and by Patiala territory elsewhere, except for a few miles on western border, where it marched with some Nabha villages. The country was a level plain, unbroken by any hill or stream, but varied only by sand drifts occurring in all directions. The chief town of Malerkotla was divided into two parts, Maler and Kotla, which were united by the construction of Moti Bazar. The former was founded by Shaikh Sadruddin and the latter by Bayazid Khan in 1656. The principal buildings were the residence of

the ruling chief, an administrative block in Kotla and the tomb of Shaikh Sadruddin. *Imperial Gazetteer of India, Provincial Series: Punjab*, vol. II, pp. 398-400.

78. Khwaja Niamatullah bin Khwaja Habibullah al-Harvi, *Tarikh-i Khan Jahani wa Makhzan-i Afghani*, Persian text, ed. Syed Muhammad Imamuddin, Dacca: Asiatic Society of Pakistan, 1962, vol. II, pp. 787-8.
79. Members of the families of Haidar Shaikh's descendants (*khalifas*) have preserved a large stock of stories about their progenitor. These tales, which were not related by other inhabitants of Malerkotla, tended to emphasize Haidar Shaikh's spiritual power over worldly authority. Ahmad, who served as a revenue collector (*nambardar*) and whose father and grandfather were Sufis, was a prominent source of such stories. It was Ahmad who narrated this particular story. Anna Bigelow, *Sharing the Sacred: Practicing Pluralism in Muslim North India*, New York: Oxford University Press, 2010, pp. 46-7.
80. Ibid., p. 47.
81. Ibid.
82. Nawab Iftikhar Ali Khan, *History of the Ruling Family of Sheikh Sadruddin Sadar-i Jahan of Malerkotla (1449 AD to 1948 AD)*, ed., R.K. Ghai, Patiala: Punjabi University, 2000, pp. 1-10.
83. The ancient name of Banur was Pushpa or Popa Nagari or Pushpavati (the city of flowers). Once it was famous for pefume distilled from Chambeli gardens. As observed in the early twentieth century, the ruins surrounding Banur testified to its former importance. The tomb of Malik Sulaiman, the father of the Syed ruler Khizr Khan, was found here. Mentioned in Babur's memoirs, Banur became a subdistrict (*mahal*) of the government of Sirhind under Akbar. *Imperial Gazetteer of India, Provincial Series: Punjab*, vol. II, p. 303.
84. Official papers, which were in the possession of the ruling family of Malerkotla, have incorporated the story of the horse, but have recorded the name of Bahlol Lodi instead of Sikandar Lodi. Remaining elements of the story – gift of the horse, its slaughter and consumption by the followers of the Shaikh, the Sultan's attempt to recover the horse and the Shaikh's miracle of showing more than a hundred horses – have been repeated. Bahlol Lodi became a disciple of the Shaikh and offered his daughter in marriage to him. Three years after securing the throne of Delhi, Bahlol Lodi passed through Malerkotla and solemnized the marriage of his daughter Taj Murassa Begum with the Shaikh. Nawab Iftikhar Ali Khan, op. cit., pp. 4-5.
85. Nawab Iftikhar Ali Khan, op. cit., pp. 6-8.
86. Bigelow, *Sharing the Sacred: Practicing Pluralism in Muslim North India*, pp. 33-4.
87. Nawab Iftikhar Ali Khan, op. cit., pp. 11-13.
88. Ibid., pp. 15-22.
89. Salim Mohammed, 'Shrine of Shaikh Sadruddin at Malerkotla: History, Politics and Culture,' in *Sufism In Punjab: Mystics, Literature and Shrines*,

Making and Breaking of Political Structures 433

   ed., Surinder Singh and Ishwar Dayal Gaur, New Delhi: Aakar Books, 2009, pp. 363-5.
90. Ibid., pp. 366-70.
91. Bigelow, *Sharing the Sacred: Practicing Pluralism in Muslim North India*, pp. 177-82.
92. Nizamuddin Ahmad, II, pp. 788-9.
93. Ibid., p. 788.
94. Rai Sehra directed the servant to cut the throat of a lamb with his knife in a corner of the house and to bring the blood in a cup after heating it. When the servant carried out the order, Rai Sehra drank off the cup, resulting in a fake illness.
95. Nizamuddin Ahmad, II, pp. 789-90.
96. Ibid., pp. 790-1.
97. Sultan Husain attacked the fort of Shorkot, which was held by Ghazi Syed Khan. The latter advanced 10 leagues and, after fighting bravely for a while, fled to Bhera. His followers continued to resist the besiegers, hoping for reinforcements from Bhera, Khanewal and Khushab that were in the possession of Syed Khani nobles. Failing to secure any help, they surrendered the fort and went to Bhera. Sultan Husain settled the affairs of Shorkot and, besieging the fort of Khanewal, captured it from Malik Majhi Khokhar, who was a representative of Ghazi Syed Khan. Nizamuddin Ahmad, II, pp. 792-3.
98. Nizamuddin Ahmad, II, pp. 791-5.
99. The Thattawa tribe controlled the greater part of the area between Bhakkar and Thatta. Considering themselves as descendants of Jamshed, the Thattawas were superior to other tribes in bravery and administration. The two Thattawa chiefs were angry with Jam Nanda, the Samma ruler of Sind, who also regarded himself as a descendant of Jamshed and backed another faction of the Thattawa tribe. Nizamuddin Ahmad, II, pp. 795-6.
100. On behalf of Multan, its *wazir* Imad ul-Mulk Tawalak claimed that the region had given rise to a number of eminent Sufis and scholars, who had earned unprecedented fame in Hindustan. This statement was made in retaliation to the arrogance of Sultan Muzaffar of Gujarat, who felt that the entire revenue of Multan could not finance a single building matching the palaces of Gujarat. It was argued that God had distinguished each kingdom with some excellence, which was respected in other kingdoms. The states of Gujarat, Deccan, Malwa and Bengal were known for their fertility and materials of enjoyment. Yet the kingdom of Multan had produced great men (Sufis and scholars) who were honoured wherever they went. Nizamuddin Ahmad, II, pp. 797-8.
101. Ibid., pp. 799-802.
102. Ibid., pp. 802-4.
103. Ibid., pp. 805-6.
104. Ibid., pp. 810-11.

105. Guru Arjan Dev, ed., *Sri Guru Granth Sahib*, Original text with English and Punjabi translations, Manmohan Singh, Amritsar: Shiromani Gurudwara Prabandhak Committee, 2nd edn., 1981, p. 145.
106. Ibid., pp. 468-9.
107. Ibid., p. 1288.
108. Ibid., p. 1191.
109. Ibid., pp. 471-2.
110. Ibid., p. 360.
111. Ibid., pp. 417-18.
112. Ibid., p. 417.

CHAPTER 7

Islamic Spirituality in Southeast Panjab

South of the Satluj, the towns of Hansi and Panipat emerged as centres of Islamic spirituality during the middle of the thirteenth century. Baba Farid had established a Chishti seat at Hansi, situated on the Delhi-Multan route and the headquarters of a revenue assignment (*iqta*), which was once entrusted to Ghiasuddin Balban. Shaikh Jamaluddin Hansavi and his successors nourished this establishment with care and commitment. At Panipat on the Delhi-Lahore route, Bu Ali Qalandar set up a hospice and shaped a tradition of opposition to the Islamic orthodoxy. Both Shaikh Hansavi and Bu Ali Qalandar employed their pens to record mystical ideas, while their popularity is epitomized in shrines that have survived upto the present. An equally significant development was the arrival from Kaliyar of the Sabiris, who worked from Panipat throughout the Sultanate period, and went on to establish new seats at Shahabad and Thanesar. The Sabiri tradition, extending from Shaikh Alauddin Ali Ahmad Sabir to Shaikh Abdul Quddus Gangohi, percolated into several hagiographies only centuries after the demise of the early masters. During the second half of the fifteenth century, Malerkotla rose to prominence owing to the efforts of a Suhrawardi exemplar Shaikh Sadruddin.

The Chishti Seat of Hansi

Shaikh Jamaluddin Hansavi (d. 1261) was a prominent disciple of Baba Farid. A descendant of Imam Abu Hanifa, he had served as a sermonizer (*khatib*) before devoting himself to mysticism. Baba Farid took pride in the spiritual excellence of Shaikh Hansavi. He often said that Jamal was his beauty and that he wished to revolve around his head. It was on account of his deep attachment to Shaikh Hansavi that Baba Farid spent twelve years of his career as a Sufi at Hansi.[1] The fame of Shaikh Hansavi had spread to different parts of northwestern India. Shaikh Bahauddin Zakariya was said to have written to Baba Farid, offering to exchange all his disciples for Shaikh Hansavi and proposed an immediate settlement of the matter. Rejecting the proposal, Baba Farid asserted that Jamal (Shaikh Hansavi) was his beauty and that a deal could be finalized in case of property, but not in case of Jamal (beauty).[2] Not surprisingly, Baba Farid made Shaikh Hansavi an integral part of his organizational activities. Whenever he conferred a certificate of succession on a disciple, Baba Farid directed him to visit Hansi and show the document to Shaikh Hansavi for approval. In the case of one unnamed disciple, Hansavi tore up the document on the ground that it was secured by exerting undue pressure on the preceptor. Deeply frustrated at this unexpected outcome, the man returned to Ajodhan and, showing the torn letter, sought assistance of his mentor. Baba Farid expressed his inability to intervene in the matter, because he could not sew what had been torn by Shaikh Hansavi.[3] On the other hand, the experience of another distinguished disciple of Baba Farid, Shaikh Nizamuddin Auliya, was quite happy. When Shaikh Nizamuddin showed his certificate of succession to Shaikh Hansavi, the latter treated the visitor with kindness and said:

Khudai jahan ra hazaran sipas
Keh gauhar sapurde ba-gauhar shanas

Thousands of thanks to the Lord of the world
For assigning the jewel to one who understood its value.

After this pleasant experience, Shaikh Nizamuddin recalled a change in the attitude of Shaikh Hansavi towards him. When he came to Hansi before his succession, Shaikh Hansavi would stand by way of respect; but after he earned his succession, Shaikh Hansavi did not stand. Shaikh Nizamuddin began to wonder why. Shaikh Hansavi explained. Now that Shaikh Nizamuddin had received the succession, the two had become equal in status. A relationship of love had been established between them and they had become one. So it was not appropriate for Shaikh Hansavi to stand in his own honour.[4] In the circle of Baba Farid's disciples, Shaikh Hansavi was remembered for his gentleness and hospitality. On one occasion, Shaikh Nizamuddin went to Hansi to meet his friend. It was the time of prayer on a cold winter morning. Shaikh Hansavi turned to the visitor and recited the following couplet:

Ba-raughan gau andareen roz khanak
Neko bashad harisa wa naan tanak

Cooked on a cold day in ghee of cow's milk
It is good to eat harisa and crisp baked bread.

Shaikh Nizammuddin felt that speaking of something which was not there was like whispering about an absent person. Shaikh Hansavi replied that he had already asked his servants to bring these dishes and soon after these were served in trays. This apparently minor incident is understandable if read with another incident. Once at Ajodhan, a man was invited by Baba Farid to join him for meals. When the loaves of bread were brought, Baba Farid instructed that they be placed on the ground. The guest said it would have been better if there were a tablecloth (*sufrah*). Baba Farid drew a design on the ground with his index finger and asked the guest to treat it as a tablecloth. Baba Farid did not fail to remark that the man was yet a novice and had just begun his spiritual journey.[5]

As soon as Shaikh Hansavi became a disciple of Baba Farid, he began to follow the Chishti principle of poverty and starvation in letter and spirit. His attendant, a woman of piety known as Madar-i Mominan, often travelled from Hansi to Ajodhan and carried messages of her master to Baba Farid. Once, Baba Farid asked her about the activities of his disciple. The woman replied, 'Ever since he has entered the circle of your discipleship, he has snapped all ties with worldly matters. He has renounced his job as a sermonizer (*khatib*) as well as his material possessions. Indeed, he is voluntarily facing starvation and performing a variety of austerities.' Baba Farid was satisfied at the state of his disciple and remarked that he was leading a happy life.[6] Even when Shaikh Hansavi established himself as a mystic in his own right, he continued to adhere to the spiritual path of his mentor. On one occasion, Shaikh Nizamuddin stopped at Hansi on his way to Ajodhan. Shaikh Hansavi, who was not able to meet the expenditure of his hospice, requested his friend to inform Baba Farid about his financial difficulties and to seek his prayer for the necessary remedy. Baba Farid reflected, then replied, 'When a spiritual territory (*wilayat*) is assigned to anyone, it becomes incumbent on him to turn it towards himself.'[7] In other words, the solution of Shaikh Hansavi's travails did not lie in mobilizing larger material resources, but in dedication to the spiritual welfare of the people with greater vigour. Shaikh Nasiruddin Mahmud (the leading disciple of Shaikh Nizamuddin Auliya) was asked to identify the solace of the king of the hereafter (Sufis). He replied that this consolation lay in diverting one's heart to God in absolute terms. While admitting that the spiritual accomplishments of Shaikh Hansavi were famous, he felt that these were less virtuous than those of the prophets.[8]

In accordance with a practice current among the Sufis, a preceptor gave advice (*wasiyat*) to a disciple who embarked on a journey. If the preceptor himself gave the advice, if unsolicited, the advice was considered a blessing. If he did not do so, then the disciple made a formal request to that effect. Once, Shaikh Hansavi wished to travel southwards from Ajodhan along with a group of disciples, including Shaikh Nizamuddin and Shamsuddin Dabir. Baba Farid directed him to keep Shaikh Nizamuddin happy during the course of the journey. Accordingly, Shaikh Hansavi (as also Dabir) treated Shaikh Nizamuddin with kindness. The group reached near Agroha, where a friend of Shaikh Hansavi, whose name was Miran, served as the administrator. This man welcomed the visitors and spent a lot of money on hospitality. Shaikh Hansavi gratefully acknowledged the kind gestures of the host and sought his permission to resume their journey. During those days, the area had not received its share of rainfall and the people had been suffering on account of the drought. Miran declared that he would permit the visitors to leave only when it rained. Shaikh

Hansavi did not say anything, but inwardly turned his attention towards the problem. Before the night was over, it rained so heavily that the area was covered with water. Next morning, every one was found to be happy. In order to show their gratitude to Shaikh Hansavi and his companions, the people arranged for their transport as well as luggage. From a village near Agroha to Hansi, the group covered the distance on horses. Unfortunately, Shaikh Nizamuddin was separated from the rest owing to a recalcitrant horse and an upset stomach.[9] The entire episode, besides pointing to the miraculous powers possessed by Shaikh Hansavi, shows that he commanded respect among the people of his spiritual domain (*wilayat*) including lower bureaucracy of the Delhi Sultanate.

Shaikh Hansavi had developed a deep love and intimate friendship with Shaikh Abu Bakr Tusi, who had established a beautiful hospice (*khanqah*) on the Jamuna, adjacent to Indarpat. This man possessed several qualities of saintliness, but his mystical engagement had nothing to do with the Haidaris. The affectionate relations between Shaikh Hansavi and Shaikh Tusi had been brought about by the former's disciple Maulana Husamuddin Indarpati. Whenever Shaikh Hansavi came to Delhi with the object of paying homage at the shrine of Shaikh Qutbuddin Bakhtiar Kaki, he had a meeting with Shaikh Tusi. Since Indarpati regarded these occasions as a blessing, he organized a lavish feast in honour of Shaikh Tusi and his friend. Interestingly, Shaikh Nizamuddin was also present in these meetings. Once, Shaikh Hansavi came to visit Shaikh Tusi. Indarpati, who was then in the village Kilokheri on the bank of the river, came out to welcome the guest. The two were separated by the river. Shaikh Hansavi enquired about his white falcon (Shaikh Tusi). In response, Indarpati stated that Shaikh Tusi had decided to perform the Haj. Shaikh Hansavi asked Indarpati to meet Shaikh Tusi on the other side of the river and communicate the following couplet:[10]

It would be much better to sacrifice one head at your feet.
It would be even better if there were a thousand heads instead of one.
Make the cave of your abode like Abu Bakr Siddiq.
It is only in the cave that Abu Bakr is Abu Bakr Muhammadi.

Endowed with a creative mind, Shaikh Hansavi produced a large corpus of Persian poetry that runs into two lithographed volumes. But his masterpiece is *Mulhimat* (Divine Inspirations), a small book of aphorisms in simple and catchy Arabic. In the words of Bruce Lawrence, 'Like the *Usul al-Tariqah* of Hamiduddin Suwali Nagauri, the *Mulhimat* of Jamaluddin Hansavi must have served a propaedeutic function in the expansion of the new silsilah.'[11] In the first half of the thirteenth century, Shaikh Shihabuddin Suhrawardi's treatise *Awarif ul-Maarif* was avidly taught in the Sufi estrablishments in Panjab. The *Mulhimat*, though composed in Arabic like the *Awarif*, differed from Shaikh Suhrawardi's prestigious work in many respects. Specifically addressed to the novice, it consisted of a series of instructions that were presented in an accessible idiom. It identified the qualities of a genuine seeker, who assumed the garb of a true lover engaged in the search of his Beloved. Shaikh Hansavi was quick to draw parallels from the struggle of legendary lovers, while he was conversant with the mystical thought of Khwaja Hasan Basri and Abu Saeed Abul Khair. He underlined relations between the seeker and his mentor, emphasizing the inner meanings of a variety of rituals that were seen as the hallmark of Sufism. Adding a personal touch, he opened every argument by addressing the seeker as Ahmad, who was none other than himself.

Shaikh Hansavi drew a distinction between three types of people: the seeker of the world (*talib al-duniya*), the seeker of the hereafter (*talib al-aqiba*) and the seeker of God (*talib al-maula*). These three categories displayed different characteristics. The seeker of the world was arrogant, base and avaricious. Deprived and chained, he was also condemned and spurned. The seeker of the hereafter was wise, auspicious and wealthy. Treading the right path, he was befriended, forgiven and exalted. The seeker of God was perfect, laudable and secure. Being a master and chief, he was ranked higher than all others. Seekers of the world were the most numerous, seekers of the hereafter less so and seekers of God were few. Similarly our Shaikh drew a distinction between ascetics (*zahid*) and gnostics (*arif*). The ascetic renounced the world for the hereafter, cleansed the exterior with water and traversed the spiritual path. He perpetually endeavoured to come out of his self and continuously strove to behold God. The gnostic renounced the world for God and purged his interior of carnal desire associated with Satan. By focusing his gaze on the Creator of earth and heaven, he reached his destination. The vocation of a gnostic comprised six elements. When he remembered God, he felt elated; when he remembered his own self, he considered it worthless; when he saw signs of God, he acknowledged them; when he inclined towards sin or lust, he reprimanded himself; when he remembered God, he congratulated himself, and when he recalled his sins, he sought forgiveness. The gnostic transcended the world, emerged out of his self and saw the beauty of the Beloved for ever. A gnostic was known by three signs – his food was that of a sick person; his sleep was that of saints; and his crying was that of a woman whose son had died.[12]

Every human being was endowed with good and bad qualities. The good ones could be preserved by submission (*taat*) and devotion (*ibadat*), while the bad ones could be removed by spiritual exercises (*riyazat*) and contemplation (*mujahidat*). This object could be achieved by means of prayer (*salat*), which personified a collection of all devotional acts (*majmua al-taat*) and treasure of worship (*makhzan al-ibadat*). The most crucial element in prayer was the absorption of the heart. In fact, prayer was like a body and absorption was like the soul. Prayer was the highest of all devotional acts and the key to felicities (*miftah al-saadat*). It could be maintained only by believers with absolute faith, and devout Muslims. A person gifted with blessings, felt inspired to offer prayer. If his heart was fully absorbed in prayer, he acquired the felicity of supplication (*lazzat al-munajat*). Prayer was like an eye whose light was absorption and this absorption, in turn, was like the light embedded in the verses of the Quran. Such an absorption in prayer was experienced by Hazrat Musa at the mountain of Toor. A prayer without absorption was comparable to moon from which light had disappeared, as well as food, which did not have the basic ingredients of oil and salt. When God held a person in the ambit of his guidance, He inspired him to pray. But when God was angry with a person, he pushed him into sinful acts. Next in importance to prayer was remembrance of God (*zikr*), which was sweetness for the tongue (*halwat al-lisan*) and felicity for the heart (*rahat al-jinan*). Remembrance was like a furnace for the heart and proof of friendship. The three letters of the word remembrance (*zikr*) stood for sagacity, intelligence and feeling. Remembrance was rewarded with purification of the heart, elimination of the carnal self and sensitivity of feeling. Remembrance was of two kinds. Remembrance of man stood for repentance and return to God, while remembrance of God meant the acceptance of one's repentance. A person who remembered God at night received happy tidings. A person who spent the night in sin received bad tidings.[13]

There were two types of people – those who were given to the gratification of self (*ashab al-nafus*) and those who were spiritually awakened (*arbab al-qulub*). Those who craved for self sought to satisfy their carnal desires. As their hearts underwent decay, they were separated from God and deprived of His mercy. Associating with the profane led to loss, as the company of self culminated in a wound. The self was as dangerous as a mad dog and its domination was more detrimental than Satan. In fact, such people were as good as dead. On the other hand, the spiritually awakened possessed healthy hearts and were close to God. Engrossed deeply in the Lord of the two worlds, they were forgiven their lapses. They were human beings in the real sense, as they had succeeded in suppressing the self. Three letters comprising the word man (*rajl*) stood for devotion, liberality and commitment to good deeds. A real man was one who gave away what he received in the way of God without hoarding, and made the worship of God incumbent on himself as long as he lived. He did not derive any benefit from gold and silver, because they were no better than stones in his eyes. One whose belly was full performed the journey of the world (*safar al-duniya*) and one who remained hungry performed the journey of the hereafter (*safar al-aqiba*). Excessive consumption was the fare of the world, while accepting hunger was provision of the hereafter. Therefore, one who ate less was honoured by all. Food itself was of two kinds – that of the self and that of the heart. The former included eatables, while the latter comprised remembrance of God who was the creator (*zikr khaliq al-makhluqat*). Absolute faith in God (*tawakkul*) lay in giving up the pursuit of livelihood. This was the way of those who were noble and it was a characteristic of prophets. This kind of faith was born out of Islam. It was nothing but calmness, with no trace of unrest. Faith meant replacing material means by mental repose – a state free from anxiety.[14]

Shaikh Hansavi has examined the nature of love (*ishq*), the state of the lover (*ashiq*) and obstacles in the pursuit of the Beloved. Love was a fire which was lighted by the fuel of passion and burnt in the breast of the lover. The word love comprised of three letters of the alphabet that reflected affliction, hardship and exhaustion respectively. These three forms of suffering manifested in the person who fell in love. Yet his heart experienced exhilaration by the excess of love. Love itself was of two kinds, that of the common (*shauq al-awwam*) and that of the elect (*shauq al-khwass*). Love of the common was associated with houris and palaces, while that of the elect was focused on the Lord who was forgiving (*rab al-ghafur*). Love was a great destroyer, as it uprooted homelands (*watn*) and razed homes. It turned the wise into restless and brought immense torment. It was an ailment which did not have a cure and, since the physician was helpless, recovery from it was impossible. A lover was bound with the anguish of heart and rope of friendship. As the door of calamity was open to the lover, his blood was shed by the sword of love (*saif al-ishq*). It was imagined that the lover and Beloved were two spirits that had entered one body. When anyone saw the lover, he also saw the Beloved and vice versa.

Unfortunately, love and reason were not found together in one heart. When the king of love dominated, reason fled. A person who fell in love was deprived of happiness and plunged into a sea of woe. He was buried under the weight of sorrow and his breast was loaded with pain. It was not possible for him to be happy when he was separated from his Beloved. He was like a fish that had fallen in the pit of fire. His state was similar to that of Majnu, who was stricken with madness on being separated from Laila.[15] For him, the separation from his Beloved was like poison, whereas a union with Him was an antidote. In other words, the life of a lover was synonymous with union, but separation amounted to death. In these circumstances, the lover had no alternative but to face hardship and resign himself to the will of the Beloved. If he could develop the faculty of patience, it could prove as effective as prayer.[16]

In the view of Shaikh Hansavi, the role of the spiritual preceptor (Shaikh) was indispensable in any discussion on Sufism, an exercise comparable to the salt in food, light in darkness and spirit in the body. A disciple (*murid*) was bound to hold his preceptor in reverence, which was unconditional and deep. He subjected his will to the will of his preceptor. He absorbed in his mind whatever was inculcated by the preceptor and also acted upon it as long as he lived. During the course of his training, he adorned his exterior with good qualities and corrected any evil disposition by contemplation (*muraqba*). Since the hair on his head appeared as a veil (*hijab*), getting it shorn served as an act of devotion and piety (*iradat wa sawab*).[17] He was required to remain engaged in remembrance of God (*zikr*) and other religious obligations day and night. He should regulate his life on the basis of strict rules of discipline. He should learn to see without eyes, hear without ears, speak without tongue, hold without hands and walk without feet. In other words, he should plunge into his avocation with such commitment that he became a stranger to his surroundings and channelized his natural abilities towards the spiritual quest. He should separate himself from his self (*nafs*) so that his spiritual status rose above fellow beings and djinns.

A disciple should not oppose his preceptor in word or deed. If he did so, it meant that he was lacking in his devotion towards him. If anyone levelled false allegations against a preceptor (or his successor) he suffered loss both in this world and hereafter. If anyone offended a preceptor or his successor, this act amounted to offending God and His messenger. When a disciple went to his preceptor's place, he should not look right and left, but sit with head bowed and eyes closed. If the disciple sat in front of him, he should focus his mind and attentively listen to his advice. When the disciple walked with the preceptor, he remained behind. He should neither be ahead of him, nor on the left or right, because doing so amounted to disrespect. If the disciple looked at the preceptor or looked right and left, without being attentive, it was a show of bad manners leading to the loss of all benefits. A disciple who did not obey his preceptor was rejected in the mystic path (*tariqat*).[18]

Generally common people identified Sufis by their woollen garments (*suf*) and staff (*asa*). In Shaikh Hansavi's discussion, emphasis has been laid on their inner meanings and implied conditions. The three letters comprising the word wool (*suf*) denoted purity, fidelity and self annihilation. The saint (*faqir*) who possessed these qualities reaped the benefits of saintliness. The saint who put on a woollen garment only for fame (*shohrat*) and embellishment (*zeenat*) was forced to weep over his self. The saint who wished to overpower his self should wear the woollen garment and, in so doing, follow the practice of Hazrat Isa.[19] Wearing it for the purpose of acquiring fame was forbidden. A woollen robe (*khirqah*) should be worn by a disciple only with the permission of his mentor (Shaikh) and, with the understanding that, it had no importance of its own and it was the preceptor's order that carried weight. Wearing a woollen garment should be accompanied by purifying the heart. Otherwise, the wearer would be a Sufi in the eyes of the common people, not in the eyes of God. Abu Saeed Abul Khair held that a woollen robe (*khirqah*) was a shroud (*kafn*) of the living,[20] heritage of the prophets and saints (*miras al-anbiya wa al-auliya*), weighing balance of religion and a mark of believers (*alamat ahl al-yaqeen*). It served as a covering of faults and key of the Unseen. It symbolized purity of both the worlds and terror for the dissolute.

As regards the benefits of carrying the staff (*asa*), Shaikh Hansavi mentioned its six qualities as identified by a famous mystic named Hasan Basri.[21] In Sufi practice it was a weapon against dogs and snakes, a support for the weak, a distress for the dissembler (*munafiq*), and an addition to virtuousness. It was believed that if anyone had a staff, the Satan ran away from him and the seditious stood in his fear. That it had thousands of benefits has been shown in an episode concerning Hazrat Musa.[22] When asked what he carried in his right hand, he replied that this was his staff on which he relied to drive his goats and perform many other tasks related to spiritual gains.[23]

During the course of their spiritual quest, the Sufis followed a number of rituals and practices. Each one of them had two aspects, an outer and an inner. The ordinary people felt satisfied only by focusing on the outer aspect, while the Sufis concentrated their minds on the inner aspect. Shaikh Hansavi uncovered the distinction between these two aspects of religious practice and provided a number of examples to illustrate his point. In his understanding, there were two kinds of bath, that of the Shariat (*ghusl al-sharia*) and that of the Tariqat (*ghusl al-tariqa*). In the former, one poured water over the head and body. In the latter, one pleased the preceptor (Shaikh) after committing a sin. In a similar manner, the ablution (*wuzu*) was of two types, that of the Shariat and that of the Tariqat. The former comprised washing one's face, hands and feet with the water of a well or pond. The latter involved bathing the heart with the water of devotion and passion for God. Solitude (*tajrid*), which was often recommended for contemplation, was of two types, external (*suri*) and internal (*maanvi*). In the former, observed by beginners, one removed clothes from one's body. In the latter, associated with the adept, one's mind was cleansed of base qualities and bad habits. In this kind of solitude, the seeker (*salik*) divested his mind of lustful thoughts and subjected it to spiritual exercises (*riyazat al-mujahidat*). The pursuit of asceticism (*tajrid*) required that the heart be distanced from all forms of creation (*al-makhluqat wa al-maknunat*) and turned towards the Creator of heaven and earth. The practice of seclusion (*uzlat*) brought seven benefits. It protected the creation from him. It averted his gaze from what was forbidden. It prevented his ears from listening to what was false. It restrained his tongue from backbiting and foul words. It made him unmindful of moving about. It ensured his perpetual engagement with devotion and prayer. It involved him in the love of God. Travel, the opposite of solitude,[24] was of two kinds viz. outer and inner. The first one meant a journey through villages and towns, while the second one implied moving through the heart and cutting the trees of desires and whims.[25]

Friction with the Rulers

After the death of Shaikh Jamaluddin Hansavi, the Chishti seat of Hansi continued to flourish under his lineal descendants, but it came under the influence of Ajodhan and Delhi. This transition occurred in specific circumstances. Shaikh Hansavi was survived by two sons. Though the elder one was endowed with wisdom and intelligence, his perpetual absorption in higher spiritual states made him appear insane.[26] The younger son Khwaja Burhanuddin was a child. His nurse, known as Madar-i-Mominan, took the boy to Ajodhan. Baba Farid showered him with affection and received his allegiance (*bait*). He not only enrolled him as a disciple, but also conferred his spiritual succession (*khilafat*) on him. On this occasion, he granted a prayer carpet and staff to him and thus formalized his appointment as the head of the Chishti spiritual domain (*wilayat*) of Hansi. These two items had been originally gifted by Baba Farid to Shaikh Hansavi and had now been brought by the nurse to Ajodhan. The step had apparently been taken in anticipation of a final settlement of succession at Hansi. Once this had been done, Baba Farid declared Khwaja Burhanuddin to be his shadow like his father and advised him to live under the tutelage of Shaikh Nizamuddin Auliya. The nurse doubted if the incumbent could carry the onerous responsibilities as he was still a child (*bala*). Baba Farid allayed her apprehensions by saying that even the full moon was small on the first night and grew to its fullness on the fourteenth night (*Punnu ka chand bhi bala hota hai*).

In accordance with the advice of Baba Farid, Khwaja Burhanuddin went to Delhi every year and received instructions from Shaikh Nizamuddin Auliya. However, even after reaching adulthood and acquiring numerous virtues, he did not enrol disciples. He could do so because a Sufi of the eminence of Shaikh Nizamuddin Auliya was there. Owing to his modesty, he did not lie on the cot in the living space (*jamaat khana*) of his mentor's hospice at Delhi. However, on such occasions, he invariably wore fine clothes and anointed himself with perfume, because this was the proper conduct while meeting a spiritually accomplished saint. He repeated this act as many times he met his mentor in a day.[27]

Shaikh Qutbuddin Munawwar, the son and successor of Khwaja Burhanuddin, had been brought up in an environment imbued with mysticism and therefore had developed an early interest in the discipline. Following the footsteps of his father, he trained under the tutelage of Shaikh Nizamuddin Auliya. Interestingly, he completed his training at the same time as Shaikh Nasiruddin Mahmud (who later became popular as Chiragh-i-Delhi) and also received his certificate of succession (*khilafatnama*) on the same day. In accordance with prevailing conventions, Shaikh Nizamuddin Auliya summoned Shaikh Munawwar and, after giving him the document and suitable instructions, directed him to offer the double prayer (*dogana*). Shaikh Nasiruddin Mahmud was then asked to undergo the same exercise. Shaikh Nizamuddin Auliya asked them to congratulate each other for receiving their mandates of succession and to embrace each other. The mentor made it clear that they were equal like brothers and that there was no difference between them on account of any difference in their respective periods of discipleship. The ceremony over, Shaikh Nasiruddin Mahmud suggested to his colleague that they should share the advice (*wasiyat*) given by their mentor, so that both of them benefited. Shaikh Munawwar did not accept the proposal, saying, 'The instructions of the spiritual master are secret, which have been revealed to this slave. This secret cannot be divulged to anyone else. Your secret is for you, whereas mine is for me.'[28] Shaikh Nasiruddin Mahmud agreed that the parting advice of the Chishti examplers to their disciples differed from case to case and that its content was possibly determined by the ability and aptitude of each as an individual.

Before Shaikh Munawwar departed for Hansi, Shaikh Nizamuddin Auliya gave a copy of the manuscript of *Awarif-ul-Maarif* to him and related the background of this gesture. The manuscript had been originally given by Baba Farid to Shaikh Jamaluddin

Hansavi (the grandfather of Shaikh Munawwar) when the latter received his certificate of succession. During the course of Shaikh Nizamuddin Auliya's visit to Hansi,[29] Shaikh Hansavi presented this manuscript to his friend and requested, 'I give this valuable manuscript along with all the blessings of our mentor. I hope that when one of my sons comes to you, you will not deprive him of the worldly and religious beneficence possessed by you.' Amir Khurd has stated that the then living descendant of Shaikh Hansavi, Shaikh Nuruddin, had preserved this manuscript with reverence.[30] The Chishtis of Hansi treated the manuscript as a sacred treasure and family inheritance. It served as a link of the Chishtis of Hansi with Ajodhan on the one hand and with Delhi on the other.

Shaikh Qutbuddin Munawwar was a mystic of high order. His personality was marked by knowledge, wisdom, love, abstinence and sorrow. He did not believe in ceremony and artificiality. He remained unaffected by crowds and noise. He kept away from people who were worldly. Following the footsteps of his ancestors, he remained immersed in the remembrance of God (*zikr*). He was content with whatever was received from the divine source. He avoided any contact with the powerful and privileged. He remained confined to his hereditary abode and left it only to offer Friday prayer or visit the tombs of his forefathers. It was another matter that the people living in the surrounding areas visited Hansi to benefit from his spiritual excellence. His eloquence had such a mesmerizing impact on the listeners that the fire of spiritual love was ignited in them. He loved his preceptor Shaikh Nizamuddin Auliya with the intensity of his entire being. On hearing just his name, Shaikh Munawwar would begin to weep with such passion that even the members of the gathering would follow the suit. He would feel the presence of his mentor even when the latter was physically absent. Acting in conformity with the Chishti practice, he enthusiastically participated in musical sessions (*sama*). His presence was noted at the death anniversary of his mentor, held at the mausoleum of the great Sufi in Delhi. It was also attended by fellow saints like Shaikh Nasiruddin Mahmud and Shaikh Shamsuddin Yahya. The chorus had such a deep impact on Shaikh

Munawwar that he started weeping and tears flowed through his beard like genuine pearls. In this state of ecstasy (*wajd*), he began to place his head on the feet of other members of the assembly and, while doing so, repeatedly intoned:

Zinda am man ba-yaad shaikh bale
Jan-i man yad shaikh shud aare
Yes, I am alive in the remembrance of my shaikh,
My life has become a remembrance of my shaikh alone.

Amir Khurd, who was present in this assembly, nurtured fond memories of Shaikh Munawwar's joyous state as well as his reference to the spiritual secrets of Shaikh Nizamuddin Auliya. On this occasion, Shaikh Munawwar was staying in a building adjacent to the dome of late Khwaja-i Jahan. Amir Khurd, whose father had sent food for Shaikh Munawwar, was deeply impressed on finding that the saint's face reflected his love soaked interior. While relishing the food, Shaikh Munawwar kept on smiling and said to Amir Khurd, 'Many times I have eaten meals cooked by your grandmother who was a disciple of Baba Farid. Since we have claims on each other, we must strengthen our mutual relations. I look forward to divine forgiveness in accordance with a Prophetic tradition, which stated that a person who ate food with a forgiven one is also forgiven.'[31] This episode, on the one hand, underlined the Chishti saint's humanism and, on the other, showed his proximity to the family of Amir Khurd.

True to the Chishti tradition, Shaikh Munawwar was kind to a fault and provided material help to the needy. In this context, there were two cases which provided insight into the social attitude of the Chishti order in general and Shaikh Munawwar's interaction with different social groups in particular. In the first incident, a Qalandar suddenly appeared before Shaikh Munawwar when the latter was engaged in meditation. Acting without any provocation, the Qalandar began to hurl abuses on the Shaikh. The next moment, he paused with the hope of receiving some alms. Keeping his cool, Shaikh Munawwar started giving him one item after the other. The Qalandar refused to be satisfied. When his meanness crossed all limits, Shaikh Munawwar asked him to spend what he had tied to his waist. A disciple Syed Kamaluddin began to grapple with the Qalandar. A purse, which had been tied to the Qalandar's girdle, opened and several silver coins (*tankas*) fell out. According to the second incident, Khwaja Kafur and three companions had been jailed by the contemporary ruler for an unspecified crime. The prisoners had suffered to such an extent that they lost all hope of escaping with their lives or preserving their property. Convinced that they could be saved only by the prayers of a saint, the four sent an emissary to Shaikh Munawwar and requested him to pray for their welfare. They took care to conceal the fact of their punishment and imprisonment. The emissary travelled to Delhi and persuaded Shaikh Munawwar to do the needful. The saint offered a prayer and declared that the three persons would secure their freedom, but the fourth one (who incidentally was a disciple) would not be released as the journey of his life had come to an end. The emissary returned and related the good news to the four persons. After a few days, the prophecy turned out to be true. Three prisoners were released from jail, while the fourth breathed his last.[32] These incidents showed that the Chishtis went out of their way to help people in distress, even though the beneficiaries did not always nurture honest intentions.

Amir Khurd has provided us with the context in which Shaikh Munawwar was offered a grant of two villages by Muhammad bin Tughluq. This offer was made neither to encourage the Shaikh to continue his spiritual activities, nor to improve the management of his hospice at Hansi. In fact, the Sultan had been giving his ear to false reports communicated by people who were envious of the Shaikh. The Sultan did not like what he heard and therefore wished to proceed against the Shaikh. Since he did not have a suitable excuse, any direct action against the Shaikh was not possible. He decided first to entangle the Shaikh in worldly matters and then to punish him by employing state power. In pursuance of this plan, he prepared a royal order (*farman*) granting two villages to the Shaikh. He deputed Qazi Kamaluddin, the Sadr-i Jahan, with specific instructions to use every device to persuade the Shaikh to accept the said sinecure. Having arrived in Hansi, the Qazi wrapped the document in a handkerchief and concealed it in his sleeve. He did not wish to reveal the purpose of his visit just at the beginning of the meeting. When the Shaikh learnt about the arrival of the Qazi, he came out and sat at the spot which had been sanctified by the presence of Baba Farid. The Qazi placed the order in front of the Shaikh and conveyed the Sultan's sentiments of affection. The Shaikh, while refusing to accept the grant, quoted the precedent of Baba Farid. Sultan Nasiruddin Mahmud (r. 1246-66) and Ghiasuddin Balban, during the course of their visit to Multan and Uch, had offered a grant of two villages to Baba Farid, who said, 'Our senior mentors had never accepted such offers. There are many others who stand in need of these. The grant should be given to them.'

Shaikh Munawwar did not stop at reiterating the Chishti position regarding financial assistance from the state. He admonished the royal emissary in strong language. The Qazi was reminded that he, in addition to holding the office of Sadr-i-Jahan, was also a preacher for the Muslims. If someone deviated from the practice of his spiritual teachers, it was his duty to stop him from such a conduct and give him suitable advice. But he was not expected to encourage the act. Ashamed, the Qazi apologized and took his leave. On meeting the Sultan, the Qazi described the spiritual eminence of the Shaikh in such an effective manner that the Sultan's mind was cleared of misgivings about the Chishti saint of Hansi.[33] However, the Sultan's new state of mind did not last long, as the following episode showed.

Once Muhammad bin Tughluq encamped at village Bansi, which was situated at a distance of 4 *kos* from the town of Hansi. He sent Nizamuddin Nadarbari, who was a personification of tyranny, to inspect the fort of Hansi. While this officer was performing the task, he reached the house of Shaikh Munawwar and felt surprised at the failure of the saint to call on the Sultan. While presenting his report to the Sultan regarding the state of the fort, he complained that Shaikh Munawwar, who was a disciple of Shaikh Nizamuddin Auliya, had not cared to pay the customary visit to the Sultan. Conscious of the royal privilege, the Sultan sent an arrogant person Hasan Sarbarhana to bring Shaikh Munawwar to his presence. Hasan reached Shaikh Munawwar's house and, after offering salutation and shaking hands, conveyed the Sultan's summons. Shaikh Munawwar, who was taken by surprise, wished to know if he had any right in the invitation. Replying in the negative, Hasan asserted that he was under royal orders to escort the saint to the Sultan. Shaikh Munawwar was shocked at the answer and declared that he was accepting the summons against his will and, addressing the members of his family, said that he was leaving them under the care of God. Placing the prayer carpet on his shoulder and carrying the staff in his hand, Shaikh Munawwar set out to meet the Sultan. When Hasan discerned the signs of spirituality on the saint's forehead, he requested him to ride on one of the horses. Shaikh Munawwar refused the offer as he possessed the strength that was needed to walk. On the way, he sought leave to pay homage at the tombs of his ancestors. Having secured the permission, he stood at the edge of the graves and respectfully submitted, 'I am not leaving your sacred precincts by my own free will, but I am being carried from here by force. I am leaving my dependents without the means of expenditure.' As soon as he emerged from the graveyard, he saw a man holding some money in his hands. The man said, 'I had taken a vow and, since it has been fulfilled, I have brought this offering for you as a token of my gratitude.' Shaikh Munawwar accepted the offering and asked the man to deliver it to his family, which did not have anything for their maintenance.

Thus freed from worries regarding his household, Shaikh Munawwar left Hansi and covered the distance of 4 *kos* upto Bansi on foot. The Sultan was informed about the arrival of the saint, while Hasan Sarbarhana related his personal observations about him to his master. Owing to the arrogance of power, the Sultan did not show the courtesy which was due to the visitor. Instead of inviting the saint for a meeting, he abruptly left for Delhi. It appeared that the Sultan avenged himself for the humiliation he might have felt at the failure of Shaikh Munawwar to honour him by a visit at Hansi.

On reaching Delhi, the Sultan again summoned Shaikh Munawwar to his presence. The Shaikh left for Delhi, but he had apprehensions regarding the impending meeting in view the recent unpleasantness. He said to the Sultan's cousin Firoz Shah,[34] who held the post of Naib Barbak, 'We are saints. We are not familiar with the customs of the royal courts and the manner of conversing with kings. We would act in accordance with your advice.' Referring to the misinformation spread by the vested interests, Firoz Shah replied, 'Some people have put in the mind of the Sultan that you do not pay any regard to kingly authority and royal protocol. It would be appropriate for you to conduct yourself with equanimity and gentleness.' When the Shaikh entered the precincts of the royal palace, his son Shaikh Nuruddin panicked on seeing large crowds of high ranking nobles and their aristocratic bearing. The Shaikh assured him that the real greatness belonged only to God, so that the boy overcame his fear of the royal court and saw the mighty nobles as docile goats.

When the Shaikh reached the stipulated place, the Sultan made another attempt to slight the visitor and began to practice with his bow. As soon as he saw the signs of saintliness on the Shaikh's forehead, the Sultan changed his attitude and began to show respect. During the formal handshake, the Shaikh held the Sultan's hand in an unusually tight grip. The author of *Siyar-ul Auliya* observed that the Sultan, who sought to bring the saints of God under his sword through sheer tyranny, turned into a devotee from the core of his heart. Complaining in a mild tone, the Sultan said, 'I came to your town, but you did not give me your advice. Nor did you honour me with a meeting.' The Shaikh replied, 'First take a look at my town of Hansi and then cast a glance at this son of a saint of Hansi. I do not consider myself fit to meet the kings. I am residing in a corner, but engaged in praying for the welfare of the king and Muslims. Kindly treat me as helpless.' The Sultan's attitude was softened by this reply. He wished to know the Shaikh's immediate desire which could be fulfilled. The Shaikh stated that his object was three fold – to serve God, to serve the legacy of his ancestors and to serve his spiritual guide Shaikh Nizamuddin Auliya. This was a most cogent articulation of the Chishti mystic ideology and, by implication, the attitude of Chishtis towards the state, which had been making a brazen display of hegemonic pretensions.[35]

Amir Khurd would have us believe that the Sultan was deeply

impressed by Shaikh Munawwar on account of his fearless disposition, a powerful handshake and spiritual excellence. The Sultan also blamed the people who, out of jealousy, had conveyed false reports about the Shaikh. In order to make amends for his wrong judgement and seal a new relationship, the Sultan sent Firoz Shah and Ziauddin Barani with a gift of one lakh *tankas* for the Shaikh. As expected, it was unthinkable for the Shaikh to accept such a large amount of cash from the ruler of the Delhi Sultanate. The Sultan sent the emissaries a second time with a gift of 50,000 *tankas*. On this occasion too, the Shaikh stuck to his guns. The Sultan was perplexed. He feared that his credibility would be undermined in the eyes of the nobles and Sufis, besides the people at large. The Sultan, with the object of retrieving the prestige of the state, deputed Firoz Shah and Ziauddin Barani to persuade the Shaikh to accept the gift of cash. After much discussion, the amount was brought down to 2,000 *tankas*. The two representatives pleaded their inability to inform the Sultan that the Shaikh would not accept even a sum of 2,000 *tankas*. Still adamant, the Shaikh asked, 'What would a mendicant, who needed just two seers of *khichri* and a little clarified butter, do with thousands of *tankas*?' In the end, the Shaikh accepted the amount of 2,000 *tankas* in order to erase any traces of unpleasantness and meet the importunities of sincere friends. This unsolicited charity (*futuh*) was fragmented into four parts for distribution – one portion for the tomb of Shaikh Nizamuddin Auliya, second for the tomb of Shaikh Qutbuddin Bakhtiar Kaki, third for Shaikh Nasiruddin Mahmud and the last one for different individuals.[36]

Shaikh Nuruddin, the son and successor of Shaikh Qutbuddin Munawwar, was the spiritual guide of the historian Shams Siraj Afif. While managing the Chishti hospice of Hansi, he followed the precedents of his ancestors in remaining aloof from the ruling elite. This became evident from a visit of Sultan Firoz Shah Tughluq (r. 1351-88) to Hansi and his meeting with Shaikh Nuruddin.[37] As the Sultan reached the vicinity of the hospice, the Shaikh wished to come out and welcome the royal visitor. The Sultan, out of respect, insisted that the Shaikh should not descend from his seat (*sajjadah*). After the customary exchange of pleasantries and handshake, the two men designated as two kings chosen by the sublime court, engaged in conversation. The Shaikh delivered a sermon like an eminent mystic, while the Sultan spoke like a ruler. The latter stated, 'I have founded the city of Hissar Firoza for the benefit of Islam and comfort of the people. If the Shaikh resides in the new city, a hospice will be built for him and adequate grant will be provided for its maintenance. The town of Hansi is just 10 *kos* from there. Owing to the Shaikh's blessings, Hissar Firoza will be saved from calamities, besides becoming populated and prosperous.' The Shaikh asked if this was a royal command or whether he had a choice. The Sultan pleaded his inability to issue an order to the Shaikh who was free to take a decision. In response, the Shaikh expressed his intention to continue residing at Hansi which was the place of his ancestors and it had been bestowed on them by Baba Farid and Shaikh Nizamuddin Auliya. The Sultan admitted that it was proper for the Shaikh to stay in Hansi and hoped that Hissar Firoza would also flourish owing to his blessings. The Sultan's hope was adequately realized. Afif would have us believe that when Timur plundered the Muslims and Hindus of Delhi, the people of Hansi and the part of Hissar Firoza that had been administratively merged with Hansi, remained safe as they constituted the spiritual domain of Shaikh Nuruddin and therefore enjoyed the blessings of God.[38]

Bu Ali Qalandar and His Masnavi

It is difficult to reconstruct a sober account of the life of Bu Ali Qalandar, owing to the near absence of reliable contemporary evidence and profusion of miraculous stories in later hagiographies. In particular, there are difficulties in establishing his parentage, chronology of career, allegiance to existing Sufi orders and the name of his mentor. He was said to have been the son of Fakhruddin Iraqi, the Sufi poet who lived in Multan under the tutelage of Shaikh Zakariya.[39] It was more certain that he lived in the late thirteenth and early fourteenth century, as some events linked him to the Khalji rulers, Shaikh Nizamuddin Auliya, Amir Khusrau, Shamsuddin Turk Panipati and Sharfuddin Yahya

Maneri. The author of *Akhbar ul-Akhyar* has rejected the tradition according to which Bu Ali Qalandar had offered allegiance (*bait*) to Khwaja Qutbuddin Bakhtiyar Kaki or Shaikh Nizamuddin Auliya. Since, unlike most mystics, he did not join any spiritual preceptor, he was categorized as an Uwaisi, i.e. one who was instructed by the spirit (*ruhaniyat*) of a spiritual master. According to a popular tradition, Bu Ali Qalandar stood for twelve years in a river waiting for a spiritual guide and, during this period, the fish nibbled away the flesh on his calves. An old man, who revealed his identity as Hazrat Ali, helped him emerge out of water and communicated some divine secrets. Bu Ali Qalandar offered a prayer in gratitude to God and kissed the feet of Hazrat Ali and, in view of this, earned the suffix of Bu Ali (fragrance of Ali) to his name Shah Sharfuddin.

In contrast to the Uwaisi tradition, Abul Fazl has sought to place the career of our saint in a more conventional mould. Writing on the authority of the saint's autobiographical account, Abul Fazl stated that he studied in Delhi under the care of several scholars and, after receiving their permission, served as a teacher and judge for twenty years. On receiving an unexpected call from God, he threw his books into the Jamuna and set out on travels. While in Roumelia, he met Shamsuddin Tabrezi and Jalaluddin Rumi, who presented him with a robe, a turban and many books. However, he threw the books into a river in their presence and returned to settle in Panipat.[40] During this phase of his life, he might have adopted the path of Qalandars. He discarded the typical Qalandari garb of the perpetual wanderer and went on to establish a hospice at Panipat in line with the distinguished Chishtis of Panjab and Delhi. Yet he did not distance himself from his association with the Qalandari path, as confirmed by a permanent addition of a second suffix to his name, Qalandar. As such, it became understandable that he be recognized as a prominent representative of a distinct offshoot of the Chishti order, Chishtiyya Qalandariyya.

Like other Sufis, Bu Ali Qalandar was reputed to possess miraculous powers. Hagiographies attribute a large number of incredible feats to him. Many of them were too outlandish to be accepted, but they provided subtle insights into his contribution to Islamic spirituality, his relations with diverse sections of society (contemporary rulers, fellow mystics and ordinary folk) and the construction of his memory by posterity. If the hagiography was any indication, Bu Ali Qalandar was a colourful figure who exercised wide influence, so that the doors of his hospice were open to one and all. Let us take a quick look at some of his miracles. On one occasion, while sitting on the top of a wall, he made it move up and down as if it was offering salutation to a mendicant. On another occasion, he caused the Jamuna to recede 7 miles from its course, because the fish had injured his legs during penance. He succeeded in infusing fresh life into a servant's son, who had died for disobeying the saint. He forced a marriage party to disappear for creating intolerable noise, but brought it back after it agreed to make an offering of three maunds of provisions (*faqiri niyaz*) for his hospice. His blessings enabled a number of barren women to bear sons, as he gave them betel leaf chewed by him. He became directly instrumental in converting a Hindu boy Amar Singh to Islam along with his entire clan, so that the convert was able to marry within his kinship group and also secure his parental property.[41]

Bu Ali Qalandar was held in high esteem by Sultan Alauddin Khalji (r. 1296-1316), who expressed his feelings by constructing a mausoleum for him. A deep bond of affection had grown between him and Prince Qutbuddin Mubarak Khalji. But the Prince, it was believed, died for violating the saint's order of throwing away the leftovers of his food. The Prince was buried within the precincts of the hospice and, the saint, after his death, was laid to rest alongside in accordance with his passionate desire. It was believed that the members of the Tughluq royal family (Ghiasuddin Tughluq, Muhammad bin Tughluq and Firoz Shah Tughluq) paid a visit to the hospice and Bu Ali Qalandar expressed his joy at the sight of three kings eating together from the same platter. Not only this, Bu Ali Qalandar prevented Sultan Ghiasuddin Tughluq from consummating his marriage with a woman who happened to be his (Sultan's) own daughter. Bu Ali Qalandar and Shaikh Nizamuddin Auliya had a lot of mutual regard, as the two exchanged views on Islamic mysticism. He was visited by Amir Khusrau, the greatest Persian poet of the times, and left a deep impact on him by his own verses. His blessings were said to have contributed to the spiritual eminence of two contemporary Sufis, Shaikh Sharfuddin Yahya Maneri and Lal Shahbaz Qalandar. It was claimed that Bu Ali Qalandar assumed the form of a lion in the presence of a mystic Shaikh Jalaluddin, who was passing through the Bhagwati jungle in the vicinity of Panipat. Since he did not wish to frighten the visitor, he resumed the human form and received the loving attention of four lions. He developed a special relation with Shaikh Shamsuddin Turk, a spiritual successor of Shaikh Alauddin Ali Ahmad Sabir. The latter was said to have sent a disciple to the saint with a message, 'If you see Bu Ali Qalandar riding a tiger, ask him that a tiger should live in the jungle.' The disciple, on seeing the saint in this condition, conveyed the message. In response, Bu Ali Qalandar left the town and went into the jungle. This miraculous story showed that he did not oppose the arrival of Shaikh Shamsuddin Turk to Panipat and, instead of harbouring any rivalry, indicated that both could exist in the same spiritual domain (*wilayat*).

It was not surprising that the ways of Bu Ali Qalandar should have given offence to the orthodox elements. There were instances when he came into conflict with the Muslim theologians. Abdul Haq Muhaddis Dehalvi has recorded one such incident. Since Bu Ali Qalandar did not pay any attention to his physical appearance, his moustaches grew beyond the permissible limits. His disciple noticed the transgression, but could not muster the courage to ask his master to trim it down to the proper length. Maulana Ziauddin Sunami, who was a strict adherent of the Shariat as well as a Mufti (interpreter of canonical law), took the matter in his own hands. He went up to Bu Ali Qalandar and asked for a pair of scissors. He held his beard with one hand and trimmed his moustaches to permissible length. Interestingly, Bu Ali Qalandar was not offended. From that day onwards, he often kissed his beard and declared, 'It has been caught in the path of the Shariat.'[42] However, his sense of humour did not rule out another clash with the orthodoxy. He happened to see a beautiful woman (the wife of his servant) and, slipping into a long trance, discontinued his normal food and prayers. When anyone inquired about his dramatic change, he merely repeated a single phrase, 'Only God is faultless. The rest is all lust (*be aib zat allah ki, baqi hawas*).' Maulana Ziauddin Sunami confronted Bu Ali Qalandar and tried to bring him to the right path. But the saint argued that he, being intoxicated (*mast al-mast*), was exempted from the obligation of prayers. He went on to assert his superiority by working a miracle. He agreed to offer the prayer only if the Mufti could bind him with a rope by his miraculous ability. When this was done, Bu Ali Qalandar unwound the rope and thus embarrassed the Mufti. However, he relented and offered the prayer while the jurist acted as the leader (*imam*) for the occasion. The Mufti finished the task, but found that Bu Ali Qalandar continued in the same state. On being asked to explain his strange conduct, the saint turned the tables on the Mufti by revealing that even he (the Mufti) did not have his heart in the prayer, as he was constantly worried about his newly born foal who could fall into a pit of grain.

The Mufti, who had repeatedly been put to shame, tried to retrieve his credibility. Securing the support of the local clerics and common people, he prepared a decree (*mahzarnama*) in which Bu Ali Qalandar was accused of violating the tenets of Islam and was directed to fall in line with the Shariat. Bu Ali Qalandar expressed his helplessness on the grounds that he was in a state of intoxication, that this state was a gift of God and that he was merely following God's will. He received the support of Khwaja Ali Ansari, but the Mufti filed a case in the court of the *qazi*. Accepting the plea of the Khwaja, which itself was based on a Quranic verse, the *qazi* ruled that the accused was not bound by the Shariat on the issue of prayer, as he was not in his senses. The accused was exonerated of the charges, while the Mufti was put to shame.[43]

Fortunately for us, Abdul Haq Muhaddis Dehalvi has included a section (*maktubat*) in his biographical sketch of Bu Ali Qalandar. Structured in the form of sixteen pieces of advice, the saint laid down the fundamental postulates of his mystical thought. His aim was to instruct the seeker, who was repeatedly addressed as 'Oh Brother' and who stood at the threshold of his spiritual journey. He touched upon a variety of themes – the beauty of creation, the quest of the lover for the Beloved, the damaging impact of earthly pleasures and the concept of heaven and hell – that were connected with one another. He urged the seeker to open his eyes and see the manner in which God had created the world out of sheer love and, in the process, constructed an amazing spectacle. God concealed his love for the creation in every tree and imparted every fruit with a distinct taste. But He did not let this fact be known to the tree itself. He injected sweetness in sugarcane as well as various types of fragrance in musk deer, sea horse and sandalwood. But He did not let these plants and animals know that they were endowed with these bounties. It had to be understood that the creation appeared before humankind in different shapes and forms, yet it was able to discern the same divine element in each of them.[44] One might take a piece of jaggery and fragment it into a hundred balls. Further, one might mould these balls into different forms and give them different names. So long as these objects retained shapes and names, they appeared entirely distinct from one another. Once these objects were combined into one, they lost their individual identity and the single ingredient remained, i.e. a piece of jaggery.[45]

A seeker was required to gain true knowledge which, in fact, involved becoming familiar with one's own true self. Once this was achieved, the secrets of love were automatically revealed to him. The seeker must become a lover and seek the Beloved in himself, so that immense beauty was reflected in the mirror of his heart. The seeker had to realize that it is God who, owing to His mercy, had saved him from selfishness and filled his heart with love and thus made him see the magnificence of beauty. As soon as he was able to discern love, he became a true lover of the Beloved. He must recognize that God had created the Beloved in his (seeker's) image and that He had placed the Beloved inside the seeker, so that he was guided on the right path. He must understand that God (Beloved) had created him out of His love for him, so that he was able to observe His beauty in the mirror of his heart, to make him a confidant of His secrets and thus to assert His presence in his glory.[46]

He is that Beloved who is coveted by all.
He is the same who has covered His face with your sheet.
Why should we go to the jungle owing to the grief of separation,
Because the Beloved is very much in your embrace.

It was incumbent on the seeker to become a true lover and to focus perpetually on the beauty of the Beloved. He must view the day of judgement as the domain of Prophet Muhammad and this world as that of the devil. He must endeavour to discover the cause underlying the existence of these two domains, each of which was the antithesis of the other. He must identify his baser instincts (*nafs*) and soul (*ruh*), the former for understanding the nature of this world (*duniya*) and the latter for comprehending the import of the day of judgement (*akhirat*). God is constantly engaged in cleansing the mirror of the seeker's heart, so as to reveal His beauty to him and to reassure the love stricken lover that He is really the Beloved. The seeker was expected to fill His heart with the love and beauty of the Beloved and, immersing himself entirely in this love, overlook everything else. Further, he must try to discern the happenings in the unseen world and to conduct himself in accordance with this rare form of knowledge.[47]

Bu Ali Qalandar came down heavily against attachment to the material world and gratification of senses. When man was overpowered by his baser instincts, he was entangled in the mundane matters of this world and fell into the depths of degradation. While enjoying the physical pleasures of life, he was not aware of his inner plight. He was merely attracted to the outward glitter of his physical environment. Oblivious of his real loss, he failed to distinguish between right and wrong. In this state, he did not know what to love and what to shun. His condition became so irreversible and unredeemable that he refused to fear death and the day of judgement. He became blind to the fact that the true Beloved (God) exercises unquestioned sovereignty over this world and that He is free to impose His will in his vast kingdom. Only when struck with misfortune, he realized that his miserable condition was caused by his own impure thoughts and baser instincts. The visible beauty of this world was, in fact, the beauty of infidelity (*kufr*). Whoever fell in love with this world had, in reality, adopted the beauty of infidelity (*husn-i kufr*) as his beloved. Only the true lover could discriminate between the two kinds of beauty – sublime and false, divine and worldly. However, it was possible for him to extricate himself from the worldly trap if he came across a spiritual mentor, who was not only kind and sympathetic, but who also made him understand the real nature of the physical world.[48]

In an insightful analysis of a wide range of Sufi literature, Bruce Lawrence has drawn our attention to the works of Bu Ali Qalandar. In his view, two of them, *Hukmnamah* and *Hikmatnamah*, are spurious. But the other two, *Masnavi* and *Maktubat*, have all the markings of authenticity. These compositions are concise and direct, besides retaining a lyrical softness even when the poet's mood became sardonic.[49] He writes, 'Bu Ali Qalandar storms the world of literary conformity, just as his reclusive but chiding presence must have affronted the comfortable Muslim saints of the Punjab. He is fresh, outrageous and uncompromising.'[50] These traits were forcefully reflected in the verses of his *Masnavi*. A perusal of its text shows that he discerned God in the beauty of plants and animals. A seeker could approach God by developing a relation of intense love, provided he shunned material temptations and practiced abstinence. He was deeply concerned about the moral decadence of the society in general and warned the seekers against the charlatans who posed as Sufis. However, the entire poem deserved a closer look.

According to our poet, when the seeker suppressed his worldly passion, the picture of the Beloved was reflected on the mirror of his heart. When the person of faith (*ahl-i yaqeen*) opened his eyes, he saw the beauty of the Beloved in every direction, besides feeling His presence in the inflamed notes of every melody. Whatever became visible was nothing but the essence of God (*zat-i haq*). God is present not only on the earth and in the sky, but also where nothing exists. He is found in every particle, whether manifest or concealed. The Beloved shows His splendour (*jalwa*) in everything. The seeker needed to be vigilant if he wished to experience the divine presence.[51] He was required to know that God possesses unmatched creative power. God had created innumerable forms, whether the mystic saw them as attractive or repulsive, blissful or baneful, good or bad. God had created rain, lightning and springs. He had created the darkness of night and the light of sun and moon. He had created stones, diamonds, gems and pearls. He had created water, fire, and air. He had created living creatures like birds, fish, snakes, ants and lions. Such was His creative power that he used merely a drop of water to generate a pearl in a seashell (*sidaf*). The treasure of His secrets was discerned in the mine of life.[52] In His role as the Beloved, God had conferred specific qualities on flowering plants that fascinated the medieval poets. Hyacinth (*sumbul*) acquired its intricate pattern from His curls. Water lily (*lala*) acquired its stains from His face. The fir tree (*susan*) employed a hundred tongues to describe His eminence. The rose bud (*ghuncha*) blossomed into a flower out of its yearning for Him. The flower of narcissus (*nargis*), which was afflicted with divine love, opened the inner eye and placed the golden cup in the silvery palm. The cypress tree (*saru*), owing to its impressive height, received a rich green foliage from head to toe. The nightingale (*bulbul*) and dove (*qamri*) lamented their distinct voices and raised much noise in the garden but, in doing so, they appeared to sing God's praise. When the musical notes emanated from the rebeck (*rubab*) and harp (*chang*), the pain springing from the listener's heart singed his chest.[53]

Har che bini dar haqiqat jumla u ast
Shama wa gul wa parwana bulbul ham az ust
Har che ayad dar nazar az juz wa kul
Bum sehra bulbul bostan wa gul[54]

In reality everything that is observed with the eye
Flame, flower, moth and nightingale had come from Him.
Whatever came within the vision whether complete or part
Includes land, desert, nightingale, garden or flower.

Since God is beautiful, He remains present in the heart of the seeker who, however, is unaware of this reality and wanders in confusion.[55] He was expected not to love anyone other than God. He had to recognize that God is his greatest benefactor. God not only provides him with necessities of life, but also confers a number of boons on him. On the one hand, God provides him with the means – eyes, ears, nose and tongue – to enjoy the senses. On the other hand, God reveals the hidden secrets (*asrar nihan*) to him. Unfortunately, the seeker is unmindful of God's kindness. He does not realize that God, in spite of His position as the Beloved of the world (*mashuq majaz*) gazes at him with pride (*naaz*) as if He is Himself the lover. The seeker, who goes in pursuit of the Beloved, transforms his entire self into an eye and sees the face of the Beloved. If the inner eye of the seeker opens, he realizes that the Beloved is Himself in love with him and that He is present in him like the life in his body. In fact, God's desire for the seeker is greater than that the seeker has for God. If he fails to look at God with the proper gaze, his vision is blocked even if God remains unveiled. The seeker, while engaged in his pursuit of God, is advised to die before his death. If he sacrifices his life for his Beloved, the Beloved manifests (*jalwagar*) Himself in his self.[56]

The seeker is further instructed to see himself with the eye of the Beloved. The union of the seeker and the Beloved is a moment of joy. If the seeker is unable to feel happy, he can undertake mourning of separation (*matam hijran*). It is important for the seeker to realize that the abode of His beloved is only a step from him (*manzil janan bud yak gam tu*). What is equally favourable, his cup is overflowing with the wine of mystical knowledge (*badah-irfan*). He is required to drink the cup of love every moment and take a step forward to unite with the Beloved. In such a situation, a person, who is as insensitive as a stone, cannot remain unaffected. However, sometimes the fault lies with the seeker who is not able to avail of the opportunity. His condition is that of a hunter, whose bow is full of arrows and who had spotted the hunted animal, but his arrows miss the target. Therefore, the seeker has to open the eye of his heart, so that he is able to see the face of the Beloved in every direction. The need is to possess an eye that can discern the splendour (*jalwa*) of the Beloved in every form of creation. The face of the Beloved is not concealed. Yet the seeker does not succeed in his aim as his eye does not have the ability to see and his cold heart does not have the passion needed for the grand vision. His condition is as miserable as the ass that is stuck in mud. So long as he remains attached to worldly desires (*nafs*), his eye of faith (*chashm-i yaqeen*) remains blind to the existence of God. So long as he does not develop the instinct to succeed, he will repent at his dismal state until the day of judgement (*hashr*).[57]

The love (*ishq*) of the seeker for the Beloved is characterized by passion and intensity. So long as the lover retains his own existence, he is unable to merge with the Beloved. Once he erases his own existence, the possibility of his union with the Beloved opens up. The lover seeks to acquire such nearness to the Beloved that he does not feel separate from Him even for a moment. The lover prays for the love of the Beloved to injure his heart in a manner that he ceases to live. He wishes being pulled towards the Beloved as he himself has lost the way. He hopes that his heart, which has withered owing to separation from the Beloved, can be revived by his love. A lover, whose heart is illuminated by the light of love (*nur ishq*), receives fresh life for all times owing to the kindness of the Beloved. Since this love is true and sublime, it is not profane or superficial. It has nothing to do with physical penance – like standing upright with head down and feet up – that fascinates others and brings fame. Such love can not be compared with the actions of worldly lovers: Majnun who excelled in pursuit of physical love, Laila who was driven by her intense longing (*niyaz*), Shireen who underwent unprecedented suffering, or Farhad who struck his own head with a hammer (*tesha*). A true lover does not pick flowers of different varieties, nor sees himself in different roles. Instead he endeavours to enter the house of unity (*khanah-i wahdat*) and loose himself in the quest for union with the Beloved.[58]

The lover needs a heart that leads him to the Beloved with the musical instrument of love (*saz ishq*). This love displays extraordinary characteristics and, in this sense, it is a rare phenomenon. It can tear the apparel of life (*jama-i hasti*) and fly without wings. It can lead the lover to omnipresent God (*la makan*). It can impart perfection to reason. It can push the seeker to a state of madness. It can raise the lover above the distinction between piety and evil. It can push the lover to the state of intoxication (*halat-i mastaan*) and forgetfulness (*framoshi*). However, the wine of love is different from the alcoholic beverage, which causes only a momentary inebriation. For the lovers, it means nothing but the pain received from the Beloved. In an effort to trace the origin of love (*asl ishq*), one is led to conclude that it is the Beloved who imparts the beauty of life to love. When the beauty of the Beloved gazes at itself, He is attracted to Himself and causes the manifestation of love. This love, like that of Jibrail,[59] is the ascension of beauty (*miraj husn*). It places a hundred crowns on the head of the lover. It enables the lover and Beloved to merge into each other, so that everything else cases to exist.[60]

Once the seeker becomes familiar with the secrets of love (*asrar-i ishq*), he ought to surrender himself to love and embark on its quest in the right earnest. This task cannot be performed by the ignorant (*kham tabiyan*) and sensual (*bu ul-hawas*). A seeker, who loses his life in the path of love, receives a fresh life every moment from the other world.[61] Fortunate is the seeker, who plunges into the gamble of love (*qimar-i ishq*) and, losing everything, achieves union with the Beloved. Since the seeker adopts the path of abstinence and faith (*zuhd wa taqwa*), he needs to suppress his worldly desires. His heart becomes oblivious of both the worlds so that, owing to his preoccupation with the reality (*haqiqat*), discards all that is profane (*majaz*). Since he has spent a large part of his life in negligence, he is bound to make the best use of the remaining part that is relatively smaller. His life is like the water of a canal (*ab ju*) which, having flowed out of its channel, can not flow back into it. In this situation, the seeker has to overpower his worldly passion and expel evil thoughts from his heart. He must ensure that every hair of his body transforms into a tongue that repeats the name of God (*zikr-i khuda*).[62]

The followers of Bu Ali Qalandar appeared to have been curious about the meaning of piety and abstinence (*zuhd wa taqwa*), terms that figure frequently in discussions on the nature of Sufism. This issue has been assigned a considerable importance, having been taken up right in the beginning of the Masnavi under reference and treated separately from other themes related to Sufism. In the opinion of Bu Ali Qalandar, a seeker (*mard-i faqir*), who adopted the path of piety and abstinence, scrupulously kept away from the ruling elite. He did not compromise his dignity (*abroo*) in return for his basic needs. He shunned the company of the rich (*sohbat ahl-i dul*) and withdrew into a corner. He did not go to the door of the king and did not even see his face, even if he was offered the treasure of Qarun and even if he faced death due to starvation.[63] He should sacrifice his head, but should not give away his self-esteem (*namus*). He should not covet the food of others like a fly, because a bitter taste was better than the sweetness of the sherbet made from rose. The best course for him was to feed only at the dining table of solitude (*khwan qanaat*), so that he did not feel guilty of disobeying God. He should refuse to come out of his self-imposed loneliness and avoid any attachment to the world.[64]

The greatest human weakness was worldly passion which, in turn, generated the greed for wealth and ambition for power. If one looked at fire from a distance, it appeared like a garden. In reality, it was nothing but a burning furnace. The same was the case with wealth. If a person did not possess wealth, he should not complain of poverty. After all, wealth did not bring any virtue in its train. The wealthy did not have mercy in their hearts. They employed deceitful means to acquire their riches. They did not hesitate to inflict inhuman cruelty in order to grab wealth, power and status. The brothers of Yusuf of Kinaan threw him alive in a well out of sheer enmity.[65] One who wore a golden crown on his head did not tolerate anyone else. In the footsteps of Nimrod,[66] he was likely to turn away from God and loose his sense of mercy. An increase in wealth led to a corresponding increase in greed. A person, who fell in love with wealth, ceased to have affection for his kith and kin. The rulers, in their passion for wealth and power, deemed it just to kill their own fathers and brothers. No powerless mendicant (*gada-i benawa*) had ever claimed the seat of God for himself. Wealth not only generated arrogance, but also led to the denial of religion. When a person was overpowered by the love of this world, his heart became as hard as stone and his eye of faith (*chashm-i yaqeen*) became blind and, ultimately, the doors of religion were closed to him. So long as a person lived in the company of worldly passion (*nafs kafir*), his life was vulnerable to the fire of hell (*atish-i dozakh*). If he was a man of courage, he could destroy this worldly passion and, in this struggle, he was assisted by the strength of his knowledge and action (*ilm wa aml*).[67]

Bu Ali Qalandar expressed anguish at the prevailing moral degeneration. He observed that a number of virtues, which constituted the foundation of any society, had disappeared leading to a moral crisis. We did not come across love, loyalty and friendship any more. Shame had departed from the eyes. The disposition of the people, who were known for the nobility of their character, had undergone a change. A disturbance had occurred in the domain of gentleness (*diyar-i hilm*), while a famine had struck the kingdom of charity. The field of love and loyalty (*mehr wa wafa*) had dried up. The sword of miserliness had cut the tree of beneficence (*shajrah-i ihsan*). Courage had flown away from this earth like the rare fabulous bird (*anqah*). Both the king and beggar had lost the quality of courage. Those distributing charity had been transformed into starving mendicants. Productivity had gone out of agriculture. Compassion had been erased from the hearts, as the human beings had become as stern as stones. Love was not visible in the hearts of wives and sons, while the daughters quarreled with their mothers. As pious habits disappeared from the world, the nature of human beings became as foul as that of an impure dog. Taken together, these symptoms were the signs of the impending day of judgement. The moral crisis could be overcome only if the human beings discarded their greed for material gains.[68]

Bu Ali Qalandar was concerned about the waywardness of the seeker engaged in making and breaking vows. Such a person often felt guilty for his past conduct and promised to make a fresh start in life. He promised to wash his heart with the water of repentance. He vowed to injure his heart with the thorn of God's love and, in pursuit of this aim, decided to suppress his carnal desires and extraneous thoughts. He promised to offer the obligatory prayer (*namaz*) only after performing the ablution (*wuzu*) with the blood of his heart. However, these promises were short lived. As soon as the night fell, he succumbed to his carnal desires. He was drowned in a colourful spectacle which was dominated by the moon faced bartender (*saqi*), cups of pure red wine, melodious voice of the singer (*mutrib*), sweet sounds of the harp (*rabab*) and bewitching beauty of the beloved. If the means of pleasure were freely available during the night, he spent his money carelessly and enjoyed momentary happiness. However, if the means of pleasure were not available, he remained in a state of depression until morning.[69]

The case of such a seeker was similar to that of a woman whose chastity could not be guaranteed by her covering sheet (*ismat-i bibi bud be chadar*). Since he remained a slave to his weaknesses, he was constrained repeatedly to break his promises. On the one hand, he ignored meditation (*ibadat*) and, on the other, he kept company with lasciviousness (*shahwat*). In fact, he was more depraved than Iblis.[70] His habit was akin to the impure dog that fed on the dead and ran across the streets and jungles. His disposition was like that of a donkey who wandered without any aim. It was from him that the devil (*shaitan*) had learnt the craft of deceit and betrayal (*makr wa fareb*). Such a shameless person could not sleep in peace, as death was chasing him. Yet all was not lost for him. Before it was too late, he could fall in love with the Beloved and thus become the ruler of the kingdom of life. If he broke free from the stranglehold of worldly passion, he could achieve his spiritual aims in the future (*aqibat*). If he wished to know the divine secrets (*sirr-i haq*), he needed to shut his eyes, ears and lips. In other words, he had to suppress the gratification of his senses.[71]

As Bu Ali Qalandar observed the social environment, he found that some Sufis were fake. Maintaining the outward appearance of a Shaikh, such a person did not possess any spiritual quality. He wore an old woollen cloak (*kuhna dilq*), a jacket (*jubba*) and a turban (*dastar*). Apart from a comb and toothbrush, he held a rosary (*tasbih*) in his hands. He was always surrounded by disciples and attendants (*khadims*) who ran all around like him. Carrying out a false propaganda in his favour, they claimed that he was a mystic of the time (*shaikh zaman*), who had already achieved the high spiritual state of annihilation and subsistence (*fana wa baqa*) and his ultimate object was to climb to the highest state of spirituality (*lahut*). He boasted of his miracles to trap innocent men and women in the net of his fraudulent spirituality. He delivered moralistic sermons (*waaz goi*), but did not follow these in his own life. While offering the obligatory prayer, he sat on the prayer rug (*mussalla*) and, closing his eyes, turned his face towards the holy city of Mecca. But his heart hovered around petty worldly matters.

He did bend in prostration (*sajda*), but he did not rub his forehead in humility, nor did he see with the eye of faith (*chashm-i yaqeen*). His prayer only aimed at inducing people to recognize him as a man of faith, piety and abstinence (*muttaqi parhezgar wa parsa*). Therefore, he was advised to look at his own faults, to discard his hypocrisy and to undertake a flight towards his origin (*parwaz su-i asl*).[72]

Such a mystic claimed to be a Sufi, but his heart was not pure. He took pride in his ancestry (*asl wa nasb*) and hankered after fame. He raised his hands in supplication (*dua*) for people, but he did so only with the hope of monetary gain. He forced the people into his subordination by promising to stand as an intercessor (*shafi*) for them before God. He claimed to be a Shaikh merely by keeping the Quran in his armpit and holding a rosary in his hand. He was so presumptuous that he compared himself with the doyen of spiritual masters Bayazid Bistami (d. 874). There were serious doubts about his faith in Islam, as he was guilty of making idols and worshipping them. That was why the light of God (*nur-i khuda*) did not enter his heart and the secrets of God (*asrar-i khuda*) had not been revealed to him. In fact, he was stuck in the mud like a mindless ass.[73] Such a mystic could have emerged from this impasse only if he had broken the idols and demolished the idol house (*butkhana*) and followed this action by constructing a new Kaaba like Khalilullah.[74] However, his biggest failing was greed and ambition (*hirs wa hawas*). Though he had been getting his share of worldly goods, yet he failed to adopt the path of contentment (*qanaat*).[75]

This world was like an old woman (*pir zaal*) who, by her deceit, had reduced the old and young to a state of desperation. The mystics had divorced her a hundred times, because anyone who fell in love with her became defiant towards God. All young men ought to heed what Jalaluddin Rumi had stated on the basis of his experience: it was not possible to desire God as well as this mean world at the same time, because this object was not achievable and it was tantamount to madness. Hazrat Ali discarded worldly pleasures and, in consequence, ruled the kingdom of Prophet Muhammad (*wali mulk-i nabi*) because he had kicked away this old woman.

On the other hand, Yazid took this old woman in marriage and went on to destroy true religion and massacre the innocent. One who partook from the dining table of Yazid came to grief.[76] Anyone who received the help of this old woman lost both worlds. Once the veil was removed from the face of this world, hatred was generated against this old woman. As soon as anyone saw the ugly face of the old woman, it became necessary for him to seek the protection of God.[77]

Arrival of the Sabiris

During the period under study, the Sabiri branch of the Chishtis disseminated the principles of Islamic spirituality in southeast Panjab. However, modern writings have tended to concentrate on the Chishti lineage extending from Khwaja Muinuddin Chishti to Shaikh Nasiruddin Mahmud. The contribution of the Sabiri branch, which flourished on both sides of the Jamuna – Panipat, Shahabad, Kaliyar and Gangoh – has been largely ignored. According to a leading authority, the disciples and devotees of Shaikh Alauddin Ali Ahmad Sabir failed to write his biography. During the seventeenth and eighteenth centuries, hagiographical literature appeared on his life with profuse details, but allegedly relied on miracles and hearsay.[78] However, in case of this lack of contemporary evidence, one could fall back on the later works as a last resort. The following discussion, which aimed at filling large gaps in the role of the Sabiris, is based on the the writings of Allah Diya Chishti, Abdul Rahman Chishti and Muhammad Akram Quddusi.

Shaikh Alauddin Ali Ahmad Sabir was the son of Baba Farid's elder sister Bibi Hajira. His father Syed Abdul Rahim Abdul Salam was a native of Baghdad and, after a prolonged sojourn in Herat, travelled to Panjab. He stayed with Shaikh Jamaluddin Sulaiman (Baba Farid's father) and studied traditional subjects. He married Bibi Hajira and, accompanied by her, returned to Herat where he established himself as a teacher. The couple was blessed with a son named Alauddin Ali Ahmad. The child was born mystic. He consumed little food, often repeated God's name and spent entire nights in prayer. At the age of five, he lost his father.[79] His mother travelled all the way to Kahtwal and placed the boy under the care of Baba Farid. He was thus initiated into the spiritual pursuits. In addition to involvement in obligatory prayers and hard penance (*mujahida*), he managed the community kitchen (*langar*) where nearly 300 people ate twice a day. As for himself, he did not consume even a single grain from the common stock and relied on the leaves and fruit found in the neighbouring jungle. His mother, during the course of a visit, complained to Baba Farid regarding her son's poor physical condition. The lad intervened to explain that he had been ordered to distribute food to the needy, but he had not been asked to partake of it himself. Baba Farid was impressed at his nephew's commitment to the Chishti principles and, conferring the title of Sabir (the patient one), enrolled him as a disciple. From then onwards, Sabir intensified his spiritual quest and, owing to his solitude (*tajrid*) and self annihilation (*istaghraq*), began to experience divine epiphanies (*tajalli*) and divine light (*anwar-i ilahi*). However, his exalted spiritual state began to show traits of wrath (*jalal*), so that none could enter the confines of his spiritual world. As a result, he could not assume the responsibilities of a married life with his cousin (Baba Farid's daughter), failed to get his succession certificate (*khilafatnama*) approved by Shaikh Jamaluddin Hansavi and was unable to take charge of the spiritual domain (*wilayat*) of Delhi.[80]

In these circumstances, Baba Farid issued a new succession certificate to Shaikh Sabir and sent him to establish a new spiritual domain at Kaliyar, a pleasant town situated in the foothills beyond the Jamuna. On reaching Kaliyar, Shaikh Sabir began to deliver sermons (*rushd wa hidayat*) at the Jama Masjid and, owing to his erudition and enthusiasm, left a deep impression on the congregation. The local notables, who were led by the prayer leader (*imam*) Qazi Tabarruk and the administrator Raees Qiwamuddin, placed obstacles in the path of Shaikh Sabir. They objected to his attempt at assuming leadership of prayer (*imamat*) at the Jama Masjid and seeking the allegiance (*bait*) from the Muslim community. They treated Shaikh Sabir's presence as a threat to their social domination and, after mobilizing a majority of the Muslims behind their cause, adopted a hostile attitude towards this outsider.[81] Finding himself at the receiving end, Shaikh Sabir sought the advice of Baba Farid. The veteran mystic assured Shaikh Sabir that once the spiritual domain of Kaliyar had been assigned to him, he had full authority to take any measure deemed necessary on the ground.[82] Matters came to a head when Shaikh Sabir was denied a decent place to sit for prayer in the Jama Masjid. According to hagiographical sources, Shaikh Sabir caused a series of tremors and a collapse of the mosque, leading to the death of all those who were present. Soon after, he caused the destruction of the town, first by a massive fire and then by a deadly plague. He withdrew to a neighbouring forest and began to live among the wild animals. He undertook hard penance, which involved constant fasting and standing still while holding the branch of a Golar tree. Baba Farid sent a disciple Shamsuddin Turk to bring him back to normal state. The visitor assumed the task of serving Shaikh Sabir in a variety of ways – assisting in ablutions, providing boiled fruit of the Golar tree and building a hut for shelter. Having softened the rigours of his austerities, Shaikh Sabir accepted Shamsuddin Turk as a disciple and began to treat him like a son. This disciple lived with his mentor till the end of latter's life.[83]

The spiritual quest of Shaikh Sabir was manifested in the practice of solitude (*tajrid*), starvation (*faqa*), absorption (*jazb wa istaghraq*), penance (*mujahida*) and wrath (*jalal*). It was difficult for anyone to approach him. Though he had mastered traditional and esoteric knowledge, yet he did not teach the Islamic law (*shariat*) and mystical path (*tariqat*) to the ordinary people. His life was characterized by extreme simplicity. His apparel consisted of a sheet (*tehband*) around the waist, a shirt (*kurta*) and a cloak (*khirqa*). The last piece of overgarment was of orange colour (*gul izmani*), which was known to the followers of the Sabiri order as Sabiriyya. While at Ajodhan, he wore a turban and green band (*sabz imamah*) but, on shifting to Kaliyar, he remained bare headed and bare footed. Fond of composing and reciting Persian verses (sonnets and couplets), he employed Ahmad as his nom de plume (*takhallus*), but later on substituted it by Sabir.[84] It has been claimed that he was held in great regard by Shaikh Nizamuddin

Auliya and his disciples. When Amir Khusrau returned to Delhi after paying a visit to Kaliyar, Shaikh Nizamuddin Auliya kissed the poet's hands and eyes as these had been blessed by the touch of Shaikh Sabir.[85] In spite of this display of mutual comraderie between the two branches (Sabiri and Nizami) of the Chishti order, there was a marked difference in their practice of the spiritual path. This became evident when Baba Farid's audition party (Qawwals) related its experiences at Delhi and Kaliyar. In Delhi they found themselves in the midst of a large number of people, enjoyed sumptuous meals and received rich awards. In Kaliyar, however, they found themselves in the midst of a deserted jungle, where they could not meet Shaikh Sabir for five days and even failed to get the minimal amount of food. The Qawwals were constrained to revise their judgement when Baba Farid explained, 'Nizamuddin took care of your worldly needs (*duniya*), while Alauddin sought to handle your hereafter (*aqibat*). But owing to your misfortune, you could not appreciate the superiority of the latter.'[86]

The author of the *Mirat-ul-Asrar*, while identifying the reasons for opposition to Shaikh Sabir at Kaliyar, has built a strong case in his (Shaikh Sabir's) favour. He has argued that the spiritual practices of Shaikh Sabir conformed to those of eminent mystics and, in fact, these were superior in several ways. In his view, the roots of the opposition of some clerics and Sufis of Kaliyar lay in Shaikh Sabir's inclination towards the Qalandars and association with the Abdals. Owing to this tendency, Shaikh Sabir was so deeply immersed in inner purification that he did not pay attention to outer ornamentation. This conduct was in line with the Prophetic tradition according to which the real saints of God had neither any fear nor any sorrow. In fact, this was the method followed by the majority of saints (*qutb abdal*) of every age and the same was reflected in the spiritual states of Shaikh Shamsuddin Tabrezi and Shaikh Fakhruddin Iraqi. The companions of Shaikh Sabir were fearless in living upto this ideal. The level of spiritual accomplishment of the Sufis made them immune to the praise or reproach of the people. If any Sufi, owing to lack of courage, paid attention to the response of the people, he fell from his spiritual state.

Shaikh Nizamuddin Auliya also believed that the aspirant (*salik*) was unable to approach higher spiritual states if there was even a trace of concern for the people. The genuine Sufis were rightly treated as the descendants of the prophets, because their words and deeds conformed to the divine revelation (Quran) and they did not deviate from the injunctions of the prophets. Since they did not violate this position in their (inner and outer) conduct and always searched for the divine object in all forms of creation, they remained entirely free from any kind of sin. Since Shaikh Sabir was one of these saints, he acquired a considerable fame and a large number of followers. The local clerics and Sufis, who were motivated by sheer jealousy, joined hands and conspired to harm Shaikh Sabir, leading to negative consequences as mentioned above.[87]

Abdul Rahman Chishti has tried to show, on the authority of Baba Farid, that Shaikh Sabir's spiritual state was more exalted than that of Shaikh Nizamuddin Auliya. When Baba Farid directed Nizamuddin Auliya to take charge of the spiritual domain of Delhi, he formally advised him to undertake penance (*mujahida*), to always give to others and to avoid receiving anything, so that God would not make him dependent on anyone. However, Baba Farid did not give any advice (*wasiyat*) to Shaikh Sabir. Instead, he merely asked him to go as he would enjoy himself (*ba-ro bhogha hawa hi karo*). According to a well entrenched practice among Sufis acclaimed for their piety, when a disciple reached the stage of perfection and optimized his faith in divine contemplation (*iman mushahida haqiqi*), which amounted to proximity with God, he did not require any advice. Abdul Rahman Chishti admitted that the advice could be interpreted in different ways, depending on the meaning assigned to just one word (*bhogha*). The word in question had at least three meanings – (i) comforts of the world and the hereafter; (ii) the lustre of majestic beauty that was showered on the seeker at the different stages of his spiritual journey and (iii) the intense attraction of God that was experienced by the seeker during contemplation, so that he felt immersed in sublime joy or shone like lightning owing to his passion. Each of these three meanings is suitable as they faithfully reflect Baba Farid's blessings for Shaikh Sabir. According to a different view, the best form of comfort (*rahat*) was amazement (*tahayyur*), experienced by a perfect Sufi (*arif kamil*) when absorbed (*fana*) in the oneness of God (*tauhid*) in a manner that he was lost to himself and his state was similar to sleep. In fact, Prophet Muhammad prayed to God to increase his sense of wonder.[88]

During the course of his training at Kaliyar, Shamsuddin Turk was directed by Shaikh Sabir to join the army of the Delhi Sultanate. He participated in the siege of Chittor, where the Sultan (Ghiasuddin Balban or Alauddin Khalji) was supervising operations. It was found that the ropes of tents had decayed due to the prolonged siege and heavy rains. The soldiers needed a large quantity of yarn for making rope. They went into a neighbouring village and pressurized the inhabitants to part with their yarn. In order to protect the people from harassment, a local Sufi offered to do the needful. He placed a single roll of yarn in a pot and, covering its head, gave it to the soldiers. They were asked to pull one end of the yarn through a small hole in the pot. The soldiers were able to pull out long lengths of yarn from the pot. The Sultan paid a visit to the Sufi and requested him to pray for his victory. The Sufi advised the Sultan to seek the help of a saintly person who was present in the camp and revealed how he could be discovered. During a stormy and wet night, all tents would collapse except the one in which a lamp would be seen burning.

According to another version, a water carrier (*saqqa*) discovered Shamsuddin Turk who possessed miraculous powers. The water carrier, while desperately looking for fire required in the military kitchen during the mighty storm, saw a lamp burning only in one of the tents. He was amazed at the site as lamps in the entire camp had been blown out by the strong wind. Anyhow, he borrowed the fire and delivered it at the kitchen. Next morning, he set out in the same direction to satisfy his curiosity. He saw the same man (Shamsuddin Turk), who had lent the fire, performing ablutions at a pond near his tent. When this man left the place, the water carrier was astonished to find that the entire pond had frozen into ice, while water was warm only at a small spot. After washing his hands and feet, he narrated the miracle to the nobles.

The news reached the Sultan, who rushed to Shamsuddin Turk and sought his intervention for victory. The Sultan was advised to lead an assault on the fort and, as a result, it was occupied.[89] Shaikh Sabir nominated Shaikh Shamsuddin Turk as his principal successor (*khalifa*) and, after communicating the spiritual insights received from Baba Farid, sent him to establish a Chishti hospice at Panipat. The incumbent expressed his reservation about shifting to Panipat, which had been under the spiritual care of a distinguished Sufi named Bu Ali Qalandar. Shaikh Sabir allayed these doubts by stating that the time of Bu Ali Qalandar had come to an end and that he would leave Panipat as soon as he reached there. Three days after the death of Shaikh Sabir, Shaikh Shamsuddin arrived in Panipat and, owing to the lack of any place to stay, sat besides a wall. He filled a cup with milk and, placing a flower on top, sent it to Bu Ali Qalandar. He wished to convey that the spiritual domain of Panipat had been assigned to him, that his functions as a Sufi would in no case interfere in the existing arrangement under the senior saint and that he would himself stay in the place like a flower on the surface of milk.[90] In spite of this friendly gesture, Bu Ali Qalandar picked up his goods and prepared to leave the town. An attempt was made to stop him by a young devotee, who was a seller of sweetmeats (*halwa farosh*). Bu Ali Qalandar explained his resolve to look for another destination as Panipat had been handed over to another person. Identifying the newcomer, he revealed that the man, with specific features and wearing the leather apparel of Qalandars, was sitting besides a wall in a particular street. When the boy reached the spot, he saw a royal falcon being protected by two lions. Dazzled by the radiance of the scene, the boy turned back and reported that it was no longer appropriate to stay in the town. In these circumstances, his mentor left Panipat and settled in village Bodha Khera where he died shortly after.[91]

Shaikh Shamsuddin acquired popularity due to his ability to help the needy. Any person, who was in distress owing to any reason, had only to recite his name 'Ya Shamsuddin Turk' one lakh times, either alone or collectively. When this method was put to test, it was found that a wish was fulfilled even before the figure reached one lakh and sometimes even before it reached fifteen or twenty thousand. The recitation of the saint's name proved particularly effective in problems related to livelihood. Allah Diya Chishti, the author of *Siyar-ul-Aqtab*, was so confident about the efficacy of this remedy that he offered an open invitation to the people to go in for it. As the only condition, the concerned person was required to undertake the recitations with a clean body and pure heart. He could then place his petition before God through the mediation of Shaikh Shamsuddin. The beneficiary, after securing the solution of his problem, made a simple offering comprising baked bread and semolina pudding in accordance with his means. This practice was common among the community to which Allah Diya Chishti belonged.[92] His account of three miraculous deeds of the saint provides some insight into the attitude of the Sabiris towards the problems of the ordinary people.

According to the first story, a certain widow was in dire need of money to arrange the marriage of her daughter. Shaikh Shamsuddin, who learnt about the cause of her distress through his inner faculties, sent his horse to her. She was directed by a voice from the unseen world to sell the horse and use the proceeds to meet her needs. She abided by the advice and overcame her difficulty. Interestingly, Shaikh Shamsuddin could provide assistance even several centuries after his death in 1317. Shaikh Yusuf narrated the following experience to Allah Diya Chishti. One night, Shaikh Yusuf went to Kamil Bagh and took his bath at a well. He was terrified on seeing thousands of devils near the wall of a mosque. At first, the devils had faces of children but, after a while, assumed the form of pigs and bears. On being attacked by these creatures, he sought divine protection by reciting 'Ya Shamsuddin Turk.' He saw a man who had a radiant face and was riding a horse. This mysterious person ordered the devils to leave the garden and guided Shaikh Yusuf on the road leading to the city. When Shaikh Yusuf asked the stranger to reveal his identity, he learnt that he was Shaikh Shamsuddin who had appeared in the hour of crisis. On his way to the city, Shaikh Yusuf was waylaid by the same devils. He again recalled the name of Shaikh Shamsuddin. This time, the saint recited sacred words over water and sprinkled it on the face of the victim who recovered his composure. In yet another instance, Shah Ala (the mentor of Allah Diya Chishti) was saved from an enemy who had appeared with a sword in his hand. When Shah Ala went to pay homage at the tomb of Shaikh Shamsuddin, a hand emerged from the grave. This hand was found to be the same that had pushed away the enemy.[93]

Shaikh Jalaluddin Panipati, the principal successor of Shaikh Shamsuddin Turk, came from an aristocratic background. His family appears to have enjoyed extensive land grants and possessed vast material assets comprising goods, camels and horses. A handsome man, he paid a lot of attention to his physical appearance and lived in great comfort. He was fond of riding Arab horses, wearing fine clothes and rubbing perfume on his body. It was in this state that he had appeared before the hospice of Shaikh Shamsuddin Turk. The Shaikh, who was impressed by the looks of the young man, attracted him by the force of his inner qualities. Jalaluddin alighted from his horse and, placing his head at the feet of the saint, enrolled himself as a disciple. Though he undertook hard spiritual exercises during the course of his training and often sank into absorption (*istaghraq*) typical of Qalandars,[94] yet he did not give up the aristocratic habits of his youth. His love for hunting continued unabated. After every ten or fifteen days, he rode into wilderness of the desert. He remained engaged in hunting for ten days at a stretch. A huge quantity of food became available and numerous companions were invited to the dining place. At home, he maintained a large establishment where food was cooked for one thousand persons every day. If the number fell short of this figure, servants fanned out in the streets and bazaars, so as to collect people for the communal meal. A large variety of dishes were cooked and these were served in covered trays. Shaikh Jalaluddin was invariably present in these gatherings, but did not eat anything.[95]

On one occasion, Shaikh Ahmad Abdul Haq (a prominent disciple of Shaikh Jalaluddin) was invited to a feast by some of his companions. He was shocked to find alcoholic drinks along with other items of food on the dining cloth. He felt so offended that he went to his mentor and, returning his turban of discipleship (*kulah-i iradat*), left the town for the jungle. However, on being guided by a supernatural source, he retraced his steps to the hospice. Shaikh Jalaluddin received him with affection, conferred on him a new turban and explained the divine secrets. Treating him like an honoured guest among other disciples, he organized a sumptuous feast in which all types of culinary delights and intoxicating liquors were laid. As all the disciples sat to eat, Shaikh Jalaluddin advised Abdul Haq to avoid anything which was distant from the oneness of God. Abdul Haq was transported to another world and felt the manifestation of supreme oneness, as his heart was cleansed of every thing except divine unity.[96] According to an anecdote, a person named Ahmad Qalandar lived in the Lakhi Jungle. He used to serve the saintly persons wherever they were found. Once he invited a number of such people over a feast. But the invitees withdrew their hands from the food, as there was some meat of animals which had been forbidden. As if by miracle, such animals rose and walked away. Ahmad Qalandar, while seeking forgiveness, confessed to have done the evil deed only to identify the perfect among the saints. He became a disciple of Shaikh Jalaluddin and, after receiving the succession certificate, left for Multan.[97]

Right from his childhood, Shaikh Jalaluddin enjoyed affectionate relations with Bu Ali Qalandar. He had the good fortune of being addressed as son by the elderly saint, who availed of every opportunity of meeting him. Once he learnt that Shaikh Jalaluddin had gone to his agricultural lands. Bu Ali Qalandar mounted his horse and reached the spot. Shaikh Jalaluddin brought a vessel of fresh grams for the horse. Bu Ali Qalandar asked him to find if the horse wished to eat it. In response to this remark, the horse said that he had just consumed the grain and was feeling satiated. Shaikh Jalaluddin was surprised at the horse who could speak like human beings. Bu Ali Qalandar, who was impressed at Shaikh Jalaluddin's kind gesture, declared that he would be blessed with a large number of descendants who would be as numerous as the grain in his stock. Since the prophecy turned out to be true, Shaikh Jalaluddin came to be known as Nuh-i Sani.[98]

According to another anecdote, once Shaikh Jalaluddin (probably before he adopted the spiritual path) was going somewhere on his horse. As soon as Bu Ali Qalandar saw him, he exclaimed, 'A good horse and a good rider.' At that very moment, Shaikh Jalaluddin fell into a state of ecstasy and, severing his worldly connections and renouncing a luxurious life, embarked on a spiritual journey which continued for forty years.[99] In fact, it has been claimed that Shaikh Jalaluddin had an ardent desire to enroll himself as a disciple of Bu Ali Qalandar. On one occasion, he met Bu Ali Qalandar and pleaded that the spiritual secrets might be revealed to him. However, Bu Ali Qalandar did not accede to the request and, instead, predicted that his spiritual aims would be fulfilled by a person who would arrive from Kaliyar.[100] This prophecy, like the previous one, turned out to be true. The inclusion of these stories in the Sabiri lore tended to dismiss any rivalry between the Sabiris and a popular Qalandari spiritualist. In fact, they underscore the positive role of Bu Ali Qalandar in promoting the activities of Sabiris in southeast Panjab. This development did not match the earlier situation when Bu Ali Qalandar was constrained to leave Panipat to make way for Shaikh Shamsuddin Turk, the mentor of Shaikh Jalaluddin.[101]

Shaikh Jalaluddin has earned the credit of affecting a reconciliation between the Sabiris and the Chishti seat of Hansi. This positive development occurred in the following circumstances. Once Shaikh Jalaluddin was travelling to Hansi along with a group of Sufis. Shaikh Jamaluddin Hansavi, who had been living under the curse of Shaikh Alauddin Ali Ahmad Sabir, received an order from the divine source. He was asked to meet Shaikh Jalaluddin whose prayer could revive his lineage. He sent an invitation to the Sufis through a servant. The visitors accepted the invitation and, leaving their luggage under the protection of Shaikh Jalaluddin, entered the town. On being asked, they admitted that they had left behind a dervish to look after their belongings. Shaikh Hansavi requested them to send a companion to bring the youngman, as he was particularly interested in him. When Shaikh Jalaluddin reached the place, Shaikh Hansavi recognized him by the signs he had seen in a vision. He received the guest with all marks of respect and, providing him a comfortable seat, served food to all.

After taking the meals, the Sufis offered a prayer in gratitude and took their leave. Shaikh Hansavi persuaded Shaikh Jalaluddin to stay back.[102] He narrated an unfortunate incident involving the tearing of his shawl by Shaikh Sabir. He also recalled Baba Farid's statement which prophesied the revival of the Chishti seat of Hansi by a disciple of the late Shaikh Sabir. Accepting the plea, Shaikh Jalaluddin offered a prayer in a manner that the spiritual order of Shaikh Jamaluddin Hansavi was revived. When Shaikh Jalaluddin joined the group of Sufis, he was shown greater respect than before. The Sufis were constrained to change their attitude on seeing the consideration with which Shaikh Jalaluddin was treated by the host and also his role in reviving the local branch of the Chishtis. Earlier they had made Shaikh Jalaluddin carry their luggage on his shoulders. Afterwards they restrained themselves from extracting this tedious labour and instead began to serve him in different ways. One day, he insisted on carrying the luggage as it was his turn to do so. He had his way in spite of protests. As he walked ahead with the luggage, it was found that the luggage floated at a level higher than the top of his head. His companions were amazed at the miracle.[103]

Shaikh Jalaluddin and his spiritual successors (*khalifas*) empathized with the peasantry and, employing their miraculous powers, fought state oppression. Once he was travelling towards the east and halted in a village. He found that the entire population intended to flee as the local administrator was demanding the land tax even though the harvest had failed. Of course, they would not migrate if they were able to pay the governmental dues. In an attempt to help the villagers, the Shaikh purchased the entire land of the village from them and sealed the deal in official documents. In the evening, he asked the villagers to bring iron. They brought various types of iron implements that were found in their homes. He placed the metallic tools in a burning furnace and, at midnight, quietly slipped out of the village. Next morning, the villagers discovered that the pieces of iron had turned into pure gold. They paid their tax with ease. Their descendants, who were in the possession of the precious metal, were found to be prosperous even in the early seventeenth century.[104]

In another instance, the landholders (*zamindars*) of Bandoli, complained to Shaikh Jalaluddin that a flooded Ganga threatened to submerge their village in two days. The Shaikh wrote a letter to his spiritual successor Shaikh Behram (who was based in village Ramadah), asking him to go to Bandoli and stay on the bank of the Ganga. Shaikh Behram went to the place along with the affected people and settled at the site. He affixed a pole in the ground as a result of which the river receded two *kos* and never advanced towards Bandoli. Shaikh Behram lived in the village for the rest of his life and provided spiritual guidance to the inhabitants. His tomb became a source of medical remedy for the sick. It was believed that a bath in the neighbouring well provided instant cure to the sick.[105] Shaikh Behram might have led the people in making arrangements to protect the village from the floods of the Ganga. These stories acknowledge the identification of Shaikh Jalaluddin with the poor people inhabiting the rural areas. It appears that the descendants and dependants of Shaikh Behram, owing to their influence in the locality and popularity of the shrine of the saint, had acquired a land grant in Bandoli. In 1647, they got into a major conflict with Mirza Muzaffar, the governor of the Mughal province of Delhi, who made an unsuccessful bid to confiscate their land grant. Employing the miraculous power of the shrine of Shaikh Behram, they taught a bitter lesson to the governor and secured an increase in the sinecure.[106]

Towards the end of his days, Shaikh Jalaluddin wished to transfer a part of his life to Syed Jalaluddin Bokhari, a prominent Suhrawardi saint of Uch. His desire was motivated by two factors – firstly, the life of Shaikh Bokhari was nearing its end and, secondly, he was a namesake. Before he could finalize his plan, he sought the opinion of his two sons, Shaikh Abdul Qadir and Shaikh Shibli. The former did not agree with the proposal of his father and, instead, suggested that they (the sons) be permitted to make this sacrifice. However, the latter asked his father to go ahead as his action would benefit a friend. In the end, Shaikh Jalaluddin gave a practical shape to this idea and bade farewell to his family. He took Abdul Qadir with him and, assisted by a miraculous journey, arrived in Delhi. He appeared before Shaikh Bokhari who was on the verge of his death. He offered salutations and made a sign with his ten fingers, so that Shaikh Bokhari immediately felt an improvement in his condition.

Sultan Firoz Shah Tughluq, a disciple of Shaikh Bokhari, came to enquire about the health of his mentor. Shaikh Bokhari informed the Sultan that his brother Shaikh Jalaluddin had come all the way from Panipat and transferred ten years of his life to him, so that he had regained his health. Deeply impressed at this outcome, the Sultan went to meet Shaikh Jalaluddin and expressed his gratitude. He availed of this opportunity to test the piety of the Sabiri saint. The Sultan wanted to know if he had seen God. The Shaikh replied that the Shariat ruled out the direct vision of God. Pleased at the reply, the Sultan offered a gift (*nazr*) of a tray full of diamonds. The Shaikh refused to accept the costly gift on the ground that he, being a Sufi, did not have the guards to protect the valuables and that these things had been created only for the rulers. Feeling disappointed at this curt reply, the Sultan tried to present the gift to the son of the Shaikh. Since this young man was deaf and dumb, he wished to know the purpose of the gift. He was told that the gift comprised diamonds that were employed to fill the stomach and wear clothes. Feeling offended, the youth explained through signs that the One who had created the stomach would also fill it and therefore the diamonds were of no use.[107] As the tearful Sultan left the place, he ordered his servants to scatter the diamonds at the Shaikh's door. This order was carried out. Even three centuries after this incident, someone or the other was able to find a diamond at the spot. As soon as Shaikh Bokhari regained his health, he came to Panipat and visited the hospice of Shaikh Jalaluddin. Here he performed spiritual austerities (*chillah*) for forty days and received blessings of the Shaikh. In fact, this particular site could be recognized even in the times of the author of *Siyar-ul Aqtab*. Having undergone this experience, Shaikh Bokhari left for Uch where breathed his last (3 February 1384).[108]

The above development went a long way in raising the stature of Shaikh Jalaluddin in the Sufi circles as well as the ruling class. This was reflected in the following incident involving four important persons, the Sultan Firoz Shah Tughluq, his nephew

Fateh Khan, Shaikh Jalaluddin, and Syed Jalaluddin Bokhari. The last named had brought a sacred imprint of the foot of Prophet Muhammad from Kaaba. In a solemn agreement between the Sultan and Fateh Khan, it was decided that whoever of the two died first would have the privilege of keeping the sacred imprint on his chest at his burial. The Sultan backed out of the promise after his meeting with Shaikh Jalaluddin. He asserted his claim over the sacred imprint and asked Fateh Khan to give up his desire in exchange for an alternative wish. Disappointed at the Sultan's attitude, Fateh Khan went to Panipat in order to seek the help of Shaikh Jalaluddin. On reaching the hospice, he tied his horse at the gate and tried to enter the cell (*hujra*) of the Shaikh. Shaikh Zeena, who was guarding the gate, warned him not to enter as he would not return safely. Fateh Khan declared that he would enter safely and return in the same condition. Shaikh Zeena challenged that if Fateh Khan returned safely, he would tear his own clothes and, if he did not, the other would tear his. As soon as Fateh Khan appeared before the Shaikh, the latter told him to go and take what he desired. On emerging out of the cell, Fateh Khan declared that he had returned unharmed. When Shaikh Zeena stated that he had brought his death along with him, Fateh Khan retorted that this was precisely his wish and he had achieved the same. On his way back to Delhi, Fateh Khan rested under a tree and, covering himself with a sheet, breathed his last. The Sultan, acting in accordance with the agreement, placed the sacred imprint on his chest that was seen even in the times of Allah Diya Chishti. It was the miraculous intervention of Shaikh Jalaluddin that fulfilled the desires of his devotees.[109]

In the Sabiri tradition, Shaikh Jalaluddin is remembered for working several miracles. It was believed that he frequently travelled to Mecca and offered his prayers under the leadership of Prophet Muhammad. On these moments, he was not found in Panipat. He wished to offer the Friday prayer at the sacred site, but he was advised by the Prophet to do so at the tomb of Syed Mahmud. It was believed that the Shaikh's wife, who was illiterate, began to rapidly read the Quran immediately after her marriage; the miracle was brought about by the Shaikh's physical touch.[110]

On one occasion, the Shaikh saw an old woman who was drawing water from a well with painful effort. Filled with pity, he pulled out the bucket from the well and filled her pitcher. Subsequently the woman was freed from her tedious work, because the pitcher never became empty. On another occasion, an alchemist (who often visited the Shaikh's son) asked the Shaikh to learn alchemy from him. In response, the Shaikh spat on the wall and its plaster turned into pure gold (*talai khalis*).[111] According to a popular story, a spark of light burnt on the grave of his spiritual successor Shaikh Nizamuddin and people visited the village of Siyam to witness the amazing spectacle. Shaikh Jalaluddin declared that the deceased did not need light as he had merged into the divine, that the display brought a bad name to the saints and that the phenomenon did not exist at the mausoleum of the Prophet. As soon as the Shaikh uttered these words, the spark of light sank into the grave.[112] According to another tale, Shaikh Jalaluddin, travelling through the hills, met a Jogi who gave him a philosopher's stone. As the Shaikh threw it into the river, a quarrel erupted between the two. The Jogi descended into the river and found that there were several stones similar to his own. He brought out his own stone along with another one and emerged out of water. The Shaikh stated that the men of God ruled over land and sky, that miraculous stones were produced out of the dust of their slippers and that they did not need such stones. Overwhelmed by the Shaikh's argument, the Jogi converted to Islam and, enrolling himself as a disciple, reached the rank of a saint.[113]

Looking East

By the end of the fourteenth century, the Sabiri branch of the Chishtis was firmly established in Panipat. During the next two centuries, the lineal descendants of Shaikh Jalaluddin held the spiritual succession (*sajjadgi*) in their hands without any break. Unfortunately, our principal source, *Siyar ul-Aqtab*, provides only brief notices about them. All of them were distinguished for their learning, quest for spiritual excellence and training of disciples. They were also remembered for their ability to perform miracles.

Khwaja Shibli (d. 1448), the son of Shaikh Jalaluddin, could not make use of his feet owing to paralysis, but stood for several watches during the ecstasy induced by musical sessions. His uncle Shaikh Idrees dissuaded him from this practice, as a public exhibition of miracles was remote from their family conventions and therefore even an occasional indulgence had to be discarded. When Khwaja Shibli conferred a boon on Malik Ujhi (an Afghan who had retrieved the Shaikh's rosary from a group of Qalandars) that his arrow would never go waste, the prediction turned out to be true when an arrow, which was shot up in the sky, fell down after piercing the body of a snake.[114] Khwaja Abdul Quddus (the son and successor of Khwaja Shibli) was credited with saving the village of Jhajpur (in the *pargana* of Panipat) from a massive fire by giving a timely warning for the inhabitants to shift their cattle and goods.[115] Shaikh Abdul Kabir Auliya (d. 1540), the son and successor of Khwaja Abdul Quddus, was tested for his piety by the contemporary ruling class. Three royal guests, Sultan Sikandar Lodi, his *wazir*, and Malik Mahmud, imagined three different dishes in their minds, while the Shaikh produced exactly the same for each one of them. But the host refused to accept the Sultan's offer of a grant of two villages for the attendants of the shrine. However, he accepted the *wazir's* offer of one village and also the daughter of Malik Mahmud in marriage.[116]

During the early sixteenth century, the Sabiri establishment of Panipat was embroiled in a major dispute, which spilled over to Delhi and even led to violence. Shaikh Usman Zinda Pir succeeded his father Shaikh Abdul Kabir Auliya as the head (*sajjadah nishin*) of the Sabiri hospice. He had three brothers, Shaikh Husain, Shaikh Ruknuddin and Shaikh Mahmud, who appeared to have accepted his elevation. But his position was vigorously challenged by his nephews Shaikh Nuruddin and Shaikh Munawwar. The discord assumed such a large proportion that it reached the court of the Delhi Sultanate. The contemporary ruler Ibrahim Lodi (r. 1517-26) was constrained to travel all the way to Panipat and undertook an investigation into the dispute. It was found that the majority of stake holders – the mother of Shaikh Usman, his disciples, his brothers and prominent citizens of Panipat – extended willing support to the incumbent. But owing to unknown reasons, Ibrahim Lodi was inclined towards the nephew Shaikh Nuruddin. Both sides seemed to have pressed their respective claims but, in the end, the spiritual successorship was divided into two parts – one half under Shaikh Usman and the other half under Shaikh Nuruddin. The Sultan's decision failed to bring peace between the warring factions and the underlying hostility raised its ugly head on the day of Id. Contrary to local convention, the annual procession was led by two palanquins (*chandol*). A fight erupted on the question of precedence i.e. which one of the two should be in the front and which one should follow it. Partisans of the two groups entered into a physical clash and, during the course of violence, Shaikh Nuruddin fell on the ground and withdrew to his house. On the other hand, the palanquin of Shaikh Usman reached the Idgah in the splendour of victory. Since that day, he began to enjoy the support of a majority of the people and the spiritual succession remained in the hands of his descendents. During the subsequent years, the rival palanquin did not appear and the tension subsided. As the spiritual authority of Shaikh Usman was established, his personal intervention led to an amicable settlement of all disputes. It was another matter that his son Shaikh Nizam failed to follow his advice regarding a wrongly constructed well, which ultimately collapsed as if by miracle.[117]

Shaikh Ahmad Abdul Haq (1374-1434), who was undoubtedly the most distinguished disciple of Shaikh Jalaluddin Panipati, established a vibrant Sabiri Chishti centre at Rudauli.[118] His grandfather Shaikh Daud had received a land grant from Sultan Alauddin Khalji and spiritual training from Shaikh Nasiruddin Mahmud Chiragh-i Delhi. His son Shaikh Umar had been blessed with two sons, Shaikh Taqiuddin and Shaikh Ahmad Abdul Haq. The elder one migrated to Delhi where he established himself as a teacher. The younger one was inclined towards mysticism and, inspired by the example of a pious mother, engaged in long hours of devotion. As he shifted to Delhi, his brother introduced him to a number of theologians one after the other. Since he was averse to theological subjects, he began to look for mystical knowledge. This search brought him to Panipat where he became a disciple of

Shaikh Jalaluddin. Political disturbances caused by Timur's invasion, a personal streak of restlessness and an insatiable hunger for spiritual advancement forced him to live in different parts of Hindustan. After his sojourns at Sunam in Panjab and Bhakkar in Sind, he returned to Panipat where he taught his mentor's son who headed the hospice.[119]

Turning towards the east, he travelled all the way to Bengal where he had a frustrating encounter with Shaikh Nur Qutb-i Alam. After a short interaction with two holy men (*majzub*) in Bihar, he came to Awadh where he served as an attendant at a local graveyard. Continuing his passion for hard penance, he stayed in a specially dug grave for six months. As the stories of his austerities and miracles spread in all directions, he acquired a considerable fame. Finally he returned to his native place Rudauli and lived here till the end of his life. He attracted the attention of Sultan Ibrahim Sharqi of Jaunpur, who offered a lavish grant of four villages and 1,000 *bighas* of land. The Shaikh, acting in conformity with the early Chishti practice, declined the offer. Similarly, he rejected another royal offer of a gift for his son-in-law and, out of anger, tore the document to pieces. According to his logic, a God who provided for the large establishment of the Sultan, could also meet his humble needs.[120]

Shaikh Ahmad Abdul Haq had extensive knowledge about the spiritual states of past Sufis and made an effective use of this during the course of his sermons. In his view, Mansur ul-Hallaj had made a childish mistake in revealing the divine secrets, whereas mature Sufis could swallow an ocean of such truths without any discomfort. Similarly, he did not agree with the view that the world had become empty of the pious and that the vessel of honey had become the abode of sheep. Even in his own times, true seekers of God were benefited from their association with Prophet Muhammad just like the latter's companions. The Shaikh had devised a difficult course for the training of his disciples. Even before the formal enrollment, a novice was required to spend several years in spiritual exercises and manual work in the hospice, including drawing water and serving in the community kitchen. He buried Shaikh Qudwatuddin in the ground for a fortnight before awarding the certificate of succession and spiritual domain of Barnawa.¹²¹

Shaikh Ahmad Abdul Haq claimed that the aspirants, who came within his mystic circle, remained unaffected by the fire of hell comprising polytheism and disunion (*shirk wa firaq*). He was confident that those who had lived under his tutelage could never deviate from his loyalty towards himself and never be misguided into the trap laid by others. Sufis who took pride in their revelations and miracles (*kashf wa karamat*) exposed themselves as childish in the comprehension of mysticism. The Chishti masters had identified as many as fifteen stages (*maqamat*) in the path of mysticism. Out of these, the revelation-cum-miracles constituted only the fifth one, which was revealed to the seeker in the plane of bliss (*alam-i jabrut*). A majority of seekers got stuck at this stage. It was only when he covered the remaining ten stages that the plane of absolute truth (*alam-i lahut*) was revealed to him and, at this juncture, revelation-cum-miracles were rendered irrelevant. This was the stage of surrender to the will of God when the seeker became absorbed in the divine unity (*ahadiyat*) in a manner that he was lost to himself and failed to find his own self. This was the condition of those who had covered all the stages of the mystical path and reached the ultimate destination of divine unity. At this ultimate stage, their annihilation and merger into the Supreme Being manifested an acute perception of God's reality. It was on account of this state that the Shaikh as well as his sons and disciples were characterized by a perpetual self-annihilation. This was the most exalted of all spiritual states, with none being higher than this. Not surprisingly, the Shaikh continued to exercise his spiritual power (*tasarruf*) even after his death from the recesses of his grave and, in this sense, played a role similar to such eminent Chishti saints as Muinuddin Chishti, Qutbuddin Bakhtiyar Kaki, Fariduddin Ganj-i-Shakar and Nizamuddin Auliya.¹²²

Shaikh Ahmad Abdul Haq remained in a perpetual state of absorption (*istaghraq*) and kept away from the crowd. Since he treated 'Haq' as the most perfect expression of God's numerous names and attributes, this word was employed most frequently in his mystic circle. When the time for obligatory prayers arrived, his disciples informed him by repeating the word thrice. When he went to the mosque to offer the Friday prayer, his disciples walked ahead chanting the word. In fact, he advocated its use as the new form of greeting each other in place of the customary salutation. In his hospice, he used two different cells for solitary contemplation, one representing his beauteous disposition (*jamal*) and the other personifying his wrathful nature (*jalal*). Such was his fondness for musical sessions that, on one occasion, he gifted his maidservant to the Qawwals. For some time, he prepared a cauldron (*deg*) and placed it on the road for the people to satisfy their hunger. He discontinued the practice as it brought undue popularity to him and he would not assume the role of God as the supreme provider. He employed his miraculous power which enabled a disciple to meet Prophet Muhammad in a vision.[123] Similarly, he revived the life of a disciple who, contrary to his mentor's advice, had opted for death; it was only with his permission that the disciple breathed his last. The Shaikh's generosity was matched by his anger and, for this reason, earned the name of Shaikh Ahmad Qattal (murderer). When Duheja, the zamindar of Narah, attacked Rudauli, the Shaikh diverted him by a miracle towards Karansa where he was killed in an encounter with his counterpart. The Shaikh was instrumental in shifting the entire tribe of the former zamindar of Bahreela to the villages of Kora and Tehlora. When the Shaikh's son-in-law was imprisoned without any reason by the local administrator of Rudauli, Malik Zakku, he not only caused the death of the culprit, but also offered the last prayer (*namaz-i janazah*) for the burial.[124]

Towards the close of our period, the Sabiris received a fresh lease of life while Shaikh Abdul Quddus Gangohi (1456-1537) lived at Shahabad near Ambala for over three decades. A descendant of Imam Abu Hanifa, he belonged to a family of devout scholars, who had received a land grant near Rudauli from the Sharqis of Jaunpur. At a relatively young age, he abandoned his study of conventional learning and turned towards spirituality. He entered the hospice of Shaikh Ahmad Abdul Haq and, while performing menial tasks, began to receive guidance from the spirit of the famous Sabiri saint and thus became his Uwaisi. He assumed discipleship under Shaikh Muhammad (the grandson of Shaikh Ahmad Abdul Haq) and went on to marry the sister of his mentor.[125] He also benefited from the company of Shaikh Piyare, a senior inmate of the hospice. He attracted a number of Afghan soldiers into his mystical circle. At the invitation of the Afghan noble Umar Khan Sarwani, he migrated to the town of Shahabad near Ambala in 1491 and resided here for more than thirty years. In 1524, he was persuaded by another Afghan noble Usman Karrani to shift to Gangoh (40 miles southeast of Shahabad across the Jamuna), where he lived till the end of his life. During the Lodi-Mughal warfare, he fell into the hands of the Mughals, who dragged him from Panipat to Delhi. Later on, he developed cordial relations with the new Mughal ruler Humayun.[126]

In matters of religious practice, Shaikh Gangohi was an ardent follower of Prophet Muhammad and the Shariat. He was so strict in observing the religious rites that he did not tolerate even the slightest deviation from the righteous path (*sirat-i mustaqim*). At the onset of his religious life, he channelized his energies towards supererogatory prayers (*nawafil*), besides the regimen of obligatory devotions. He performed eight hundred units (*rakats*) of prayer, four hundred during the day and four hundred during the night. After reciting the Fatiha and Surat, he practiced breath control alongwith silent remembrance of God. He repeated the exercise during the three postures of standing, genuflexion and prostration. Sometimes he spent the entire night in performing the double prayers (*dogana*). At other times, he recited the loud remembrance (*zikr-i jahri*) from the time of Isha and continued it till daybreak. So strong was the degree of his concentration and trust in God that he remained unaffected by unfavourable conditions – extremes of weather and presence of reptiles and insects – in his cell. He undertook forty-day retreats on a regular basis. Emulating Shaikh Ahmad Abdul Haq, who contemplated in a grave for six months, he observed complete isolation in the hole of a tamarind tree for the same duration. Following in the footsteps of the Chishti elders like Baba Farid, he often resorted to the inverted prayer (*namaz-i maakus*). From the time of Isha, he suspended himself upside down and, returning to the normal posture at daybreak, offered the morning prayer (*fajr*). During such austerities, he experienced the state of absorption, annihilation of annihilation (*fana al-fana*) and subsistence in God (*baqa ba-allah*). At this moment, a supernatural being congratulated him for achieving a union with the Almighty.[127]

A characteristic feature of Shaikh Gangohi's mystical pursuit was the *sultan-i zikr*, a term applicable to the impact of devotional practices. As a manifestation of this impact, a seeker became oblivious of his physical existence and climbed to the state of self-annihilation (*fana al-fana*) and subsistence in God (*baqa ba-allah*). In this condition, he felt that his temporal being was merged into the Supreme Being. This phenomenon had been explained in *Risala-i Makkiya* by Shaikh Najmuddin Kubra. Sometimes, it held the seeker in an overpowering grip and, without displaying any outward sign, it ended in calmness akin to sleep. At other times, it appeared in the form of light and, owing to its great power, subjected the seeker to varying degrees of trembling depending on his endurance. His bodily existence was shaken to effacement, as alluded to in the chapter related to earthquake (*sura-i zalzala*) in the Quran (99: 1-3). As the seeker was drenched in the rain of a mysterious lustre, his being was permeated by 18,000 worlds in different forms. This was his state in the plane of absolute truth (*alam-i malkut*), which induced him to feel amazed and bewildered. His heart received the knowledge of divine mysteries, while his human traits were replaced by divine qualities. He heard sounds of different types and, thinking of resurrection, lost control over his soul. His heart turned into the divinely ordained tablet (*lauh-i mahfuz*) on which God recorded the transactions of humankind. It began to receive revelations about the sublime truths that were similar to the revelations of the prophets.[128]

Normally a seeker felt the *sultan-i zikr* between sleep and waking when his outer senses were dilute. When he gained experience in it, the distinction between sleep and waking receded, so that he faced it while alert. In the beginning, he was terrified by the encounter. Frequency of the occurrence dissipated his fear and he began to anxiously anticipate the event. In this state, he became unaware of his worldly surroundings, but retained his own consciousness and knew that he was being overpowered by the *sultan-i zikr*. On some occasions, he became entirely devoid of consciousness and reached the stage of supreme annihilation (*fana al-fana*). In one of his traditions (Hadis), Prophet Muhammad stated that sometimes he received the revelation of the Quran in the form of the ringing of a bell, which was difficult to endure. Sometimes, he saw the physical form of the angel who spoke to him and he memorized the words. While receiving the revelation, drops of perspiration appeared on the Prophet's forehead, though the weather was extremely cold. The ordeal was attributed to the rise of body's temperature that overpowered the outer chill. The words revealed to the Prophet were known as *wahi*, while those revealed to the saints were termed as *ilham*.[129]

A specific method of *sultan-i zikr* was recommended for all categories of seekers including the ordinary and the select. When a seeker learnt the entire technique from his mentor and immersed himself in this exercise, he underwent a critical transformation. As the sound of *zikr* entered his heart, this organ was driven to a movement that gradually permeated his whole body. Just as sound echoed from a dome, the sound of *zikr* reached his ears and produced a pleasant sensation. Owing to the strength of the *zikr*, its dominance increased and various sounds were heard including that of a bell. When this dominance went beyond its limits, it assumed the form of *sultan-i zikr*. While hearing the sound of lightning, his body trembled and he became unconscious. Sometimes, he envisioned lights from different sources like sun, moon and stars.

It was difficult to describe the unique episode in words, though it could be recognized through its signs and symptoms. A seeker overpowered by his passion, struggled to sharpen his perception of divine secrets. His condition was similar to a tree that was violently shaken in a storm and a man who was caught in a flooded river. The impact of *sultan-i zikr*, which first appeared in the heart, spread to other parts of the body. The sound, which was emitted from these parts, rose independently and perpetually attracted the attention of the seeker. Bereft of words, this sound was the most exalted form of contemplation, which reflected all dimensions of mystical knowledge as well as divine light. As the sound progressed in proportion to increase in the epiphanies, it was endowed with words. This phenomenon, as embodied in the beginning of the Quran, indicated that words were external and sound was internal.[130]

The above phenomenon has been viewed in comparison to the experience of Prophet Muhammad in the cave of Hira. After listening to this sound, he experienced a joy that was beyond description. The quality of his hearing was transformed into the quality of vision, while the angel Jibrail appeared on the scene. As and when he concentrated his attention on this sound, the words of God were revealed to him, even though his body endured severe pain. This contemplation on the sound was extremely significant for the seeker who, by this practice, could achieve salvation from his physical being. Sometimes his body was transformed into ears, so that every hair could hear the sound. At other times, it was turned into eyes, so that every hair could see the reality in true perspective. Such a state was achieved only with hard work based on courage, aptitude and long life. Not surprisingly, Prophet Muhammad took forty years to attain the status of Prophet. However, the Sufis were not unanimous on various aspects of the *sultan-i zikr*. They differed on the sequence of hearing and seeing that was associated with revelation. Thinkers also differed on the nature of sound (grinding mill, humming bee, cannon, clarinet and tambourine) accompanying a revelation that culminated, after appropriate austerities, into a thunderous situation that was a clear sign of the *sultan-i zikr*. Evidently, the phenomenon had to be understood in accordance with one's aptitude and disposition.[131]

Shaikh Gangohi drew a distinction between two types of hunger, low (*safli*) and sublime (*alavi*). He held that the former was found in all the animals. When they were born and the animal soul entered them, they began to move and experienced warmth. As they felt the pangs of hunger, they developed the need for food. Owing to this low category of hunger, they were not able to make any spiritual progress. In contrast to the animals, the humans were endowed with sublime hunger. On taking birth, they travelled from the realm of invisibility to that of love, and from the world of movement to that of stagnancy. At this stage, the unity of God was revealed along with innumerable divine secrets, including the reality of prophethood. As a beginning of the world of unity, this was the stage of human soul and it was designated as the plane of bliss (*alam-i jabrut*). Though this was an exalted state, yet its power of proximity was inadequate and did not guarantee enough benefits. Associated with the human soul was the plane of absolute truth (*alam-i malkut*), which offered the knowledge of lower self and promised proximity to the praise of God. Here the manifestation of love did not progress, nor did it reach the peak of divine knowledge. As a result, the seeker was reduced to a mere physical being engaged in consumption and, having suffered a deficiency in knowledge, failed to distinguish between binaries – reality and metaphor, unity and multiplicity, right and wrong, presence and absence. In this predicament, the lover grasped the skirt of the Beloved.[132]

Shaikh Gangohi went on to argue that the human being, by his very nature, was permeated by this hunger. Hotter than the fire of hell, this feeling transformed impure hunger into pure hunger, bondage into freedom and human into divine. It was through this hunger that man reached God. This ability was found only in humans, because the animals were governed solely by their physical needs. Even the angels and souls, who had been placed in the category of the sublime beings (*alavi*), failed to progress beyond their given state, as they had been deprived of this hunger. This hunger was, in fact, a fire that fuelled any movement. The power of fire also resided in the seeker's love and pain. Continuing in this vein, Shaikh Gangohi classified hunger into three levels. The first, being physical, was satisfied by the consumption of food and drink. The second, associated with the pain of love, was satisfied by the blood of the liver and chips of straw. The third was connected with the Beloved, and its food comprised the perfections of beauty and virtue. According to a verse, the incomparable God was the lover of his own beauty and, therefore, served as the beholder of His beauteous persona.[133]

Endowed with a wide outlook, Shaikh Gangohi absorbed ideas

from the non-Islamic spiritual traditions. He was intimately familiar with the content of *Amritkunda*,[134] which he communicated to his disciple Shaikh Sulaiman. This text perceived human body as a microcosm of the universe and emphasized the discipline of three elements – body, senses and mind – through the regulation of breath. In his own work entitled *Rushdnama*, Shaikh Gangohi demonstrated that Ibn-i Arabi's unity of being (*wahdat ul-wujud*) was identical with the philosophy of Gorakhnath. For him, the union of Shakti and Shiva, as the basis of three worlds, was similar to the inverted prayer (*salat-i maakus*) of the Sufis. Its Yogic equivalent was a regressive exercise (*ulti sadhna*) involving the reversal of human bodily functions. The Shaikh found it appropriate to rely on terms – *alakh niranjan, onkar, sahaj* and *sabad* – from the Yogic terminology. Alakh Niranjan, like Khuda, was the unseen Lord who had created the different worlds, while Onkar was the transcendent Absolute who was approached through remembrance (*zikr*). Sahaj, which was the state of perfect equilibrium and led to ontological immortality, was akin to the Sufi ideal of subsistence in God (*baqa*). As the undefinable word, Sabad was realized by installing truth in the heart through contemplation. In the eyes of Shaikh Gangohi, Ibn-i Arabi's *wahdat ul-wujud* did not differ from Gorakhnath's concept of absolute truth (*parbrahma*), which was beyond origin, destruction, imagination, names and forms. This theme of unity was comprehended by looking at the different forms of water – vapours, clouds and rain. The Sufi theory of creation, as revealed by God to David ('I was a hidden treasure and I wished to be known; so I created the creation so that I might be known.'), was identical with the Yogic theme of divine will. The Shaikh's frequent allusion to the heart as a mirror was also based on the ideas of Ibn-i Arabi and Gorakhnath.[135]

Shaikh Gangohi has paid a considerable attention to the yogic technique of breath control (*pas-i anfas*), with reference to the role of three types of breath. According to a significant statement, the first breath (*prana*) came out upwards, the second breath (*apana*) went downwards and the third breath (*samana*) came out of the whole body along the roots of the hair. A Sufi practitioner was required to transform these three breaths into a single one, which was subsequently turned back. Departing from the standard Yogic explanation, the Shaikh held that the third breath was not engendered by the first two, but it operated in the human frame before joining. The three corners (*trikuti*), according to the Yogic parlance, stood for the junction of three cords – *ida*, *pingala*, and *susumna* – that served as conduits for the three breaths. Sometimes, the Shaikh conceived of the junction as a penultimate circle above the eyebrows and, at other times, situated it in the navel. Irrespective of the location of the junction, it was a void that expressed the final liberation. Designated as the fundamental base (*muldwara*), it meant the crown of the head, which was the abode of the brain and a receptacle of the seminal fluid. Owing to the movement of the breath, the seminal fluid turned into clear water and suffused through the whole body. In other words, the reversed breath went back in the opposite way and spread through the interior. As the body of the seeker became subtle, he received the illumination of divine mysteries and experienced the state of annihilation.[136]

NOTES

1. Amir Khurd, p. 188; Abdul Haq Muhaddis Dehalvi, *Akhbar ul-Akhyar*, Urdu translation, Subhan Mahmud and Muhammad Fazil, Delhi: Noor Publishing House, 1990, p. 151; Abdul Rahman Chishti, *Mirat ul-Asrar*, vol. II, Urdu translation, Wahid Bakhsh Siyal, New Delhi: Khwaja Hasan Sani Nizami, 2010, p. 231.
2. Muhammad Ghausi Shattari, *Gulzar-i Abrar*, Persian text, ed. Muhammad Zaki, Patna: Khuda Bakhsh Oriental Public Library, 2nd rpt., 2001, p. 44; Khaliq Ahmad Nizami, *Tarikh-i Mashaikh-i Chisht*, vol. I, Karachi: Oxford University Press, rpt., 2007, p. 203.
3. Amir Khurd, pp. 178-9; Muhammad Ghausi Shattari, *Gulzar-i Abrar*, p. 44; Abdul Rahman Chishti, *Mirat ul-Asrar*, vol. II, p. 231.
4. Amir Khurd, p. 179.
5. FF, Faruqi, pp. 152-3; Lawrence, p. 144; Abdul Rahman Chishti, *Mirat ul-Asrar*, vol. II, p. 233.
6. Amir Khurd, pp. 180-1; Abdul Rahman Chishti, *Mirat ul-Asrar*, vol. II, p. 232.
7. Amir Khurd, p. 180.
8. Ibid., p. 180.

9. Ibid., pp. 179-80; Abdul Rahman Chishti, *Mirat ul-Asrar*, vol. II, p. 232.
10. Amir Khurd, pp. 181-2; Abdul Rahman Chishti, *Mirat ul-Asrar*, vol. II, p. 233.
11. Bruce B. Lawrence, *Notes from A Distant Flute: Sufi Literature in Pre-Mughal India*, Tehran: Imperial Iranian Academy of Philosophy, 1978, p. 38.
12. Jamaluddin Ahmad Hansavi, *Mulhimat wa Ahwal wa Asar*, ed. Sardar Ali Ahmad Khan, Lahore: Sang-e-Meel Publications, 2005, pp. 11-20. (hereafter cited as *Mulhimat*).
13. Ibid., pp. 3-10.
14. Ibid., pp. 28-35.
15. Laila and Majnun fell in love in their school in northern Arabia. Laila's parents took her away from school. Majnun, in his sorrow, became a wanderer. His father could not unite the lovers in marriage. He was instead married to the daughter of a chief. He fled into the jungle and lived among wild animals. His parents died in grief. Laila, on hearing a rumour of Majnun's death, died of shock. Majnun, who joined her funeral, jumped into the grave and held her body. The two were buried in the same grave.
16. Hansavi, *Mulhimat*, pp. 20-8.
17. In accordance with a practice followed by Baba Farid, a seeker who enrolled himself as a disciple and took the oath of allegiance, had his head shaved. It was believed that the act erased all traces of arrogance and pride. FF, Faruqi, pp. 424-5; Lawrence, pp. 346-7.
18. Hansavi, *Mulhimat*, pp. 67-72.
19. Isa is the Quranic name of Jesus. The Quran refers to him in 15 Surahs and devotes to him 93 verses, the foundation for Muslim Christology. Various traditions, containing additions from apocryphal gospels of the childhood of Jesus from Muslim Christian literature, have enriched this Christology and, in certain respects, brought it nearer to the Christian traditions. Islamo-Christian polemic has tended through the years to harden the positions. Most of these positions have become classic and are found unchanged in present day Muslim writings. E. Van Donzel et al., eds. *The Encyclopaedia of Islam*, vol. IV, Leiden: E.J. Brill, 1990, new edition, p. 81.
20. Abu Saeed Abil Khair (967-1049) made a major contribution to the theory and practice of Sufism. Born in Maihana, he studied at Merv and Sarakhs, before finally moving to Nishapur. He vindicated the realization of Mansur al-Hallaj and expanded the horizons of Islamic sprituality by adopting a joyful life after achieving enlightenment. While emphasizing the inner dimension of the Quran, he underlined the secondary status of the canonical law. He was a strong advocate of musical sessions, but rejected the necessity of Haj. Opening his hospice to the common people, he made it a centre of spiritual training and social service. For his controversial acts, he narrowly escaped trial at the Ghaznavid court. Shuja Alhaq, *A Forgotten*

Vision: A Study of Human Spirituality in the Light of the Islamic Tradition, vol. I, New Delhi: Vikas Publishing House, 1997, pp. 161-74.

21. Hasan Basri (642-728), the son of a freed slave, became a famous Sufi. Born in Madina, he settled in Basra where he acquired fame for his learning. During the reign of Umayyads when intellectual activity was at a low ebb, he became a lighthouse that attracted a wide circle of students. He taught Islamic law, theology and Sufism. He was a link in the transmission of many Hadis, having known several companions of the Prophet in Madina. Most of Sufi initiatic chains passed through him. He left no writing, but was frequently quoted widely by others. Cyril Glasse, *The Concise Encyclopaedia of Islam*, London: Stacey International, rpt., 2004, p. 173.

22. Musa was the Prophet who led the Israelities out of slavery in Egypt. The Quran records him having been placed in a basket, being taken into the house of Pharaoh, his encounters with the court magicians, the plagues sent against Egypt when Pharaoh refused to let the Israelites go, the parting of the sea, the drowning of Pharaoh's army, Musa's forty days on the mountain, the receipt of the Tablets of Law and striking of his staff against a rock in the desert to obtain water. In the Quranic account, Musa set down tablets containing God's commandments, rather than breaking them after discovering the Israelites worshipping the golden calf. John L. Esposito, ed., *The Oxford Dictionary of Islam*, Karachi: Oxford University Press, rpt., 2007, p. 206.

23. Hansavi, *Mulhimat*, pp. 79-88.

24. Sufis did not regard travelling as mandatory, but it was recommended for suppressing the carnal self. Undertaken in accordance with a variety of rules, it began with proper resolution and aimed at acquiring knowledge and meeting peer Shaikhs. It enabled the seeker to separate from his kith and kin, to practice solitude and to read verses on the oneness of God. At the outset, he bade farewell to brothers of the hospice. He offered prayers on arriving and leaving a station. Carrying a few essential articles, he bathed on entering a city. Shaikh Shihabuddin Umar bin Muhammad Suhrawardi, *Awarif ul-Maarif*, pp. 42-8.

25. Hansavi, *Mulhimat*, pp. 72-8.

26. Shaikh Nizamuddin Auliya, who personally knew this elder son, asserted that when he was in control of his senses, he made sublime statements that were beyond the capacity of most sane people. Once he said, '*Al ilm hijab all al-akbar*,' which meant that knowledge was different from absolute truth (*haq*) and something unconnected with absolute truth was nothing but a veil over truth. The Shaikh recognized him as a frenzied spiritual lover. Amir Khurd, p. 184.

27. Amir Khurd, pp. 182-4.

28. Ibid., pp. 248-9.

29. It appeared that Shaikh Hansavi would have passed on the manuscript to his spiritual successor. But he restrained himself from nominating one of

his two sons to this position, as the elder one had turned a frenzied lover (*majzub*) and the younger one was a minor. As a temporary arrangement, he gave it to his colleague-brother Shaikh Nizamuddin Auliya, so that it could be preserved as a trust till a suitable descendant assumed the headship of the Hansi hospice after his death. The manuscript was not to be treated in the category of such personal possessions of Sufis like patched robe, prayer rug, staff and sandals, which were granted to a disciple nominated as the principal successor. Tanvir Anjum , 'Sons of Bread and Sons of Soul: Lineal and Spiritual Descendants of Baba Farid and the Issue of Succession, in *Sufism in Punjab: Mystics, Literature and Shrines*, ed. Surinder Singh and Ishwar Dayal Gaur, p. 68.
30. Amir Khurd, pp. 249-50.
31. Ibid., pp. 255-7.
32. Ibid., p. 251.
33. Ibid., pp. 250-1.
34. Barbak was the master of ceremonies at the court. He maintained the dignity of royal functions. He marshalled nobles in accordance with their rank. His assistants (*hajibs*), who stood between the king and his subjects, introduced visitors to the Sultan. All petitions were presented to the Sultan through the chief of assistants. Since the post commanded great prestige, it was reserved for princes of the royal blood or the most trusted noble. Ishtiaq Husain Qureshi, *The Administration of the Sultanate of Dehli*, p. 61.
35. Amir Khurd, pp. 252-4.
36. Ibid., pp. 254-5.
37. By then, two developments had taken place. Firstly, the arid tract of southeast Panjab had witnessed agrarian expansion owing to the provision of canal water and, at the same time, Hissar Firoza had emerged as a vibrant urban centre. Secondly, the political dispensation had overcome its apprehensions about the Chishtis of Hansi and had been trying to build bridges with different Sufi networks. In these circumstances, it was not surprising that Firoz Shah Tughluq should pay a visit to Shaikh Nuruddin. As discussed in Chapter 3, the state at this stage was forging alliances with local elements and, therefore, tried to fraternize with the Sufis and, if possible, to absorb them into the political structure.
38. Afif, pp. 132-3.
39. The claim, if made by Bu Ali Qalandar or during his lifetime, explained his identification as a Qalandar. The account of his virtues, including lack of attachment to a band and sedentary life in a particular locality, made him fit the category of a Majzub. His exemption from ritual duties of Islam was traced to an anecdote, wherein he performed seventy ablutions for several nights after experiencing seventy orgasms in a night. Simon Digby, 'Qalandars and Related Groups: Elements of Social Deviance in the Religious Life of the Delhi Sultanate in the Thirteenth and Fourteenth

Centuries,' in *Islam in Asia,* vol. I *(South Asia),* ed. Yohanan Friedmann, Jerusalem: The Magness Press, The Hebrew University, 1984, pp. 101-2.
40. Abul Fazl, *Ain-i Akbari,* vol. III, English translation, H.S. Jarrett and Jadunath Sarkar, New Delhi: Oriental Books Rprint Corporation, 3rd edn., 1978, p. 410.
41. This section has been reconstructed on the basis of stories of Bu Ali Qalandar's miraculous feats that have been culled from hagiographical accounts. Kumkum Srivastava, *The Wandering Sufis: Qalandars and Their Path,* Bhopal: Indira Gandhi Rashtriya Manav Sangrahalaya & New Delhi: Aryan Books International, 2009, pp. 147-63.
42. Abdul Haq Muhaddis Dehalvi, *Akhbar ul-Akhyar,* pp. 269-70.
43. Srivastava, *The Wandering Sufis: Qalandars and Their Path,* pp. 150-2.
44. Abdul Haq Muhaddis Dehalvi, *Akhbar ul-Akhyar,* pp. 280-1.
45. Ibid., p. 282.
46. Ibid., p. 281.
47. Ibid., p. 282.
48. Ibid., p. 283.
49. Lawrence, *Notes from A Distant Flute: Sufi Literature in Pre-Mughal India,* p. 79.
50. Ibid., p. 82.
51. Shah Sharfuddin Bu Ali Shah Qalandar, *Masnavi,* ed. Muhammad Muslim Ahmad Nizami, Delhi: Kutubkhana Naziriyya, 1963, p. 20 (hereafter cited as Masnavi).
52. Ibid., p. 25.
53. Ibid., pp. 23-4.
54. Ibid., p. 25.
55. Ibid., pp. 25-6.
56. Ibid., pp. 40-1.
57. Ibid., pp. 42-4.
58. Ibid., pp. 31-2.
59. Jibrail was the angel who was believed to be the medium of the revelation of the Quran to Prophet Muhammad. He has been mentioned only twice in the Quran by name i.e. in Surah-i Baqarah (11: 91) and Surah-i Tahrim (lxvi: 4). He was supposed to have spoken in a few other verses. In the Islamic tradition, he has been referred to as the Supreme Spirit, the Honourable Spirit, the Holy Spirit and the Faithful Spirit. Thomas Patrick Hughes, *Dictionary of Islam,* p. 133.
60. Masnavi, pp. 33-4.
61. The couplet was somewhat similar to the one attributed to the Iranian Sufi, Ahmad-i Jam. While repeatedly listening to the latter in a musical session, Shaikh Qutbuddin Bakhtiar Kaki breathed his last. *Kushtagan-i khanjar-i taslim ra / Har zaman az ghaib jan-i digar ast* (Those slain by the submission's dagger / Each moment find new life from beyond.) Carl W.

Ernst and Bruce B. Lawrence, *Sufi Martyrs of Love: The Chishti Order in South Asia and Beyond*, New York: Palgrave Macmillan, 2002, p. 16.
62. Masnavi, pp. 35-7.
63. Karun occurred in the Quran at xxviii: 76-82, xxix: 38 and xl:25. Along with Haman, he was an unbelieving minister of Firaun in oppressing the Israelites. He behaved proudly towards Musa and his people, owing to his immense wealth, which he believed to have been given to him for his knowledge. He made a great display of his wealth and was swallowed up by the earth with his palace. He was an example of those who preferred the fleeting wealth of this world to gaining alms, humility, righteousness and abiding riches given by Allah in the world to come. M.T. Houtsma et al., eds., *The Encyclopaedia of Islam*, vol. II, Leiden: E.J. Brill, 1927, pp. 780-1.
64. Masnavi, pp. 6-7.
65. The story of Yusuf, the Joseph of Bible, was narrated with concise beauty in Surah-i Yusuf of the Quran. A favourite son of Yaqub, he was sold into slavery and brought to Egypt. He was taken as a slave in the household of Potiphar, a great man of the country. He was so handsome that women of Egypt, on seeing him, cut their hands with serving knives. The wife of Potiphar made advances to Yusuf. He resisted and tried to escape. His innocence was proved by the fact that his shirt was torn at the back. Nevertheless, he was put into prison and released after many years for correctly interpreting Pharaoh's dreams. His brothers came to him for food during a famine. His shirt sent to his father restored Yaqub's sight which had been lost for weeping for the loss of his son. Cyril Glasse, *The Concise Encyclopaedia of Islam*, London: Stacey International, rpt., 2004, p. 487.
66. Nimrod has been mentioned in the Quran (ii: 260 and xxi: 68-69) with reference to his persecution of Abraham. He created a massive fire in Kusa, where he tried to burn alive Abraham, who was miraculously saved by Jibrail. According to Jewish tradition, Nimrod imprisoned Abraham for ten years. He raised a huge tower to heaven, with the aim of seeing Abraham's God, but suffered a great fall. In a battle against Abraham, Nimrod and his forces were destroyed by a swarm of gnats that was sent by God. Thomas Patrick Hughes, *Dictionary of Islam*, pp. 433-4.
67. Masnavi, pp. 16-18.
68. Ibid., pp. 38-9.
69. Ibid., pp. 27-8.
70. Believed to be descended from Jann and named as Azazil, the devil or Iblis was said to possess authority over the animal and spirit kingdoms. When God created Adam, the devil refused to prostrate before him and therefore he was expelled from Eden. He was sentenced to death, but upon seeking a respite, he obtained it until the day of judgement when he would be destroyed. According to the Quran, the devil was created of fire, while

Adam was created of clay. Thomas Patrick Hughes, *Dictionary of Islam*, p. 84.
71. *Masnavi*, pp. 28-30.
72. Ibid., pp. 8-11.
73. Ibid., pp. 12-13.
74. Khalilullah, meaning the friend of God, was the title given to Abraham in the Quran (iv: 24). It was believed that Abraham, during the times of scarcity, tried to acquire corn from Egypt through a friend. He sent a few servants for this purpose, but his friend did not help and made excuses. The servants, who were ashamed of returning empty handed and, to conceal their faulire from neighbours, filled their sacks with fine sand. Abraham was depressed, but Sarah found flour in the bags and set about making bread. She believed that the flour had been sent by the friend in Egypt, but Abraham declared that the supply had come from his friend God Almighty. Thomas Patrick Hughes, *Dictionary of Islam*, p. 269.
75. *Masnavi*, p. 14.
76. Yazid bin Muawiya was the second Umayyad caliph (c. 680-3). He continued the form of his father's rule, which depended on relations between the caliph, his governors and tribal notables in provinces. His caliphate marked the beginning of a crisis, commonly reffered to as fitna, so that the Umayyads came close to losing the caliphate. He faced continuing opposition from Abdullah bin Zubair and Husain bin Ali, both then in Madina. In a battle at Karbala, Husain died fighting against Yazid's governor of Iraq, Ubaidullah bin Ziyad. Tradition was hostile to Yazid for the death of Husain, attack on the two holy cities of Arabia and burning of Kaaba. P.J. Bearman et al., eds., *The Encyclopaedia of Islam*, vol. XI, Leiden: Brill, 2002, pp. 309-10.
77. *Masnavi*, pp. 14-15.
78. Khaliq Ahmad Nizami, *Tarikh-i Mashaikh-i Chisht*, vol. I, pp. 251-52; the same difficulties have been reiterated in Carl W. Ernst and Bruce B. Lawrence, *Sufi Martyrs of Love: The Chishti Order in South Asia and Beyond*, p. 118.
79. Alam Faqri, *Tazkira Hazrat Ali Ahmad Sabir Kaliyari*, New Delhi: Farid Book Depot, 2005, pp. 38-48.
80. According to hagiographical narratives, Shaikh Sabir travelled all the way to Hansi to get his succession certificate signed by Shaikh Jamaluddin Hansavi. He offended his host by a series of mistakes – failing to alight from his horse after entering the hospice, insisting on signatures in poor light and miraculously removing darkness by lighting his fingure like a candle. Shaikh Hansavi refused to sign the document as he felt that Shaikh Sabir's quick temper rendered him unfit for holding the spiritual territory of Delhi. In retaliation, Shaikh Sabir cursed that Shaikh Hansavi's spiritual eminence would soon be terminated. On learning of the incident, Baba Farid admitted his inability to sew what had been torn by Shaikh Hansavi.

Allah Diya Chishti, *Siyar ul-Aqtab*, Urdu translation, Syed Muhammad Ali Joyea Muradabadi, Karachi: Oxford University Press, 2011, pp. 147-8; Abdul Rahman Chishti, *Mirat ul-Asrar*, vol. II, pp. 275-6.
81. Alam Faqri, *Tazkira Hazrat Ali Ahmad Sabir Kaliyari*, pp. 84-95.
82. Allah Diya Chishti, *Siyar ul-Aqtab*, p. 148.
83. Allah Diya Chishti, *Siyar ul-Aqtab*, pp. 149-50; Abdul Rahman Chishti, *Mirat ul-Asrar*, vol. II, pp. 278-9.
84. Alam Faqri, *Tazkirah Hazrat Ali Ahmad Sabir Kaliyari*, pp. 119-22.
85. Ibid., pp. 108-9.
86. Ibid., pp. 124-6.
87. Abdul Rahman Chishti, *Mirat ul-Asrar*, vol. II, pp. 277-8.
88. Ibid., p. 280.
89. Allah Diya Chishti, *Siyar ul-Aqtab*, p. 152. According to another source, Shaikh Shamsuddin himself rode up to the fort on a horse and, placing his chest against the gate, uttered the name of God in a loud voice. As a consequence, the gate fell down and the victorious army gained its much awaited entry. On the same day, Shaikh Sabir passed away at Kaliyar and Shaikh Shamsuddin left Chittor in order to arrange the burial of his mentor. Alam Faqri, op. cit, pp. 114-15.
90. Allah Diya Chishti, *Siyar ul-Aqtab*, p. 152.
91. Abdul Rahman Chishti, *Mirat ul-Asrar*, vol. II, pp. 351-2.
92. Allah Diya Chishti, *Siyar ul-Aqtab*, p. 151.
93. Ibid., p. 154. Here, it has been added that a prominent noble of Muhammad Shah, Umdat ul-Mulk Safdar Jang, was a desendant of Shaikh Shamsuddin Turk. When this noble was travelling to Kabul, where he had been appointed as the governor, he passed through Panipat. He learnt from one of his followers that the tomb of the Shaikh was found in the town. Safdar Jang, who became emotional, asked for the location of the tomb. He went to the place and, after offering the prayer (*fatiha*), stated that he was a descendant of the Shaikh and even showed the genealogical table to those present. The descendants of the Shaikh were found in the town at that point of time.
94. Abdul Rahman Chishti, *Mirat ul-Asrar*, vol. II, p. 439.
95. Allah Diya Chishti, *Siyar ul-Aqtab*, p. 156.
96. Abdul Rahman Chishti, *Mirat ul-Asrar*, vol. II, 439-40; this episode has been described with minor differences and more details in Allah Diya Chishti, *Siyar ul-Aqtab*, pp. 160-1.
97. Allah Diya Chishti, *Siyar ul-Aqtab*, p. 160.
98. Ibid., p. 156.
99. Ibid., p. 157.
100. Ibid., p. 159.
101. Shaikh Jalaluddin Panipati took concrete steps to develop friendly relations with neighbouring Sufis, particularly in cases where some friction had

Islamic Spirituality in Southeast Panjab   507

been existing, e.g. with the Chishtis of Hansi, Bu Ali Qalandar and Syed Jalaluddin Bokhari. This was a strategy not only for survival, but also for consolidation and expansion of the Sabiri branch of the Chishtis, who had been quite active from the middle of the thirteenth century onwards.

102. Allah Diya Chishti has wrongly identified this Chishti saint of Hansi with Shaikh Jamaluddin Hansavi (d. 1261), who had died in the lifetime of Baba Farid. If Shaikh Jalaluddin Panipati lived in the late fourteenth century, was a contemporary of Syed Jalaluddin Bokhari and died in 1403 as mentioned by Allah Diya Chishti, then he (Shaikh Jalaluddin Panipati) must have met a descendant of Shaikh Jamaluddin Hansavi.
103. Allah Diya Chishti, *Siyar ul-Aqtab*, pp. 157-8.
104. Ibid., pp. 157-8.
105. Ibid., p. 162.
106. Ibid., pp. 162-3.
107. This episode was somewhat similar to the experience of Shaikh Qutbuddin Munawwar and his son Shaikh Nuruddin when the two met Sultan Muhammad bin Tughluq. The narrative aimed to show that the Sabiris were in no way less than the Chishtis of Hansi in their attitude towards the state and wealth.
108. Allah Diya Chishti, *Siyar ul-Aqtab*, pp. 164-6.
109. Ibid., pp. 165-6.
110. Ibid., p. 159.
111. Ibid., p. 164.
112. Ibid., p. 163.
113. Ibid., pp. 158-9.
114. Ibid., pp. 168-9.
115. Ibid., p. 170.
116. Ibid., pp. 171-2.
117. Ibid., pp. 173-4.
118. Said to have been founded by a Bhar chief Rudra Mal, the town of Rudauli was situated in Ramsanehighat tahsil and Barabanki district of United Provinces. It contained two shrines of Muslim saints, viz., Shah Ahmad who was entombed alive for six months and Zohra Bibi who recovered her sight miraculously by visiting the shrine of Salar Masud Ghazi at Bahraich. Large fairs were held at each of these. *Imperial Gazetteer of India*, vol. XXI, p. 338.
119. This became a precedent, as the offspring of Shaikh Jalaluddin enrolled themselves under the tutelage of Shaikh Ahmad Abdul Haq's descendants, who were based in Rudauli. In this manner a lasting link was established between the Panipat and Rudauli seats of the Sabiris. They were schooled in the spiritual curriculum which was developed for conventional and mystical learning by Shaikh Ahmad Abdul Haq. Abdul Rahman Chishti, *Mirat ul-Asrar*, vol. II, p. 444.

120. Abdul Rahman Chishti, *Mirat ul-Asrar*, vol. II, pp. 522-30; Abdul Haq Muhaddis Dehalvi, *Akhbar ul-Akhyar*, pp. 403-8.
121. Abdul Rahman Chishti, *Mirat ul-Asrar*, vol. II, pp. 535-8.
122. Ibid., pp. 539-41.
123. Ibid., p. 532.
124. Ibid., pp. 533-8.
125. Ibid., pp. 561-3. According to popular belief, when Shaikh Gangohi decided to leave Rudauli in search of a living mentor, Shaikh Ahmad Abdul Haq physically emerged from his tomb. He owned Shaikh Gangohi as his own and, directing him to stay put in Rudauli, revealed the mystical perfections of his grandson Shaikh Muhammad. This hint was enough for Shaikh Gangohi, who followed it in letter and spirit.
126. Simon Digby, 'Abd al-Quddus Gangohi (1456-1537): The Personality and Attitudes of an Indian Sufi,' *Medieval India: A Miscellany*, vol. III, Bombay: Asia Publishing House, 1975, pp. 2-11.
127. Abdul Rahman Chishti, *Mirat ul-Asrar*, vol. I, p. 563; Muhammad Akram Quddusi, *Iqtibas ul-Anwar*, pp. 615-16.
128. Muhammad Akram Quddusi, *Iqtibas ul-Anwar*, pp. 616-18.
129. Ibid., pp. 621-2.
130. Ibid., pp. 623-4.
131. Ibid., pp. 624-6.
132. Abdul Haq Muhaddis Dehalvi, *Akhbar ul-Akhyar*, pp. 465-7.
133. Ibid., p. 467.
134. Originally written in Sanskrit, *Amritkunda* (Pool of Nectar) has been translated into Persian, Arabic, Turki and Urdu. It dealt with a variety of practices, which were neither distinctively Indian, nor restricted to Yoga e.g. fasting, vegetarianism and celibacy. It stressed breath control to maximize inhalation for achieving long life, besides discussing physiological techniques for purification of human body, with reference to bodily postures and chakra meditations. Besides quotes from the Quran and Hadis, the text includes several terms from Islamic religious practices including Sufism. Carl W. Ernst, 'Islamization of Yoga in the Amritkunda Translations,' *Journal of the Royal Asiatic Society*, Third Series, vol. 13, no. 2, July 2003, pp. 217-20; also see, Yusuf Husain, 'Haud al-Hayat: The Arabic Version of Amritkund,' in *On Becoming an Indian Muslim: French Essays on Aspects of Syncretism*, ed. M. Waseem, New Delhi: Oxford University Press, 2003, pp. 63-74.
135. Saiyid Athar Abbas Rizvi, *A History of Sufism in India*, vol. I, pp. 335-41.
136. Simon Digby, op. cit., pp. 46-9.

CHAPTER 8

The World of the Zamindars

The story of Hir and Ranjha has been the most popular folktale of Panjab. The narrative was set in the second half of the fifteenth century when the authority of the Delhi Sultanate had declined and, as a result, local chiefs had gained in political influence and material resources. The plot revolved around the pursuit of love by the protagonists, with particular reference to the dominance of patriarchal forces. Though the available versions differ in matters of detail, its major landmarks were essentially common. Ranjha, the son of a zamindar of Takht Hazara, abandoned his home in protest against the unfair distribution of ancestral lands. During his wanderings, he fell in love with Hir, the daughter of a zamindar of Jhang Siyal. He worked as a herdsman for Hir's family in order to pursue his love. While he grazed buffaloes and played on the flute, Hir and her friends would come to meet. When the matter came out in the open, the Siyals married Hir to a Khera youth of Rangpur Khera. Hir refused to consummate the marriage, while Ranjha went to Tilla Balnath and became a Jogi. He gained access to Hir and, with the help of Hir's sister-in-law Sehti, eloped from the village. Unfortunately they met a tragic end at the hands of their opponents. A different version related that they were united by the intervention of a just local potentate, while still another held that they left for Haj.

Damodar Gulati was the first to versify the tale in Panjabi. He claimed to have set up a shop at Jhang Siyal during the reign of Akbar. It is, however, difficult to believe that he was a contemporary of the lovers and witness to events in their lives. Apparently Damodar has grafted a century-old story to his own times, with the aim of imparting authenticity to his narrative. Long before he took up his pen, the story had entered the collective memory in northwestern India. This has been attested by Baqi Kulabi (d. 1579) who,[1] while preparing a Persian account of the tale, asserted that the story (*afsana*) had caused an uproar (*ghogha*) in Hind, as it was found on every tongue.[2] Shah Husain (1539-99), the famous Sufi poet of Lahore, employed episodes from the tale as metaphors for expressing the love of a seeker for the divine. In this cultural environment, Damodar produced the first ever account of the story in Panjabi (western dialect) in over 960 stanzas of four lines each. In the following pages, an attempt is made to present this narrative, while staying close to the text. It throws light on several aspects of medieval Panjab. The countryside was controlled by powerful zamindars, who relied for support on their respective clans. On the one hand, they organized agricultural production and reared large herds of cattle and, on the other, they aggressively sought to amplify their power. Patriarchal in character, the clans used every device to impose their will on members. In these conditions, the lovers survived with the assistance of supernatural forces as well as spiritual entities like the Sufis and Jogis.

Alliance between the Siyals and Kheras

Jhang town was under the notables (*abdaleen*) of the Siyal clan.[3] The place enjoyed prosperity, reflected in its large population of buffaloes and cows. Chuchak, who was its chief (*sikdar*), exercised his power over the land and rivers. He received his income from a variety of sources and, thus, challenged the authority of Akbar. He was blessed with four sons – Khan, Pathan, Sultan and Bahadur. As the boys grew older, they did not recognize any superior power. Kundi (the wife of Chuchak) had grown somewhat old, but she gave birth to a beautiful daughter named Hir. Before she entered her teens, she attracted offers of betrothal. As the father and sons pondered over the matter, they hoped to expand their clout in the locality.[4] If she were married in the country of the Afghans, their sway would extend beyond the Indus. If she were offered in marriage to Akbar, they would acquire the right of assessing the land revenue.[5]

The Siyal men assembled and advised Chuchak to find a suitable match for Hir. Chuchak revealed that two messengers, a Brahmin and a Doom, had been sent by the Kheras with a written proposal for marriage. The Siyals declared, 'There is no reason to decline the offer of the Kheras. This is a divine opportunity to form a grand relationship, which would be useful in the future.' Chuchak secured the concurrence of the women folk and implemented the collective decision of the Siyal clan. The Brahmins and Dooms of the village hosted the visitors.[6]

After eight days, Chuchak summoned a meeting of the Siyals. In accordance with a collective decision, the two emissaries were given a three-piece apparel and a horse each.[7] Chuchak conveyed a message to the Kheras, congratulating them for the impending alliance, which was expected to enhance the fortunes of both the clans. The Khera chief Ali was overjoyed at the acceptance of the proposal by the Siyals. He gave orders for the circulation of the good news. Drums were beaten and messengers were dispatched to summon the Khera clansmen. The Khans assembled and, following a discussion (*maslat*), decided to visit Jhang Siyal, so as to formalize the betrothal. Preparations were made for a large convoy. A number of goods, including horses and cash, were collected. Weapons were stacked in the wooden slings (*behangi*) meant for luggage. Also present was a colourful party of jesters, pipers, singers and dancers. The Khans, who were the lords of the land (*bhoyen de khawind*) left for Jhang Siyal, while the local populace converged to see the magnificent spectacle.[8]

Waiting for the arrival of the Kheras, Chuchak made the requisite preparations. The meeting hall (*dalan*) was given a fresh coat of clay plaster, mattresses and sheets were spread. All types of provisions – ghee, sugar, grain, flour, liquor and fodder – were gathered. The Siyals welcomed the guests in the midst of music and dance. The festivities transformed the site into the court (*akhada*) of Indra.[9] The party was brought to the meeting hall, where the brave warriors, who were masters of land and rivers (*bhoyen nayi de sayin*), assembled. As the cups of liquor circulated, the balladeers sang the epical tales (*vaaran*).

Next morning, the jesters and singers commenced the day with their performances. The Siyals distributed alms among the beggars, who offered blessings (*asees*) in return. Chuchak sat among the Siyal clansmen and decided that, in addition to a camel and horse, each guest be given a turban and gold based apparel (*siropau sunehri*). The Kheras were served food and presented gifts.[10] Chuchak came forward and, unfolding his turban around his neck, pleaded in humility: 'I have released Taazi horses on the land. I have created many enmities in the world. But I have threshed the earth with my sword, forcing everyone to submit before me. This exalted Khan (*khan salamat*) has never bent on any occasion. It was only now that Hir has induced me to submit.' Reciprocating these sentiments, Ali clasped the hand of Chuchak. This act formalized the betrothal ceremony and sealed the proposed marriage alliance between the Siyals and Kheras.[11] Thus far, the prospective bride and bridegroom were conspicuous by their absence. After the departure of the Kheras from Jhang Siyal, an identical ritual, which involved the girl and the boy, was held in both the households. Dooms sat to sing and felicitations poured in.[12] Kundi, the mother of Hir, summoned all the girls. She prepared a dessert (*kheer*) of rice, milk and sugar. As she gave the first morsel to Hir, she also made an offering of gold ornaments weighing one maund.[13] As soon as the Kheras reached their village, a similar ritual was held, with the boy and his mother in the centre of the proceedings. The process of betrothal was sealed.

Conflict between Two Clans

Noora, a Jat of the Sambhal clan,[14] held a zamindari in the neighbourhood of the Siyals. He had a magnificent boat (*berha ajab*) built for himself and appointed Luddan, a Jhinwar by caste,[15] as his boatman (*malah*). But the relation between master and servant turned sour in a dramatic manner. One day, a group of zamindars appeared on the scene and, with the help of Luddan, inspected the boat. Outraged at the intrusion, Noora abused Luddan and gave him a sound beating. Unable to digest the insult, Luddan ran away with the boat and escaped to the zamindari of the Siyals. Crying in a loud voice, he sought protection from a brave chief (*raath*) engendered by a noble woman.[16] Hir, who was sporting with a large troupe of her friends on the Chenab,[17] took Luddan in the protection of the Siyals. He asked Hir to call her elders, as the Sambhals could launch an attack on the Siyals. Hir, who was acting as the Siyal chief, threw a challenge, 'Curse the father and grand daughter of Noora. Why are you afraid? If some people dare to raid, I will kill them where they stand. I will call my father and uncles only if an Akbar-born himself leads the attack.' Having taken the boat in her custody, she got it anchored on the Siyal dock.[18]

As soon as the news of the events reached Noora, he was filled with rage. His existence and authority had been challenged as never before. People asked: 'Why has a turban been tied on your head? Why should your name prevail? The Siyals had captured your boat and it is in their firm possession.' He summoned the leading men (*raath*) of his clan and resolved to punish the Siyals. In his view, the Siyals were flirting with death, thirsting for blood and itching for the taste of iron. He sent a Doom to the Siyals with a letter in which he demanded the return of the boat and custody of Luddan, failing which he would use force to recover his rightful possession. Chuchak, who was conducting the business of his chiefdom in the assembly (*sath*), lost his temper. On reading the letter, the Siyals fell on the Doom, whose face was blackened and who was thrashed with shoes. Noora was left with no choice but to fight the Siyals in order to recover his property, servant and honour. He mobilized his men and saddled 360 horses.[19] Raising the slogan of 'Ali Ali,' the Sambhals rode through 6 leagues at night.[20] They aimed at capturing the boat, tying Luddan with ropes and retreating in a swift move and, in the process, avoiding any armed encounter with the Siyals. They would resort to fighting only if they met any resistance from the enemy. While the Sambhals galloped in the darkness, the normal arrangement of nature was disturbed. As soon as Luddan heard the sound of hooves, he warned Hir of the impending danger.

The girls ran from the banks of the Chenab to their houses and prepared for a contest. They tied gray shawls round their bodies and armed themselves with swords and shields. Luddan advised Hir to call her father and brothers, but she rejected the plea. Irritated at this cowardly suggestion, Hir ordered Luddan to go away, lest she should kill him. She asked him to watch from a distance as the girls routed the intruders. In a quick discussion on the spot, Hir unfolded the plan of making a frontal assault on the Sambhals. The Sambhals were astounded on seeing a group of young girls armed to the hilt and ready for battle. When the hostilities began, Hir ducked the blow of Noora Chaddar (not to be confused with Noora Sambhal) and, in a quick counter attack, knocked him down from his horse. Before retaliating, she shouted: 'Do not run away, O Jatta. Now it is my turn.' Hassi, the closest friend of Hir, asked Hir to be more cautious because, if something happened to her, the band would be left without a leader. Justifying her action, Hir asserted that it would be matter of shame for a chief (*sikdar*) to remain at the rear in battle. Since human life was in the hands of God, she would not undermine the position of the other members of the band. In her view, the Sambhals were the aggressors and their own existence had been threatened by the attack. God had provided them with an opportunity to prove themselves and their bravery in battle would earn universal praise. As the men watched in amazement, the girls fell upon the enemy while crying 'Ali Ali.'[21]

The Siyal girls, crawling forward like iguanas (*gohs*), blocked the arrows with their shields. As the swords flew in all directions, corpses fell and limbs bled. The girls fought like headless mendicants (*jogianian*) who were notorious for drinking blood.[22] Hir herself killed twelve men, while eight girls lost their lives. The morale of the Siyal girls kept on rising and, imbued with a furious killer instinct, they gained an upper hand. The Sambhals lifted the reins to turn back and release arrows in defense, but the Siyal girls allowed them to retreat. The Sambhal chief Noora saw the defeat staring at him. He ordered his men to retreat, leaving the boat and Luddan behind. After all, getting killed at the hands of a bunch of girls would be the worst of humiliations. Throwing a direct challenge to Noora Sambhal, Hir asked him not to flee. Noora Sambhal was constrained to admit that the girls were as brave as the Siyal knights. If the girls had fought in this manner, one could imagine how their parents would fight.[23] Hir directed her companions to cover their faces with veils and to refrain from hurling taunts on the vanquished. They had to realize that the bearded ones had taken to flight, but had lost their honour in the process. She ensured that the corpses of the enemy were dragged and thrown in the river. However, when she saw the mortal remains of her companions, she was overcome with emotion. As she mourned their death, she held them close to her chest and had them buried.[24]

As the people of Jhang Siyal heard of the violent episode, they assembled in a central place. Hir's brothers confronted their sister. They wanted to know the reason of being kept in the dark about the development. Did she think that her brothers had died? They wished to go after the Sambhals immediately. Fabricating a credible story, Hir stated, 'Someone has conveyed a false report to you. In fact, some starving herdsmen (*bhukhe chak*) came from some where and laid their hands on the creepers. The girls threw them out without much effort. Thereafter, we did not see anyone. Should I ask some one to tell you that it was Akbar who attacked us?' The Siyals had no choice but to disperse. As soon as Hir was seen alone, Luddan approved her action of dispersing the contingent (*kattak*) of intruders. Free from all worries, he resumed his duties as the boatman.[25]

Rupture in the Zamindari Household

Mojam, who belonged to the Jat clan of Ranjhas,[26] was a great lord of land and rivers. He was blessed with a son Dhido, who was an epitome of physical beauty and beacon of miraculous powers. As the child grew up to boyhood, the fame of his charm spread in all directions. Parents of girls began to send proposals for marriage. However, his three brothers (Tahir, Zahir and Jeevan) were jealous of Dhido and the attention he was getting.[27] They were helpless so long as their mother was alive. When she died, Mojam began to keep Dhido close to himself. The three brothers feared that they would be deprived of the hereditary chiefdom (*sikdari*) if Dhido were allowed to live. They conspired to kill Dhido outright.

Mojam considered ways of securing the life and future of Dhido. He decided to seek the daughter of Yaqub Khan Waraich, a prominent chief (*wadda aha raath*),[28] as a match for Dhido. He sent a Brahmin and Doom to negotiate the alliance. He dictated the letter without letting anyone get wind of his shrewd move.[29]

The two emissaries travelled for three days and, on meeting Yaqub Khan Waraich, delivered the letter. Yaqub summoned the members of his clan (*qabila*) and sought their opinion on the proposal. Expressing their approval, the clansmen offered their own daughters as well.[30] They were equal partners in the process of developing relations between clans through the matrimonial alliances. In accordance with the prevailing custom, the emissaries were hosted for eight days. On the advice of his clansmen, Yaqub gave gold necklaces (*tarag*) to the two emissaries, who were seen off with respect. When they reached Takht Hazara, they conveyed the happy tidings to Mojam. Ceremonial drums (*tamak dhol*) were played and goods were distributed among the large clan (*bahut jamiat lashkar*).[31] Shocked beyond words, the brothers became desperate. Forced to act quickly, Mojam decided to place Dhido in the protective custody of the Waraich chief, who had been tied in the bond of kinship. He again sent the Brahmin and Doom to Yaqub in order to fix the marriage. Sensing the cause of Mojam's urgency, Yaqub sent the desired knotted strings (*gandhiyan*), which indicated the final date of marriage. As soon as Mojam received the knotted strings, he intiated elaborate arrangements for Dhido's marriage.[32]

Mojam sent invitations to his brothers and other relatives through messengers. He accumulated huge stocks of grain, flour, sugar and clarified butter. Drums, trumpets and pipes were kept in readiness. Dhido, who was just ten years of age, was placed in ceremonial seclusion (*maiyan*). His body was rubbed with perfumed paste (*watna*) and colourful henna (*mehandi*). He wore golden bangles on his wrists, danglers in his ears and a ring in his nose. The curled tresses of his long hair fell on his shoulders like snakes. His face shone and his eyes flashed. But when seven days remained before the wedding, Mojam died suddenly and goods were plundered.[33] Emboldened, the three brothers considered different ways of killing Dhido – administering poison or slaying in sleep and casting his body in the river. On second thoughts, they abandoned the plan to kill Dhido owing to the fear of rousing suspicion and getting caught. Therefore, they decided to divide their ancestral landed estate as well as the internal and external wealth into four parts. By doing so, they could demonstrate to the world that they just intended to live separately and cultivate the respective shares of their common inheritance.[34]

Shocked at the turn of events, Dhido appealed, 'O Tahir. You are in the place of our father. I do not know the ways of the world. I am just a suckling child. You are the keeper of honour.' The three brothers, who drew from the ancient theoretician Chanakya, advised him to earn his livelihood by working like Jats. He was asked to pick up the spade and hoe to uproot the weeds from his land. Though he was young in age, yet Dhido understood that his brothers had already expelled him from the ancestral legacy.[35] Therefore, he declared his resolve to leave the village: 'The land is yours and the water is yours. You brothers have divided every thing. My hands and feet are red with henna. How can I wield the spade? With the death of Mojam, your affection for me ended and there is no place for me in the lands of the Chenab. Fate does not let me stay here. Moreover, I am being chased by the tax collector (*muhassil*).'[36]

When Dhido left Takht Hazara, the people of the village congregated in the streets. In their view, Mojam's death had set the ball rolling, as the three brothers dispossessed Dhido of his inheritance and, separating him from his roots, made him homeless.[37] The women of Takht Hazara, while sympathizing with Dhido, felt that his marriage had been blocked by the death of Mojam. The common view (*lokachari*) and popular whispers (*cho cho*) clearly indicated that the brothers were huddled in counsel (*maslat*) and hatched a conspiracy to eliminate Dhido, who would surely be murdered.[38] Dhido, who sensed the evil designs of his brothers, slipped out at midnight without any means of expenditure (*kharch*). He carried two valuable possessions, a staff (*khundi*) and flute (*vanjhli*). In spite of his depressing mental state, he looked handsome and impressive in his physical appearance.[39]

A fugitive from his home in Takht Hazara, Dhido walked day and night. He reached an unknown place and settled in a mosque to spend the night.[40] Some young girls, who were going to fetch water, saw him. Sardara, who was the daughter of a Jhinwar, fell for him. Before the encounter could proceed, a group of Jats appeared on the scene. Dhido turned pale, fearing that they might be his brother's spies deputed to kill him. However, his fears turned out to be unfounded.[41] In response to a question, Dhido told them that he had become a traveller to save his life, as his brothers had conspired to kill him after their father's death. Meanwhile, Sardara went home and told her mother that she would marry Dhido or elope with him. After intitial reluctance, she gave her consent on seeing Dhido. She was deceived into believing that the visitors were Jhinwars bound for Multan and that Dhido was one of them. The men agreed to her proposal of Dhido-Sardara marriage in lieu of a sumptuous meal. The woman went home and arranged the provisions that were carried to the mosque.[42] The Jats felt guilty of making Dhido a pawn in realizing their immediate aim. They admitted having told a lie just to fill their stomachs. Shocked at the behaviour of the Jats, Dhido admonished them for their deceit and, in protest, did not join in their feast.[43] He refused to be a party to the fraud on a simple Jhinwar woman and would not play with the life of an innocent young girl.

Dhido departed from the mosque and walking through the wilderness, entered a habitation at the edge of a town. He reached the house of an old couple, who gave him food to eat and bed to sleep. Next morning, the hosts asked about Dhido's identity (caste, clan and father), having guessed that he had forsaken his native place (*vatn*) owing to a dispute. Dhido, who had learnt from his bitter experience at the mosque, refused to reveal his identity and, snapping all social ties, became a homeless wanderer. The Khan invited Dhido to settle as a cultivator in the village. He offered to provide all the basic needs – camel, mare, mule, buffaloes, cows and wells along the silting land. He would even fix his marriage with one of his sisters or nieces. Dhido felt indebted to the old couple for their hospitality and warmth, but refused to entangle himself in worldly matters. He promised to settle in the village only after returning from a pilgrimage (*ziyarat*) to the sacred tombs of the saints.[44] Bidding farewell to the old couple, Dhido again embarked on his journey through the jungle, valleys and moors. He reached the hereditary domain (*sik*) of the Siyals and, sitting in contemplation on the Chenab, started playing the Rag Bambiha on his flute. He was wonderstruck on seeing a boat moving towards the bank. A group of five saints, the Panj Pir,[45] who were sitting in the boat, was charmed by the melody of the flute. As the boat docked, the Panj Pir alighted and sat on the bank. Dhido, who was joined by the saints, narrated his tale of woe and followed it up by playing the Rag Lalit on his flute. Pleased, each saint conferred a boon on him and bestowed Hir in his lappet. At the same time, they appeared before Hir in a vision and instructed her to accept Ranjha as her partner, who had been tied to her lappet. They sealed this union by offering milk to the two and departed.[46]

Having spent the night on the bank of the Chenab, Ranjha woke up and boarded the beautiful boat. He told Luddan that he was a traveller (*sailani*) observing the world and that his only companions were a staff and flute.[47] As the music rose from his flute, a number of wild animals – tigers, leopards, pythons and cobras – were attracted to the site. Elevated to ecstasy, Luddan offered valuable gifts – buffaloes, cows and two women – to Ranjha. But he would not permit Dhido to rest in the boat out of the fear of Hir. A daughter of Chuchak and sister of Pathana, she did what pleased her. She had subjugated the four rivers. Drawn like a bow, she prowled to hunt. She did not fear Akbar, having rendered the Mughals powerless. Feeling dejected, Ranjha admitted that he did not have any claim, document or plough. He was merely the master of a mat and fire, with no interest in a luxurious bedstead. The argument had the desired effect and Luddan allowed him to sleep on the bed.[48]

Hir, who was flying high on a swing, was shocked to find a stranger lying on her bed. She leapt into the river and swam towards the boat along with her companions. They had armed themselves with branches of trees to deal with the intruder. Hir directed her rage at Luddan and asked if he had inched towards his grave by treating the stranger as a chief greater (*rath dadhera*) than herself. Luddan defended himself by referring to the stranger as a saint (*wali khasm da poora*) who was fully devoted to God and whose words never ended in error.⁴⁹ Rejecting the request of such a spiritually endowed person would have brought harm to her. Unimpressed by his defence, Hir gave a severe beating to Luddan who, with his body covered with blood, became half dead. As soon as the girls saw Ranjha's moonlit forehead, they were instantly ensnared by his beauty. When he leapt out of the boat, Hir held his arm in a strong grip and asked him to play on his flute. In response to the lilting notes, all living beings, including animals and plants, arrived for a pilgrimage (*ziyarat*) and prostrated themselves as if offering the salutations of Id.⁵⁰

Luddan asked Ranjha to stop his music, lest someone should die. He located Hir and, kneading her limbs, tried to revive her from a trance. Rising from a swoon, Hir declared that she had found in Ranjha a partner she was looking for. Putting her shawl round her neck and bending double till her hands touched her feet, she apologized to Luddan and gave him a gift of two buffaloes. He reminded Hir that he had permitted Ranjha to sleep on the bed, because he was a suitable (*laik*) match for her. Ranjha and Hir, along with her 360 friends (*saheliyan*), sat on the bank of the Chenab. The two lovers looked into each other's eyes and, without uttering a word, felt that they had been placed into the lot of each other by the saints (*piran*). Some girls began to take a romantic interest in Ranjha and wished to marry him. Another disapproved their rash manner, as it had put the honour of the zamindars (*rathayen*) at stake. Veero advanced her own suitability, because belonging to the menial caste (*kameyani*) of the Dooms, she would be a proper match for this poor load carrying slave (*gand gahir ghulam*) like Ranjha.⁵¹ At this moment, class and caste became crucial. Since Ranjha was seen as a poor and homeless vagabond, he could not be married to the daughter of any zamindar. Hence the claims of the lowly placed Doom girl.

Hir was assailed by a range of depressing thoughts. Ranjha would not be able to prolong his stay in village Chuchakana or her parents would not accept their relationship or one of her friends could claim Ranjha. Her closest friend Hassi enabled her to devise a plan of action. They brought all the Siyal girls to the bank of the Chenab, but made them stay at the swings. As Hassi stood guard, the two lovers met in the boat and locked themselves in a sexual union.[52] Hir underwent a dramatic transformation and assumed a new social identity. She declared to Ranjha, 'Let no one call me Hir. Nor call me as one of the Siyals. Having erased caste and craft (*jat sanaat*), I have become the maid of a herdsman. I am not the daughter of Chuchak and my mother. I am now tied to your lappet, if you accept this Jat girl.' She put her shawl round her neck and touched Ranjha's feet. Through this physical gesture of absolute submission, she swore eternal love (*ishq*) for Ranjha, which had conferred a new consciousness on her. She broke the tradition with one stroke and, having discarded all pride, reduced herself to the dust of earth. She was dyed in Ranjha's red colour, just as Ranjha himself had been dyed in red by the saints (Panj Pir).[53] In their love, sexuality and spirituality merged into each other, creating a new identity, both social and religious.

Grazing Buffaloes in the Meadows

As the romance graduated from one stage to the other, the conventional roles were reversed. Hir assumed the dominant role of a lover, while Ranjha accepted the passive position of the beloved. Hir formulated a plan to integrate Ranjha into the socio-economic life of Jhang Siyal. She made him familiar with the geographical layout of the place, identifying the major landmarks including the ancestral meeting place (*sath babbani*) where three types of tree – banyan, fig and sirises – were found. She instructed him on the manner he should conduct himself during his first meeting with her parents. He must walk slowly, speak softly and ask only for water. Covering his face with the lappet of his turban, he should speak little.[54] On reaching her house, Hir told her mother that she had found a herdsman (*chak*) who possessed numerous virtues. Every morning, he would get up and graze the buffaloes. Owing to his charisma (*barkat*) grass would not dry up, buffaloes would not drop their calves, they would not catch the mouth and foot disease and there would be plenty of rainfall. Soon after, Ranjha presented himself before Chuchak, who was sitting in the common assembly (*sath*). Speaking in unison, all the Siyals asked Ranjha the place from where he had come. Ranjha agreed to answer all queries, provided his hunger and thirst quenched. Hir served him food comprising sweetened bread, milk, cream and ghee. As she moved a fan over his head, she mumbled several auguries and effected many omens. Wrapping a scarf round her neck, she declared: 'You are my lord and I am your subject (*raiyat*), just like an iron nail fixed in a hoe. My shame (*lajja*) is in your hands and I am your votive offering.'[55]

After eating the simple fare, Ranjha went up to the Siyals and introduced himself, 'My name is Dhido and I am the son of Mojam. My caste is Ranjha who belong to Takht Hazara. No body leaves his native place (*vatn*) without a dispute. After the death of Mojam, my brothers gave me much pain. They even wanted to kill me. Therefore, I came to you.'[56] Chuchak was willing to give not only a simple protection to Ranjha, but he was inclined to settle him as a cultivator on his land. This was indicated by the package, which was offered by Chuchak in his capacity as the local zamindar. This package, apart from a plough and well in the riverine land, comprised unspecified number of camels, horses, cows and buffaloes. He would be free to sow and reap himself. As a concrete and definite incentive, he would not pay land tax to any higher authority. Ranjha politely declined the attractive offer, but proposed to be employed as a herdsman.[57] Ranjha would not work as a farmer because the task was quite back-breaking and would extract much of his energy and time. He lacked the toughness and experience that was required to grow crops.[58] On the contrary, the work of grazing cattle was not only less demanding, but it would open up numerous opportunities of pursuing his love, far from the prying eyes of the villagers. That was why Hir was herself keen on employing Ranjha as a herdsman (*chak*).

Before taking a final decision in the matter, Chuchak summoned his Siyal clansmen and chief herdsmen for consultations. He informed the gathering that Ranjha was inclined to work as a herdsman, but was not willing to settle as a cultivator in spite of several incentives. At first the Siyal clansmen ridiculed the idea of wasting a herd of buffaloes by placing it in the hands of an immature boy. The heads of the herdsmen offered a solution. They felt that it was possible to accommodate Ranjha in the zamindari, as a number of projects were under construction. There were eighty four herdsmen (*chaks*) in the zamindari. They would dry the bogs (*khubbar*) in the pond (*chappar*). They would fill the gaps in the embankments, wherever the structure had sunk.[59] It appears that a new servant could be employed only in consultation and with the approval of the managers of the servants. They were duly consulted by the zamindar on the recruitment of a new servant. This was not a rule legally binding on the zamindar. It appears to have been only a matter of procedure, which was sanctioned by practice in the rural areas.[60] This would enable the managers to wash away an earlier stigma of laziness. A servant could be assigned more than one task, depending on the changing needs of the farm, as understood by the zamindar. Thus Ranjha, who was employed as a herdsman, could also be deputed for other jobs that were unrelated to the grazing of buffaloes.

The candidate for a post was duly tested for the skill required for a particular task. The test was carried out in a discreet manner, so that even the candidate did not know about it. As soon as the Siyal clansmen and heads of servants granted their approval, Chuchak publicly announced the terms of Ranjha's appointment. Buffaloes would be placed under his charge. In compensation, he would be given sweet bread (*mitha tukkar*) in the morning and evening. On the next Thursday, he would make his debut with the buffaloes. Having settled the matter, Chuchak put Ranjha to a discreet test. He was offered a dish of slow-boiled milk, sweet bread and fine flour.[61] As soon as Ranjha took the first morsel (*nivala*) in his mouth, he flew into a rage and shouted that he was fed the milk of a miscarried buffalo (*turooi*).[62] Chuchak expressed his amazement. How could Ranjha discern the quality of milk? Was he a spiritual guide (*pir*) or true saint (*wali sachawan*) who could convey messages from the other world? Did he see a dream or possess miraculous power or learnt the truth from someone? Ranjha was clear and accurate in his reply. It was the third pregnancy of the buffaloe, who was auburn of colour and had a white spot on her forehead. She had dropped a six month old female calf and, while the herdsman (*majhi*) was away, struggled in the moor (*bela*) and swallowed the placenta (*jeer*). Not copulated since then, it was her milk which had been fed to Ranjha. Impressed with Ranjha's veterinary skills, the assembly unanimously approved his appointment. Chuchak, who was happy at acquiring a singular herdsman (*chak navela*), celebrated the occasion by having the drums beaten.[63]

Once Ranjha took charge of his duties, people began to speculate about him. How could such a good-looking and gentle person accept the lowly position of a herdsman? The girls, in particular, wished to be attached to him in love or matrimony. Serving as a herdsman, Ranjha applied unique methods. He built a raised seat and, digging a hole in earth, lit a smouldering fire. He also built a raised platform (*jallar*) in order to keep an eye on his flock. Whenever the buffaloes were escorted to the moor and back to the village, he played a Rag on his flute.[64] In response, the buffaloes clustered around him just as the Gopis were attracted on hearing Krishna's flute in the Vrindavan.[65] The wild animals, too, converged on the scene as if they were on a pilgrimage (*ziyarat*). He lived in harmony with them. The buffaloes, while being milked in their sheds, were found gentler than before. The prominent men of Jhang Siyal praised Ranjha in the presence of Chuchak. He was spoken of as a perfect saint (*wali hai poora*) who need not be tested. Contrary to the past practice, he drove the buffaloes to the moor at night and brought them back at dawn, both at a time when the wild animals were out of their dens. The herdsmen, who were jealous of this rootless upstart (*bemuniyadah*), feared the end of their livelihood. They conspired to kill him at midnight in the moor and throw his corpse in the river. On a dark night, as many as eighty four herdsmen set out for the moor, carrying double edged swords on their shoulders. They managed to locate Ranjha who was sitting in deep contemplation (*dhiyan*). The attackers unsheathed their weapons and, crying 'Ali Ali,' rushed forward.

They were astonished on seeing a detachment of armed men, who wore black robes and rode black horses. The assailants were struck with panic. When they took to flight, they were caught in a stampede. Many of them were killed, while others had broken limbs. Those who remained alive slipped back in stealth. The desire of the conspirators ended in a disaster.[66] The wailing women of the bereaved families complained to Chuchak, who summoned the herdsmen to know the details of the violent episode. The herdsmen admitted that they planned to eliminate Ranjha. But a group of black-robed warriors on black steeds chased them away. Chuchak was convinced that Ranjha was endowed with divine blessings (*barkat*). Dejected, the herdsmen declared that a fraudster had snatched their bread and that they would be forced to grow grass and produce wood. When their opposition subsided, Ranjha came to virtually rule over the moors like a sovereign. He continued to handle the buffaloes in his own unique way. He had acquired intimate knowledge about every nook and corner of the place. He had gained the friendly intimacy with wild animals.[67] In Damodar's portrayal, Ranjha was not only an innovative herdsman, but also a saint with supernatural powers.

Devices of Patriarchy

When Ranjha had grazed buffaloes in Jhang Siyal for two months, his love affair with Hir became popular gossip (*chocho*). Moving about with untied hair, she carried for Ranjha a packet of food – bread crushed in clarified butter and sugar (*choori*) – which was prepared by Hassi. Hir's companions warned Hir to restrain her steps, lest Chuchak should learn about the goings on. In responding to her friends, Hir revealed the advanced stage of her love. When she was a virgin (*kanj kuwari*), she had played with dolls. When she took Ranjha as her husband after the ceremonial rounds (*laavan*), nothing came into her heart. Since she had acquired a perfect spiritual guide (*kamil murshid*), she did not need anything else. Her friends were free to enjoy themselves with the boat and swings, while she was dedicated to her lord (*sayin*)

Ranjha. The girls were astounded at this brazen admission.[68] In a short time, the news of Hir's love affair circulated freely in the eighty-four villages of Chuchak's *zamindari*. They wanted Hir to be strangled for bringing about a major calamity. The women of the Siyal clan and the three daughters-in-law (wives of Hir's brothers) met the mistress of the house, Kundi. They complained that Hir had disgraced the Siyal clan, while she had remained oblivious of the scandal. Diverting the real issue to local politics, Kundi asked the women to return to their houses. As her mind turned to the stigma of Hir's scandal, she felt like consuming poison. The women decided to speak directly to Hir on her return and dispersed.[69]

When the daughters-in-law confronted Hir, they questioned her relations with the herdsman, pointed to the high status of her father and brothers, besides referring to her betrothal among the Kheras. Hir became angry, as it did not behove the Khan's family to believe something without seeing it. Kundi reminded Hir of the family's high status and big influence. Her father and father-in-law were lords of lands and rivers. Her father had contested the authority of Akbar and controlled the seven routes. He had subjugated all his rivals. But now she could only think of killing herself. Rejecting all the charges as lies, Hir asserted that she was a virgin and knew nothing about physical intimacy. She argued that Ranjha arrived in Jhang Siyal owing to the decree of fortune, but the Siyals had no respect for him. Kundi expressed her fear that Ranjha could be killed by Hir's brothers and this death would spell the doom of the Siyals. Kundi started crying and fainted.[70] In her view, Hir's relation with Ranjha was not sanctioned by the social norms and, therefore, it was impermissible. On the other hand, Hir held that her relation with Ranjha was pure and beyond reproach. It was impossible to reconcile these two positions.

One day Chuchak was supervising the construction of an embankment, where he had put all the inhabitants of the town (*qasba*) to work. On hearing Hir's intimacy with Ranjha from an uncouth man (*ganwar*), he became depressed. His state of depression was not related to routine matters of his chiefdom (*zamindari*). He had not entered into a fresh dispute; the tracks of any investigation did not reach his abode; he did not encounter any new enmity; he had not hurt anyone; he did not nurture any evil intention and Emperor Akbar was not marching in hot pursuit. At this moment, his mind was assailed by the talk of Hir's association with Ranjha. Kundi argued that they should not accuse without seeing, particularly in case of a virgin who was protected by her father and brothers. Chuchak requested his elder brother Kaido to pursue Hir into the moor and bring a true report of her activities. Kaido was reluctant to undertake this task, because he could loose his life at the hands of Hir. Known to be bold and aggressive, she did not fear even the military might of Akbar.[71]

Kaido went to the moor and kept a careful watch. Hir arrived on the scene with the bowl of food on her head. She touched Ranjha's feet in reverence and, picking up the dust, put it on her face and forehead. She stood before Ranjha with folded hands. He asked her to get milk. Hir picked up a vessel and left to get milk. Wearing the garb of a beggar, Kaido sought alms (*bhikhiya*) from the herdsman. Ranjha treated him with respect and gave him the sweetened crumbs. Kaido returned to Chuchak and presented the alms as evidence of Hir's intimacy with Ranjha. He asked the Siyals not to keep their daughters in their houses; either they should be drowned in rivers or their heads should be chopped off. Chucak, while showing the sweetened crumbs to Kundi, expressed his anger at the rich food being provided to a mere servant, whereas he himself never ate anything like that. In an attempt to defend Hir, Kundi stated that she had herself prepared the sweetened crumbs, while girls had poured extra butter on them as they intended to make an offering to Khwaja Khizr. Chuchak was not convinced.[72] When Hir returned with the vessel of milk, she realized that her uncle (*taya*) Kaido had come to spy on them. She feared that their love affair, which was concealed from view, would be blown into a mighty blaze. Failing to control her rage, she torched Kaido's hut which, along with all its goods, was reduced to ashes. She further threatened to pull out the hair on his head, break his leg which was still intact, drink his blood and finally kill him. Shocked beyond words, Kaido intended to survive either by shifting his loyalties or by migrating to Rajoa Syedan[73]

One day Chuchak went to the moor and saw the two lovers sleeping on the platform (*jallar*). Hir climbed down and walked away. Chuchak delivered two blows of a cane (*kamchi*) on Ranjha, who was banished from Jhang Siyal. As Ranjha was walking away, he began to play on the flute. Chuchak heard the lilting notes and slipped into ecstasy (*masti*). Surprisingly, the cattle as well as the wild animals followed in the footsteps of Ranjha. In spite of Chuchak's efforts to push them back, they became even more insistent on sticking to their beloved herdsman. Chuchak succeeded in persuading Ranjha to resume his duties, but only after making numerous entreaties and recognizing him like his own sons.[74] When Chuchak returned to his home, the entire Siyal clan (*kul qabila*) had assembled to know the truth. Chuchak could not publicaly admit that whatever was being verbally circulated was factually true. Too embarrassed to speak to them, he shared his agony with Kundi. After consultations, they decided to immediately organize the marriage of Hir with the Khera boy. Any further delay would merely add to their disgrace. Acting secretly, Chuchak called several workers and assigned different tasks. The preparations could not, however, remain secret, as this was the only topic that was talked about in Jhang Siyal.[75]

Kundi confronted Hir and admonished her for making the herdsman her beloved and roaming with him. There was no talk in every home other than this affair, which had blackened their faces. Therefore, they had decided to marry her to the Khera youth at the earliest. Rejecting the decision, Hir declared that water had flowed to merge in water and nothing was left behind. She wanted to know who had arranged her marriage with the Khera. Kundi argued that they had found the best match in the Kheras who were incomparable. In fact, lakhs like the Siyals were available to them, there being no shortage of suitable alliances for them. Hir asserted that she had pledged her head to the one with whom her conjugal tie was an absolute truth. Kundi argued that Ranjha could be accepted as her husband only if her parents agreed. A number of distinguished persons had tied Hir's knot with the Khera youth, who had been written in her destiny. Since they had retained her beloved herdsman in employment, she must accept her match with the Kheras. Hir asserted that her betrothal with Ranjha was fixed even before Adam and Eve. In fact, this bond had been blessed by the eminent saints (*wadde wali sahib de sadiq*) of God. Kundi tried to strike fear in the mind of Hir, while referring to the Khera's potential for violent revenge and their possibility of forcibly taking her away as a rightful claim. People would cease to bear daughters who brought shame to their clan.[76]

As part of the preparations for the marriage, Chuchak sent knotted strings to the Kheras, who were delighted. In Chuchak's house, festivities started and drums were placed. Kundi received felicitations from one and all. The people of the locality felt happy. Beggars arrived in such large numbers that they could not be accommodated. Hir and Ranjha, who were together in the moor, expressed anguish at the proposed celebrations that kept them out. The moment provided an opportunity for the lovers to reflect on their relationship. Ranjha declared that he was not a long standing herdsman, but he was the son of a chief. Since his heart had been captured by Hir, he accepted the position of a herdsman (*chak*) and, as a consequence, underwent much suffering and degraded the name of his father. Hir recognized Ranjha as a perfect spiritual guide (*kamil murshid*). She treated herself as a humble disciple, who was attached to his feet. Averse to being forgotten, discarded or misguided, she wished to die at his feet. Ranjha feared that no one would care for him once she was married. Confused and disoriented, Hir reaffirmed her undying love for Ranjha and consigned the Kheras to hell. On returning home, Hir found the girls singing, flour being ground and goods being crafted. But she remained aloof.[77]

The Siyals sat in council to finalize preparation for the oil ceremony. The task was difficult in view of the recalcitrance of Hir who was ready to pounce on anyone. If the Siyals failed to nab her and send her as a bride, they would be proved as liars and degraded in the society. Since Hir was not likely to sit for the pre-wedding ritual (*maiyyan*), the Siyals formed a contingent plan. A number of males of the clan hid where Hir was eating. As soon as she had washed her hands, her brothers tried to lay their hands on her. Hir leapt back and asked her brothers to keep away and treat her as the chief's daughter. She would go herself, wherever she was needed. But she would not let them touch her body, which had already experienced the touch of Ranjha. Having failed to use force against her, the Siyals decided to poison Hir at night and, in her place, fix her niece as the bride. Duly cooked by Kundi at night, poisoned food was eaten by Hir who remained unaffected by the poison.[78] She alleged that her brothers, who had failed to pin her down physically, had violated her purity through poison. But this poison was overpowered by those who nurtured perfect love (*kamil ishq*). Her relatives, adhering to a customary practice, confined her to a room. She told her closest friend Hassi, who was a witness to this patriarchal oppression, that she was bearing all this for the sake of the perfect spiritual guide (*kamil murshid*). Addressing her mother, she refused to allow the application of henna on her hands, because she had only one heart that she had given to Ranjha. What would she give to the Kheras? She was not a camel of the Baloch that prostrated at every door. She was segregated from her companions and forcibly rubbed with the ceremonial pastes. For people, this practice was associated with marriage, but for Hir it was a funeral rite.[79]

On the appointed day, the marriage procession of the Kheras, which comprised all relatives, departed for Jhang Siyal. A variety of horses – white, gray speckled and golden (*nukre neele ablak peele*) – were tastefully decorated. With their pommels covered with velvet, tasseled necklaces hung from their necks. There were ponies meant to be offered as presents. A large volume of gifts, particularly fabrics, bed clothes and cash, were carried on camels and Kashmiri ponies. The procession was led by decked horses with banners and emblems. Entertainment was provided by jesters, singers and dancers (*bhand bhagtiye aur kanjariyan*). Drums and pipes emitted musical notes, while falcons and hawks were flown in the air. The marriage procession – men, animals and goods – was so large that even the earth found it difficult to bear its weight. Back in Jhang Siyal, Chuchak did not leave any stone unturned. In addition to innumerable mattresses and quilts, he had arranged for ample stocks of grain, rice, ghee and sugar. In their wealth and prestige, the two chiefs, Chuchak and Ali, were not inferior to Akbar.[80]

In the moors, Ranjha became a soft target of sarcastic attacks by the rival herdsmen. They drew his attention to the arrival of the Kheras in a marriage procession. Hir would leave the village after the solemnization of her marriage. Who would then feed him with sweetened breadcrumbs and butter? He was guilty of snatching away their cattle. It was heard that he could be killed on the spot. Refusing to be provoked, Ranjha replied that fortune had brought him to Jhang Siyal and he would remain there till his daily bread (*rizq*) was guaranteed. He could leave the Siyals without any hitch, as he had not signed any written agreement with them. He had no quarrel with anyone, as he had not ploughed the edge of anyone's field. The herdsmen, without relenting, taunted that he was thinking of leaving only after the master was sending away Hir, whereas earlier he was happily consuming milk and cream (*dudh malai*). He had enlarged his body by eating the sweetened breadcrumbs without bothering about any profit or loss. He had moved across the moors the whole day with a carefree swagger, without ever caring to respond to their calls. Since he had now come into their grasp, he would surely be punished. He was without any roots and without any argument. Yet it was not the end of the world for him. If the Kheras had snatched Hir from him, he would return to Takht Hazara, provided the herdsmen left him unharmed. He was merely imploring his fellow herdsmen with humility, while they were unjustly inclined to kill him. If he had taken anything from Jhang Siyal, they were free to take it back from him.[81]

During the pre-wedding rites, Hir raised a clamour and cried. She refused to take food and water. She had enjoyed herself in the moors, but there was none to feed her in her own house. The men folk of the place, particularly her three brothers and four maternal uncles, were convinced that Hir would undermine their honour. They unanimously decided to kill Hir at night and replace her by Pathan's daughter on whose hand the bridal string (*gana*) was tied. Chuchak directed Hassi to sleep away from Hir, as the latter was to be killed at night. In her sarcastic reply, Hassi argued that the murderous plan would register the honour of Siyals and prestige of his chiefdom. She asked to be killed before snuffing out the life of Hir. Hassi wasted no time in conveying this exchange to her friend. Rejecting the threat offhand, Hir asserted that she could not be tied by the patriarchal norms and that one who was under Ranjha's protection could not be killed. At midnight, the uncles and brothers advanced to perform the evil deed. However, they saw Hir guarded by black robed warriors sitting on black horses. Taken by surprise, the assailants fell unconscious with locked jaws. A wailing Kundi, in an attempt to revive her brothers and sons, poured water in their mouths to unlock their jaws. The Siyals, who were caught between fire in the front and a wall at the back, beat a retreat.[82]

Next morning, the marriage procession of the Kheras arrived in the midst of fanfare, drums and banners. As the chiefs descended in a garden, the people of the locality came out to see the grand spectacle, but Hir was crying in her dark corner. Chuchak sent trays of sweets through the hands of servants. All eyes were focused on the bridegroom who wore a gold threaded saffron dress, with his face covered by a chaplet (*sehra*) of flowers. When Ranjha went forward to have a glimpse of the bridegroom, the girls recognized him and recalled that he was Hir's sweetheart. Ranjha felt giddy but climbed on a bull (*sandh*) to watch the proceedings.[83] At this point of time, a short meeting took place between Hir and Ranjha. It was arranged through the efforts of a Doom girl in dramatic circumstances. On seeing Ranjha, Hir adopted a humble posture by pulling her long scarf around her neck and touched his feet. While embracing him, she addressed him as Lord Dhido Ranjha, owner of the entire land (*kul zamin da khawind*) and perfect mentor (*kamil murshid*). She asked him why she had been imprisoned when she had already sacrificed everything for him. She had no refuge other than him. Ranjha, who was carrying an injured foot, admitted that their relation was virtually over, as she would go with the Khera and he would leave for Takht Hazara. Before the meeting could proceed, Hir was dragged back into the house, while Ranjha returned to the moor.[84]

In the house of Chuchak, a Brahmin was summoned to conduct

the ritual. He asked Kundi to call Hir as the auspicious time might pass and the Khans were keenly watching. Holding the wedding threads (*mauli*) in his hand, he received offerings from the gathering including the family of Hir's parents-in-law. In return, he showered his blessings and prayed that their wealth might increase. As Hir appeared on the scene, Kundi advised her to keep quiet, while the Brahmin conducted the ritual. But Hir did the opposite. She declared that she had only one heart which she had given to Ranjha and, therefore, she would not let any stranger touch her. Since she had gained a perfect master (*kamil murshid*) in Ranjha, she would permit only him to offer the auguries. Hir's parents had no choice but to summon Ranjha. When he appeared on the scene, Kundi asked him to tie the first wedding thread (*gana*) on Hir's wrist. Hir could not restrain herself, as she was engulfed in a flood of emotion. She fell at his feet and gave vent to her feelings. She asked Ranjha to tie the ceremonial thread wherever he liked. She knew no one except her lord mentor (*murshid sayin*) Ranjha. She kept him in her thoughts day and night (*athe pehar*), without wasting a single breath. He was free to mould her in accordance with his desires. The Brahmin asked Kundi why Hir was being forced to marry someone against her wishes. He had seen with his own eyes all he had been hearing and, thus, confirmed all the facts (*kul haqiqat*). Kundi paid a bribe (*vaddi*) to the Brahmin and purchased his silence. Everyone felt that the marriage ceremony was over and that Hir would be soon made to sit in the palanquin.[85]

The stage had been set for the marriage ceremony (*nikah*) in accordance with Islamic injunctions.[86] All males sat on wicker mats (*khara*) including the bridegroom. The *qazi* ordered that the girl be brought there. A group of people – mother, brothers and uncles of Hir – got up to do the bidding. Hir warned them not to touch her, as she would conduct herself on her own. She refused to accept that these close relatives were her well wishers (*mehram*). She could rely only on Ranjha, whom she recognized as her lord (*sayin*). She wrapped a shawl around herself and came to sit on the spot marked for her. The ceremony had no meaning, as she had accepted Ranjha as her husband long back. The *qazi* asked Hir two questions – if she needed a representative (*vakil*) in accordance with the legal provision and to speak loudly for every one to hear if she accepted the son of Ali (Sahiba) as her husband. Hir felt offended for being treated as immature and deficient. She clarified that she did not need any representative, as she was neither dumb nor deaf. She declared that Ranjha had been bestowed on her by higher powers and that her mother could be attached to the Khera instead of her. Her male relatives sealed her mouth, so that she did not utter another word. Repeating 'Let us go' in a chorus, they created a false impression as if Hir had given her consent for the marriage. They forcibly tied the end of her shawl to that of Sahiba, so that the customary rounds (*laavan*) could be conducted. She told her father that force would not achieve anything, as she was already married and no longer a virgin.[87]

The Siyals and Kheras decided that the couple should consummate the marriage without any delay.[88] Appropriate arrangements were made for the occasion. When the Khera arrived like a victorious conqueror, a furious Hir rushed at him like a tigress and delivered a mighty slap on his face. Hir cried that she had been touched by someone who was not intimate with her, i.e. a stranger. Addressing the Khera as her brother, she wanted to know where he had seen Ranjha. Since the Khera was looking for an opportunity to save himself from further humiliation, he slipped away on the excuse of searching for Ranjha. He reached the place where the marriage party had encamped. His relatives were keen to know his experience with Hir, who was unique in every way. The Khera declared that the girls had played a trick on him, that they had placed a kicking mare instead of his wife and that the animal had damaged his teeth.[89]

After spending the night, the marriage party of the Kheras prepared to leave. The Siyals gave a large dowry comprising of horses, camels, ponies, bedclothes, goods and cash. The zamindars made sure that all the servants were satisfied with their gifts. When the food was ready, the servants came to invite the guests. As the Khans sat in the lounge, they consumed cups of liquor which flowed freely and, when they were intoxicated, they asked for more of it.[90] In accordance with the directions of Chuchak, the dowry was laid on the cots. A great variety of ornaments were brought by the servants in two-maund pans; beds and chairs were gilded with silver and woven with the golden thread; three sets of clothes as well as the bedspreads were made of silk. Apart from heavy jewellery and beaded bracelets, there were receptacles (*surmedani*) studded with rubies. Drums made of silver and showing signs of antiquity were on display. There were mountains of cooked food, while people assembled from seven directions. Each member of the marriage party was given golden clothes and white bowls. As instructed by the Kheras, their servants packed the goods (*asbab*) in sacks fastened at the top.[91]

Chuchak went into consultation with the Siyals in strict privacy (*khilwat*). They discussed the manner in which Hir could be put in the palanquin, which was likely to be a great calamity (*qehar qahari*) in view of Hir's recent behaviour. Their outstanding concern was to send Hir along with the Kheras without any ruckus. Her mouth could be stuffed with cotton or her hands could be tied behind her back, only to be pushed into the palanquin. Chuchak, who was agonized at the proposed violence on his own daughter, started crying. At the advice of Kaido, they decided to send Ranjha as an escort with a drum on his head, as this would erase the huge stigma (*kalank*) built into the marriage.[92] When told that Hir would not leave without him, Ranjha fell into a trap. A drum was placed on his head and he was made to sit near the palanquin. The bridegroom reached the spot on his mare. Kundi advised Hir to sit in the palanquin with happiness in her heart, as the entire marriage party was watching and the honour of the Siyals was at stake. Hir lost her temper and shouted at Kundi. She even asked her mother to sit in the palanquin so that she herself watched the spectacle (*tamasha*). She cursed Kundi in abusive language and labelled her as a swallower of children. Since she was a harbinger of death, she must die and her brothers too must meet their end. When Kundi informed Hir that they were sending Ranjha along with her, she was immediately reconciled with her mother. Ready to leave her parental home for good, Hir declared herself as a traveller (*musafir*) as her bread (*rizq*) in her parental home had terminated. As she began to bid farewell, everyone started weeping. Hir gently requested her mother to allow Ranjha to sit in the palanquin along with her. Kundi advised Hir to be patient and satisfy herself with the fragrance of Ranjha, lest a physical contact between the two caused a scandal.[93]

Clouds of sadness descended on the girls' common (*aatan*) and courtyard of every house. Hir embraced the girls one by one. Even Hir's mother started crying and felt that she should have given her daughter in marriage to Ranjha. Men folk of the two clans, including prominent chiefs and brave warriors, said farewell to each other. Chuchak took the centre stage and highlighted his achievements as a powerful zamindar. He had subjugated the Chaddars and earned the enmity of the Nahars, so that none dared to oppose him. He had never bowed to anyone, but had done so only then for the sake of Hir. Ali, the Khera chief, reciprocated these sentiments. For him, Hir was his honoured lady (*sahibiyani*) and Chuchak was his lord (*sir sayin*). Saying this, he touched the feet of Chuchak who raised him up.[94]

While the marriage party undertook its return journey, the Kheras spoke of only one aim – how to avenge themselves for the damage done to their honour. They were of the unanimous view that Ranjha ought to be killed. All of them, one by one, began to attack Ranjha who was a soft target. He was not only kicked and pushed, but was also cursed and abused. Since a great enemy was in their grip, they would kill him on the spot. Before sunset, the party set up a camp and tied the horses to pegs. Preparing a meal of sweetened breadcrumbs, they ate their fill. Hir, who was hungry and crying, refused to eat and cursed a nurse (*dai*) who tried to feed her by a ruse.[95] When the Kheras began their journey the next morning, they resumed the ill treatment of Ranjha. On the one hand, he suffered the humiliation of seeing Hir being carried away by the Kheras and, on the other hand, he suffered sharp blows on his naked body. Damning the Kheras, Hir exclaimed that her bond with Ranjha had been snapped, but even the Kheras would not get anything as they had been deceived forever. This provoked the Kheras who, acting in groups as well as individually, unleashed a fresh onslaught on Ranjha, whose body was covered with blood and wounds. In his misery, Ranjha reasoned with the Kheras in the name of God. Instead of beating him illegally, they should chop off his head. Kheras considered the ways of eliminating Ranjha to wash off the dishonour. They would slash his head with a sword and throw his body in the river. This idea was dropped, as the herdsmen of Chuchak were accompanying them and the guilt would permanently stick to them. Ranjha was sent after the buffaloes into the river to be drowned.[96]

As the convoy reached the river, the Kheras embarked on a boat. But they did not allow Ranjha to climb on the excuse that there was no space for him. He was ordered to push his way across the river along with the buffaloes. Ranjha ridiculed the Kheras for their inability to kill him, as they feared punishment at the hands of justice. In a state of utter misery, Ranjha invoked the Panj Pir. When they appeared to him, he made his complaint. He had not himself acquired Hir, but it was they who had conferred her on him. They had enabled him to climb to the top and then withdrew the ladder. The saints revealed that they had deliberately brought this punishment on him, so that he could become illumined (*raushan*). Let him descend into the river, as they took the responsibility for his safety. Ranjha created soulful melodies (*bambiha*) on his flute. As a result, turtles and crocodiles emerged on the surface, while oars fell from the hands of boatmen. The marriage revellers and horses were intoxicated, as the boat swayed towards the south.[97]

The marriage party reached Rangpur Khera. Hir was made to wait in a garden, while preparations were afoot in the house of Ali to receive her. As people turned out to offer felicitations, the women folk took up the customary rituals. When the mother-in-law touched her forehead with that of Hir, she was dumb founded by the radiance of her face. While performing omens, she offered a morsel of sweetened breadcrumbs to Hir. Instead of being pleased at the gesture, Hir pulled up her mother-in-law for making undue noise (*dhum*). Refusing to swallow the morsel, she shocked everyone by revealing her love for Ranjha in the moors. Amidst confusion, the Khera women came in to play the game of 'Ring in Buttermilk' (*lassi mundari*). Hir announced that she would play only with Ranjha and that she would break the teeth of Khera if he dared to come. In another audacious move, she asked the assembly to congratulate her for having Ranjha as her bridegroom. While a commotion arose, a frustrated mother-in-law cancelled the ceremony. She turned her ire against Ali, who had been hasty to form an alliance which had destroyed their peace. He had failed to recognize a woman who was a terror even for wild animals and monsters.[98] Ali summoned the members of the Khera clan and a collective resolution (*mata*) was passed. It was decided that Ranjha be killed, dragged and thrown in the river. Only then the stigma (*kalank*) on the name of the Kheras would be washed off. But this work had to be done on the same day. Being alerted, Ranjha fled from Rangpur Khera at night and, jumping into the river, crossed over to safety by dawn.[99]

Ranjha entered the boundary of Jhang Siyal. He reached the meadows where he had grazed buffaloes, played on the flute and sank in the love of Hir. He encountered a group of girls who wished to know the cause of his despair. He replied that he was a homeless wanderer and ill-starred person whose cargo had been plundered. The girls asked him to settle in the moors again. They would build a shelter for him. Since he was the same Ranjha and they were the same girls, fresh love would bloom for him. Ranjha declined the offer as it was impossible to live in the moors without Hir. He went to the same old tree platform (*jallar*) and, touching his forehead, kissed the place. His heart, which was attached to each and every site, was filled with pain. As he played on the flute, a number of girls, including Hassi, converged there as if the Gopis were responding to the call of Krishna. Ranjha narrated his tale of woe, particularly the murderous conspiracy of the Kheras. The girls offered to recreate his happy days that revolved round the moors, boats and the dwelling. Ranjha would not live in any place that was imbued with Hir's memory. Since the girls could not imagine a life without Ranjha, they wished to go along with him wherever he went. But they were unable to change his resolve.[100]

After a gap of twelve years, Ranjha returned to Takht Hazara. He was shocked to find that his brothers nurtured the same old hostility towards him. With a view to reassure them, he clarified that he had not come to claim his share in the ancestral land. He had been engaged in mendicancy (*faqiri*) for twelve years and had come only to see his native place. He was not demanding anything from them, nor was he advancing any claim. The three brothers, however, had a bigger grudge against Ranjha. He had blackened the face of their illustrious father Mojam as well as their clan. He had taken employment with the Siyals as a herdsman and, while serving as a menial, he had been digging wells and constructing palaces. He had followed marriage parties with a drum on his head and thus shamed his brothers. Ranjha was quick to see the wide difference between himself and his brothers. He was just a mendicant (*faqir*), while Tahir was a lord (Khan). He had come to his own country by invoking Tahir's exalted authority, but had no demands. His humble expectations had ended in disaster. No one belonged to anyone, as kinship and affection had disappeared.[101] On meeting his three sisters-in-law, Ranjha refused to say anything about Hir as her memories would bring him close to death. However, Ranjha felt happy on meeting a few old friends who treated him like a brother. They offered to arrange for his stay in the village by building a thatch, spreading a straw mat and putting a hedge round the enclosure; they would place two water pitchers and two smoking pipes (*chillams*). They met in the village common (*dara*) and sat in a blissful assembly (*majlis*) day and night.[102]

It may be recalled that when Mojam was alive, he had fixed the marriage of Ranjha with the daughter of Yaqub Khan Waraich. The marriage did not take place owing to the death of Mojam and the deceit of his elder sons. Now Yaqub heard that Ranjha had returned to Takht Hazara. Accompanied by the members of his clan, he reached the village. The visitors met Tahir and Zahir (the two elder sons of Mojam). Yaqub began with a sarcastic remark, 'O Khans. Your brother has arrived. It is true that Mojam was blessed with your brother. He has raised the reputation of your family by being called the herdsman. To discuss these matters, all prominent persons have assembled.' Tahir retorted that the matter could be sorted out as the plaintiff (*muddai*) had come back to Takht Hazara. The two sides, the Ranjha brothers and the Waraichs, faced each other in the assembly, but both did not like Ranjha, though for different reasons. Yaqub accused Ranjha of disgracing his brothers. Ranjha protested against these harsh words, but asked the Waraichs to state the exact nature of their suit. Yaqub clarified that they did not come on a pilgrimage to see his face. They came to Takht Hazara only to find if the marriage would take place or the engagement would be broken.[103] Ranjha asked the Waraichs to marry their daughter anywhere, as he himself had no claims in this regard. Focusing on the wide social distance between the Waraichs and himself, Ranjha stated that the masters of land and rivers could not be the masters of the mat and fire. Since the betrothal was formally cancelled in the presence of witnesses, the Waraichs prepared to leave.[104]

Fearing that the departure of the Waraichs would be a blot on the Ranjha clan, the brothers persuaded the visitors to stay for meals. Jeevan, the third of the Ranjha brothers, arrived on the scene and assumed charge of the proceedings. His intervention, which was apparently pre-decided by the brothers among themselves, proved decisive. Endowed with the skills of diplomacy and oratory, Jeevan spoke to the Waraichs, 'O Khans. Listen to what we say. We are in kinship (*sakke*) with each other. Even in the past there had been many matrimonial alliances (*saak*) between us. We are intertwined (i.e. the clans of Ranjhas and Waraichs) like thick ropes (*une soo vaan niyayin*). Since the son of Tahir is here, let us clinch the matter. Otherwise there is no honour in our relationship.' Yaqub, alluding to the bitterness of the past experience, assumed a high moral ground. Earlier too, they had been given assurances in the betrothal with the youngest of the Ranjha brothers. Though they had come personally, yet they were met with refusal. This episode did not provide any solace. Shifting the blame to Ranjha, Jeevan argued that if one person turned out to be foolish, he must be treated as dead. No one was bound to him. In contrast, the Ranjhas and Waraichs were intimately related to each other since long like the thick rope. Their mutual intercourse did not need any investigative review.[105] The three brothers, bound by common interest, publicly disowned Ranjha. The two clans, in spite of tensions in the past, revived their kinship as both would gain in political and social terms.

In Takht Hazara, preparations were made for the marriage of Tahir's son. A Brahmin was sent to the Waraichs with knotted strings, confirming the day of the marriage ceremony. Much attention was paid to decorate horses of different breeds. The members of the marriage party turned out in bright apparels, giving boost to their pride. Someone advised Tahir to take along Dhido. The task was not easy, as the brothers had publicly disowned Dhido a second time. Therefore, accompanied by the entire clan of the Ranjhas, Tahir went to the village common, and invited Dhido to join the marriage party. Dhido declined the invitation as a number of questions would be raised leading to their loss. Tahir employed the skill of persuasion and declared that if he did not go, then the entire party of Ranjhas would not leave. He was also the progeny of Mojam and, therefore, he occupied the same place as the father of the bridegroom. Dhido's resistance collapsed and he gave his consent.[106] The three Ranjha brothers, who were squarely responsible for destroying the life of Dhido, were able to put up a façade of unity to wash off the guilt of injustice against their brother.

Ranjhas and Waraichs, all brave warriors, assembled in a garden. The girls, in an attempt to identify the bridegroom, saw the handsome Dhido, who had been disinherited by his family. The girls, who were enamoured of Ranjha, told the bride that she was extremely unfortunate in failing to marry him. The bride, while cursing Hir for taking away Dhido from her, raised a clamour for seeing him so that her longing could be satisfied.[107] As soon as he entered, he was recognized as the light of spiritual excellence (*azmat ki rushnai*). The bride cornered Ranjha and wished to know her fault (*taqseer*) that prevented their union. Ranjha created a false image of himself, claiming to be ignorant and good for nothing (*makhattu*). It was not proper for him to marry someone's daughter when he had no means to feed her. What was worse, he did not have any strength (*quwwat*) in his body and could not lift anything heavy. Anguished at his evasive reply, the Waraich bride gave expression to her pent up feelings,

You possessed all the strength in Jhang Siyal. You brought a bad name to your father by grazing buffaloes and carrying a drum on your head. It is only when Hir went with the Kheras that you retraced your steps to Takht Hazara. You made humble supplications for Hir, but she did not come into your hands. When the herdsmen made your life miserable, you resorted to renunciation (*udasi*). It was only when you lost Hir that you began to pose as worthless (*makhattu*). You adopted this name when my turn came. Day and night, I gazed at the door and wept at my misery. My hair changed colour, but I remained full to the brim in beauty. You may be after someone else's right, but I will not surrender mine.

Upset at these allegations, Ranjha asked the woman (*bibi*) to leave his lappet, as they had no claims on each other. She had shown lack of shame in bringing him there. She should have thought of his brothers and other people. Tahir admonished Ranjha for usurping the place of a lawful bridegroom. Ranjha explained how he fell into a trap laid by the bride whom he treated as a sister. He extricated himself from an embarrassing situation and fled to Takht Hazara to his relief.[108]

Lovers in Struggle

At Rangpur Khera, the Kheras called a meeting of close relatives. Ali, the chief, asked them to give some counsel (*maslat*) on the fate of Hir, who had brought a major affliction (*zehmat*) on them. After considering a number of options, they came round to the view that she be killed at the earliest to remove the stigma from their faces. Owing to the intervention of Ali's wife, the Kheras resolved (*mata*) to place Hir in segregation. Accordingly, Hir was shifted to the granary as a neighbour of Ali's daughter Sehti. Here the premises was large and rooms isolated. Hir's room was poorly furnished, as it was provided with only a reed stool and torn mat. Her food (*ahar*) comprised only desire (*sik*). Sehti approached Hir with great affection in order to win her confidence. She asked the cause of the grief (*ranjish rog*) of Hir, who was physically declining with every passing day. A fire was smouldering in her while she was hiding it. Hir was reluctant to open up. She had no confidant, as her closest kin – father, mother and brothers – had forsaken her. Moreover, her mind was in disorder owing to constant weeping. Someone, who was afflicted like her, could appreciate the agony of her heart.[109] Sehti, in order to extract Hir's secret (*bhed*), narrated her own love affair with Ramu, a Brahmin. Hir anticipated that Sehti could support her in the future. With her consent, Hir saw the lovers joined in physical intimacy. Soon after, Hir became an emissary between them, conveying the messages of one to the other. Since the veil between them was lifted, Sehti asked Hir to reveal her sorrow. Overcoming her earlier reluctance, Hir described the entire story of her love for Ranjha, the agony of her separation and the tension in her organs. Her troubles would end if someone were sent to bring Ranjha. Sehti felt that Hir should have revealed her pain earlier. Hir entreated that past be forgotten, and her lord be united with her, lest she should die.[110]

Sehti called Ramu and sent him to Takht Hazara. The kind of love shared by him and Sehti also existed between Hir and the herdsman. He was urged to convey all kinds of afflictions (*dukh*) being suffered by Hir. Before leaving, Ramu asked Hir for her message as well as a sign (*nishani*) that would lend credibility to the messenger. In response, Hir identified the landmarks in the moors on the banks of the Chenab, where her love flowered. Since Ranjha was her perfect mentor (*kamil murshid*), she sought his loving attention to acquire eternal truth and firm faith. Her love (*preet*) with Ranjha was similar to that of Dasrath's son with Sita and Nand's son with the daughter of Brikh Bhan. She was full of defects (*auganhari*), but begged forgiveness for her sins. Ramu, having absorbed Hir's message in his limbs, embarked on his long journey on foot. Walking for two days and covering a distance of 40 leagues, he reached Takht Hazara on the third day.[111]

Ramu took shelter in the house of a local Brahmin and concealed his real object. During his conversation with the hosts, he learnt about the local agricultural conditions, besides Mojam and his sons. He was told that the rains and crops had been in accordance with the times. There was plenty of prosperity (*chokhi barkat*) during the days of Mojam. Things were not bad even at that time. Each of Mojam's three sons surpassed the others in progress. The fourth son had become a master of mat and fire (*sathar dhooyen sayin*). He lived among the Siyals till Hir did not marry. When she was married among the Kheras, he returned to Takht Hazara.[112] Having acquired a sufficient information, Ramu came to the village common. He waited for an opportunity to speak to Ranjha when all others had left. Ranjha, who was curious about the stranger, offered to arrange for his stay and food. Ramu, unable to control his emotions, declared that he had come to meet him and that he had been sent by Hir with a message for him. Ramu enumerated the sites of Ranjha's love – the new boat, the boatman Luddan, river Chenab and the ferry of Chuchkana. He also referred to the love of Hir and Ranjha in the moors, the dense shisham, the bald fig, grazing of buffaloes, an abode on the platform and sweetened breadcrumbs brought by Hir.[113]

Ranjha, who feigned ignorance about the sites, revealed his identity. Vowing to lay down his life for Hir, Ranjha urged Ramu to narrate the facts (*haqiqat*) about her. Ramu related that she did not have a drop of blood or a layer of flesh. Like a smouldering fire that alternatively burnt and kindled, she hung between life and death. Ranjha was galvanized into action. Putting his own amulet (*trag*) round Ramu's neck, he begged him to return quickly and ask Hir to wait for Ranjha who was also on his way. Deciding to renounce Takht Hazara again, he burnt his thatch and broke his pitchers. At midnight, he slipped out of the village.[114]

Walking to the Jhelam and climbing the hills, Ranjha reached Tilla Jogian. He presented himself before Sidh Bagai, the chief of the Jogis. The Jogi, who was enamoured of his good looks, asked a number of questions about his country, condition and object. Ranjha, while dissociating himself from any place or parentage, requested to be enrolled as a Jogi. Sidh Bagai declared the candidate as unfit for the pursuit, as he was too worldly (*hoshnaq*) and was used to the food cooked by his mother. Ranjha fell at the feet of Sidh Bagai and, resumed his entreaties. He had taken the shelter (*sharani*) of the master, whose favour had enabled the people to swim across the world. If Gopichand and Bharthari could take Jog,[115] so could a poor man (*gharib*) like him. Sidh Bagai tried to dissuade Ranjha from his resolve. In his view, the pursuit of Jog was difficult and its mysteries were intricate. Jog meant begging to eat and sleeping on the mat. He could consider his case if he truthfully described his background.

Ranjha revealed that his country was Takht Hazara. He was the son of Mojam. Owing to adversity (*vakht*) he was separated from his home. He went to the district of the Siyals. When Hir was married in the country of the Kheras, he was put to great trouble (*kaziya*). When he could not think of anything, he came under the Jogi's protection (*saam*). Astonished at this admission, Sidh Bagai sought the view of his disciples before taking any final decision.[116] The disciples replied in the negative, as Ranjha had not dug out any forgotten matter. The master was the mentor of the entire Tilla and did not have dearth of disciples. Sidh Bagai overruled the plea and, considering the high pedigree (*aseel*) of the candidate, admitted him into the path of Jog. Having received the sanction, Ranjha was transformed into the light of spiritual excellence (*azmat ki rushnai*). Ranjha fell at the feet of Sidh Bagai and sought his permission to leave for alien lands and rivers, where his work lay. The mentor and disciple fell at each other's feet. Assuming a strange garb (*kapad ajab*) – saffron robes, rings in ears and ashes on forehead – Ranjha descended from the Tilla.[117]

The Jogi reached the outskirts of Rangpur Khera. This place, referred to as the village of Sehti, was large and pleasant. The Jogi established himself on the bank of a river. Clearing the ground with a spade, he spread his mat and lit a fire. Rani Sehti was the first to see the Jogi, who appeared like a sun descending on earth. Endowed with a face like the moon and eyes like the flame, his youth was full of luster. Imagining herself as a mother separated from her son, she was curious to know why he he had adopted Jog. The Jogi replied in the idiom of his path, 'I fell from above and was destroyed on the earth. I have no place which I can call my own. If I had any antecedents or future, I would have informed you. Mother! I am a mendicant (*darvesh*) who has come to beg at your door.' Sehti, while knowing that the Jogi was in fact Ranjha, tried to expose his new garb.[118] She wished to know where was his sainthood (*faqiri*) on three occasions – when he got Luddan beaten, when he carried the drum (*tamak*) on his head and when he gave sweetened breadcrumbs to Kaido. Offended at the bad words (*mande sukhan*) and taunts (*taane*), he wondered at the woman who knew all his travails and passed insightful messages promising to cure his malady. Admitting that she was speaking the truth, Ranjha fell at her feet and placed himself under her protection (*saam*).[119] Sehti revealed that Hir was in her house, that she had learnt everything about their love and that she had sent Ramu to him. Ranjha started crying and declared that his honour (*lajj*) was in her hands. Sehti assured that she had assumed the responsibility of the honour of both in her hands and, in the process, put at stake the honour of 900 turbans of her parental home. Here she was referring to the men of the Khera clan, who were settled in the *zamindari* headed by her father Ali. Ranjha spent the night at the riverbank after lighting a fire. Sitting in the posture of a Jogi, he covered his face and did not speak to anyone.[120]

The Jogi found that Hir had been reduced to a physical wreck. Always sunk in a trance like an opium addict (*posti*), she was consumed by the sorrow of separation from Ranjha. When the Jogi appeared before her, he begged for alms (*bhikhya*), as he was hungry. Since she consumed her own longing and sighs, she could give only hunger (*bhukh*) in charity. While the Jogi gave his blessings (*aseesan*), Hir poured millets into his lap. Jogi spilled the millets on the floor. Hir ordered the Jogi to leave forthwith. Soon she smelt a familiar fragrance and felt that the Jogi was none other than Dhido Ranjha. She must confirm the identity of the visitor.[121] The Jogi offered to give her medicinal herbs if she related the cause of her sorrow. Upset at the Jogi for trying to intrude into her private space, she raised doubts about his credentials as Jogi. His looks did not match his pursuit. He appeared to belong to the ruling class (*ahl muluk*). It was strange that he had thrust rings by slitting his ears and did not feel horrified at the sight of blood. He must be an impostor, who ensnared women and deceived children.[122]

The Jogi countered all the objections raised by Hir. A Jogi for seven generations, he had travelled down from Bhutan, Multan, Narwar Kot and Kirhana. His spiritual master Sidh Bagai had forbidden him from using his tongue and eyes. It was in Hir's interest to reveal her inner pain, so that he could suggest a suitable remedy. He had come only to beg for alms. If she did not wish to give anything, he would leave after delivering his sermon (*adesh*)[123] There was a stalemate between the two contenders, as neither was willing to blink. At this moment, the Panj Pir informed Hir that Dhido had come in the garb of a Jogi and that she must meet him.

Resuming her interrogation of the Jogi, Hir asked questions about his native place, country and river where he dwelt. She also asked him about his spiritual mentor who, after enrolling him, bored his ears and gave lessons (*sikh*) on the new path. Ranjha revealed his identity and suffering. Hir flew like a falcon towards Ranjha and took him in a tight embrace.[124] They exchanged their thoughts on the benign role of Sehti. Ranjha returned to the riverbank and established himself as a Jogi. Spreading his mat, he lighted a fire and covered his face.

On the third day, Sehti met Hir and expressed her happiness on seeing her. The condition (*halat*) of Hir had improved and her complexion had changed. Hir acknowledged the grace (*sadka*) of Sehti in her recovery to health. Addressing her as mother (*bebe*) and queen (*rani*), Hir asserted that Ranjha came on his own and set her on fire. Sehti confirmed the presence of Ranjha, but warned Hir to keep quiet and not let anyone see him. Hir had rightly identified her problem, but the same had afflicted Sehti also. Sehti claimed (like she did in presence of Ranjha) that for the sake of Hir, she had brought 900 turbans to shame (*sun Hire main taindi khatir, nau sau pagg lajjai*). Sehti shared the next part of her plan with Hir. They would quarrel with each other and exchange angry abuses (*gaal*). They must fight until the bitter end, so that the people gathered there.[125]

At dawn, the two sisters-in-law came out in the courtyard to start the sham fight. More than exposing each other, they heaped insults on the family of the opponent. Sehti said that the Kheras had become a laughing stock for brining a unique daughter-in-law, who had taken a harsh revenge (*nivatta*) from them. People like Hir's father were their workmen (*kammi*) and Hir was a mean bitch (*kamini kutti*) who had started this wrangle (*siyapa*). Her father was so rich that gold had been used as mortar (*kandhi gil sona*) in the walls of his house. On the other hand, Hir questioned Sehti's claim of a distinguished parentage and plentiful wealth. Hir had been living there for the last thirty-five months, but she was neither given food, nor cared for. It was futile to praise the greatness of Sehti's father, as his son was of no use after marriage. This father could not be rich, as Hir was given only a broken reed stool. The Kheras had usurped even what Hir's father Chuchak gave her.[126]

At the end of this friendly confrontation, Sehti appeared before her father and complained that her brother did not get Chuchak's daughter, but instead married a lowly slave girl (*goli*). In spite of this injustice, she asserted that Hir must be given all she received from her father if she agreed to cohabit with her husband (*Hir vassan te aayi*). In his displeasure, Ali sent a large number of goods including bags, utensils, buffaloes, cows, bedsteads, mattresses and blankets. Hir arranged the goods in their respective places, making decorations (*saj*) and inserting hanging pegs. Sehti offered to provide more goods that she might desire. As the time for cohabitation drew near, the Kheras began to receive felicitations (*vadhai*) and a jubilant Hir performed all the household tasks.[127] As soon as Sahiba entered her apartment, Hir ran away from him like a gazelle as he was not her consort (*be mahram*). A horrified Sehti asked her if she had been scared by fairies, demons or ghosts. Sehti told him that he had made a mistake by coming there and that he could come only when she signalled. Sahiba quickly slipped out. When Hir returned, she stepped inside only after everything had been washed and purified (*pak*).[128]

Sehti held a meeting (*majlis*) with Hir and chalked out a plan for the future. They came to the edge of a sesamum field. Hir was made to lie on the ground and, applying the turmeric paste, a needle was pierced in her ankle so that blood oozed out. Sehti started crying that Hir had been bitten by a snake when she was about to assume her conjugal responsibilities. The entire village, including women, rushed to the site. Ali sent horsemen to bring a healer (*mandri*) found anywhere. Sehti suggested the name of the Jogi, who had revived three men, who had died of snakebite.[129]

People had seen the Jogi living at the ferry (*pattan*) for a while. A large number of people, led by Ali and other chiefs, marched to the site. With shawls round their necks, they requested the Jogi to save the life of their bride (Chuchak's daughter) who had been stung even when their debts were unpaid. The Jogi, who kept his back towards the crowd, did not give any response. After the entreaties of Ali failed to move the Jogi, Sehti led a group of women to try their luck. Sehti declared that the Jogi remained detached from the world and absorbed in his ecstasy. Since he was a perfect ancient sage (*sidh pir puratan*), his intervention was necessary to save the bride, who could not be allowed to go waste. The Jogi referred to the nature of the world, the tendency of snakes to bite and the suitability of incantations as remedy. He, followed by a procession of women and girls, walked to the victim. As soon as he saw Hir, he turned back and revealed that the assailant was not an ordinary serpent, but the rare one with a crown, so that the treatment was difficult. If he could revive the dead, insisted Sehti, he could cure one who was breathing. Agreeing to start his job, the Jogi said that hard work had to be done on the woman (*bibi*) involving innumerable *mantras*. She would be placed in a solitary house (*ikalla kotha*), which none might peep through. A woman, who cried a lot, would remain in attendance for service (*khidmat*). If a treatment of forty days (*chillah*) worked, the problem could be controlled.[130]

A bed was brought to Sehti's house. As the Jogi entered, all the doors were bolted. The lovers, who had been separated for thirty-five months and nine nights, were united. Sehti asked them to enjoy themselves, as nothing would be found lacking. She offered all possible help, even if she had to sacrifice her own life. She would cook whatever lord (*sayin*) Ranjha desired. She herself prepared sweetened breadcrumbs, rice dessert, buffalo's milk, butter, cream, buttermilk, fruits and dates. The moon faced slaves of love, with eyes illumined like flames, did nothing but eat, drink and laugh. They also played on the bed. After every eight days, the parents-in-law of Hir, accompanied by the entire Khera clan and other residents of the village, arrived at the venue of treatment and enquired about the state of the patient. Sehti did not permit anyone to enter. On every occasion, she cooked up a new answer that satisfied the enquirers. For example, she said that lakhs of snakes crawled inside, that the one who stung the victim was not one of them, that the Jogi recited incantations without placing his feet on the ground and that there was a slight improvement in Hir's condition. Sehti found it increasingly difficult to cope with the situation. She could not befool the people for all the times.

She could not see any alternative shelter for the lovers who were entirely dependent on her support.[131]

The lovers failed to see any way to extricate themselves from a difficult situation. When a week was left for the expiry of the forty days' treatment, parents-in-law and the clan again appeared at the door. Sehti informed them that Hir would be released from the ordeal after a week. They should make preparations for giving a ceremonial bath to Hir in the midst of joyous celebrations. When five days elapsed, a breach (*sanh*) was made in the wall at night and, as the day dawned, the lovers escaped. They travelled at a fast pace through thick vegetation but, owing to darkness, came to the same spot repeatedly. Next morning, Sehti covered the hole with material for fuel, while the fugitives ran through the countryside and covered 15 leagues. Concealing themselves during the day, they resumed their journey at night. On the third day, a procession of villagers marched towards Sehti's house. In the midst of song and dance, alms were distributed on the way. Sehti, who was sleeping on her bed at the door inside, did not respond. A boy climbed on the wall and, awakening Sehti, removed the latch. Sehti told her father that a large number of snakes in the courtyard had passed on the poison to her, so that she had been lying in a swoon for the last three days, unaware of Hir. When the people rushed inside, they were shocked to find that two persons had run away through the breach and that the Jogi was none other than the herdsman.[132]

As the scandal came into full view, the Kheras were outraged. They saddled their horses and, urging the ferry to be closed, prepared to catch the fugitives at the earliest. They wished to know from Sehti the direction in which the runaways had gone, but she vaguely pointed towards the north. The Kheras, having covered two stages, passed through wastelands and wild growth. Thirsty for blood, they just wanted to kill the Jogi. Whenever they met anyone, they enquired about a good looking Jogi and a young girl. A group of men who had seen the two – both appearing as the light of spiritual excellence (*azmat ki rushnai*), though both were in deep love with each other – wished to know the motive of the enquiry. Angered by the reply, the Kheras moved on. They met a group of girls who, being enamoured of Hir, affirmed the passionate attraction between the two. Hir and Ranjha, who had no strength left in them, stopped on hearing the hooves. Ranjha wanted Hir to kill him, as the Kheras were likely to inflict a cruel death. Hir said that he was her lord (*sahib*) and she was his slave. He should not put the helpless (*aajiz*) to test, as he had moulded situations in his favour in the past. Ranjha sensed the arrival of the blood thirsty Kheras and feared an attack sooner than later.[133]

Zamindari Custom of Providing Sanctuary

The two lovers, who were being relentlessly pursued by the Kheras, entered the territories of a powerful clan of Jats, the Nahars. At this particular time of the year, the Nahars were engaged in harvesting a crop of lentils (*maanh*). On seeing them from a distance, the lovers hastened with strong steps. They weighed the limited options before them and decided to seek sanctuary with the Nahars. Taking the initiative, Hir told her story. Moved by the plight of the lovers, the Nahar chief took them under his protection. He made a formal declaration (*hukmi*) of his commitment including the offer to put his own life at stake. Since he had not surrendered even the dogs who came under his protection, he could not ignore the fugitives who were born in the families of zamindars (*raathan jaye*). He would not surrender them even if he was required to confront Emperor Akbar. Assuming responsibility of fighting against the enemies of people who were aliens to them, the Nahars began preparations for any exigency, including death. They harnessed their horses and took out their weapons.[134]

The Kheras reached the scene and exchanged greetings (*salaam*) with Nahars. The Kheras pointedly asked if they had seen a Jogi along with a woman (*mehri*). The Nahars told a plain lie. Since they were harvesting the lentils, they advised the Kheras to go ahead and make their enquiries. As for themselves, the Nahars asserted their deep involvement in the moors and their aversion to anything false. The Kheras were disappointed at the reluctance of Nahars to speak the truth.[135] Though they were physically exhausted after a long chase, yet they could discern the fugitives in the eyes of the Nahars. They asked the Nahars to reveal the whereabouts of the fugitives with friendliness, failing which they would pick up their weapons. Accepting the challenge, the Nahars announced, 'Even if the fugitives are not here, we admit that they are here. We have nothing to fear. We are not sparrows sitting on dead trees that would fly away. We do not even surrender the dogs who come to us for protection. In this case, we have zamindars (*raath*) who have come to us. Your horde (*kattak*) seems to be larger. But the size of our small contingent will increase soon.' The warriors drew swords from scabbards and, raising the cry of 'Ali Ali,' fell upon one another. Heads were smashed like earthen pitchers and corpses started falling. The battle was fought in two phases, as the two sides summoned reinforcements mid way. In all, fourteen Kheras and eight Nahars were killed.[136]

The Syeds of Rajoa,[137] who were passing by in a palanquin, stopped on hearing the cries of battle. They found that the two warring clans, the Kheras and Nahars, were entangled in an armed encounter, while sending out demands for additional support. They discontinued their journey and, making an effective intervention, separated the two adversaries. They made the combatants sit on the ground and explain the cause of their enmity and clash. Ali, the Khera chief, described the sequence of events. In the view of Nahars, the fugitives arrived from somewhere and came under their protection. They did not even surrender dogs who took shelter with them. It was not possible for them to refuse asylum to the offspring of chiefs. It was not proper to hand them over to their opponents, as such a move would blacken their (Nahars') face. The Syeds held both the chiefs guilty of improper actions and responsible for getting their young men killed. They were advised to travel 22 leagues to reach Kot Qabula and to fight a legal battle. The claim over the woman had to decided by the *qazi* in a trial.[138]

As a result of the mediation,[139] conflict was doused. The two warring hordes marched into the village of the Nahars. Sixty Nahars converged on the scene in anticipation of a fresh armed encounter. The Nahars made arrangements for providing food to the Kheras, who encamped at the village for the night.[140] Hir and

Ranjha, who had remained concealed for obvious reasons, were escorted under the protection of the Nahars. As soon as Hir saw the Kheras, she fell into a rage. She condemned Ali for mobilizing armies (*faujan*) against two helpless persons and thus displaying his utter lack of shame. But she showered fulsome praise on the Nahars for providing shelter to the fugitives in the face of heavy odds. Hir's verbal attack (*sukhan*) provoked the Kheras to target a quiet Ranjha. They accused him of treacherous conduct in stealing away the bride, but hiding his crime behind the cover of a shawl as well as silence. They threatened to eat his raw flesh and drink his blood. Hir flared up and shouted back, 'O Khera. You have been bad since antiquity (*qadimi bhaira*). How can you, a mean Jat, dare to admonish us? I will burn the faces of all the Kheras for reviling us in our presence.[141]

The truce between the Nahars and Kheras was short lived. Differences erupted again on the treatment of the fugitives. The Nahars had lodged the two in an isolated house (*kotha hik ikalla*). The Kheras accused the Nahars of enabling Hir to stay with the herdsman (*chake naal bahai*). Nahars asserted that their action was based on what they had seen in the first instance.[142] They had found the two with their arms round each other. It was not proper (*munasib*) for them to disjoin one from the other. The Khera chief Ali demanded that Hir be sent to a female quarter (*zenana*). The whole world knew that a thief (*chor charoka*) had been chasing her for a long time. The Nahars not only rejected the proposal of separating the fugitives from each other, but they were willing to stand by this decision with all their might. The Nahars were not legally empowered to drive a wedge between the two, as they could not inflict any pain on those who were under their protection. In any case, the Kheras were going to Kot Qabula in order to pursue their claim in a court of law. The Nahars would support anyone who was able to get Hir through a legal verdict.[143]

The people of the village took a keen interest in the dispute and, out of sheer curiosity, wished to see the lovers at close quarters. A group of Nahar girls came to see Hir and Ranjha. While serving them food, they were overwhelmed by their beauty. They exclaimed that Ranjha was a suitable partner for Hir and that God (*sayin*) had rightly willed their union. The people argued that the Kheras had perpetrated a great calamity (*qehar*) by chasing the lovers with an armed retinue (*lashkar*). The Kheras were deeply embarrassed by the barrage of taunts, but thought it prudent to keep quiet. In the morning, both sides prepared to leave and saddled their horses. Asked to explain the object of their proposed journey, the Nahars said that they would serve as good companions for the Kheras (*sathi sahih tusade*). Being confident of the propriety of their action and holding the custody of the fugitives in their hands, the Nahars explained: 'Friends. It is not proper for us to hand over these two persons to you. You may kill them on the way, but we are guided by the spirit of compassion (*tars*). We will present them before the judge (*qazi*), jurist (*mufti*) and administrator (*hakam*). We will hand over Hir in accordance with the decision of the law (*shariat*).'[144]

A large convoy of people marched towards Kot Qabula. Nahars and Kheras rode on their high bred steeds, while the non-partisan persons ran ahead. The two lovers, with their faces covered in the folds of their shawls, were placed at the head of the entire group. The Khera youth Sahiba, who had been married to an unwilling Hir, lost his cool on seeing the two lovers together. Wailing at the pitch of his voice, he accused Hir of devising tricks to acquire the herdsman. On the other hand, Hir came out strongly in favour of Ranjha during the course of a verbal spat. Addressing Sahiba, who was supposed to be her husband, Hir shouted, 'O wretched Khera. May your face be burnt. I sacrifice myself for Dhido. When love (*ishq*) was being distributed, you were not given any share. You are as useless as the string which rotates the churn (*madhani*). Do not dare to speak again. You wretched Khera. Your father is a shifty man.' In the midst of his howling, the Khera cursed, 'You bitchy wench (*kutti ranne*). May you neither live nor die. You have become a keep of the herdsman. You openly go about fornicating (*kardi rajj haram*).'[145]

In accordance with a premeditated plan, the Kheras fell upon the two lovers. They overpowered Ranjha and grabbed Hir by the arm. The Nahars, who tried to prevent this physical assault, argued, 'This is not proper (*munasib*). Men do not enter into an altercation with women. You two (the plaintiff and accused) will face each other soon. Let every one keep quiet till we reach Kot Qabula.' The Kheras did not challenge the reprimand, in view of the reinforcement of sixty men to the retinue of the Nahars. Hir accused the Kheras of making false statements. She claimed to be under the protection of a perfect mentor (*kamil murshid*) and a true lord (*sacha sahib*) from the beginning to the end. He was her husband and she his wife.[146]

Clans and Lovers in the Qazi's Court

The convoy reached Kot Qabula at the time of evening prayer and, tying horses in the stables, prepared to spend the night. The men, including the Nahars and Kheras, formed a circle (*ghera*) around the two detainees (*bandhuye*). Damodar claimed to have been present on the occasion and even helped the lovers to sit in comfort, with the object of saving them from any humiliation. Every one took the meals and slept in a circle. Next morning, the litigants entered the *kachehri* and remembered God (*sayin*) in this hour of reckoning. News had already spread in Kot Qabula about the arrival of Hir (the daughter of Chuchak, the chief of Jhang Siyal) along with herdsman to argue her case. Virtually the entire population of the town (*qasba*), assembled at the court to see the spectacle with their own eyes. Qazi, *mufti*, *hakim* and *qanungo* took their seats. The Qazi asked the litigants to advance their pleas, so that these could be scrutinized on the basis of Shariat.[147]

Ali, the Khera chief, stated,

Listen to our petition (*arz*). Our debts have been mounting ever since we brought Chuchak's daughter as a bride. We had performed all ceremonies of the wedding in the most appropriate manner. We heard the scandal about the herdsman, but we did not know the exact facts. We made him carry the kettledrum on his head. In a secret move, Hir pretended to be bitten by a snake and, therefore, withdrew herself into a room. The Jogi assumed the garb of a healer (*mandri*) and eloped with her after making a breach (*sann*) in the wall. It is we who have hauled him here. Please ask the Nahars why they have given protection to the two.

The Nahar chief explained that they were harvesting a crop in their field when two persons appeared from somewhere. When they learnt the true facts, their sense of honour was roused and they offered sanctuary to them. They did not refuse shelter even to the dogs. The visitors, being the offspring of zamindars, possessed dignity. She (Hir) would go with the person to whom she had been betrothed. The Nahars did not have any interest of their own. They were willing to accept the verdict of the judge and, thus, withdraw their support to the fugitives, if any.[148]

The Qazi, while framing the charges against Hir, enumerated her transgressions of both the legal injunctions and social norms. He praised her for possessing a number of virtues, but also drew her attention to what the Lord (*sahib*) had ordained. She took pride (*maan*) in her association with Ranjha, who belonged to someone else as a matter of right (*haq paraya*). She was guilty of bringing shame on her father and destroying the honour (*adab*) of her brothers. The information about her affair had spread (*jag dhandora*) all over the world. Hir's defence against the charges was based on love and not on law. In her view, since the Qazi had not tasted the sweetness of love, he was not competent to sit in judgement over the case. Her love for Ranjha could be traced to remote antiquity. In fact, it originated at a time when God created the world. The marriage (*nikah*) of the hearts was solemnized by God and this was beyond the jurisdiction of the Qazi.[149] Being offended by this explanation, the Qazi declared that Hir had come with the aim of raising a quarrel. Her contention was based on falsehood, whereas the truth would prevail in the end. She was reminded of her arrival as the bride of the Kheras, a fact which was known to the whole world. Her relation with the Khera youth was sanctified by the Shariat, which did not take cognizance of love (*ishq*).

On the other hand, Hir stuck to her guns. She expressed doubts about the legal credentials of the Qazi and, therefore, asked him to give statements based on truth. He was guilty of taking his task lightly and did not know the secrets of love. She cursed the lineages of those who forbade what was lawful. She would not relinquish her relationship with Ranjha, even if she was rendered without caste. At this moment, the *qazi* lost his temper. He dubbed Hir as an infidel (*kafiryani*) who was guilty of blasphemy. Her passion (*chetak*) for Ranjha was illicit and it had brought her clan into disrepute. She was threatened with punishment for speaking improper (*namaqul*) words. She was warned to control her tongue, lest she should repent during her penance. Hir expected the Qazi to be fair towards her, particularly because he too had a daughter (*peton jayee*). Standing in the dock and facing trial, she was clear about the issues in dispute and nothing was concealed from her. If she was punished for adhering to the truth, there was nothing more agreeable to her. She was willing to enter the grave while being alive, provided the *qazi* quoted a similar precedent from his legal experience.[150]

The Qazi was angered by Hir's firm stance and spirited defence. He reminded her that a large number of people (*janj alam*) had joined the marriage procession. But if she denied her marriage with the Khera youth, she could be subject to a public beating and, in the process, she was likely to die while being alive. He could not accept her contention because he was aware of her intimacy (*ashnai*) with the herdsman (*chak*). Hir, who refused to be cowed down by threats, expressed doubts about the professional competence and ethical standards of the Qazi. In fact, she poked fun at the manner in which the Qazi was conducting the trial. He was not only ignorant of the facts of the case, he also did what pleased him. Since he was enticed by worldly illusions (*maya*), he exposed himself to infidelity (*kufr*). After all, the whole world knew that she belonged to Ranjha and none else. The Qazi repeated that the whole world knew that Chuchak had married her among the Kheras, who had brought a sizeable marriage party and had incurred a large expenditure. But she, being afflicted with love, made defiant speeches and abandoned all sense of shame. Hir made an attempt to overwhelm the Qazi by invoking the omnipotent God and the reigning Mughal emperor, besides referring to her own high social background. She expected the Qazi to fear God (*sache khudai*) particularly because his own daughter could meet a fate similar to hers. Akbar had put in place a strong administration (*raj dhadera*) which had conferred the office of Qazi on him. As for herself, she was not an ordinary young woman, but the daughter of a zamindar.[151]

The Qazi recognized the fact that Hir was the daughter of a powerful zamindar (*raath vadhera*). But she did not live up to the expectations of the contemporary society, as she was not ashamed of her bad conduct. Irrespective of her (controversial) life in her parental village, she was made to accompany the Kheras as a bride. But it was the height of shamelessness on her part to have stealthily run away from their village. She was advised to return to her husband's house with honour, failing which she would be forced to do so. Hir upbraided the Qazi for threatening to use force, while everyone (*sab lukai*) knew that only Ranjha was her rightful (*haq*) husband. She accused the Qazi of failing to provide justice as he had taken a bribe (*vaddhi*), but had the audacity to show legal texts (*kitab*) as the basis of his contentions. The Qazi lost his temper on account of Hir's accusations of bribery and uncouth speech (*be adab alaye*). Addressing Hir as a shameless woman (*ran besharmi*), he threatened to chop off her nose and ears for adhering to the unlawful (*haram*) instead of the lawful (*halal*), for refusing to abide by the God's law (*shara khudai*) and repeatedly bringing the herdsman (*chak*) into the legal proceedings.

Hir believed that her crime of love for Ranjha did not merit the punishment of chopping bodily parts. In her view, such a punishment should be meted out to those who indulged in clandestine love (*yaari chori*) and those who grabbed another's right (*haq paraya*). Since she and Ranjha belonged to each other, there could be no question of a second marriage (*beya nikah*). Speaking sarcastically, she argued that she had been hearing of the Khera with her ears, but had never seen him with her eyes. The Qazi felt intrigued that Hir had spent a married life of three years with the Khera. Yet she allowed herself to be carried away by her father's herdsman who, in spite of his hunger and homelessness, appeared again on the scene. Hir was quick to catch the Qazi on the wrong foot and, in the process, gave evidence of repudiating her marriage with the Khera. She argued, 'During the last thirty-five months and a half, I have not eaten the salt of the Kheras. I did not wear any clothing other than the scarf (*chhipri*) received from my parents. I swear on whichever oath you wish, I have not allowed the Khera to come anywhere near my bed. But my face acquired radiance (*lali*) as Ranjha showed his face.[152] At this moment, the Qazi turned his ire against Ranjha. He asserted that Ranjha was a thief in the eyes of the Shariat. In fact, the people would testify (*ugahi*) that he was a long standing thief (*chor charoka*) who had been chasing Hir for a long time. Hir's legally wedded husband was the Khera who would not leave her by any means. It was not clear why she should leave her husband (*haq*) for a paramour (*yaar*). Hir felt it necessary to come out in support of Ranjha and to assert the purity of her love and legitimacy of their relationship. Claiming to understand the nature of their mandate (*sanad*) of love, she traced their love to earliest of times (*nehun charoka*) when she was a suckling infant and writhed in her cradle, while there was none to comprehend her agony. Since she was conscious of her individuality (*vast*), she disowned both her father Chuchak and father-in-law Ali. While the trial was in progress hundreds of people gathered at the court. Every day they had been hearing of the two lovers, but now they availed themselves of the opportunity of seeing them with their own eyes. They were amazed at the ability of Hir to answer all questions that were posed to her by the Qazi.[153]

In another attempt to persuade Hir to change her mind, the Qazi invoked her superior social background. He argued that she ought to remember whose daughter and whose daughter-in-law she was. Her father and father-in-law were not only lords of land and water, but they were also linked to the mighty Mughal emperor Akbar. Since the Qazi had a high regard (*adab*) for them, he did not order Hir to be beaten. He had been trying his best to ensure that she did not kill herself. Hir refused to be impressed by the power and wealth of the two zamindars which, in any case, was acclaimed in all directions. She would prefer to throw these riches in the fire, because they did not guarantee her love. The Qazi, feeling exasperated, could no longer show any favour towards the two Khans. He ordered Hir's hands to be tied behind her back. He declared that he would not release her till she admitted that she was the daughter-in-law of the Kheras (*nonh khereyan di*), a fact which was known to the whole world.

Fearing that she had lost the case, Hir made one last attempt to salvage her position. She asserted that the story of her love was unique, as it could not be narrated (*akath kahani*). Her love was older than creation. It predated even the mythical stone tablet (*lauh kalam*), the canopy of heaven and throne of God. It happened when there was no earth, sky, sun, moon or water. Only a small glow existed within a bigger light. If there was anyone who belonged to that period, Hir could have presented him as a witness. Since this was physically impossible, Hir appeared to have given up the fight. Ranjha, who was wearing the garb of a Jogi, was brought in front of the Qazi for interrogation. The Qazi spoke harshly, 'You were a herdsman of Chuchak. When did you assume asceticism (*jog*)? You appear to be an illegitimate offspring of some herdsman. What a garb you are wearing?' The Qazi did not wait for any answer, but had Ranjha's hands tied behind his back. Feeling extremely dejected, Hir made her last statement in the court. Her story was intricate (*aukhi eh kahani*). It could be understood only by someone who was an intimate (*mehram*), i.e. one who could comprehend the rules of love. Even if someone tried to explain it in fullest detail, no one would believe it. Her own tongue had been sealed (*mohar zaban kari*). Since she was rendered dumb, her thoughts could be understood only by the dumb (*gunga*). She meant to say that the entire trial was a farce. The long verbal exchanges were futile. Only if the nature of love had been understood, justice could have been done.[154]

In accordance with the Qazi's judgement, Ranjha was whipped in full public view.[155] His arms were raised above his head, as the whip landed on his body. Hir could not bear the sight of Ranjha being punished in this fashion. She rushed forward and clasped (*jaffa*) him to her chest. While thus blocking the blows, Hir appealed in the name of God to stop the whipping. She demanded that Ranjha's entire punishment be given to her, so that she was able to share half of the pain. The court found it impossible to continue the whipping. The gathering laughed at the helplessness of the concerned functionaries. Hir was physically separated from

Ranjha. An official named Abul Fateh intervened. Questioning the thrashing of the convicts, he ordered that Hir be immediately handed over to the Khera chief Ali. This would save the legal dispensation from further embarrassment. After all, there was no need to ask for any witness (*shahid*) when the facts of the case were known and the judgement had been pronounced.[156]

Damodar claimed to be present on the scene when the judgement was implemented. As soon as Hir came into the custody of the Kheras, a rope was tied round her waist and she was made to walk ahead of the horses. Some partisans of the Kheras continuously attacked her with stones and sticks, while some others used their legs. Feeling the painful jerks of the rope, Hir spoke to the Khera chief Ali. She would not entreat the brutish Jat (*siyada jatta*) to stop her ill treatment. She felt as if these blows had been inflicted by Ranjha and, therefore, offered to sacrifice her life for him. The more did she confront her tormentors, the more was she got beaten by the Khan. Her body was covered with blood and hair were mingled with dust. This did not deter Hir from continuing her tirade against the Kheras. Again addressing Ali as a brutish Jat, she affirmed Ranjha as her spiritual mentor (*murshid*) whose mysteries could not be discerned by anyone. It was merely Ranjha's work which was being done by the Khera chief. She was dragged by the rope and her clothes got entangled in a thorny bush, but the Kheras did not show any mercy towards her. In response, she warned Ali and his son of the impending revenge, which would be taken by her spiritual mentor who would not spare them at all.[157]

Justice through Supernatural Means

All of a sudden, a fire irrupted at the gate of Kot Qabula and quickly spread across the town. The inhabitants, while crying in desperation, tried to douse the flames. But these efforts produced the opposite results, as the water turned into oil. They also tried to determine the cause of the fire. They felt that the ruler Adli Raja did not dispense justice and that the concerned officers, owing to their greed for money (*dirman*), had received a bribe. The angry inhabitants rushed to the administrator (*hakim*) and the judge (*qazi*). They posed several questions. How was it that a flourishing town was converted into a blazing inferno? What answer would they give if Akbar sought their explanation? The inhabitants who converged in a single large body, were filled with anger. In their view, it was the Jogi's appeal (*jogi parcha laya*) against the Qazi's verdict which had engulfed the town in the huge fire. The Qazi and *mufti*, who stood in opposition to the people, felt amazed at the fury of nature. Failing to elicit a favourable response from the administrator, the people sought forgiveness from the Jogi. They appealed to him to employ his miraculous power to stop the fire and, at the same time, to send an armed body to bring back the Kheras. The Qazi found himself in the dock and was constrained to reverse his recent judgement. He explained that he had delivered his verdict on the basis of facts, which were placed before the court. But no one knew the will of God, who was empowered to dispense the ultimate justice. Therefore, Hir would belong to the person who would extinguish the fire.[158]

The assembly of the people categorically attributed the fire to the Qazi's wrong judgement. In their collective opinion, the Qazi had wrought a great calamity (*qehar*) by handing over Hir to the Kheras. Hir belonged to the Jogi by right. The injustice inflicted by the Qazi on the Jogi was solely responsible for the destruction of the town, while the Jogi had shown a lot of patience all through. In fact, the assembly of people cried (*sabha kook khaloi*) that this was the cause of the unfortunate incident. As Damodar witnessed a tense scenario with his own eyes, the people took the initiative in their own hands. While they fell at the Jogi's feet and sought his intervention to restore normalcy, they persuaded the Qazi to dispatch an armed contingent to intercept the Kheras on the way and haul them back. Turning towards the Qazi, they ridiculed him for throwing away the sprig (*bumbal*) which could have grown into the tree of love. They asked him to retrieve this very sprig, so that he could earn some merit (*sobha*) as well as their blessings (*aseesan*).[159]

In accordance with the orders of the local authorities based in Kot Qabula, a party of soldiers intercepted the Kheras and hauled them back. None except Hir could understand that the situation had been reversed owing to the miraculous power of the herdsman (*azmat chak vikhai*). With her morale shooting up, she was filled with fresh energy. Without letting the horses of the Kheras come near her, Hir tied her loincloth (*kachhota*) and ran with big strides. She was elated at the thought that her honour had been protected by the Lord. When the convoy reached Kot Qabula, it found its passage blocked by fire. Nobody could think of any solution to the predicament. During their onward journey, the Jogi had enabled them to go unharmed though the fire. How could they proceed further? At this moment, it was Hir who displayed her miraculous power. She stood before the fire and moved her hands. Instantaneously, a path was made through the raging flames and Hir guided the entire *lashkar* across it.[160]

When the convoy entered the town of Kot Qabula, the *qazi* explained to Ali the circumstances in which he was constrained to modify his decision. He had delivered the original verdict by taking into account whatever was visible (*zahir dittha aha*) and on the basis of the Shariat. But nobody was familiar with the hidden mysteries (*batin baat*). Therefore, it was decided that Hir be taken as a rightful due by the person who could put out the fire. Ali realized that the tables had been turned on them and it was advisable to abandon their claims on Hir. He admitted that the two lovers were inseparable. The Kheras would leave the place immediately as it was impossible to stay there any longer. On seeing the flames, the Kheras assumed an attitude of detachment (*udasi*), while their leading men (*mahajan*) saw an imminent demise of their fortunes. The people of Kot Qabula threatened to burn the Kheras who had brought a calamity (*bala*) on the town (*vast*). In this situation of widespread panic, the people appealed to the Jogi to save them. In response to the plea, the Jogi stood up with folded hands and appealed (*arz*) to the Panj Pir to have mercy on the entire town and put out the fire. As the flames subsided, the people bowed before the Jogi.

The populace of the town, including the judge, jurist and administrator, appeared before the Jogi. With shawls round their necks and hands on their feet, they declared that they were his creatures (*bande*) and beseeched him to settle in the town. Paying homage to the Jogi for showing great miraculous power (*azmat*), they admitted that Hir belonged to him by right (*haq*). In these circumstances, the Jogi and Hir were united with each other. When the herdsman displayed his miraculous power, the entire populace of the town, including its government officers, came to offer respect to him as if they were undertaking a pilgrimage (*ziyarat*). All were unanimous in demanding that the Kheras must be beaten, expelled and humiliated in such a manner that they were not seen in the town again. Accordingly, the Kheras suffered this treatment.[161]

The life of Kot Qabula witnessed a new beginning. The fragrance of musk spread across the town. Adli Raja recognized the importance of justice. As the roses bloomed, the sandalwood walls emitted a pleasant perfume. Every inhabitant of the town felt happy. It was 1529 of the Bikrami era. The rule of Akbar became strong with every passing day. Hir and Ranjha, now united with each other, left the town while showering their blessings, as all the disputes had ended. The inhabitants of the town, who came to bid farewell, beseeched them to settle in the place. They offered to build a new house (*dalan*) and meet all their desires. However, the lovers took their leave and left towards the south, hoping to establish a new abode for themselves.[162] Damodar claimed to have travelled along with them. When they had covered a distance of 3 leagues, five horsemen in black robes appeared from the other world (*ghaib*) and, addressing Hir, said, 'You would not have become illuminated without undergoing this experience.' They disappeared and never seen again. The tale of Hir thus came to an end. There has never been a love (*ishq*) of this kind. Damodar concluded his narrative by stating that he had brought to an end what he had taken up, that it was something which was known to the three worlds and that he had written what he had seen. His name was Damodar Gulati and he had settled at Jhang Siyal in the domain of Chuchak.[163]

NOTES

1. Native of a town in Badakhshan, Baqi Kulabi spent a long time in India and died during the rebellion of Masum Khan Kabuli. Endowed with a natural talent for poetry, the specimens of his couplets underlined the physical and mental affliction of the poet due to pain in separation from the beloved. While asserting that his worth had not been recognized, he complained about the greed of his beloved for gold and silver. Abdul Qadir Badauni, *Muntakhab ut-Tawarikh*, vol. III, English translation, Wolseley Hague and B.P. Ambashthya, Patna: Academica Asiatica, 1973, p. 270.
2. Damodar Gulati, *Hir Damodar*, Panjabi text, ed. Jagtar Singh, Patiala: Punjabi University, rpt., 2000, p. 6 (hereafter cited as Damodar).
3. The Siyals were descendants of Rai Shankar, a Punwar Rajput, who resided near Allahabad in the east. On his death, dissensions in his family drove his son Siyal to migrate to Panjab. During his wanderings, he received Islam at the hands of Baba Farid, who prophesied that his progeny would rule the tract between Jhelam and Chenab. They mainly settled in southern portion of Jhang district along the left bank of the Chenab between confluences of the Jhelam and Ravi. The Siyals were described as large in stature and rough of disposition. Fond of cattle rearing, they cared little for agriculture. They observed Hindu ceremonies like the Kharral and Kathia. They did not keep their woman in Pardah. Denzil Ibbetson, *Panjab Castes*, pp. 147-8; H.A. Rose, *A Glossary of the Tribes and Castes of the Punjab and North West Frontier*, vol. II, pp. 417-18.
4. These possibilities were rooted in the changes in the Delhi Sultanate during the fourteenth century. As the old rural aristocracy (*rais, ranas and rawats*) was destroyed, a new class of intermediaries (*chaudhuris*) was created for the extraction of land revenue. This new class was created by assimilating elements from the older aristocracy and some village headmen. Tapan Raychaudhury and Irfan Habib, eds., *The Cambridge Economic History of India*, vol. I: *c. 1200-c. 1750*, New Delhi: Orient Longman, rpt., 2004, p. 57.
5. Damodar, stanza nos. 2-6, pp. 77-8.
6. Ibid., stanza nos. 7-10, p. 78.
7. The Brahmins were the most numerous caste in Panjab, outnumbering all except the Jats and Rajputs. Their proportion to total population reached its maximum where people were entirely Hindus, e.g. in the hills, submontane areas and Jamuna tract. They decreased gradually from east to west, disappearing in the western plains. Their function and position being sacerdotal in character, they were consulted on omens and auspicious dates, besides officiating at ceremonies. They were seen as grasping, quarrelsome and overbearing. In their avarice, they were placed alongside the Dum, Mulla and Bhatt. Denzil Ibbetson, *Panjab Castes*, Patiala: Languages Department, Punjab, rpt., 1970, pp. 215-18.

8. Damodar, stanza nos. 11-20, pp. 78-9.
9. Indra was the god of thunder, who overcame drought and darkness, bringing water and light. He was also the god of warfare and used thunderbolt as his weapon. The world of Indra was filled with sidhas, charans, apsaras, gandharvas, brahmrishis and other deities. As celestial plants and fragrant air marked the Nandana grove, his grand assembly (*sabha*) boasted of a richly adorned court, glittering chariots and enchanting music and dance. Roshen Dalal, *Hinduism: A Alphabetical Guide*, pp. 164-5.
10. Damodar, Stanza Nos. 21-9, pp. 80-1.
11. Ibid., Stanza Nos. 30-2, p. 81.
12. The two words Doom and Mirasi were absolutely synonymous. The former was a Hindu name, while the latter was Muslim and Arabic. Apart from serving as genealogists for different agricultural castes and outcaste tribes, they also performed as musicians and minstrels. Assigned an exceedingly low social position, they recited genealogies at weddings and similar occasions. They were notorious for their exactions, which were made under threat of lampooning ancestors of their clients. Denzil Ibbetson, *Panjab Castes*, pp. 234-35.
13. Throughout territories of the Mughal Empire, the customary Indian scale of weight treated a *man* as equal to 40 *sers*. Before Akbar, a *ser* was equal to 22 *dams* in weight. In the beginning of this reign, the *ser* was raised to 28 *dams* in weight and before writing of the *Ain-i Akbari*, it was raised to 30 *dams* in weight. Since a *dam* was equal to 322.7 grains, a *ser* of 28 *dams* was equal to 51.63 lbs. or 23.44 kg. and a *ser* of 30 *dams* was equal to 55.32 lbs. or 25.11 kg. Irfan Habib, *The Agrarian System of Mughal India 1556-1707*, New Delhi: Oxford University Press, 2nd revd. edn., 1999, pp. 420-1.
14. Sambhals have been listed as a clan of Muslim Jats in Montgomery district, engaged in agriculture. H.A. Rose, *A Glossary of the Tribes and Castes of the Punjab and North West Frontier*, vol. II, Patiala: Languages Department, Punjab, rpt., 1970, p. 351.
15. Jhinwars were included among menials who worked as watermen, boatmen and cooks. They were known as Jhinwar in east Panjab where they were largely Hindu and as Machhis in west Panjab where they were mostly Muslim. They were most numerous in central and westren districts of the province, which were traversed by the great rivers and where they assisted in agricultural labour. Besides supplying water in houses and at social functions, they carried palanquins and other burdens. As true village menials, they received customary dues for their services. Denzil Ibbetson, *Punjab Castes*, pp. 303-6.
16. Damodar, Stanza Nos. 40-9, pp. 82-4.
17. Originating in China, the Chenab passes through Chamba and reaches Kishtwar. Here it is joined by the Bhaga arriving from Tibet, so that it is known as the Chandrabhaga. Flowing through Rohtal, Jammu and Akhnoor, it enters the plains. From here it fragments into eighteen

The World of the Zamindars 567

branches and, after 12 *kos*, rejoined at Bahlolpur. It goes through Sialkot, Sodhra and Wazirabad, where it pierces the highway and moves through Buriana, Bhutamaral, and Hazara. At Chiniot, it passes through two large hills. Near the town of Jhang Siyal, the native place of Hir, it merged with the Jhelam. Sujan Rai Bhandari, *Khulasat ut-Tawarikh*, Persian text, ed. M. Zafar Hasan, Delhi: G and Sons, 1918, pp. 77-8.

18. Damodar, Stanza Nos. 57-9, p. 85.
19. Ibid., Stanza Nos. 62-9, pp. 85-6.
20. For comparison, one might turn to medieval Europe where the onus was on the wronged individual to avenge himself through vendetta. For him, it was the most sacred of duties, a moral obligation and a point of honour. A feudal lord, joined by his kinsmen and vassals, directed vengeance not only against the culprit, but against any of his relatives. While seeking pardon, it was not only the guilty, but his kinship group that paid the compensation and offered a collective apology. Similarly, the victim and his kinsmen received the indemnity. Marc Bloch, *Feudal Society*, vol. I: *The Growth of the Ties of Dependence*, English translation, L.A. Manyon, New Delhi: Asha Jyoti Booksellers & Publishers, rpt., 2006, pp. 183-4.
21. Damodar, Stanza Nos. 70-89, pp. 87-9.
22. Aghoris were a sect of ascetics known for their abominable practices. They ate human flesh and filth, using human skulls as vessels. They were associated with Tantric rites of Shaivas, the worshippers of one of the forms of the Mother Goddess. They smeared their bodies with ash from funeral piles, wore strings of human skulls around their necks, wove their hair into a matted braid, clothed their loins in tigerskin and carried a bell that was rung incessantly. Found largely in eastern India, they wandered from one pilgrim centre to the other. James Hastings, ed., *The Encyclopaedia of Religion and Ethics*, vol. I, Edinburgh: T and T Clark, 1967, pp. 210-12.
23. Damodar, Stanza Nos. 90-9, pp. 89-91. The poet wished to convey that the Siyal girls, who were brought up in the lap of luxury, wore silk and ate nuts. As beautiful nymphs of heaven, they ought to have settled in matrimony. It was to their credit that they were fighting like their male counterparts and laying down their lives, while trying to assert a point of honour, which was the lifeblood of *zamindari*. Unique in every way, the Siyal girls did not play the conventional role imposed by patriarchal norms and demolished the male bastion of *zamindari*, which was based on military prowess.
24. Damodar, Stanza Nos. 100-1, p. 91.
25. Ibid., Stanza Nos. 102-5, pp. 91-2.
26. According to surveys of 1883 and 1892, the Ranjhas were a tribe of Rajput status, chiefly found in eastern uplands of Shahpur and Gujarat between the Jhelam and Chenab. In small numbers, they have crossed both rivers into the Jhelam and Gujranwala districts. They were for most parts returned as Jats, except in Shahpur. They might be described with accuracy as of Jat status. However, they were Bhatti Rajputs. In Gujarat, they claimed a

Qureshi origin as descendants of Abu Jahl, the Prophet's uncle. Following death of Abu Jahl's son, they migrated to the Kirana Bar. But they retained many Hindu customs. Subsisting mainly on agriculture, they were peacable and well disposed section of population. In physique, they resembled their neighbours, Gondals, with whom they freely intermarried. Denzil Ibbetson, *Panjab Castes*, p. 148; H.A. Rose, *A Glossary of the Tribes and Castes of the Punjab and North West Frontier*, vol. II, p. 323.

27. Damodar, Stanza Nos. 107-09, p. 92.
28. The Waraich were one of the largest Jat tribes of Panjab. In Akbar's time, they held two-thirds of the Gujarat district, though on less favourable terms than those allowed to the Gujjars who held the remainder. In the nineteenth century, they held 170 villages in the district. They had crossed the Chenab into Gujranwala, where they held a tract of 41 villages. Almost entirely Muslim, they retained all their tribal and many of their Hindu customs. They married in the best local tribes. Ibbetson, *Panjab Castes*, pp. 114-15.
29. Damodar, Stanza Nos. 110-15, pp. 92-3.
30. Ibid., Stanza Nos. 117-19, pp. 93-4.
31. Ibid., Stanza Nos. 120-1, p. 94.
32. Ibid., Stanza Nos. 122-9, pp. 94-5.
33. Ibid., Stanza, Stanza Nos. 130-6, pp. 95-6. Though Damodar has not mentioned the names of the culprits who forcibly took away the goods that had been collected for the marriage function, yet it might be surmised that this crime was the handiwork of the selfish and cruel brothers of Dhido. This incident, besides other factors, utterly demoralized Dhido and he was driven to think of leaving his home.
34. Damodar, Stanza Nos. 137-9, pp. 96-7.
35. Waris Shah has given three reasons for Dhido's departure from Takht Hazara. He was given a bad patch of land in the wake of division of property. He was subjected to taunts by his brothers. His sisters-in-law picked up a quarrel with him. In the end, his brothers did try to stop him from leaving the house, but they did not succeed. Waris Shah, *Hir Waris Shah*, Panjabi text, ed. Piara Singh Padam, New Delhi: Navyug Publishers, rpt., 1998, Stanza Nos. 11-31, pp. 62-6.
36. Damodar, Stanza Nos. 140-3, p. 97.
37. Damodar would have us believe that a few travellers came from the north to Jhang Siyal and, since they were quite familiar with Mojam's family, they described the superlative qualities of Ranjha in glowing terms. As the poet's curiosity was aroused, he travelled all the way to Takht Hazara after covering the distance in three stages. He claimed to have met Ranjha, who was sad and restless due to a series of problems. The poet hinted at acquiring accurate information about Ranjha's departure from his village. Damodar, Stanza Nos. 144-6, p. 97.
38. Ibid., Stanza Nos. 150-2, p. 98.
39. Ibid., Stanza no. 153, p. 98.

40. Waris Shah has described an unpleasant encounter between the Mullah and Ranjha. The Mullah lashed out at Ranjha not only for playing on the flute in the precincts of the mosque, but also for his un-Islamic outward appearance as manifested in long hair and a waist covering hanging below the ankles. In retaliation, Ranjha condemned the Mullah for his hypocritical religious orientation, fake piety and penchant for illicit sex. The Mullah, by invoking the Islamic jurisprudence, threatened Rajha with physical punishment for failing to abide by Islamic injunctions regarding prayers and physical bearing. He ordered the traveller to leave the mosque after spending the night. Waris Shah, *Hir Waris Shah*, Stanza Nos. 33-41, pp. 66-8.
41. Damodar, Stanza Nos. 155-7, p. 99.
42. Ibid., Stanza Nos. 158-67, pp. 99-100.
43. Ibid., Stanza Nos. 168-70, pp. 100-1.
44. Ibid., Stanza Nos. 179-80, p. 102.
45. In the version of Waris Shah, the Panj Pir (Khwaja Khizr, Baba Farid Shakarganj, Shaikh Bahauddin Zakariya, Syed Jalaluddin Bokhari and Lal Shahbaz Qalandar) appeared to Ranjha on the first day of his work as a herdsman. On a second occasion, they appeared before the two lovers and advised them to be steadfast in love and trust in God. On the third occasion, impressed by Ranjha's soulful music on the flute, they conferred Hir on him and placed her under the care of one of them, i.e. Syed Jalaluddin Bokhari. Waris Shah, *Hir Waris Shah*, Stanza Nos. 79-80, 106-7, 117-20, pp. 77, 83-4, 86-7.
46. Damodar, Stanza Nos. 181-7, pp. 102-3.
47. Ibid., Stanza Nos. 188-90, pp. 103-4.
48. Damodar, Stanza Nos. 191-8, pp. 104-5. According to Waris Shah, Luddan refused to take Ranjha across the Chenab as he had no money. Ranjha played on the flute and charmed a crowd, including the two wives of Luddan. When Ranjha jumped into the river, he was brought back by Luddan's wives and allowed to rest in the boat owned by Hir. Waris Shah, *Hir Waris Shah*, Stanza Nos. 43-7, p. 69.
49. At this stage, Ranjha proved himself as a genuine mendicant. He was a homeless wanderer. He played music and attracted wild animals. He had no possessions other than a staff and flute. He disregarded social hierarchy. He did not have economic transactions with anyone. He associated himself with the mat and fire. These were the characteristics of many other contemporary saints, who were engaged in spiritual pursuits.
50. Damodar, Stanza Nos. 201-10, pp. 105-6. The two major festivals of the Muslim calendar, Id ul-Azha and Id ul-Fitr, were marked by special prayers, serrmons, family gatherings and charitable acts. The former was celebrated at the end of Haj on the tenth of Zilhijj when unblemished animals were sacrificed. The latter was celebrated at the end of the fasting month of Ramzan on sighting of the crescent moon. It required alms giving prior to morning prayers. John L. Esposito, *The Oxford Dictionary of Islam*, p. 131.

51. Damodar, Stanza Nos. 211-20, pp. 107-8.
52. Ibid., Stanza Nos. 221-7, pp. 108-9. In his account, Waris Shah did not refer to sexual intercourse between the protagonists. Rather, the two exchanged their feelings for each other. Ranjha voiced his doubts about Hir's steadfastness in love. On the other hand, Hir made a number of promises and took an oath of fidelity for Ranjha in the name of Khwaja Khizr. She asked him about his tribe, clan and native place, so that he could be employed by her father as a herdsman. Waris Shah, *Hir Waris Shah*, Stanza Nos. 59-69, pp. 73-5.
53. Damodar, Stanza no. 229, p. 109.
54. Ibid., Stanza Nos. 230, p. 109.
55. Ibid., Stanza Nos. 231-6, pp. 109-10.
56. Ibid., Stanza no. 238, p. 110.
57. Ibid., Stanza Nos. 239-40, p. 111.
58. Cultivation of land demanded a huge input of labour, time and energy. In a single year, there were normally two major crops, Rabi and Kharif. The preparation of soil needed several rounds of ploughing that were accompanied by levelling and fertilizing. Before sowing, the seeds required a special treatment to check disease. Besides major cereals and commercial crops like sugarcane and cotton, a farmer grew a variety of vegetables and fodders. After harvesting, the grain had to be treated for being preserved till the next crop. Hamida Khatoon Naqvi, *Agricultural, Industrial and Urban Dynamism under the Sultans of Delhi 1206-1555*, New Delhi: Munshiram Manoharlal, 1986, pp. 15-18.
59. Damodar, Stanza Nos. 244-7, pp. 111-12.
60. In his version, Waris Shah did not involve the Siyal clansmen and heads of herdsmen in the process of employing Ranjha. It was only Chuchak who interrogated Ranjha, while Hir virtually answered all the questions, as if she was the legal representative of the candidate. In accordance with this account, Ranjha was employed only to graze the buffaloes, and not to perform any other task on the landed estate. Waris Shah, *Hir Waris Shah*, Stanza Nos. 70-7, pp. 75-7.
61. Damodar, Stanza Nos. 248-9, p. 112.
62. Ibid., Stanza No. 250, p. 112.
63. Ibid., Stanza Nos. 251-5, pp. 112-13.
64. Ibid., Stanza Nos. 256-61, pp. 113-14.
65. Gopis were herdswomen, many of whom left their homes, children and husbands to dally with Krishna on the Yamuna. Imagining holding Krishna's hand, they engaged in a circular dance, which probably aimed at promoting fertility in cattle and plants. It was believed that Krishna multiplied himself many times and danced between each pair of Gopis. This idyllic picture of divine Krishna with Gopis symbolized the abstract relation of the deity to his devotees. It was a drama perpetually enacted in the heart of every votary. Margaret and James Stutley, *A Dictionary of Hinduism: The*

The World of the Zamindars 571

Mythology, Folklore and Development (1500 BC–AD 1500), Bombay: Allied Publishers, 1977, p. 101.
66. Damodar, Stanza Nos. 265-72, pp. 114-15. Waris Shah was silent about Ranjha's conflict with other herdsmen, particularly their consistent opposition to him and an attempt to kill him. He was also silent on Ranjha's innovations in the grazing of buffaloes in the moor and village. On the other hand, Damodar has paid a lot of attention to these two aspects in the life of the protagonist.
67. Damodar, Stanza Nos. 273-7, p. 116.
68. Ibid., Stanza Nos. 278-82, pp. 116-17.
69. Ibid., Stanza Nos. 283-92, pp. 117-18. According to Damodar's narrative, before Hir and Ranjha fell in love with each other, both had been separately betrothed – Hir with a youth from the Khera clan and Ranjha with the daughter of Yaqub Khan Waraich. According to Waris Shah, Hir first fell in love with Ranjha and, after the affair became a scandal, she was forcibly married to Saida Khera in response to a proposal from the Kheras. In fact, the Waraichs are conspicuous by their absence in the plot constructed by Waris Shah.
70. Damodar, Stanza Nos. 293-304, pp. 119-20.
71. Ibid., Stanza Nos. 305-18, pp. 120-2.
72. Ibid., Stanza Nos. 319-25, pp. 122-3.
73. Ibid., Stanza Nos. 326-35, pp. 123-5.
74. Damodar, Stanza Nos. 336-48, pp. 125-7. Unlike Damodar, Waris Shah has provided details of letters between Ranjha's brothers and Chuchak as well as between Ranjha's sisters-in-law and Hir. Here an attempt was made by Ranjha's brothers and their wives to explain their previous conduct and to bring Ranjha back to Takht Hazara. However, their demand was rejected by the other side on the basis of a different reading of Ranjha's circumstances. Waris Shah, *Hir Waris Shah*, Stanza Nos. 158-70, pp. 97-100.
75. Damodar, Stanza Nos. 349-56, pp. 127-8.
76. Ibid., Stanza Nos. 357-79, pp. 128-32.
77. Ibid., Stanza Nos. 380-7, pp. 132-3.
78. Waris Shah has delved at length into the severe reprimands issued to Hir by her parents and brothers, with reference to the threat of inflicting a variety of physical tortures on her. He has also described the Qazi's futile attempts to pull Hir back into the conventional patriarchal mould. However, Waris Shah did not point to the actual attempt to poison Hir and the plan to replace her by her niece in a wedlock with the Khera boy. Waris Shah, *Hir Waris Shah*, Stanza Nos. 108-16, pp. 84-6.
79. Damodar, Stanza Nos. 392-401, pp. 134-5.
80. Ibid., Stanza Nos. 388-91, pp. 133-4.
81. Ibid., Stanza Nos. 402-7, pp. 135-6.
82. Ibid., Stanza Nos. 408-16, pp. 136-7.
83. Ibid., Stanza Nos. 417-29, pp. 137-9.

84. Ibid., Stanza Nos. 430-4, pp. 139-40. Reflecting on the defeat of Ranjha in his fight against the Kheras, Waris Shah has conceived the situation in terms of an eternal conflict between the weak and strong, poor and rich. Speaking on behalf of Ranjha, he strongly condemned the Jats in general and the Siyals in particular. They have been caricatured as thugs, who sold off their daughters to strangers even if they were married. Their women were alleged to prefer thieves to men of piety and even led their daughters into bigamous relationships. Waris Shah, *Hir Waris Shah*, Stanza Nos. 223-7, pp. 114-15.
85. Damodar, Stanza Nos. 435-41, pp. 140-1. As as shown by Damodar, Hir made two attempts to scuttle her forced marriage with the Khera youth. Twice she succeeded in bringing Ranjha to the marriage venue and, in full public view, she declared him as her bridegroom. She even went to the extent of touching his feet and embracing him. Acting boldly and intelligently, she provided an opportunity to the Siyals to reverse their decision. She did not succeed, because the marriage party of the Kheras had arrived. Moreover, her niece could not substitute her, as she herself was still alive.
86. *Nikah* as the marriage contract in Islam was based on four conditions – (i) consent of the marriage guardian (*wali*), (ii) agreement of the woman, (iii) presence of two witnesses of manifest rectitude and (iv) an offer and immediate acceptance expressed in terms of marriage by two persons of full legal competence, neither of them being a woman. These persons might be the husband and the marriage guardian or their authorized representatives. Abu Hamid Muhammad Ghazzali, *Adab al-Nikah*, English translation, Muhtar Holland, Kuala Lumpur: Dar ul-Wahi Publications, 2012, pp. 62-3.
87. Damodar, Stanza Nos. 442-6, pp. 141-2.
88. The Kheras took this step, because they knew that the marriage ceremony was illegal, as Hir had not given her consent. She could run away while being taken from Jhang Siyal to Rangpur Khera. By consummation of the marriage, they would put a seal of legitimacy on the ceremony and also erase the claim of Ranjha on her.
89. Damodar, Stanza Nos. 447-54, pp. 142-3.
90. In medieval France, a lawful marriage among the elite was arranged in advance, besides being lavish and public. The future wife was ceremonially bestowed (betrothal) and then ceremonially conducted to the marriage bed (nuptials). Not far from the marriage chamber, a large crowd kept up a long and noisy party, having gathered to certify the physical union, to rejoice at it and through its own brimming pleasure to capture the mysterious gifts needed to make the marriage fruitful. Georges Duby, *The Knight, the Lady and the Priest: The Making of Modern Marriage in Medieval France*, p. 44.
91. Damodar, Stanza Nos. 455-60, pp. 143-4.
92. Ibid., Stanza Nos. 461-8, pp. 144-5.
93. Ibid., Stanza Nos. 469-77, pp. 145-6. Hir was deceived into believing that Ranjha had been allowed to stay at Rangpur Khera. But this was only a ploy

The World of the Zamindars   573

to ensure her smooth departure from Jhang Siyal. Evidently, the patriarchal forces resorted to three successive devices to separate the lovers for good. At the outset, they tried to exert mental pressure by invoking the principle of clan honour as well as the religious authority of the *qazi*. In the second stage, they thought of using violence to kill her. Failing in both the moves, they finally resorted to deceit and apparently succeeded in achieving their object, little anticipating the resilience of the lovers.

94. Damodar, Stanza Nos. 478-9, 484-5, 491-3, pp. 147-9.
95. Ibid., Stanza Nos. 494-502, pp. 149-50.
96. Ibid., Stanza Nos. 503-9, pp. 150-1. Damodar has taken a lot of interest in the acute maltreatment of Ranjha at the hands of the Kheras. However, in Waris Shah's account, Ranjha has been shown as escorting the cattle sent as Hir's dowry to Rangpur Khera, but without any harassment from the Kheras.
97. Damodar, Stanza Nos. 512-16, pp. 151-2.
98. Ibid., Stanza Nos. 517-25, pp. 152-3.
99. Ibid., Stanza Nos. 526-7, pp. 153-4.
100. Ibid., Stanza Nos. 528-50, pp. 154-7.
101. Ibid., Stanza Nos. 551-5, pp. 157-8.
102. Ibid., Stanza Nos. 556-9, p. 158.
103. Ranjha, having discarded kinship ties and property claims, reasserted his new identity as a mendicant (*faqir*). The Waraichs would not give their daughter in marriage to Ranjha in this new incarnation. Ranjha's voluntary withdrawal from the betrothal had rendered their task easy, but the cancellation of the betrothal had to be formalized only by the two clans. In fact, the stakeholders were required to follow the same procedure as was adopted when the betrothal was contracted during the time of Mojam. Among the land owning groups, the individual did not have freedom of action. Where an individual wished to go against his clan, he had to pay a very heavy price like Ranjha.
104. Damodar, Stanza Nos. 560-7, pp. 158-9. Clear about his new social identity, Ranjha highlighted the vast difference between himself who, as an ascetic, was tied to fire and mat, and his brothers and Waraichs, who were tied to landed property and related worldly affairs, particularly the relative position of Jat clans.
105. Ibid., Stanza Nos. 567-71, pp. 159-60.
106. Ibid., Stanza Nos. 572-7, pp. 160-1.
107. Ibid., Stanza Nos. 578-83, pp. 161-2.
108. Ibid., Stanza Nos. 584-97, pp. 162-4. While dealing with three hostile elements – his brothers, the Waraichs and their daughter – Ranjha conducted himself like a true saint. Though he had been the target of unwarranted criticism, yet he refused to enter into any confrontation and, in the process, displayed exemplary fortitude and gentleness.
109. Damodar, Stanza Nos. 598-602, 616-17, pp. 164-76.

574   *The Making of Medieval Panjab*

110. Ibid., Stanza Nos. 622-36, pp. 168-70.
111. Ibid., Stanza Nos. 637-44, pp. 170-1.
112. Ibid., Stanza Nos. 646-52, pp. 171-2.
113. Ibid., Stanza Nos. 654-63, pp. 172-4.
114. Ibid., Stanza Nos. 664-7, p. 174.
115. These two prominently figured in the traditions of Nath Yogis alongside spiritual masters like Gorakhnath, Machhandar Nath, Jalandhar Nath and others. Their tales have been sung by wandering minstrels in a vast area exrending from Panjab to Bengal. Gopichand was said to have been the son of Rani Mainavati and Raja Manikchandra of Bengal. Bharthari, said to be the ruler of Ujjain and elder brother of Vikramaditya, was the uncle of Gopichand. Placed in different circumstances, both renounced their royal positions and adopted the path of the Nath Yogis. Ann Grodzins Gold, *A Carnival of Parting: The Tales of King Bharthari and King Gopi Chand as Sung and Told by Madhu Natisar Nath of Ghatiyali, Rajasthan*, New Delhi: Munshiram Manoharlal, rpt., 1993, pp. 57-70.
116. According to Waris Shah, Balnath refused to initiate Ranjha in the path owing to his privileged background and aristocratic bearing. On hearing Ranjha's tale of woes and sincere intent, Balnath relented. The senior disciples revolted against Balnath, accusing him of favouritism and physical attraction towards the novice. They beat up the master, destroyed the hermitage and threatened to leave. Balnath, having suppressed the opposition, enrolled Ranjha as a Jogi after shaving his hair, boring his ears and smearing ash on his body. In his sermon, Balnath explained the doctrines of his path, emphasizing the practice of celibacy. Since Ranjha resolutely argued against celibacy, Balnath conferred Hir on him like the Panj Pir. Waris Shah, *Hir Waris Shah*, Stanza Nos. 253-84, pp. 122-31.
117. Damodar, Stanza Nos. 668-80, pp. 175-6.
118. Waris Shah has recorded an acrimonious debate between Ranjha and Sehti. The latter questioned the credentials of the mendicant as a Jogi. He was a peasant wearing a saintly garb to cheat innocent women. He was ignorant of the Yogic philosophy and meaning of its symbols. She threatened to expose him and expel him from the village after a severe beating. In his spirited defense, Ranjha revealed his knowledge of Hindu philosophical systems and his ability to cure diseases through occult powers. Though he regarded men as superior to women in thought and action, he was willing to cure Hir of her affliction. In the end, Sehti begged Ranjha to treat her sick sister-in-law. Waris Shah, *Hir Waris Shah*, Stanza Nos. 333-83, pp. 147-62.
119. Damodar, Stanza Nos. 706-15, pp. 180-2.
120. Ibid., Stanza Nos. 716-19, pp. 182-3.
121. Ibid., Stanza Nos. 720-9, pp. 183-4.
122. Ibid., Stanza Nos., 731-2, 734-5, 737, 740, 742, pp. 184-6.
123. Ibid., Stanza Nos. 730, 732-3, 736, 739, 741, 743, pp. 184-6.

The World of the Zamindars 575

124. Ibid., Stanza Nos. 744-51, pp. 186-8.
125. Ibid., Stanza Nos. 752-9, pp. 188-9.
126. Ibid., Stanza Nos. 760-7, pp. 189-90.
127. Ibid., Stanza Nos. 768-73, pp. 190-1.
128. Ibid., Stanza Nos. 774-9, pp. 191-2.
129. Ibid., Stanza Nos. 780-9, pp. 192-4.
130. Ibid., Stanza Nos. 790-800, pp. 194-5.
131. Ibid., Stanza Nos. 808-22, pp. 196-9.
132. Ibid., Stanza Nos. 840-5, pp. 202-3.
133. Ibid., Stanza Nos. 846-57, pp. 203-5.
134. Ibid., Stanza Nos. 858-63, pp. 205-6.
135. The Kheras listened patiently to the explanations of the Nahars, but did not believe what they were told. Since they understood that the Nahars were in no way inferior to them, they did not level a direct allegation of complicity in the flight of the lovers. Rather they tried to win over the sympathy of the Nahars in order to apprehend the fugitives.
136. Damodar, Stanza Nos. 864-71, pp. 206-7. Damodar would have us believe that he was present on the scene while hiding behind two plants and a reed bush (*naun damodar chhap khalota / do boote ikk kahi*).
137. Syeds were regarded as the descendants of Prophet Muhammad through his daughter Fatima. Owing to this, every Syed was supposed to be brave, truthful and pious, besides possessing every other noble quality. The Mongol ravages forced a large number of Syeds to migrate to Hindustan. They received land grants from the Sultans of Delhi and exaggerated respect from the Muslims in general. Beyond the meridian of Lahore, they formed a larger proportion of population, being the largest of all in the Salt Range and Pathan frontier. They constituted a smaller element of population in the eastern half of Panjab. As landowners and cultivators, the Syeds were known for their incompetence. Kunwar Muhammad Ashraf, *Life and Conditions of the People of Hindustan*, New Delhi: Munshiram Manoharlal, rpt., 1970, pp. 100-1; Ibbetson, *Panjab Castes*, p. 222.
138. Damodar, Stanza Nos. 872-8, pp. 207-8.
139. In medieval western Europe, the church tried to curtail violence by invoking the horror of bloodshed, while the traditional notion of peace played its part. The state took such steps as drawing a distinction between lawful reprisals and plain brigandage, limiting number and nature of wrongs which could be expiated in blood, forestalling private vengeance that threatened public peace, compelling hostile groups to conclude peace treaties of armistice or reconciliation under arbitration of courts. Marc Bloch, *Feudal Society*, vol. I: *The Growth of the Ties of Dependence*, p. 182.
140. The Nahars had earned the ire of the Kheras for a number of hostile actions – giving shelter to the two fugitives, failing to give any information about them, refusing to surrender them to the Kheras, fighting an armed encounter to protect them and lodging them together for the night. These

576   *The Making of Medieval Panjab*

anti-Khera steps could be attributed to the unwritten *zamindari* code of chivalry, which was observed in letter and spirit.

141. Damodar, Stanza Nos. 879-83, pp. 208-9.
142. The Kheras objected to the lodging of Hir and Ranjha together, because the arrangement negated their claim on their bride. In contrast to this legalistic stance, the Nahars accorded legitimacy to the relationship of love between the fugitives, to which they were a witness.
143. Damodar, Stanza Nos. 884-7, p. 209.
144. Ibid., Stanza Nos. 888-93, pp. 209-10.
145. Ibid., Stanza Nos. 894-7, pp. 210-11.
146. Ibid., Stanza Nos. 898-9, p. 211.
147. Ibid., Stanza Nos. 900-3, pp. 211-12.
148. Ibid., Stanza Nos. 904-6, p. 212.
149. Hir asserted that she was married to Ranjha, but this marriage was different from the conventional ones. In the latter case, the marriage was merely an alliance between two clans and this had nothing to do with love or emotions in the two hearts.
150. Damodar, Stanza Nos. 907-12, pp. 212-13.
151. Ibid., Stanza Nos. 913-16, p. 214.
152. Ibid., Stanza Nos. 917-22, pp. 214-15.
153. Ibid., Stanza Nos. 923-6, pp. 215-16.
154. Ibid., Stanza Nos. 927-32, pp. 216-17.
155. The whipping of the lovers indicated that the *qazi* might have held them guilt of fornication (*zina*) i.e. sexual intercourse between man and woman who were not married to each other. The sentence required four witnesses to prove the offence. The Quran (XXIV:2) stipulated fornicators to be punished with one hundred lashes. All Sunni schools of jurisprudence advocated stoning if the offender was adult, free, Muslim and had previously enjoyed legitimate sex in matrimony. P.J. Bearman et al., eds., *The Encyclopaedia of Islam*, vol. XI, Leiden: Brill, 2002, New Edition, p. 509.
156. Damodar, Stanza Nos. 933-5, p. 217.
157. Ibid., Stanza Nos. 936-41, pp. 217-18.
158. Ibid., Stanza Nos. 942-6, pp. 218-19. It must be noted that the *qazi* did not reverse his decision. Rather he reopened the case and, after a review in the wake of people's intervention, left it open for the future, i.e. a miracle. In this sense, the *qazi* partly changed his original verdict.
159. Damodar, Stanza Nos. 947-8, p. 219.
160. Ibid., Stanza Nos. 949-51, pp. 219-20.
161. Ibid., Stanza Nos. 951-8, pp. 220-1.
162. Unlike Damodar, Waris Shah has concluded the story on a tragic note. According to him, Hir, after securing a favourable verdict from Raja Adli, refused to accompany Ranjha to Takht Hazara, lest she be seen as a woman who had been abducted. As the lovers went to Jhang Siyal, the Siyals

welcomed Ranjha and agreed to solemnize his marriage with Hir, provided he arrived with a marriage party from Takht Hazara. Ranjha left for Takht Hazara and, in his absence, the Siyals poisoned Hir. When a messenger carried the news to Ranjha, he died of a shock. Waris Shah, *Hir Waris Shah*, Stanza Nos. 609-24, pp. 231-5.

163. Damodar, Stanza Nos. 960-63, pp. 221-2. Damodar's narrative indicates that the *qazi's* decision was undone by a combination of two forces – earthly and divine. The people, who were convinced that the fire was caused by an unjust verdict, demanded its reversal and came out in support of the victims. Ranjha employed his miraculous powers by invoking the Panj Pir and put out the fire. A similar wondrous ability was also shown by Hir, who made a path through the raging fire and enabled the soldiers to penetrate through it. Thus, three entities – people, saints and God – succeeded in overpowering the oppressive alliance of medieval state and zamindars.

CHAPTER 9

Conclusion

For five centuries (1000-1500), Panjab witnessed sporadic warfare owing to annexations, invasions and rebellions. In the wake of the Ghaznavid rule, the region acquired greater linkages with the lands beyond the Indus. With the rise of the Delhi Sultanate, it became home to a bulk of immigrants, who were pushed out from their homelands in Mongol ravages. The new regime, having overcome the barriers to its existence, adopted diverse ways of consolidating its power. In due course, the situation became ripe for some local elements – tribal chiefs, zamindars and Sufis – to associate with the state, which had attained stability and strength. The mercantile networks, owing to the perennial demand for quality horses, learnt to survive in all conditions. Concomitant with these developments, a cultural transformation had been taking place owing the institutionalization of Sufi establishments. Evidence of these historical changes was found in a variety of primary documentation – official chronicles, Sufi literature (manuals, biographies, discourses and poetry), and folklore.

On the eve of the Ghaznavid invasions, Panjab was fragmented into a number of small principalities. It was not difficult for Sultan Mahmud (r. 999-1030), equipped with a superior military machine, to overpower them. The relatively larger Hindushahi state offered dogged resistance to the Ghaznavid onslaught but, in the end, faced complete extinction. Sultan Mahmud, mindful of his designs in central Asia and Gangetic plain, annexed (1022) a large part of Panjab to the Ghaznavid empire. The Sultan and his ministers, while entrenched in Ghazni, took a keen interest in the affairs of Panjab and received detailed reports from Lahore. The Ghaznavids consolidated their sway in the region by recruiting local elements, particularly in the army. Yet they found it extremely difficult to exercise their authority for any considerable period. The division of administrative functions between civil and military officers did not prove workable and led to numerous conflicts. The dual government was abolished in favour of a single powerful governor, who was usually a royal prince and was assisted by a team of departmental heads. Time and again, the local potentates managed to remove the Ghaznavid officers and recover their territories. On one occasion, they even besieged Lahore. Local tribes, particularly the Jats and Gakhhars, availed every opportunity of offering violent opposition. Ghaznavid rule was undermined by revolts of governors posted in Lahore, the power struggles in Ghazni and expansion of the Saljuqids. Even a fragile control over Panjab enabled the Ghaznavids to extract wealth of the Gangetic plain and take refuge in Lahore during times of crisis back home. Ghaznavid Panjab, owing to the development of cultural and economic ties with Afghanistan, was increasingly drawn into the vortex of the larger Islamic world. The poet Masud Sad Salman, the mathematician and astronomer Abu Raihan Alberuni, and the scholarly mystic Syed Ali bin Usman Hujwiri became the pioneers of the most sublime manifestations of the Islamic culture.

Like the experience of the Ghaznavids, the Ghorid advance into Panjab took almost three decades (1175-1206) to bear fruit. The remnants of the Ghaznavid rule and Rajput polities were wiped out, while the stubborn resistance of the Khokhars and Jats was overcome. Since Sultan Muizzuddin did not formalize any administrative arrangement that would function after his death, a triangular conflict irrupted among three of his governors – Qutbuddin Aibak, Nasiruddin Qubacha, and Tajuddin Yaldoz – to control the Indian possessions of their master. Shamsuddin Iltutmish, who took the place of Aibak, succeeded in defeating the other two contestants. He established his sway over entire Panjab, except the northwestern extremity that had passed into the hands of the Qarlughs. Iltutmish symbolised his success by posting his son Nasiruddin Mahmud at Lahore. In a royal mandate, the princely governor was advised to patronize the Syeds and clerics, cherish the subordinate officials and protect the peasantry. It was doubtful if these ideals were realized, because the new ruling class was entangled in recurring internal convulsions. During a period of nearly three decades (1236-66), as many as five Sultans were raised to the throne, while prominent military commanders (*muqtis*) rose in revolt. The insurrections affected the revenue assignments (*iqtas*) of Lahore, Multan, Bathinda, Hansi and Sunam. The problem assumed an alarming proportion with the involvement of high ranking grandees at Delhi. Very often, the Sultans found themselves virtually helpless in dealing with powerful nobles who possessed large retinues, extensive territories and unbridled ambitions.

Arid southwestern Panjab, particularly Multan, has played a prominent role in the period under study. Besides being a major entrepot of long distance trade on the Delhi-Qandhar route, it nurtured the growth of the Suhrawardi order. Ever since the early days of the Delhi Sultanate, it was in the hands of nobles who stood out for their ability. Four successive governors of Multan – Nasiruddin Qubacha, Kabir Khan Ayaz, Izzuddin Balban Kishlu Khan and Sher Khan – were Turkish slave officers and prominently figured in the chronicle of Juzjani. Remaining at loggerheads with the Delhi-based dispensation, they exercised a freedom of action and nurtured ambitions of sovereign power. It was true that they bore the brunt of invasions led by the Mongols, Khwarizmians and Qarlughs. With their military exertion, they blocked the eastward advance of these powers and, in this sense, contributed to the consolidation of the fledgling Delhi Sultanate. However, they did not hesitate to seek the support of the Mongols in order to pursue their personal interests, extracting better terms from their masters in Delhi. Ghiasuddin Balban terminated this virtual blackmail by appointing his son Sultan Muhammad as the governor of Multan.

During the thirteenth century, the Delhi Sultanate found it difficult to establish its control in Panjab, owing to the intrusion of Mongols, Khwarizmians, and Qarlughs. Jalaluddin Mangbarni, the Khwarizmian prince, succeeded in creating a political space for himself with the help of a Khokhar chief. He conducted predatory raids on Multan and made substantive territorial gains at the expanse of Qubacha. Though he failed to contract an anti-Mongol alliance with Iltutmish, yet he left a longer legacy in the form of a Qarlugh principality on the northwestern edge of Panjab. As for the Mongols, they destroyed Lahore in a major attack in 1241 and, forcing its governor to flee, exposed the weakness of the frontier defences. In addition to recurrent intrusions up to the Beas, they gave shelter to the disgruntled grandees of the Delhi Sultanate like Izzuddin Balban Kishlu Khan, Sher Khan, and Prince Jalaluddin Masud. In this manner, they brought much of western Panjab under their sphere of influence, forcing the Delhi regime on the defensive. Ghiasuddin Balban (r. 1266-86) posted his sons on the frontier marches, chastised the Khokhars, rehabilitated Lahore and collected horses from the tribal areas. He also opened negotiations with the Mongols and Qarlughs, but his moves could not enlarge the territory of Delhi Sultanate. In fact, the death of Sultan Muhammad in a military disaster against the Mongols exposed the chinks in military arrangements in the frontier provinces and limited benefits of diplomatic ties with Halagu, the founder the Ilkhanid empire. The unprecedented frequency of Mongol invasions in the first decade of the fourteenth century induced Alauddin Khalji (r. 1296-1316) to overhaul the military organisation including expansion of the army, regulation of horse trade, and manufacture of armaments. Sher Khan and Zafar Khan, two generals who displayed conspicuous bravery in fighting the Mongols, are lionised in the contemporary chronicles. Jalaluddin Khalji and Ghazi Malik, owing to their military services on the frontier, succeeded in acquiring the throne of Delhi and founding new dynasties.

During the thirteenth century, Panjab was a scene of political confrontation and recurrent warfare. A number of tribes – Jats, Khokhars, Bhattis, Minas, Mandahars and others – offered stiff resistance to the new Turkish regime, while the zamindars did not collaborate in the collection of tribute. The growing Sufi networks, with the exception of the Suhrawardis, remained aloof from the ruling class. Towards the beginning of the fourteenth century, the political confrontation as well as the cultural distances between different social elements began to wane, paving the way for mutually beneficial relationships between the contenders for power. The local elements, emerging in the centre stage of politics, positively responded to the overtures of the state representatives. On its part, the Delhi Sultanate felt encouraged to adopt new strategies of state formation. The process was initiated by Ghazi Malik who, during his long service in Panjab, acquired intimate knowledge of the regional social structure. Endowed with a possible Jat ancestry, he developed alliances with diverse social elements: a Bhatti Rajput zamindar of Abohar, the Khokhar chiefs of the Salt Range, and the shrine of Baba Farid at Pakpattan. He was also reported to have excavated a canal in his territorial jurisdiction, indicating a serious interest in agrarian expansion. In due course, these measures constituted a political model that was emulated in the second half of the fourteenth century.

What was begun by Ghazi Malik on a small scale was applied by his nephew on a wider canvas. Firoz Shah Tughluq (r. 1351-88), owing to his passion for hunting, had acquired a considerable familiarity about the Panjab countryside, particularly the area lying to the south of the Satluj. Aided by this knowledge, he wove alliances with powerful zamindars, who possessed military resources and held a key to the extraction of land tax. Walking in the footsteps of his uncle, he cemented these alliances with strategic marriages. At the same time, he conferred lavish land grants on prominent Sufis and revived the Sufi establishments (*khanqahs*) that had fallen on bad times. Such linkages enabled the Delhi Sultanate to embark on a project of irrigation-based agrarian expansion in two arid zones, cis-Satluj tract and Multan. In the first mentioned area, over half a dozen canals were dug from the Satluj, Jamuna, Ghaggar and Kali. The canals did much more than supplying water to the newly developed city of Hissar Firoza. Earlier the farmers raised only the monsoon (*kharif*) crop, but with the availability of irrigation facilities, they also cultivated the winter (*rabi*) crop including wheat and two varieties of sugar cane. As suggested by Barani, groups of pastoralists, who lived in clusters of bullock carts (*talwandi*) and perpetually shifted from one place to the other in search of water, settled as sedentary cultivators. Arrival of canals raised the subsoil water, making it possible to dig wells and obtain water from a depth of only four yards. Since Afif's description was limited to two canals, Rajabwah and Ulughkhani, he has identified only a few places – Hansi, Jind, Dhatrath, and Tughluqpur – that benefited from the facility. Taking into account the canals mentioned in the *Tarikh-i Mubarakshahi*, it appeared that the improvement embraced a much larger area that included Ambala, Mustafabad, Shahabad, Thanesar, Kuhram, Samana, Kaithal, Tohana, Jamalpur, Ahroni, Sarsuti, Khanda, Atkhera, Agroha, Barwala, Hansi, and Hissar Firoza. The increased agricultural production was manifested in stocks of grain in the countryside. It was worthy of note, Timur penetrated through the agriculturally improved lands and looted these very heaps of grain.

On assuming charge as the governor of Multan, Ain ul-Mulk Mahru found that the economy was in a dismal condition. As a large number of inhabitants had migrated, the cultivated area had reduced to a tenth of the better times. While a number of taxes had been abolished, the expenditure had risen owing to the liberal financial support to the needy. The inflow of land revenue and income of the land grantees had gone down due to a slump in the grain prices. In these circumstances, Mahru dealt with the competing claims of three classes: army, theologians, and lower bureaucracy. He gave priority to the maintenance of soldiers above others, because the fear of armed intervention kept the external enemies at bay and forced the zamindars and peasants to pay their taxes. However, the religious classes – Syeds, clerics, and Sufis – were compensated with grain for any fall in their income from land grants. Financial obligations of such beneficiaries were reframed in order to encourage the reclamation of barren lands. Besides agriculture, the provincial administration kept a close watch on the commercial activities. When it was found that the merchants and artisans were engaged in regrating (*ihtikar*) of essential commodities (ghee, cloth, sugar, and fuel), the governor made an effective intervention to protect the interests of the common people including soldiers, preachers and the destitute. He purchased such goods at prices paid by the regrators and arranged their sale at reasonable prices. However, he was sensitive to the grievances of the people against his subordinates, who were accused of oppression. He remained in correspondence with local Sufis regarding highhandedness of petty functionaries.

In a significant statement, Mahru has claimed that economic revival in Multan was a personal achievement of Firoz Shah Tughluq. The claim was not off the mark, because the kind of agrarian expansion undertaken by the Sultan in southeastern Panjab was replicated in the Multan region. The project was possibly implemented during the governorship of Mahru, as the related evidence was found only in his letters. We come across the names of five canals – Nasirwah, Qutbwah, Khizrwah, Qabulwah, and Hamruwah. Nothing was known about the sources and routes of these canals, but the available information is categorical on two points: financing of their excavation and the role of local beneficiaries. In case of large rivers, money was spent from the public treasury, though the ruler could turn to the common people in the event of any shortfall in funds. In case of the above canals, the cost of construction and maintenance was borne by the beneficiaries including the chiefs and peasants. In fact, the provincial administration secured the active cooperation of the village headmen in constructing and maintaining the canals. Those who willingly performed this role were rewarded, while those who refused to do so were liable to punishment, including exile and death.

Ibn Battuta, who travelled through Panjab in the winter of 1333-4, has left an account of the conditions prevailing in the region before the implementation of the canal-based agrarian expansion. Since Multan was an entrepot of long distance trade, Muhammad bin Tughluq (r. 1325-51) abolished all taxes on merchandise except the alms tax (*zakat*) and a tenth of the produce. The provincial governor, while conducting official business in an open court, was surrounded by a judge (*qazi*), preacher (*khatib*) and military commanders. One of his functions was to recruit soldiers, who were tested for their skill in archery and riding. He issued orders to lodge foreigners in houses set aside for the purpose. A postal superintendent (*malik ul-barid*), who reported to Delhi all events in Multan and its dependencies, communicated the arrival of foreigners and escorted them to the governor. In view of the special rules for foreigners, they were permitted to enter India only if they wished to stay. Following their consent, they were required to sign a bond in the presence of a judge and notary. For the benefit of high-ranking foreigners, the Sultan deputed a special team comprising a chamberlain and police commander. These officers provided security, purchased provisions from the market and arranged meals all along the way. The visitors made it a point to call at the Sufi shrines in Multan and Ajodhan, besides paying respects to the spiritual heads. Ibn Battuta took forty days to travel from Multan to Delhi. The major towns – Uch, Abohar, Sarsuti and Hansi – were populous and prosperous, while the countryside was productive. However, the roads were not safe. In the outskirts of Abohar, Ibn Battuta's caravan was attacked by eighty armed robbers and, in the ensuing encounter, twelve assailants were killed.

Regarding the development of Islamic spirituality in Panjab, we consider two aspects. Firstly, modern scholarship has tended to concentrate on the establishment of Sufi lineages in southwestern Panjab, while similar developments across the Satluj have been pushed into the background. When Baba Farid and Shaikh Bahauddin Zakariya were giving shape to the Chishti and Suhrawardi spiritual regimes, three towns across the Satluj – Hansi, Panipat and Kaliyar – were emerging as vibrant centres of Islamic spirituality. Baba Farid's close disciple Shaikh Jamaluddin Hansavi and his lineal descendants nurtured the Chishti seat of Hansi. Towards the east, Bu Ali Qalandar chose Panipat as the space for his unorthodox activities. The town acquired further prominence when Shaikh Shamsuddin Turk and his successors contributed to the rise of the Sabiris, a branch of the Chishtis founded near Saharanpur by Baba Farid's nephew Shaikh Alauddin Ali Ahmad Sabir. Our second aspect was related to the rich crop of literature, which was produced in different genres and languages all over the region under study. If Shaikh Ali bin Usman Hujwiri explained the fundamentals of Sufism in Persian, Shaikh Jamaluddin Hansavi accomplished the same task in Arabic, but from a Chishti standpoint. Baba Farid expressed his thoughts in Panjabi poetry, while Shaikh Bahauddin Zakariya compiled prayer formulae that formed the bedrock of the Suhrawardi path. Fakhruddin Iraqi and Bu Ali Qalandar, who understood divine love in the garb of physical love, chose the medium of Persian verse. The discourses of Shaikh Nizamuddin Auliya, as recorded by Amir Hasan Sijzi, and the Chishti history chronicled by Amir Khurd were largely inspired by Sufism in Panjab. The sermons of Syed Jalaluddin Bokhari were collected in nearly half a dozen works, while the same concerns were reflected in the writings associated with Shaikh Abdul Quddus Gangohi. The legacy of this large body of literature produced in Panjab percolated into the mystical lyrics of Shah Husain as well as the first versification of Hir-Ranjha by Damodar Gulati.

Viewed from the angle of chronology, the growth of Islamic spirituality appeared in four distinct phases. In the first phase, the picture was somewhat hazy owing to the lack of appropriate evidence. We come across a few charismatic individuals, who were commemorated in oral tradition as well as the oldest shrines in the region. During the second phase, the Sufi orders established their hospices (*khanqahs*) at a number of places – Ajodhan, Multan, Uch, Hansi, Panipat, Shahabad, and Kaliyar – where disciples were trained and devotional exercises were crystallized. In the third phase, Islamic spirituality assumed a popular dimension with the emergence of shrines (*dargahs*) as centres of pilgrimage (*ziyarat*) and institutionalisation of rituals associated with sacred days. At the same time, Sufi establishments in southwest Panjab bowed to the Delhi Sultanate and, receiving diverse forms of patronage, became a part of the political structure. In the last phase, the major Sufi networks became dormant and even slipped into hibernation. Not surprisingly, two Suhrawardi masters did not hesitate to assume political power. In contrast, the Sabiris consolidated their hold in southeast Panjab and, showing great energy and dynamism, added fresh ideas to the Chishti path.

The history of Sufism in Panjab began with the cult of Baba Haji Rattan, which is embedded in the oral tradition. Evidence is clearer in the case of Shaikh Ali bin Usman Hujwiri (d. 1072). He had widely travelled in the Islamic lands and had acquired extensive knowledge of Islamic spirituality He was remembered for producing a major treatise (*Kashf ul-Mahjub*) on the subject and the evolution of his shrine as a landmark in the cultural landscape of Lahore. By writing this book, he aimed to dispel the prevailing ignorance about Sufism as a discipline. Half of his work was devoted to an account of Sufi orders and leading spiritual masters, while the other half dealt with theoretical underpinnings and practical aspects of Sufism. He argued that knowledge of God and His oneness could be acquired through divine favour, not through human effort. He laid emphasis on inner meanings of devotional pursuits – offering prayers, adherence to poverty, wearing distinct garments, and travelling – so that the seeker made genuine spiritual progress. Recommending musical sessions only for the beginners, he underscored the hierarchical nature of emotional states. He advocated the principle of sobriety (*sahv*) as opposed to intoxication (*sukr*) in relation to God and, therefore, rallied behind Shaikh Junaid Baghdadi, but disapproved the doctrines of Shaikh Bayazid Bistami and Mansur ul-Hallaj. During the thirteenth century, *Kashf ul-Mahjub* might have been included in the curriculum of the Chishtis and Suhrawardis, though it was not specifically mentioned as such. In the early fourteenth century, it emerged as one of the books on Sufism that were in great demand in the city of Delhi. During the Mughal period, its merit was recognised in the Sufi circles, while a number of leading Sufis cultivated devotional ties with the shrine of Hujwiri. Allama Iqbal believed that Hujwiri had breathed fresh life into the dust of Panjab. In the present times, however, the Pakistani establishment has incorporated the cult of Hujwiri in its nationalist ideology.

Though Baba Farid (1175-1265) did not travel in Islamic lands and trained under Khwaja Qutbuddin Bakhtiar Kaki in Delhi, he acknowledged the unspecified connection with the Chishti masters of Chisht (Afghanistan). After a long stay in Hansi, he established himself at Ajodhan where he lived till the end of his life. He concentrated his energies on organizing a Sufi lodge (*khanqah*), training of disciples and promoting an abstemious living based on hard spiritual exercises. The inmates, while conforming to the demands of community life, shared the responsibility of multifarious tasks. Relying essentially on unsolicited charity (*futuh*), the hospice opened its doors to all sections of society, from rulers and merchants to travellers and mendicants. The disciples, who lived in the place for varying periods, demonstrated their firm commitment to the Chishti spiritual path, but their spiritual progress depended on their own aptitude. So intense was their reverence for Baba Farid that they regarded a visit to his tomb as meritorious as Haj. An erudite scholar and eloquent teacher, Baba Farid structured his curriculum on the *Awarif ul-Maarif* and *Tamhid ul-Muhtadi*, besides supervising recitations from the Quran. On the completion of training, he issued a certificate of succession (*khilafatnama*) which, aside from noting the abilities of the disciple, offered advice on his future role as a Sufi in a new spiritual domain (*wilayat*). The devotional aspect of his spiritual path comprised a regimen of prayers modelled on the life of Prophet Muhammad. He held supererogatory prayers in congregation and popularized the recitation of the Surah-i Fatiha. As for austerities, he had performed the inverted forty days' retreat (*chillah makus*) under appropriate conditions. Fond of quoting poetic couplets and attending musical sessions, he was averse to receiving financial donations from the state. As recorded in the Chishti discourses, he came out in support of the distressed and, in doing so, did not hesitate to use his miraculous powers. Undoubtedly, such stories were designed to assert his authority as a charismatic spiritual master. His immense popularity among all classes of people was attested by the huge crowds of visitors, who thronged his hospice to pay homage and receive amulets.

Baba Farid was the first Sufi of Panjab to have expressed his teachings in the language of the people among whom he lived. Employing imagery from his locality and an idiom of simplicity, he adopted the tone of a persuasive teacher. Across the subsequent centuries, his verses acquired such sanctity and universality that they were collected by Guru Nanak and included in Sikh scripture by Guru Arjan Dev. He believed that the search for God, who is the sole nourisher of humankind, was a desirable pursuit. However, it was beset with obstacles, as the path was narrow and the journey was long. A seeker, while submitting to God, was bound to perform Islamic observances including ablutions and prayers. After minimizing his physical needs, he was advised to be as humble as grass and as patient as trees. The ideal course for him was to follow his mentor who, like an astute boatman, felt concerned about the safety of passengers. The relation of the seeker with God was akin to the conjugal tie between a wife and her husband. In the absence of a sexual union, she suffered from the pangs of separation, only to realize that these were integral to love. The seeker needed to understand the transitory character of the world, as even the members of the ruling elite, who possessed unlimited wealth and exercised unquestioned power, ultimately sank into the grave. Since old age caused degeneration of the body, the seeker was advised to turn towards God in his youth. As his death was inevitable, his actions in this world served him in the court of God.

Shaikh Bahauddin Zakariya (1182-1262), a contemporary of Baba Farid, laid the foundation of the Suhrawardi order in Multan. Endowed with a spiritual genealogy going back to Shaikh Shihabuddin Suhrawardi of Baghdad and a long sojourn in west Asia, he commanded a prestige denied to most members of the Indian religious elite. However, his work in Multan revolved around his involvement in contemporary politics, his acquisition of wealth, and his emphasis on the outward form of Islamic rituals. His support to Shamsuddin Iltutmish in preference to Nasiruddin Qubacha may have landed him in controversy, but he compensated for his political leanings by saving the inhabitants of Multan in times of political turmoil. His extensive hospice was maintained with income from ample land grants and offerings from rich merchants. Strict in his understanding of religious observances, he sometimes found himself in unpleasant situations, including serious differences with the head of a local seminary. It was true that two of his disciples – the devout Hasan Afghan and the maverick poet Fakhruddin Iraqi – went a long way in confirming his credentials as a distinguished spiritual master. In two works, Shaikh Zakariya developed the content of spiritual exercises prescribed in addition to the ritualistic prayers and fasts. In the *Khulasat ul-Arifin*, which was interspersed with Quranic verses, the Shaikh conceived the heart as the main organ for spiritual cleansing and primary site for realizing God. In another work entitled *Al-Auard*, the Shaikh designed the content of several remembrances of God (*zikr*), each suited for a specific occasion.

The development of the Suhrawardi order in Multan during the middle of the thirteenth century could not be detached from the contribution of Shaikh Fakhruddin Iraqi (1213-89). Arriving from Hamadan to Multan with a band of Qalandars, Iraqi became a disciple and son-in-law of Shaikh Bahauddin Zakariya. During a stay of twenty-five years in the city, he composed mystical songs that were sung in the taverns of the city. Annemarie Schimmel, who heard these songs outside the mausoleum of Shaikh Zakariya, attributed the popularity of the Suhrawardi order in west Asia to the poetry of Iraqi. The mystic poet held that God, who fashioned all forms of creation in forty days, is omnipotent and sovereign. His word was revealed to Prophet Muhammad who reached within two bows of the divine presence. A seeker converted his heart into a mirror, which reflected the divine light. The seeker, who was fundamentally a lover, was set apart from society, as he possessed a number of rare qualities. He sacrificed himself at the altar of love like the legendry lovers of yore. He was charmed by the beauty of the Beloved who, acting like an astute hunter, fired the fatal arrow towards him. Since love was an incurable malady, he bore pain with joy and prayed for the aggravation of his sickly condition to prove his fidelity. He visualized the Beloved as a beautiful woman, whose loveliness had put the sun to shame. He was madly attracted towards the different parts of her body – face, forehead, eyes, eyebrows, lips, and waist – that were endowed with indescribable sensuousness. A lover could even be attracted towards a handsome boy, because this experience reminded him of God's incomparable creative power and intensified his spiritual urge. In the final analysis, love was essentially a quality of the Creator that underscored a unity between lover, love and beauty.

With the demise of the founders of the two major Sufi orders, the second phase of Sufism gave way to a third. One of the most important decisions, which was unanimously taken by the sons and disciples of Baba Farid, was the choice of Shaikh Badruddin

Sulaiman as the head of the Chishti hospice at Ajodhan. Shaikh Sulaiman's lineal descendants not only retained this position during the subsequent centuries, but they were also integrated into the political structure of the Delhi Sultanate. They were appointed to important positions during the reign of Muhammad bin Tughluq (r. 1325-51). What happened to the lineal descendants of Baba Farid through his progeny other than Shaikh Badruddin Sulaiman? Since they were denied any share in the legacy of Baba Farid, they shifted to Delhi and lived under the fraternal care of Shaikh Nizamuddin Auliya. After receiving spiritual training from the Shaikh, some of them stayed on at the hospice, while others migrated to distant places like Malwa, Devagiri and Telengana. Interestingly, the Delhi Sultanate did not pay any attention to these lineal descendants of Baba Farid who were associated with Shaikh Nizamuddin Auliya. Here, we are particularly reminded of Baba Farid's son-in-law Shaikh Badruddin Ishaq. Though he had played a significant role in the organization of the Ajodhan hospice, yet after the demise of his mentor, he felt constrained to leave the place and shift to the local Jama Masjid, where he gave lessons on the Quran. After his death, his two sons came to Delhi, where they were brought up by Shaikh Nizamuddin Auliya. Coincidentally, the fate of Shaikh Badruddin Ishaq was also shared by the son-in-law of Shaikh Bahauddin Zakariya, Shaikh Fakhruddin Iraqi. Evidently, the death of a Sufi master caused ruptures in the family and scattered its members to different places, while a son-in-law was the first casualty.

After the demise of Baba Farid (d. 1265), his followers shifted a major part of their devotion to his shrine, which had begun to evolve as a leading sacred centre. The hereditary spiritual head (*sajjadah nishin*), known as the Diwan, brought the neighbouring clans to cultivate the lands grants received from the Tughluqs. In the shrine, the institutionalization of rituals brought these clans in the fold of what has been designated as 'theatre Islam'. The link between the shrine and the clans was continuously strengthened as the sons of the Diwans began to marry into the families of the clan chiefs. Of the twenty-two marriages listed in *Jawahar-i Faridi* by Muhammad Ali Asghar Chishti, the Diwans took thirteen brides from the Khokhars, five from the Bhattis, three from the Rajputs and one from the Dhudis. What was worthy of note, the Diwans did not hesitate to take brides from the families of Khokhar chiefs (Shaikha and Jasrath) as well as their progeny who had been in rebellion against the Delhi Sultanate for long periods. One of the Diwans, Shaikh Tajuddin Mahmud, organized marriages of his five sons and one grandson with four Khokhar women, one Rajput and one Dhudi. He himself had married the daughter of Rai Qutba, a Rajput.

The shrine complex at Pakpattan comprised three structures that sheltered the tombs of Baba Farid and his lineal descendants, besides a mosque. Every day, a set of ceremonies was observed, wherein a functionary called *chiraghi* performed a number of duties. A little before the Maghrib prayer, the Shajrah-i Chiragh, which included the names of Chishti masters, was recited. The *chiraghi* lighted the lamps that were placed besides the tombs, before he moved to lead the Maghrib prayer. Some devotees observed a vigil through the night and remained absorbed in contemplation. Before dawn, the outer gate was opened and the covering over Baba Farid's tomb was replaced, while the entire place was cleaned. On the occasions of annual festivals – Miraj Sharif, Shab-i Barat, the month of Ramzan and Lailat ul-Qadr – the daily schedule was modified in response to special needs and increase in the number of pilgrims. Id ul-Fitr was marked by a public display of the relics of Baba Farid. The most important annual festival was his death anniversary, which was held from 25 Zilhijja to 6 Muharram. During these days, the spiritual head of the shrine, the Diwan, played a central role in a series of observances. Besides the commemoration of Hasan and Husain, musical sessions (*sama*) were held and sugar was distributed. In memory of the installation (*dastar bandi*) of Baba Farid's first successor, saffron-dyed muslin strips were tied around the Diwan's turban. The southern door of Baba Farid's mausoleum, which was known as the Bahishti Darwaza, was unlocked and devotees were allowed to pass through for two evenings and nights. In the early twentieth century, as many as 40,000 pilgrims availed of this opportunity during one night. In the concluding rite, the Diwan led his followers in emptying pitchers of water on the tomb, which was rubbed with a paste of sandal and perfume. According to the judgement of Ziauddin Barani, three eminent Sufis – Shaikh Nizamuddin Auliya, Shaikh Alauddin and Shaikh Ruknuddin Abul Fateh – two of whom lived in southwestern Panjab, had brought about a fundamental transformation in the religious life of the Muslims by the early decades of the fourteenth century. They were emulated by the Muslims at large for their arduous spiritual exercises and high moral character. Under their benign influence, thousands of people abandoned their immoral activities and included prayers in their daily routine. A large number of aspirants wished to enrol under their mentorship. Seen as kings of religion (*shahan-i deen*), they were believed to have prevented natural calamities and the Mongol invasions. The credibility of Islam increased, as the rules of the Shariat and Sufism were observed in all directions. In the city of Delhi, Shaikh Nizamuddin Auliya opened the doors of discipleship to all social classes, particularly functionaries of the Khalji regime ranging from nobles to slaves. Becoming devout in their religious life, the Muslims avidly turned to prayers and recitations of the Quran. Streams of devotees made a beeline for the Shaikh's hospice at Ghiaspur and sought answers to their queries on spiritual matters. There were lively interactions between the old and new disciples. Vigils were maintained during Ramzan and on Fridays, while musical sessions were held in every quarter once in three or four weeks. There was an increase in the demand for books on Sufism, while the sale of devotional paraphernalia went up. This substantive transformation in the religious life of Muslims in Delhi must have also taken place in southwestern Panjab, particularly owing to the influence of Shaikh Alauddin and Shaikh Ruknuddin Abul Fateh.

It is difficult to weave an account of the successors of Shaikh Bahauddin Zakariya, owing to the paucity of contemporary evidence. Shaikh Nizamuddin Auliya, who has referred frequently to Shaikh Zakariya in his discourses, did not show any interest in his lineal descendants. Fazlullah Jamali, who was affiliated to the Suhrawardi order, confined himself to miraculous stories about them. In this situation, Abdul Haq Muhaddis Dehalvi filled the gap to some extent. From him we learn that Shaikh Sadruddin Arif produced a short work entitled *Tasrif-i Jaduli*, which was studied in the seminaries for a long time, while his conversations were compiled in *Kanuz ul-Fawaid* by a disciple named Khwaja Ziauddin. That the Shaikh walked in the footsteps of his illustrious father is indicated by his recognition of the profession of faith as a fort and the three methods of entering it. He laid equal stress on the need to emulate the Prophet as well as the benefits of remembrance of God (*zikr*). Again, it was Dehalvi who drew our attention to an account of Shaikh Ruknuddin Abul Fateh in the *Fatawah-i Sufiyah* by a disciple and a collection of his discourses entitled *Majma ul- Akhyar*. In the last mentioned work, the Shaikh held that quality was superior to form in man, as it determined his fate in the afterlife. He delved into the consequences of good and bad actions, besides drawing a distinction between impurities of the body and mind. In an important statement, he held that a Shaikh needed to possess three things – money, knowledge and spiritual states – to perform a meaningful role in the society. However, in his actual life, a Shaikh acquired prominence on account of three types of concern – involvement in local politics, close relations with the reigning Sultan and an intimate friendship with Shaikh Nizamuddin Auliya.

Shaikh Ruknuddin visited Delhi twice during the reign of Alauddin Khalji and three times during that of Qutbuddin Mubarak Khalji. From Alauddin Khalji, he received a sum of 2 lakh *tankas* on his arrival and 5 lakh *tankas* on his departure. The Shaikh distributed the entire amount among the needy on the same day. Whenever he went to meet Qutbuddin Mubarak Khalji, he collected the petitions of the people on his palanquin. He presented these applications, one by one, before the Sultan and left the palace only when the royal order had been inscribed on each of them. The views of his brother, Maulana Ilmuddin Ismail, were sought by Sultan Ghiasuddin Tughluq on the indulgence in musical sessions by Shaikh Nizamuddin Auliya. These observations went a long way in finalizing the verdict in the case. Shaikh Ruknuddin was one of the dignitaries, who went to Afghanpur to welcome Sultan Ghiasuddin Tughluq and, if Jamali was relied upon, the Shaikh foresaw the tragic accident and warned the Sultan to leave the newly constructed pavilion. The family of the Shaikh extended active support to Sultan Muhammad bin Tughluq during the punitive expedition against the rebellious governor Bahram Aiba Kishlu Khan. The Shaikh's brother Shaikh Imamuddin laid down his life for the Tughluq regime in a battle fought near Abohar. The Shaikh, acting on behalf of the inhabitants of Multan, prevented the Sultan from carrying out a massacre in the city. The Shaikh and his nephew Sadruddin (the son of the deceased Shaikh Imamuddin) received grants of a hundred villages each for two purposes: as a means of their personal livelihood and to enable them to administer food in the hospice of Shaikh Bahauddin Zakariya.

In the above circumstances, the Suhrawardi order passed under the control of the Delhi Sultanate. A succession dispute at the premier hospice reached the court of Muhammad bin Tughluq. The Sultan, having accepted the will of Shaikh Ruknuddin, upheld the claims of his grandson Shaikh Hud. What was interesting, the Sultan decreed that Shaikh Hud be provided a feast at every station from Daulatabad to Multan, besides official banquets at Delhi and Multan. Shaikh Nuruddin of Shiraz was deputed to escort Shaikh Hud to Multan, where he was installed as the head of the Suhrawardi establishment. The princely treatment of Shaikh Hud must be attributed to the need of the Tughluq regime to win over the Suhrawardis at a time when the Chishtis of Delhi and Hansi had been alienated from it. However, the Delhi Sultanate was constrained to proceed against Shaikh Hud for misappropriating the income from his land grant. He was arrested and, after an interrogation by the Sultan, was put to death. In this context, the refusal of Syed Jalaluddin Bokhari, the leading Suhrawardi saint of Uch, to accept the guardianship of forty Sufi shrines of Sind, became understandable. The tension between the Suhrawardis and Delhi Sultanate continued well into the fourteenth century. During his expedition to Thatta in 1365, Firoz Shah Tughluq did not visit the mausoleum of Shaikh Bahauddin Zakariya, whereas he made it a point to pay homage at all the Chishti centres. This episode, argued Qamar ul-Huda, meant a loss of influence by the Suhrawardi order in the region. Though the Suhrawardi spiritual masters held the office of Shaikh ul-Islam, yet they could not persuade the Tughluq rulers to provide them with support.

The setback to the Suhrawardis was only temporary. Writing in 1350, Fazlullah Majawi described the vibrancy of the Suhrawardi hospice at Multan. A large complex of buildings, it was home to hundreds of inmates, servants and visitors. Its busy schedule included perpetual recitations of the Quran, intonations of the remembrance of God (*zikr*), prayers, fasting, vigils, teaching and learning. This trend might have inspired the sister Suhrawardi establishment at Uch, where Syed Jalaluddin Bokhari (1308-84) led a powerful revival of the order. The Shaikh had travelled extensively in west Asia and, having learnt the Islamic sciences from renowned scholars, received as many as forty-six robes (*khirqahs*) from six leading Sufi orders of his times. Widely read and extremely erudite, he established a seminary where he took classes and employed teachers. He was held in high regard by Firoz Shah Tughluq, while his mediation was sought to settle political matters in Sind as well as local issues in southwestern Panjab. A close examination of his discourses has enabled Amina M. Steinfels to reconstruct his mystical path. His training of a seeker was based on the twin foundations of knowledge (*ilm*) and action (*amal*), while precedence was given to knowledge, particularly the study of Islamic jurisprudence. The boundaries between Sufism and jurisprudence collapsed, while the respective roles of Sufi and Alim were intertwined. The acquisition of knowledge of Islamic jurisprudence was followed by action, which comprised a variety of devotional practices. In addition to obligatory prayers, the Shaikh prescribed recitations of Quranic verses, supplications and remembrance of God, which was implanted in the disciple's heart by the mentor, who had received it from his elders through a chain of transmission. While enrolling an aspirant, the Shaikh formed a bond of brotherhood, while the investiture included a request for forgiveness, a statement of repentance and request to God for opening the disciple's heart. The Shaikh prepared a list of the apparels bestowed on disciples in accordance with their spiritual states and virtues. He was conscious of the negative features of audition, but permitted the practice under strict conditions. He accepted land grants from Firoz Shah Tughluq for the maintenance of his hospice and benefit of worshippers, while holding that the source of donations determined the head of expenditure.

We have seen that southwest Panjab gained prominence owing to the establishment of the Chishti and Suhrawardi orders. But other areas of Panjab did not lag behind in nourishing the growth of Islamic spirituality. During the thirteenth century, southeast Panjab witnessed the rise of Hansi and Panipat as vibrant centres of Sufism, though they have received little attention from modern scholars. It is not difficult to explain this imbalance in modern scholarship on the subject. While facing several political and military challenges in southwest Panjab, the Delhi Sultanate extended liberal patronage to the Sufi establishments of Pakpattan, Multan and Uch which, on their own, had acquired strong roots and social influence in the locality. The political influence commanded by the hospices of southwest Panjab was faithfully reflected in the official histories. Leading chroniclers – Ziauddin Barani, Shams Siraj Afif, Abdul Malik Isami, and Ibn Battuta – not only acknowledge the eminence of the spiritual masters, but also highlight the benevolent attitude of the ruling class towards the charismatic mystics. To an extent, this partiality was clearly inscribed in the Sufi biographies and discourses. In comparison, the Delhi Sultanate did not worry about its control over southeast Panjab. The tract was situated close to the capital and had remained relatively free of political disturbances. Thus, the rulers entrenched in Delhi did not place it on their list of priorities until the middle of the fourteenth century. The ruling class could afford to ignore the Sufis of the area and, therefore, did not anticipate political dividends in patronage of any kind: cash allowances, construction of mausoleums, endowment of shrines with land grants, and providing jobs to the scions of Sufi families. Not surprisingly, the apathy of the state was replicated in the official histories as well as Sufi literature. Shaikh Jamaluddin Hansavi and Bu Ali Qalandar, who were denied adequate space in the contemporary sources, thought it prudent to wield their own pens. The early Sabiris fared no better, because their memory was retrieved several centuries after they had gone into oblivion.

Early in the thirteenth century, Hansi developed as a seat of Chishti mysticism, because Baba Farid lived here for twelve years along with his disciple Shaikh Jamaluddin Hansavi. After the departure of Baba Farid for Ajodhan, Shaikh Hanṣavi and his lineal descendants (Shaikh Burhanuddin, Shaikh Qutbuddin Munawwar and Shaikh Nuruddin) nourished the hospice even when they faced internal difficulties and state repression. The ball was set rolling by Shaikh Hansavi when he wrote a book in Arabic entitled *Mulhimat*. Meant to be a guidebook for young aspirants, it elaborated the cardinal principles of Islamic spirituality from a Chishti perspective. In his view, a majority of people in this world were engrossed in gratifying their carnal desires and, therefore, they were distant from God. A minority was formed by the spiritually awakened, who suppressed their lower self and gained proximity to God. The gnostics (*arif*), who renounced the world, were superior to the ascetics (*zahid*), who renounced the world for the hereafter. In his pursuit of love (*ishq*), the lover was afflicted by an incurable ailment. His misery was similar to that of Majnu who was stricken with madness on being separated from Laila. Of all the devotional acts, the most superior was prayer (*salat*), provided it was based on the absorption of the heart in it. Next in importance was the remembrance of God which resulted in purifying the heart, destruction of the carnal self, and sensitivity of feeling. A disciple, who was bound by the strict rules of discipline, bore unconditional reverence for his mentor. The Sufis were associated with certain visible symbols, but their inner significance was crucial. The same was true of obligatory rituals. These guidelines, as laid out in the *Mulhimat*, illumined the path of Chishti aspirants.

The successors of Shaikh Hansavi not only adhered to the principles enunciated by Baba Farid and Shaikh Nizamuddin Auliya, but also stood against political pressure. Shaikh Qutbuddin Munawwar, the grandson of Shaikh Hansavi, was an outstanding exponent of the Chishti path and, therefore, deserved a closer attention. Knowledgeable and eloquent, he kept away from the crowds and remained immersed in the remembrance of

God. He bore intense emotional attachment to his mentor Shaikh Nizamuddin Auliya and the family of Amir Khurd. Having cultivated a deep interest in musical sessions, his ecstatic states were remembered in the Chishti circles for long. Like Baba Farid, he refused to accept a grant of two villages from Muhammad bin Tughluq. He distributed a cash offering of 2,000 *tankas* among the needy, because he believed that a mendicant did not need anything more than a *ser* of boiled rice-lentil (*khichri*) and a little clarified butter. He agreed to meet Muhammad bin Tughluq only when he was convinced that he was doing so against his wishes. In a categorical statement on the Chishti mystical ideology, he identified his objectives as serving God, the legacy of his ancestors, and his spiritual guide Shaikh Nizamuddin Auliya. His son and successor Shaikh Nuruddin followed his teachings in letter and spirit. Shaikh Nuruddin refused to shift to Hissar Firoza from Hansi, which had been the spiritual domain of his grandfather Shaikh Burhanuddin and father Shaikh Qutbuddin Munawwar, and it had been bestowed on them by Baba Farid and Shaikh Nizamuddin Auliya. The refusal of the Chishtis of Hansi to be assimilated into the political structure stood in sharp contrast to the collaborative attitude of the contemporary Chishtis of Ajodhan, including Shaikh Alauddin and his successors.

Bu Ali Qalandar, the Chishti-Qalandari saint of Panipat, lived during the late thirteenth and early fourteenth century. He is remembered through his incredible deeds and clashes with the Muslim orthodoxy. Some of his mystical ideas have been preserved in sixteen precepts (*maktubat*) that were compiled by Abdul Haq Muhaddis Dehalvi. He held that the divine element was embedded in all forms of creation and that the humankind was fashioned out of God's love for it. The seeker could experience God's beauty on the mirror of his heart, provided he detached himself from the material world and gratification of senses. These thoughts, along with other themes, have also been elaborated in verse (*masnavi*) by Bu Ali Qalandar. He asserted that God's beauty was manifested in the physical attributes of plants and animals. God is Himself in love with the seeker, who was only a step away from Him. He had only to sip the wine of mystical knowledge (*badah-i irfan*) and open the eye of his heart to see the face of the Beloved. He did not need to undergo arduous austerities, as his love was different from the suffering of the legendary lovers like Laila, Majnu, Shireen, and Farhad. The wine of love was nothing but pain received from the Beloved. Since every moment of life was valuable, it could not be wasted in negligence. The spiritual pursuit, which was based on piety and abstinence (*zuhd wa taqwa*), demanded the rejection of rulers and riches. Social life was plagued by moral degeneration, which induced the people to waste money on carnal pleasures. Still another problem was posed by fake Sufis, who befooled the people with outward symbols of piety and thrived on the false propaganda of their sycophantic disciples. Slaves of greed and ambition (*hirs wa hawas*), their devotions lacked sincerity and their faith in Islam was doubtful.

From the middle of the thirteenth century, the Sabiri branch of the Chishtis became active on both sides of the Jamuna. Acting under the direction of Baba Farid, his nephew Shaikh Alauddin Ali Ahmad Sabir established a Chishti seat at Kaliyar (near Saharanpur and beyond the Jamuna) that grew into its Sabiri branch. Shaikh Sabir, who faced relentless opposition from a dominant section of the local Muslim community, was known for his solitude (*tajrid*) and absorption (*istaghraq*). Hagiographic writings have adopted a number of strategies to legitimise the position of the Sabiris. A conscious effort was made to show that Shaikh Sabir's way, which was based on inner purification and fearlessness, conformed to divine revelation (Quran) and Prophetic traditions. At the same time, the Sabiris were said to be in line with the spiritual states of eminent mystics like Shaikh Shamsuddin Tabrezi, Shaikh Fakhruddin Iraqi, and Shaikh Nizamuddin Auliya. The rooting of the Sabiris in Panipat was facilitated by the benevolent attitude of Bu Ali Qalandar, who not only shifted out of the town, but also treated the Sabiri newcomers with exemplary affection. Though the Sabiri spiritual path markedly differed from that of their Nizami counterpart in Delhi, they maintained a spirit of brotherhood with them. At the popular level, the Sabiris gained acceptance owing to their ability to help the needy. The wishes of the people could be fulfilled if they recited the name of 'Ya Shamsuddin Turk' a few thousand times. Shaikh Jalaluddin made effective interventions to protect the peasantry from state oppression and also brought about a reconciliation with the Chishtis of Hansi. Shaikh Ahmad Abdul Haq (1374-1434), who lived in different towns of Panjab and ultimately developed a Sabiri hospice at Rudauli, envisaged a fifteen stage spiritual journey that culminated in divine unity (*ahadiyat*) and perpetual annihilation (*istaghraq*). Shaikh Abdul Quddus Gangohi (1456-1537), who lived at Shahabad (between Thanesar and Ambala) for thirty years, articulated the concept of sublime remembrance (*sultan-i zikr*) and, while proposing the Yogic technique of breath control, perceived an identity between Ibn-i Arabi's unity of being (*wahdat-ul wujud*) and Gorakhnath's philosophy.

In the middle of the fifteenth century, the writ of Delhi Sultanate was restricted to a radius of twenty leagues from its capital. The Syed rulers failed to exercise their authority and stem internal strife among the nobles. They were unable to appoint governors in different parts of the kingdom and, if at all they did, these officers failed to perform their duties. In Panjab, the death of Jasrath Khokhar in 1442 did not revive the authority of the central government in the region. Bahlol Lodi, who was entrenched in Sirhind as an independent ruler, brought the vast area from Lahore to Panipat under his sway. In these circumstances, the tracts beyond the Ravi went under the control of traditional rural magnates, the zamindars. Supported by their respective clans, they wielded undisputed power in their vaguely defined enclaves comprising several villages. They organized agriculture, dried marshes, and raised embankments. They permitted outsiders to settle as farmers, providing means of cultivation, and concessions in land tax. They maintained large herds of cattle and employed scores of herdsmen. A zamindar measured his prosperity in terms of the size of cattle population. He perceived his power through his military resources. Chuchak, the Siyal chief who had eighty-four villages in his *zamindari*, claimed to have earned the enmity of Nahars and Chaddars. Hailed as the lord of land and rivers, he controlled seven routes passing through his territory and derived his income from a variety of sources. He was audacious enough to challenge the authority of the Delhi-based emperor. He did not bow to anyone until the marriage of his daughter Hir forced him to submit to the Kheras. Ali, the Khera chief, could muster a retinue of 900 clansmen. His daughter Sehti, while helping her sister-in-law Hir to elope, admitted putting at stake the honour of 900 turbans. However, the zamindars did not hesitate to ill-treat their servants and bribe the priests.

A zamindar was entirely dependent on his clan to play a multifarious role in the society. He invested a considerable time in the village common (*sath*), where he held consultations (*maslat*) with his clansmen on all matters. When the Siyals deprived Noora Sambhal of his luxury boat and boatman, the loss was seen as an affront to his entire clan. In the ensuing armed conflict with the Siyals, twenty men lost their lives. The warring zamindars were not perturbed, as this kind of violence was common. Even in personal and peaceful matters, the decision was not taken by the zamindar, but by his clan (*mel kutumb*). The members of a clan took unanimous decisions on proposals for marriage, besides the gifts for emissaries and members of the marriage party. The Siyals collectively dealt with Hir's refusal to marry the Khera youth. Having failed to coerce or poison her, they decided to replace her by her niece. The Kheras collectively dealt with the situations caused by Hir's recalcitrance, snake bite and elopement. The Kheras saw Ranjha as a common enemy and, subjecting him to repeated beatings, discussed ways of killing him. More telling was the case of Yaqub Khan Waraich whose daughter had been betrothed to Dhido years back. In a joint meeting between the Ranjhas and Waraichs, the betrothal was cancelled and his nephew replaced Dhido. It was stated that the changes could not snap the long standing ties between the two clans, who were intertwined like thick ropes. With the aim of gaining legitimacy, the zamindars provided sanctuary to the distressed and, with the help of their clans, defended such actions. However, the clans recognised the authority of the *qazi's* court and spiritual entities.

Among zamindars, matrimonial bond was established in two stages, betrothal and wedding ceremony. At the outset, the family of the boy or girl sent a written proposal through two emissaries, a Brahmin and a Doom. During their stay of eight days, they were lodged with their caste brethren. On their departure, each of them was given a gift of three-piece apparel, gold necklace and horse. When they conveyed the news of acceptance to their patron, a feast was held amidst distribution of goods. The zamindar, at the head of a long convoy, went to the village of his counterpart to formalize the betrothal. Apart from horses and camels, the procession comprised jesters, musicians, singers and dancers. The guests were received in a big meeting hall, where balladeers sang epical tales and alcohol was served. Next morning, with a horse and camel as the main gifts, each guest was individually given a turban and gold based dress. The two chiefs clasped their hands and thus sealed the alliance. In the two households, the mother in respect of the boy or girl conducted the identical ritual of happy omens (*shagan*). A few weeks before the marriage, the father of the bride or groom sent messengers to the other side with knotted strings (*gandhiyaan*), fixing the date of the wedding. During the oil ceremony (*maiyyan*), the bride was rubbed with perfumed paste (*vatna*) and her hands were dyed with henna (*mehandi*). A Brahmin conducted the rite of auguries (*shagan*) by tying the first wedding thread (*gana*) on the wrist of the bride. From the groom's side, the marriage party went in a grand procession comprising horses, banners and musicians. In the bride's house, the *qazi* conducted the Islamic marital rite (*nikah*), which was followed by the customary Hindu rounds (*laavan*). Next morning, the bride's family displayed a rich dowry, while the guests consumed endless cups of liquor. After a tearful farewell, the bride sat in a palanquin and left with the marriage party. At the destination, her mother-in-law performed the omen of revealing the bride's face. Surrounded by womenfolk, the newly-weds played the game of 'Ring in the Buttermilk'(*lassi mundri*), which aimed at creating physical familiarity between the two as a prelude to the consummation of marriage.

As regards their attitude to marriage and sexuality, the Jat clans were intensely patriarchal in social practice. They did not permit their adolescent children to choose their partners. They frowned upon love, as the act did not have parental sanction. The close relatives of Hir – father, mother, brothers, uncles and sisters-in-law – subjected her to different forms of oppression. Her movements were watched; allegations were hurled at her; she was threatened with physical punishment, and attempts were made to kill her. Her parents fixed her marriage with the Khera and carried out a number of marital rites, though she registered her strong opposition at every step. The Kheras, while returning to Rangpur Khera with an unwilling bride Hir, gave a severe beating to Ranjha and even decided to murder him. During the trial at Kot Qabula, the *qazi* charged Hir of rejecting a marriage validated by the Shariat, for maintaining illicit relations with a herdsman and bringing a bad name to two powerful zamindars. In the wake of the Qazi's verdict, the Kheras subjected the lovers to merciless blows. On the other hand, the lovers relied on spiritual entities (Sufis and Jogis), friendly zamindars and ordinary people to sustain their fight against patriarchy. The Panj Pir appeared to them in difficult times and offered crucial support. Sidh Bagai, the chief Jogi at Tilla Balnath, brought Ranjha into the path of Jog and, making him a disciple, enabled him to meet his beloved. Hir treated Ranjha not only as a lover, but as a spiritual preceptor (*kamil murshid*). Both the lovers, while facing the law and wrath of the Kheras, displayed miraculous powers and, therefore, were hailed as lights of spiritual excellence (*azmat ki rushnai*). With this supernatural ability, they extinguished a big fire at Kot Qabula, undid a dubious legal verdict, and punished their opponents. Ultimately, they united with each other.

 Slipping back in time, we find that during the course of his invasion (1398-9), Amir Timur marched up and down in a manner that his route roughly assumed the shape of the letter 'W'. Crossing the Indus, he travelled southwards to Ajodhan and then turned southeast to target Bhatner. From here, he marched towards the northeast and touched Samana, from where he turned southwards and reached Delhi. Leaving the capital, he penetrated through the hills and, after attacking Jammu, turned west to cross the Indus. The Delhi Sultanate, paralysed by internal strife and having lost the support of landed gentry, failed to offer suitable resistance to the invaders. The local chiefs, who were struck with fear, rushed to pay homage to the warlord. The people, who were left to fend for themselves, fled from their villages and travelled long distances to save their lives. Southeast Panjab suffered the most, as Timur marched through it twice – Bhatner to Samana and Samana to Delhi – during his whirlwind onslaught. This area, having benefited from canal irrigation and agrarian expansion, had gained in settlement and productivity during the last few decades. Timur paid a lot of attention to this tract, as it promised a rich dividend. Apart from huge heaps of grain, Timur seized fodder, cattle, and human captives. As could be feared, socio-economic activities were entirely dislocated. However, Timur was considerate towards the Muslim religious elites including Syeds, theologians and Sufis. He did not show any greed for precious metals and, therefore, did not desecrate Hindu religious centres at Thanesar, Haridwar, Kangra, and Jawalamukhi. In the northern hills, he carried out widespread deforestation in order to lay roads for the passage of his vast army. Since the paths were narrow, he divided his soldiers into small segments in order to attack isolated hamlets. Inhabitants came out to defend their cultivated fields and humble abodes. But, owing to lack of support from their chiefs, did not engage in fighting the well equipped adversary.

During a period of half a century after the departure of Timur, Panjab witnessed intense political turmoil, which was defined by localised tussles and recurrent warfare. At the outset, a conflict broke out between two leading nobles, Khizr Khan and Mallu Iqbal Khan, for control over Panjab. Emerging from his base in Multan and Dipalpur, Khizr Khan brought the entire cis-Satluj tract under his sway and, after the death of Sultan Nasiruddin Mahmud, ascended the throne of Delhi on 6 June 1414. The Panjab officers were engaged in suppressing the revolt of the Turkbachas in Sirhind and the distrurbance of a fake Sarang Khan in the foothills of Hoshiarpur and Ropar. However, it was Jasrath Khokhar who dominated the political stage of Panjab for nearly two decades (1421-42). Many a times, he descended from his mountainous stronghold beyond Sialkot and ravaged the plains of Panjab including Lahore, Jammu, Kangra, Jalandhar, Ludhiana, Ropar, and Bajwara. During his military campaigns, he targeted the senior officers who held revenue assignments (*iqtas*) in different districts as well as the local chiefs who supported them. At one time, he had grandees like Zirak Khan and Sikandar Tohfa in his custody. He not only killed Rai Bhim, the chief of Jammu, but also plundered the zamindaris of Rai Kamal Muin and Rai Firoz Muin. A short span of four years (1430-33) became critical for Panjab, because three diverse elements in the form of a local chief, a disaffected noble and a foreign invader – Jasrath Khokhar, Faulad Turkbacha and Shaikh Ali – became active at the same time and even collaborated with one another. At the end of protracted fighting, Faulad Turkbacha was killed in Bathinda and Shaikh Ali was dislodged from Seor, whereas Jasrath Khokhar survived for another decade. If the authority of the Delhi Sultanate was not erased from Panjab, it was because Sultan Mubarak Shah took the affairs of Panjab in his own hands and, apart from rehabilitating the city of Lahore and supervising the military operations at different fronts, transferred governors from one place to the other. A lot of good work was done by officers like Zirak Khan, Sikandar Tohfa, Mahmud Hasan, Islam Khan Lodi, Yusuf Sarwar, and Nusrat Khan. In spite of its difficulties, the Delhi Sultanate was vibrant enough to command the support of local chiefs like Rai Bhim of Jammu, Rai Dulchin Bhatti, Rai Ghalib of Kalanaur, Rai Daud of Jalandhar, Rai Kamal Muin of Ludhiana and Rai Firoz Muin of Bathinda. Yahya Ahmad Sirhindi, who belonged to the area affected by political disturbances, was personally familiar with the locality and thus recorded the events in a sober account.

Following the collapse of the Syed regime, the Delhi Sultanate survived as a polity for another seventy-five years, as it availed the opportunities of experimenting with new modes of building power structures. The roots of Afghan power in Panjab lay in the pastoral-nomadic Afghan society organised on the kinship basis, the Afghan dominance in the Indo-Central Asian horse trade, and immigration of the Afghan tribes to different parts of northwestern India in search of employment. Islam Khan Lodi, who held the *iqta* of Sirhind, mobilized an armed contingent of 12,000 Afghans, most of whom comprised his clansmen. He also secured suitable *iqtas* for his brothers who lived with him. He had a number of sons, but he chose his nephew Bahlol Lodi as his successor through a will. After his death in 1431, his followers were divided into three camps. Since the Delhi Sultanate viewed the convergence of Afghans in Sirhind with suspicion, it sent a punitive expedition under Sikandar Tohfa and Jasrath Khokhar against them. A substantial number of Afghans were killed in violation of a promise of safety. Bahlol Lodi was convinced that the Afghans could survive only if they assumed power in Delhi. Acting with tact and caution, he earned the trust of the Syed ruler and occupied large areas in Panjab including Lahore, Sirhind, Sunam, Samana, and Hissar Firoza. Striking at the right moment, he overturned the Syed regime and inaugurated on 19 April 1451 the first Afghan state in India. However, Guru Nanak, who lived during the times of the Lodi rule, condemned the regime from top to bottom for being oppressive and incompetent.

At this time, two Suhrawardi Sufis emerged as rulers in different sets of circumstances. Shaikh Sadruddin (Haidar Shaikh), who established a hospice at Malerkotla, married the daughter of Bahlol Lodi and, with the help of a dowry of sixty-nine villages, converted his position as a land grantee into a zamindar. He consolidated his hold over a semi-autonomous principality by entering into matrimonial relations with the zamindars of Kapurthala and Tohana. This approach to politics was similar to the marriages of the spiritual heads of the Chishti shrine at Pakpattan, who pioneered the practice of taking brides from the clan chiefs dominant in the countryside. Moving to Multan, it was found that local inhabitants and zamindars persuaded Shaikh Yusuf Qureshi, a descendant of Shaikh Bahauddin Zakariya, to assume the reins of the government. He strengthened his rule by marrying the daughter of the Langah chief Rai Sehra. Ousted from the seat of power by his father-in-law, he shifted to Delhi. Bahlol Lodi gave his daughter in marriage to the son of Shaikh Yusuf Qureshi, but could not reinstate the Sufi as the ruler of Multan, despite a military intervention. In any case, the assumption of power by the two Suhrawardis, who were related to Bahlol Lodi, underlined the significance of Sufis in the political life of Panjab.

During the period under study, the Ghaznavids and Ghorids

annexed Panjab to their expanding empires. They could not consolidate their rule owing to the disaffection of governors and resistance of local tribes. It was only during the fourteenth century that the local elements, including the zamindars and Sufis, collaborated with the Tughluq regime in the passage to a higher stage of state formation, which brought about canal irrigation and agrarian expansion. The process of political consolidation and economic development was disrupted by Timur's invasion, necessitating novel modes of building fresh power structures. In western Panjab, the Jat clans vied with one another to gain supremacy in their localities and fought their way under powerful zamindars, who claimed to be the lords of land and masters of rivers. Concomitant with these political developments, Islamic spirituality became firmly rooted in the cultural soil of Panjab. Operating through numerous manifestations of piety – hospices (*khanqahs*), shrines (*dargahs*), prayers, remembrance of God, recitation of the Quran, fasts, spiritual exercises, annual festivities, musical sessions, mystical poetry, and wondrous stories – the Sufis gained religious legitimacy and social prestige. In some cases, they were assimilated into the state structure through a system of patronage, which included land grants, honorific titles, and administrative positions. The Sufis (Panj Pir), by coming out in support of the socially distressed, earned popular adulation and, in the process, carved out a distinct place for themselves in the collective memory. With the passage of times, Islamic spirituality became the backbone of the culture of Panjab. Given the evidence at our disposal, three entities – the representatives of the state, zamindars and Sufis – played a dominant role in the medieval society. Since their paths often crossed those of one another, their relations were marked by varying degrees of agreement, confrontation and indifference. Common to them was the urge to gain legitimacy for their position in society. They perpetually endeavoured to attain this objective by sponsoring different forms of documentation – official chronicles, mystic literature, and oral traditions – corresponding with their respective roles, resources, and self-images.

Bibliography

Primary Sources

Abdul Hamid Muharrir Ghaznavi, *Dastur ul-Albab fi Ilm ul-Hisab*, English translation, Shaikh Abdur Rashid, *Medieval India Quarterly*, vol. I, nos. 3 & 4, 1950.

Abdul Haq Muhaddis Dehalvi, *Akhbar ul-Akhyar*, Urdu translation, Subhan Mahmud and Muhammad Fazil, Delhi: Noor Publishing House, 1990.

Abdul Malik Isami, *Futuh us-Salatin*, English translation, Agha Mahdi Husain, vols. I & II, Bombay: Asia Publishing House, 1967 & 1976.

Abdul Qadir Badauni, *Muntakhab ut-Tawarikh*, vol. I, English translation, George S.A. Ranking and B.P. Ambashthya, Patna: Academica Asiatica, rpt., 1973; vol. III, English translation, Wolseley Hague and B.P. Ambashthya, Patna: Academica Asiatica, rpt., 1973.

Abdul Rahman Chishti, *Mirat ul-Asrar*, Urdu translation, Wahid Bakhsh Siyal, New Delhi: Khwaja Hasan Sani Nizami, 2010.

Abdullah, *Tarikh-i Daudi*, Persian text, ed. Shaikh Abdul Rashid and Iqtidar Husain Siddiqui, Aligarh: Aligarh Muslim University, 1969.

Abu Hamid Muhammad Ghazzali, *Adab al-Nikah*, English translation, Muhtar Holland, Kaula Lumpur: Dar ul-Wahi Publications, 2012.

Abu Najib Suhrawardi, *Kitab Adab-i Muridin*, English translation, Menaham Wilson, entitled *A Sufi Rule for Novice*, Cambridge: Harvard University Press, 1975.

Abu Nasr Muhammad bin Muhammad al-Jabbar Utbi, *Tarikh-i Yamini*, English translation, *History of India as Told by its Own Historians*, ed. H.M. Elliot and John Dowson, vol. II, rpt., Allahabad: Kitab Mahal, n.d.

Abu Raihan Alberuni, *Kitab ul-Hind*, English translation, Edward C. Sachau, entitled *Alberuni's India*, rpt., New Delhi: Rupa, 2002.

Abul Fazl Baihaqi, *Tarikh-i Subuktgin*, English translation, *History of India as Told by its own Historians*, ed. H.M. Elliot and John Dowson, vol. II, rpt., Allahabad: Kitab Mahal, n.d.

Abul Fazl, *Ain-i Akbari*, vol. III, English translation, H.S. Jarrett and Jadunath Sarkar, New Delhi: Oriental Books Reprint Corporation, rpt., 1978.

Ahmad Muin Siyahposh Alavi, *Siraj ul-Hidaya*, Persian text, ed. Qazi Sajjad Husain, Delhi: Indian Council of Historical Research, 1983.

Ain ul-Mulk Ainuddin Mahru, *Insha-i Mahru*, Persian text, ed. Shaikh Abdul Rashid, Aligarh: Aligarh Muslim University, 1954.

Alauddin Ata Malik Juvaini, *Tarikh-i Jahan Gusha*, English translation, John Andrew Boyle, entitled *The History of the World Conqueror*, vol. II, Manchester: Manchester University Press, 1958.

Ali bin Usman Hujwiri, *Kashf ul-Mahjub*, English translation, Reynold A. Nicholson, Delhi: Taj Company, rpt., 1982.

Allah Dia Chishti, *Siyar ul-Aqtab*, Urdu translation, Syed Muhammad Ali Joeya Muradabadi, Karachi: Oxford University Press, 2011.

Amir Hasan Sijzi, *Fawaid ul-Fuad*, English translation, Ziya ul-Hasan Faruqi (entitled *Spiritual and Literary Discourses of Shaikh Nizamuddin Awliya*), New Delhi: D.K. Printworld, 1996; Bruce B. Lawrence (entitled *Nizam Ad-Din Awliya: Morals for the Heart*), New York: Paulist Press, 1992.

Amir Khurd, *Siyar ul-Auliya*, Persian text, Delhi: Matba-i Muhibb-i Hind, 1885.

Amir Khusrau, *Khazain ul-Futuh*, English translation (entitled *The Campaigns of Alauddin Khalji*), Mohammad Habib, in *Politics and Society during the Early Medieval Period: Collected Works of Professor Mohammad Habib*, vol. II, ed. K.A. Nizami, New Delhi: People's Publishing House, 1981.

―――, *Miftah ul-Futuh*, Persian text, ed. Shaikh Abdul Rashid, Aligarh: Aligarh Muslim University, 1954.

―――, *Tughluq Nama*, Persian text, ed. Syed Hashmi Faridabadi, Aurangabad: Matba Urdu, 1933.

Damodar Gulati, *Hir Damodar*, Panjabi text, ed. Jagtar Singh, Patiala: Punjabi University, rpt., 2000.

Dara Shukoh, *Safinat ul-Auliya*, Urdu translation, Muhammad Waris Kamil, Deoband: Sabir Book Depot, n.d.

Fakhr-i Mudabbir, *Tarikh-i Fakhruddun Mubarak Shah*, Persian text, ed. D. Denison Ross, London: Royal Asiatic Society, 1927.

Bibliography 611

Fakhruddin Iraqi, *Kulliyat Fakhruddin Iraqi*, Persian text, ed. Nasreen Muhatshim, Tehran: Intsharat Zawwar, 1392 AH.

Firoz Shah Tughluq, *Futuhat-i Firoz Shahi*, Persian text, ed. Shaikh Abdul Rashid, Aligarh: Aligarh Muslim University, 1954.

Ganeshdas Badehra, *Rajdarshani*, English translation, Sukhdev Singh Charak and Anita K. Billwaria, Jammu: Jay Kay Book Store, 1991.

Guru Arjan Dev, ed., *Sri Guru Granth Sahib*, Original text with English and Panjabi translations, Manmohan Singh, Amritsar: Shiromani Gurdwara Prabandhak Committee, 2nd edn., 1981.

Hamid bin Fazlullah Jamali, *Siyar ul-Arifin*, Persian text, Delhi: Rizvi Press, 1893.

Hamid Qalandar, *Khair ul-Majalis*, Persian text, ed. Khaliq Ahmad Nizami, Aligarh: Aligarh Muslim University, 1959.

Ibn Battuta, *Rehla*, English translation, Mahdi Husain, entitled *The Rehla of Ibn Battuta: India, Maldive Islands and Ceylon*, Baroda: Oriental Institute, 1976.

Jamaluddin Ahmad Hansawi, *Mulhimat wa Ahwal wa Asaar*, ed. Sardar Ali Ahmad Khan, Lahore: Sang-e Meel Publications, 2002.

Khwaja Niamatullah bin Khwaja Habibullah Harvi, *Tarikh-i Khan Jahani wa Makhzan-i Afghani*, Persian text, ed. Syed Muhammad Imamuddin, vol. II, Dacca: Asiatic Society of Pakistan, 1962.

Khwaja Nizamuddin Ahmad, *Tabaqat-i Akbari*, vol. I, English translation, B. De, Calcutta: The Asiatic Society, rpt., 1973; vol. III, English translation, B. De and revised by Baini Prashad, Delhi: Low Price Publications, rpt., 1990.

Minhaj-i Siraj Juzjani, *Tabaqat-i Nasiri*, English translation, H.G. Raverty, 2 vols., rpt., New Delhi: Oriental Books Rprint Corporation, 1970.

Muhammad Akram Quddusi, *Iqtibas ul-Anwar*, Urdu translation, Wahid Bakhsh Siyal, Lahore: Ziaul Quran, 1993.

Muhammad Ali Asghar Chishti, *Jawahar-i Faridi*, Urdu translation, Fazluddin Naqshbandi Mujaddidi, Pakpattan: Maktaba Baba Farid, n.d.

Muhammad Ghausi Shattari, *Gulzar-i Abrar*, Persian text, ed. Muhammad Zaki, 2nd rpt., Patna: Khuda Bakhsh Oriental Public Library, 2001.

Muhammad Qasim Hindu Shah Firishta, *Tarikh-i Firishta*, Urdu translation, Abdul Rahman and Abdul Hayy Khwaja, 2 vols., Lahore: Al-Mizan, 2004.

Nur Ahmad Chishti, *Tahqiqat-i Chishti*, Lahore: Al-Faisal Nashiran wa Tajiran Kutb, 2001.

Shah Sharfuddin Bu Ali Shah Qalandar, *Masnavi*, Persian text, ed. Muhammad Muslim Ahmad Nizami, Delhi: Kutbkhana Naziriya, 1383 AH.

Shaikh Fariduddin Masud Ganj-i Shakar, *Shalok*, Panjabi text and English translation (entitled *Hymns of Sheikh Farid*), Brij Mohan Sagar, Amritsar: Guru Nanak Dev University, 1999.

Shaikh Rizqullah Mushtaqi, *Waqiat-i Mushtaqi*, Persian text, ed. Iqtidar Husain Siddiqui and Waqar ul-Hasan Siddiqi, Rampur: Rampur Raza Library, 2002.

Shaikh Sikandar bin Muhammad urf Manjhu bin Akbar, *Mirat-i Sikandari*, Persian text, ed. S.C. Misra and M.L. Rehman, Baroda: The Maharaja Sayajirao University of Baroda, 1961.

Shams Siraj Afif, *Tarikh-i Firoz Shahi*, Persian text, ed. Maulavi Wilayat Husain, Calcutta: Asiatic Society of Bengal, 1890.

Sharfuddin Ali Yazdi, *Zafar Nama*, Persian text, ed. Muhammad Ilahdad, vol. II, Calcutta: Asiatic Society of Bengal, 1888.

Shihabuddin Umar bin Muhammad Suhrawardi, *Awarif ul-Maarif*, English translation H. Wilberforce Clarke, New Delhi: Taj Co., rpt., 1984.

Sujan Rai Bhandari, *Khulasat ut-Tawarikh*, Persian text, ed. M. Zafar Hasan, Delhi: G. and Sons, 1918.

Syed Alauddin Ali Husaini, *Jami ul-Ulum*, Persian text, ed. Qazi Sajjad Husain, Delhi: Indian Council of Historical Research, 1987.

Tajuddin Hasan Nizami, *Taj ul-Maasir*, English translation, Bhagwat Saroop Goel, Delhi: Ibn Saud Dehalvi, 1998.

Waris Shah, *Hir Waris Shah*, Panjabi text, ed. Piara Singh Padam, rpt., New Delhi: Navyug Publishers, 1998.

Yahya bin Ahmad bin Abdullah Sirhindi, *Tarikh-i Mubarak Shahi*, Persian text, ed. M. Hidayat Husain, Calcutta: Asiatic Society of Bengal, 1931.

Ziauddin Barani, *Tarikh-i Firoz Shahi*, Persian text, ed. Sir Syed Ahmad, Aligarh: Aligarh Muslim University, 2005.

Secondary Sources: Books

Alhaq, Shuja, *A Forgotten Vision: A Study of Human Spirituality in the Light of the Islamic Tradition*, New Delhi: Vikas Publishing House, vol. I, 1997.

Allsen, Thomas T., *Culture and Conquest in Mongol Eurasia*, Cambridge: Cambridge University Press, 2001.

Bibliography 613

Anjum, Tanvir, *Chishti Sufis in the Sultanate of Delhi 1190-1400: From Restrained Indifference to Calculated Defiance*, Karachi: Oxford University Press, 2011.

Ashraf, Kunwar Muhammad, *Life and Conditions of the People of Hindustan*, 2nd edn., New Delhi: Munshiram Manoharlal, 1970.

Aslam, Muhammad, *Malfuzati Adab Ki Tarikhi Ahmiyat*, Lahore: Idarah-i Tahqiqat-i Pakistan, 1995.

Auer, Blain H., *Symbols of Authority in Medieval India: History, Religion and Muslim Legitimacy in the Delhi Sultanate*, New Delhi: Viva Books, 2013.

Baldick, Julian, *Mystical Islam: An Introduction to Sufism*, London: I.B. Tauris & Co., rpt., 2000.

Bearman, P.J. et. al., eds., *The Encyclopaedia of Islam*, vol. XI, Leiden: Brill, 2002.

Bigelow, Anna, *Sharing the Sacred: Practicing Pluralism in Muslim North India*, New York: Oxford University Press, 2010.

Bloch, Marc, *Feudal Society*, vol. I: *Growth of the Ties of Dependence*, English translation, L.A. Manyon, rpt., New Delhi: Asha Jyoti Booksellers & Distributors, 2006.

Boivin, Michel, *Artefacts of Devotion: A Sufi Repertoire of Qalandariya in Sehwan Sharif, Sind, Pakistan*, Karachi: Oxford University Press, 2011.

Bosworth, Clifford Edmund, *The Later Ghaznavids: Splendour and Decay (The Dynasty in Afghanistan and Northern India 1040-1186)*, Edinburgh: Edinburgh University Press, 1963.

———, *The Ghaznavids: Their Empire in Afghanistan and Eastern Iran 994-1040*, Edinburgh: Edinburgh University Press, 1963.

Chittick, William C. and Peter Lamborn, *Fakhruddin Iraqi: Divine Flashes*, New York: Paulist Press, 1982.

Dalal, Roshen, *Hinduism: An Alphabetical Guide*, New Delhi: Penguin Books, 2010.

Digby, Simon, *War Horse and Elephant in the Delhi Sultanate: A Study of Military Supplies*, Oxford: Oxford Monographs, 1971.

Donzel, E. Van et al., eds., *The Encyclopaedia of Islam*, vol. IV, New Edition, Leiden: E.J. Brill, 1990.

Douie, James, *The Panjab, North-West Frontier Province and Kashmir*, Delhi: Low Price Publications, rpt., 1994.

Droge, A.J., *The Quran: A New Annotated Translation*, New Delhi: Oxford University Press, 2013.

Duby, Georges, *The Knight, the Lady and the Priest: The Making of*

Modern Marriage in Medieval France, English translation, Barbara Bray, Chicago: University of Chicago Press, 1983.

Ernst, Carl W. and Bruce B. Lawrence, *Sufi Martyrs of Love: The Chishti Order in South Asia and Beyond*, New York: Palgrave Macmillan, 2002.

Ernst, Carl W., *Eternal Garden: Mysticism, History and Politics in a South Asian Sufi Centre*, New Delhi: Oxford University Press, 2nd edn., 2004.

Esposito, John L., *The Oxford Dictionary of Islam*, rpt., Karachi: Oxford University Press, 2007.

Faqri, Alam, *Tazkira Hazrat Ali Ahmad Sabir Kaliyari*, New Delhi: Farid Book Depot, 2005.

Frembgen, Jurgen Wasim, *At the Shrine of the Red Sufi: Five Days and Nights on Pilgrimage in Pakistan*, Karachi: Oxford University Press, 2011.

Glasse, Cyril, *The Concise Encyclopaedia of Islam*, rpt., London: Stacey International, 2004.

Gold, Ann Grodzins, *A Carnival of Parting: The Tales of King Bharthari and King Gopi Chand as Sung and Told by Madhu Natisar Nath of Ghatiyali, Rajasthan*, New Delhi: Munshiram Manoharlal, rpt., 1993.

Habib, Irfan, *The Agrarian System of Mughal India 1556-1707*, New Delhi: Oxford University Press, 2nd revd. edn., 1999.

Habib, Mohammad and Khaliq Ahmad Nizami, eds., *A Comprehensive History of India*, vol. V: *The Delhi Sultanate (AD 1206-1526)*, rpt., New Delhi: People's Publishing House, 1982.

Habib, Mohammad, *Sultan Mahmud of Ghaznin*, 2nd edn., New Delhi: S. Chand & Co., 1967.

Habibullah, A.B.M., *The Foundation of Muslim Rule in India*, 3rd revd. edn., Allahabad: Central Book Depot, 1976.

Hamadani, Agha Hussain, *The Frontier Policy of the Sultans of Delhi*, Islamabad: National Institute of Historical and Cultural Research, 1989.

Hasrat, Bikrama Jit, *Dara Shikuh: Life and Works*, New Delhi: Munshiram Manoharlal, rpt., 2013.

Hastings, James, ed., *The Encyclopaedia of Religion and Ethics*, vol. I, Edinburgh: T and T Clark, 1967.

Houtsma, M.T. et al., eds., *The Encyclopaedia of Islam*, vols. II & IV, Leiden: E.J. Brill, 1927 & 1934.

Huda, Qamar-ul, *Striving for Divine Union: Spiritual Exercises for Suhrawardi Sufis*, London & New York: Routledge Curzon, 2003.

Hughes, Thomas Patrick, *Dictionary of Islam*, rpt., New Delhi: Rupa, 2007.

Husain, Agha Mahdi, *The Rise and Fall of Muhammad bin Tughluq*, rpt., Delhi: Idarah-i Adabiyat-i Delli, 1972.

Ibbetson, Denzil, *Panjab Castes*, Patiala: Languages Department Panjab, rpt., 1970.

Imperial Gazetteer of India, *Provincial Series: Punjab*, 2 vols., Calcutta: Superintendent of Government Printing, 1908.

Islam, Riazul, *Sufism in South Asia: Impact on Fourteenth Century Muslim Society*, 2nd edn., Karachi: Oxford University Press, 2003.

Jackson, Peter, *The Delhi Sultanate: A Political and Military History*, Cambridge: Cambridge University Press, 1999.

Javed, Qazi, *Punjab Key Sufi Danishwar*, Lahore: Fiction House, 2005.

Karamustafa, Ahmet T., *God's Unruly Friends: Dervish Groups in the Islamic Middle Period 1200-1550*, Oxford: Oneworld Publications, rpt., 2007.

Khan, Nawab Iftikhar Ali, *History of the Ruling Family of Sheikh Sadruddin Sadr-i Jahan of Malerkotla (1449 AD to 1948 AD)*, ed., R.K. Ghai, Patiala: Punjabi University, 2000.

Kumar, Sunil, *The Emergence of the Delhi Sultanate 1192-1286*, Ranikhet: Permanent Black, 2007.

Lal, Kishori Saran, *Twilight of the Delhi Sultanate*, rpt., New Delhi: Munshiram Manoharlal, 1980.

Latif, Syad Muhammad, *History of the Punjab: From the Remotest Antiquity to the Present Time*, New Delhi: Eurasia Publishing House, rpt., 1964.

Lawrence, Bruce B., *Notes from A Distant Flute: Sufi Literature in Pre-Mughal India*, Tehran: Imperial Iranian Academy of Philosophy, 1978.

Manz, Beatrice Forbes, *The Rise and Rule of Tamerlane*, Cambridge: Cambridge University Press, 1989.

Mirza, Muhammad Wahid, *The Life and Times of Amir Khusrau*, Delhi: Idarah-i Adabiyat-i Delli, rpt., 1974.

Misra, S.C., *The Rise of Muslim Power in Gujarat: A History of Gujarat from 1298 to 1442*, New Delhi: Munshiram Manoharlal, 2nd edn., 1982.

Mojaddedi, Jawid A., *The Biographical Tradition in Sufism: The Tabaqat*

Genre from al-Sulami to Jami, Richmond (Surrey): Curzon Press, 2001.

Moreland, W.H., *The Agrarian System of Moslem India*, New Delhi: Oriental Books Reprint Corporation, 2nd edn., 1968.

Multani, Farhat, *Auliya-i Multan*, Multan: Kutbkhana Haji Niyaz Ahmad, 1980.

Naqvi, Hamida Khatoon, *Agricultural, Industrial and Urban Dynamism under the Sultans of Delhi 1206-1555*, New Delhi: Munshiram Manoharlal, 1986.

Nasr, Seyyed Hossein et al., eds., *The Study Quran: A New Translation and Commentary*, New York: Harper One, 2015.

Nazim, Muhammad, *Sultan Mahmud of Ghazna*, 2nd edn., New Delhi: Munshiram Manoharlal, 1971.

Nigam, S.B.P., *Nobility under the Sultans of Delhi*, New Delhi: Munshiram Manoharlal, 1968.

Nizami, Khaliq Ahmad, *On History and Historians of Medieval India*, New Delhi: Munshiram Manoharlal, 1983.

_____, *Religion and Politics in India during the Thirteenth Century*, new edn., New Delhi: Oxford University Press, 2002.

_____, *Tarikh-i Mashaikh-i Chisht*, vol. I, rpt., Karachi: Oxford University Press, 2007.

_____, *The Life and Times of Shaikh Nasiruddin Chiragh-i Delhi*, Delhi: Idarah-i Adabiyat-i Delli, 1991.

_____, *The Life and Times of Shaikh Nizamuddin Auliya*, New Delhi: Oxford University Press, new edn., 2007.

Nizami, Moin Ahmad, *Reform and Renewal in South Asian Islam: The Chishti Sabris in 18th-19th Century North India*, New Delhi: Oxford University Press, 2016.

Prasad, Ishwari, *History of the Qaraunah Turks in India*, vol. I, rpt., Allahabad: Central Book Depot, 1974.

Qadiri, Muhammad Ayub, *Makhdum-i Jahaniyan Jahangasht*, Karachi: Idarah Tahqiq wa Tasnif, 1963.

Qureshi, Ishtiaq Husain, *The Administration of the Sultanate of Dehli*, rpt., New Delhi: Oriental Books Reprint Corporation, 1971.

Qureshi, Samina, *Sacred Spaces: A Journey With the Sufis of the Indus*, Ahmedabad: Mapin Publishing & New Delhi: Timeless Books, 2009.

Rashid, A., *Society and Culture in Medieval India (1206-1556)*, Calcutta: Firma K.L. Mukhopadhyay, 1969.

Raychaudhuri, Tapan and Irfan Habib, eds., *The Cambridge Economic*

Bibliography 617

History of India, vol. I: *c. 1200-c. 1750*, rpt., Hyderabad: Orient Longman & Cambridge University Press, 2004.

Rizvi, Saiyid Athar Abbas, *A History of Sufism in India*, vol. I, New Delhi: Munshiram Manoharlal, 1978.

Rose, H.A., *A Glossary of the Tribes and Castes of the Punjab and North West Frontier*, vol. II, rpt., Patiala: Languages Department Panjab, 1970.

Sahu, Kishori Prasad, *Some Aspects of North Indian Social Life (1000-1526)*, Calcutta: Punthi Pustak, 1973.

Schimmel, Annemarie, *As Through A Veil: Mystical Poetry in Islam*, London: Oneworld Publications, rpt., 2001.

_____, *Mystical Dimensions of Islam*, rpt., New Delhi: Yoda Press, n.d.

Shaikh, Samira, *Forging a Region: Sultans, Traders and Pilgrims in Gujarat 1200-1500*, New Delhi: Oxford University Press, 2010.

Sharma, R.S. & K.M. Shrimali, eds., *A Comprehensive History of India*, vol. IV (AD 985-1206), New Delhi: People's Publishing House, 1992.

Sharma, Sunil, *Amir Khusrau: The Poet of Sultans and Sufis*, Oxford: One World, rpt., 2009.

_____, *Persian Poetry at the Indian Frontier: Masud Sad Salman of Lahore*, New Delhi: Permanent Black, 2000.

Shokoohy, Mehardad and Netalie H. Shokoohy, *Hisar-i Firuza: Sultanate and Early Mughal Architecture in the District of Hisar, India*, London: Monographs on Art, Archaeology & Architecture, 1988.

Siddiqui, Iqtidar Husain, *Authority and Kingship under the Sultans of Delhi (Thirteenth and Fourteenth Centuries)*, New Delhi: Manohar, 2006.

_____, *Indo-Persian Historiography up to the Thirteenth Century*, New Delhi: Primus Books, 2010.

_____, *Perso-Arabic Sources of Information on the Life and Conditions in the Sultanate of Delhi*, New Delhi: Munshiram Manoharlal, 1992.

Sikand, Yoginder, *Sacred Spaces: Exploring Traditions of Shared Faith in India*, New Delhi: Penguin Books, 2003.

Singh, Fauja, ed., *History of the Punjab*, vol. III (AD 1000-1526), Patiala: Punjabi University, 1972.

Singh, Pritam, *Sri Guru Granth Sahib Wale Sekh Farid Di Bhal*, Amritsar: Singh Brothers, 2010.

Srivastava, Kumkum, *The Wandering Sufis: Qalandars and Their Path*, Bhopal: Indira Gandhi Rashtriya Manav Sangrahalaya & New Delhi: Aryan Books International, 2009.

Steinfels, Amina M., *Knowledge before Action: Islamic Learning and Sufi Practice in the Life of Sayyid Jalal al-Din Bukhari Makhdum-i Jahaniyan*, Columbia (South Carolina): The University of South Carolina Press, 2012.

Strothmann, Linus, *Managing Piety: The Shrine of Data Ganj Bakhsh*, Karachi: Oxford University Press, 2016.

Stutley, Margaret and James Stutley, *A Dictionary of Hinduism: The Mythology, Folklore and Development (1500 BC–AD 1500)*, Bombay: Allied Publishers, 1977.

Suvorova, Anna, *Muslim Saints of South Asia: The Eleventh to Fifteenth Centuries*, Abingdon, Oxon: Routledge Curzon, 2001.

Thapar, Romila, *The Penguin History of Early India*, rpt., New Delhi: Penguin Books India, 2002.

Thomas, Edward, *The Chronicles of the Pathan Kings of Delhi*, New Delhi: Munshiram Manoharlal, rpt., 1967.

Tripathi, R.P., *Some Aspects of Muslim Administration*, Allahabad: Central Book Depot, rpt., 1974.

Wink, Andre, *The Making of the Indo-Islamic World*, vol. II: *The Slave Kings and the Islamic Conquest (11th-13th Centuries)*, New Delhi: Oxford University Press, rpt., 1999.

Secondary Sources: Articles

Anjum, Tanvir, 'Sons of Bread and Sons of Soul: Lineal and Spiritual Descendants of Baba Farid and the Issue of Succession', in *Sufism in Punjab: Mystics, Literature and Shrines*, ed. Surinder Singh and Ishwar Dayal Gaur, Delhi: Aakar Books, 2009.

Aquil, Raziuddin, 'Miracles, Authority and Benevolence: Stories of Karamat in Sufi Literature of the Delhi Sultanate', in *Sufi Cults and the Evolution of Medieval Indian Culture*, ed. Anup Taneja, New Delhi: Indian Council of Historical Research & Northern Book Centre, 2003.

———, 'Episodes from the Life of Shaikh Farid-ud-Din Ganj-i-Shakar', *International Journal of Punjab Studies*, vol. X, nos. 1 & 2, 2007.

———, 'Conversion in Chishti Sufi Literature (13th–14th Centuries)', *The Indian Historical Review*, vol. XXIV, nos. 1-2, 1997-8.

Askari, S.H., 'Wit and Humour in the Works of Amir Khusrau', in *Life and Times of Amir Khusrau*, ed. Zoe Ansari, New Delhi: National Amir Khusrau Society, n.d.

Bira, Shagdaryn, 'The Mongol Empire', in *History of Humanity:*

Bibliography 619

Scientific and Cultural Development, vol. IV: *From the Seventh to the Seventeenth Century*, ed. M.A. Al-Bakhit et al., Paris: Unesco & New York: Routledge, 2000.

Chaudhuri, Nupur, 'A Vanished Supremacy: The Qiyamkhanis of Fatehpur-Jhunjhunu', in *Popular Literature and Premodern Societies in South Asia*, ed. Surinder Singh and Ishwar Dayal Gaur, New Delhi: Pearson Longman, 2008.

Dabashi, Hamid, 'Historical Conditions of Persian Sufism during the Seljuk Period', in *The Heritage of Sufism: Classical Persian Sufism from its Origin to Rumi 700-1300*, ed. Leonard Lewisohn, Oxford: Oneworld Publications, 1999.

Digby, Simon, 'Abd al-Quddus Gangohi (1456-1537): Personality and Attitudes of an Indian Sufi', *Medieval India: A Miscellany*, vol. III, Bombay: Asia Publishing House, 1975.

—————, 'After Timur Left: North India in the Fifteenth Century', in *After Timur Left: Culture and Circulation in the Fifteenth Century North India*, ed. Francesca Orsini and Samira Shaikh, New Delhi: Oxford University Press, 2014.

—————, 'Qalandars and Related Groups: Elements of Social Deviance in the Religious Life of the Delhi Sultanate of the Thirteenth and Fourteenth Centuries', in *Islam in Asia*, vol. I (*South Asia*), ed. Yohanan Friedmann, Jerusalem: The Magnes Press, The Hebrew University, 1984.

Eaton, Richard M., 'The Political and Religious Authority of the Shrine of Baba Farid', in *Essays on Islam and Indian History*, New Delhi: Oxford University Press, 2000.

Ernst, Carl W., 'Islamization of Yoga in the Amritkunda Translations', *Journal of the Royal Asiatic Society*, Third Series, vol. 13, no. 2, July 2003.

Habib, Irfan, 'Economic History of the Delhi Sultanate: An Essay in Interpretation', *The Indian Historical Review*, vol. IV, no. 2, 1978.

—————, 'Society and Economic Change: 1200-1500', Seminar on Social and Economic Change in Northern India (Typescript), University of Kurukshetra, Kurukshetra, 1981.

—————, 'Technological Changes and Society: 13th and 14th Centuries', Presidential Address, Section II, *Proceedings of the Indian History Congress*, Varanasi, 1969.

—————, 'Jatts of Punjab and Sind', in *Essays in Honour of Dr. Ganda Singh*, ed. Harbans Singh and N. Gerald Barrier, Patiala: Punjabi University, 1976.

———, 'The Social Distribution of Landed Property in Pre-British India: A Historical Survey', in *Essays in Indian History: Towards A Marxist Perspective*, New Delhi: Tulika, 1995.

Habib, Irfan, and Faiz Habib, 'Mapping the Canals of Firoz Shah (1351-88)', Indian History Congress, 77th Session, University of Kerala, Thiruvananthapuram, 28-30 December 2016 (Typescript).

Habib, Mohammad, 'Chishti Mystics Records of the Sultanate Period', in *Politics and Society during the Medieval Period: Collected Works of Professor Mohammad Habib*, ed. Khaliq Ahmad Nizami, New Delhi: People's Publishing House, 1974.

Horovitz, J., 'Baba Ratan: the Saint of Bathinda', in *Notes on Punjab and Mughal India: Selections from Journal of the Punjab Historical Society*, ed. Zulfiqar Ahmad, Lahore: Sang-e Meel Publications, 2002.

Husain, Yusuf, 'Haud al-Hayat: The Arabic Version of Amritkund', in *On Becoming an Indian Muslim: French Essays on Aspects of Syncretism*, ed. M. Waseem, New Delhi: Oxford University Press, 2003.

Irving, Miles, 'The Shrine of Baba Farid Shakarganj at Pakpattan', *The Panjab Past and Present*, vol. VII, pt. 2, October 1973; first published in the *Journal of the Punjab History Society*, no. 1, 1911.

Jackson, Peter, 'Jalal al-Din, the Mongols and the Khwarizmian Conquest of Panjab and Sind', in *Studies on the Mongol Empire and Early Muslim India*, Farnham, Surrey (England) and Burlington (USA): Ashgate, 2009.

———, 'The Dissolution of the Mongol Empire', in *Studies on the Mongol Empire and Early Muslim India*, Farnham, Surrey (England) and Burlington (USA): Ashgate, 2009.

Jauhri, R.C., 'Ghiathud-Din Tughluq: His Original Name and Descent', in *Kunwar Muhammad Ashraf: An Indian Scholar and Revolutionary 1903-1962*, ed. Horst Kruger, New Delhi: People's Publishing House, 1969.

Khan, Ibadur Rahman, 'Historical Geography of the Punjab and Sind', *Muslim University Journal*, vol. I, no. 1, July 1931.

Kumar, Sunil, 'Assertions of Authority: A Study of the Discursive Statements of Two Sultans of Delhi', in *The Making of Indo-Persian Culture: Indian and French Studies*, ed. Muzaffar Alam, Francoise Nalini Delvoye & Marc Gaborieau, New Delhi: Manohar, 2000.

———, 'Ignored Elites: Turks, Mongols and Persian Secretarial Class in the Early Delhi Sultanate', in *Expanding Frontiers in South Asian and World History: Essays in Honour of John F. Richards*, ed. Richard M. Eaton et al., New Delhi: Cambridge University Press, 2009.

———, 'Trans-regional Contacts and Relationships: Turks, Mongols and the Delhi Sultanate in the Thirteenth and Fourteenth Centuries', in *Turks in the Indian Subcontinent, Central and West Asia: The Turkish Presence in the Islamic World*, ed. Ismail K. Poonawala, New Delhi: Oxford University Press, 2017.

Lawrence, Bruce B., 'The Early Chishti Approach to Sama', in *Islamic Society and Culture: Essays in Honour of Professor Aziz Ahmad*, ed. Milton Israel and N.K. Wagle, New Delhi: Manohar, 1983.

Mohammed, Salim, 'Shrine of Shaikh Sadruddin of Malerkotla: History, Politics and Culture', in *Sufism in Punjab: Mystics, Literature and Shrines*, ed. Surinder Singh and Ishwar Dayal Gaur, Delhi: Aakar Books, 2009.

Nizami, Khaliq Ahmad, 'Some Aspects of Khanqah Life in Medieval India', in *Studies in Medieval Indian History and Culture*, Allahabad: Kitab Mahal, 1966.

Parihar, Subhash, 'The Dargah of Baba Haji Ratan of Bathinda', *Islamic Studies*, vol. 40, no. 1, 2001.

Sabir, Aneesa Iqbal, 'Suhrawardi Mysticism in South-Western Punjab: Contribution of Syed Jalaluddin Bukhari Makhdum-i Jahaniyan', in *Sufism in Punjab: Mystics, Literature and Shrines*, ed. Surinder Singh and Ishwar Dayal Gaur, Delhi: Aakar Books, 2009.

Siddiqui, Iqtidar Husain, 'The Qarlugh Kingdom in the Thirteenth Century: Liaison Between Mongols and Indian Rulers in Medieval India', in *Medieval India: Essays in Diplomacy and Culture*, New Delhi: Adam Publishers & Distributors, 2009.

Singh, Surinder, 'Book Review', of Sunil Kumar, *The Emergence of the Delhi Sultanate, 1192-1286*, Ranikhet: Permanent Black, 2007; *The Medieval History Journal*, vol. 13, no. 1, April 2010.

———, 'Dynamics of Statecraft in the Delhi Sultanate: A Reconstruction from the Letters of Ainul Mulk Mahru', *Proceedings of the Indian History Congress*, 61st Session, Calcutta, 2001.

———, 'The Making of Medieval Punjab: Politics, Society and Economy c. 1200-c. 1400', Presidential Address, Medieval Section, *Proceedings of the Punjab History Conference*, 40th Session, 14-16 March 2008.

Talbot, Cynthia, 'Becoming Turk in the Rajput Way: Conversion and Identity in an Indian Warrior Narrative', in *Expanding Frontiers* in *South Asian and World History: Essays in Honour of John F. Richards*, ed. Richard M. Eaton et al., New York: Cambridge University Press, 2013.

Tazeem, Mohammad, 'Theory and Practice of Islamic Mysticism: An Exposition by Ali bin Usman Hujwiri', in *Sufism in Punjab: Mystics, Literature and Shrines*, ed. Surinder Singh and Ishwar Dayal Gaur, Delhi: Aakar Books, 2009.

Wink, Andre, 'On the Road to Failure: The Afghans in Mughal India', in *Islamicate Traditions in South Asia: Themes from Culture and History*, ed. Agnieszka Kuczkiewics, New Delhi: Manohar, 2013.

Zilli, Ishtiyaq Ahmad, 'Early Chishtis and the State', in *Sufi Cults and the Evolution of Medieval Indian Culture*, ed. Anup Taneja, New Delhi: Indian Council of Historical Research and Northern Book Centre, 2003.

Index

Abdul Haq Muhaddis Dehalvi 22, 24-5, 318, 594, 599, 459-60
Abdul Malik Isami 20, 93, 112, 126, 364
Abdul Malik Ismail 364
Abdul Rahman Chishti 18, 26, 472, 476
Abdul Rahman Jami 25, 193
Abdullah (Mongol) 107
Abdullah (Chronicler) 21
Abdullah Karatigin 47, 49
Abdullah Rumi 181, 188-9
Abdullah Yafai 343, 366
Abohar 21, 177, 215, 223-4, 227, 234, 239, 242, 249, 251-2, 288, 323, 582, 585, 595
Abu Bakhr 234, 242
Abu Bakr 369-70
Abu Bakr Kharrat 189
Abu Nasr M. Utbi 19
Abu Nasr Parsi 61
Abu Raihan Alberuni 19, 44, 579
Abu Saeed Abul Khair 440, 445, 500
Abul Fateh Daud 42
Abul Fazl 457
Abul Fazl Baihaqi 19, 52
Abul Fazl bin M. Khattali 131-2
Aden 179-80, 342-3, 353-4
Adil Khan 370
Adli Raja 561, 564
Afghanistan 40, 44, 72, 84, 86, 94, 128-9, 132, 206, 228, 234, 371
Afghans 510, 606-7
Afifuddin Matari 342-3
Agroha 438-9, 583
Ahmad Chap 106

Ahmad Mashuq 314-15
Ahmad Niyaltigin 19, 47-50, 52-4
Ahroni 377, 583
Ain ul-Mulk Mahru 21, 31, 229, 266-73, 275-84, 293-4, 356-7, 583
Ajmer 40, 42, 56-7, 65, 129, 149, 151
Ajodhan (Pakpattan) 23-4, 59, 149-50, 153-6, 158, 169, 171-7, 223, 232-4, 242-3, 246, 262, 288-9, 297-305, 311, 361-2, 370, 375-6, 386, 436-8, 447, 474, 582, 585-7, 591-2, 597-9, 604, 607
Akbar 21, 509-10, 513, 515, 519, 526-7, 531, 551 557, 559, 562, 564, 566
Akhbar ul-Akhyar 26, 31, 457
Akhtiaruddin Aitigin 81
Akhtiaruddin Altuniya 81
Akhtiaruddin Qaraqash 81, 87-8
Alaghu 107
Alam Khan 421-2
Alauddin Bahram Shah 78
Alauddin Jam Juna 356-7
Alauddin Jani 80
Alauddin Khalji 20, 107, 109-15, 125, 581, 222, 224, 226, 265, 268, 275, 287, 321, 331, 335-9, 458, 477, 489, 594
Alauddin Masud Shah 81, 89-90
Alauddin Muhammad bin Tekish 76
Alauddin Shah 406, 416
Al-Aurad 22, 185, 187
Alhaq, Shuja 15
Amir-i Akhur 81, 88
Amir-i Hajib 81

Ali (Khera chief) 511-12, 531, 534, 536-8, 542, 546, 548, 552-3, 555, 559-63, 602
Ali Aryaruq 19, 46-8
Ali Asghar Chishti 303-4, 591
Ali Beg 111
Ali bin Rabia 58
Ali bin Usman Hujwiri 14, 21, 30, 131-47, 205, 207, 210, 579, 585-7
Ali Karmakh 64
Ali Sultan Tawachi 374, 381
Allah Dad 374, 376, 380
Allah Diya Chishti 18, 26, 472, 479-80, 486
Allahdad Kaka Lodi 399, 401
Ambala 259, 266, 492-3, 583
Amir Hasan Sijzi 22, 99, 332, 586
Amir Husain 329, 364
Amir Khurd 24, 26, 233, 288, 298, 300, 324-5, 361, 586, 599, 449-51, 454
Amir Khusrau 20, 22, 99, 102, 104-5, 111-13, 221, 224, 228, 301, 456, 458, 475
Amir Muzaffar 400-1
Amir Shah Malik 373-4, 380-1
Amritkunda 498, 508
amulets (*tawiz*) 175-6, 297, 349
Anandpal 41-4, 46
Anhilwara 64, 78
Anjum, Tanvir 15
Anushtigin Balkhi 56
Anushtigin Hajib 58-9
Aqsanqar 88
Aquil, Raziuddin 15
Arabia 234
Arghons 403-5, 410, 413, 419, 425, 431
Arkali Khan 106
Asandi 377
Attock 29, 115, 128
audition (*sama*) 99, 142-5, 169-70, 188, 309, 322-3, 326-7, 331-2, 352-3, 449, 492
Auer, Blain H. 14
Aurangzeb 414
Awarif ul-Maarif 16, 155-6, 185-6, 205, 327, 343-4, 588, 440, 448-9

Ayat ul-Kursi 167, 187
Azerbaijan 94, 123

Baba Farid 16, 22-6, 30-1, 59, 147-58, 161-77, 189, 205-6, 210-12, 214-6, 223, 232-3, 242-3, 246, 261, 288-9, 375, 409, 435-8, 447-8, 452, 472-8, 491, 493, 500, 507, 565, 582, 585, 587-92, 598-600
Baba Haji Rattan 18, 30, 127-31, 586
Babdujah 273
Babu Rajab Ali 18
Babur 419, 422, 424-5, 432
Badakhshan 25
Badaun 177, 242-3, 250, 288
Badaun 83
Badruddin Ishaq 150, 154, 156, 169, 175, 215, 298, 303, 361, 591
Badruddin Sulaiman 211, 298, 303, 306, 590-1
Bagar 67
Baghdad 16, 95, 129, 146, 178, 366, 472
Bahadur 510
Bahadur Nahir 369
Bahawalpur 311
Bahlol Lodi 21, 32, 255-6, 396, 402-6, 409-12, 431-2, 601, 607
Bahram Aiba Kishlu Khan 228, 231, 322-3, 595
Bahram Khan Turkbacha 386
Bahram Shah 60, 62-3, 118
Bairam Khan Turkbacha 386-7
Bajwara 388, 399, 401, 605
Balochis 417
Baniyan 94
Banur 410, 432
Baqi Kulabi 510, 565
Baradus 231
Baran 81, 86
Bathinda 18, 39, 65-6, 72, 78-9, 81-4, 95-6, 109, 127-9, 394-5, 398-401, 429, 580, 606
Bayazid Bistami 23, 145, 209, 332, 471
Beas 28, 41, 90, 93, 98, 108, 272, 370-1, 374, 384, 390-6, 398, 400, 581
Benares 50, 52

Bhakkar 77-8, 234, 266, 393, 422, 433, 490
Bhandari, Sujan Rai 148, 223
Bharat 41
Bhardwaj, Ajay 18
Bharthri 544, 574
Bhatner 96, 256, 356, 375, 377, 604-5
Bhattis 96, 304, 425, 581, 592
Bhera 39, 41, 433
Bhimpal 43-4
Bibi Hajira 472
Bibi Mangi 410-11
Bibi Naila (Kadbanu) 224-5
Bigelow, Anna 17
Bihishti Darwaza 302, 306, 310-11
Biji Rai 42
Binban 83, 85, 87, 93-4
Bokhara 156, 177, 182, 237, 340, 404
Bokharis 421
Brahmins 43, 55, 57-8, 243, 421, 424, 511, 516, 532-3, 540, 543, 565, 603
Bu Ali Qalandar 22, 26, 33, 217, 435, 456-63, 467, 469-70, 478, 481-2, 502, 507, 585-6, 597, 599-600
Bughra Khan 97-8
Bul Qasim Hakim 46, 48-9
Bulle Shah 148

Central Asia 11, 46, 94, 127, 346
Chaddars 536, 601
Chamba 39
Chanakya 517
Chandardat 41
Chauhan, Karam Chand 254, 256
Chauhans 39, 118
Chaul-i Jalali 372, 385
Chenab 28, 33, 39, 41, 48, 68, 72, 80, 90-1, 272, 280, 373, 384-5, 391-3, 421, 428, 430, 513, 517, 519-21, 543-4, 565-7, 569
Chhat 388, 410
Chilla Makus 167, 212
Chingez Khan 76-7, 107, 228, 372
chiraghi 307, 309
Chishtis 14-5, 17, 25, 30-31, 205, 233-4, 289-90, 298, 307, 309, 321, 333, 335, 342-3, 349, 352, 365, 450-1, 454, 457, 472, 475, 478, 491
Chuchak (Siyal chief) 510-13, 521-32, 534-7, 548, 555, 557, 559-60, 564, 570, 601
Chuchkana 520, 544
Chutang 260
Cis-Satluj 79, 259, 388, 414, 582, 605

Dadbeg 279, 295
Dailamis 48-9
Damascus 193
Danganah 277, 280, 295
Dara Shukoh 364, 414
Daraban 410
Darrah 59
Darrera 254
Dastarbandi 302, 310
Data Ganj Bakhsh 131
Daulat Khan 386-7
Daulat Khan Lodi 422
Dava Khan 108
Debal 64-5, 77, 89
Delhi 12, 20-1, 24-5, 28-31, 40, 42, 44, 118, 65-6, 68, 71, 77, 79-82, 85-7, 90-6, 98, 101, 105, 108, 110-15, 119, 121, 123, 125-6, 149-50, 156, 158, 167, 171, 175-7, 190-1, 205, 210, 222-3, 226, 228-32, 234, 240, 244-8, 250-1, 255-8, 261, 263-5, 275, 277, 279-80, 283-4, 289, 291, 295, 298-303, 318, 320-3, 326-7, 331, 333, 335-6, 338, 354, 356-60, 365, 369-70, 378, 380, 385-7, 389-92, 394-5, 399-400, 402-6, 412, 416-17, 419-20, 422, 431-2, 435, 447-8, 451, 453, 456-7, 473, 475-6, 484, 488-9, 493, 505, 575, 580-1, 584-5, 600
Delhi Sultanate 13-14, 20, 29, 32, 63, 76-7, 80, 83-4, 86, 90-1, 93-6, 98, 102, 106, 108, 113-14, 122-4, 131, 149, 221, 223-4, 226-8, 234, 248, 250-1, 255, 267, 270, 274, 276-7, 291, 294, 303-4, 333-4, 337-8, 359, 369, 378, 389, 394-5, 397, 401-2, 409, 413, 420, 439, 455, 477, 488, 509, 565, 601, 606-7

Dhankot 420
Dhatrat 260, 265, 583
Digby, Simon 13
Diler Khan 109
Dinarkotah 55
Dindar Muhammad 88
Dipal Hari 55
Dipalpur 20, 79, 96, 102, 110, 114-15, 126, 221-2, 249, 232, 246, 249, 251, 259, 283, 295, 300, 302, 370-2, 374-7, 385, 390, 392-3, 396, 400-2, 406, 605
Diwan 302, 309-11
Doab 95-6, 370-1, 384, 386-7
Dooms 511-13, 516, 520, 532, 565-6, 603
Dorbei Doqshin 76, 84, 178

Eaton, Richard M. 16
Ecstasy (*wajd*) 143-4, 450
Egypt 335, 337
Ernst, Carl W. 17, 158

Fakhruddin Gilani 180
Fakhruddin Iraqi, 22, 30, 191-5, 202, 206, 456, 475, 586, 589-90, 600
Fakhruddin Juna 230-1
Faqih Bassal 343
Faqih Saliti 56
Farhad 466
Fasus ul-Hikam 193
Fatawa-i Sufiyyah 339-40
Fateh Khan 397
Fateh Khan (s/o Firoz Tughluq) 359, 486
Fatehabad 260, 265, 377, 386,
Fatehpur 386-7
Fatimid caliphate 39
Faulad Turkbacha 394-6, 398-9, 401, 606
Fawaid ul-Fuad 22-5, 332
Fazlullah Majawi 339, 596
Firishtah 222
Firoz Shah Langah 421
Firoz Shah Tughluq 20, 21, 31, 225-7, 232-3, 245-52, 254-64, 266, 268, 272, 277, 280, 282-4, 289-90, 292-5, 334-5, 353, 356-8, 360, 367, 369, 378, 402, 427, 429, 454-6, 458, 485, 502, 582, 584, 595-7
Firozabad 259-61, 378, 380, 387
Firozi slaves 369-70
Firozpur 29, 260, 381, 387

Gakkhars 42, 579
Ganga 50, 62, 381-2, 428, 484
Gangoh 311, 472, 493
Garmsir 87
Gazrun 342-4
Ghaggar 29, 259-60, 265, 292, 377, 582
Ghaggar Plain 28
Ghalib Khan 369, 371
Ghaznavids 15, 39-46, 55-7, 578-9, 607
Ghazni 15, 18, 19, 40, 47-8, 52, 54-68, 71-2, 76, 85-7, 95-6, 118, 129, 132, 177, 207, 578-9
Ghiasuddin Balban (Ulugh Khan) 20, 82-4, 86-7, 90-4, 95-8, 101, 106, 121, 123-4, 214, 222-3, 297, 392, 435, 452, 580-1
Ghiasuddin Tughluq (Ghazi Malik) 20, 25, 30, 114, 126, 250-1, 256, 266, 289-90, 302, 319, 322, 326-9, 333, 363-4, 369, 458, 477, 581-2, 595-5
Ghor 76, 84, 87, 118-19
Ghorids 15, 62-5, 70-1, 607
Ghuzz 101
Giri 55-6
Gobind Rai 65-6
Gopichand 544, 574
Gopis 524, 538, 570
Gorakhnath 128-9, 498
Guga 129, 206
Gujarat 25, 108, 252-4, 280, 291, 295, 371, 433
Gul Chand 228, 230-2
Gulati, Damodar 509, 525, 555, 561-2, 564, 568, 572-3, 575-7
Guru Arjan Dev 158
Guru Gobind Singh 130
Guru Nanak 130, 158, 423, 607
Gwalior 42

Habib, Irfan 12-13, 226

Index

Habib, Mohammad 14, 45-6
Haidaris 248, 439
Haikan 378
Haj 342
Hajib Tughantigin 62
Halaku 82-3, 87, 92, 93-5, 107, 122-3, 581
Hamadan 191
Hamid bin Fazlullah Jamali 24, 192-3, 217, 314, 322, 362-4, 366, 593, 595
Hamid Khan 406, 431
Hamid Multani 336-8
Hamid Qalandar 23-4
Hamruwah 272-3, 584
Hanafi school 342, 346
Hansi 24, 26, 32, 54-7, 66-7, 79-80, 84, 149, 167, 171, 176, 210, 230-1, 234, 244, 247-8, 256, 259-62, 265, 289, 370, 435-9, 447-9, 452-6, 482, 502, 505, 507, 580, 583, 585-7, 595, 597-9, 601
Harni Khera 259
Hasan Afghan 190-1, 589
Hasan Maimandi 47, 49, 51
Hasan Qawwal 328
Hassi 514, 521, 525, 530-2, 538
Hazrat Ali 103, 319, 457, 471
Hazrat Isa 445, 500
Hazrat Musa 441, 445, 501, 504
Hejaz 177, 342-4
Herat 87, 193, 329, 472
Himalayas 28
Hindushahis 20, 39-41, 43-4, 578
Hindustan 46-7, 49, 51, 61-2, 65, 75, 94-6, 102, 112, 114, 154
Hindustanis 71
Hir 509-15, 519-22, 525-39, 541-64, 570-2, 574, 576-7, 602-4
Hissar Firoza 254-63, 265, 369-70, 387, 394, 406, 456, 502, 582-3, 599, 607
Hoqutar 85
Hoshiarpur 388, 605
Huda, Qamar ul- 16
Humayun 25, 493
Husain 102-3, 124
Husain bin Kharmil 64

Husain, Agha Mahdi 226
Husam Khan 405-6

Iblis 470, 504
Ibn Battuta 31, 222, 224, 234-8, 240-5, 288-9, 300, 333, 363, 365-6, 584
Ibn Hajar 127
Ibn-i Arabi 15, 193, 343, 349, 498
Ibrahim Lodi 488-9
ijaz 183-4
Ilmuddin Ismail 320, 363, 594
Ilyas Afghan 380
Imad ul-Mulk 268, 333-4, 357
Imaduddin Raihan 83
Imam Abu Hanifa 274, 435, 492
Imam Ghazzali 166, 203, 209
Imam Malik 274
Imam Muhammad Idris 274
imlak 71
Indo-Panjab Plain 28-9
Indra 511, 566
Indrapat 155, 439
Indus 28, 41-2, 45, 56, 58, 62, 71, 85-7, 91, 108, 111, 116, 125, 128, 234, 288, 292, 371-2, 378, 385, 510, 578 604
Iqbalmanda 112-13
iqta 79, 92-3, 97-8
Iraq 25, 83, 94-5
Isfahan 191
Islam 42, 68, 73-4, 103, 107, 129-30, 133, 147-8, 191, 218, 245, 251-3, 255, 257, 261, 272, 291, 302, 304, 307, 331, 335-6, 338, 350, 355, 360, 398, 409, 412, 424, 430, 443, 456, 458, 460, 471, 487, 565, 572
Islam Khan Lodi (Sultan Shah Lodi) 388-90, 392, 396, 402-5, 393-4, 397, 399-400
Islam, Riazul 15
Islamic jurisprudence (*fiqh*) 342, 344, 346, 352
Islamic spirituality 435, 457-8, 472
Islamization 16, 409
Izzuddin Balban Kishlu Khan 81-4, 86, 92-3, 121, 580-1
Izzuddin Muhammad Salari 78, 80-1

Index

Jackson, Peter 13, 223
Jahan Shah 382
Jahangir 414
Jaipal 40-2
Jalaluddin Khalji 105-7, 125, 223, 581
Jalaluddin Mangbarni 76-8, 84-6, 178, 372, 580
Jalaluddin Rumi 15, 193, 457, 471
Jalandhar 39, 41, 61, 83, 108, 370, 388-90, 391-4, 396, 398-401, 606
Jalor 228-9
Jam Bayazid 420-22
Jam Ibrahim 420
Jam Juna 295
Jamaluddin Ali Khalji 93-4
Jamaluddin Masud 83-4, 86, 91-2, 581
Jamaluddin Yaqut 81
Jammu 39, 63-4, 370, 383-4, 391-3, 428, 605-6
Jamuna 15, 23, 28, 44, 55, 66, 111, 206, 257-61, 263, 265, 292, 378, 380, 382, 386, 439, 457-8, 472-3, 493, 582, 600
Janjuhas 106
Jankar Khan 90
Jaspal Sehra 91
Jasrath Khokhar 32, 304, 373-4, 389-95, 398-403, 405, 431, 592, 601, 607
Jat clans 302, 304
Jats 15-16, 19-20, 29, 33, 45, 52-3, 56, 63, 66-7, 96, 116, 222-3, 377, 512, 515, 517-18, 521, 551, 553, 561, 565, 572-3, 579, 581-2, 603, 608
Jawahar-i Faridi 303, 591
Jawaliqs 320
Jeddah 180
Jeevan 515, 540
Jhajjar 426
Jhang Siyal 509-12, 515, 521, 524-6, 528, 530-1, 538, 541, 555, 564, 567-8, 572-3, 576
Jhelam 28-9, 41, 44, 55, 68-70, 91, 108, 272, 372-3, 395-8, 400, 544, 565, 567
Jhinwar 512, 518, 566
Jibrail 195, 219, 467, 496, 503-4
Jind 260, 265, 583
Jinjan 374

Jog 544-5, 560
Jogi 487, 509, 544-51, 555, 560, 562-4, 574, 602-4
Junaid Baghdadi 132, 135-6, 145-6, 209, 332, 355, 363
Junaidis 145

Kaaba 132, 170, 190, 218-19, 327, 486
Kabak 111-12
Kabir Khan Ayaz 80-1, 87, 580
Kabiruddin (s/o Iraqi) 192-3
Kabul 40, 44, 54, 85, 118, 128, 149, 393, 395-7, 404
Kahtwal 149, 473
Kahun Raj 399
Kaido 527, 535, 545
Kaithal 81, 84, 106, 257, 166, 377, 583
Kalanaur 392-3
Kali 259, 261, 582
Kalima-i shahadah 188, 208
Kalinjar 40, 42, 44
Kaliyar 26, 33, 311, 435, 472-5, 477, 482
Kamal Badhan 388
Kamal Khan 394, 397
Kamal Taj 273, 276, 282
Kamaluddin Masud Sherwani 179-80
Kambohs 283-4
Kanauj 40, 42
Kapurthala 411, 413
Karbala 102-3, 428
Karman 71, 85
Karnal 26, 29, 259-60
Kashf ul-Mahjub 30, 132, 205, 332, 587
Kashmir 39, 43-4, 51, 63, 85, 129, 206, 372, 390, 414, 426, 428
Kashshaf 183, 216
Kat Karor 420
Kavi Jan 254, 291
Khair ul-Majalis 23-5
Khairuddin Khani 389, 397
Khalilullah 471, 505
Khaljis 65, 71, 84
Khan Jahan Maqbul 357-8
Khan, Hasan Ali 17
Khanewal 420, 433
Khan-i Khanan 230-31

kharaj 71
Kheras 509, 511-12, 526, 528-32, 534-8, 541-3, 545-58, 560-4, 571-2, 575-6, 602, 604
khirqah 351-2
Khizanat ul-Fawaid 345-6
Khizr Khan (s/o Alauddin Khalji) 226
Khizr Khan 32, 256, 357, 368, 371, 385-8, 402, 429, 432, 605
Khizrabad 265, 405
Khizrwah 272, 584
Khokhar Bhikan 68
Khokhars 20, 29, 63-4, 67-70, 75-7, 88, 91, 95-6, 108, 119, 223, 227-8, 230-2, 304-5, 390, 392, 395, 579-82, 592
Khudawandzada Qiwamuddin 236-8
Khulasat ul-Arifin 22, 185-6
Khurasan 25, 44, 54-5, 60, 63, 83, 87, 114, 118, 146, 177, 190, 222-3, 228, 236-7, 258, 278, 289, 374, 425
Khurasanis 71
Khushab 433
Khusrau Khan 227, 229-32, 293, 329
Khusrau Malik 63-4, 68
Khusrau Shah 63
Khwaja Ali Andrabi 388-9
Khwaja Burhanuddin 447, 598-9
Khwaja Hasan Basri 440, 445, 501
Khwaja Khizr 129, 527
Khwaja Muinuddin Chishti 17, 24-6, 147, 149, 151, 205, 211, 335, 472, 491
Khwaja Nizamuddin 297
Khwaja Nizamuddin Ahmad 19, 21
Khwaja Qutbuddin Bakhtiar Kaki 24, 149, 167, 169, 175-6, 179, 184, 210-12, 331, 439, 455, 457, 491, 503, 587
Khwaja Shibli 488
Khwaja-i Jahan 245, 247, 266, 370
Khwarizm 67, 76
Khwarizmians 30, 65, 72, 75-7, 80, 84-5, 580
Kitab ul-Hind 19
Kohistan 71
Kopla (Haridwar) 381-2, 428
Kot Karor 177
Kot Qabula 553-5, 561-4

Kotla 371
Krishna 524, 538, 570
Kuhram 66-7, 71-2, 79, 84, 109, 111, 257, 266, 583
Kujah 92
Kullu 39
Kumar, Sunil 13, 223
Kundi 510, 512, 526-30, 532-3, 535-6

Lahore 29-30, 39, 41, 44, 46, 48-50, 52, 54, 56-63, 64-5, 68, 71-2, 76, 79-80, 82-4, 87-9, 91-2, 95-6, 102, 114, 118, 131-2, 147-9, 210, 222, 226, 275, 280, 295, 370, 384, 390-3, 396, 398-402, 405-6, 575, 578-81, 587, 601, 605, 607
Lahrawat 231
Laila 443, 466, 500
Lal Shahbaz Qalandar 217, 459
Lamaat 193
Lamghan 39-41
Langahs 417-21, 607
langar 302
Lawrence, Bruce B. 17, 440, 463
Lodi Afghans 12, 33, 402, 404, 423-5
Loni 378
Luddan 512-15, 519-20, 544-5, 569
Ludhiana 370, 389-91, 431, 605-6

Macauliffe, M.A. 158
Madar-i Mominan 437, 447
Madina 25, 117, 325, 327, 342-4, 366
Mahmud Hasan 391-7, 399-400, 606
Mahmud Khan Langah 421-3, 427
Majnu 443, 466, 500
Makran 78
Malerkotla 17, 32, 406, 408-9, 412-14, 431-2, 435, 607
malfuzat 22
Malik Arsalan 62
Malik Ayaz 44
Malik Bahram 402
Malik Barbak Bektars 98
Malik Chajju 106
Malik Firoz 403, 405
Malik Firoz Ali 369

Malik Hoshang 244
Malik Kafur 111-12, 126
Malik Kalu 391, 395, 397
Malik Khas Hajib 283-4
Malik Mardan Daulat 353, 357, 368, 402, 429
Malik Mughalti 229
Malik Raja 400
Malik Rajab 392
Malik Sohrab Dudai 420
Malik Sulaiman 368, 429, 432
Malik Yaklakhi 229
Malik Yusuf Sarwar 394, 397, 399-400
Malik Ziauddin Tulaki 65-6
Mallu Iqbal Khan 256, 371, 378-9, 385, 386, 402, 605
Malner 408
Mandahars 96, 106, 123, 581
Mandkakur 52
Mangu Khan 82-3
Mangutah 89-90
Mannu 384
Mansar 383
Mansur al-Hallaj 146-7, 210, 219, 490
Mansura 72
Mansurpur 80, 85, 259
Marigalah 56
Masud Sad Salman 54, 60-1, 118, 579
Masudabad 234, 244-5
Maulana Nur Turk 149
Maulana Shamsuddin Turk 335-8
Maulana Sirajuddin Savi 106
Maulana Ziauddin Sunami 460
Mecca 25, 127-8, 130, 145, 155, 168, 177, 180, 190, 193, 244, 324, 327, 342-4, 353-4, 366, 470, 486
Meerut 380-1
Mewat 95
Minas 96, 581
Minhaj-i Siraj Juzjani 14, 20, 63, 65, 88, 90-2, 122-3, 580
Mir Jakar Zand 422
Mirat ul-Asrar 27, 475
Mirat-i Sikandari 250-2
Mirza Kamran 423
Miyan Mir 147

Mojam 515-17, 522, 539, 541, 543-4, 568, 573
Mongke 86, 123
Mongols 11, 30, 75-7, 80-1, 83-4, 86-98, 100-15, 122, 126, 149, 178-9, 222-3, 225, 228, 248, 279-80, 287, 295, 318, 331, 575, 578, 580-1, 593
Morocco 238-41, 244, 289, 335, 366
Mote Rai Chauhan 254-6
Mubarak Shah 390-401, 606
Mufassal 184
Mughals 413, 423, 425-6, 493, 519
Muhammad Akram Quddusi 18
Muhammad Bahalim 62
Muhammad Bayazid Khan 414, 431
Muhammad bin Qasim 226-7
Muhammad bin Tughluq 16, 225, 232-8, 242-5, 248, 250-1, 257, 282, 287-8, 295, 301-2, 322, 332-5, 342, 355-6, 363-5, 451-5, 458, 507, 584, 591, 595, 599
Muhammad Halimi 56
Muhammad Qasim Hindu Shah Firishta 19, 222
Muhammad Shah (Sultan) 403, 405-6
Muhammad Shah Lur 229
Muizzuddin Bahram Shah 81, 87, 121-2
Mulhimat 33, 440, 598
Multan 14-16, 21-2, 24-5, 30-2, 39-40, 42-3, 45-6, 56, 58, 62, 64-5, 67-8, 71, 77-84, 86-7, 89-90, 92-3, 97-102, 104, 106, 121, 123, 109-10, 112, 116, 149, 153, 169, 171, 176-7, 177-83, 188-93, 216, 221, 228-9, 234-7, 239, 245-6, 266-9, 271-2, 275, 277-80, 282-4, 287-8, 294-5, 299, 311, 314, 317-18, 322-3, 326-7, 329, 332-7, 339-41, 350, 353, 356, 358-9, 361, 370-4, 385, 427, 429, 386-7, 393-9, 401-2, 410, 416-23, 433, 435, 452, 456, 481, 518, 546, 580-6, 589-90, 595-7, 605, 607
muqtis 79, 93

Nagarkot (Kangra) 43, 57-8, 369, 382, 394, 605
Nagaur 81-2

Index

Nahars 536, 551-6, 575, 601
Naib-i Mamlikat 81
Najibuddin Mutawakkil 154, 156, 171, 361
Nandanah 41, 43, 69-70, 72, 76, 79, 85
Nangrahar 56, 85
Nasiruddin Aitmur 78
Nasiruddin Mahmud (r. 1246-66) 20, 22, 81-4, 91-2, 93, 96, 121, 171, 176, 214, 452, 455
Nasiruddin Mahmud (r. 1394-1412) 370, 379, 385-7, 426
Nasiruddin Mahmud (s/o Iltutmish) 20, 29, 72-5, 579
Nasiruddin Muhammad 86
Nasiruddin Muhammad Qarlugh 83, 93-4
Nasiruddin Qubacha 70-2, 76-7, 78, 80, 84-5, 119, 178-9, 185, 579-81, 589
Nasirwah 272-3, 583
Nath yogis 128
Nawahun 359-61
Nimrod 468, 504
Nishapur 20, 49-50, 117
Nizam ul-Mulk Junaidi 78, 80
Nizami, Khaliq Ahmad 13-14, 158
Nizami, Moin Ahmad 17
Noora Chaddar 514
Noora Sambhal 512-14, 602
Nur Ahmad Chishti 147
Nusrat Khan 399, 606
Nusrat Shah 371, 386, 426

Ogetai 85

Paila 383
Panipat 33, 371, 378, 399, 405, 435, 457, 459, 472, 478, 482, 485-90, 493, 585-6, 597, 599-601
Panj Pir 519, 521, 537, 546, 563, 569, 574, 577, 604, 608
Panjab 11, 13-16, 18-21, 25-6, 28-30, 32, 39, 41, 43-52, 54, 56-63, 64-5, 67, 70-2, 75-8, 79-81, 84-6, 89, 91, 93-6, 98, 105, 107-11, 113, 118-19, 127, 131, 147-8, 156, 185, 205, 221, 223, 227,
232-4, 245-6, 248, 257, 272, 280, 284, 295, 327, 330-1, 337, 369-71, 377, 384, 386-91, 393-4, 397-402, 406, 409-10, 413-17, 420, 422-3, 440, 457, 463, 472, 490, 509-10, 565-6, 568, 574, 578-82, 584, 585-8, 593, 596-7, 600-1, 604-8.
Pasrur 77
Pathan 510, 531
Persia (Iran) 25, 78, 85, 89, 191, 234, 343, 426
Peshawar 41-3, 55, 58, 64-5, 72, 85
Pir Muhammad 371-5, 381-2
Pratiharas 39, 118
Prince Bahram 51
Prince Majdud 54-6, 60
Prince Shahrukh 381
Prince Shirzad 61
Prithviraj Chauhan 65-6
Prophet Muhammad 124
Prophet Muhammad 14, 18, 24, 26, 73, 127-31, 139, 143, 145, 152, 166, 184, 195-6, 203, 208-9, 214-16, 219, 264, 274, 279, 307, 312, 319-21, 324-7, 336-8, 343, 347-51, 357, 360, 368, 377, 429, 462, 471, 477, 486-7, 490, 492-3, 495-6, 501, 503, 575
Prophetic traditions (*hadis*) 16, 127, 135, 138, 140, 143, 157, 177, 182, 184, 186, 205, 208, 300, 312, 325, 335-7, 341, 343-5, 349, 354-5, 450, 475, 495, 501, 508

Qabulpur 391
Qabulwah 272-3, 584
Qalandars 151, 173, 191-2, 215, 217, 248, 349, 450-1, 457, 475, 478, 480, 482, 488, 502-3, 590
Qamar ul-Huda 185
Qandhar 314
Qaramathians 1, 14, 39, 42-3, 56, 64, 118
Qaraunahs 101-2, 222, 228
Qarlughs 30, 80, 84-5, 93, 579-81
Qasur 108, 395-6
qawwali 302

Qawwals 18, 169, 177, 309-10, 323, 328-9, 352, 475, 492
Qazi 533, 555-60, 562, 573, 576
Qazi Asiruddin Khwarizmi 317-18
Qazi Hamiduddin Nagauri 169
Qazi Kamaluddin 451-2
Qazi Shirazi 46-52
Qazi Shuaib 149
Qiwam Khan 256, 387
Qiyam Khan 255-6
Qiyamkhanis 291-2
Quran 130, 155, 177, 183, 186, 188-91, 195, 197, 205, 217-18, 248, 271, 278, 298, 300-1, 308, 312, 314-18, 327-8, 331, 339-40, 343-5, 347-8, 362-3, 410, 441, 471, 476, 486, 494-6, 500, 508, 575-6
Qutb Khan 403, 405
Qutb ul-Mulk 234-6
Qutbuddin Aibak 66-8, 70-2, 119, 579
Qutbuddin Kashani 182, 185
Qutbuddin Mubarak Khalji 114, 222, 321, 323-4, 326, 364, 458, 594
Qutbwah 272, 584
Qutlugh Khan 82-3, 92
Qutlugh Khwaja 108-10, 113

Rag Bambiha 519
Rag Lalit 519
Rai Bahram Bhatti 411
Rai Bhim 391-3, 606
Rai Bhiru Bhatti 225-6
Rai Daud 370, 386-8, 606
Rai Dulchin 375-6
Rai Firoz Muin 390, 392, 395-6, 398-400, 429, 606
Rai Ghalib Kalanauri 393
Rai Hinu Bhatti 386, 394, 397
Rai Juljain Bhatti 369-70, 386, 397, 606
Rai Kalu 102
Rai Kamal Muin 369-70, 386, 390, 429
Rai Rattan 382
Rai Sangin 76
Rai Sehra 417-18, 433, 607
Rai Tamachi 357

Raja Bhoj 130
Raja Mal Dev 428
Rajabwah 258, 265, 583
Rajasthan 64, 71, 119
Rajoa Syedan 527
Rajputs 65, 304-5, 377, 428, 565, 592
Ram Rai 55
Ramu Brahmin 542-5
Rana Mal Bhatti 223-5, 252, 256, 291
Rana Shatra 76
Rangpur Khera 509, 537-8, 542, 545, 572-3, 604
Ranjha (Dhido) 509, 515-47, 551, 553-61, 564, 568-74, 576-7, 602-4
Ranjhas 515, 522, 539-41, 567, 602
Ravi 28, 88, 90, 103, 272, 280, 391-2, 396, 398, 422, 427, 565, 601
Rawalpindi 28
Rizvi, S.A.A. 15
Roh 404
Rohtak 230, 387, 426
Ropar 260, 388-91, 605
Rudauli 311, 489-90, 492, 507-8
Ruknuddin Firoz Shah 79, 121, 123
Rushdnama 498
Ruzbihan Baqli 204, 219

Saadi Shirazi 99
Sabiris 435, 472, 479, 482, 487, 507, 585-6, 597, 600
Sad Salman 54, 60
Sadharan 226, 250-53, 256
Sadhaura 260
Sadhu 226, 250-1, 256
Sadhu Nadira 387-8
Sadruddin Banbhaniya 280, 295, 356-7
Safedun 260, 265
Sahiba Khera 509, 528-9, 532, 534, 548, 553-4, 556-9, 571-2, 604
Sahij Rai 228, 231
Saifuddin Hasan Qarlugh 82, 85-7, 89
Saifuddin Kuchi 80
Saifuddin Suri 63
Sajjadah Nishins 305
Sakambri 39

Index

Saldi 108
Sali Bahadur 83, 90-2
Saljuqids 55, 59-60, 62-3, 118, 579
Salt Range (Koh-i Jud) 29, 64, 68, 76-7, 85, 91, 95, 106, 108, 223, 228, 279, 372, 385, 575, 582
Samana 66, 71-2, 79, 95, 97-8, 106, 108, 110-11, 114, 228-9, 257, 259, 266, 295, 369-71, 377-8, 383, 386-9, 393, 399-401, 404, 406, 431, 583, 604-5, 607
Samarqand 235, 237, 372, 380, 382, 390, 427
Sambhal 83
Sambhals 512-15, 566
Sanquran 71
Sarang Khan 370-2, 384, 388-9, 429, 605
Sardara 518
Sari Nuyin 94
Sarki (Khokhar) 68
Sarsuti 66, 79, 90, 230-2, 234, 243-4, 246, 249, 259-60, 265, 275, 289, 377, 394, 583, 585
Sarwar ul-Mulk 392
Satan 441-2, 445
Sati 289
Satluj 15, 28, 84, 108, 258-60, 292, 370, 375, 388-91, 396, 410, 435, 582, 585
Sehti 509, 542-3, 545-50, 574, 602
Sehwan 68, 77
Seor 395, 397, 400-1, 606
Sewi 417-8
Shafi school 342
Shah Husain 147, 510, 586
Shah Husain Arghon 422-3
Shahabad 33, 435, 472, 492-3, 583, 586, 583, 601
Shahin Khan 403
shahnas 83, 85
Shahnawaz 374
Shaikh Abdul Quddus Gangohi 26, 435, 492-4, 496-9, 508, 586, 601
Shaikh Abu Bakr Tusi 439

Shaikh Ahmad Abdul Haq 26, 480-1, 489-93, 507, 601
Shaikh Ala 480
Shaikh Alauddin 232-3, 243, 246, 262, 283, 288, 290, 298-303, 306-7, 309, 311, 330-1, 363, 593, 599
Shaikh Alauddin Ali Ahmad Sabir 26-7, 150, 435, 459, 472-8, 482, 505-6, 585, 600
Shaikh Ali 393-401, 429-30, 606
Shaikh Ali b. Usman Hujwiri 14, 21, 30, 131-47, 205, 207, 210, 579, 585-7
Shaikh Badruddin Ghaznavi 150, 167, 169, 184, 211
Shaikh Bahauddin Zakariya 16, 22-3, 25, 30, 91, 176-92, 205, 215-16, 222, 246, 311, 313-14, 316, 322-3, 326-34, 340-1, 345, 349-50, 353, 364, 416, 419-20, 422-3, 436, 456, 585-6, 589-1, 593, 595, 607
Shaikh Behram 484
Shaikh Budh 315-6
Shaikh Burhanuddin Araj 242-3
Shaikh Hasan 410-11, 413, 415
Shaikh Hud 332-5, 365, 595
Shaikh Husain Zinjani 132, 392
Shaikh Iku Timur 373-4
Shaikh Imaduddin 323-5
Shaikh Isa 411-13, 415
Shaikh Jalaluddin Panipati 459, 480-90, 506-7, 601
Shaikh Jalaluddin Tabrezi 149, 179
Shaikh Jamaluddin Hansavi 22, 32-3, 245-6, 282, 289, 358, 435-40, 443-9, 473, 482-3, 502, 505, 507, 585, 597-8
Shaikh Jamaluddin Uchi 245-6, 282, 341, 358, 366
Shaikh Musa 411-12, 415
Shaikh Najmuddin Kubra 493
Shaikh Nasiruddin Mahmud 17, 23, 212, 246, 289-90, 321-2, 342, 363, 366, 438, 448-9, 472, 489
Shaikh Nizamuddin Auliya 22-4, 115, 150-8, 169-71, 175-7, 211-12, 233, 246, 248, 261, 288, 290, 297, 300,

303, 311, 314, 321-33, 361, 364-5, 436-9, 447-9, 452, 454-8, 474-6, 491, 501-2
Shaikh Nuruddin (Sabiri) 489
Shaikh Nuruddin 247, 261-2, 289, 372-4, 376, 428, 449, 454-6, 502, 507
Shaikh Qutbuddin Munawwar 246-7, 261-2, 289-90, 448-55, 507, 598-9
Shaikh Raziuddin 281-3
Shaikh Rizqullah Mushtaqi 21
Shaikh Ruknuddin Abul Fateh 222, 236, 246, 288, 299-300, 315, 318-27, 330-2, 341-3, 350, 357, 359, 363-4, 410, 431-3, 593-5
Shaikh Sadruddin (Haidar Shaikh) 17, 32, 406-16, 431-2, 435, 607
Shaikh Sadruddin Arif 25-6, 180-4, 192-3, 311-18, 335, 341, 350, 365, 594
Shaikh Sadruddin Qonawi 193
Shaikh Samauddin 24, 25
Shaikh Shamsuddin Turk 456, 459, 474, 477-80, 482, 506, 585,
Shaikh Shamsuddin Yahya Maneri 456, 459
Shaikh Shihabuddin Suhrawardi 16, 178, 188, 215, 345, 347, 440, 589
Shaikh Tajuddin Mahmud 305
Shaikh ul-Islam 185, 193, 233, 301-2, 330, 334-5, 342, 342
Shaikh Usman Harwani 212
Shaikh Usman Zinda Pir 488
Shaikh Yusuf Gardez 334
Shaikh Yusuf Qureshi 416-21, 607
Shaikha Khokhar 304, 370, 373, 381, 383-5, 389, 592,
Shajrah-i Chiragh 307, 309
Shams Khan 369
Shams-i Siraj Afif 21, 24, 222, 224, 227, 247, 257, 259-62, 264-5, 272, 294, 455, 583, 597
Shamsuddin Dabir 438
Shamsuddin Iltutmish 14, 68, 72, 75-7, 78-9, 81, 85, 90, 96, 112, 119, 121, 228, 579, 581, 589
Shamsuddin Kurt Ghori 82, 90-2
Shamsuddin Tabrezi 457, 475

Shansbanis 64, 118-19
Sharfuddin Ali Yazdi 21, 259, 375
Shariat 71, 74, 247, 270, 275-6, 278, 283, 290, 294, 319-20, 331, 336, 345-6, 355, 360, 365, 446, 459-60, 474, 485, 493, 502-4, 555-6, 558-9, 563, 604
Sher Khan 81-4, 92, 96-7, 106, 115, 121, 171, 580-1
Sherwanis 410
Shihab Afif 224-5, 227
Shihabuddin Tamimi 372-3 \
Shiraz 342-3, 353-4
Shireen 466
Shorkot 422, 430, 433, 272
Sialkot 29, 64-5, 79, 389, 605
Sidh Bagai 544-6, 604
Sikandar bin Manjhu 253-4
Sikandar Lodi 25, 407-8, 412, 420, 422, 432, 488
Sikandar Shah 372, 426, 428
Sikandar Tohfa 391-3, 396, 398-403, 405, 606-7
sikdar 510, 514-15
Sinanuddin Chatisar 77-8
Sind 14, 39, 56-8, 64-5, 67, 71-2, 80, 85-6, 92, 94-5, 100, 111, 116, 222, 228, 230, 234-5, 279-80, 293, 295, 342-3, 393, 433, 490, 595-6
Sipahsalar Rajab 222-6, 251-2
Siraj ul-Hidaya 345-6
Sirhind 21, 32, 259-60, 386-91, 392-3, 402-3, 405-6, 409-10, 412-14, 601, 605-6
Siri 109-10, 113
Sirmur 83, 369, 259-60
Sitpur 420
Siwaliks 28-9, 62, 95, 112, 382-3, 402
Siwistan 85, 89, 108, 153, 245, 266
Siyal, Wahid Bakhsh 17
Siyals 509-15, 519, 521-3, 526-32, 534-5, 539, 543-4, 565, 567, 572, 576-7, 601-2
Siyar ul-Aqtab 26, 479, 485, 487
Siyar ul-Arifin 25, 31
Siyar ul-Auliya 24-6, 298, 454
Sodhra 80, 90-2

Index

Sonepat 55
South Asia 11
Steinfels, Amina M. 16, 342, 596
Subuktgin 40-1
Suhrawardi hospice 417, 419
Suhrawardis 14, 16-17, 25, 30-1, 33-5, 178, 188, 191-2, 215, 234, 300, 322, 333-5, 338, 340, 342, 352, 361, 421, 580-1, 586
Sukhpal 42
Sulaiman Shah 381
Sultan 510
Sultan Abdul Rashid 58-9
Sultan Bahu 147
Sultan Husain Langah 420-1, 423, 433
Sultan Ibrahim 59-61
Sultan Mahmud (r. 1405-12) 256
Sultan Mahmud (Ghazni) 40-7, 50-1, 58, 60, 62, 117, 578
Sultan Masud (III) 61
Sultan Masud 47, 49-52, 54-6, 59-60
Sultan Maudud 56, 58-9
Sultan Muhammad (r. 1388-94) 369
Sultan Muhammad (s/o Balban) 20, 22, 95, 97-104, 123, 192, 271, 317, 580
Sultan Muhammad Shah 401-2
Sultan Muizzuddin 13, 29, 63-8, 70-2, 118-19, 178, 226, 271, 579
Sultan Qutbuddin Langah 418-9, 421
Sultan Raziya 80-1, 86, 121, 131
Sultan Shah Khushdil 369
Sultan Zain ul-Abidin 129, 206
Sultan-i zikr 494-6
Sumras 100
Sunam 79-80, 84, 95-7, 257, 327, 387, 406, 490, 580, 607
Surah-i Fatiha 167, 187
Surah-i Ikhlas 18
Surah-i Kafirun 188
Syed Ahmad Kabir 341
Syed Jalaluddin Bokhari 16, 17, 31, 252-3, 281, 295, 340-60, 366-8, 429, 484-6, 507, 586, 595-6
Syed Muhammad Kirmani 297, 361
Syed Nasir 254-5

Syed Raju Qattal 343, 360, 366
Syed Salim 394
Syed Usman Marwandi 99, 124
Syeds 71-3, 373, 375-80, 398, 579, 583
Syeds of Rajoa 552, 575

Tabaqat-i Nasiri 20
Tabrez 94
Tahir 515, 517, 539-42
Taifuris 145
Tair Bahadur 88
Taj Murassa Begam 410, 413, 415, 432
Taj ul-Maasir 20, 66-7
Tajuddin Abu Bakr Ayaz 80, 89
Tajuddin Arsalan Khan 83
Tajuddin Hasan Nizami 20, 67-9, 119
Tajuddin Yaldoz 70-2, 579
Takht Hazara 509, 516-18, 522, 531-2, 538-44, 568, 571
Taks 252-3
Tamar (Mongol) 100
Tamar Khan 97
Tamhid ul-Muhtadi 155, 157
Tarain 80
Targhi 100, 113, 126
Tarikh-i Firishtah 11
Tarikh-i Firoz Shahi 20, 263
Tarikh-i Masudi 19
Tartaq 111
Tatar Khan 371
Tatar Khan Lodi 420
Taziks 80
Thakurs 425
Thanesar 43, 56-7, 95, 226, 250-1, 253, 266, 294, 311, 435, 583
Thatta 245-6, 289, 356-7, 367, 433
Thattawas 420, 433
Tilak 50-4
Tilhar 391, 393-4, 399
Tilla Balnath (Tilla Jogian) 29, 509, 544-5, 604
Timur 21, 32, 256, 261, 291, 371-85, 390, 402, 404, 426-8, 456
Tirhara 370
Tohana 377, 411-13, 583, 607
Tomars 39

Transoxiana 228
trans-Satluj 84
Trilochanpal 43-4
Tughan Rais Turkbacha 388-90, 429
Tughluqpur 377, 381, 583
Tughluqs 12, 20, 30, 222-3, 232-4, 284, 322, 335, 591, 608
Tulamba 373, 390, 427, 396, 398, 400
Turan 404
Turkbachas 388
Turkistan 82, 86-7, 91-2, 222
Turkomans 50, 52-4
Turks 66, 71, 425

Uch 29, 64-5, 71, 77-83, 86, 89-90, 118-19, 149, 167, 171, 176, 178, 181, 210, 228, 234-5, 245, 252, 276, 282-3, 295-6, 313, 340-1, 343-4, 353, 356, 358-9, 361, 371, 373, 386, 417, 420-1, 429, 452, 484-5, 585-6, 595-7
Ujjain 42, 130
Ulugh Khan (Khalji commander) 108, 110
Ulughkhani 258, 265, 583
Umar Khan Sarwani 493
Umdah 183-4
unasked charity (*futuh*) 297, 455
Urs 309
Ushaqnama 22
ushr 71
Uwaisi 457, 492
Uzbeg Tai 85

Wahdat ul-wujud 498

Waihind 15, 25, 42, 55
Wajihuddin Usman Sunami 327-9
Waraichs 516, 539-41, 568, 571, 573, 602
Waris Shah 568-74, 576
West Asia 341-2, 355
Wink, Andre 13

Yahya Ahmad Sirhindi 21, 259-60, 397, 430, 607
Yaminis 64
Yaqub Khan Waraich 516, 539-40, 571, 602
Yazid 472, 505
Yoga 129
Yusuf of Kinaan 468, 504
Yusuf Zulaikha 196, 217, 219

Zafar Khan (s/o Sadharan) 252-4, 291
Zafar Khan 108-10, 113, 125, 581
Zahir 515, 517
zakat 277, 280, 294-5
Zamakhshari 183, 206, 216
zamindari 526, 546, 551, 567
Zamindars 11, 27, 31, 33, 250-1, 253-4, 256, 269, 410-4, 509-10, 520, 522-3, 534, 536, 551-2, 556, 558-9, 577, 601, 603-4, 607-8
Ziauddin Barani 14, 20, 96, 98, 100, 102, 106, 112-15, 224, 260, 263-4, 300, 330-1, 338, 356, 455, 582, 593, 597
zikr 185-8, 313, 347, 350, 442, 444, 449
Zirak Khan 387-9, 391, 393-4, 397, 399-400, 606
Zu ul-Nun Misri 135, 143